The Debt Crisis in the Eurozone: Social Impacts

The Debt Crisis in the Eurozone: Social Impacts

Edited by

Nicholas P. Petropoulos
and George O. Tsobanoglou

CAMBRIDGE SCHOLARS PUBLISHING

The Debt Crisis in the Eurozone: Social Impacts,
Edited by Nicholas P. Petropoulos and George O. Tsobanoglou

This book first published 2014

Cambridge Scholars Publishing

12 Back Chapman Street, Newcastle upon Tyne, NE6 2XX, UK

British Library Cataloguing in Publication Data
A catalogue record for this book is available from the British Library

ISBN (10): 1-4438-5630-4, ISBN (13): 978-1-4438-5630-0

TABLE OF CONTENTS

Part II. Micro- and Macro-Social Impacts on Eurozone Countries under Austerity Regimes

Part III. Migration, Migration Attitudes and Religion in Countries under Austerity Regimes

Conclusions and Recommendations

PROLOGUE

The production and publication of every book has its history. The impetus for this volume came from the "Disaster, Conflict and Social Crisis Research Network" (DCSCRN) of the European Sociological Association. The RNs are urged by the ESA to organize interim conferences, on themes relevant to the purposes of the RN. The Network usually concentrated on "natural" and "technological" disasters, although a focus on "social crises" was also a central objective of its professional repertory. Following the breakout of the economic crisis in the Eurozone, especially in Southern Europe and Ireland, with its extensive impact on citizens of these societies and its evolution into an "humanitarian crisis" in some of these countries—that brought to memory the conditions of the Great Depression—the Network decided to focus on the "social crisis" dimension and organize an interim meeting with the following theme: "The Debt Crisis in the Eurozone: Social Impacts". The conference took place on the island of Lesvos (Mytilene), 13-14/09/12, and attracted more than 30 academics/researchers participants (speakers) from Greece, Spain, Turkey, Germany, UK, USA, New Zealand, Finland, Russia, France and Switzerland, i.e. from the entire spectrum of "debt-" and "non-debt-ridden" countries. For the needs of the current volume, selected papers were written up and updated by the authors.

The volume is organized into five parts, following the structure of "causes", "responses" and "new structures", though admittedly some of the chapters could also be included in more than one part, depending upon interpretation. Part I deals with the political-economic dimensions/bases of the debt crisis and consists of five chapters. Chapter 1, by Prof. Brigitte Young (See "Contributors" at the end of the text) explores the role of "rule-based" German "ordoliberalism" and the "monetarist-supply" bias in the debt crisis. Chapter 2, by Prof. Magnus Ryner, focuses on the "disastrous" consequences of the European Monetary Union financial capitalism on the Eurozone members. Chapter 3, by Prof. Georg Vobruba, describes how the adoption of the "common currency" led to the Europeanization of distributional conflicts and the emergence of a complex conflict structure. In turn, he describes how this new constellation of conflicts is open to "populist exploitation" or can present a challenge for the development of a new European society. Chapter 4, by Profs.

Sotiris Chtouris and DeMond Miller, arguing from a Bourdieuian perspective, analyzes the role of social, human, natural, cultural and economic capital, as well as their interrelationship in causing or solving the "economic" crisis. Finally, Chapter 5, by Josua Gräbener, focuses on one of the crisis-ridden countries, Italy, using both quantitative and qualitative data; Gräbener examines how ESF and its European Employment Strategy for worker training, with the different agendas of the employers, can reinforce north-south regional fragmentation and thus exacerbate the crisis.

Part II consists of four chapters that deal with the macro- and micro-impacts of the debt crisis and focus on Greece, the EZ country worst hit by the recession. Chapter 6, by Prof. Dennis Smith, adopts a historical-comparative and typological approach for comprehending the contrasting coping tactics, strategies and collective reactions of Greek and Irish people to the "humiliation" attendant to the bailout system. Dr. Dionyssis Balourdos, the author of Chapter 7, also focuses on the country level, employs a variety of quantitative methods (e.g., trend and cluster analysis) and a multi-dimensional conception of poverty, to assess the impact of the crisis on poverty risk as well as on "old" and "new" categories of poverty in EU countries—and especially in Greece which, as said above, is the hardest hit of the debt-ridden countries. Chapter 8, by Dr. Joanna Tsiganou, relying on the European Social Survey (ESS) micro-sociological data (2002, 2005 and 2010 rounds), and comparing Greece with the EU-27 as a whole, assesses the impact of austerity programs on interpersonal trust, trust in sociopolitical institutions and sense of security while simultaneously making a critical note on the application of anomie theory. The last Chapter (9) of Part II, by Prof. Joanna Despina Bergiannaki, based on a review of the relevant literature and on clinical experience, applies the classical notions of post-traumatic stress symptoms/reactions—that we usually associate with "natural" or "technological" disasters and humanitarian emergencies such as wars, terrorism and hostage situations—to the economic-financial crisis.

Part III concentrates on the relation and/or the impact of the economic crisis on migration processes and intergroup relations. Chapter 10, by Profs. Nikolaos Nagopoulos and Konstantinos Rontos, evaluates the impact of the economic and social crisis on the labour market and migrant integration, as well as the impact of a large number of non-documented migrants on the Greek labour market and its implications for the current EU policy implementation at a time of crisis. The next three chapters, on the micro-sociological level of analysis, are based on data from the European Social Survey (ESS). Chapter 11, by Dr. Stefania Kalogeraki, tests the relevance of the well-known "realistic group conflict theory", using the 2004 (pre-crisis) and 2011 ("post"-crisis) rounds of the ESS and *Anovas,* as a framework for the prediction of native (majority) and migrant ("minority") intergroup attitudes. Chapter 12, by Dr. Katerina Iliou, also assumes the immediately above theory and takes into account the debt crisis and the "disproportionate large inflow of migrants"; Iliou uses data from four Rounds of ESS (2001/02-2010/11), a time-series analysis of fluctuations in personal perceptions of social trust, institutional trust, subjective well-being, human values and political affiliation (interest, participation, ideology and allegiance), as well as an inter-correlation analysis, to draw conclusions on the impact of the crisis on "negative attitudes" toward immigrants. The authors of the last Chapter (13), Dr. Theoni Stathopoulou and Prof. Anastasia Kostaki, use two rounds of ESS data (2009 and 2011) and regression analysis to account for variations in interpersonal trust, institutional trust, tolerance for immigrants, homophiles and "political extremes" in two of the debt-ridden countries—Greece and Spain; a plethora of "independent" variables (e.g., sex, education, religion indicators, living in a big city, feelings about household income, ESS round, etc.) are used as potential explanatory variables. The Stathopoulou and Kostaki chapter complements the Tsiganou chapter and expands the types of target groups.

Part IV focuses on the impact of the debt crisis on political processes, and especially on the *indignados* movements in Spain and Greece. Chapter 14, by Ignacía Perugorria and Prof. Benjamín Tejerina, relies on qualitative methods—ethnographic and depth interviews with indignados; following a dissection of the 15M into its principal axes (cognitive, emotional and relational), the authors describe the process of synchronizing divergent 15M identities. The author of Chapter 15, Prof. Alberto Cotillo, works within the context of macro-politics and views the 15M as a "withdrawal" from institutional politics; using a time-series analysis of the political situation and the economic situation and a multi-dimensional conception of "political disaffection" within various categories of ideological proclivity, he explores the source of the increasing disaffection in Spain during the last decade (2002 to 2012). The last Chapter (16) of Part IV, by Dr. Nicholas Petropoulos, deals with the *indignados* of Greece. Relying both on qualitative (e.g., participant observation, content analysis) and quantitative (e.g., Greek social surveys) methods, he arrives at a sociopolitical profile of the indignados, accounts for the mass phenomenon and draws out its short- and long-term effects.

The last part of the volume, Part V, presents *some* of the alternatives that could constitute an answer to the debt crisis, affecting not only

Greece, but also other debt-ridden countries. In Chapter 17, Prof. George Tsobanoglou, after a review and analysis of the social impact of the debt crisis on the Greek economy, as well as an analysis of the idiosyncrasies of the Greek labour market, discusses the established and emergent forms of "assembling sociality" and "social economy" as possible therapeutic alternatives for the current crisis. The authors of Chapter 18, Christos Kanellopoulos and Dr. Sotiria Liakaki, after an exhaustive review of the international and Greek situation, analyze the concept of "full citizenship" and its implications for the distribution of social resources; furthermore, they analyze the shortcomings of the Greek social insurance system and recommend that Greece pay more attention to the Scandinavian model. Chapter 19, by Dr. Antti Silvast, based on documents and textual analysis, compares the concepts of "critical infrastructure" in the U.S., the E.U. and Finland, with special reference to economic institutions and banking systems; in turn, he takes a more in-depth longitudinal look at the Finnish situation pointing out some of its limitations from the perspective of integrated disaster management. In Chapter 20, Prof. George Gantzias occupies us with the new technologies, the "info-communication landscape" and "Global Info-Cash" (GIC); in addition, he describes how the adoption of the "digital transactions/payment culture" could help the debt-ridden countries of Southern Europe to emerge from the crisis.

The Editors would like to point out that two of the chapters, Chapter 4 by S. Chtouris and D. Miller, and Chapter 5 by J. Gräbener are theoretical and/or empirical observations of cross-cultural research work in progress. They nonetheless provide significant analytical perspectives to the economic crisis and constitute an impetus for further substantive discussion with the authors. In any case, in a scientific community, even the "completed works" are essentially works in progress.

To document the impact of the crisis, the text relies on graphic presentations (diagrams, graphs, photos etc.). The Editors would have liked to print these in the original four colors. However, the costs would be forbidding, especially at a time of crisis, and our main concern was to reach wider audiences of social scientists and policy-makers. Following consultation with the CSP, the authors were instructed to invest their graphic presentations with a variety of symbols, types of lines, and the labels for the various statistical groups, and assess their legibility by doing a black and white print-out before submitting their contribution. We hope that these techniques mitigate the problem.

As the solutions to the debt crisis confronting Southern European countries are not exhausted in Part V, the volume closes (Chapter 21) with conclusions and policy recommendations drawn from all, if not most of, the contributions. A number of the authors contributed to the text of this chapter. However, the order of presentation does not necessarily follow the order of the chapters. It is the hope of the Editors and all the contributors to this volume that the recommendations will not fall on the deaf ears of policy makers.

Before ending this Prologue, the Editors would like to acknowledge the contributions of the main factors in the production of this volume. First, the European Sociological Association which contributed to the funding of the Lesvos midterm conference. Second, the "Disaster, Conflict and Social Crisis Research Network"—especially the Coordinator, Murat Balamir; the Vice-Coordinator, Nina Blom Andersen; the economic liaison with ESA, Susann Ullberg; and the web manager, Antti Silvast—for its logistic and IT support. Third, the members of the mixed consultation committee from Aegean University and DCSCRN (Sotiris Chtouris, Murat Balamir, Maureen Fordham, Anastasia Zissi, George Tsobanoglou and Nicholas Petropoulos) for the initial selection of conference papers. Fourth, the University of the Aegean for its professional auspices and its logistic support to the conference. Fifth, the Lesvos Chamber of Commerce for the venue of the conference. Sixth, the "Krishan and Vicky Joshi Foundation" of Dayton, Ohio, for the funding of the keynote speakers and the registration fees of conferees from debt-ridden Southern European countries (Greece and Spain). Lastly, but not least, our links with Cambridge Scholars Publishing: Carol Koulikourdi, Author Liaison and Commissioning Editor, for her guidance, patience and understanding; Amanda Millar, Typesetting Manager and Keith Thaxton, Typesetter, for their technical assistance in text formatting; Adam Terry for the design of the dust jacket and Sean Howley for his promotion efforts. Above all, our thanks to Cambridge Scholars Publishing and its Management who gave us the opportunity to reach wider audiences of social scientists, crisis managers and policy makers.

Nicholas P.Petropoulos, Ph.D.
George O. Tsobanoglou, Ph.D.
Athens, 17/01/2014

PART I.

THE EUROZONE CRISIS: REGIONAL, INTERNATIONAL, POLITICAL-ECONOMIC AND SOCIAL DIMENSIONS

CHAPTER ONE

THE ROLE OF GERMAN ORDOLIBERALISM IN THE EURO CRISIS

BRIGITTE YOUNG
UNIVERSITY OF MUNSTER

"Germany destroyed itself – and the European order – twice in the twentieth century. It would be both tragic and ironic if a restored Germany, by peaceful means and with the best intentions, brought about the ruin of the European order a third time".
(Joschka Fischer, former German Foreign Minister)

Abstract

The paper argues that the German belief in the rule-based ordoliberal doctrine is a major agenda setter of Eurozone crisis management. Ordoliberalism, also known as the Freiburg School, rejects government intervention championed by Keynesians to shore up indebted countries, since this would violate the independence of the European Central Bank to follow its mandate of price stability. This position was ideologically defended in the so-called economist dispute between German ordoliberals and Post-Keynesian economists debated in highly prestigious German newspapers in the summer of 2012. This debate is important for several reasons. First, it demonstrates the deep divisiveness within the German economic profession representing the ordoliberal tradition of the Freiburg School with its emphasis on a rule-based monetarist supply-side model and the Post-Keynesian ideas with their focus on demand-led growth. Secondly, the debate brings to the fore the many veto points and institutional frictions within the domestic German decision-making process resulting in the much criticized lack of coordination of Euro crisis management. In the concluding part, the article discusses some strategies to resolve the crisis. It argues for a deepening of the Eurozone with a political, banking, economic and fiscal union which would permit executive decision to be accountable to European citizens. Most surprising in this design of an institutional framework is the missing link of a "Social Europe". The asymmetry between the model of "Market Europe" and the model of "Social Europe" means that social policy is largely left to member states with very different capacities to protect citizens from economic and financial market failures.

An introduction to crisis politics in the Eurozone

The present financial and economic crisis has split the Eurozone not only along geographical lines among northern current account surplus and southern deficit countries[1], the fissure also reflects a deep ideological rift in how to resolve the financial and sovereign debt crisis in the Eurozone. Under the leadership of Germany, the current account surplus countries of Finland, Austria and the Netherlands call for strict austerity rules to reign in fiscal deficits of the highly indebted Eurozone states (the so-called GIIPS of Greece, Ireland, Italy, Portugal and Spain). The pressure for strict household consolidation has only limited support among other European nations. In fact, many European government and political leaders, as well as president Barack Obama and the Canadian prime minister Stephen Harper, have criticized Germany for its single-handed pursuit of austerity measures, its strict legal approach to the ECB mandate of monetary stability, and its export model which has contributed to the macroeconomic asymmetries in the Eurozone.

Keynesian economists have pointed to the pro-cyclical nature of the mandated austerity programs for indebted peripheral countries, since these policies leave no room for discretionary fiscal policy. Countries are in a no-win situation: they confront unsustainably high budget deficits, but the austerity measures are most likely to harm aggregate demand and may aggravate the fiscal deficits of debtor nations even further (Heise 2012). Recent data on GDP declines in the Eurozone seem to support the Keynesian position. Even the economically strong northern states have registered a fall in GDP due to the economic slow-down in peripheral countries. German economic growth shrank 0.2 percent in Q2 compared with the previous Q1, while the economies of Greece, Spain, Italy and even Finland contracted sharply (FT, 15.8.2012: 4).[2]

Although European political and financial leaders have met nineteen times for summit meetings to resolve the Euro crisis since the first Greek bailout measure was agreed in May 2010, the crisis is by far not over and will occupy Eurozone leaders throughout 2013. While there has been some leveling-off in the skyrocketing interest rate hikes on sovereign bonds for some peripheral countries, the rating agencies have continued downgrading European states and banks.[3] The economic turmoil has already led to the fall of governments in Ireland, Greece, Italy, Spain, Portugal, Holland and France. The replacement of political leaders in Italy and Greece (until the Greek election in spring 2012) with unelected technocrats was greeted with euphoria by the financial markets, but alienated many citizens. European citizens are losing trust in their elected leaders and in the legitimacy of the European Union (Scharpf, 2012). The result is a rise in populism and revolt in countries whose citizens are told that there is no alternative to the austerity measures championed by Germany and its allies to regain the trust of the financial markets (Leonard and Zielonka, 2012). The Occupy movement which started in the United States but has since found followers in many places around the globe is a further indication of the frustration of ordinary people about political decisions to socialize the costs, and privatize the benefits of the financial sector. In a German *Spiegel* interview, Mario Monti, the head of the technocratic caretaker government of Italy until his resignation in December, warned about the increasing resentment of Italians (this is also happening in other countries) "against the EU, against the Euro, against the Germans, and sometimes even against Chancellor Merkel" (*Der Spiegel*, 2012: 44). Many analysts see the Eurozone at a cross-road between complete disintegration and deep structural reforms of the economic governance structure of the European Union.

The inability of European leaders to arrive at a coordinated reform agenda is not just a failure of individual leaders of the Eurozone, it signals the structural flaws of the European Monetary Union and its economic (non)governance system. Setting monetary policy at the European level while leaving fiscal policy in the hands of individual member states was a huge gamble from the inception of the European Monetary Union, and may have worked during "normal" economic times, but became the Achilles heel during the financial crisis. Namely, the inability of economic leaders to arrive at authoritative political decisions has deteriorated the credit conditions in the Eurozone. This "executive deficit" is less the result from "inadequate decisions than from an absence of decisions when they were needed" (Véron, 2012: 1). Four years into the crisis and the slow pace and fragmented process of decision-making has exacted huge long-term political costs.

As the borrowing costs of Italian and Spanish government bonds started to reach unsustainable levels in the late spring of 2012, and speculation increased about the possible exit of Greece from the Eurozone, the European leaders finally decided at their Brussels summit meeting in June 2012 (lasting into the early morning hours) to sign up for "more Europe" by agreeing to transfer some national sovereignty to four new

European institutions consisting of a fiscal union, a banking union, an economic union and a political union. While these results were hailed by many government leaders and the financial media across and beyond Europe as a true break-through, it started one of the most virulent debates among German economists: whether the banking union would result in the mutualisation of European debt and would thus violate the mandate of the Maastricht Treaty. The former member of the ECB-Executive Board, Otmar Issing, even warned that "forming such a union would be the end of the nation state" (Issing, 2012).

This emotional and vitriolic debate started with a protest call drafted by Walter Krämer, economist at the University of Dortmund, which then was co-signed by the renown director of the Munich ifo-Institute, Hans-Werner Sinn. The *Economist Streit* was launched in the *Frankfurter Allgemeine Zeitung,* on July 5, 2012, was entitled "Dear Fellow Citizens" and was subsequently signed by about 200 German economists (Sinn and Krämer 2012). The public memo was immediately met with counter-responses by other renown German economists, signed also by many hundred economists, arguing that economists around Hans-Werner Sinn lacked impartiality and did not even understand a banking crisis. However, the criticism was not restricted to the German economic profession; many star foreign economists also took issue with the ideological arguments of Krämer/Sinn and their supporters (FT 9.7.2012; *The Economist,* 2012).

This debate, which in the meantime has found critics but also supporters across the German political party spectrum, the media and civil society groups, is important for several reasons. First, it demonstrates the deep divisiveness within the German elite and among economists representing the ordoliberal tradition of the Freiburger School with its emphasis on a rule-based supply-side model and Keynesian ideas with their focus on demand-led growth. While Keynesianism has never gained a really strong foothold among German economists or in the state bureaucracies, Keynesian ideas have become stronger since the start of the global financial crisis in 2008. Given the aggressive and emotional debate played out for weeks in the public media, it is not surprising that in the meantime only 27 percent of Germans believe Greece should stay in the Eurozone, against 54 percent who said it should leave (FT, 3.9.2012: 1). Nevertheless, this debate is the first real public discussion on the future of the European Union, which was until now an elite project discussed behind closed doors without any democratic accountability. Secondly, the divisiveness brings to the fore the many veto points and institutional frictions within the German decision-making process which has resulted in the much criticized incremental steps taken to resolve the Euro crisis. The reactive and uncoordinated mode of crisis resolution has largely been associated with Angela Merkel and her small-step approach to the crisis. Analysts have warned about the fragmentation and the renationalization of Euro politics since the Euro crisis and that Merkel's hesitant intervention has made the rescue packages for peripheral countries more expensive since the uncertainties in the Eurozone markets drove the credit default swaps and yields on government bonds to ever greater heights (Young and Semmler, 2011).

The rule-based system of ordoliberalism

Despite the many institutional players in the German domestic arena which Hall and Soskice (2001) have identified as part of the coordinated market economies of the "Rhenish" model, and which other authors have adapted as a framework to explain the different approaches to financial regulation (see Zimmermann 2010; Mügge 2006), I argue that the German belief in the rule-based ordoliberal doctrine is a major agenda setter to prevent a coordinated decision-making process in the Eurozone as a whole. Ordoliberalism, also known as the Freiburger School, rejects government intervention championed by Keynesians to shore up indebted countries, since this would violate the independence of the European Central Bank to follow its mandate of price stability. This "ideological edifice behind German orthodoxy" (Dullien and Guérot, 2012: 2) is strongly entrenched in German tradition and is unlikely to change even if there was a transfer of power to a SPD/Green coalition in 2013.

Namely, ordoliberalism is geared to long-term solutions of establishing a political framework, an *Ordo,* in which market forces can work efficiently. The present international demand for political intervention in fiscal and monetary policy to stabilize the Euro crisis is contrary to the long-term goals of ordoliberals to establish a legal system through treaty changes to force countries to adhere to strict fiscal discipline and for automatic sanctions if the constitutional framework is violated (Berghahn and Young, 2012; Dullien and Guérot, 2012). Ordoliberalism has its antecedents in the 1930s, and was influential after World War II in the development of the Social Market Economy of Ludwig Erhard. Its most influential leaders are Walter Eucken, Franz Böhm, Wilhelm Röpke, Alfred Müller-Armack and Alexander Rüstow (Sally, 1996; Bonefeld, 2012; Berghahn and Young 2012; Young, 2013). In the present Euro crisis resolution scenario, the influence of ordoliberalism is most evident in the German position on price stability and its defence of the independence of the Central Bank. The German Bundesbank was created and reflects the rule-based approach of an *economic order,* within which economic processes take place (Sally 1996: 235). After World War II, the Freiburgers argued for the primacy of currency policy. For Walter Eucken, monetary policy was the constituting principle of the *Ordnungspolitik:* "All efforts to institute a competitive market economy will fail as long as price stability is not guaranteed" (cited in Issing, 2000: 1). However, the goal of a sound monetary system was not just to guarantee price stability. Equally important are the rules for sanctions against any transgression of such price stability. The purpose is to rule out any discretionary space for politicians to intervene in monetary policy (Young, 2013).

The dilemma of the German Chancellor

Angela Merkel faces now a huge dilemma. While she clearly sided with the ordoliberal austerity orthodoxy since the outbreak of the debt crisis and rejected Keynesian demands to use the ECB's "firepower" to safeguard the monetary transmission to the real economy, she now welcomes the ECB's "Outright Monetary Transaction" (OMT) program of bond-buying as a useful short-term measure. This is trying to square the circle, since Germans trust Angela Merkel (at least, until now) as the defender of monetary stability characterized in the caricature of *the Swabian housewife.* A more cynical reading of her not publicly coming to the rescue of Jens Weidmann, the president of the German Bundesbank, to defend his no-vote against the ECB decision, is that Merkel can no longer count on the Chancellor's majority in pushing through any further rescue measures in the German Bundestag; thus she accepts the ECB's bond buying scheme in order to gain time. That the German government faced a near mutiny among many CDU-rebels and the Bavarian sister party (CSU), as well as among the coalition partner of the FDP, was to be expected.

Given this emotional polarization in Germany between those that are nostalgically looking backward to the time of the DM when German ordoliberals guarded the stability of the money in the Bundesbank and the others who are trying to shift the debate away from this introspective understanding of the Euro crisis blaming either the debtor countries or feeling victimized "as the paymaster of Europe", Chancellor Merkel will find it difficult to gather support for a political union, and possibly even for a constitutional Convention, given that Otmar Issing, a representative of the ordoliberal orthodoxy, has decried the entire project as "an idea worthy of satire" (Issing 2012). The ordoliberals are deeply disappointed in Merkel. There is even talk in CDU circles that Germany should try to push for a veto right in the ECB (n-tv 7.9.2012).

A "market union" without a "social union"?

Essentially, there are only two possible strategies left to resolve the crisis: either to return to national currencies in the entire EU area and be subject to the volatility of highly speculative currency markets, or laying the groundwork for deepening the Eurozone with a political, banking, economic and a fiscal union with the goal to regain the political space at the transnational level lost to global market forces (Habermas et al., 2012). It has dawned on many political and economic leaders that a break-up of the Eurozone would be a costly calamity. And the biggest loser will be Germany, if the Eurozone fails (Cameron, 2012). This may be one reason why Angela Merkel has taken the strong lead for *more Europe.* At the same time, it has also become apparent that the institutional design of the EMU is deeply flawed, and needs the "E" as in economics in addition to the monetary in EMU as Jean-Claude Trichet pointed out in his acceptance speech of the 2011 *Karlspreis* in Aachen, which is awarded to persons/leaders who champion the European idea.

The only possible way forward is to design an institutional framework which allows executive decisions to be made which are democratically accountable to Europe's citizens. This means also that the European Parliament has to be empowered to control executive decisions. Making the European Parliament more representative is all the more important since the German Constitutional Court has cited in 2009, and cited again in its decision on 12 September 2012, that Berlin cannot surrender fiscal power to Europe in the absence of democratic representation in Brussels. The same lack of accountability is also evident in the European Council consisting of heads of states and leaders of government. These political leaders report back to their national citizens, but "the Council as a whole is accountable to no one" (Véron, 2012: 4). While the European Commission is on paper, at least, accountable to the European Parliament, in the early phase of the debt crisis the Commission was largely ignored by the heads of states and the leaders of government (Young and Semmler, 2011). The same lack of democratic accountability is also found in the two intergovernmental institutions, the Eurogroup made up of national finance ministers and the Economic and Financial Affairs Council (ECOFIN) composed of the Economic and Financial Ministers of the 27 member states. However, nothing harmed the trust of citizens as much as the disregard for the French and Dutch no-vote on the European Constitution in 2004, which was then repacked in the Lisbon Treaty in 2007. A similar fate befell the Irish voters who first rejected the Lisbon Treaty in 2008, and were subsequently asked to change their vote in 2009. Nicolas Véron is absolutely right in asserting that "[T]he democratic shortfall has been widely cited as a factor in the rise of populist anti-European parties in recent elections in several member states" (Véron, 2012: 4).

The first step to more democratic accountability has been made with the proposal on 26 June 2012 for a political, economic, fiscal, banking union with different but interdependent tasks. This truly forward-looking proposal issued by the president of the European Council, Van Rompey, addresses not just the technical fixes of a fragile banking system, the lack of European supervision of banks, the break-down of interbank and cross-border lending, the lack of economic competitiveness in the Eurozone, the increasing risk of sovereign bonds, it also addresses the democratic deficit and loss of trust in the European project (Euro Area Summit Statement, 2012; European Council, 2012). None of the proposed individual unions will be legitimate without the political union providing the umbrella to ensure democratic accountability The four building-blocs are divided into different problem solving mechanisms.

A banking union would entail a common framework for banking supervision, crisis resolution, and deposit insurance. A fiscal union would include the creation of a commonly issued debt instrument to meet investors' demand for a credit-risk-free asset (or ("Eurobonds").... accompanied by adequate central controls on national budgetary choices. A competitive (or economic) union would monitor, assess and coordinate structural reform policies at the national and European levels, including in areas that have high impact on the potential development of high-growth firms in Europe such as insolvency legislation, financial regulation, service sector regulation and labor law. A political union would make the European Parliament genuinely representative and able to exert due democratic control of relevant executive functions (Véron, 2012: 5-6).

At the outset, most of the details were provided for the banking union. The Euro Area Summit Statement dated 29 June 2012 "affirms that it is imperative to break the present vicious circle between bank and sovereigns" on the "condition that an effective single supervisory mechanism is established". The proposals are to be considered on the basis of Article 127(6) for a single supervisory mechanism. Once a single supervisory mechanism is established, it will be possible to recapitalize banks directly rather than having to rely on the state to provide the liquidity. Perhaps not unexpectedly, Wolfgang Schäuble objected in the *Financial Times* (31.8.2012) that a European supervisor would not be able to supervise all of the 6,000 banks in the Eurozone. It has since been agreed that the ECB should only have supervisory power over the largest banks and exclude the German public banks, savings banks, and mutual banks from European supervision. This means that these banks would remain under national jurisdiction and should a bank fail it could not be closed down by the European supervisory authorities. As a result, the banking oversight is once again split between Europe and national authorities.

Most surprising is not what has been suggested to create a democratically accountable executive framework, but rather what is missing. Namely, the present European legitimacy crisis is also a crisis of the missing "Social Europe". Faced with financial crisis and huge sovereign debt levels, citizens suspect that the EU will promote further a "Market Europe" at the expense of a "Social Europe" based on solidarity and social integration (Scharpf, 2012; Negt, 2012). As Liebert (2011) argues, the Treaty of Lisbon has strengthened the economic dimension of the EMU greatly, but has made little advancement towards a supranational social welfare regime based on economic solidarity. Instead, it has divided the competences of social policy between the EU and the member states. While the Treaty of Lisbon has strengthened fundamental rights, specifically in the social area, the double asymmetries between a "Social Europe" based on soft law and a "Liberal Market Europe" based on hard facts, means that social policy is largely a matter of member states. The near financial meltdown and the subsequent debt crisis in Europe have opened a political and analytical space to question the model of a "Market Europe" of the past two decades. There is widespread public awareness that the near meltdown of the world economy and the drastic economic decline in many European peripheral countries have exacerbated the poverty of many people. The casino capitalism that began in Wall Street and The City and copied in many financial centers in Europe has been pushed back, but the economic and social problems it created are far from having been solved (Berghahn and Young, 2012). As a new political union process matures, it is imperative for a democratic Europe to strengthen the social dimension governing the European Monetary Union.

Notes

[1] The current account surplus countries include Germany, Austria, Holland, Finland, Luxemburg, while deficit countries include Ireland, Spain, Greece, Cyprus, Portugal, and Italy.
[2] Greece contracted about 7 percent in 2012, compared to the IMF forecast of 4.7 percent. Even Finland, a staunch supporter of austerity measures, declined by 1 percent in the Q2 of 2012.
[3] See the satirical memorandum about a Plan B for Chancellor Merkel in the event of a break-up of the euro area, published as lead article in *The Economist,* The Merkel memorandum, 11 August 2012.

References

Berghahn, V. and Young, B. (2013). 'Reflections on Werner Bonefeld's 'Freedom and the strong state: On German ordoliberalism and the continuing importance of the ideas of Ordoliberalism to understand Germany's (contested) role in resolving the Euro Zone crisis', in *New Political Economy,* vol. 18, no. 5, pp. 768-778.

Bonefeld, W., (2012). 'Freedom and the strong state: On German ordoliberalism', *New Political Economy*, vol. 17, no. 5, pp. 633-56.

Cameron, D. (2012). 'Why the Eurozone will survive?'. Written presentation for the American Political Science Conference, Sept 2012, personal communication.

Der Spiegel, (2012). 'Eine front zwischen Nord und Süd', No. 32, 6 August, pp. 44-46.

Dullien, S. and Guérot, U. (2012). 'The long shadow of ordoliberalism: Germany's approach to the Euro crisis'. Policy Brief, February, London: European Council on Foreign Relations.

Euro Area Summit Statement 2012: 29 June, Brussels.

European Council (2012). 'Towards a genuine economic and monetary union', Report by the President of the European Council Herman Van Rompuy, Brussels, EUCO 120/12.

Financial Times (2012). 'Eurozone close to second slump', 15 August, p. 4.

—. (2012). 'Germans write off Greece', 3 Sept., p. 1.

—. (2012). 'Weidmann isolated as ECB plan approved', 7 Sept., p. 2.

Financial Times Deutschland (2012). 'Eichengreen gegen Sinn: Deutscher Aufruf empört Starökonomen'. 9 July.

Guérot, U. (2012). 'He who comes too late is punished by life', *European Council on Foreign Relations*, 11 July, Available:

http://ecfr.eu/blog/entry/he_who_comes_too_late_is_punished_by_life [20 July 2012)

Habermas, J. Sigmar, G,., Bofinger P., and Nida-Rümelin, J. (2012). 'Einspruch gegen die Fassadendemokratie', *Frankfurter Allgemeine Zeitung,* vol. 4, no. 8, p. 33.

Hall, P. and Soskice, D. (2001): *Varieties of capitalism*, The Institutional Foundation of Comparative Advantage. Oxford: Oxford University Press.

Heise, A. (2012). 'Governance without government or: The Euro crisis and what went wrong with European Economic Governance', Discussion Paper,. ISSN, 1868-4947/32. Zentrum für Ökonomische und Soziologische Studien. Universität Hamburg.

Issing, O. (2000). 'Walter Eucken: Vom Primat der Währungsunion', Vortrag: Freiburg Walter Eucken Institut, 17 March, Available: http://www.ecb.int [20. September 2000].

Issing, O. (2012) 'Europe's political union is an idea worthy of satire', *Financial Times*,www.ft.com, [29 July 2012].

Leonard, M. and Zielonka, J. (2012). 'A Europe of incentives: How to regain the trust of citizens and markets', June, London: European Council on Foreign Relations.

Liebert, U. (2011). 'Reconciling market with social Europe? The EU under the Lisbon Treaty', in Schiek, D., Liebert, U. and Schneider, H. (eds.), *European Economic and Social Constitutionalism after the Treaty of Lisbon*. Cambridge: Cambridge University Press, 47-73.

Mügge, D. (2006). 'Reordering the marketplace: Competition politics in European finance', *Journal of Common Market Studies*, ωol. 44, no. 5, pp. 991-1022.

Negt, O. (2012). *Gesellschaftsentwurf Europa*. Göttingen: Steifl/ifa

Sally, R. (1996). 'Ordoliberalism and the social market: Classical political economy from Germany', *New Political Economy,* vol. 1, no. 2, pp. 233-257.

Scharpf, F. (2012). 'Erosion der delegitimation in der EU durch eine soziale Krise'. Thesen. Presentation at the Summer Symposium, 'Soziales Europa unter den Bedingungen der Krise', 21 August, University of Düsseldorf,.

Schäuble, W. (2012). 'How to protect EU taxpayers against bank failures?', *Financial Times*, 31 August, p.7.

Sinn, H.-W. and Krämer, W. *(2012). Protestaufruf. Der offene Brief der Ökonomen im Wortlaut', Frankfurter* Allgemeine Zeitung. Wirtschaft. 7 July.

The *Economist* (2012). 'German economists. In a momentous tiff. Germany's economists bicker publicly about the euro crisis', 4 August, Available: www.economist.com/node(/21559964/ [10 August 2012].

Véron, N. (2012). 'Challenges of Europe's Fourfold Union'. Prepared statement before the U.S. Senate Committee on Foreign Relations: Subcommittee on European Affairs. Hearing on 'the Future of the Eurozone: Outlook and Lessons', 1 August 2012, pp. 1-7

Young, B. and Semmler, W. (2011). 'The European sovereign debt crisis: Is Germany to blame?', *German Politics and Society*, vol. 29, no. 1, pp. 1-24

Young, B. (2013). 'Neoliberalismus - Laissez-Faire – Ordoliberalismus', in Wullweber, J., Behrends, M., and Graf A. (cds.), *Theorien der internationalen Politischen Ökonomie*, Wiesbaden: VSA (forthcoming)

Zimmermann, H. (2010). 'Varieties of global financial governance? British and German approaches to financial market regulation', in Helleiner E., Pagliari, S. and Zimmermann, H.(eds.), *Global finance in crisis*, London/New York: Routledge, pp. 121-136.

CHAPTER TWO

THE EUROPEAN MONETARY UNION: AN UNFOLDING DISASTER?

J. MAGNUS RYNER
KING'S COLLEGE LONDON

Abstract

Far from being the result of some error or mistake, the Eurozone crisis is the consequence of the over-determined ideology and interests that shaped the monetary union in the first place. Eurozone crisis management continues to be shaped by these interests and attendant ideology, with dire social consequences as documented in other chapters of this volume.

Introduction

The notion of unfolding is nowadays normally eschewed in the social sciences, and for good reasons. It is seen as resting on a particular outmoded 19th century evolutionary conception of temporality. As Andrew Sayer suggests (1992: 122), conceptions such as these rest on assumptions about intrinsic and extrinsic closure of social systems that only rarely obtain. In other words, the identities and external conditions of social objects are rarely as stable as evolutionary conceptions presuppose. Hence, the postulate of evolutionary mechanisms that generate predictable effects are in most instances implausible. Not the least, the capacity of social agents to reflect on their social existence and their capacity to learn are invoked in that regard.

Yet, it is advisable not to forget the basic structuralist insight that a measure of elision and repression is a necessary precondition of social life (e.g. Eagleton, 1991). This may give socio-economic and socio-political processes a degree of determinacy and even a teleological quality after all. Here, I suggest that this is the case with the unfolding disaster that is the

European Monetary Union, which, in the last few years, has manifested itself as the Eurozone crisis.

In making this argument, I will begin by outlining the broad contours of Eurozone crisis management as it crystallized in 2012. The objective here is to register the elision in question[1]. I will then account for the unfolding disaster, starting with an analysis of the conjuncture that the Eurozone has found itself after the G20 Summit in London in 2009 and then proceeding to a broader historical-structural level, where I account for the co-determining ideology and interests that have shaped the Eurozone.

Eurozone crisis management

By January 31, 2012, the European Council had agreed to the so-called Fiscal Compact (European Council, 2012). Together the so-called "Six Pack", the "Euro Stability Plus" Agreement, and the Europe 2020 long-term reform agenda, these were the *quid pro quo* for the so-called European Stability Mechanism (ESM) and the precondition for the massive injections of liquidity into the European banking system that the ECB administered under its so-called Long Term Refinancing Operations (LTRO).

The Fiscal Compact is an attempt to resuscitate and firm up the 1996 Growth and Stability Pact (GSP), which in turn sought to lock in the fiscal Maastricht Convergence Criteria once the Euro had been launched. Here, it is worthwhile to recall that the GSP had been broken by France and Germany in November 2003, when overly anaemic growth rates had undermined their capacity to meet the 3 percent deficit target. Since that time—when the Council refused to enact disciplinary measures—the GSP had been a fudge, and the Fiscal Compact most certainly removes any ambiguities about norms and rules pertaining to fiscal rectitude. Compared to the 3 percent norm of the GSP, in the Fiscal Compact, structural deficits of member states may not exceed 0.5 percent of GDP. This norm can only be infringed in "deep recessions" and "exceptional circumstances". When member states exceed the 0.5 percent threshold—and it is worthwhile to note that at the time of the inception of the Fiscal Compact only Finland and Estonia had not exceeded 0.5 percent—the Excessive Deficit Procedure is activated automatically. This is in contrast to the GSP, when a qualified majority vote was required to activate it (and hence it was not activated in the case of France and Germany in 2003).

When in the Excessive Deficit Procedure, member states are required to enter into Economic Partnership Programmes with the EU. These are to be detailed descriptions of macroeconomic *as well as structural* reforms to be undertaken by the member state in question. Progress reports on the implementation of the Economic Partnership Programmes are to be regularly submitted to the European Commission and the Council for surveillance and endorsement. Notably, the Economic Partnership Programmes are to be encoded in EU law, with all that that entails in terms of Direct Effect, Supremacy of EU law and State Liability. Claims of infringement can be made by the European Commission or any other member state, and should the ECB find the offender guilty, then a penalty of up to 0.1 percent of GDP is to be paid into the ESM.

Whilst these norms and rules cannot be faulted on their clarity, they have been subject to criticism well beyond the usual suspects of heterodox economists and critical political economists, to include significant segments of pundits in the financial press. The concern can be summarised in a basic question: From where is final effective aggregate demand going to come in the Eurozone? The Eurozone crisis is a metamorphosis of the global financial crisis that started in US subprime housing markets in 2007, and started when state bailouts transformed private debt into public debt in an effort to save the financial system from meltdown. This, however, put the public debt of some countries, namely Portugal, Italy, Ireland, Greece and Spain, under stress as the confidence in their capacity to service their debt waned resulting in a deteriorating balance of payments and a spread in bond yields, which further increases costs of servicing the debt and hence undermines confidence further. The EU crisis management regime envisages a simultaneous reduction of both private and public debt, and hence balance can only be ensured in the form of massive balance of payments surpluses. But how are the so-called PIIGS going to achieve this, when it would require the elimination of a relative unit labour cost disadvantage of 20 percent with the German economy, which has an inflation rate of 1 percent? This can only happen through deflation, which is certain to lead to a collapse of public revenues, which in turn reinforces a debt trap. The classical adjustment mechanism in such a situation is devaluation of the currency, but it is of course exactly this that is not possible in a monetary union. It is nevertheless the objective need for a devaluation that has been undermining the credibility of the euro in financial markets. Hence, the recurring pattern of inadequate political agreements followed by further financial turbulence. To date only massive ECB interventions now also in sovereign bond markets (so called "Outright Monetary Transactions" or OMTs)—a process which has taken EMU way beyond the intention and spirit, if not the letter, of the Maastricht Agreement—have prevented a meltdown. Whilst these interventions by the ECB have calmed the waters for the moment, we are far away from institutional equilibrium as the current and fraught process of a banking union indicates.

The conjunctural context

The aforementioned, and ultimately unsustainable, crisis management measures only make sense with reference to the strange conjuncture that the Eurozone has experienced since 2009, when the London G20 Summit redressed the most acute symptoms of the global financial crisis. It set the stage for an export-led recovery in northern EU member states, namely in Germany, Austria, Netherlands and the Nordic countries, with a strong high-value manufacturing sector, niche services or even raw materials sector. These member states managed to take advantage of demand-pull from emerging economies that at least temporarily and partially offset the shortfall of American demand as the US underwent its own adjustment process. Their export-led recovery made it possible to dissociate the emerging troubles in the southern member states of the Eurozone from the financial crisis, and made it possible to evade hard questions about the extent to which design flaws of the Eurozone had been contained only because of the financial bubble. It short, it made it possible to represent the crisis through stereotyped tropes about lazy and corrupt southerners and as one of lack of competitiveness.

But to assume that the emerging markets are ready to take over America's role, as the consumer and balancer of accounts of last resort for the Eurozone, is fanciful. Whilst developments in Asia have been remarkable over the last couple of decades, these economies are not ready to replace America, and there are strong indications that the demand pull of the last couple of years is itself based on an unsustainable bubble (*The Economist*, 2012). Consequently, problems of anaemic and uneven growth in the Eurozone and the evident impossibility of maintaining a monetary union without fiscal transfer mechanisms will continue to haunt the Eurozone.

The Eurozone: Flawed premises, self-serving interests and power

This brings us back to the ideological elisions that underpinned, provided the rationale, and legitimated the Maastricht design of the Eurozone as well as the interests that these serve.

The chief of these is the Efficient Market Hypothesis. The idea that it would be possible to sustain a monetary union on the basis of a supranational monetary policy based on the sound money principle, whilst keeping fiscal policy intergovernmental, was based on hubristic faith in the self-equilibriating powers of the single European market that was being created for goods, labour, but above all financial services. Nowhere is this more clearly manifested than in the Sapir Report (2003), which articulated the intellectual rationale for the Lisbon Agenda. According to the Sapir Report, self-regulating financial markets, flanked by flexible labour markets, will allocate capital rationally to business investments in high-tech and high value-added sectors. This would not only make Europe, in the infamously immodest language of the Lisbon Agenda, the most dynamic and competitive part of the world, endogenous optimal currency area theory also predicted that it would automatically resolve the (non-) optimum currency area problem (e.g. Frankel & Rose, 2002).

Hence, it can be recalled that the accumulated current account deficits in Southern Europe were not until recently a source of concern. Blanchard and Giavazzi (2002), for instance, saw them as the natural consequence of capital inflows and in the long run they would balance themselves out. The underlying premise was that market actors were taking advantage of price-competitive factor endowments in Southern Europe and that in the long run, investments would make these economies more competitive presumably by savings flowing into high tech investments via efficient disintermediated financial markets a la the Sapir Report. That these financial resources rather fed a real estate bubble that burst is a fact that refutes the efficient market hypothesis and which undermines the premises of the Maastricht Design of the EMU. It is above all the implications of this destruction of capital that we are currently living with, and the incidence of the cost is born disproportionally and outrageously by the most vulnerable in Europe's periphery.

From this perspective one can pass the same verdict on the Fiscal Compact as was once passed on the last Bourbon King of France in the wake of the 1830 Revolution: they have forgotten nothing and learnt nothing. It is, however, also from this perspective that the Fiscal Compact and the other crisis management measures become further intelligible. From this intellectual perspective, given that markets remain imperfect (as Polanyi, 1957, reminds us they are bound to do so), the problem resides in imperfect implementation. Hence, the remedy is more of the same failed policies: further privatizations, further market flexibility, but now also even firmer constraints on fiscal policy (e.g. Issing, 2012). This is a paradigm that never opens itself up for falsification, and hence is very reminiscent of totalitarian reasoning (Patomäki, 2013). The objective of the measures does not seem to be above all about restoring macroeconomic balance but rather to, a la Naomi Klein's (2007) notion of "shock doctrine", use the crisis as an opportunity to move the limits of the possible even further towards a logic for the commodification of social life.

The prevalence of these ideas in policy-making circles is not *sui generis.* From the pioneering work of Kees van der Pijl (1984) to the recent award-winning volume by Jamie Peck (2011), there is now a weighty political economy literature that quite appropriately has categorised them as forming a neoliberal paradigm which, with local variations, serves as rationale for a finance-dominated transnational capitalism. If Fordist capitalism of the immediate post-World War II period was based on the integration of mass production and mass consumption underwritten by productivity growth through collective bargaining regimes and welfare state expansion, then finance-led capitalism draws on information technology to return to a more classical capitalism of labour market flexibility and privatisation. Final aggregate demand has been maintained through an alternative mechanism, namely the extension of debt underwritten by the increase of asset values (e.g. Montgomerie, 2008). However, by the mid-2000s, expanded reproduction had taken market actors into ever riskier segments; hence, the depth of the financial crisis, which spread through the complex packaging of securitized financial products.

But there is also a geopolitical angle to this story, which underlines the tendency towards disaster in the Eurozone. Both Fordist and finance-led capitalism were sustained through US hegemonic leadership although the modalities of leadership were very different (Cafruny & Ryner, 2007). Whereas, US leadership in the Fordist period was based on support and granting a degree of autonomy to other social formations (the Marshall Plan, capital market regulation provisions in Bretton Woods), leadership in the finance-dominated period was more narrowly self-interested, and based on displacing externalities from the US to other parts of the world (see also Henning, 1994). Finance-led capitalism rested in that regard on the Dollar as a reserve currency and the unique manner in which global financial markets were made in the image of the specificities of the American social settlements, assigning a central role to retail finance, home ownership and private pensions (e.g. Seabrooke, 2001; Konings, 2011). European business interests were progressively integrated into these capital circuits, but were then at the same time partially dislocated from the specificities of European capitalism, based on different more coordinated forms of innovation, more public forms of social insurance. There was, in other words, a lack of institutional complementarity between finance-dominated capitalism and European institutions that resulted in

Europe sharing US vulnerabilities but not its dynamism (Stockhammer, 2008). This was further compounded by uneven development and the weakness of EU institutions in dealing with them. Nicos Poulantzas presciently anticipated these developments (1974) and predicted that it would make it increasingly difficult to maintain social cohesion in Europe.

Conclusion

Other contributions in this volume document the immense human costs, and dire social consequences of Eurozone crisis management, as well as the anatomy of the destabilising social conflicts that these have generated especially in Southern Europe. The standard establishment response to such findings are to acknowledge them, but only as an unfortunate consequence of necessary adjustments, which in the long run will put Europe on a more prosperous footing. Here, I have questioned such arguments. I have suggested that it is symptomatic of an economistic rationality that has been found wanting. Indeed, there are good reasons to see this rationality as part of the problem that has generated the Eurozone disaster. At the same time, ideas do not float freely. This is a rationality that resonates with dominant interests in finance-led capitalism, which crisis-management seeks to rescue, consolidate and deepen. It could be reasserted in a peculiar conjuncture after the London Summit in 2009, which sharply divided the Eurozone into a northern core and a southern periphery.

To reduce this disparity, a number of critical policy recommendations are indicated. Among these can be included: (1) a reduction of the power and size of the financial sector, including measures already in the Euromemorandums 2011/2012 (e.g., promote separate commercial and investment banks, ban most derivatives, post all securities trading in public platforms, set up non-profit banks, tax financial transactions, establish public-owned credit-rating agencies) (2) the implementation of a common EU macro-economic policy (e.g., ECB as a lender of last resort and creation of EU-wide fiscal transfer mechanisms that require an expansion of the EU budget to 10% of GDP) (3) the adoption of an EU-wide incomes policy based on productivity-growth in deficit countries and above productivity-growth in the surplus countries—the percentages to be determined. The latter has been proposed by researchers at the tripartite WSI/Hans Bockler Foundation meeting in Dusseldorf (2004). Beyond these, there should be provisions for debt audits and selective defaults, as well as for the use of structural funds to promote high-tech investments, especially in the energy renewables—the urgency of which was brought home to the author during the 2012 conference on island of Lesvos.

Notes

[1] With his concept of "commodity fetishism", Karl Marx offered a powerful account of how elision works in economic relations to produce a degree of determinacy. The Frankfurt School rescued this concept from evolutionary theories, and for instance Adorno and Benjamin analysed its permeation in the cultural sphere. Whilst it is beyond this essay to elaborate the point, the analysis of policy-ideology that I offer here is based on the complex interplay between commodity fetishism and *Vergesellschaftung*—a very particular conception of "socialisation" that Marx as well as Weber elaborated upon in *The Grundrisse* and *Economy and Society* respectively (see van der Pijl, 1998; Sohn-Rethel, 1971).

References

Blanchard, O. and Giavazzi F. (2002). 'Current account deficits in the Euro area: The end of the Feldstein-Horioka Puzzle?,' MIT Department of Economics Working Paper 03-05.

Cafruny, A. and Ryner, M. (2007). *Europe at bay: In the shadow of US hegemony,* Boulder: Lynne Rienner.

Eagleton, T. (1991). *Ideology,* London: Verso.

European Council (2012). *Treaty on stability, Coordination and governance in the Economic and Monetary Union,* Brussels: European Council.

Frankel, J. and Rose, A. (2002). 'An estimate of the effect of common currencies on trade and income,' *The Quarterly Journal of Economics* , vol. 117, no.2, May, pp. 437-66.

Henning, R. (1994). *Currencies and politics in the United States, Germany and Japan,* Washington DC: Institute for International Economics.

Issing, O. (2012). *Wie wir die Euro retten und Europa stärken* , Kulmbach: Börsenmedien.

Klein, N. (2007). *The shock doctrine: The rise of disaster capitalism,* New York: Penguin.

Konings, M. (2011). *The development of American finance,* Cambridge: Cambridge University Press.

Montgomerie, J. (2008). 'Bridging the critical divide: Global finance, financialisation and contemporary capitalism,' *Contemporary Politics,* vol. 14, no. 3, October, pp. 233-52.

Patomäki, H. (2013) *The great Eurozone disaster,* London: Zed Press.

Peck, J. (2011). *Constructions of neoliberal reason* , Oxford: Oxford University Press.

Polanyi, K. (1957). *The Great Transformation,* Boston: Beacon Press.

Poulantzas, N. (1974). 'Internationalisation of capitalist relations and the nation state,' *Economy and Society, vol.* 2, no. 1, July, pp. 145-79.

Sapir, A. et. al. (2004). *An agenda for a growing Europe: The Sapir Report,* Oxford: Oxford University Press.

Sayer, A. (1992). *Methods in the social sciences: A realist approach,*2nd edition, London: Routledge.

Seabrooke, L. (2001). *US power in international finance: The victory of dividends,* Basingstoke: Palgrave Macmillan.

Sohn-Rethel, A. (1971). *Materialistische erkenntniskritik und vergesellschaftung der arbeit,* Berlin: Merve.

Stockhammer, E. (2008). 'Some stylized facts on the finance-dominated accumulation regime,' *Competition & Change, vol.* 12, no. 2, June, pp. 184-202.

The Economist (2012). 'Emerging markets: Dream on?', Available: http://www.economist.com/node/21559336 [21 July 2012].

Van der Pijl, K. (1984). *The making of an Atlantic ruling class,* London: Verso

—. (1998). *Transnational classes and international relations,* London: Routledge.

CHAPTER THREE

THE EUROPEANIZATION OF DISTRIBUTIONAL CONFLICTS WITHIN THE EUROCRISIS

GEORG VOBRUBA
UNIVERSITY OF LEIPZIG

Abstract

What impact has the Eurocrisis on the emerging European society? In order to deal with this question the chapter focuses on the significance of conflicts for social integration. Introducing the common European currency means abandoning the exchange mechanism and intensifying competition, hence replacing indifference between the people of different countries by cooperation and conflict. At present, conflicts simultaneously taking place within single nation states as well as between them cause a complex conflict constellation. This constellation is open to populist political exploitation, but it is also likely to spur the emergence of a European society.

I. Introduction: The common currency and the emergence of a complex conflict structure

The Eurocrisis unfolded in 2009 and is still unsolved. In the course of the crisis not only remarkable economic differences among the Euro-member states became manifest, but also serious distributional conflicts emerged. We observe conflicts and dispute within several member states as well as between them. Think of protests against wages cuts, against unemployment, or against cuts in the welfare systems which are directed against national governments. And there are protests against austerity policies and the loss of national sovereignty directed against the European Union and other member states. Simultaneously, we face protest and opposition to remissions of debts and to different attempts to create a so-called fiscal and transfer Union. This opposition might be less noisy, but it is important anyway. It is represented by some newspapers, by several groups taking the fiscal pact as a cause for action at the constitutional court, by some parties in several middle and North European countries.

It is this connection between economic disparities and social tensions that makes the crisis of the common currency appear as a severe challenge for European integration as a whole. It becomes clear at first sight that this constellation is a challenge not only for politics but also for sociology. The reason, in a nutshell, is that the Eurocrisis made relationships between the people (or between groups of actors) in the EU manifest and revealed a remarkable potential for conflict. Concurrently, a complex and unclear conflict structure became visible. This makes orientation in theory and practice complicated.

II. Conceptions of social conflict through time

Social conflict is a key concept in order to understand modern society. Thus, it doesn't come as a surprise that the development of Sociology is centered on social conflict.

Sociology is a relatively young scientific discipline. It dates back to the second half of the 19th century, and its development was triggered by manifold experiences of rapid and fundamental social change particularly in Europe at that time. Contemporaries perceived the outcome of the social change towards capitalist industrial societies as an overall disorder, pre- or proto-sociological observers reacted with blueprints of new kinds of order. One might think of Riehl and his attempts to reconstruct the traditional family, of Tönnies and his focus on *Gemeinschaft*, of Durkheim and his interest in values and solidarity as conditions of the stability and cohesion of a society. But think also of Marx and his theory of a transition from disordered capitalism to the new order of a (*Gemeinschafts*-like) classless society. These first generations of sociologists were observing conflicts but focusing on stability.

The stability-oriented sociology, culminating in the seminal work of Talcott Parsons, centered on the question: what the elements of a system contribute to the stability and reproduction of this system. In all these approaches, conflicts are seen as risky and mainly as a deviation. From this results a preference of values over interests and the hope that society can be integrated by normative consensus. Habermas' "Theory of communicative action" might be seen as the last and most elaborated approach in this general perspective.

A rivaling approach dates back to Georg Simmel. He focused on social relations as the basic principle of society, and in particular on social conflict as an important expression of it. And what is more, in his famous chapter "Der Streit" in his book "*Soziologie*", first published in 1908 (Simmel, 1992), he emphasized that quarrels not only have to be taken as normal in modern society, but also that they have an important impact on society: First of all, quarrels represent a certain kind of social integration, for they establish a closer relationship than mutual indifference would. Thus, quarrels contribute to social integration. They are fueled by social tensions but also contribute to their dismantling. Second, quarrels transcend the bipolarity of social relations. And finally, and perhaps most important, quarrels trigger social change. They lead to new arrangements, becoming manifest in new institutions and providing new opportunities and new restrictions. Thus, without quarrels social change and progress are hardly possible.

At least in German sociology, Georg Simmel remained the only important theorist of social conflict for decades. Admittedly, in the 20th century there was an intense debate in the tradition of Karl Marx, focusing on conflict rather than on its outcome, the classless society. On the one hand, this debate influenced more political economy than sociology, and on the other hand, it was preoccupied by a particular conflict pattern, namely the struggle of classes. Conflict theory as a core element of a sociological theory of society reemerged after Talcott Parsons' stability-centered approach was attacked by the very young and so self-confident Ralf Dahrendorf. Dahrendorf (1959) conceptualized social conflict without *a priori* ticking to the conflict between labour and capital. He made the point that even in a capitalist class society various kinds of cleavages of interest, and thus different conflicts, have to be taken into account.

It is exactly in this respect, that the Eurocrisis represents a challenge as well as an opportunity for Sociology: Analyzing new patterns of conflicts emerging in the Eurocrisis promises both a better understanding of the potential impact of the crisis on the further European integration and an understanding of the relationship between social conflict and the development of a new European society. In order to make this clear, it is necessary to have a closer look into the logic and the development of the Eurocrisis.

III. The Eurozone: From a win-win to a win-lose situation

From its very beginning it was clear that the common currency is a "technically and politically … highly complex experiment" (Padoa-Schioppa, 1994: 163). It was obvious that the Eurozone is far from being an optimal currency area. But political actors at that time expected economic pressure to spur on less productive members of the Eurozone, hence equalizing competitiveness and standards of living. And indeed, for ten years it looked like the Eurozone economic development would meet these expectations. The good experiences with the euro fuelled the public opinion that European integration and the common currency in particular are a positive sum game, serving the interests of everybody. Conflict was hardly an issue (see the debate between Bach, Rhodes, Szalai and Vobruba, 2003; see also Marks and Steenbergen, 2004). Nevertheless, these good experiences were deceptive. What happened?

Between around 2000 and 2008 the credit costs all over the Eurozone narrowed remarkably. The difference between the interest rates in the Euromember states—the so called spread—almost disappeared (SVR 2010). This led to a constant flow of cheap money into the less productive Euromembers, either via private credit or via public debt. Permanent export surpluses in high productive Euromembers provided a steady supply of capital for less productive members. As a consequence, the banking sector expanded and standards of living rose, for imports could be easily financed. It is worth to note that for almost one decade this constellation suited different interests. It offered chances for export, it provided an opportunity for investment, it dampened distributional conflicts and facilitated governing, and it raised the living standards almost everywhere. Ironically, just workers in highly competitive export countries took relatively less advantage from this constellation, for a high degree of wage discipline and relevant deregulation were seen as necessary in order to support the export-oriented economy. With the subprime crisis and the collapse of Lehman Brothers, things changed almost overnight (European Commission, 2009; Preunkert and Vobruba, 2012).

What are the relevant characteristics of the Eurocrisis (see also Vobruba, 2012)? The crisis started as a problem between banks and debtors. Then it turned out that at least some creditors were "system relevant". This means that their problems not only had consequences for themselves, but were also threatening to contaminate other economic actors or even national economies as a whole. The overwhelming importance of this sudden realization and its impact on the way the crisis was handled is obvious, as "contagion" soon became the leading metaphor in the Eurocrisis (Vobruba, 2012a).

As soon as these problems no longer were problems just between creditors and debtors, the constellation of actors in the crisis changed from a two to a three poles structure. In other words, the States became guarantors and were involved in the crisis. At the latest, the Eurocrisis had turned into a political and social problem. As a consequence of the crisis and the way it was handled, two phenomena fundamentally emerged. First, it appeared that the monetary volume in virtual circulation exceeded by far what was really there. And second, several vicious circles were triggered off. Rising credit rates led to soaring public deficits and thus even higher credit rates. Unsound credit practices brought the banks to the verge of collapse, forcing governments to bail them out, exponentially increasing public deficits in the process. Austerity measures, instituted in order to bring public deficits under control, led to shrinking GDPs, thus increasing the public debt ratio, even if debts themselves were diminishing in absolute terms.

IV. From "political" conflicts between nations to "distributional" conflicts between peoples

At this point, the relation between the common currency and distributional conflict becomes clear. Imagine a situation without the euro. Trade between countries with different levels of productivity would lead to an export surplus, mirrored by a strong demand for the exporting country's currency. This would eventually lead to a revaluation of the exporting country's currency, and to a devaluation of the importing country's currency. Devaluation implies a shrinking purchasing power (because of comparatively high prices for imported goods) at home, but an increase in purchasing power for people from "hard currency" countries, who would enjoy cheaper imports and tourism services from the less competitive countries. All in all devaluations provide a competitive advantage for less productive economies. In this constellation—two countries, two currencies—the currency exchange mechanism works as an interrupter of interdependencies. It creates a constellation of economic trade without social entanglements, leading to transnational social indifference and nationally framed social conflicts.

Nevertheless, some caveats have to be added: first, this is not to say that transnational trade does not cause distributional conflicts at all. In less productive countries, rising prices for imported goods might lead to discontent and claims for higher wages, thus spurring inflation. In more productive countries, wage discipline aiming to secure exports also might cause dissatisfaction. But all these conflicts unfold within each country, not between them. From the point of view of an export country, an abrupt and strong devaluation might appear as an illegitimate advantage that could provoke retaliation. But these are political conflicts between countries, not distributional conflicts between people across borders.

V. Distributional conflicts: Toward higher EU integration?

A relevant conclusion can be drawn. The decisive moment was, when third players came into the game. As soon as the states were (or felt) forced to function as guarantors, the problems between investors and debtors changed into complex relations between the economic and the political system; between tax payers, welfare recipients, financial institutions, etc. in different countries. Thus, as I already mentioned, unclear cleavages and conflicts came into being. Of course, I cannot offer more than a rough woodcut. But perhaps a basic structure of it can be identified (see Figure 3-1).

Figure 3-1. Class cleavages before and after the adoption of the common currency

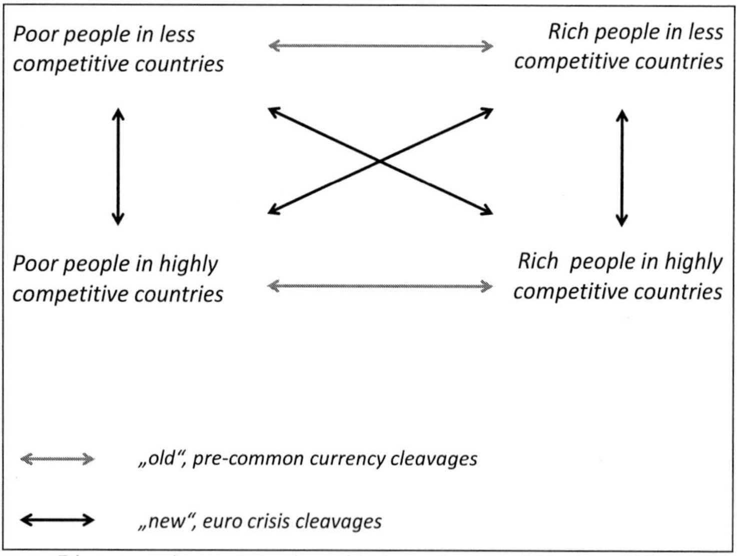

Source: Diagrammatic representation with the assistance of Francesca Montemaggi, Cardiff University, UK.

Admittedly, this is an oversimplification in many respects. It ignores all nuances between "rich" and "poor", as well as, say, the possibility of individually highly competitive enterprises in a less competitive economy (and vice versa). But as a first approximation to systematising a complex constellation, this scheme seems to be quite useful. It demonstrates that the constellation which comes with the common currency triggers conflicts that follow neither a logic of class, nor a logic of nation.

The scheme reveals one main characteristic of the Europeanization of distributional conflicts: namely, that the conflict constellation entails two dimensions. The European Union faces (a) conflicts about the frame of conflicts (Fehmel, 2010) and (b) new patterns of distributional conflicts.

Conflicts about the frame of conflicts in the crisis

Conflicts about the frame of conflicts are about the question, who has to take part in a conflict. The rhetoric of "contagion" (Vobruba, 2012a: 72ff.) indicates that even countries at a bigger distance are involved in the Eurocrisis, and that they are forced somehow to invest in its solution. "Contagion" triggers self-interested aid: I help you because otherwise your problem will become my problem. A rivaling but less influential interpretation focuses on building a "firewall". The metaphor of the firewall indicates the attempt to distance oneself; to place oneself outside the crisis.

Conflicts about the frame of conflicts lead to "unbounded cleavages" (Bach, 2006), obviously causing severe problems of protesters against austerity politics to find the appropriate target for their protest, as for instance, banners carried at the occasion of demonstrations at Syntagma Square (Athens, Greece) reveal (Petropoulos 2012).

New patterns of distributional conflicts

Most likely is the development of triangle-constellations. Triangle conflict constellations are difficult to survey both for participants and for observing sociologists. Triangle-constellations are likely to unfold, because conflicts unfold simultaneously between different groups within the national frame, as well as between different economies (represented by their nations). At present, all organized interests at the European level, be it business, workers or voters, are too weak to overcome national rivalries. Thus, far from a revival of class conflict, the common currency led to a new constellation in which economic and political disparities between national societies are carried out as conflicts between the poor(er) parts of these societies. In other words, the complex conflict constellation is open for populist exploitation.

VI. Summary and conclusions

Let me summarize. The introduction of the euro meant abandoning the exchange mechanism between the national currencies. It is often said that European integration proceeds "without society" (Bach 2008), that integration at the institutional level is deepening without any progress at the societal level. And in this respect, the introduction of the common currency is seen as a prominent case in point. But consider this: The common currency has sparked intensified cooperation and conflict in a wider institutional frame. Never in history had there been such close relations between member states and people in the EU, nor had there ever been such a strong sense of mutual dependence (albeit not of solidarity) within Europe.

In the course of the Euro crisis, it has turned out that with the loss of the currency exchange mechanism, indifference was to be replaced by quarrel. This causes a complex conflict constellation, because the European Union in its present shape is hardly prepared to regulate distributional conflicts at the European level, due to the lack of a genuinely European public sphere (Hepp et al., 2009) as well as to conflict regulating European institutions. But in the light of a conflict theoretical approach, it also can hardly be ignored that the present conflict constellation is a remarkable step towards social Europeanization. It is an element in the construction of a European society (Vobruba, 2012b) and able to be seen as temporary. Therefore, we have to deal with the Europeanization of distributional conflict not as a danger but as a manifestation of a society in the making, though the present conflict constellation bears political danger. Denying this conclusion would imply a definition of society which equates it with the absence of conflicting interests, thus identifying social integration with harmony–which would be an absurd claim, at least in the modern world.

References

Bach, M. (2006). 'Unbounded cleavages. Grenzabbau und die Europäisierung sozialer Ungleichheit', in Eigmüller, M. and Vobruba, G. (eds.), *Grenzsoziologie. Die politische Strukturierung des Raumes.* Wiesbaden: VS, pp. 145-156.

—. (2008). *Europa ohne Gesellschaft. Politische Soziologie der Europäischen Integration,* Wiesbaden: VS.

Dahrendorf, R. (1959). *Class and class conflict in industrial society,* Stanford: Stanford University Press.

European Commission (2009). Directorate General Economic and Financial Affairs, *Economic Crisis in Europe: Causes, Consequences and Responses.* European Economy No. 7/2009.

Fehmel, T. (2011). *Konflikte um den Konfliktrahmen.* Wiesbaden: VS.

Hepp, A. et al. (2009). 'Europe beyond the crisis? Citizens' (re)actions on the multi-segmentation of the European public sphere', in Carpentier, N. et al. (eds.), *Communicative approaches to politics and ethics in Europe,* Tartu: Tartu University Press, pp. 69-84.

Marks, G.; M. and Steenbergen, R. (eds.) (2004). *European integration and political conflict,* Cambridge: Cambridge University Press.

Mundell, R. A. (1961). 'A theory of optimal currency areas', *American Economic Review*, vol. 51, no. 4, pp. 657-665.

Padoa-Schioppa, T. (1994). *The road to monetary union in Europe,* Oxford: Clarendon Press.

Petropoulos, N. (2012). 'A Socio-Political Profile and the Political Impact of the Greek Indignados: An Explanatory Study', Paper presented at the Conference 'The Dept Crisis in the Eurozone: Social Impacts', 13-14 September, Mytilene, Greece.

Preunkert, J. and Vobruba, G. (2012). 'Die Eurokrise. Konsequenzen der defizitären Institutionalisierung der gemeinsamen Währung, in Kraemer, K. and Nessel, S. (eds.), *Entfesselte Finanzmärkte. Soziologische Analysen des modernen Kapitalismus,* Frankfurt a. M, New York: Campus, pp. 201-223.

Simmel, G. (1992). *Soziologie.* Frankfurt a. M.: Suhrkamp.

SVR (2010). 'Sachverständigenrat zur Begutachtung der gesamtwirtschaftlichen Entwicklung', *Jahresgutachten 2010/2011. Chancen für einen stabilen Aufschwung.* Wiesbaden.

Vobruba, G. (2004). 'The enlargement crisis of the European Union', *Journal of European Social Policy*, vol. 13, no. 1, pp. 35-49.

—. (2012). 'A complex conflict constellation: Distributional conflict in the euro crisis'. Available: http://www.opendemocracy.net/author/georg-vobruba [15 October 2013]

—. (2012a). *Kein Gleichgewicht. Die Ökonomie in der Krise,* Weinheim, Basel: Beltz-Juventa.

—. (2012b). 'The Social Construction of the European Society', in Dahms H. and Hazelrigg, L. (eds.), *Theorizing modern society as a dynamic process.* Emerald: Bingley, UK, pp. 263-279 .

CHAPTER FOUR

SOCIAL ACCUMULATION OF VALUE FOR ECONOMIC RECOVERY–RESEARCH MODEL (SAVER)

SOTIRIS CHTOURIS
UNIVERSITY OF THE AEGEAN
AND DEMOND SHONDELL MILLER
ROWAN UNIVERSITY

Abstract

The recent economic and social crisis, which has affected particularly hard the South European countries, raises the urgent question about the ways of achieving economic and social sustainability in both national and regional economies. In Greece, as well as in other South European countries, during the past decade, we witnessed a series of precursor phenomena to the current crisis. Indeed, the current economic crisis is the culmination of a long process of social, cultural and human capital gradually declining, in the framework of the southern welfare model, provoking a strong internal imbalance in the total value stock but also a consequent decline of societal trust in economic activity as such. The research model "SAVER" is inspired by Leontief's (1986) analysis and measurement of economic input and output (Input/Output I/O). This model, *mutatis mutandis,* will be used to evaluate total input and output in relation to different forms of capital, namely, Social, Cultural, Human, Natural and Economic, in order to measure the Total Social Value Stock at both individual and regional levels. A central hypothesis is that a thriving social organization requires an optimal and sustainable balance within the Total Social Value Stock. Social accumulation of values and the growth of Total Social Value Stock can lead to economic recovery in Greece and the South European countries that have been severely affected by recession and unemployment. The development of a Total Social Value Stock in society will also constitute an adequate response to counteract the spread of political right-wing extremism in Greece ("Golden Dawn") which is largely based on organized groups and communities with criminal practice and negative ("dark") social capital.

Introduction

A thriving social organization requires an optimal and sustainable balance within the *Total Social Value Stock (TSVS)*, as well as among different forms of capital that constitute it: Economic (Real, Financial), Social, Cultural, Human and Natural Capital. The research model is inspired by Leontief's (1986) analysis and measurement of economic input and output (Input/Output I/O). This model, *mutatis mutandis*, will be used to evaluate total input and output in relation to different forms of capital, in order to measure the *Total Social Value Stock* at both individual and regional level. The proposed research model uses mixed available methodology, namely, quantitative and qualitative, to gain insight into the highly heterogeneous and complex phenomenon of *capital transformation* and the generation of a *socioeconomic regional optimum*: Analysis and documentation of links in the chain of transformability and amelioration of different capital forms in the context of economic crisis. How social accumulation of values and growth of *Total Social Value Stock (TSVS)* can lead to economic recovery, as well as social and economic integration of young people in Southern Europe.

1. Transformability and amelioration of different capital forms in the context of an economic crisis

The recent economic and social crisis, which affects particularly hard the South European countries, raises the urgent question about the ways of achieving economic and social sustainability in both national and regional economies. The current economic crisis, which has been identified mostly as sovereign debt crisis and oversized public and private loans (state and households), also raises a crucial question, namely, how important values such as social solidarity and social cohesion can be preserved in these countries, in such a precarious economic environment, when powerful central powers of political and economic adjustment no longer function. The disintegration of the protective framework for national and regional economies, along with weak European economic cooperation, have generated not only social and political uncertainty but also a rapidly deteriorating process for countries such as Greece, Spain and Portugal that are not deemed to have an adequate level of competitiveness (Bennett,

2008; WEF, 2012). This degradation has come mostly from the reduction and devaluation of the productive workforce (Caffet et al., 2011:10), the sharp increase of unemployment, the malfunction of all state institutions, disputes over salaried work and working rights, the longstanding deficit of social capital in South Europe (Putnam, 1993; Maratou, 1999; Christoforou, 2003; Orpheas, 2005; Chtouris, 2006) and, last but not least, the pervading black economy/corruption phenomena, especially in countries such as Greece and Italy. At the same time, following the major economic melt-down that the global financial markets (Chtouris, 2004) triggered in the US and in Europe and in spite of the fact that the whole financial construction proved to be extremely irresponsible and self-serving, national governments resolutely set the course of their economic policies towards the goal of servicing public debt and balancing national budgets at all costs, namely, by imposing drastic austerity policies applied horizontally on all citizens. For the last two years, at least in Greece, the austerity programme has not managed to improve not even one of the problematic economic indicators; on the contrary, it has led to a deepening economic recession, high rates of unemployment, heightened political dissent, disintegration of political credibility and a sharp degradation of traditional social and political values. A characteristic feature of this development is the marked devaluation of human capital, especially that of young people, accompanied by dramatic increase of youth unemployment rates (Eurostat, European Commission "Youth in Europe", 2009) which, in December 2011, surpassed 51,1% in Greece, for the ages 15-24 and 28,7% for the ages 25-34 (ElStat, 2011), while in the third term of 2011, youth unemployment in Spain was 47,8%, in Portugal 29,9% and in Italy 28,2% (Eurostat, 2012). It is also a fact that entire regional economies have suffered a long deindustrialization and marginalisation process, depending more and more on external loans and imports. This has been the result of longstanding economic policies that relied on the production of goods and services that were not directed to cover real economic and social needs, but were mostly the result of cheap money circulation through multiple leverage of financial capitals.

In this context, demand for permanent consumer goods—a classic example being that of housing—developed vigorously in the last decades, since loan capitals and their derivatives via financial engineering (Neftci, 2008) were promptly available to consumers, mostly in the USA, Ireland, Iceland, and Spain, but also in South European countries, where productivity faltered and commercial deficit skyrocketed; in Spain it reached 4.4% of GDP, in Portugal 10.4% of GDP, while in Greece it climbed to 12.3% of GDP (Caffet et al. 2011: 9). Practices that in the past were considered at the limit of legitimacy were transformed, during the decades of 1990 and 2000, to undisputed economic policies, dominating the financial markets (Ferguson, 2010). As a result, households and national governments alike resorted to excessive borrowing, resulting in the accumulation of staggering debt. In the same context, in countries of South Europe such as Greece, Spain, Italy and Portugal, economic activity and political systems adjusted to the oversupply of cheap financial capital, thus allowing for the shrinking of their productive basis. Economic growth relied mostly on encouraging unbridled consumption on behalf of the middle classes, as well as on economic reliance on tertiary sector activities. This development produced a catalytic and deleterious effect on value relationships in the fields of production, reproduction and cultural structure at both national and international levels (Chtouris, 2004; SCDD, 2012). The economic system had to face the disintegration of the entire value context and the entailing conflict and strife among institutions and actors identified with them (Chtouris, 2008, 2006). Today, at the core of the current crisis are issues of legitimization of both parliamentary democracy and capitalist economy; indeed, the main challenge for western democratic systems has always been the safeguarding of an acceptable living standard for the general population, without exclusions. However, economic growth and production, during the last two decades at least, were guided mainly by a logic of circular expansion of financial values, at both national and global level, via financial engineering (Neftci, 2008) and, to a much lesser extent, by actual demand and satisfaction of economic and social needs. During this time, the financial value system disengaged itself from any other value system such as social and cultural capital, labour and human capital, as well as the preservation of natural capital. Undeniably, the current economic crisis has led to further environmental degradation, namely, overexploitation of vital and non-renewable resources, as debt servicing and deficit reduction override any other policy goal. Indeed, recently, a series of outrageous environmental measures have been taken by the government such as legalization of illegal housing and buildings, public infrastructure works with no accompanying environmental impact studies, private energy companies taking over alternative energy projects with no established environmental criteria, etc.

2. How the social accumulation of values can lead to economic recovery and social and economic integration of young people

We have witnessed in Greece, as well as in other South European countries, during the past decade, a series of precursor phenomena to the current crisis (Matsaganis, 1999; Arts and Gelissen, 2002; Aassve et al., 2006): sharp decline of social capital—already at low levels—(Putnam, 1993; Christofourou, 2003), low participation of cultural capital in everyday practice (Chtouris, 2012), as well as misplaced and asymmetric investment in human capital, mainly in the public sector, with no link to actual production needs. In contrast to traditional and pre-modern economies where these forms of capital found themselves in relative equilibrium (Chtouris, 1990, 2000; Chtouris and Papageorgiou, 2009), these new emerging forms of economic relations seem to be subordinated, almost exclusively, to the dominance of financial capitals, thus severely curtailing the role of all other forms of capital in social organization.

One could say, as further interpretation, that the current economic crisis is the culmination of a long process of social, cultural and human capital gradually declining in the framework of the southern welfare model (Ferrera, 1996), provoking a strong internal imbalance in the total value stock but also a consequent decline of societal trust in economic activity as such. Furthermore, a host of parallel phenomena such as a sharp increase of non-productive consumption (Steger, 2002), a lack of social control and social solidarity coupled with an absence of effective regulation to combat endemic corruption and black economy, further weakened the ability to set forward individual and collective strategies that would foster economic growth.

As a result, now, more than ever, South European youth—and more specifically Greek youth—seems to be increasingly excluded from any possibility of securing for itself participation in this value stock or securing any chance to create new values (economic, social, cultural). At the same time, these societies face an acute problem of radical de-legitimization of their political system, due to the pervasive influence that systemic corruption exercises on society as a whole. Indeed, scandals and large scale corruption during the administrations of Costas Simitis, Costas Karamanlis and Sylvio Berlusconi, manifest themselves via unlawful networks (Chtouris, 2004) involving party leaders, government or party officials, multinational corporations (e.g., Siemens) and the Church (e.g., Vatopedi, Greece). It is worth noting that an unspecified number of public servants and public administrations are also deeply entangled in these networks. The emergence of new forms of public political protest—a sort of hybrid activist movement such as the *"Indignados"* or other forms of spontaneous youth protest—do not seem to constitute collective vehicles that can bring about significant social change and reform (Chtouris & Zissi, 2012).

This development makes it all the more necessary to explore new methods and forms of policy intervention in order to restore balance among different forms of capital, aiming at restoring social cohesion and social well-being in the framework of recovery efforts in South European countries. The above reflection touches on the main concern of this research model, as well as its main working hypothesis: *A thriving social organization presupposes an optimal and sustainable balance within the Total Social Value Stock (TSVS) and among the different forms of capital that constitute it: Real, Social, Cultural (*Chtouris, 1990; 2000; 2009*), Human and Natural* (Chtouris, 2009) *while the Financial capital is found in a functional and productive relation to all the above.*

The proposed research model intends to explore the formulation and empirical documentation of a general social theory of *Total Social Value Stock (TSVS)*, according to which the inflows and outflows balance is to be checked in order to ensure that basic living needs are covered, while preserving both ecological sustainability and social cohesion. More significantly, integration of young people in the overall strategic economic and social development process is of paramount importance.

While we plan to work with concrete theoretical models in mind, pertaining to the New Theory of Capital (Waldstrom and Svendsen, 2008; Svenddsen, 2010), we plan to expand them so as to formulate a comprehensive inflows/outflows and accumulation model of the different forms of capital (economic, social, human, natural) based on empirical data. Most importantly, our aim is not only to formulate an integrated *theoretical* model but also to be able to propose specific policies that foster young people's social and economic integration, as well as their capability to confront the economic and social crisis in South European countries.

3. Analysis of social structure and social functions through a comprehensive capital model

Historically, interpretation of social structures and functions that are inspired by a central notion draw their origin from Marx's Capital theory. In spite of several empirical problems that have emerged in relation to the above mentioned theory, Marx's idea to consider the Capital as the central structural element of social formation, but also as a generating and mediating factor in all social functions and relationships, gave the opportunity to macro-social and macro-economic analysts to formulate important theories that for a long time retain significant validity regarding their exegetic ability. At the same time, modern social and economic science developed important complementary theories, at the medium- and micro-levels, aiming at revealing theoretically and empirically important social phenomena that seem to be directly or indirectly linked to other forms of social values, but not necessarily in direct connection to economic capital. Marx, in the first part of his Capital theory, makes a distinction between use-value and exchange-value. Based on this distinction, Marx suggests that, similarly, labour, as value, can be accumulated as exchange-value losing its initial use-value. (Marx, 1890: 42*). "Diese Dinge stellen nur noch dar, daß in ihrer Produktion menschliche Arbeitskraft verausgabt, menschliche Arbeit aufgehäuft ist. Als Kristalle dieser ihnen gemeinschaftlichen gesellschaftlichen Substanz sind sie Werte – Warenwerte"* (Marx, 1890*: 42).*

The complexities of the Capital theory, in its modern transformation and development, seemingly originate from a difficulty to explain dimensions of social and economic reality that are determined by different forms of value and value prototypes, mainly in the field of social reproduction. Thus, several theories were developed during the second half of the twentieth century, namely, by Bourdieu on Social and Cultural Capital (Bourdieu, 1987), by Coleman (Coleman, 1988) and Putnam (1993, 2004) on Social Capital, as well as by Becker (Becker, 1964) on Human Capital. Indeed, there was a need to formulate different theoretical norms for different forms of value that are produced and diffused in a different way, not determined solely by the economic capital or its visible form, the financial capital. Furthermore, one significant difference is that these forms of value have a different internal constitution and different functions as far as their accumulation and convertibility are concerned.

Using the comprehensive capital model, our intention is to make a synthesis of the different types of capital into a general theory of social value deposit, a new reference concept, similar to Marx's concept of capital, mainly through integration of the different qualities (types of capital) in a comprehensive model that will include them in the form of a *Total Social Value Stock (TSVS).* This theoretical effort aspires to deal, not only on a theoretical level, but also on the basis of systematic empirical research, with difficulties that both Marxist theory and modern theoretical approaches have faced, namely, the distribution of different forms of capital. A necessary precondition for the success of such an effort is the formulation of a valid model that will describe and evaluate internal interconnections, as well as convertibility and functions of all known forms of capital, in the context of this *Total Social Value Stock*.

4. Links and transformability in the context of measuring Total Social Value Stock (TSVS)

There are various modern approaches concerning issues of capital convertibility, namely, of social and cultural capital into economic capital (Svendsen et al. 2010; Chtouris, 2010, 2012). These efforts point to an analysis of specific conditions under which social capital can be transformed and transferred in a way that this change will be visible and measurable. Studying the issue at the micro-level we observe that these transformations are achieved either via a parallel activation of formalized systems (Svendsen et al., 2010) or through direct reference to specific territorial contexts, where social and collective action is capable of creating specific value transfers. Public spaces, for example, such as squares, apart from being symbolic places for similar repetitive actions, also attract business activities, as their cultural capital accumulates (Chtouris, 2009).

The pattern for measuring the flow of TSVS is based on the model constructed by Leontief (1986), namely, an analysis of inputs and outputs (I/O) of economic sectors in the framework of the national economy. Looking forward to a similar hypothesis on assessment and measurement of total outputs and inputs of various types of capital, our aim is to define *Total Social Value Stock (TSVS)* at both an individual, a local and other aggregated levels (Regions, Organizations, Social movements etc). In the first phase of the research, this model will be developed by using empirical research data. Research will be conducted in eight selected regions of Southern Europe with different systems (Lucas, 1988) for economic and social development. Specific production mode and transformation processes of different types of capital will be documented via administration of questionnaires and qualitative tools of research, at individual level, for a long time span, in order to create a credible analytical context. More specifically, we plan to assess all types of capital that present collective aspects and, as such, have a direct impact on the generation and development of *Total Social Value Stock (TSVS)* at a regional level. Measurement of six different types of capital will be conducted at the individual level and this will serve as a basis for the evaluation of the *TSVS* following aggregation at the regional level. Moreover, questionnaires will be designed to include both simple and composite variables that register general preconditions for the presence of different types of capital, as, for example, Carpiano (2007)

Figure 4-1. Comprehensive Capital Model: Input-Output Value Table (I/0)

Capital Forms	**1.Physical**	**2.Financial**	**3 Social**	**4. Cultural**	**5.Human**	**6.Natural**	**Total Output**
1.Physical							
2. Financial							
3.Social							
4. Cultural							
5.Human							
6. Natural							
Total Input							

has described in relation to the individual antecedents of acquired social capital (structural elements of social capital), as well as processes that relate to norms and values prevailing at the regional level and which have an impact on the transformation of these types of capital. Finally, the respondents will be asked to evaluate different categories of Social Capital Stock that they have at their disposal. In this context, the specific strings of capital conversion in time and space (Bourdieu, 1986: 252-255; Svendsen, 2010: 631) will be registered at the micro-level; furthermore, this analysis will be supplemented by qualitative research, namely, by focus groups organised in the same regions. As far as the formulation of hypothesis and the analytical patterns of transformation processes are concerned, we will be assisted in our work by research that has been conducted in relation to conversion of social capital into human capital (Heller 1988, 1996; Ostrom, 2000; Dinda, 2002, 2008) and, more generally, on the role of productive consumption (Gradstein & Justman, 2000).

While we plan to work with concrete theoretical models in mind, pertaining to the New Theory of Capital (Waldstrom and Svendsen, 2008; Svendsen, 2010), we also plan to expand them so as to formulate a comprehensive inflows/outflows and accumulation model of the different forms of capital (economic, social, human, natural) based on empirical data. Most importantly, our aim is not only to formulate an integrated *theoretical* model but also to be able to propose specific policies that foster young people's social and economic integration as well as their capability to deal with economic and social crisis in South European countries.

Our goal is the empirical substantiation of the *Total Social Value Stock (TSVS)* in which the balance of the value inputs and outputs will explain the prospect of incorporation of young people into professional business and social life.

5. The origin of capital concepts and their possibility of being measured

a. Economic capital

According to Marx's theory (1890), economic capital largely consists of the accumulated value of human labour. This accumulation presents some specific characteristics, as it takes place via its socialization in the means of production while, at the same time, being appropriated by one part of society, namely, the bourgeoisie.

Capital formation is directly related to the creation of a class structure, as well as the establishment of an exploitative system, bringing about social dependence of the weakest. In this sense, capital mediates in all social processes transposing its inner logic into them, thus creating social inequality, social control and social alienation (Bottomore, 1998). Thus, capital shapes or abolishes any form of collectivity that is not compatible with its inner logic. Without going into an in depth analysis of Marxist theory, we can consider that Capital represents accumulated value that determines any form of action, provided that said action is meant to reproduce the accumulation process. Social inequality and social exploitation, in this sense, are not the primary goals of this process; they are its byproducts. Marx's theory regarding labour-generated value presents considerable affinities with Adam Smith's older theoretical perception; indeed, Adam Smith considered capital to be a form of labour saved up in visible, tangible objects, bound to produce future revenues (Smith, 1976: 330). There is, however, a fundamental difference in their assessment of capital's function in the production process and market. While Marx ascribes to capital a unique dynamic and defining role, Adam Smith proposed that the economy's "invisible hand" places individual expectations to the service of the common good. In modern economic theory, the concept of capital is split into two: (a) *physical* (real capital), namely, capital assets such as production means (machinery, buildings, tools and all forms of infrastructure) and (b) *financial capital*, namely, liquid money funds, cash money, deposits, bonds, shares, etc. New financial instruments that investment banks and credit institutions have been circulating around the globe such as derivatives, Credit Default Swaps (CDS) and the like belong to this kind of capital (Robison 1996; Arrow, 2000: Robison et al., 2002). For our research purposes, we differentiate financial values, between those that are produced in the framework of production processes and consumption and financial values that are produced by financial engineering and leverage, thus creating appropriate synthetic values (Neftci, 2008: 18).

b. Cultural capital

Cultural capital is the value accumulated by an individual based on cultural qualities and practices. According to Bourdieu, the accumulation of cultural capital on an individual basis starts with childhood, when parents have their children socialize on various cultural levels, i.e., language, cultural aptitudes, preferences, as well as cultural and overall knowledge (Bourdieu, 1984). In the final, theoretical proposal by Bourdieu, cultural capital is constructed as a value at the individual level. Also, Bourdieu argues that cultural capital is neither transmittable nor distributable among members of a community. According to Bourdieu, cultural capital is the main means to construct and legitimize processes of choice and exclusion between the highbrow culture of the upper social class and the culture of the labor class, and, therefore, it constitutes a vehicle which imposes and legitimizes the structures reproducing social inequality (Bourdieu, 1984; Lamont and Lareau, 1988).

Bourdieu, in his analysis of the various forms of capital, distinguishes cultural capital, based on individual knowledge, skills, educational and professional qualifications, from economic capital (money, property, etc.), and social capital which is based on individual networking as well as participation in groups, associations and institutional organizations. Seen from a hierarchical perspective, an individual is placed in a social milieu according to the range of all forms of capital available to him, thus acquiring the respective position, symbolic capital and social recognition (Bourdieu, 1986: 257). Thus, the combination of those three forms of capital, at the individual level, defines the social dynamics of an individual in a milieu. According to Bourdieu, recording all forms of capital allows us to understand the structure and functioning of the social world. "It is in fact impossible to account for the structure and functioning of the social world unless one reintroduces capital in all its forms and not solely in the one form recognized by economic theory" (Bourdieu, 1986: 242).

Further on, Bourdieu (1986) conceptualizes three forms of cultural capital: (a) *institutionalized* cultural capital (acquiring qualifications from formal institutions) (b) *objectified* cultural capital and (c) *embodied* cultural capital in its fundamental state as it involves a process of self-representation and life style. Cultural capital is present in its highbrow forms as a refined "taste" in art, literature or poetry, and it is often associated with upper social class; in its lowbrow forms, it involves learned skills, abilities and knowledge. Not all forms of cultural capital can be transmitted instantaneously, as it is the case with property or money. Measuring cultural capital, due to its intangible and abstract form, is problematic; therefore, "there is no standard way of measuring the concept of cultural capital" (Robson, 2009: 109). We intend to concentrate our research efforts on measuring cultural capital in its institutionalized form, namely, as comparable certificates of individual cultural competence and not to extend our measurement to other more fuzzy forms of cultural capital.

This decision is based on the assumption that the institutionalized form of cultural capital is the one that affects mostly the transformation process of cultural capital into other forms of capital through work and participation in economic activities.

c. Social capital

The initial premise postulated by Bourdieu (1986) on cultural, and, primarily, on social capital, laid the foundations for an overall theory on Social Capital in the context of social and political sciences. Coleman (1990) and Putnam, introduced a new dimension to the theory, maintaining, however, some basic characteristics of Bourdieu's original theory (1977), i.e., those characteristics that link social capital with social networks and relations of social trust. Although the interrelation among the aforementioned thinkers is not clearly documented (Portes, 1998), there is no doubt that social links and social networks, irrespectively of economic exchange relations, constitute a common ground of convergence for all theoretical models on Social Capital. Coleman (1998), in an article on the importance of social capital in the establishment of human capital, currently deemed as classic, defines social capital as a factor which facilitates relations of trust and collaboration among all acting agents, both at the micro-social level and at the level of their collaborative networks in general. Although Coleman does not provide us with an explicit definition of social capital, he indicates its role so as to promote better coordination, communication, and mutual exchange at the socioeconomic level. According to Coleman, social capital, in its capacity as an element of social structure, is definitely the most difficult to comprehend in the theoretical model. «The various entities which construct social capital such as trust, obligations, sanctions and information channels are directly linked to social organization» (1990: 302).

Social capital, in Bourdieu's original theory, is described more clearly, as «the totality of active or potential resources linked to the possession of a network of permanent relations—more or less institutionalized—of acquaintance and mutual recognition». Social capital, in contrast to cultural capital, is sustained more by specific connections and networks, and sets as a prerequisite the mobilization of resources to the benefit of the individual linked to them.

Despite certain variations in Bourdieu's theory on social capital, the previous quote always remains central, in a sense that social capital is considered as a resource to be possessed and used on an individual basis. In fact, Bourdieu argues that this resource is usually appropriated by the members of the upper class and "highbrow" culture, precisely as is the case with cultural capital. However, one might express some criticism here regarding Bourdieu's theory, since it does not include some kind of provision as to the possession of capital by collective acting agents, nor as to its creative use by the less favoured. Ultimately, however, Bourdieu's theoretical proposal on social capital, even though concise, gives leeway to research for a collective dimension in social capital.

Furthermore, according to Bourdieu, social capital is the means in order to define delimitations among social groups and networks, primarily via individual action of their members, but, equally, via institutional or diffuse representation of the total field, embodied by individuals with prestige and symbolic power (Bourdieu, 1984: 55-58). In this context, individual benefit is the outcome of transaction and solidarity relations within a network, but also an outcome of common symbolic references to people and institutions. When one considers this aspect of social capital, i.e., shared control of entry in a network, as well as acquisition of some kind of right to network representation, a link is established between individual strategy and collective action. In this sense, as Bourdieu argues, there is an internal cohesion as well as a «total social capital»: «The volume of social capital possessed by a specific agency depends on the range of the network of connections it can mobilize effectively, as well as on the volume of (social, cultural or symbolic) capital appropriated by each and every one of them linked to it»; and he continues the same thought by stating that «the network of connections is the outcome of social investment strategies, consciously or unconsciously orientated to the institution or the reproduction of social relations to be used directly, in the short or in the long run..., for the transformation of symptomatic relations... into concurrently necessary and selective relations» (Bourdieu, *op.cit.*). One could say that, in this manner, social capital is a product of individual strategy and informal collective reciprocity derived from a network of connections. Thus, social capital oscillates between individual choice and its collective embodiment in social structures (Portes, 1998), primarily residing, however, in the individual. At the same time, limits to mutual understanding among group members are linked to transactions and events (dinners, banquets, weddings), but they are also linked to rights and obligations, which act as constructing agents for the network and social capital therein.

Coleman (1998: 109) examined the ways social capital is transformed into human capital, arguing that an individual's family and community background involves three different resources, namely, social, human and pecuniary capital. Pecuniary capital can provide tangible, real resources for the success of the interested party. Human capital derives from the academic level, namely, parental education, thus forming the cognitive capital of the descendants, and, finally, social capital, which is vital for the intellectual growth of the descendants. The family's social capital is constituted by parents/children relations, and it allows for the diffusion of the parental generation's human capital to the next generations.

In all theoretical proposals that followed suit, on social and cultural capital, even in the most known proposal by Putnam (2000), there is no relevant idea as to the social and cultural capital organization and formation via common symbolic practices and cultural events, but what is even more important, there are no proposals regarding the processes of accumulation and transformability of Social Capital in other forms of capital (Chtouris, 2010, 2012). However, these processes are present, as a strong tradition, in the construction and cohesion of human community at all times and in all cultures. What has also been lacking is a micro-sociological and psychological examination leading to identification with space and social networks, which, in turn, lead to the social capital construct and its transformation in other forms of capital.

d. Human capital

It was mainly Gary Becker (1964) from the Chicago School of Economics who introduced human capital in economic and social theory. According to Becker, human capital is considered as a means of production, as it is the case with economic (real) capital. Investment in education, training or medical insurance for employees constitutes a return on investment in the form of further performance in labour. In that sense, human capital is yet another real capital, the only difference being that it is directly linked to specific employees, and, therefore, it cannot be transmitted. as is the case with real or financial capital. As various forms of real capital have different growth cycles, human capital also becomes, on a long-term basis, a significant factor in economic development that eventually may lead to a return of our investment (Mamuneas, 2006). Furthermore, it is quite evident that it constitutes a more long-term investment on individuals, albeit in a social context. Trans-generational accumulation of human capital improves the next generations' capacity to provide more qualified and specialized work. In this research, we are focusing on the forms of human capital which relate to the acquisition of professional competences, and not on formal education which is under the umbrella of cultural capital.

e. Natural capital

Natural capital is an important factor in ensuring quality of life and as such constitutes the necessary precondition for sustainable development.

The creation of models that record the relationship between natural capital and quality of life provides a stricter definition of sustainable development through explicit characterization and classification of natural capital (Collados and Duane, 1999:441). Moreover, natural capital plays an important role in ensuring the necessary conditions for the acquisition and use of other forms of capital, namely, cultural, human and social capital, as well as ensuring internal balance among them. Indeed, ensuring the physical space for undertaking any sort of action or social relationships is of paramount importance; public space (Chtouris, 2009) is a prerequisite in order to develop other forms of capital such as cultural and social capital, allowing for their accumulation at individual and collective levels. Measurement of natural capital, in the context of SAVER-proposed research is undertaken in a twofold approach: (a) as an indicator of natural capital existing in the research area and (b) as individual use of natural resources independently of the specific place of use. In this context, we plan to trace the paths that lead to the parallel development of other forms of capital and the TSVS through utilization of natural capital resources. Ecological economist Daly (1996) understands "natural capital" as a factor in commodity production. However, such a limitation curtails development possibilities for businesses and regions to maintain a satisfactory living standard. The value of the natural capital stock has declined significantly during the past century because of human economic practices, but investment in human and natural capital is possible even when financial resources are scarce. There are examples of initiatives that workers have undertaken in order to build upon their own skills and knowledge so as to work within the resource opportunities and constraints at hand, being able to transform negative cycles of poverty and resource degradation into positive cycles of knowledge expansion and forest re-growth. Wangari Maathai (Maathai, 2007). suggests that a new development paradigm—one centered on investments in human and natural capital—may constitute a viable alternative to conventional approaches. The effects of investment on natural capital to promote sustainable development can be traced at regional and local levels; in the long run, they have significant influence on individual quality of life, as well as on economic and cultural capital. *Our hypothesis is that total individual capital stock can increase or decrease over time through the improvement or degradation of natural capital and other capital forms in the neighborhood/locality/region.*

6. Main research questions and TSVS-specific ontological quality

The formation and weight of the individual value stock internal ratios relate to the essential, everyday life experiences of people, and as such, they acquire, *pro rata,* the same ontological existence as work does in Marx's and Lukacs' (1986:12) theories; it constitutes an important defining parameter of social existence, transcending definitions specific to economic capital, money or other forms of relations linked to social and cultural capital. At the same time, it seems that, for social subjects, it constitutes an element of self-realization in each and every historical time. This is becoming all the more manifest today, especially through the reversal of value relations and the unilateral imposition of the "financial values" dynamics in everyday life, in work assessment, as well as in the tangible production of goods. We have been witnessing unique social phenomena and a deregulation of individual identity and existential entity in the social milieu where financial engineering prevails. This constitutes an *in vivo* lab, enabling us to study the reversals brought about by this lack of equilibrium. On the other hand, the depreciation of work's ontological foundation and value (Marx, 1973: 610-12), among numerous social groups, undermines society's cohesion. In this context, the main aims of the research model are the following:

1. The research team's main question involves the ways through which different types of capital values (social, cultural, human, economic), networks, as well as different social ties (Granovetter, 1973) associated with them, affect social and professional integration and entrepreneurial activities of young people.
2. Different kinds of transformative processes take place in both social and cultural capital, i.e., bonding to bridging social capital (Lin, 2001), as well as social capital to economic capital and Value Stock. We plan to explore how these forms associate themselves with successful transitional processes, mainly of young people, that is, from formal education to professional and social integration and successful economic activity. Moreover, we intend to explore forms of cultural capital and the way they contribute to social integration through political activism, voluntarism and creative networking.
3. The research team plans to explore the transformative role played by different forms of capital values and TSVS in the formation process of social identity and agency: what kind of political

practices are associated with its collective form (Giugni & Lorenzini, 2010), how they affect social integration and social cohesion and *vice versa* (Sobel, 1993).

4. The impact of economic crisis on transitional processes, i.e., education to work and nascent entrepreneurship; furthermore, what kind of coping practices, along different capital formations, are developed especially by young people themselves, as well as their immediate social environment, in order to address problems such as unemployment, long waiting periods out of work or protracted stay within their nuclear family of origin.
5. An important research topic is the weight and importance of each form of capital in order to unlock the process of economic development. It is also necessary to illustrate the temporal sequence and priority that should be given to investment (economic, political and intangible) for the development of each form of capital separately.

7. Conclusion and policy recommendations

Policy recommendations for the implementation of a large scale development program such as a new "Marshall Plan", in Greece—and South European countries in general—should take into account the country's proven inability to absorb resources transferred exclusively in the form of financial aid. Indeed, this has been demonstrated by the failure of European Union aid programs, that have been consistently implemented since the '80s, to transform the economic base of the Greek economy. Apart from the characteristic introversion of the Greek economy and its structural weaknesses, the biggest problem that has been identified concerns lack of human and social capital, as well as absence of social control over institutions of public administration and the economy. Corruption, lack of transparency, low participation and unaccountability in local, regional and national administration, as well as pervasive and generalized clientelism, are the main factors for loss and mismanagement of financial resources. Unlike proposals that support a full neo-liberal policy, namely, non-interference of the state in society and culture, as well as a breakdown of social institutions, this project proposes increased investment to be directed to the revival of local and urban communities, based on reciprocity, solidarity, social control and cooperative production. This is a way through which different kinds of capital value (social, cultural, human, financial), networks and various social relations associated with them, affect social and labour integration, as well as the creation of business opportunities, especially for the young who suffer more from the economic and social crisis. Social accumulation of values and the growth of Total Social Value Stock can lead to economic recovery in Greece and the South European countries that have been severely affected by the financial crisis. The development of a Total Social Value Stock in society will also constitute an adequate response to counteract the spread of political extremism in Greece ("Golden Dawn" fascist party) which is largely based on organized groups and communities with criminal practice and negative ("dark") social capital.

References

Arts, W. and Gelissen, J. (2002). 'Three worlds of welfare capitalism or more?, A state-of-the art report', *Journal of European Social Policy,* vol. 12, no.2, pp. 137-158.

Aassve, A., Iacovou, M. and L. Mencarini, (2006). 'Youth poverty and transition to adulthood in Europe', *Demographic Research,* 15, 21–50, 2006. Available: http://www.demographicresearch.org/Volumes/Vol15/2/ [12 June 2013].

Arrow, K.J. (2000). 'Observations on social capital', in Dasgupta, P. (ed.), *Social capital: A multifaceted perspective,* The World Bank, Herndon, pp. 3–5.

Becker G. S. (1964, 1993). *Human capital. A theoretical and empirical analysis, with special reference to education,* 3rd edition, Chicago: University of Chicago Press.

Bennett H., Escolano, J., Fabrizio, S., Gutiérrez, E., Ivaschenko. I., Lissovolik, B., Moreno-Badia, M., Schule, W., Tokarick, S., Xiao, Y., and Zarnic, Z. (2008). 'Competitiveness in the Southern Euro Area: France, Greece, Italy, Portugal and Spain', *IMF, Working Paper* /08/112.

Bourdieu, P. (1986). 'The forms of capital', in Richardson, J. (ed.) *Handbook of theory and research for the sociology of education,* New York: Greenwood, pp. 241-258,

—. (1984). *Question de sociologie*, Paris: Minuit.

—. (1977). *Outline of a theory of practice,* Cambridge: Cambridge University Press.

Bottomore, Tom, ed., (1998). *A dictionary of marxist thought*, Oxford: Blackwell.

Caffet J.-C., Castillo, J., and Thellier, C. (2011). 'Can southern Eurozone countries correct their external imbalances?', *Economic Research NATI*XIS, 30 May. No.388

Carpiano, R. M. (2007). 'Neighborhood social capital and adult health: An empirical test of a Bourdieu-based model', *Health &Place,* vol. 13, no.3, pp. 639-655.

Christoforou, A. (2003). 'Social capital and economic growth: The case of Greece', Presented at the 1st LSE PhD Symposium on Modern Greece, 'Current Social Science Research on Greece', 21 June 2003, London School of Economics.

Chtouris, S. (1990). *Die andere Gegenwart. Kreta, Tradition und Moderne der europäischen Peripherie('Tradition and modernity in the European periphery')* Kassel:GHK.

—. (1992). *Complex processes of social exclusion and the role of the family in social protection.* Athens: Praxis.

—. (2000). *Music crossroads: Lesvos 19th & 20th century*, Athens: Exantas.

—. (2004). *Rational symbolic networks* (Orthologika Symvolika Diktya), Athens: Nissos.

—. (2008). 'Social Capital. The missing link coping with environmental and social risks', Paper presented in European Parliament Conference, 'Are we prepared?', 12 November 2008 Brussels, .

—. (2009). 'The spatial dimension of social and cultural capital', *Synchrona Themata (*Modern Issues Journal*)*. January March, vol. 209, no. 105, pp. 209-220.

Chtouris, S. and Zissi, A. (2012). 'Youth and place. Constructing ways of being in the world', in Tsoukala, K., Conenna, C., Daniil, M., and Pantelidou, C. (eds.) *Youth and space,* Thessaloniki: School of Architecture, Aristotelian university of Thessaloniki.

Chtouris, S., Zissi A. and Rontos K. (2006). 'The state of youth in contemporary Greece', *Young: Nordic Journal of Youth Research*, vol. 14, no.4, pp. 309-322.

Chtouris, S. and D. Papageorgiou (eds), (2009). *Music crossroads: Lemnos 20th and 21th Century*, Athens: ION.

Coleman, J.S. (1988). 'Social capital in the creation of human capital', *American Journal of Sociology,* 94, S95–S120.

—. (1990). *Foundations of social theory.* Cambridge MA: Harvard University Press.

Collados, C. and Timothy P. D. (1999). 'Natural capital and quality of life. A model for evaluating the sustainability of alternative regional development paths', *Ecological Economics*, vol. 30, pp. 441–460

Daly, H.E. (1996). *Beyond growth: The economics of sustainable development*, Boston: Beacon Press.

De Leeuw E. (2005). 'To Mix or Not to Mix Data Collection Modes in Surveys', *Journal of Official Statistics,* vol. 21, no. 2, pp. 233–255.

Dinda, S. (2008). 'Social capital in the creation of human capital and economic growth: a productive consumption approach', *The Journal of Socio-Economics,* vol. 37, pp. 2020-2033.

Du Bois R., Plug W. and Stauber B. (2002). 'Youth policy and participation. Potentials of participation and informal learning for the transition of young people to the labour market: A comparison in ten European regions', Research Project YOYO, Co-ordinated by IRIS Tübingen, Tübingen: IRIS Working Paper 2.

ELSTAT (2011). *Labour Force Survey, monthly results.* Athens 2011, Available: www.statistics.gr [10 June.2013].

European Commission (2009). 'European research on youth supporting young people to participate fully in society', European Research Directorate-General for Research, Socio-economic Sciences and Humanities, *EC Policy Review*, EUR 23863 EN.

Eurostat, European Commission (2009). 'Youth in Europe. A statistical portrait', *Publications Office of the European Union*/ISBN 978-92-79-12872-1, Luxembourg; Eurostat Unemployment Statistics 2009, Available:
http://epp.eurostat.ec.europa.eu/statistics_explained/index.php/
Unemployment_statistics [15 June 2013].

European Social Survey (2003), Available:
www.europeansocialsurvey.org [20 June2013].

Ferguson, C. (2010). *Inside Job, A d*ocumentary Film produced by Audrey Marrs and Charles Ferguson, released 16 May 2010 [Cannes] and distributed by Sony Pictures Classics.

Ferrera, M. (1996). 'The 'southern model' of welfare in social Europe', *Journal of European Social Policy,* vol. 6, no. 1, pp. 17–37.

Gradstein, M. and Justman, M., (2000). 'Human capital, social capital, and public schooling', *European Economic Review,* vol. 44, pp. 879–890.

Granovetter, M. S. (1973). 'The strength of weak ties', *American Journal of Sociology*, vol.78, pp.1360-1380.

Greenbuam,T.L. (1993). *The practical handbook and guide to focus group research*. Lexington, MA: Lexington Books.

Grootaert C., Narayan D., Nyham J. and Woolcock M. (2004). *Measuring social capital. An integrated questionnaire,* New York: World Bank.

Giugni M. and Lorenzini J. (2010). 'Employment situation, social capital, and political participation: A survey of unemployed and precarious youth in Geneva', Paper for the seminar, 'Economic/Social Exclusion and Collective Action: Asia and Europe Compared', 16-17 September 2010, Limerick, University of Geneva.

Heller, P. (1996). 'Social capital as a product of class mobilization and state intervention: Industrial workers in Kerala, India', *World Development,* vol. 24, no.6, pp. 1055-1071.

Kilpatrick, S., Johns, S., Mulford, B., Falk, I. and Prescott, L. (2002). 'More than an education: Leadership for rural school-community partnerships', RIRDC Publication No. 01/, RIRDC Project No. UT-31A

Lamont, M. and Lareau A. (1988). 'Cultural capital: Allusions, gaps, and glissandos in recent theoretical developments', *Sociological Theory* , vol.6, no. 2 pp. 153-168.

Leontief, W. W. (1986). *Input-output economics.* 2nd ed., New York: Oxford University Press.

Lorenzini J. and Giugni M. (2010). 'Youth coping with unemployment: The role of social support', University of Geneva, Paper for the YOUNEX Swiss Workshop,"Youth, 'Unemployment, Precariousness, and Exclusion in Switzerland', University of Geneva, Geneva,

Lin, N. (2001). *Social capital*, Cambridge: Cambridge University Press.

Lucas Jr., R.E. (1988). 'On the mechanics of economic development', *Journal of Monetary Economics*, vol. 22, pp. 3–42.

Lukacs Georg. (1986). Zur Ontologie des gesellschaftlichen Seins. Erster Band. Werke Band 13. Darmstadt: Luchterhand. Available: (http://www.archive.org/search.php?query=Zur%20Ontologie%20des %20gesellschaftlichen%20Seins) [20 June 2013]

Mamuneas, T.P. (with Ketteni E., Savvides A. and Stengos T.) (2007). 'Is the financial development and economic growth relationship nonlinear?' *Economics Bulletin,* vol. 15, no. 14, pp. 1-12,

Mamuneas, T.P. (with Savvides, A. and Stengos, T.) (2006). 'Economic development and the return to human capital: A smooth coefficient semiparametric aspproach', *Journal of Applied Econometrics* vol. 21, no. 1, pp. 111-132.

Mamuneas, T.P. (with Kalaitzidakis, P. and Stengos, T.) (2002). 'A specification analysis of cross-country growth regressions', *Empirical Economics*, vol. 27, no.4, pp. 645-656.

Maratou-Alipranti, L. (1999). 'Inter-generational relations in the modern era: theories, trends and practices', *Greek Review of Social Research, v*ols. 98-99, pp. 49-76.

Marx, K. (1995). *Capital: A new abridgement,* New York: Oxford University Press.

—. (1973). *Grundrisse,* London: Penguin.

—. (1890). *Das Kapital.*Vierte Auflage, Available: http://www.archive.org/details/KarlMarxDasKapital.pdf [22 June 2013].

Maathai, W. (ed.), (2002). *The green belt movement: Sharing the approach and the experience*, New York: Lantern Books, New York.

Maathai, W. (2007). *Unbowed: A memoir*. New York: Anchor Books.

Matsaganis, M. (1999). 'Support of low incomes and the poverty trap', *Greek Review of Social Research, vol.*100, pp.65-78.

Morgan, D. (1997). *Focus group as qualitative research,* 2nd edition, Thousend Oaks Ca: Sage

Narayan, D. Cassidy, M.F. (2001). 'A dimensional approach to measuring social capital: development and validation of a social capital inventory', *Current Sociology,* vol. 49, no. 2, pp. 59–102.

National Statistics Service of Greece, (N.S.S.G.) *Population Census,* 1951-2001. Available: www.statistics.gr [10 June2013].

—. *Labour Force Research.* 1988-2002. Available: www.statistics.gr [10 June.2013].

—. *Labour Force Research.* 2002, Available: www.statistics.gr [10.6.2013].

Neftci S. (2008). *Principles of fnancial egineering*, Amsterdam, Boston: Academic Press.

ORPHEAS, (2005). *Topiki Stratigiki gia tin Anaptixi gia tin Apasxolishi kai tin Aiforia*, (Local Strategy for development, employment and sustainability, Scientific Director and Editor, Sotiris Chtouris, EU, North Aegean Region, Mytilini: University of the Aegean.

Ostrom, E. (2000). 'Collective action and the evolution of social norms'. *Journal of Economic Perspectives,* vol. 14, no. 3, pp. 137-158.

Pohl, A., Stauber, B. and Walther, A. (2007). 'Youth - actor of social change. Theoretical reflections on young people's agency in comparative perspective', Interim discussion paper for the UP2YOUTH project Institut für Regionale Innovation und Sozialforschung', *IRIS Arbeitspapiere* 1, Tübingen : IRIS.

Portes, A. (1998). 'Social capital: its origins and applications in modern sociology', *Annual Review of Sociology,* vol. 24, pp. 1–24.

Putnam, R. (1993). *Making democracy work: Civic traditions in modern Italy*, Princeton, NJ.: Princeton: University Press.

—. (2000). *Bowling alone, the collapse and revival of American community*, New York: Simon & Schuster.

Robison, L. J., Schmid, A. A. and Siles. M. E. (1996). 'Is Social Capital Really Capital?', *Review of Social Economy*, vol. 60, no. 1, pp. 1–2

Robson, K. (2009). 'Teenage time-use as investment in social capital'. in Robson, K. and Sanders, C. (eds.), *Quantifying Theory: Pierre Bourdieu*, Springer: Dordrecht, pp. 105-124.

SCDD-Laboratory, University of the Aegean (2012). 'Social groups with xenophobic attitudes', European Integration Fund for the Third Country Nationals–Annual Programme 2009, Action 2.3/09, Priority 2, *A Report for the European Commission and the Greek Ministry of Interior, Decentralization and E–Government,* Mytilene [Scientific Director: Chtouris, S.]

Smith, A. (1976). *The wealth of nations: An inquiry into the nature and causes of the wealth of nations,* Oxford: Clarendon, Press.

Sobel, R. (1993). 'From occupational involvement to political participation: An exploratory analysis', *Political Behavior*, vol. 15, pp. 339-353.

The World Economic Forum (WEF) (2012). *The Global Competitiveness Index 2011-2012. Ranking,* Available : http://www.weforum.org/issues/global-competitiveness [30 June 2013].

Steger, T.M. (2002). 'Productive consumption, the intertemporal consumption trade-off and growth', *Journal of Economic Dynamics & Control*, vol. 26, pp. 1053–1068.

Svenddsen, G.L.H., Kjelden, C. and Noe, E. (2010). 'How do private entrepreneurs transform local capital into economic capital? Four case Studies from rural Denmark', *Journal of Socio-Economics,* vol. 39, pp. 631-644.

Waldstrom, C. and Svendsen, G.L.H. (2008). 'On the capitalization and cultivation of social capital: towards a neo-capital general science?', *Journal of Socio-Economics, vol.* 37, no.4, pp. 1495–1514.

Woolcock, M. and Narayan, D. (2000). 'Social capital: Implication for development theory, research and policy', *The World Bank Observer*, vol 15, no 2, pp. 225-49.

CHAPTER FIVE

THE ITALIAN NATIONAL DEBT CRISIS: JUST ANOTHER ARGUMENT TO PULL TOWARD TERRITORIAL FRAGMENTATION? SOME [CONTRADICTORY] EVIDENCE FROM LOMBARDY'S LIFE LONG LEARNING POLICIES[1]

JOSUA GRÄBENER
UNIVERSITY OF GRENOBLE, PACTE RESEARCH CENTRE

Abstract

The Eurozone debt crisis and the austerity measures have put public authorities under strong pressure. Facing significant financial resources reduction, the Lombardy regional authority has sought to use the European Social Funds (ESF) for employees' training, in cooperation with the Italian Fondi Paritetici Inteprofessionali (FPI), that are Labour-Capital Joint Management Commissions. The FPI collect and mutualize the employers' compulsory training taxes and implement training projects; by doing so, these collective actors contribute to the regulation of the labor market.. The analysis of the cooperation between the private and public actors of regulation through ESF constitutes the object of this study, which has a threefold task: First, it assesses the theoretical implications of Putnam's legacy for research on public-private partnerships in Italian regions. Second, it evaluates the very argument of regional differentiation using the case of adult education. On the one hand, the fragmentation argument is confirmed. Lombardy experiences higher rates of employers' membership in the FPI than other parts of the country. Yet, on the other hand, when it seeks to share funds with the FPI, the Regional Council services face an ambivalent reception. To understand that paradox, pinpointing the contradiction between ESF's general skills ambition and employers' specific skills demands is insufficient. Third, the article develops the argument that other variables need to be taken into account. To do so, the literature on the tensions surrounding the logic of membership in business associations, is mobilized, together with scholarship on the strategic usages of Europe. Eventually, the Lombardy case study is compared with France. The comparison allows the identification of the common trends in the practices of FPI facing EU norms: avoidance, inertia through strategic usages and reframing, or adoption. The probability, to develop one or the other trend, depends on the status of the training tax, alternatively considered as a continuation of employees' wages or as a part of employers' investment. The status of the training tax is in turn explained by a set of three variables that can shape further research: the degree of competition amongst business associations and FPI, the skills strategies stemming from sector collective bargaining, and the discourses held by interviewees on employers' autonomy.

Introduction

The European Social Fund (ESF) was established in 1957 in the Treaty of Rome. It is the "main tool for creating more and better jobs in Europe" (ESF website). As a public-funded investment for lifelong learning, the ESF stipulates the conditions for its beneficiaries. It aims to curb the dynamics of employers' under-investment in workers skills, and especially transferable skills, a phenomena that has been well documented (Johansen, 2002). By doing so, the ESF also nourishes the ambition of a win-win game where workers and employers interests can be reconciled. At the same time, the ESF is well-known for being difficult to obtain and process, from a technical point of view, in line with other European funds. However, when it comes to implement the transferability objective instead, it is rather flexible, mainly because of the high heterogeneity across countries, regions and sectors regarding skills identification and regulation. Whereas the administrative accountability rules of the ESF are set up at the EU-level, the substantial objectives are defined at the domestic level (Sanchez Salgado, 2013). Indeed, when it comes to welfare state reforms and social policies, European member states are still left with an important room of manoeuvre to implement EU strategies, according to the more recent literature on the usages of Europe (Graziano, Jacquot and Palier, 2011). In the case of continuous training for employees, that flexibility can partly be explained by the large diversity of labour markets across European member states, and the methodological challenge of measuring skills and occupation through common categories (Chauvel, Chenu, and Oberti, 2002).

The gap and double-standard used for the two policy clusters raise a large number of questions. First, is it possible to compare different actors using ESF for continuous training, despite of these differences? Second, if one chooses to do so, do the inequalities in the access to ESF match with the differentiated usages of this resource? Third, if, instead, one chooses not to compare regions but sectors, then what should be taken into account to assess compliance with EU rules not only from the point of view of the administrative rules but also as concerns the substantive objectives? From a critical perspective, this analysis raises a paradox: if employers and workers benefit from the ESF, then why does it still face major challenges of implementation? Doesn't it question the extent to which all stakeholders want "better jobs and greater social cohesion"? This article argues that the major obstacle to ESF substantive objectives' implementation is the unwillingness of private enterprises to abandon degrees of freedom in human resources management and to delegate part of their decision-making to market-economy coordination structures. But, since such public subsidies are also welcome to foster training, the coordination actors (in charge of training projects implementation and subsidies collection) seek to reduce much of the substantive constraints attached to the ESF. Consequently, there might be a significant tension between at least three different agendas: first, the promotion of transferable skills in the ESF agenda; second, the somewhat short-term demands of the employers, usually willing to train the workers in a merely productivity enhancement perspective (and potentially reluctant to certifications demands); third, the agenda of collective actors in charge of training. Italy constitutes a privileged vantage point from which to analyse these tensions, as one of the "PIIGS" States (PIIGS stands for Portugal, Italy, Ireland, Greece and Spain) that has been harshly hit by the Eurozone crisis and austerity measures. While unemployment is on the rise, adult training becomes a highly sensitive issue. In Italy, ESF has been used by the State to complement labour market public policies from the very beginning, and long before the Eurozone crisis. I argue that what has changed with the crisis, is the relation to the private coordination actors.

The research question set here is: under which conditions and how do labour-market collective regulation actors use the ESF, and what does it say about the way they arbitrate between contradictory demands? To answer this question, this article focuses on the intermediate level of these collective actors in Lombardy, a northern region. Lombardy has been chosen because it offers a good point of view on both setς of rules mentioned above. It has very good rates of ESF absorption, and is characterized by the fact that the Regional Council is willing to share ESF resources with Labour-Capital Joint Management Commissions. More specifically, this article stems from an on-going research on the reactions to and usages of EU labour market priorities by employers' associations, based on two case studies: Lombardy in Italy and Rhône-Alpes in France. EU labour-market priorities are approximated through the ESF, and the employer's associations with Labour-Capital Joint Management Commissions (FPI). For each case study, the documentation consists of three steps. First, the historical evolution and the legal framework for organizing Continuous Vocational Training have been contrasted with the communication of these Labour-Capital Joint Management Commissions with their members, based on a sample of six out of 20 FPIs. Second, semi-structured interviews (one to three hours) have been conducted with forty employees of the FPIs, along with twenty employees of training centres and public administrations. The interviews were supplemented by the analysis of the partnership agreements concluded with the public authorities to obtain ESF. Third, the training programmes and budgets were compared across the FPIs in the two case studies; this qualitative study was supplemented by quantitative data on the results of ESF-subsidized training on the levels of qualification and job security for the employees. While significant progress has been made on the first and the second steps during the two first years of the research, the third type of data has been more difficult to obtain and will be addressed during the third year. As such, this article presents intermediary results of a research project that should be completed within 2014. Since the research question changed significantly throughout the field investigation (and as such, obeyed more to an inductive than to a deductive logic), this work represents a major opportunity to capitalize on the early exploratory steps.

Section 1 briefly covers the historical and theoretical grounds that led many scholars to consider the usages of ESF by regional authorities, using mostly a regional differentiation perspective. It stresses the interest but also the more questionable dimensions of such a framework and presents the organizations considered in the case study. Section 2 consists of a more systematic focus on the Continuous Vocational Training segment of Lombardy's Lifelong Learning (hereafter LLL) policies. It proves that indeed large differences can be noteworthy across Italian Regions, and must be taken into account since they affect the nature of initiatives taken by public authorities, and the strategies adopted by labour-capital commissions. Section 3 seeks to balance such observations and to solve the paradox of private actors more or less willing to use public funds. It argues that the major explanation is based on the degree of freedom in human resource management wanted for the members. The conclusion attempts to synthesize the main findings, to consider the implications for a cross-national comparison, and to suggest a reconsideration of the variables that should shape further research.

I. ESF as a tool for regional differentiation?

The theoretical frameworks used to approach the usages and the impacts of the ESF are predominantly grounded in European integration scholarship. Most authors distinguish the top-down and the bottom-up dimensions when it comes to europeanizing public policies through that financial instrument, just as in other public policy fields (Brunazzo, 2007). Research on the top-down aspect of the ESF has been very well documented: it is an instrument with numerous impacts on domestic employment policies, contributing to their "activation", not only according to national but also sub-national specificities (Verschraegen, Vanhercke and Verpoorten, 2011). Partly in line with conclusions on the factors of fit or misfit of national structures to European pressures, authors have sought to identify factors of facilitation and/or limitation of harmonization. When it comes to ESF, some authors have concluded that some countries and regions are better prepared than others to adapt to European requirements. For instance, in the case of Italy, there is a rich body of literature showing that southern regions face more difficulties to implement the priorities than the northern ones, for multiple reasons, amongst which administrative inefficiencies and lack of cooperation with private actors (see Milio, 2007; for a comparison with Spain, see Roller, 2001). These two aspects will be examined more closely in this section, arguing that they require analytical tools that do not match with our empirical investigation and call for other research models. The two aspects mentioned above are partly inspired by Robert Putnam's major book, "*Making democracy work: Civic traditions in modern Italy*", published in 1993. At a time when regional governments were increasingly empowered, he developed arguments to understand the variations in the efficiency of regional authorities. According to Rayner (1998), Putnam's work represented a hidden apology of the free market against public administrations that are *ex ante* accused of being inefficient. Nonetheless, Putnam's insights are interesting: he shows that instead of having a linear evolution of societies from the very old and traditional societies (*Gemeinschaft*) towards the more modern and atomized societies (*Gesellschaft*), there are frequent cohabitations between the two situations, and "modern" areas (in an industrial sense) can also be more civic, thanks to well-established powerful organizations. Thus, he reconciled the economic and cultural "performances", by showing that advanced industrial areas can also be better structured than archaic peasant societies.

In other words, capitalism's development did not necessarily presuppose individualism. On the contrary, it can be based on the stronger cooperation between actors, which can be stimulating according to the latest political economy theory, especially when it comes to workers' training. Robert Putnam suggests that there is a strong correlation between civic society and institutional performance, even in a dialectic way: the more individuals tend to cooperate with each other and dedicate themselves to the common good, the more the institutions they target may be better, because the latter can rely on the citizens' experience which in turn empowers the people. Such insights also echo the literature on the relation between business associations and the State: there is a relationship of mutual dependence. While the State often needs business associations to run its public policies, business associations partly benefit from the privileged relation to the State to legitimize themselves in front of their members (Grote and Schneider, 2006).

Consequently, there might be a virtuous circle of horizontal participation, collective efficiency and empowerment, but also a vicious circle of authoritarianism, inefficiency and immaturity. To measure the regional administrations' so-called "efficiency", Putnam elaborated 12 indicators that are important to quote since many of them are also useful to obtain European Social Funds and to give an orientation to Continuous Vocational Training trends. For instance, regarding the indicator "government stability and quick legislative process", Rubio Barceló (2007) shows that the lack of it had put Lombardy at risk of losing large amounts of ESF. Other indicators have to be considered such as agricultural spending; public statistics and information services since the ability of having their own information makes public authorities more autonomous against the easy influence of private interest groups; innovative legislation and reform efforts; care facilities (3 indicators); bureaucratic reactivity; industrial policy tools; housing and urban development. These 12 indicators helped him to form an "index of institutional performance" and to assign a score to the different regions. In a more or less systematic manner, the southern Regions received a very low score and the northern ones a higher one.

This difference was explained by Putnam mainly through the historical cleavage, juxtaposing a "clientelistic" Mezzogiorno, with vertical relations between public authority and society, to a Northern area with horizontal and symmetrical relations. In this view, the North economic and political interests are well structured, thus putting the regional government under pressure to be transparent and "efficient". Under the pressure to be transparent and efficient, employers and their representatives seek efficient public infrastructure, availability of investments, as well as incentives for long-term planning. As a consequence, such research ultimately suggests an increasing differentiation of public policies across the country and more explicitly a territorial fragmentation, largely fed by political autonomy discourses. Moreover, unequal trends in workers' and employers unions' membership across the regions have an impact on the potential access to LLL possibilities that are both an opportunity for skills upgrading and later reconversion for the workers as well as a productivity rise for the companies (Streeck, 2012). However, a growing literature showed that promoting virtuous LLL practices is largely depending on the types and density of workers' and employers' representatives, as well as on the willingness of the public authorities and, eventually, on the cooperation among these different actors (Culpepper 2003; for a latest synthesis, see Busemeyer and Trampusch, 2012).

Although Putnam's contribution is crucial in understanding the differences across Italian regions (particularly when it comes to assessing their articulation with private interests), it suffers from several problems. To begin with, it continues to work within a state-centric approach, where diminished importance is given to social partnership. Moreover, there are several normative problems that make his demonstration very fragile. First, the explicit linkage made between civic culture and institutional performance suggests that a positive correlation exists, *ceteris paribus*, between them. But by doing so, he reifies the very "civic culture" that is hardly objectifiable. Second, the very idea of "democracy" is merely legitimated on the basis of elections (the 1948 Constitution already seeks to empower Regional Executives by direct elections) but he does not really address the existent literature on the role of interest groups in democracy. Empirical investigations have instead shown that without explicit and well-organized workers' and businesses' representatives, what often happens is that informal business influence takes place, for which both the rules and the effects are hard to understand. In addition, very little importance is given to the economical dimensions (e.g., the size of the enterprises). Indeed, these problems stem probably from the very epistemological perspective chosen by Putnam who seeks to explain "success" or "failure" of some public institutions through the single factor of people's "civic virtue".

To sum up, while Putnam offers a highly profitable heuristic device to understand macro-political dynamics, it does not help to fully understand a specific public policy sector, especially when the actions are negotiated with public actors whose interests are antagonistic. Robert Putnam shows the importance of previous experiences in the field of cooperation, especially between guilds or mutual-help societies, to foster economic growth: these experiences could be capitalized and then appropriated by the regional executives. So, he somehow underlines the role of already existing traditions to maintain powerful efficient public structures, which is paradoxical in view of the previously analysed assumptions. The main theoretical issue in Putnam's positions lies in his strong opposition between "cooperation" and "clientelism". Such a difference is much exaggerated and politically constructed with academic justifications (Briquet, 2006); furthermore, it lacks the necessary subtlety to interpret the complex situation and dynamics observed empirically. But above all, Putnam concludes that in the southern regions the citizens' political participation in the public sphere is essentially done through political parties that very much rely on the clientele's vertical relations, whereas in northern areas, the political participation is taking place in a horizontal, cooperative manner. However, once again, the applicability of these assumptions is hard to prove since public, union, market tutelary relations are often mixed and hardly distinguishable. To put it clearly, it seems to correspond to a political and "common sense" agenda rather than to an academic one.

This has several theoretical implications for current research. Using Putnam's framework to understand the politics of ESF usages in Italian regions would suggest that a successfully implemented European Employment Strategy (EES) would primarily rely on two elements. First, it would rely on the willingness of the regional authorities to cooperate with private actors. Second, a successful implementation of the ESF would rely on the ability of the associated private actors to provide appropriate information and then efficient social networks to legitimize the public policies. Indeed, research on the conditions of compliance with EU norms shows that trade unions and employers' associations do play a significant role for the implementation of EU rules (Falkner et al., 2004); they can be facilitators but also veto-players.

The present article argues that although such dynamics are largely verified in the field of Continuous Vocational Training policies fed by the ESF, empirical evidence in a northern Italian region suggests that other dimensions need to be taken into account. When private actors do not participate in public-led initiatives, it does not necessarily stem from so-called administrative inefficiency or political power reluctance to associate partners; neither does it correspond to weak social and political networks of these actors. Evidence rather suggests that private actors are not necessarily interested in being helped with public resources because it would force them to slightly change the agenda of their members. Yet, this relation to members is very central to the study of business associations:

employers' organizations have to deal not only with the challenge of influence, but also with the difficulty of membership (Schmitter and Streeck, 1999; Schneider and Grote, 2006). This literature is also central for the understanding of the tensions and the contradictions that can exist between the employers' organizations and the public administrations.

In Italy, the State has sought to use the expertise of trade unions and employers' organizations to reinforce the collective skills formation system (Croce and Montanino, 2007). Enterprises pay a « training tax » to the National Social Security Institute (INPS: Istituto Nazionale di Previdenza Sociale). Then, there are two possibilities. If the employer has chosen a given FPI (Fondi Paritetici Interprofessionnali/Labour-Capital Joint Management Commission) where unions and business associations are equally represented, the INPS redistributes the collected tax directly to the chosen FPI. If the employer has not chosen an FPI, the INPS redistributes the tax to the regional administration under whose authority the employer is. As a consequence, large numbers of enterprises do not benefit from collective training projects built by the FPIs and depend on public initiatives. According to many interviewees, the problem was (and partly still is) revolving around the training supply, primarily oriented by the offer (training centres' proposals, following public authorities' guidelines), instead of around the demand; this would frequently end in a misfit between skills' demands and skills' offers. To reverse such a tendency, the national government and the regional authorities seek to increase the rates of membership for the FPIs.

The main argument developed by the authorities takes the form of a causal chain. The more members the FPI have, the more training will be provided to workers, the more responsive and competitive the economy will be, and the less unemployment there will be. Such a causal chain has been widely encouraged and appropriated by Italian scholars and by the FPI actors, as we discovered in our interviews and internal documents reading. However, for the purpose of this research, focusing on the usages of Europe, it will be shown that these public-private interactions need to be seen more closely, in order to assess the role of different factors within the examined mechanisms and understand the diversity of reactions to the EU claim of "more and better jobs".

The purpose of section 1 was to identify the main trends and implications of the much-used argument of administrative and civil society capacity for understanding the domestic uses of ESF for continuous vocational training. But such a view underestimates the diversity of membership practices within each of the FPI. This analysis assumes that the diversity of practices is lower across the Italian regions than across the

FPI within the same region. Section 2 therefore insists on the appropriateness of the Lombardy Region as a space with favorable conditions for State-FPI cooperation.

II. A territorial fragmentation equally affecting Regional Authorities and FPI?

In the light of the assumptions criticized above, one can only try to question the reason of important variations in the implication of Labour-Capital Joint Management Commissions at the regional level, e.g., in Lombardy. Lombardy, one of the richest regions in Italy, constitutes a good case study to challenge Putnam's hypothesis that regional performance depends on the strength of civic culture. Here, it is argued that beyond the "global performance" illusion, one needs to understand under which conditions well-structured actors accept to participate in public initiatives. In his work on the institutionalisation of a regional business association in Brittany during the 1950–2000 period, Fournis (2010) argues for further analytical investigations that have been for a long time a focus of political scientists on the macro-level determinants of business association collective action, where the articulation between State and market can explain the types of organization capital chooses. He underlines that such a theoretical model might be highly valuable for national history but is hardly applicable on a sub-national and in particular regional scale. To understand the mystery of the collective action reinforcement, Fournis suggests turning to a more micro-level analysis, by gauging the attitudes of their members. Indeed, according to him, "*the employers' organization is a place, among others, for the institutionalisation of a territorial political order*" (Fournis, 2010: 323, our translation). In line with the above, many interviewees taking part in our study have stressed the important differences in the Labour-Capital Joint Management Commissions' actions and opportunities across the different Italian regions, mainly reflected by their different capacities to access their members:

> "What happens in some regions cannot happen in others. Here in Milan, but also in general in Lombardy […] we can easily promote an initiative through an event to which many enterprises will come to hear us. In other Italian regions [instead], if you want to get an enterprise to know something, you need to go knock on their doors, meet them, present yourself, and solicit them. So, the ways these enterprises can be approached are quite different." *(Interview, FPI 1 Representative, Milan, 1st March 2012).*

That difficulty directly echoes the unequal rates of membership in FPI by enterprises across Italian regions. The unequal rates of membership impact in turn upon the rates of workers that can access collective projects carried out by the FPI. Training projects provided solely by employers result more frequently in narrow skills than training projects provided by collective institutions (for instance the FPI). That is even truer when contrasting projects benefiting from public subsidies and other sources. Table 5-1 seems to support the above-mentioned literature conclusions. It presents for each Region (column 1): the number of employees in the enterprises that are members of a FPI (column 2), the total number of employees (column 3), and the rates of employees benefiting from FPI services (column 4).

Table 5-1. Percentage of workers in enterprises members of the FPI, over the total amount of workers in the private sector, per region

Regions[2]	Number of employees in enterprises that are members of a FPI	Total number of employees (2009)	Rate of employees benefiting from FPI services
Piemonte	645 111	973 372	66,3
Lombardia	2 017 399	2 929 917	68,9
Veneto	835 863	1 173 396	71,2
Emilia Romagna	847 677	1 148 500	73,8
Toscana	415 588	729 657	57,0
Lazio	871 617	1 404 392	62,1
Campania	295 169	657 616	44,9
Puglia	238 678	455 453	52,4
Calabria	73 395	164 833	44,5
Sicilia	254 594	484 447	52,6
Sardegna	115 219	205 878	56,0
Total (Italy)	**7 562 016**	**11 918 316**	**63,4**

Source: Ministero del lavoro e delle politiche sociali, *Rapporto 2011 sulla formazione continua in Italia,* p. 139.

The North/South cleavage seems to be confirmed. It has tremendous impacts in terms of policy-making: a single reform may be implemented differently and have different consequences in each region. Such a difficulty is also underlined by this interviewee, as he puts it regarding the "activation" of labour market policies (including the usages of ESF for lifelong learning):

> "First of all, let's see what Monti will do. But for sure, there won't be similar interpretations in each region. Every regional space seeks to meet the expectations of those who work in the territory: it's hard sometimes to compare them! Because […] the types of work, the declared/undeclared work, or the types of work contract are very different... You need to know how to approach each of the entrepreneurs at the regional level." (*Interview, FPI 1 representative, Milan, 1st March 2012).*

In reaction to these large differences, many of the Labour-Capital Joint Management Commissions also aim to balance the resources across the regions, according to a trade union representative:

> "You need to consider that the FPI are born because there was the South problem. Hadn't there been a national structure, the South wouldn't have had anything! I mean, in the original national design [of the FPI], a part of the Northern and Central resources would go to the South, even though the South hadn't resources because it has few productive units. The construction of the FPI took place that way, because otherwise we would have had the half of Italy without resources!" (*Interview, Trade Union 2 representative, Milan, 6th June 2012*).

According to this representative, the FPI are structurally linked to a national redistribution system aimed at helping the Mezzogiorno (*L'intervento straordinario*), despite of some regional political attempts to concentrate the resources on a territorial basis. This example clearly weakens Putnam's hypothesis that private actors' strategies are primarily driven by regional political games. It was not the case; this FPI, for instance, is very well rooted in the Mezzogiorno as well as in the North (but less in the Centre). The good integration in these territories contrasted very much with the idea that should derive from the above-mentioned literature: clientelism would be opposed to civic virtue. But again, field evidence from our study seems to stress another more relevant cleavage, between politicization and market principles. For instance, the same FPI representative considers that some of the main FPI (e.g., Fondartigianato and Fondimpresa), in which the three main trade unions (CGIL, CISL, UIL) are part of the board, tend to use the FPI to expand their own membership networks both for the companies and for the workers (*Interview, FPI 4 commercialisation responsible, Roma, 27th of October 2012*). The variety and complexity of motivations across each FPI brought us to focus more particularly on the very individuals and on their own preferences. And surprisingly, the FPI defending an internal reallocation of resources would also have a critical discourse on administrative centralization:

> "We actually suffer a lot with this national organization; because we therefore lack the space for action at the regional level [...] we are trying now to obtain more autonomy [...] because indeed, and in particular for training, you cannot avoid the territorial dimension which is central. Each region has a particular economic activity and, hence, specific needs. We can find similarities with other Northern regions like Veneto, but with the South it's more difficult [...]. In each region, as the needs are different, we are asking for more autonomy, because we believe we are the ones better prepared to satisfy the industrial needs. But it seems to be a lost battle, by now!" (*Interview, Trade Union 2 representative, Milan, 6th June 2012*).

In this interview, the problem seems to be located in the internal decision-making system and alternatively in the symbolic retributions apparatus, rather than in a long-term political willingness. The very same person also implicitly opposes the FPI autonomy and the regional executive reinforcement. Interestingly, the institutional innovation for job seekers training and placement has taken place in line with the choices made for employees.

> "When the crisis reached its peak, the Italian State and the Regions, in order to finance the social safety nets (*amortizzatori sociali),* used the ESF resources. But to allow these things, the EU obliged Italy to activate the labour policies. This happened in 2009 and 2010, and again in 2011. So in Lombardy, we had agreements on *active policies*. Lombardy's regional authorities have decided to use these resources for the active policies, through a voucher system. They are the only ones to do so." *(Interview, Trade Union 1 representative, Milan, 23rd February, 2012).*

Such a choice, though currently specific to Lombardy, might be exported to other Italian regions. As Mayneris and Motchidlover (2009) have shown, the ESF competitive evaluation system, whereby local authorities can obtain more or less funding according to the objectives accomplishment, has brought competition among Italian Regions to obtain further funding. This reveals the important differences not only between the North and the South, but also among southern regions. Transparency and partnership are not equally applied according to a range of reasons (Graziano, 2007, 2010). But it has also encouraged self-improvement of the executives and good-practices sharing, for instance through the interregional structure aimed to provide collective expertise on ESF management to the different member regions, the so-called "Tecnostruttura". These institutional constraints are essential to better understand why and how the FPI are needed by regional authorities in order to absorb large amounts of ESF and to implement the EES domestic objectives.

Section 2 suggested that the cumulated evidence supports the hypothesis of a territorial fragmentation. Not only do the regions largely differ from an economic point of view, but the material inequalities are deepened by organizational inequalities. Even in the FPI themselves, many actors seem reluctant to share the resources on a national basis, following in a way the regional autonomy political agenda. However, such reluctance can be understood differently when put into comparison with the French casc, where the FPI equivalents (the French OPCA) are put under pressure by their members to redistribute the money according to each employer's amount of contributions, instead of labour-capital agreed criteria. Consequently, there is again a problem of collective action. Plus, even in the rich and well-organized regions, significant variations have appeared across the FPI, depending on a multiplicity of factors. Therefore, Section 3 focuses on the type of relationship between these collective actors and their members.

III. ESF avoidance, as a symptom of the employer's sovereignty priority?

Discussing the "social impacts" of the national debt crisis in Italy necessarily implies discussions on the individual professional perspectives and on the narrow versus broad skills debates (Streeck, 2012). Shall the skills be completely aligned to the employers' needs as expressed in some of the bargaining structures or promote qualifications that can be used in different contexts and also carry rights? This tension was raised through the description of the "poaching" phenomena. In that mechanism, small enterprises invest significantly (making sacrifices) for the training of their employees, but these employees might be later recruited for higher wages by larger companies (Cognard, 2010). The fear of poaching frequently ends up in collective underinvestment and requires the institution of collective systems regulating training investment. And here is where the articulation between territoriality, the market and relations with the public authorities becomes fully interesting. Indeed, in other FPI, the discourse is significantly different. Replying to the very same question on the eventual existence of an internal national redistribution system, those responsible for the commercial relations in an FPI, associated to the Regional

Executive, strongly disagreed, using both an overall macro-economic justification (general efficiency) and a free-market justification (freedom of choice for entrepreneurs). Both dimensions are profoundly interconnected, since the internal redistribution systems—when they exist—are structured along calls for proposals to which the enterprises can apply. Such calls carry specific representations and symbolic values on the goals enterprises should attain. In an interviewee's opinion, these calls also imply a homogeneous approach of skills needs across the country whereas in reality some enterprises might have a specific need that needs to be addressed and encouraged, even if it is expensive and unfair from a redistribution perspective:

> "But who am I to tell the enterprises what is good for them? The best person to know what the workers need, is the entrepreneur himself!". Plus, if a successful enterprise has an exciting project and needs help while others just want the training fund for useless stuff, why should we favour the latter?" *(Interview, FPI 4 commercialisation responsible, Roma, 27th of October 2012).*

This interview extract is a challenging one when it comes to theoretical interpretations, and the effort to answer the research question. On the one hand, the interviewee seeks to reduce the "pressure" and "intrusion" he could exert on the members. Such a cautiousness can be located either ideologically (to what extent should employers be regulated in their everyday practices?) and/or practically (to what extent is the membership stable in the Italian FPI, and particularly in that one?). On the other hand, when questioned on the North-South cleavage, the interviewee promotes his role of referee in front of numerous training projects: he considers himself legitimate to arbitrate whether a training project is "exciting" or "useless"'. The tension between two trends (the refusal to judge, and the promotion of judgement) raises a new range of questions: to what extent are the industrial relations and national redistribution problems connected? And is that connection equivalent in each of the FPI? These questions are central to identify and explain the different usages of ESF by Labour-Capital Joint Management Commissions.

Answering them brings us back to the fundamental point of this article on the conditions and types of cooperation between FPI and public authorities, a cooperation that can be in part observed through the instrumentation and usages of the European Social Fund. Lombardy is one of the few Italian regions that has chosen to share its ESF resources with the FPI (ISFOL, 2012). Here, the comparative research design of a broader investigation is useful. It sheds light on the general political strategy of the

Lombardy Region. The latter can be illuminated by the French case and defined as a willingness to transform the FPI into *brokers*. FPI are brokers for the Regional Council labour market policies, to the extent that they contribute to its implementation and legitimization among the employers. Until that goal is reached, Italian regional executives cumulate many roles such as prescription-buying of training courses, whereas in France the regions merely buy the courses while State-run agencies participate in the programming procedures and the stipulation of requirements. Consequently, one could expect that the FPI seek to obtain additional resources, in order to serve their members. However, documents collected from the services show that not all FPI are involved in the initiative. This raises two questions. First, which FPI are not participating, and, second, why aren't they doing so? It is assumed that answering these questions will help to explain the differential usages of ESF for training projects.

Table 5-2 is constructed on the basis of documents collected during fieldwork or available from the Regional Executives and FPI websites, as well as 20 interviews conducted in Italy from February to October 2012 (in Milan and Rome).

Table 5-2 helps us to recapitulate and to identify the main trends in the participation or not in regional calls for proposals (i.e., for cooperation), and shows unexpected results. The challenge is to interpret them. Different potential explanatory variables based on existing scholarly literature and on evidence from the interviews, as well as on a comparison with France, have been examined in this case to explain the willingness of the FPI to participate in the regional initiatives.

The first explanation that comes up is a "capacity" one. As many scholars have shown, the international organizations funding conditions are heavy and can have an impact on the very structure. The EU confirms this tendency at least through ESF, as demonstrated by Sanchez Salgado (2010). NGOs willing to obtain ESF, she shows, have to internalize the bureaucratic requirements and professionalize their activity, culminating in growing inequality between the NGOs of unequal size, as well as creating problems regarding democratic control within these organizations (stemming from the complexity and specificity of fund-raising involving professionalization and bureaucratization). In Italy, instead, at least when it comes to ESF for adult education, most of the technical assistance needed is provided by regional authorities with the potential impact on the reproduction of regional inequalities (Table 5-1). This implies that the technical difficulties might not be a relevant explanation for the lower participation of small or sectorial-specialized FPI in the call for proposals made by the region. Moreover, the size of FPI is not a positive incentive to

Table 5-2. List of Italian Labour-Capital Joint Management Commissions for employees' training: sector of interest, board organizations and involvement in Lombardy's ESF sharing initiative (as of 2011).

Labour-Capital Joint Management Commissions (FPI)	Sector of interest	Board organizations (employers and workers representatives)	Involvement in Lombardy Region ESF sharing initiative
Foncoop	Cooperative	A.G.C.I.; Confcooperative; Legacoop; Cgil; Cisl.; Uil	Yes
Fo.In.Coop	Cooperative	UNCI, Confsal	No
Fon.Ter	Tertiary	Confesercenti; Cgil; Cisl; Uil	Yes
Fond.E.R.	Religious-based private sector	Agidae; Cgil; Cisl; Uil	No
Fondimpresa	Any	Confindustria; Cgil; Cisl; Uil	No
Fondir	Companies directors	Confcommercio; Abi; Ania; Confetra; Fendac; Sinfub; Fidia	No
Fondirigenti	Companies directors (Confindustria-based)	Confindustria; Federmamager	No
Fondo Artigianato Formazione	Handicraft	Confartigianato; Cna; Casarti-giani; Cgil; Cisl; Uil; Claai	Yes
Fondo Dirigenti PMI	SME directors (Confapi-based)	Confapi; Federmanager	Yes
Fondo Formazione PMI	SME workers	Confapi; Cgil; Cisl; Uil	Yes

Labour-Capital Joint Management Commissions (FPI)	Sector of interest	Board organizations (employers and workers representatives)	Involvement in Lombardy Region ESF sharing initiative
Fondoprofessioni	High skilled workers	Consilp; Confprofessioni; Con-federtecnica; Cipa; Cgil; Cisl; Uil	Yes
For.Te.	Tertiary activity	Confcommercio; Confetra; Cgil; Cisl; Uil	No
Fondo Banche Assicurazioni	Banking and Insurance	Abi; Ania; Cgil; Cisl; Uil	No
For.Agri	Agriculture	Confagricoltura; Coldiretti; CIA; CGIL; CISL; UIL; Confederdia	No
FondAgri	Agriculture	F.Agri ; CONFSAL	No
Formazienda	Diverse sectors	Sistema Commercio e Impresa ; CONFSAL	Yes
Fondazienda	Diverse sectors	Confterziario; CIU; Conflavo-ratori	No
Fon.Ar.Com	Diverse sectors	Cifa; Confsal	Yes
Fonditalia	Diverse sectors	FederTerziario; UGL	Yes
Fondolavoro	Diverse sectors	UNSIC; UGL	No
Fonservizi	Industrial public services workers	CONFSERVIZI; Asstra; Feder-ambiente; Federutility; CGI;, CISL; UIL	No

Source: Field documents, Regional Executives, FPI websites and field interviews.

participate in the public initiatives, contrary to what the literature on administrative efficiency suggests. Instead, financial power is a strong incentive to resist European integration (Saurugger and Terpan, 2013). Fondimpresa representing half of the workers in Lombardy does not participate, whereas Fonditalia with much lower figures does (see Table 5-2). Eventually, it is obvious that there are important variations in the participation or abstention for each trade union. For instance, CGIL, CISL, and UIL may in some cases not participate, and in other FPI be involved in the cooperation; the same holds for UGL or CONFSAL. Whereas, when it comes to employers' organizations, Confindustria in its two FPI is not involved in the Region initiatives.

A second explanation could be a mismatch between the guidelines of the Region and the sectors represented by the FPI. But again, there are too many exceptions and contradictions to confirm it. For instance, one can see that being cross-sectoral or, on the contrary, specialized in a specific sector of activity, is not a relevant factor for the FPI's involvement in the public initiative. This is of highest importance as the ESF also aims at promoting access to training for low-skilled workers who are usually concentrated in some sectors of activity. Behind that second possible explanation lies a third one. What if the main determinant for usage or avoidance of ESF was not the size of the FPI or the sector-specificity, but the status given to individuals in the research? To avoid the bias of a deterministic approach that would consider interviewees as simple executioners of orders taken at a macro level, this article argues that one needs to pay attention to their representations regarding the degree of freedom private enterprises should have. That could be a stimulating explanation that allows exploring not only of the different relations to the national redistribution argument, but also the different arguments mobilized to justify their everyday activity and eventually their potential transformation because of ESF use.

The evidence gathered during the investigation invites us to be much more cautious in the way private actors are conceived. They are not necessarily fully interested in the public initiatives of resource-sharing, primarily because it might affect the role they built for themselves: a role of counselor for enterprises. When there is tension between the logic of influence and logic of membership, the latter seems to be more valued by the organizations. The role of broker for the European Employment Strategy and the Regional Authorities, comparable to the role of broker often assigned by the State to business associations (Grote and Schneider, 2006), is not always fully assumed by all FPI. In Lombardy, for instance, the Regional Authorities have tried to use the European Social Funds to support their training projects, and articulate these funds with the ones of the Labour-Capital Joint Management Commissions (FPI).

However, the social partners supposed to be involved do not all fully agree:

> "In the new agreement on active policies in 2012 produced by the Lombardy Regional Council, public resources and FPI resources are expected to be mixed. I can tell you FPIs are reluctant, more particularly Fondimpresa; they claim they want a complete autonomy in the management of their funds." (Interview, Trade Union 2 representative, 6th June 2012).

Indeed, an administrative senior staff of the above FPI's national headquarters in Rome put it very clearly during an interview:

> "We do not want to make agreements with Regions. They make their calls for applications, but we don't want to participate, because we want to stay autonomous. […] Plus, let me tell you something. If we mix our resources, we would need to comply with the accountability rules of the ESF which are so heavy. It would make our work less efficient. So in the end, just to have a bit more money, we would be less attractive […] And there is another reason, I can tell you openly: you certainly read the Italian newspapers, and you see what is going on here in the Regions. So, also for political reasons, we prefer to keep a distance with them." (Interview, FPI Headquarters, Rome, 25th October 2012).

These hesitations towards the Regional Executive reflect some research conclusions on the effects of ESF on domestic politics (Sanchez Salgado, 2013). In the case of Italy, the authors conclude that ESF can be considered as a "vincolo esterno" (external constraint) interfering not only with political institutions and arrangements but also with the very socio-economic structure, since to obtain ESF the Italian State and Regions have to comply with new consultation rules. Although Graziano and Jessoula showed that European resources are not bringing structural changes but rather help to reinforce already existing mechanisms (Graziano and Jessoula, 2011), in other public policy areas there is some evidence on the simultaneous strategic use and long-term impact of ESF on executive practices.

Conclusion and research agenda: Implications for a cross-national comparison

This article had three main objectives. After briefly recapitulating them, implications for further research will be drawn, both empirically and theoretically. In Section 1, the objective was to discuss the conclusions identified in the existing literature on ESF and Italian regions. It has been argued that instead of focusing on the conditions of success or failure in obtaining European funds from the point of view of the regional administration, a research question that is consistent with Putnam's legacy, there is much work to be done on how these resources are used in the case of training. Since that aspect is not very much explored, in Section 2, the objective was to question the homogeneity of Lombardy, a region with high ESF absorption rates. This case study is useful to challenge the views with regard to public-private partnerships in the European Employment Strategy. Section 3 unveiled the range of reactions to the public-led initiative of the Lombardy Region. Various explanations have been challenged. These observations are of highest importance for the continuation of the investigation. The sector specificity might play a significant role in explaining the diversity of usages of ESF in Lombardy, but under the crucial condition of being articulated with other relevant variables.

To best shape further research, it seems useful to compare these results with evidence gathered in France. It will help to identify other factors of differentiation that might shed light on the practices observed. In section 1, I argued that in Italy, the promotion of public-private partnership (both scholarly and institutionally) reinforced the shift from an offer-centred training system to a demand-centred system. The employers' skills demands have been increasingly legitimated in Italy, and when compared to French labour law, Italian employers seem to have much more freedom. Two major differences need to be underlined. First, the resources the FPI get from compulsory contributions (and hence the amount of resources available) are lower than in other countries with a similar collective skill formation system (for instance, 0.3% in Italy instead of 1.5% in France). This leaves room for more employer-based training, instead of collective-bargaining led training. Second, whereas in France employers are obliged to pay their contributions to an OPCA chosen through sectoral collective bargaining, in Italy employers are free to choose with which FPI they are willing to cooperate. Comparative evidence cumulated during the first 15 months of the research project suggests that this institutional difference has a tremendous impact on the relation to the members and, hence, the balance between logic of influence and logic of membership. Since the Italian FPI are very much concerned with attracting members, they are less willing to align their member's training projects with ESF substantive requirements, because it might end in a loss of loyalty. A last factor might balance that powerful, institutional trend: an individual one. The representation of the companies' legitimate space of freedom (freedom of human resource management out of external constraints) is not only directed by institutional dynamics but also by biographical properties. When it comes to that aspect, additional material is needed in order to evaluate the most relevant theoretical framework. First, it will be useful to orient the research in the path drawn by Mayntz and Scharpf (2001), with special attention given to actors *within* the institutions they work. However, albeit focusing on the individual representations, it is not yet certain whether this research meets Kohler-Koch and Larat's research agenda on the importance of previous "European socializations" for the dissemination of EU norms (2001). Indeed, most interviewees of our study have had a European experience (that is through transnational projects and/or negotiating with the supranational institutions), be it professional and/or political; in the case of the current sample (N=60), it does not have a significant effect on their attitudes.

In addition, our analysis sought to solve a paradox in the critical approaches to ESF. Many scholars have argued that the EES and the ESF serve the interests of the employers since it helps to provide an abundant qualified workforce, whereby individuals are made more "employable" instead of reducing unemployment at a larger scale (Conter, 2007). But the evidence gathered here shows how and why employers' representatives seek to avoid or considerably reframe these priorities. Such a gap needs to be addressed and explained. Further research will be shaped by the following assumption: there is a marked misfit between the EU labour-market priorities and the individual employers' skill demands. The ESF, major tool of the European Employment Strategy, is aimed at enhancing the qualifications of the workers across Europe. Hence, its usages shall favor general skills rather than specific ones. The employers' interests are rather to provide specific skills to workers. Thus, considering the difference between the two sets of rules in the ESF, the FPI play an ambivalent role in the European Employment Strategy. On the one hand, they are useful for public authorities willing to maintain high rates of ESF absorption (good compliance with administrative rules). On the other hand, at the implementation stage, they are expected to be brokers and facilitators. But this assigned role potentially contradicts their fragile relation to members (more difficult compliance with substantive rules). To sum up, this article has two main findings. First, the FPI may be brokers for the European Employment Strategy, but that role is continuously negotiated, depending on several factors. Second, these factors are numerous, ranging from public-private relations to industrial relations and perceptions of the labour market.

In Lombardy, the field of vocational continuous training for occupied workers is characterized by two major trends. On the one hand, the rapidly changing multilevel environment and the need for external resources (amongst which the ESF) has motivated the Regional Council to increase the partnerships with employers' associations and, as it has been studied here, with Labour-Capital Joint Management Commissions. On the other hand, these institutions constitute a pluralist and highly-competitive FPI system. The present exploratory study has permitted us to unveil a major dimension that helps to explain the strategic usages of European resources (Jacquot and Woll, 2010). The best approximation to understand the reactions to EU labour market norms by the FPI is the very status of the taxes they collect and use. Whether these resources are considered as a continuation of employees' wages or as a part of employers' compulsory investment, the search for public subsidies will not be equally driven. To sum up, the thesis defended here is that the more the training tax will be considered as a wage continuation by the FPI, the more they will seek to comply with the EU objectives of more qualified jobs. To defend that thesis, it will be necessary to look more closely at the training projects and the nature of the skills obtained by the workers. For each of the training projects, three main elements, identifiable in this article, should be compared: the country in which it takes place, the sector of production involved in collective bargaining between employers and employees, and the representations of the individuals regarding skills needs and the labour market. These three variables and their articulation with the literature on the usages of Europe could only be identified and articulated through an inductive research that is time-consuming. However, I argue that it was necessary to answer broader questions. Preliminary intuitions stemming from the existing literature on territorial politics as fundamental cleavages have been challenged and were eventually abandoned in the face of field evidence. Yes, in the context of the Eurozone debt crisis, the EU policy may reinforce the North-South inequalities: Table 5-1 confirms the regional cleavage. Nevertheless, according to Table 5-2 and the interviews, there is such a high differentiation of attitudes among the partners of the regional public policy that one can hardly speak about "Lombard specificity". Moreover, beyond the macro-aspect, there is a major class-related conflict that needs to be addressed and for which other theoretical tools are welcome. Otherwise, it would be difficult to explain the decisions taken in each FPI. Furthermore, even when territorial politics can be relevant, they cannot be dissociated from the wider issues transforming the sociopolitical balances such as the increasing professionalization and the increasing technological complexity of industrial relations.

Lombardy seems to represent a fruitful case study to understand both the intertwined dynamics of the ambivalent state-social partnership relations and the competition across business associations, taking place in Italy (Vatta, 2007). As such, it helps us to draw a broader picture of current transformations in the European labour market. Italian regions are heavily affected by the debt crisis and are confronted with a reduction of public resources while social needs are on the rise—a situation also confronting many public administrations in the Eurozone. ESF provides a significant opportunity to limit these difficulties. However, as has been shown in our exploratory study, its usages depend very much on the existing socio-political configurations and the nature of industrial relations.

Notes

[1] This article stems from a PhD investigation started on October 2011, on the usages of the European Social Fund for Lifelong Learning by Labour–Capital Joint Management Commissions in France and Italy, and conducted at the Research Centre PACTE (UMR 5194), University of Grenoble, France. The research is funded by the Rhône-Alpes Regional Council, France (ARC 8 – "Industrialisation et sciences de gouvernement"). The oral version of this article at the Lesvos Conference (13-14/09/2012) was funded by the PACTE Research Centre, the Institute for Political Studies (IEP) of Grenoble, and the SHPT Doctoral School. I am grateful to all funders for making this work possible, to the DCSCRN of the ESA for accepting the oral version, and to Dr. Nicholas Petropoulos for his useful comments to the oral and written versions.

[2] Eight Regions have been removed from Table 5-1, because of their smaller population and when the result was not significant. For purpose of transparency, these regions are: Valle d'Aosta, Friulia Venezia Giulia, Liguria, Umbria, Marche, Abruzzo, Molise, Basilicata.

References

Briquet, J.-L. (2006). 'Les formulations savantes d'une catégorie politique. Le clientélisme et l'interprétation sociohistorique du 'cas italien' ', *Genèses,* vol. 62, no. 1, pp. 49-68.

Brunazzo, M. (2007). 'Da policy-taker a policy-shaper: L'europeizzazione della politica di coesione dell'Italia,' *Rivista Italiana di Scienza Politica*, vol. 37, no. 2, pp. 233-260.

Busemeyer, M. R. and Trampusch, C. (ed.) (2012). *The political economy of collective skill formation*, Oxford: Oxford University Press.

Chauvel, L., Chenu, A., and Oberti, M. (2002). 'Enjeux et usages des catégories socioprofessionnelles: Traditions nationales, comparaisons internationales et standardisation européenne', *Sociétés contemporaines*, vol. 45-46, no. 1-2, pp.157-182.

Cognard, E. (2010). *Economie politique des employeurs et néo-corporatisme : Financer la formation professionnelle continue en Europe*, PhD dissertation in economics, University of Lyon.

Conter, B. (2007). 'Plein-emploi ou chômage nécessaire: La stratégie européenne pour l'emploi, entre utopie et pragmatisme', *Politique européenne,* vol. 21, no. 1, pp. 21–40.

Croce, G., and Montanino, A. (2007). 'Le rôle des politiques publiques de formation des salariés en Italie', *Revue européenne de formation professionnelle*, vol. 41, no. 2, pp. 153-167.

Culpepper, P. D. (2003). *Creating cooperation. How states develop human capital in Europe*, Ithaca : Cornell University Press.

European Social Fund website, Available: http://ec.europa.eu/esf/main.jsp?catId=278&langId=en [10 october 2013].

Falkner, G., Treib, O., Hartlapp, M., and Leiber, S. (2005). 'Why Do Member States Fail to Comply? Testing the Hypotheses Suggested in the Literature', in Falkner, G., Treib, O., Hartlapp, M., and Leiber, S. (eds.), *Complying with Europe. EU harmonisation and soft law in the member states*, Cambridge: Cambridge University Press, pp. 277–316.

Fournis, Y. (2010). 'Comprendre les institutions par le bas: L'institutionnalisation d'un patronat régional par l'action collective (1950-2000)', *Revue Française de Science Politique*, vol. 60, no. 2, pp. 319-334.

Graziano, P. (2007). 'Adapting to the European Employment Strategy? Recent development in Italian employment policy', *International Journal of Comparative Labour Law and Industrial Relations*, vol. 23, no. 4, *pp.* 543-565.

—. (2010). 'From local partnerships to regional spaces for politics? Europeanization and EU cohesion policy in southern Italy', *Regional and Federal Studies*, vol. 2, no.3, pp. 315-333.

Graziano, P., and Jessoula M. (2011). 'Eppur si muoveva... The Italian trajectory of recent welfare reforms: From 'rescued by Europe' to Euro-skepticism', in Graziano, P., Jacquot, S., and Palier, B. (eds.), *The EU and the domestic politics of welfare state reforms. Europa, Europae*, New York: Basingstoke, Palgrave Macmillan, pp. 148 – 174.

Graziano, P., Jacquot, S., and Palier, B. (eds.) (2011). *The EU and the domestic politics of welfare state reforms. Europa, Europae*, New York: Basingstoke, Palgrave Macmillan.

Grote, J. R., and Schneider, V. (2006). 'Business associations, associative order and internationalization', in Streeck W. et al. (eds.), *Governing interests: Business associations facing internationalization*, London: Routledge, pp. 1-18.

ISFOL (2012). 'XIII rapporto sulla formazione continua, annualità 2011 – 2012', Ministero del Lavoro e delle Politiche Sociali, Direzione Generale per le Politiche Attive e Passive del Lavoro, Roma.

Jacquot, S., and Woll, C. (2010). 'Using Europe: Strategic action in multi-level politics', *Comparative European Politics,* vol. 8, no. 1, pp. 110-126.

Johansen, L.-H. (2002). 'Transferable training as a collective good', *European Sociological Review,* vol. 18, no. 3, *pp.* 301-304.

Kohler-Koch, B., and Larat F. (2001). 'La dissémination du modèle communautaire de gouvernance comme processus d'adoption et d'adaptation', *Politique européenne,* vol. 2, no. 1, pp. 87-106.

Mayneris, F., and Motchidlover, J. (2009). 'Les politiques régionales en faveur du Mezzogiorno : Un changement de perspective radical', in Caracciolo, P. (ed.) *Refaire l'Italie. L'expérience de la gauche libérale (1992 - 2001)*, Paris : Ed. de l'ENS.

Milio, S. (2007). 'Can administrative capacity explain differences in regional performances? Evidence from structural funds implementation in southern Italy', *Regional Studies,* vol. 41, no. 4, pp. 429 – 442.

Ministero del lavoro e delle politiche sociali, *Rapporto 2011 sulla formazione continua in Italia.*

Putnam, R.D. (1993). *Making democracy work. Civic traditions in modern Italy*, Princeton: Princeton University Press.

Rayner, H. (1998). 'Le point de vue aérien de Robert Putnam : A propos de making democracy work', *Politix*, vol. 42, no. 2, pp. 179-204.

Roller, E. (2001). 'The Europeanization of sub-national politics: Institutional change in Andalucía and Catalonia', *Politique européenne,* vol. 2, no. 1, *pp.* 107-110.

Rubio Barceló, E. (2007). *Regional governments, territorial political restructuring and vocational education and training policies. A comparison of four cases: Catalonia, Lombardy, Valencia and Veneto*, PhD dissertation in political science, European University Institute of Florence.

Sanchez Salgado, R. (2013). 'From 'talking the talk' to 'walking the walk'': Implementing the EU guidelines on employment through the

European Social Fund', *European Integration online Papers (EIoP)*, vol. 17, no. 2, pp. 1-26.

Sanchez Salgado, R. (2010). 'NGOs' structural adaptation to funding requirements and prospects for democracy: The case of the European Union', *Global Society*, vol. 24, no. 4, *pp.* 507-527.

Saurugger, S., and Terpan, F. (2013). 'Analyser les résistances nationales à la mise en œuvre des normes européennes : Une étude des instruments d'action publique', *Quaderni*, vol. 80, pp. 5-24.

Streeck, W. (2012). 'Skills and politics: General and specific', in Busemeyer M. R., and Trampusch C. (eds.), *The political economy of collective skill formation*, Oxford: Oxford University Press. .

Vatta, A. (2007). 'Italy', in Traxler F., and Huemer G. (eds.), *Handbook of business associations, firm size and governance. A comparative analytical approach*, London; New York: Routledge, pp. 204 – 229.

Verschraegen, G., Vanhercke, B., and Verpoorten, R. (2011). 'The European Social Fund and domestic activation policies: Europeanization mechanisms', *Journal of European Social Policy*, vol. 21, no. 1, pp. 55–72.

Part II.

Micro- and Macro-Social Impacts on Eurozone Countries under Austerity Regimes

CHAPTER SIX

COPING WITH THE THREAT OF HUMILIATION: CONTRASTING RESPONSES TO THE EUROZONE CRISIS IN GREECE AND IRELAND[1]

DENNIS SMITH
LOUGHBOROUGH UNIVERSITY

Abstract

The paper begins by briefly locating the Greek and Irish bailouts during the current Eurozone crisis in a larger European and global context. The paper then considers how humiliation and the responses made by those it hurts or threatens can feed back into the political arena. The paper compares the historical development of Greece and Ireland, and their citizens' responses to episodes of actual or threatened humiliation, including the recent bailouts. Finally, some wider implications of the analysis for the European Union are explored.

I. Introduction

Humiliation can be a weapon or a wound, depending on whether one is the initiator or at the receiving end. So it is with national governments. Take the case of the reluctant bailout requests made during the Eurozone crisis by the so-called "PIIGS"—hardly an innocent acronym—and the cuts in government spending forced on them by the European Union.

Requests for help often followed several days of denial and were normally treated by the politicians who made them, or at least by their domestic parliamentary opponents, as admissions of weakness and failure. There was a strong implication in some foreign media comments, especially in North Europe, that the "PIIGS" had been exposed as unworthy and deserved to be taken down a peg or two as the price for being reckless and irresponsible.

Such comments were deeply unfair, as was the demeaning suggestion made on *Newsnight* by Jeremy Paxman, just before greeting his Greek guest, that Greece might be "vomited" out of the Euro like a "bad kebab."[2] However, two common features of humiliation are a deep sense of unfairness and inappropriateness in the eyes of the recipient, and great confidence on the part of the perpetrators that what they are doing is justified.

Humiliation cannot be reduced to sets of feelings within individuals or groups. It is an iterative social process entailing mutual engagement between perpetrators and victims. Feelings such as anger, fear and sorrow, and acts of self-defense and revenge, are interwoven with rational calculations and actions relating to material interests. The battle is on two fronts: the scramble for survival or advantage and the struggle to maintain dignity and self-respect.

When the emotional temperature is raised and fierce engagements are being fought, it can be difficult to see the bigger picture. With those considerations in mind, this paper begins by briefly locating the Greek and Irish bailouts in a wider context, noting that they have put into reverse the progress made by the EU in establishing itself as a post-humiliation regime, a kind of European "city on the hill".[3] The paper then considers how humiliation and the responses made by those it hurts or threatens can feed back into the political arena. The paper then compares the historical development of Greece and Ireland, and their responses to episodes of actual or threatened humiliation, including the recent bailouts. Finally, some wider implications of this analysis for the European Union are explored.

Protest or acquiescence?

Current transformations in the EU stem from a global crisis in the workings of capitalism. This has resulted, in large part, from the collapse of confidence in debt creation as a means of managing market transactions. To summarize, the deliberate creation of risky sub-prime debt during recent years has weakened the credit and credibility of many large banks, leading to a widespread unwillingness of banks to lend to each other. This has contributed to a double-dip recession.

Government debt levels have risen, partly so they can help their countries' banks maintain their own balance sheets. This has created an unsustainable gap between some governments' outgoings and their income. Some of the worst affected governments have sought financial help from multinational bodies such as the International Monetary Fund and the European Central Bank.

The credit crunch and the sovereign debt crisis have acted as a catalyst for increased centralization within the EU, which has long been planned, and the emergence of a more overt hierarchy of European governments, a move that has occurred with much less political preparation. A dominant coalition of "central" or "northern" powers has been able to impose its will to an increased extent upon "peripheral" or "southern" powers through the so-called fiscal treaty "on stability, coordination and governance."[4]

The EU leadership in Brussels, Berlin, and Paris evidently believe that a further consolidation of the EU's structures is needed at a time when competition between global regions is intensifying. Easier said than done. Extensions of the EU's powers over the European citizenry were easier to enact in the past when people felt more secure in their jobs, homes and futures. However, the recession has created a climate of insecurity in national electorates. It has become easier to arouse suspicion of interventions "from above" and "outside", especially when "Eurocrats" are imposing restrictions that make matters worse for many ordinary people, certainly for the foreseeable future, as they see it.

In response to this new situation, the people of Greece have protested violently, demanding the withdrawal of "the memorandum".[5] Meanwhile, in Ireland, abruptly deprived of its booming economic micro-climate as the "Celtic Tiger", the people have not revolted. Instead, they have voted by a large margin in favour of the new European treaty making strict fiscal discipline according to externally imposed rules a condition for membership of the Euro.

How do we make sense of the different ways the Greek and Irish political and business establishments and Greek and Irish citizens in general have responded to the threat of humiliation imposed upon them by the credit crunch, the bailouts, and the conditions imposed upon them from outside?[6] How will these responses feedback into the politics of the Eurozone crisis and the debate over the future of the Euro and the EU itself?

Consolidation or break-up?

The EU is hovering uncertainly between two trajectories: consolidation and break-up. The consolidation trajectory leads towards the creation of a stronger political centre. This will have increased authority over the economic policies of those member states that belong to the Euro and a greater capacity to project abroad a consolidated "European will" in matters of diplomacy and foreign affairs. The end point of that road is a kind of United States of Europe.

By contrast, the break-up trajectory leads towards the voluntary or forced disentanglement of a growing number of member states from the constraints imposed by belonging to the Euro, perhaps resulting in the abolition of the Euro as a distinct currency. The momentum generated by such a trajectory might encourage some weaker member states to raise tariff barriers that interfere with European-wide free trade. Some of the stronger members might look for long-lasting political alliances with partners outside the EU. The end point of this road is the disintegration of the European Union.

At the moment, political leaders in Brussels and Berlin, along with Paris, are mounting a strong resistance to break-up while at the same time creating the legal framework for consolidation. Others, including some within the City of London and on Wall Street, are keen to see break-up.[7]

Brussels vision or Washington vision?

If the fiscal treaty proves to be unenforceable, that will be a major reversal for the long-term game plan that took shape during the decade following the collapse of the Berlin Wall in 1989.[8] When the Euro project was agreed in 1999, the ambition was to create a stronger Europe, not just economically but politically, and harness the energy of newly reunited Germany to that task.[9] French president Jacques Chirac declared in 1999 that "The European Union itself [must] become a major pole of international equilibrium, endowing itself with the instruments of a true power." The following year Tony Blair said that "Europe's citizens need Europe to be strong and united. They need it to be a power in the world. Whatever its origin, Europe today is no longer just about peace. It is about projecting collective power."[10]

That European "collective power" was clearly intended to project globally the influence of a powerful European quasi-state in close alliance with its central bank, both of them sustained by, but also in command of, a strong European currency and a flourishing European economy. This vision is a direct challenge to the neo-liberal vision, favoured by corporate business and strongly associated with Washington DC, which wants to put multinational corporations in the driving seat where they can set the agenda of politicians and civil servants, both at home and abroad. The credit crunch and sovereign debt crisis have made it more difficult to implement either of these two visions, from Brussels and Washington respectively.

Government or private enterprise?

Meanwhile, on both sides of the Atlantic, the crisis has intensified the struggle for dominance between two interests, which have both been damaged by the current crisis: on the one hand private enterprise with its focus on profit-making, including transactional opportunities such as major currency shifts; on the other hand, government with its focus on regulation, especially the imposition of standards and procedures that enhance the state's capacity to deliver.

One very active front in this battle is the field of taxation. The European Commission has proposed a Tobin-like scheme to generate direct revenue from the EU's financial sector while, at the same time, reducing the levies paid by member states, a clear attempt to shift the burden away from governments to corporations.[11] Meanwhile, tax avoidance by business corporations is a very large-scale operation involving multiple transfers of funds through offshore tax havens. This has the overall effect of increasing corporate profits while at the same time depriving governments of revenue, thus systematically weakening states while strengthening corporations. Both Ireland and Greece (partly through its links with Cyprus) are part of the global offshore road map, on which the City of London is even more prominent.[12]

Humiliation is a weapon available to both sides in the struggle between government and private enterprise. Take the British case. Opponents of corporate power scored a substantial hit with the public grilling in the British House of Commons of Rupert Murdoch, a neo-liberal icon. Also subjected to ordeal by parliamentary committee were misbehaving senior executives of Barclays, a bank that had chosen to spurn the offer of assistance from the British government during the height of the credit crunch crisis. Meanwhile, on the other side, there is a constant stream of advocacy and speculation from the City of London about the possible collapse of the Euro. Such a collapse, perhaps precipitated by a Greek exit, would not only be a substantial profit opportunity for City traders. It would also be a major humiliation of the European Union and greatly diminish the authority of its leaders in Brussels, Berlin and Paris.

Humiliation or post-humiliation?

The European Union has always presented itself as a post-humiliation regime, a polity that respects and enforces the peaceful enjoyment of human rights within the societies and between the states that constitute it.[13] The EU's creation ended a century and a half of vengeful warfare between

France and Germany. The Union imposes high standards with respect to democracy, justice and citizenship rights upon new entrants. Liberty and equality as well as the spirit of fraternity are highly valued. For example, the principles of equality and fraternity are given institutional form in arrangements such as the EU's structural funds, which organize transfers to poorer and less developed areas.

For many national populations, joining the EU was an act of emancipation by a welcoming host, a way to put behind them a history of colonial subjection, or dictatorship, or both.[14] This was the case for post-Ascendancy Ireland,[15] post-Hitler West Germany, post-Mussolini Italy, post-Salazar Portugal, post-Franco Spain and post-Junta Greece. More recently, ex-members of the old "Eastern Bloc" joined the EU following the collapse of the Soviet Union and Yugoslavia. However, over recent years there has been a lack of fatted calves to slaughter for returning prodigal children.

In fact, humiliation has returned to Europe on a large scale during the past few years. The credit crunch and the Eurozone crisis have produced a considerable amount of forced social displacement: loss of jobs, income, status, reputation, credit and so on, not least in Greece and Ireland, our case studies. Furthermore, when, in their hour of need, the Greeks and the Irish were forced with great reluctance to ask for bailout loans to meet debt repayments falling due, they received not fraternal encouragement but paternal chastisement.

During the Eurozone crisis the EU has proved to be a heavy-handed parent, easily portrayed as a wicked stepmother. As everybody knows, the so-called *troika*—consisting of the European Commission (EC), the European Central Bank (ECB) and the International Monetary Fund (IMF)—has imposed draconian and unprecedented cuts in government spending upon the Irish and Greek governments, especially the latter.

Take another case: Slovenia. In late August 2012 there were signs that the government in Ljubljana might be forced to ask for a bailout from the EU. It is clear from the cases of Greece, Ireland and other governments that this would not be a pleasant experience. *The Economist* neatly summarized what is at stake in this case when it commented that "If Slovenia succumbs, … once again the badge of honour of joining the zone would have become a mark of humiliation" (*The Economist*, 2012; 59-60)

II. Humiliation coping tactics and response strategies

Subjection, relegation and exclusion

This is a good point to delve a little more deeply into the nature of humiliation. Stated briefly, it is forced social displacement that challenges and undermines the social identity of the displaced ones. The root cause of the distress caused to the victims is their awareness that an inferior social location and less worthy social identity are being imposed upon them, and they cannot prevent this.[16]

Humiliation is different from shame. When people feel shame, this is a mental and bodily acknowledgement that they themselves have transgressed norms that they accept. Shame feelings arise from contemplating the gap between those normative requirements and their own inadequate performance, as well as from the knowledge that others may be aware of their failings. Shame merges with guilt feelings as transgressors also acknowledge their own responsibility as authors of the shame-producing acts or characteristics.

By contrast, victims of humiliation feel transgressed *against*. Like Job their rhetorical response is, to paraphrase: "why me? what did I do to deserve this?" When humiliation happens, it is experienced as an undeserved deprivation, involving a loss or reduction of one or all of the following: *agency*, the capacity to enact one's will in the world; *autonomy*, the right to do what one wants; *security*, the expectation that one's identity and interests will be safeguarded; and *recognition*, the acknowledgement by others that one's social identity will be respected and taken into proper account.

At every level of societal existence, from an individual person to a national state, or a continental polity such as the European Union, the contours of the humiliation process are fundamentally the same. There are three "moments", which are logically or structurally related in a specific sequence (see Figure 6-1).

The first moment is *subjection*, entailing loss of autonomy and a reduction of agency for the victims, who become subordinate participants in a newly imposed hierarchy. This establishes the conditions for the second moment, which is *relegation*, whereby humiliated subordinates are pushed down the hierarchy, signaling their diminishing importance in the sight of those who rule. Relegation prepares the ground for the third moment, *exclusion*, which turns the subordinate into an outsider, deprived of recognition and protection.[17]

Figure 6-1. Three "moments" of humiliation—subjection, relegation, exclusion

I SUBJECTION ↓		
Reduction of *autonomy* and *agency*; imposition of *hierarchy*.	II RELEGATION ↓	
	Demotion within social hierarchy; diminution of *recognition* (reduction of worthiness).	III EXCLUSION ↓
		Denial of group membership, *recognition* and *security*; some *agency* and *autonomy* may be retained.

For all its idealism, the post-war European movement was given life at a moment of humiliation. It was the overwhelming preponderance of US military power that forced arrogant enemies in Western Europe to enter into economic cooperation.[18] Ironically, it was their common subjection to American lordship, to their conquest by Washington that created a sense of equality, and later increasing fraternity, between French, German, Italian and Benelux diplomats and politicians. This spirit was given institutional form through the practice of distributing the positions of European Commissioner in Brussels on an egalitarian basis amongst member countries while insisting that each commissioner should represent the interests of the EU as a whole.

Since the beginning of the "common market", as the EU was initially termed, some critics in all member countries have treated it as a transgression, an undemocratic imposition by an arrogant European Commission upon the citizens of sovereign nations, who are left relatively powerless. However, the present recession has reshaped the debate. For the first time the subterranean division, and sometimes, tension between the northern and southern members of the EU has come to the surface and taken centre stage.[19]

It is common to present the current situation as *subjection* of the EU to German interests, and to see the imposition of austerity programmes on Greece, Italy, Spain and Portugal as the *relegation* of the South to an inferior position within the EU. Greece is the object of a sustained attempt from at least some vocal commentators to implement the third moment of humiliation: *exclusion*, from the Euro and perhaps also the EU itself.

Coping tactics

Those who suffer humiliation have no choice but to acquiesce in their enforced displacement, in the first instance. Since they have been unable to prevent it from happening, they have to cope with it, for a while at least. What can they do? They typically retain some degree of autonomy and agency, which can be exploited in coping tactics such as *reversal, separation, pragmatic accommodation and surrender.* People may move between these tactics and some may be combined.

Reversal seizes the initiative in a self-dramatizing way. This may take the form of defiant compliance. This tactic parades the supposedly demeaning identity as a kind of banner, with amusement or contempt, showing that carrying this label is quite bearable. One example occurred in June 2012 when a group of Irish fans about to fly off to the European football championship displayed an Irish flag with the words: "Angela Merkel Thinks We're At Work."[20]

Another, more complex variant of reversal is the politics of victimhood. In this case, the object is to make others, including the supposed perpetrators, feel guilty, sorry or afraid because of the victim's condition. The victims may then manipulate these feelings for their own advantage. For example, they may demand help, compensation, indulgence, special understanding, privileged credence, or the right to take revenge.

A second set of coping tactics involves *separation.* By dividing themselves internally, individuals and groups are able to present a misleading persona to their masters, enemies or rivals. Behind that screen they can protect and deploy their other selves. This approach makes possible sabotage (minor acts of revenge), inner withdrawal ("The real me/us is not engaged here") and denial ("this is not happening to me/us"). Reversal and separation both have the effect of blurring and disrupting the framing power of humiliation, interrupting its attempt to reassign social identity and social location in a demeaning way.

Turning to the other coping tactics, those who adopt the tactics of *pragmatic accommodation* and *surrender* shrug their shoulders and admit: "We lost out. They won." Pragmatic accommodation means cooperating with new masters who command by right of conquest. Their new servants use the shreds of agency and autonomy they still retain to limit their chances of being hurt. They may make few demands or complaints (adopting stoicism), at least not openly (imposing self-censorship). They may go further and acknowledge the superiority of those who now command them (through real or pretended elevation of the master) and even minimize the significance of their own suffering (through real or pretended self-diminishment). By contrast, the tactic of surrender gives up the last shreds of autonomy and agency, through exhaustion and demoralization. It raises the white flag and says: "Do with us as you wish."

These initial coping tactics, driven by forced acquiescence, can only be short term. Even the attitude of surrender may be abandoned if the initial exhaustion of defeat passes. All these tactics defer resolution of a large and pressing question, which is: how can the victims of humiliation get rid of the intense discomfort—what Cannetti calls "the sting" (see Cannetti 1973, 67, 355, 360)—that has been caused by contemplating the extent of their "fall", the distance between, on the one hand, where they "really" belong and who they "really" are and, on the other hand, the social location and social identity that are being forced upon them? Coping tactics may alleviate the discomfort in the short term. Getting rid of the sting requires longer-term strategies of response.

Response strategies

Over time, short-term coping tactics are likely to merge into longer-term response strategies (see Figure 6-2). For example, two types of yielding response may be identified. One of these is *escape,* in other words, removing the object of intended humiliation (i.e., the victim) to somewhere that is out of the perpetrator's reach. Emigration is a classic instance of this strategy.

If it is to work, emigration must be more than exile, which continues the humiliation in the form of exclusion. Successful emigration must be to a better place, a promised land, a kind of paradise. So the escaping emigrants' standards and expectations are high, and their fear of failure and renewed humiliation great. Such migrants are suspicious of all neighbours, and liable to engage in pre-emptive strikes against them, repeatedly. Humiliation, for others and themselves, is liable to be renewed through such fear cycles.[21]

Another yielding response is *acceptance*, which attempts to remove the victim's objection to humiliation by agreeing that the distress and deprivation it caused was a deserved punishment. This turns humiliation into shame. But does this win the master's respect? If not, the danger is that acceptance is followed by further acts of humiliation: a victimization cycle.

There are also two challenging responses. One is *rejection*, which tries to eliminate the effects of humiliation on the capacity and morale of the victim. Rejection can take one or both of two forms. Revenge-rejection tries to "even up the score" by inflicting a counter-humiliation. The likely effect is to trigger more "incoming" humiliation and this has to be answered in turn, leading to a revenge cycle, which, like the fear cycle and the victimization cycle, perpetuates acts of humiliation into the future. Another approach is resistance-rejection, which maintains or builds up the victims' strength, reducing their vulnerability to humiliating attacks.

If resistance-rejection is successful, it may prepare the ground for the second challenging response, which is *conciliation/reform*. In this case, the intention is not to damage or destroy the humiliating person or group but to remove the causes of humiliation itself: to eliminate the condition by reforming the relationship between the parties concerned.

Conciliation/reform works best if there is a powerful third party respected and/or feared by both sides that can act as intermediary and guide, preferably with ample resources to help fund the creation of a new institutional order. So, it was after World War II when the United States made greater economic cooperation and exchange between France and Germany a precondition for Marshall Aid. The British and Irish governments played a similar role in bringing peace to Northern Ireland. In this fourth strategy, the chief danger is that truce and negotiation will not reduce distrust sufficiently to prevent the recurrence of conflict, and the renewal of humiliating acts of aggression.

Which of the coping tactics and strategic responses will be available or adopted in any particular case is likely to be greatly influenced by the practical opportunities available and the various parties' cultural resources, attitudes and habits of behaviour. Those factors are shaped by history to a great extent, and a brief historical comparison between Greece and Ireland will be useful, not only as a case study in the dynamics of humiliation but also as a stimulus to thinking about how the responses within national societies to the current Eurozone crisis may impact at the level of the EU as a whole. In the next section the object is not to produce fully-rounded analytical portraits of two societies–which would be impossible in this presentation–but to draw attention to some key differences between them which help to account for their differing responses to the threat of humiliation during the Eurozone crisis.

Figure 6-2. Response strategies

	Type of Strategy	Object of Strategy	Downside Risk
Yielding Responses	ESCAPE	To remove the **object** → of intended humiliation	Fear Cycle
	ACCEPTANCE	To remove the **objection** → to humiliation	Victimization Cycle
Challenging Responses	REJECTION: Revenge-Rejection or Resistance-Rejection?	To eliminate the **effects** → of humiliation	Revenge Cycle
	CONCILIATION-REFORM	To eliminate the **causes** → of humiliation	Distrust Cycle

III. Geo-history and geo-politics[22]

Geo-history and geo-politics have dealt very different hands to Ireland and Greece. Their monuments declare this difference. Athens has its hilltop citadel, the Acropolis, dominated by the Parthenon, which served as the fortified treasury of the ancient Athenian empire. These buildings say that Greeks have autonomy and agency, that they are not just a free people but also powerful, imperial, with a history of being leaders and overlords.[23] Greek culture, the Greek language, and Greek churchmen, merchants and officials all dominated Byzantium, the Eastern Roman Empire, and retained an important position in its Islamic successor, the Ottoman Empire.

Historically, the Greek world from the Balkans to Asia Minor and beyond was a vast beehive whose main movers and shakers were traders, military men and diplomatic fixers. Their primary loyalty was to their good name, their extended families and their localities. This way of thinking was widespread throughout Greek society at all levels. The main task of life was to pursue prosperity and honour through the market and, where possible, political bargaining. The values of the town seeped deep into the countryside along with commercialized agriculture.[24]

Many of the richest and most powerful Greeks made and invested their money outside the Greek mainland, both before and after 1832 when the sovereign Greek state came into existence. Traditionally, they had strong alliances with leading Orthodox churchmen, similarly cosmopolitan, who helped them keep their profits out of the hands of Ottoman tax-collectors, and do so with a good conscience. These tax-avoidance habits did not diminish after 1832. Nor were they confined to the rich.

By contrast, the main buildings in Ireland's capital, Dublin Castle, Trinity College and Leinster House are all symbols of past English rule, the so-called Protestant Ascendancy.[25] For centuries the "emerald isle" was trapped between the Atlantic Ocean and its much larger neighbour whose industrial strength and imperial possessions made it the most powerful in the world during the mid- and late nineteenth century. The feeling of being at the bottom of the heap entered deep into Irish popular culture. As Jimmy Rabbitts put it in the film *The Commitments* (1991), "Do you not get it lads? The Irish are the blacks of Europe" (http://www.imdb.com/title/tt0101605/quotes [16 June 2013]). However exaggerated, this very un-Greek statement expresses a common Irish attitude: proud resentment.

In Ireland, unlike Greece, the values of the countryside dominated the town.[26] The larger tenant farmers set those values. This class had established its dominance locally after the Great Famine of the 1840s, which had dispersed the landless poor, many to the graveyard, and others to England or America. Above them were the Anglo-Irish gentry living on their estates or in England.[27] There had been a very serious Irish revolt against the English crown in 1798, and since then intermittent protests against specific injustices, but the main response to subjection was pragmatic accommodation.

Not till the 1950s did the world open up for the Irish Republic, when American big business and finance capital began to look overseas in a big way and the Atlantic Ocean became a bridge and not a barrier. By contrast, the new Kingdom of Greece, born in the early nineteenth century, had from its beginning the benefit of being on a busy global crossroads in the East Mediterranean, patrolling the frontier not only between East and West, but also between North and South. For centuries, the Greeks have had widespread trading and diplomatic links and it has been advantageous for foreigners with ambitions in this strategically significant area to make bargains with them. The new state's founders made the most of this.

Nation-building and ideology

The leaders of the Greek War of Independence (1821-32) knew the Ottoman Empire was slowly crumbling and wanted a more secure political base, one under their control.[28] During the war massacres were common on both sides. The politics of victimhood were mobilized effectively by the Greek rebels and their friends, for example in several paintings made by Eugène Delacroix, one of which depicted Greece as a maiden threatened with humiliation at Ottoman hands.[29]

Then, as now, powerful business and political interests in Europe and America were ready to buy friends and influence in a territory that provided a valuable listening post in a highly sensitive region. Foreign loans flowed into Athens throughout the century, for distribution among competing factions and to pay for wars intended to detach more Greek territory from the Ottoman Empire.[30] Victorious politicians handed out positions in central government and local administration to their supporters. Patronage and clientelism ruled, a tradition that has continued. Loans were often not repaid but the foreign governments who made them, such as the French and English and, later, the Americans, were able to wield influence inside Greece. Occasionally, the government went bankrupt, most notoriously in 1893 after which an international commission moved into Athens to supervise the administration of the national budget.[31] These scenarios show that recent exchanges between Greece and the EU leadership have historical precedents.

In the early 1920s, the historical trajectories of Ireland and Greece briefly converged. At that point, each country was, for the first time, both independent and with stable territorial boundaries,[32] although both had troubled frontiers in the north.[33]

However, their national trajectories were very different. In the Greek case territorial stabilization coincided with the ejection of Hellenic forces and populations from Asia Minor, a major defeat for *Megali* idea, the dream of a greater Greece.[34] By contrast, in Ireland's case, the early 1920s were a moment of success: the end of British rule and the establishment of a Free State. During those years the Greek state was humiliated while the Irish state triumphed over past humiliations.

There was another difference. By the late 1920s, the Irish Free state had not only got rid of its foreign monarchy but also established itself as a reasonably coherent and stable parliamentary democracy under civilian control, a condition Greece did not begin to achieve for another half-century. In Ireland, there was a brief civil war (1922-3) caused by disagreement within the nationalist movement over the terms of the treaty but after that the new state was able to spend two decades settling in and settling down. During the 1930s, it had to deal with an Anglo-Irish trade war and a short-lived proto-fascist movement but progress towards stability was helped by several factors. The focus of political militancy was transferred north outside the Free State. The conservatism of rural Ireland was reinforced by Eamon De Valera's support for small-scale farming and a protectionist tariff wall.[35] The Irish state was neutral in the Second World War. Above all, Ireland inherited a highly efficient and professional civil service from the British.[36]

Meanwhile, in Greece the crown, military chiefs and political leaders such as Eleftherios Venizelos found it very difficult to make stable compromises with each other. The complexity and instability of government was increased when after 1923 it acquired an influential and discontented refugee population that soon organized itself both in commerce and politics, especially in the largest towns and in the north. The newcomers injected a new dimension of idealistic or ideological vision into Greek politics, partially filling the vacuum left by the collapse of hopes for a greater Greece. One consequence was to increase the ranks of Greek socialist and communist organizations.

By the mid-1930s, the Metaxas dictatorship had forced the Greek left underground, and it did not fully re-emerge in Greece's public arena for another four decades. That brief summary does not adequately convey the intense and prolonged trauma experienced by all Greeks during and after the Second World War from invasion through occupation to civil war. However, the main point here is that Greece's position on the frontier between East and West meant that for three decades after 1945 American influence was used to keep the left out of Greek politics while bringing prosperity to the Greek people. Marshall Aid and foreign direct investment produced a so-called "Greek miracle" during the 1950s and 1960s mainly focused on urban renewal and tourism.[37]

This state of affairs came to an end during the 1970s when the United States began looking for ways to reduce the economic burden of its overseas commitments. By that time, the European Union was beginning to seem like an alternative home for Greece, especially after that sensitive and volatile "frontier" state got rid of its military dictatorship.[38] For Greece, entry to the EU was the solution to a geo-political dilemma. For Ireland, it was the seizing of a geo-economic opportunity.

Europe and emancipation

In 1958, shortly before the Treaty of Rome was signed, the Irish government finally abandoned protectionism and began to plan for economic expansion through free trade with a new emphasis on industry and services.[39] As part of this strategy, Ireland sought membership in the EU and finally succeeded in 1973. Stable and Anglophone, Ireland proved to be a highly convenient point of entry to that trading area for American business. By the 1990s, Ireland was having its own "economic miracle", culminating in the "Celtic Tiger" years (1995-2007) during which very high levels of bank-lending to businesses and private individuals fed a property boom.

The economic story of Ireland's boom and bust is well known. Less appreciated is the change that occurred in Irish culture. For half a century, before joining the EU, Ireland had been free yet still half-trapped in the restrained postures imposed by centuries of pragmatic accommodation with British rule. Entry into Europe increased the self-esteem of the Irish, especially their professional and business elites. It also opened up popular culture to outside influences to a greater extent than before, and gave people, especially women, encouragement to stand up for their rights.

By the time the Celtic Tiger years arrived, there was a rough balance between the new expansive optimism and the defensive caution and cynicism of the old days. The Celtic Tiger years lasted a little over a decade.[40] Ten years is enough time for a family to accumulate a large number of debts and get a taste for high living, while enjoying the contrast between present luxuries and the tighter budgets of earlier years. But a decade is not long enough for old habits and attitudes to die out, so long-established Irish reactions to the threat of humiliation have sprung into life. Both of the yielding responses mentioned earlier have come into play. Escape has taken the form of emigration as young people resume the practice of looking for opportunities overseas, in Canada, Australia, South Africa and elsewhere. Acceptance is also rife. Many people feel a little ashamed of being swept up by the temptation to go deeply into debt to fulfill dreams of individual happiness they now realize were unrealistic. The boom, it now seems, was a party that got out of hand, so now, it is widely accepted, everyone must put up with a very big hangover and abide by the rules in the future.

The Greek case is very different. The demise of the military regime and the turn towards Europe provided a large political opportunity for Andreas Papandreou, the charismatic left-wing son of a formidable centrist politician. Using the Panhellenic Socialist Movement (PASOK) as his vehicle, Andreas, as he was commonly known, was able to capture the electoral initiative. He had the skills needed to win mass votes from a rapidly urbanizing population that wanted to maintain and, if possible, improve its living standards. This was a difficult challenge since growth was lower and prices higher for several years after the mid-70s.

Going into the EU gave the PASOK government access to a large amount of funding. Following Greek political practice established over the previous century and a half, these funds, bolstered by the additional financial leverage they made possible, were channeled into government contracts, financing the expansion of central and local government, and generally oiling the wheels of political influence.

The money provided incomes for thousands of people, many of them PASOK supporters, young and old adherents of left-wing politics who had a collective memory of half a century of being abused, persecuted, and excluded. Some of them had fought against the Nazis, and later the British, during the period of occupation and civil war. For such people, and their friends and relatives, the largesse supplied through PASOK was a just and long-delayed form of recompense for prolonged suffering, one to which they felt fully entitled.

This could not be said too openly. The vast expansion of the public sector was presented as the building of a modernizing technocratic and professional elite whose task was to bring about the change (*allage*) that Greece so badly needed.[41] PASOK's conservative opponents, New Democracy, criticized this rationale but maintained the system, extending it to their own supporters. The consequences of this approach for Greece's public finances are now very well known.

Comparing the Irish and Greek cases in these years, some differences stand out. One is that the system established by PASOK in the early 1980s had a quarter of a century to take root. That is long enough to implant a specific *habitus* in a whole generation, to instill a style of life and a set of perceptions. After twenty-five years of prosperity, many Greek citizens had been rescued by the expansion of the public sector, either as employees or recipients of benefits. They had buried the painful past in forgetfulness and become used to the more comfortable present (now the recent past). Axing the public sector, as is now being done, feels to them more like an amputation than a hangover.

As in Ireland, there is some evidence of acceptance and the desire to escape. For example, some Greeks are returning from the cities to the countryside ("Greek crisis forces thousands of Athenians into rural migration" (Smith, 2011: 18). However, desire for revenge is a much more prominent response in Greece than in Ireland. Politicians are physically attacked in the streets. Major public buildings are set on fire. German politicians are caricatured as Nazis in the press, a reminder of old wounds. Immigrants are beaten up. The radical right and the radical left are both resurgent. This is very different from Dublin.

The main political beneficiary seems to be SYRIZA, which may have a good chance of displacing PASOK as the main party of the left in Greece.[42] SYRIZA's insistence that the spending cuts and repayments demanded by the *troika* are impossible to make seems highly realistic, irrespective of whether or not one accepts that they are completely unjustified. It would mean reversing at a stroke political and economic practices that have been embedded in Greece for nearly two centuries, as well as expropriating a generation of articulate and well-organised citizens who have only recently come into what they see as their well-deserved and much-delayed inheritance.

IV. Where do we go from here?

A well-known Irish joke tells of an old man who was asked the question: how do I get to the city of Cork? His answer was, of course: I would not start from here. In other political and economic circumstances, one possible answer to the question of how we alleviate the pressures being placed upon Greek citizens might be: provide the external financial support needed and, at the same time, monitor the implementation of an agreed plan, over a time period that is feasible, for reforming the public sector (including the system of tax collection), promoting industrial growth and educating a new generation in the satisfactions of genuine public service.

When this is proposed the normal reply is: not enough time, not enough money. Why are the necessary time and money not being made available? The reasons are certainly complex but seem to stem in part from lack of trust and good will on many sides, a condition made worse by the playing out of humiliation dynamics. Another factor seems to be speculation that there may be benefits to certain special interests if Greece exits from the Euro.

Presumably, those possible benefits are being calculated not just by financial speculators but also by political speculators on both the left and the right. Second-guessing those calculations and evaluating them would require another paper. However, anyone who is still interested in the prospects for the European Union as a post-humiliation project advancing equality and human rights might take a deeper look at the basic roots of the crisis.

Constant complaining in the media about the failings of national politicians in the so-called PIIGS, especially in Greece, has drawn attention away from the origins of the present crisis. These lie in the neglectful and sometimes fraudulent behaviour of bankers and allied professions in and around the finance industry. This has included the practice of maximizing their returns by leveraging assets through the creation of mountains of dubious debt.[43] The result of this activity has been to throw huge extra burdens on the treasuries of those governments who came to the banks' rescue.

It is therefore difficult to accept with equanimity another very extensive activity of finance professionals. This has been to build up a massive apparatus for tax avoidance crossing national and continental borders, thus depriving those same governments of the income they need to replenish the treasuries they have emptied on the banks' behalf.

Set beside this huge attack on the public purse throughout the European Union and beyond, the failings of the Greek tax-payer come into their proper perspective. There is surely a case for giving the regulation and reduction of tax avoidance by business corporations throughout Europe a much higher prominence on the EU's agenda. It may be an even more important task than punishing the Greeks and praising the Irish.

Notes

[1] In preparing this paper I made visits to both Athens and Dublin. I am grateful for help and comments to Michael Spourdalakis, Nicolas Demertsiz, Costas Eleftheriou, and many colleagues in the Hellenic Political Science Association (whose kind invitation to speak in March 2012 gave me the chance to try out, and correct, some early thoughts), Teresa Whitaker, Mike Fitzgerald, James Wickham, Colm O'Regan, and (beyond Dublin) to many participants at the 2012 Kilkenny Comedy Festival (which I attended through the kind invitation of Ed Smith and Tami Hoffman). I would also like to thank colleagues in the European Sociological Association Research Network on Disaster, Conflict and Social Crisis for their comments on earlier versions of this paper which was initially presented at a

conference in Mytilene on the social impacts of the Eurozone debt crisis organised by Dr Nicolas Petropoulos, 13-14th September 2012.

[2] The discussion on Newsnight (31st May 2012) was between, Jeremy Paxman, BBC presenter, Paul Krugman, Nobel prize winner in economics and Giorgos Papakonstantinou, a PhD from LSE, one-time senior economist at the OECD, and an ex-finance minister in the PASOK government. Paxman's distinguished guests "swiftly slapped him down", to borrow the phrase used in the next day's *Daily Mail*. Paxman did not try to defend himself, then or later. Demeaning and diminishing others is a common tactic in political debate and all forms of power struggle, including contests over authority, legitimacy and competence. Stereotyping is one form of intended humiliation, used here by Paxman. Replying, Papakonstantinou let it be seen that he was angry but completely under control. He took issue with the analogy and said: "the Greek people are going through a lot, and deserve some respect, and I really did not find that very appropriate." Krugman followed this up by telling Paxman: "I think that was, actually, quite inappropriate, to say that the Greeks have done something terribly wrong."

[3] The reference is to the early American pioneer, John Winthrop who used this phrase in 1630, see, for example, http://www.historytools.org/sources/winthrop-charity.pdf [17 June 2013].

[4] The draft treaty text may be found at http://www.telegraph.co.uk/finance/financialcrisis/9026142/The-EU-fiscal-draft-treaty-in-full.html [17 June 2013].

[5] A copy of the memorandum may be found at http://www.scribd.com/doc/81046399/Memorandum-of-Economic-and-Financial-Policies-February-8 [18 June 2013].

[6] See, for example, "Irish treat pain of crisis like a hangover," Gillian Tett of the *Financial Times* on May 10th 2010.

[7] Two examples of many: http://www.telegraph.co.uk/finance/financialcrisis/9345635/Hedge-fund-manager-says-that-Greece-must-leave-euro-or-it-will-fail.html; http://www.dailymail.co.uk/news/article-2149193/Greece-WILL-leave-eurozone-January-1-2013-Citigroup-boss-predicts-exit-date-warns-massive-wave-contagion-Europe.html [19 June 2013]

[8] Before that date the EU was held within the embrace of the transatlantic alliance, alongside NATO. It "borrowed" the prestige and aura of strength enjoyed by its powerful ally, the United States. However, after 1989 the EU became more independent of the United States and built up its institutional apparatus, for example through the Maastricht Treaty.

[9] For one version of the historical context, see Smith and Wright, 1999a.

[10] From a speech at Elysee Palace, 4th November 1999. See www.delegfrance-cd-geneve.org/chirac041199.htm (30th May 2005; consulted 19 June 2013)). "Prime Minister's speech to the Polish Stock Exchange", October 6th 2000. See www.number-10.gov.uk/news.asp?Newsld=1341&Section1d=32 [18 June 2013] Quoted in Kupchan 2002, 151.

[11] See Ian Traynor, "EU calls for Tobin tax in a move to raise direct revenue", *The Guardian*, 29 June 2011.

[12] See, for example, Hellener, 1994; Palan, 2003; Shaxson, 2012.
[13] This was formalised in 2009 with the accession of the EU to the European Convention of Human Rights, which originally came into force under the auspices of the Council of Europe in 1953. See http://hub.coe.int/what-we-do/human-rights/eu-accession-to-the-convention [18 June 2013]
[14] See, for example, Jauregui 1999.
[15] The reference is to the so-called "Protestant Ascendancy", the domination of Irish society and politics by the British crown until the early twentieth century.
[16] Humiliation may be deliberate, or it may be an unintended occurrence. It may be experienced by an individual, in some cases marked out as a member of a specific social category, or by a group, for example an occupational or ethnic group, or a group sharing leadership responsibilities within an institution (such as an army, a church, or a national state apparatus). It may also occur within a crowd, since crowds may both impose and be subjected to humiliation.
[17] Take the case of an individual who is suffering symptoms of dementia or some other form of mental ill-health, either temporary or irreversible, but who remains perfectly capable of perceiving changes in the attitudes and behaviour of others. Their decreased ability to manage important aspects of their lives is likely to mean they fall increasingly under the control of others, some of them strangers. They lose agency and autonomy. They experience subjection. As they become less powerful and more dependent within their relationships, this may lead to increased demoralization and depression, and a worsening of their symptoms. If they become institutionalized, and increasingly under the control of strangers, the danger is that they become regarded as chronic sufferers, less interesting, and less worthy of personal attention and respect. They may suffer relegation in the pecking order. This would make them more vulnerable to denial of proper human consideration, to neglect and even abuse. Only the strongest of such victims may retain sufficient agency to exploit their remaining autonomy and complain or even rebel.
[18] See Smith 1999.
[19] For a relevant recent discussion see Thompson 2009.
[20] Later they were invited to tea in Dublin by the German Ambassador who commented: "It was such a great joke, such a perfect example of Irish humour," he said, adding "We put a lot of hope in the Irish people... they are determined to succeed, and they will recover." (http://www.bbc.co.uk/news/uk-northern-ireland-18371142; http://www.bbc.co.uk/news/uk-northern-ireland-18582740 [18 June 2013]. The ambassador, perhaps sensibly, chose to see the episode as an example of humour without acknowledging the undercurrent of derision.
[21] See Smith 2006, especially chapters 8-10
[22] By a happy chance, Ireland and Greece were both case studies in a collection edited by Margaret Scotford Archer and Salvador Giner, entitled *Contemporary Europe. Class, Status and Power*, published in 1971. Comparing the chapter on Greece with the Ireland chapter, certain similarities can be seen. In the early 1970s, in both countries manufacturing was on small-scale and agriculture remained the predominant activity. Tertiary occupations connected with the professions, tourism, shopkeeping and office work were more widely developed than manufacturing. The Church was a powerful conservative force. Political life at a

local level was to a great extent based upon patronage and the exchange of favours. Property ownership and kinship links were the main basis of inequality and social ranking, although educational qualifications were interwoven with these particularistic structures. The editors comment that "In countries where tertiary development has outstripped the emergence of a strong industrial sector (such as Ireland and Greece) there is an analogous, though less marked, tendency for open competition to follow the possession of certain status characteristics" (Archer and Giner, 1971: 48).

[23] The Roman monuments, symbols of Greek military defeat, are liable to be dismissed by Athenians as "the new stuff."

[24] The Greek small farmer's characteristics included "imitation of urban styles of life and increasing desire to migrate to the city…Rising aspirations and the development of a consumer's mentality…[and] Chronic indebtedness to urban moneylenders and state banks, etc." (Mouzelis and Attalides, 1971: 173).

[25] Leinster House, seat of the Irish national parliament, used to be the residence of the Dukes of Leinster, a branch of the Norman-Welsh Fitzwilliam dynasty.

[26] John Jackson reported that in Ireland in the early 1970s "the influence of the farm family and its dominant position of the country remain decisive", being (for example) "responsible for the institutional character of [Irish] marriage and for status attributions which continue into the urban society of Dublin and provide the basic framework for analysis" (Jackson, 1971; 204).

[27] Or Scotland, Wales or other parts of the Empire. My mother, born in Limerick, used to quote an Irish saying, "The Devil is an absentee landlord". Compare Al Pacino as the Devil in *The Devil's Advocate*: "God…is an absentee landlord!" http://www.youtube.com/watch?v=F2oq7sgBETE [16 June 2013].

[28] The context is explained in Spourdalakis 1988, 13-14.

[29] The picture is entitled "Greece on the Ruins of Missologhi". See, for example, http://www.eugenedelacroix.org/Greece-on-the-Ruins-of-Missolonghi.html [20 June 2013]

[30] Each new bit of new territory–the Ionian Islands in 1864, Thessaly in 1881, Crete, Epirus and Macedonia in 1913, and West Thrace in 1923–added to the nation-state's complexity, bringing new dialects and regional cultures.

[31] For information on this and other episodes, see Dritsas 1993.

[32] The Dodecanese Islands were added later in 1947.

[33] There were issues relating to Ulster and Macedonia, respectively.

[34] On the "great idea", see, for example, Peckham, chapter three.

[35] On St Patrick's Day 1943, De Valera told his radio audience about "The ideal Ireland that we would have, the Ireland that we dreamed of, would be the home of a people who valued material wealth only as a basis for right living, of a people who, satisfied with frugal comfort, devoted their leisure to the things of the spirit—a land whose countryside would be bright with cosy homesteads, whose fields and villages would be joyous with the sounds of industry, with the romping of sturdy children, the contest of athletic youths and the laughter of happy maidens, whose firesides would be forums for the wisdom of serene old age. The home, in short, of a people living the life that God desires that men should live." See *Oxford Dictionary of Quotations* 1999, 259.

[36] A useful survey of this period can be found in Lee, 1989, chapters 2 and 3.
[37] In 1971, Mouzelis and Attalides pointed out that "the urban prosperity achieved after the war is not an "economic miracle"—in the sense that the country develops along lines that aggravate rather than solve the social and economic problems of the country". They quote UN figures showing that before the war "Greece was the most industrialized country in the Balkans" but by 1965 it had fallen below Yugoslavia, Bulgaria and Rumania. Mouzelis and Attilides 1971, 177.
[38] The main advocate for Greek entry into Europe had been Contantine Karamalis. Papandreou had spoken against it though he subsequently swung round on the issue (Woodhouse, 1982: 104, 109; Spourdalakis, 1988: 164.
[39] A key intellectual, political and diplomatic role was played by the Irish civil servant T.K (Ken) Whitaker. Ireland's Economic and Social Research Institute is located in Whitaker Square, named in his honour.
[40] For one view of the period, see Hourihane 2000. For other analytical surveys, see, for example, O' Hearn 1998; O'Hearn 2001; Inglis 2008; O'Sullivan 2006.
[41] See Spoudalakis, chapter 5.
[42] On Syriza's rise, see Alex Doherty's interview with Michael Spourdalakis on the New Left Project website at http://www.newleftproject.org/index.php/site/article_comments/syrizas_rise [20 June 2013]
[43] Some interesting insights are to be found in Gillian Tett's highly readable *Fool's gold* (Tett, 2010).

References

Archer, M.S. and Giner, S. (1971). *Contemporary Europe. Class, status and power*, London: Weidenfeld and Nicolson.

Cannetti, E. (1971). *Crowds and power*. Harmondsworth: Penguin.

Cooper, M. (2012). *How Ireland really went bust*, London: Penguin.

Donnelly, J.S. (2002). *The great Irish potato famine,* Dublin: The History Press.

Doyle, R (1990). *The Commitments*, London: Vintage.

Dritsas, M. (1993). "Foreign capital and Greek development in historical perspective," *Uppsala Papers in Economic History*, Working paper no 10, Uppsala University, Sweden.

Hellener, E. (1994). *States and the reemergence of global finance*, London: Cornell University Press.

Hourihane, A.M. (2000). *She moves through the boom*, Dublin: Sitric Books.

Inglis, T. (2008). *Global Ireland. Same difference*, London: Routledge.

Jackson, J. (1971). 'Ireland' in Archer M.S.and Giner, S. (eds.) *Contemporary Europe. Class, status and power*, London: Weidenfeld and Nicolson, pp. 198-222.

Jauregui, P (1999). 'National pride and the meaning of Europe: A comparative study of Britain and Spain', in Smith, D and Wright, S (1999b). *Whose Europe? The turn towards democracy*, Oxford: Blackwell, pp. 257-87.

Koliopoulos, J. S. and Veremis, T.M. (2002). *Greece. The modern sequel from 1821 to the present*, London: Hurst.

Kupchan, C. (2002). The end of the American era, New York: Alfred A. Knopf.

Lapavitsas, C. et. al. (2012). *Crisis in the Eurozone*, London: Verso.

Lee, J.J. (1989). *Ireland 1912-1985,* Cambridge: Cambridge University Press.

Manolopoulos, J (2011). *Greece's "odious" debt. The looting of the Hellenic Republic by the Euro, the political elite and the investment community*, London: Anthem Press.

Mouzelis, N. and Attalides, M. (1971). 'Greece", in Archer, M.S. and Giner, S. (eds.) *Contemporary Europe. Class, status and power*, London: Weidenfeld and Nicolson, pp. 162-97.

Mokyr, J. (1983). *Why Ireland starved. A Quantitative and analytical history of the Irish economy, 1800-1850*, London: Allen and Unwin.

O Grada, C. (1989). *The great Irish famine*, London: Macmillan.

O'Hearn, D. (1998). *Inside the Celtic tiger. The Irish economy and the Asian model*, London: Pluto Press.

—. (2001). *The Atlantic economy. Britain, the US and Ireland*, Manchester: Manchester University Press.

O'Sullivan, M.J. (2006). *Ireland and the global question*, Cork: Cork University Press. *Oxford dictionary of quotations* (1999), Oxford: Oxford University Press.

Palan, R. (2003). *The offshore world. Sovereign markets, virtual places and nomad millionaires*, London: Cornell University Press.

Peckham, R.S. (2001). *National histories, natural states. Nationalism and the politics of place in Greece*, London: I.B.Tauris.

Petrakis, M. (2006). *The Metaxas myth. Dictatorship and propaganda in Greece*, London: I.B.Taurus.

Shaxson, N. ((2012). *Treasure island. Tax havens and the men who stole the world*, London: Vintage.

Smith, D. (1999). 'Making Europe—processes of Europe-formation since 1945', in Smith, D. and Wright, S. (1999b). *Whose Europe? The turn towards democracy*, Oxford: Blackwell, pp. 235-56.

—. (2001). *Norbert Elias and modern social theory*, London: Sage, pp. 134-47.

—. (2006). *Globalization. The hidden agenda*, Cambridge: Polity.

Smith, D and Wright, S. (1999a). 'The turn towards democracy' in Smith, D. and Wright, S. (eds.) *Whose Europe? The turn towards democracy*, Oxford: Blackwell, pp. 1-18.

Smith, D. and Wright, S. (eds.) (1999b). *Whose Europe? The turn towards democracy*, Oxford: Blackwell.

Smith, H. (2011), 'Greek crisis forces thousands of Athenians into rural migration', *The Guardian*, 16 June, p. 18.

Spourdalakis, M. (1988).*The rise of the Greek socialist party*, London: Routledge.

The Economist, (2012). 'Next in line', 18 August, pp. 59-60, http://www.economist.com/node/21560567.

Tett, G. (2010). *Fool's gold. How unrestrained greed corrupted a dream, shattered global markets and unleashed a catastrophe*, London: Abacus.

Thompson, R (2009). "Actor alignments in the European Union before and after enlargement",*European Journal of Political Research*, vol. 48, pp.756-781.

Veremis, T. (1997). *The military in Greek politics. From independence to democracy,* London: Hurst.

Woodhouse, C.M. (1982). *Karamanlis. The restorer of Greek democracy*, Oxford: Clarendon Press.

CHAPTER SEVEN

EFFECTS OF THE ECONOMIC CRISIS ON POVERTY IN GREECE

DIONYSSIS BALOURDOS

NATIONAL CENTER FOR SOCIAL RESEARCH

Abstract

This paper aims to identify the impact of the economic crisis on poverty in Greece, using data from the EU-SILC survey. The analysis is mainly descriptive and comparative, based on appropriate indices, trends, and policy prospects. The research questions are: How was poverty in Greece affected at the early years of the recession? Have new forms of poverty emerged? Has its severity increased? Can reliable policy answers be formulated? In Greece, the impacts of the current budget cuts and the unprecedented economic and social crisis on poverty have been considerable, even though they will be fully felt only at a later stage. What is important, however, is that the available data indicate it is not only the level of poverty that matters, but also the way in which it should be examined and interpreted. New concepts, such as "new poor", "severe poor", "near poor", "persistent poor" and "materially deprived", indicate that we are dealing with new forms of poverty, completely differentiated from the "old poor". In Greece, the poor are "financially poor" and, to great extent, "materially deprived", as a result of redistribution policies being insufficient to offset the effects of high levels of income inequality. During the crisis, social groups that are traditionally more exposed to poverty, i.e., unemployed, immigrant workers, single mothers, are joined by the "new poor": working poor, children and young people, typical male bread winner households and households with difficulties in making "ends meet". The "old poor" have become poorer and stay in poverty for extended periods of time, but at the same time, below the conventional poverty line fall people who had never been there before. Our analysis suggests that not only the "vulnerable poor" but even the "near poor" and the "new poor" groups may need to be a key focus of attention for any conception of social policy as active rather than passive; as involving social investment rather than social assistance.

1. Introduction

The Greek economy was one of the fastest growing in Europe during the 2000s. Its evolution was spectacular and financial indicators reached very high levels, especially during the 2000-2007 period. As the economic crisis rapidly expanded in 2008 (Quitini, 2010), Greece encountered serious difficulties in financing borrowing and continuing its investments. By 2009, Greece had become one of the worst affected countries in Europe. Financial debts were rising and expectations for improvement were limited. After about four years of crisis, the Greek economy seemed to be still far from recovery. GDP has been falling continuously since the beginning of the crisis in 2008 up to 2011.[1] Despite previous estimates that economic recovery will begin in 2012, it is expected that the rate of growth of GDP will not reverse before 2013. Latest data estimate a recession of more than 6% of GDP in 2012 (Ministry of Labour, Social Security and Welfare, Hellenic National Social Report 2012: 5). It is strongly expected that the recession of the Greek economy in 2012 will be deeper than projected, given that recent data (October 2012) estimate a recession of more than 7.2% of GDP.

Prior to the crisis, Greece had one of the highest at-risk-of poverty rates in the EU. On the basis of the available statistical data, no major changes are observed for the first two years the recession (2008-2010). According to the Hellenic Statistical Authority (2012: 2):

> "In 2010, 20.1% of the population was at risk of poverty, while the risk of poverty threshold is 60% of the total equivalised disposable household income. The above mentioned indicator, calculated with the same methodology, remained relatively stable during the last 15 years (1994-2009), for which there are available data, ranging from 19.5% to 23%."

Nevertheless, continuous adoption of strict austerity measures implemented by the Greek government, rising unemployment rates especially for the young population and women, cuts in wages,[2] pensions and social spending were expected to have an acute impact on the most disadvantaged members of society, as well as to push increased numbers of people living below the poverty line and middle income earners to seek the services of welfare agencies. Obviously, there is a growing need to identify a plurality of profiles of the poor towards which social policies must correspond and be targeted. Besides, due to the crisis, not only the level of poverty matters, but its composition and the way in which it should be examined as a dynamic and multidimensional phenomenon. New concepts, such as the "new poor", "severe poor", "near poor", "persistent poor" and the "materially deprived", indicate that we are dealing with new forms of poverty, completely differentiated from the "old poor".

This paper examines the effects of this crisis on poverty in Greece during the period 2008 to 2011.[3] The focus is on old and new socio-economic groups, as well as on the use of non-monetary deprivation indicators, which can help improve the identification of those experiencing poverty and understand how it comes about.

The questions to be addressed are as follows:

- How was poverty in Greece affected during the first years of the recession?
- What are the characteristics of those at risk of poverty? Who is "at risk of poverty"?
- Which types of individuals or families have been hit hardest by recession?
- Have new forms of poverty emerged? Has its severity increased?
- How do poverty rates in Greece compare to those of several other European countries, and what explains these differences?

More specifically, the paper aims:

- to describe trends in poverty incidence and evaluate the extent to which poverty has changed since 2008;
- to analyse socio-economic and demographic characteristic of the poor including the socio-economic and demographic profiles of new, transient and chronic poor;
- to illustrate and further investigate the non-monetary indicators of deprivation in the study of poverty;
- to identify country groups with similar characteristics with regard to selected poverty dimensions; and
- to provide some possible recommendations for programs and policies directed towards poverty alleviation.

Based on a series of the EU Statistics on Income and Living Conditions (EU-SILC), we aim to built a sort of poverty map with the possibility of identifying the various types of poor, in order to concretely gain a better knowledge of the poverty phenomenon itself. This perspective, on a first level, yields elementary and strongly diversified configurations of poverty, ranging from situations of "intermittent" poverty, for which the solution could be mere material aid, even of a temporary kind, to situations of extreme poverty, characterised not only by the lack of material and social resources, but especially by the presence of negative psychic factors in the poor such as feeling poor with the inability to mobilise oneself and making ends meet.

A detailed examination of poverty is limited by serious gaps and inadequacies in the available data. In particular, there is one key issue: the timeliness of data. More specifically, the data used in our analysis is derived from the EU Survey on Income and Living Conditions (EU-SILC), for the period 2008-2011. The income concept used in the analysis is annual net household disposable income, including any social transfers received and excluding direct taxes and social contributions.[4] The reference period for income covers the previous years.[5]

The second part of our study gives a short overview of the main theoretical and methodological considerations of poverty. Section three presents the development of relative income poverty over the period 2008-2011 in Greece and EU member states, by using comparative descriptive analysis. An attempt to characterize traditional and new population sub-groups particularly vulnerable to poverty in terms of their main socio-demographic characteristics—including a description of material deprivation, subjective poverty, poverty rate at different thresholds and persistent poverty rates—is the object of section four. After that, we examine the depth of poverty by using different poverty thresholds and the at-risk-of poverty rate anchored in 2008. In the same section we also present the groups exposed to persistent poverty. Section six attempts to describe the evolution of poverty and social exclusion during 2009–2011, using simple and composite measures.

Section seven shows the similarities and differences between the EU member countries, with the help of selected poverty indicators, by employing the method of cluster analysis. It will be investigated if countries seriously affected by the crisis and relatively developed countries fall within the same or different clusters, and whether poverty continued to be the common problem of all EU member countries. The last section summarizes the results of the study.

2. Theoretical and methodological considerations

The conventional view of poverty in the European Union countries[6] is based on a relative approach that refers to "*persons whose resources (material, cultural and social) are so limited as to exclude them from the minimum acceptable way of life in the Member State in which they live*" (EEC, 1985: 24). In this sense, it is a relative definition, and the primary frame of reference is the country in which one lives, while resources refer to goods, cash income plus services from public and private sources. Townsend (1979: 31) introduced a relative deprivation approach to poverty that covered a wide range of aspects of living standards, both material and social:

> "Individuals, families and groups in the population can be said to be in poverty when they lack the resources to obtain the types of diet, participate in the activities and have the living conditions and amenities which are customary, or are at least widely encouraged or approved, in the societies to which they belong. Their resources are so seriously below those commanded by the average individual or family that they are, in effect, excluded from ordinary living patterns, customs or activities."

From this starting point, poverty has two core elements: inadequate resources and inability to participate—exclusion from the minimum acceptable way of life. In the first approach, poverty causes mainly due to the lack of income (financial poverty),[7] available to individuals for meeting their needs in relation to an "ordinary" or "minimum living pattern" in the society in which they live (Nolan and Maitre, 2010: 3). The basic assumption is that an income equivalent to the poverty line gives people the ability to buy a minimum of food, housing and other necessities. In the second (direct) approach, poverty deals primarily with living conditions, underlying either a poor way of life, poor consumption standards or attitudes towards living in poverty. It is people's actual life that matters and poverty is seen as an effect of accumulated deprivation (Townsend, 1979; Mack and Lansley, 1985). As Halleröd (1995: 51) stated:

> "The direct conceptualization of poverty concentrates on the 'outcome' aspect of the poverty situation. It deals primarily with living conditions, stressing either a poor way of life or poor consumption standards or attitudes towards living in poverty."

Empirically, relative deprivation is a different source of information that supplements the information collected by the income method. It measures poor living conditions directly using non-monetary variables and/or indicators of living standards (goods and services households can consume) and goes beyond traditional measures of poverty (which is more related to the lack of resources, particularly financial resources, needed to acquire modern goods and commodities). People unable to afford certain basic items are considered to be materially deprived, emphasizing further the inadequate social participation and integration of the poor into the mainstream society. A person may be considered deprived to the extent that he or she falls below the level attained by the majority of the population or below what is considered socially acceptable. Material deprivation measures ask respondents about the ownership of items regarded as "necessities" by a majority of the population. Essentially, the absence of some items is taken to reflect deprivation and the greater the number of items absent, the greater the degree of deprivation (Townsend, 1979; Mack and Lansley, 1985; Desai and Shah, 1988; Nolan and Whelan, 1996; Godman and Myck, 2005; Willitts, 2006). Poverty measures based on this type of information are also known as consensual poverty measures. Mack and Lansley (1985) alternatively defined poverty as an enforced lack of socially perceived necessities in order to introduce the role that choice plays in the ownership of items. In this way those who cannot afford items, that the majority in society say are necessary, were defined as deprived. This approach, in terms of "enforced lack" due to financial pressures, makes the suggested indices more comparable with income poverty. In relation to EU-SILC, Guio (2005: 2) defines material deprivation as "*the enforced lack of a combination of items depicting material living conditions such as housing conditions, possession of durables and capacity to afford basic requirements.*" The material deprivation rate is an indicator adopted by the Social Protection Committee[8] which measures the percentage of the population that cannot afford[9] at least three of the following nine items:[10] to pay their rent, mortgage or utility bills; to keep their home adequately warm; to face unexpected expenses; to eat meat or proteins regularly; to go on a holiday; to have a television set; a washing machine; a car; a telephone. Severe material deprivation rate is defined as the enforced inability to pay for at least four of the above-mentioned items.[11]

Direct measures of poverty, living standards in particular, may be used in isolation or in combination with income. Muffels (1993) described income and deprivation as separate concepts in poverty measurement and concluded that they should complement each other rather than act as substitutes for each other. Ringen (1988) promotes also a compound approach because, otherwise, those with a low standard of consumption are excluded from the monetary poverty definition. Halleröd (1995) argues that direct and indirect poverty measures should be combined to produce a more robust measure. European Union's Social Inclusion Process[12] uses the following compound relative definition of poverty:

> "People are said to be living in poverty if their income and resources are so inadequate as to preclude them from having a standard of living considered acceptable in the society in which they live. Because of their poverty they may experience multiple disadvantage through unemployment, low income, poor housing, inadequate health care and barriers to lifelong learning, culture, sport and recreation. They are often excluded and marginalised from participating in activities (economic, social and cultural) that are the norm for other people and their access to fundamental rights may be restricted."

Measuring poverty using disposable incomes has been found to measure more temporary poverty, while measuring material deprivation serves to capture the severity and duration of poverty: People who suffer from a longer spell of low income are more likely to lack certain essential items, and they may also suffer more than those who are in poverty for a short period of time. For example, persistent poverty[13] may lead to and sustain other deprivations such as educational under-achievement and unemployment. The identification of the persistently poor should facilitate the design of the anti-poverty strategy, as they may need support measures different from those required by other disadvantaged groups such as the recurrently poor and the temporarily poor. Recently, in June 2010, the concept material deprivation gained in political importance, as the European Commission and all 27 Member States adopted a social inclusion target for the EU as a whole, which is based on a combination of three indicators: at risk of poverty or severely materially deprived or living in households with very low work intensity.[14]

The concept of poverty in this study uses the following dimensions:

- Relative income poverty;[15]
- Non- monetary severe material deprivation indicator; and
- Subjective poverty,[16] which is operationalised in terms of economic strain. In the EU–SILC, respondents are asked to rate the degree of financial difficulty their household experiences in "making ends meet", and households are identified here as subjectively poor if they report "great difficulty" in doing so.

These inter-related characteristics (tiers) can be used as coordinates in order to identify specific situations of poverty *while the level of poverty can be* considered to be falling if all measures are moving in the right direction. In some cases, for example, there may be a prevailing lack of social ties with respect to the scarcity of material resources, as would appear to be the case with some elderly people. In the opposite situation, when there is a marked lack of resources, we see different types of poverty and of poor people: this may be the case for certain immigrant groups in Greece.

Given the deep and continuing recession, when examining the consequences of poverty in Greece, it is important to identify a number of patterns. Firstly, the effects of poverty are usually nonlinear, meaning that the consequences of income differences *below or near*[17] poverty levels are substantially greater than comparable differences at higher income levels. Differences in outcomes for individuals or families living at 50 percent of the poverty level versus 70 percent of the poverty level are shrinking. Secondly, persistent poverty[18] can be particularly destructive, compared to short-term poverty, while other so-called secondary indices (i.e., at-risk-of-poverty rate anchored at a fixed moment in time) may be of greater importance now when compared to the past. Thirdly, many people who previously thought themselves to be secure are now falling into poverty (new poor), many of those who have been worst hit come from distinct vulnerable groups—in particular, people already experiencing poverty before the crisis (i.e., the "old poor") are falling in an even deeper poverty. Fourthly, it is important to recognize that different risk factors (e.g., low education and unemployment) are cumulative in their effects while the effects of poverty can be both interactive and cumulative.

3. At-risk-of-poverty rate and poverty threshold 2008-2011: Some descriptive statistics

The Greek economy, although booming up until 2008, showed signs of recession in 2009, as a result of the international financial crisis.[19] The strict income policy and the drastic cuts in public spending initially seem to have had only a marginal[20] impact on relative risk of poverty as there was no clear trend upwards or downwards in rates over the period 2008-2010:[21] from 20.1% in 2008 it was reduced to 19.7% in 2009 and increased back to 20.1% in 2010.[22] However, in 2011, 21.4 % of the Greek population was defined as being at risk of poverty, equivalent to 2,341,400 people. This has led to the gap between Greek and EU average rates widening over time. The gap was 4.5% points difference in 2011, when compared with a 3.7% in 2010 and 3.4% in 2009 (Figure 7-1). The relatively large increase between 2010 and 2011 for Greece is likely explained by the at-risk-of-poverty threshold decreasing by 587€, due to a fall in median equivalent disposable income from 11,963€ to 10,986€ in cash terms.[23] More precisely, Greek incomes have fallen sharply since 2010, mainly due to repeated rounds of spending cuts and tax hikes to meet the terms of a bailout from the European Union and the International Monetary Fund. We can argue that we are probably experiencing an increasing income inequality[24] and rising poverty rate, reflecting falls in real income at the bottom of the distribution, which are not fully cushioned by government support.[25]

Actually, the newest data show that the poverty rate in Greece increased dramatically: From 21.4% in 2011 it rose to 23.1% in 2012, approaching the 1994 level. This rate sets Greece at the top of the eighteen countries for which data are available until now (next comes Bulgaria, with 21.2%). During the same period, there has been a parallel increase the Gini coefficient (33.5 in 2011 and 34.3 in 2012) and the income quintile share ratio (S80/S20: 6.0 in 2011 and 6.6 in 2012), the latest data show that inequality has increased and Greece figures as the country with the highest inequality in the EU.

In 2011, the countries with the highest poverty rates in Europe were from Eastern and Southern Europe. It is also estimated that two thirds of the total poor population in the European Union lives in six countries: Germany, France, the United Kingdom, Italy, Poland and Spain. Among these, two of them—Germany and France—the rate of poverty is lower (15.8 and 14.0, respectively) than the EU average (16.9%) (Figure 7-1). Interestingly, although the poverty rate is about the same in Spain (21.8%) and Greece (21.4%), the latter has a smaller total population and the absolute size of the poor population is almost one-fifth of the poor population of the former (Figure 7-2). Over one-fifth of the total population is estimated to be poor in two of the new member states (Bulgaria, Romania), as well as in Lithuania (20%). The incidence of poverty is also higher than the EU average (16.9%) in other Eastern and Southern European countries: Italy (19.6%), Portugal (18%), Poland (17.7%) and Estonia (17.5%).

In a few countries, the decline of median incomes, on which the poverty lines are set, has automatically led to decreases in or stagnation of the risk of poverty; that was the case with Latvia and Lithuania. This apparent improvement in relative poverty may be misleading as it may reflect the fact that people with an income slightly below the poverty line may move above it although their situation has not changed or has even worsened.

Figure 7-1. At-risk-of-poverty rate in the EU-27, 2008-2011

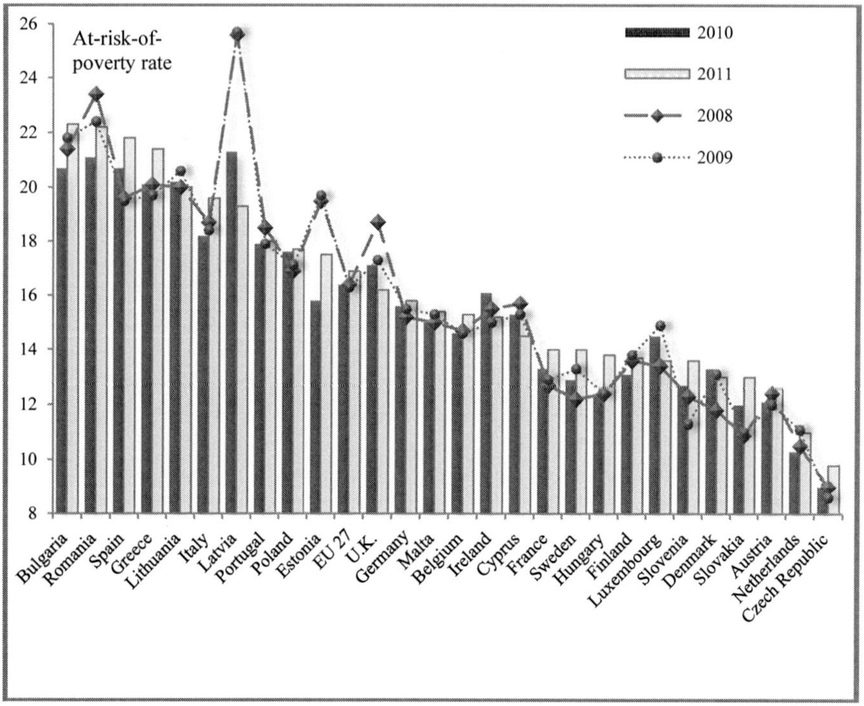

Figure 7-2. The size of the poor population and the poverty rate across European countries, 2011

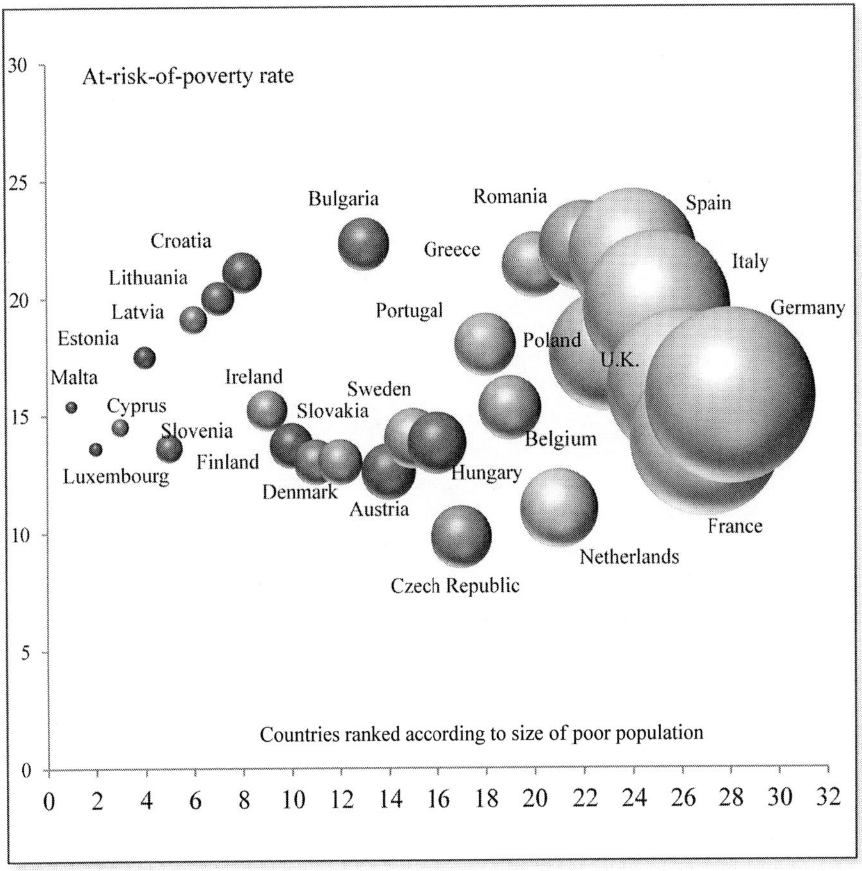

Note; Bubbles, showing the size of the poor population

4. High risk groups

Focusing on developments in terms of the risk of poverty for different groups, it is evident that the crisis has not impacted uniformly across the whole population. Social groups, that are traditionally more exposed to poverty—unemployed, immigrant workers, single mothers—although affected first, are joined by "new poor", i.e., working poor,[26] children and young people, typical male bread winner households and single households. The "old poor" have become poorer and stay in poverty for extended periods of time, but at the same time, people who have never been poor before, now fall below the conventional poverty line.

4.1. Traditional risk groups

The breadth and depth of poverty is significant as some groups are more likely than others to find themselves in poverty. The harm done to families living in poverty has lifelong consequences for them with respect to future social and economic prospects. "Traditional" risk groups are still important and are hit hardest. For the period 2008-2011, we highlight the following (Figure 7-3):

- The risk of poverty is highest for the unemployed men: risk of poverty increased from 39.5% in 2008 to 48.6% in 2011. The lack of "marketable skills" limits employment options and subsequent income potential and may be viewed as a potential cause of poverty. Unemployed women are also among the high at-risk-of-poverty groups: The rate reached 40.1% in 2010 and slightly decreased in 2011 (39.4%).
- The rate is very high for Third Country Nationals,[27] as it increased from 32.7% in 2008 to 46.9% in 2011.
- Families with children are traditionally vulnerable to poverty. Among them, most vulnerable are single parents with at least one dependent child[28] (43.2% in 2011, an increase of 16.1 percentage points in comparison to 2008 and 9.8 percentage points in comparison with 2010)[29] and large families with 3 or more children (the at-risk-of-poverty rate increased from 27.2% in 2008 to 28.6% in 2009); however, there was a decrease between 2008 and 2011 of 7.8 percentage points,[30] in contrast with what was seen in the overall population, probably due to measures designed and implemented in the previous years.
- There are strong positive relationships between income and education. As the level of education increases, income (and employment) tends to increase. Higher skilled occupations, with higher pay, typically require higher education. At the same time, having a lower income is a barrier to obtaining the higher education needed to be competitive for higher paying occupations. In Greece, the poverty risk for those with low education[31] increased from 28.7% in 2008 to 31.9% in 2011. This result also suggests that when targeting anti-poverty initiatives, a

large proportion should be aimed at those with low education levels, including those with low levels of literacy.

- Other inactive persons also score high on the at–risk-of-poverty rate (29.2% in 2011 compared to 27.3% in 2008).
- The private house rented sector is now at the poverty front line. Due to the crisis–and the difficulties in securing a steady job or sufficient income–more and more people are being forced into an insecure tenure with high housing costs and facing a high risk of poverty. The rate from 24.7% in 2008 increased to 25.9% in 2011. In turn, the high costs of housing and the dissolution of the couple or the family may force young people to return to the parental home. The proportion of young adults (aged 18-34) living with their parent(s) in Greece increased from 59.2% (2007) to 61,7% (2012).
- In 2011, members of households in sparsely populated areas (24.7%) are threatened by poverty to a greater degree than those in intermediate urbanised areas (20.4%) and in densely-populated areas (18.4%). Nevertheless, during 2008-2011 an increasing trend is documented only in the last two cases.[32]

Looking at the at-risk-of-poverty rates by gender, the rates for females have consistently been higher than those for males in Greece (and the EU average). This has to do with the fact that women still retain primary responsibility for home and family. For example, females spend more time providing unpaid care for children or elderly family members, so are more likely to take time out of work or work part time in order to enable them to provide this care. Females are also more likely to take on the economic costs of raising children. This traditional "male breadwinner/female caregiver" model, discouraged labour market participation of (married) women while strongly supporting men's work through high levels of job protection and social security rights. Actually, the at-risk-of-poverty rate fell between 2008 and 2009 for both males and females and then it followed an increasing trend. In 2011, the at-risk-of poverty rate in Greece was 21.9 per cent for females, compared with 20.9 per cent for males, while the overall EU rate was 17.2 per cent for females and 15.8 per cent for males.

Figure 7-3. Traditionally at-high-risk-of-poverty groups in Greece, 2008-2011

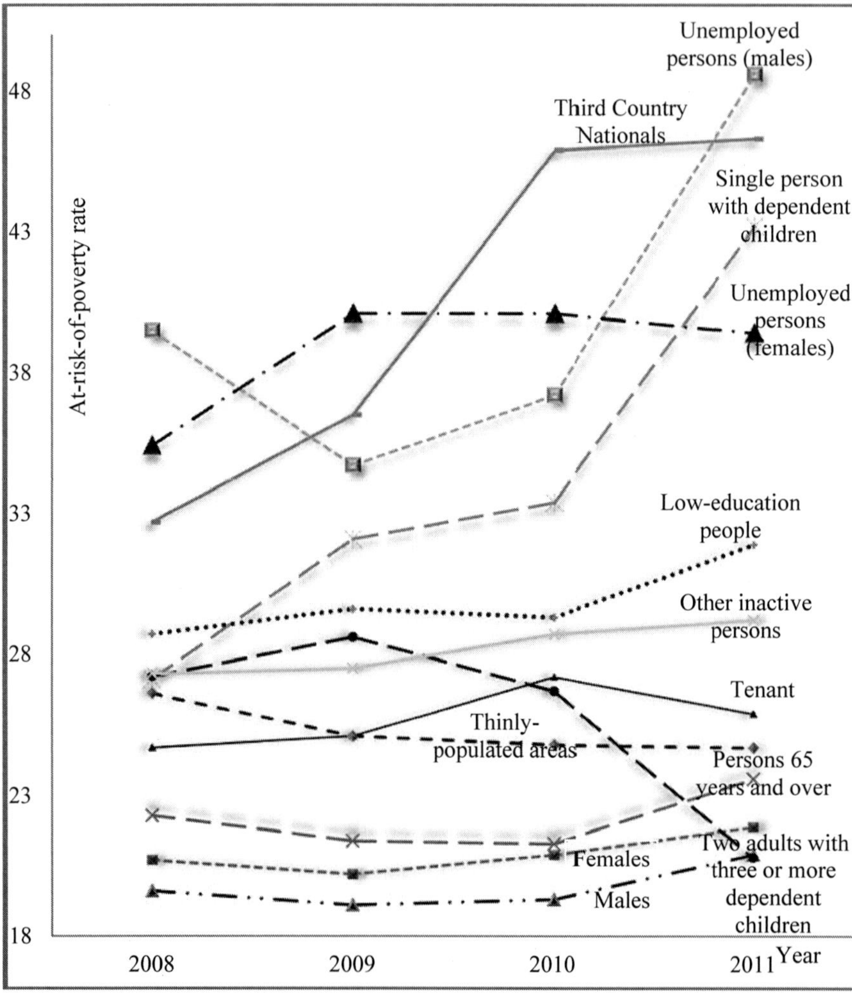

Traditionally, the elderly are also seen as a vulnerable group, because their economic wellbeing largely depends on the social protection system. In Greece, among those aged 65 and over the at-risk-of-poverty rate fell between 2008 and 2010 to 21.3 per cent (from 22.3 percent in 2008), but then increased between 2010 and 2011 to 23.6 per cent. In contrast, the average at-risk-of-poverty rate, for those over 65 in the EU, decreased significantly between 2008 and 2011 (from 19 per cent to 15.8 per cent). However, the apparent changes in the relative situation for the elderly reflect the fact that pensions have remained to a large extent unchanged during the initial years of the crisis, and have in some cases brought pensioners' income above the poverty threshold due to the changes in the total income distribution while not altering in real terms their economic situation.

4.2. New risk groups

Working poor

Salary cuts, deregulation of business, privatization of state-owned business, elimination of trade barriers, reduction/dismantling of the welfare state and restructuring the national workforce in order to increase industrial and economic flexibility eroded the middle class, creating a growing "working poor" population. Not only workers on the margins of labour markets (low educated and low skilled workers) but even skilled workers lost their jobs and they may now be at best relegated to the unskilled sector through a process of declassification, or very often into recurrent unemployment.[33] Having a job seems to be the best way out of the poverty risk, but it does not necessarily offer protection against poverty. According to the European Commission (2011: 142):

> "Having a low wage job will not, of itself, necessarily push someone into poverty, any more than having only a part time or temporary job, since family composition is also a major factor affecting the individual situation. Low wage and low labour market attachment such as a part time or temporary job, poor contractual conditions, can still result in poverty,"

In-work poverty is a complex situation as it usually refers to the overall income of a household—where at least one person works—in relation to the number of people dependent on that household income.[34] According to Crettaz (2011), it can be linked to household size and composition,[35] low work intensity[36] and low wages. In this respect, single households, as well as one-earner families, are seen to face the highest risks of poverty.[37] Many studies point out that in-work poverty is very high in almost all European countries (European Commission, 2012). In 2010, Greece (13.9%) and Romania (17.1%) had the highest rates. In 2011, the highest rates are observed in Romania (18.7%), Spain (12.2%), Greece (11.9%),[38] Poland (11.2%), Italy (10.8%), Portugal (10.2%) and Lithuania (10.1%).[39]

In-work poverty is also linked to the specific employment circumstances of individuals such as involuntary part-time work and type of contract. In Greece, 21.4% of those working part time in 2011 are at risk of in-work poverty, whereas the number declines to 10.4% for those working full time. In both cases, a decreasing trend is observed during the period 2008-2011 (Figure 7-4). Changes in the labour market have increased the number of non-permanent jobs in recent years. Recent statistics show that in 2011 the poverty risk for people on permanent employment contracts is 4.3% (5.1% in 2010), compared with 8.9% (13.4% in 2010) for people on temporary employment contracts.

In parallel with the economic pressure, as the Greek population ages, more people live in smaller households, increasingly consisting of a single person. At the same time, many young adults postpone leaving their parental home in order to find their own household.

The proportion of young adults (aged 25-29) living with their parent(s) is high in Greece (66% for men and 51% for women) while it is reported highest among the EU countries when the age group 30-34 is concerned (European Commission and Eurostat, 2011: 73). Material difficulties are the main obstacle for young people leaving the parental home. Changes in the housing and labour markets (for instance, lack of job security), or the conditions under which young people pursue their education, are some difficulties reflected in the large number of young people living with their parents even if they are employed. According to the European Commission and Eurostat (2011: 5):

> "When the recession struck, the first groups to be affected were younger people and immigrants. Governments faced increasing difficulties in balancing support for families, consolidation of budgets, assistance for young people and immigrants in a shrinking labour market, and funding for retirement schemes."

Work intensity, differences between part-time and full-time employment, permanent and temporary jobs, employees and self-employed workers

In general, the poverty risk of household members decreases when the work intensity increases.[40] In households with no dependent children, for example in 2011, 40% of the members with *very low* work intensity face poverty. This proportion declines to 30.4% in households with *low* work intensity. One of the more interesting results is that in households with children, 30% of the members of *medium* work intensity face poverty. The proportion, for households with children, increases significantly to 52.7% in households with *low* work intensity and 74.2% in households where no adult household member is at work (*very low* intensity) (Figure 7-5).[41] Thus, workers' vulnerability to poverty relates more to family income and composition than to own earnings. The presence of children in a household increases the likelihood of belonging to the working poor; the greater the number of children the higher the risk, though this risk is radically reduced in the case of dual earner households.

Demographic group and house owners

According to the latest data, among the new groups joining the ones at-high-risk-of-poverty are some new "demographic groups"[42] (Figure 7-6):

- Poverty levels of children below 18 years old rose from 23% in 2008 to 23.7% in 2011.[43]
- For young people aged 18-24 the increase was more intense, rising from 23% in 2008 to 26.9% in 2011.
- Households with one senior adult of 65 years old or over had an opposite tendency, demonstrating a slight drop in poverty levels, namely from 30.6% in 2008 to 29.9% in 2011.
- Single-person households appeared to have different trends, depending upon gender. For women, the poverty level dropped from 26.7% in 2008 to 25.8% in 2011; however, in the years between, it rose to in even higher levels (28.3% and 27.7% respectively). For men of the same category, poverty levels rose from 22.7% in 2008 to 24.3% in 2011, and demonstrated a peak similar to that of women for the years in between
- Households with two adults and two dependent children exhibited a growth in their poverty levels from 21.9% in 2008 to 24.2% in 2011.
- Households with dependent children showed a slight increase in the proportion, namely 22.1% in 2008 to 23.2% in 2011.
- Finally, households with owned dwelling also exhibited an increase in poverty levels (from 19.1% in 2008 to 20.3% in 2011), albeit demonstrating a slight decrease in the years between (18.5% in both 2009 and 2010).

To sum up, we find that, on average, child poverty in Greece is a greater problem than is the poverty of the elderly. But immigrants, unemployed persons, low educated persons and tenants, generally have the highest poverty rates. The household types most at risk of poverty were single parents with dependent children, households with dependent children and low, very low or medium work intensity, single elderly people, single females, and two-parent families with two children (See Figures 7-3–7-6). Furthermore, austerity measures and squeezed family budgets affect also many households who have their own house/dwelling as they are obligated to pay a significant portion of their income on shelter even if they have low income (Balourdos, 2012).

Figure 7-4. New at-risk-of-poverty groups (working poor: employed, type of contract, working full time-part time, employed persons except employees)

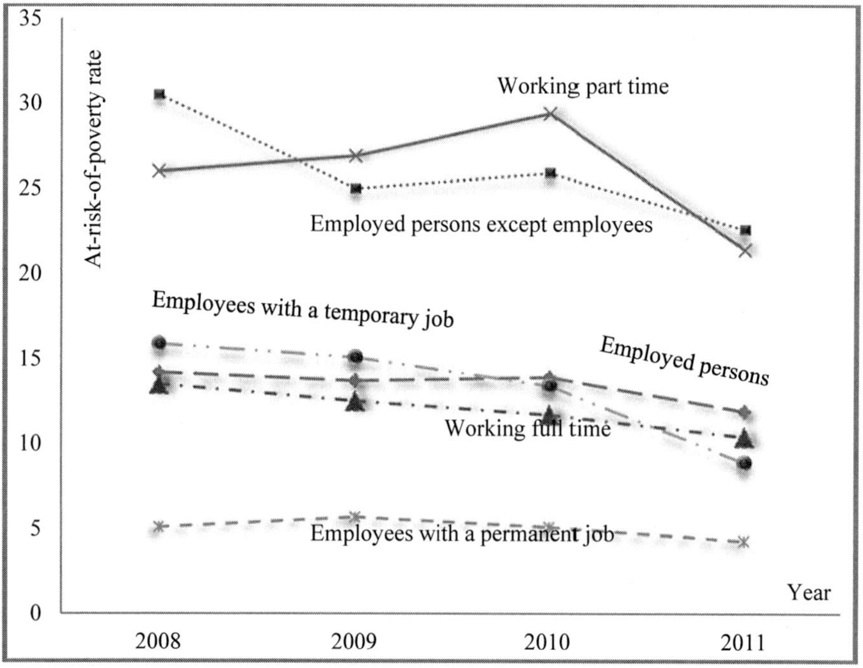

Figure 7-5. New at-risk-of-poverty groups (working poor- persons at households with dependent children and very low, low or medium work intensity)

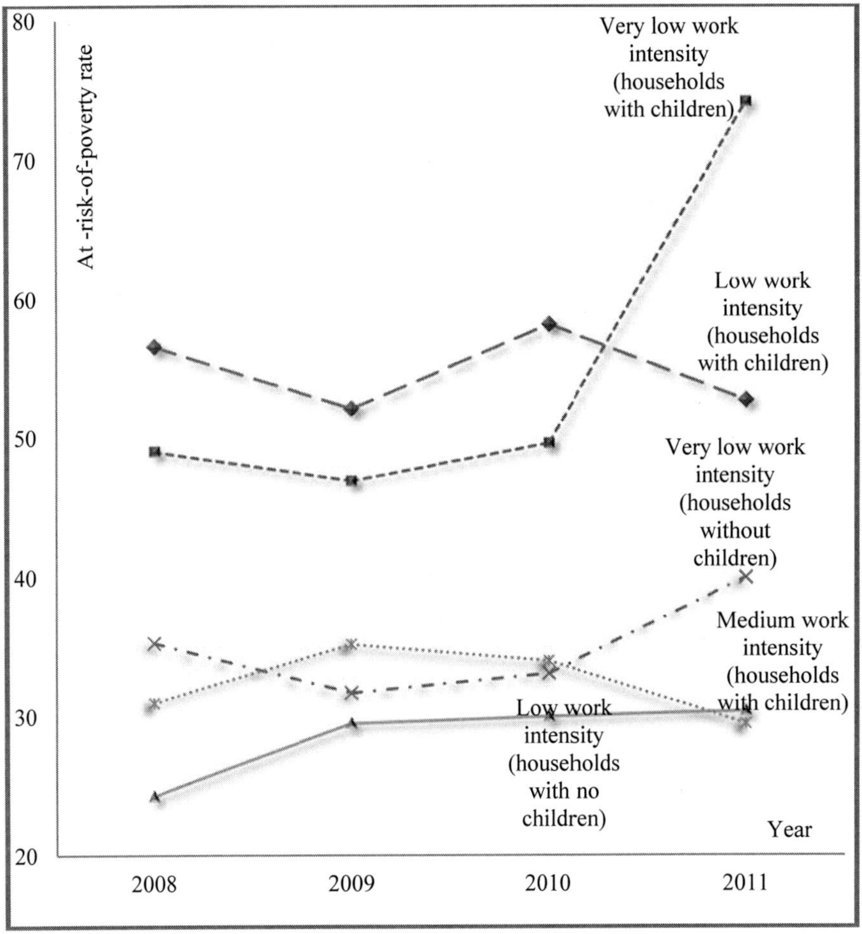

Figure 7-6. New at-risk-of-poverty groups in Greece, 2008-2011

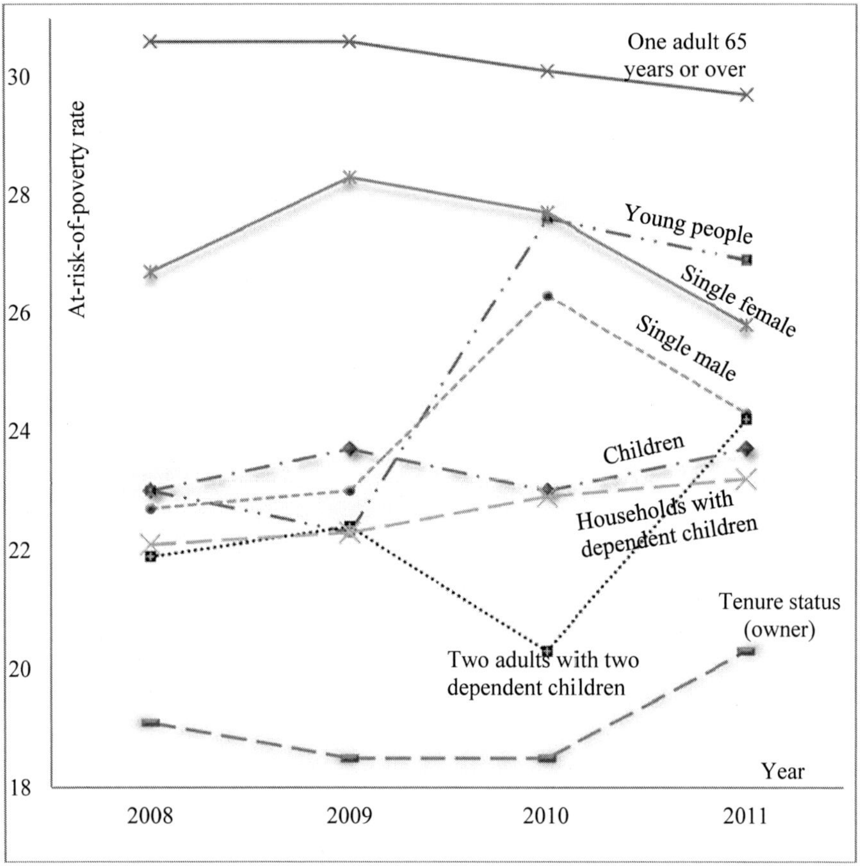

4.3. Material deprivation and subjective poverty

Other large parts of Greek society, which find it difficult to afford a meal per day, now belong to the "newly poor"; people with or without family responsibilities, who are unable to pay their mortgages or even meet more direct current needs of their households. According to the most recent data, material deprivation rate and severe material deprivation rate in Greece fluctuate in particularly high values, following a growing trend during 2008-2011; material deprivation rate climbs from 21.8% in 2008 to 24.1% in 2010 and to 28.4% in 2011, while severe material deprivation rate increases from 11.2% to 11.6% and to 15.2%, respectively. Thus, the share of people in Greece who have seen their living standards deteriorate, as measured by the level of (severe) material deprivation has increased during the reference period (2008-2011). It is very disturbing that more and more poor and non-poor individuals and households state that they face difficulties in paying utility bills,[44] arrears on hire-purchase installments or other loan payments,[45] rent or mortgage installments[46] and an inability to respond to unexpected but necessary financial expenses (Table 7-1).

The relative number of people who are materially deprived according to the latest data (2011), varies from 1.2% of the population in Luxembourg and Sweden, just under 3% in Netherlands, Finland and Denmark and over 30% for Latvia and Bulgaria (Figure7-7). There is very little relationship between the proportion measured as being deprived and the relative number at risk of poverty, in the sense of having an income below 60% of the median (Figure7-7). A number of countries that have a relatively low material deprivation rate have a relatively high at-risk-of-poverty rate—Spain and Portugal, in particular. Conversely, a number of countries with an above-average deprivation rate have a below-average risk of poverty, specifically Slovenia, Hungary and Slovakia. It is evident, therefore, that the indicator of material deprivation does not duplicate the risk-of-poverty indicator, at least across countries, but instead provides additional information about the social situation in different member states.

As the crisis has been especially severe in Greece, increases in material deprivation, the number of people who felt poor (i.e., subjective poverty) and the number of people living in jobless households is dramatic. Rising difficulties in coping with necessary expenses are also reported by the population in general, while for the poor the situation is dramatic. The number of people who declared facing difficulties in the list of economic strains[47] rose while the situation is more severe for the poor.

Self-assessed basic financial needs, i.e., the share of persons declaring that they were having great difficulty in making ends meet, increased from 20% in 2008 to 25.6% in 2011. In effect, the number of people who felt poor—in the sense that they report significant difficulties in making ends meet—was higher than the number of those with an income below the poverty threshold, and very close to the material deprivation rate and the poverty rate anchored at a fixed moment in time as Figure 7-8 and Table 7-1 show.[48]

Table 7-1. Material deprivation rate and selected deprivation items for the poor and the non-poor, Greece 2008-2011

		2008	2009	2010	2011
Material deprivation rate (3 items or more)		21.8	23.0	24.1	28.4
Material deprivation rate (4 items or more)		11.2	11.0	11.6	15.2
Inability to keep home adequately warm	poor	29.9	36.8	38.4	38.8
Inability to keep home adequately warm	non-poor	11.8	10.5	9.7	13.2
Inability to afford paying for one week annual holiday away from home	poor	73.6	76.5	83.5	87.2
Inability to afford paying for one week annual holiday away from home	non-poor	43.8	38.9	37.0	41.4
Inability to afford a meal with meat, chicken, fish (or vegetarian equivalent) every second day	poor	29.9	24.0	22.7	42.2
Inability to afford a meal with meat, chicken, fish (or vegetarian equivalent) every second day	non -poor	1.4	3.6	4.2	0.3
Inability to face unexpected financial expenses	poor	54.3	57.1	63.4	69.3
Inability to face unexpected financial expenses	non-poor	19.6	19.1	19.3	25.0
Arrears on mortgage or rent payments	poor	12.6	13.8	15.2	22.9
Arrears on mortgage or rent payments	non poor	3.7	7.3	8.9	7.7
Arrears on hire purchase installments or other loan payments	poor	17.2	15.7	17.3	22.2

		2008	2009	2010	2011
Arrears on hire purchase installments or other loan payments	non-poor	10.7	12.6	12.3	11.1
Arrears on utility bills	poor	29.5	37.1	38.0	41.3
Arrears on utility bills	non-poor	12.4	14.4	14.0	18.4

A particularly disturbing fact is the sharp increase of the population living in households with very low work intensity, signaling the danger of their long-term exclusion from the labour market (Figure 7-8). This share has risen between 2010 and 2011 (above 4.3 percentage points) in the context of worsening conditions in the labour market.

Figure 7-7. The proportion of the population severely deprived materially and at risk of poverty, 2011

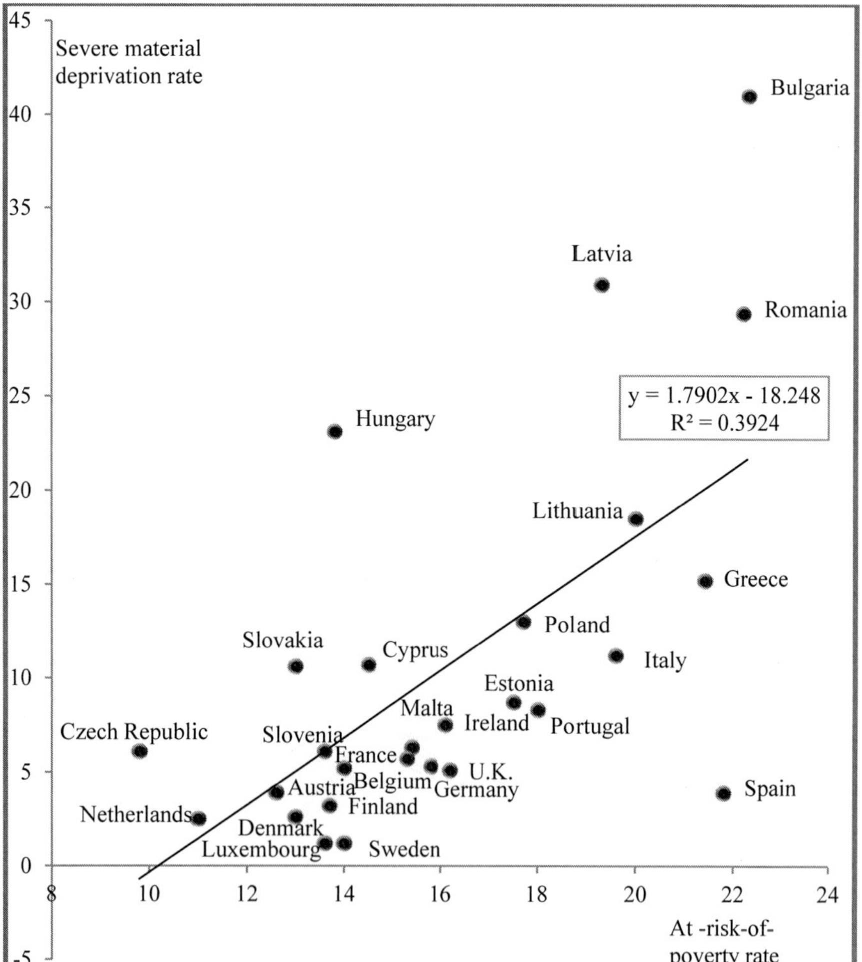

Figure 7-8. At-risk-of-poverty rate, severe material deprivation rate, people living in jobless households and "ability to make ends meet very difficult", Greece 2008-2011

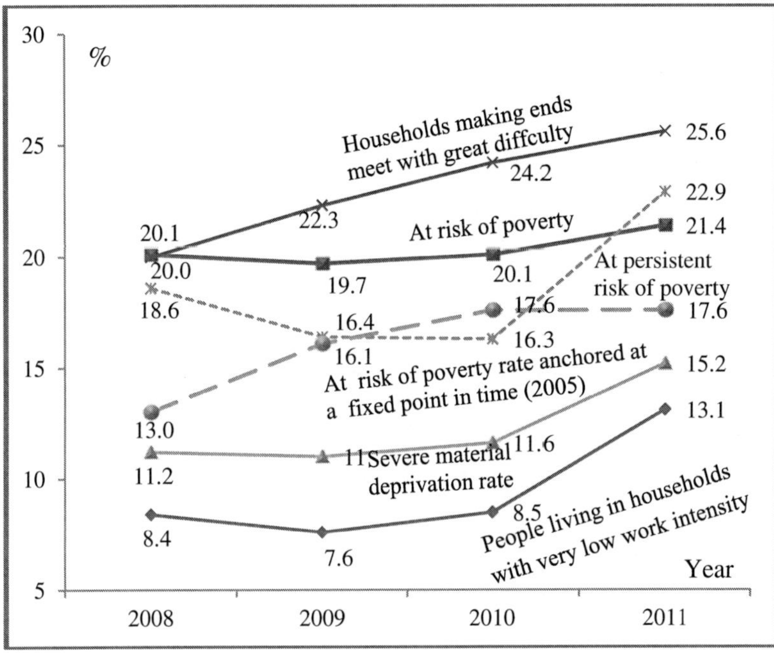

5. Dispersion around the threshold, poverty gap, poverty anchored at one point of time and persistent poverty

According to the data presented in Figure 7-9, in Greece the percentage of people who get by with less than 40% of the median equivalized income[49] slightly increased from 2008 to 2011 (from 6.7% to 8.2%). A commensurate increase of people above but close to the conventional poverty line (difference of poor at 70% threshold with 60% threshold) is recorded during 2009-2011 (from 6.7% in 2008 falls to 5.7% in 2009, climbs to 7.1% in 2010 and 7.2% in 2011). It thus becomes evident that since the beginning of the crisis, many "already" poor fell to the lowest point of the income distribution and are faced with extreme poverty. Furthermore, more non-poor have now found themselves faced with poverty, too.[50]

Figure 7-9. Poverty depth with different thresholds, Greece 2008-2011

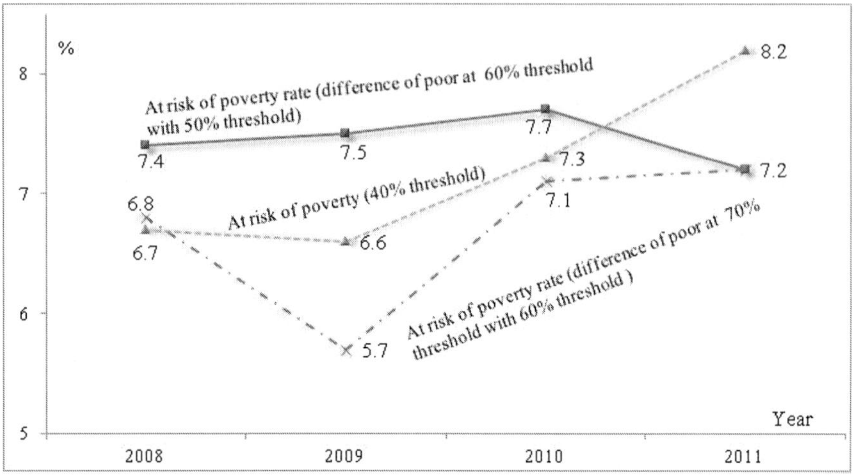

The relative gap of median income of people at-risk-of-poverty is the difference between poverty line and the median of the equivalized available income of the poor population and is presented as a percentage of the poverty threshold. In other words, it is an estimate of the income increase that poor people should get in order to reach the poverty line. For 2010, the median income of the poor in Greece was equivalent to 76.6% of the poverty threshold. That is to say that the poverty gap was 23.4%, which means that half the people (50%) subject to poverty get by with a lower income than 76.6% of the poverty threshold[51] (i.e., lower than 76.6% x 60% of the median equivalized income).[52] For 2011, the median income of the poor in Greece was equivalent to 73.9% of the poverty threshold (poverty gap 26.1%).

Among the EU member states, in 2011 the lowest gap was found in Finland (13.5%), followed by Netherlands (15.5%). That is to say that people who are at risk of poverty in these countries are to a great extent right below the poverty threshold. As a result, improving the living standards of all poor people in Finland would require less financial resources per person than in Greece where a relatively higher percentage of the population is in a worst income situation.

The at-risk-of-poverty rate for 2011, calculated according to the poverty threshold of 2008 (i.e., 60% of the 2008 median income and expressed in 2011 scores according to the adjusted consumer price index), is estimated at about 24.9%.[53] In other words, using the index of anchored poverty, there is a difference of 3.5% when compared to the conventional at-risk-of-poverty rate for 2011 (see Figure 7-12). The purpose of such a comparison is to document how the risk of poverty changes in absolute rather than relative terms; i.e., when the poverty threshold remains stable over time in terms of actual buying power.[54] In other words, 24.9% of the Greek population in 2011 would be categorized as facing risk of poverty under the conditions of 2008. Even though in most countries there is a rising trend for the period 2008-2011, in Greece there is a falling one during the years 2008-2010 (20.1%, 18.9% and 18.0%) and a sudden rise to high levels in 2011. Extremely high scores for 2011 are also documented in countries of the European South that are severely affected by the economic recession and countries that implement strict austerity policies: Spain 25.7%, Italy 21.4% and Portugal 17.9%.[55]

In 2011 the anchored at-risk-of-poverty rate in Greece exhibits significant increases, since it climbs to 24.9% and thus exceeds the at-risk-of-poverty rate (21.4%). Since the country has experienced negative income growth, the last difference in those measures suggests that at least part of the population with lower household incomes is hit from the financial recession.

We believe that these estimates are far more realistic, since we are going through a period of intense transformation, where living standards change rapidly, the poor population is severely affected, nominal incomes shrink and the prices of goods are on the rise.

Persistent risk of poverty/ long term poverty

Under the light of the current economic recession, a view on poverty based on its *duration* rather than its *prevalence* among different population subgroups is of particular importance. The situation is much more crucial and should be examined in a different way, if within a country poor people remain the same over time in comparison with a country where at least a certain share of poor people doesn't stay the same due to income mobility.[56] According to Eurostat's definition of persistent or long-term poverty, a person is considered persistently poor if he/she is classified as poor at present and has been poor for at least two of the three previous years.[57] Because of the way persistent poverty rate is defined, it must be lower than the relative conventional poverty rate. Persistent poverty rate has been given little attention, even though it is one of the main EU indicators for social integration. The information provided is significant and adds to existing information regarding transverse–instant poverty (at one given moment in time). It is widely accepted that poverty is more adverse for any single individual when he/she is poor for an extended period. According to available data for Greece (Figures 7-10 and 7-11 and other data[58], the following noteworthy trends are documented:

a) During 2008-2010, the level of persistent poverty progresses upwards: from 13% in 2008 it increases to 16.1% in 2009 and reaches 17.6% in 2010.
b) When we compare the persisting poverty index with the conventional index for poverty, we see that in 2010, from the total population of the poor about 88% were also long-term poor.
c) Large proportion of the long-term poor are also poor at the 40% of the dividing line: in 2010 one out of four long-term poor also had very low incomes, i.e., below €4.785 annually (40% of the median equivalized income threshold).
d) Concerning the distribution of population by years spent in poverty within a four-year period (Figure 7-11), we observe two opposite trends: (i) a downward for the period 2009-2010 that relates to those who are poor for one, two or three years and (ii) an opposite trend that concerns those that are at risk of poverty for the entire four year period.
e) The observed values in Greece are significantly higher than the EU-27 mean (8.7% in 2008, 8.8% in 2009 and 9.7% in 2010)
f) Children and elderly[59] (mainly women)[60] constitute the predominantly at-high-risk-of- persistent poverty groups. However, young people aged 18-24 also score very high on this index [Figure 7-10].
g) For 2010, Greece was second from the top. The highest risk was documented in Romania (18.2%), while Greece is followed by Bulgaria with a rate of 16.3%.

Figure 7-10. Persistent at-risk-of-poverty rate in Greece and the EU and among selected at-high-risk groups in Greece, 2008-2011

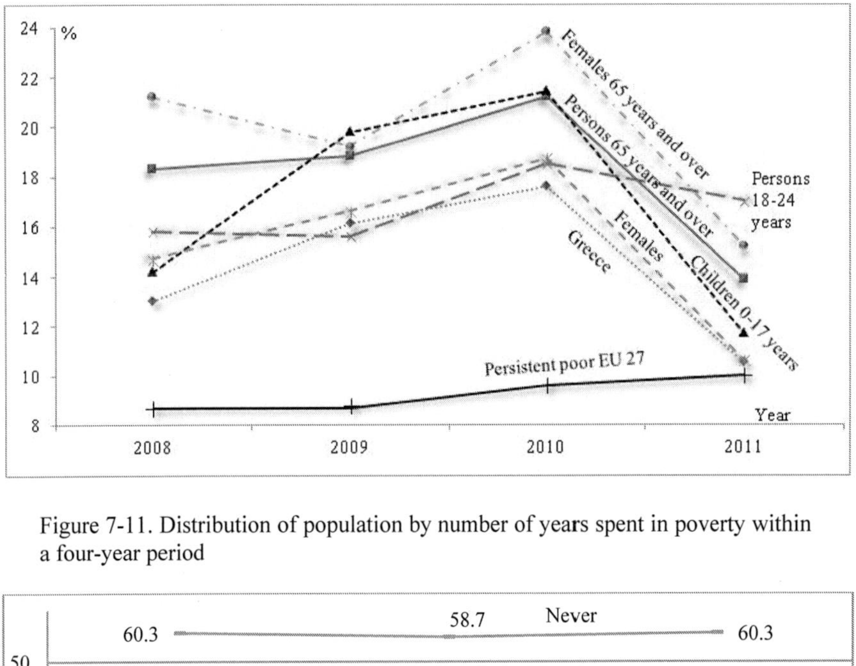

Figure 7-11. Distribution of population by number of years spent in poverty within a four-year period

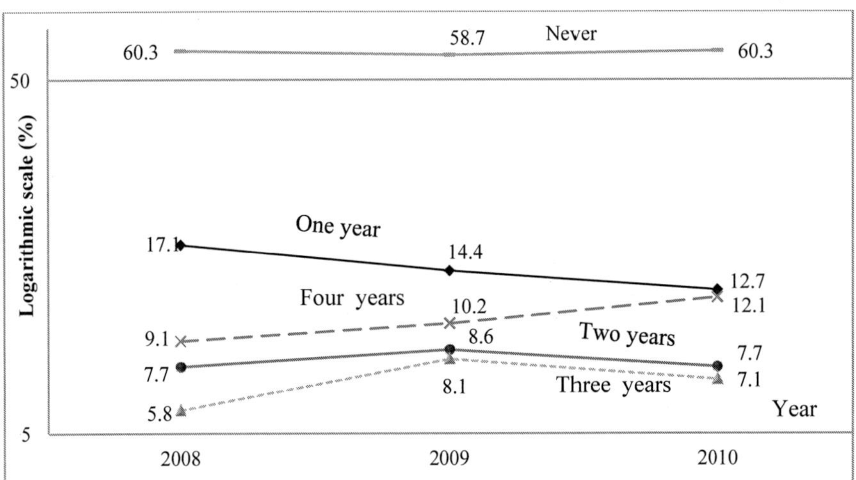

6. The evolution of poverty and social exclusion during 2009–2011: simple and composite measures

Severe material deprivation and very low work intensity are two of the three components of the Europe 2020 Poverty and Social Exclusion indicator. The third component is being at risk of poverty, the monetary element of poverty and social exclusion. People are considered to be at riskof poverty or social exclusion if they face at least one of the three risks (Eurostat 2012b). The latest developments for the years 2009, 2010 and 2011—subject to data availability—show that the proportion of the population at risk of poverty or social exclusion increased in Greece by 3.4 percentage points (Figure 7-12). However, in the majority of the EU countries we see similar increases, while by far the largest increases occurred in Bulgaria (7.5 percentage points in 2011) [data not shown]

Figure 7-12. Evolution of selected poverty, deprivation and social exclusion indices, Greece 2008-2011

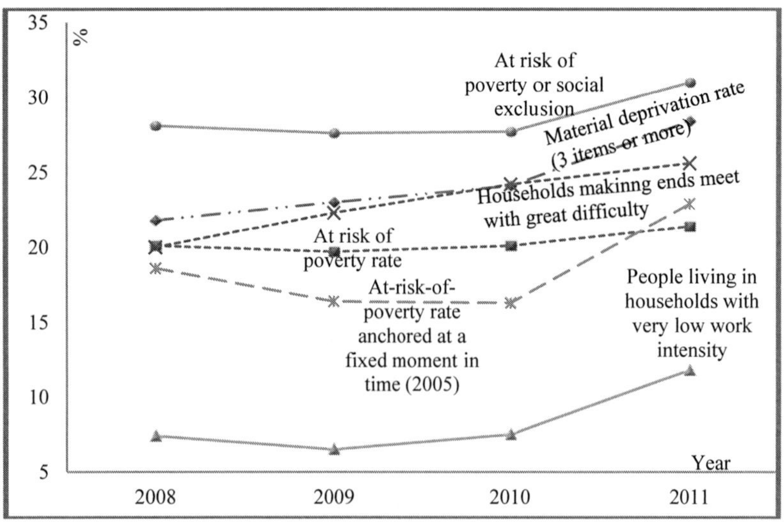

Another important conclusion is that almost all indices show an upward trend in Greece. It is obvious that austerity measures and regressive taxation measures can only serve to widen poverty and social exclusion.

Economic shocks could cause severe harm to unemployed, children and other vulnerable groups, through at least two channels: first, through lower household incomes (i.e., resulting from loss of jobs, asset depletion, tighter credit conditions, etc.); and second, through more limited access to public services due to tightening government budgets and social spending. If the at-risk-of-poverty rate is compared before and after social cash transfers, it becomes obvious that social policy plays a moderating effect on the poverty risk in Greece. The 2011 poverty risk would increase from 21.4% to 44.9% in the absence of all social transfers and to 24.8% if pension payments were excluded.[61]

7. Cluster Analysis

The aim of this section is to demonstrate the similarities and differences (grouping) between EU member states through cluster analysis, on the basis of selected socio-economic indicators. What will be examined is whether: (a) founder and relatively developed countries fall within the same clusters, (b) serious changes in groups are experienced in the beginning and after the crisis periods (defined here with the two distinct time points 2008 and 2011), and (c) poverty continues to be the common problem of some or all EU member states.

The indicators included in the analysis are: At-risk-of-poverty rate (after social transfers), severe material deprivation rate, persons living in households with very low work intensity,[62] the at-risk-of-poverty threshold (in €) in order to reflect different income levels across countries,[63] poverty before social transfers[64] and the subjective poverty indicator (ability to make ends meet with great difficulty).

Clusters were initially produced using Ward's Method, which is a hierarchical technique, in order to analyse country-level indicators and to identify country groups that are similar to each other. As Table 7-2 shows, for 2011 there are four distinct clusters.[65] The *first* and biggest cluster, with Belgium, France, Ireland, Netherlands, Germany, Austria, Finland, Sweden, Cyprus, the UK and Italy, is characterized by an above-average share of low work intensity rates (except Cyprus and Sweden),[66] at-risk-of-poverty rates below or around the EU average, and below EU average (10%) share of people suffering from severe material deprivation (except Italy and Cyprus). The countries in this cluster enjoy a better social situation when compared to the rest of EU with most aspects taken into account (this is clearly seen by the high levels of the poverty threshold). The weakness in some of these countries is low work intensity: in other words, a high share of people living in jobless households or in households with little labour market engagement (Belgium 13.7%, Germany 11.1%, France 9.3%, Italy 10.4%, U.K. 11.5%, Finland 9.8%, Sweden 6.8%, and Cyprus only 4.6%). However, in this "work-poor" or "better than average" group, two countries which are characterized by a high at-risk-of-poverty rate and severe material deprivation are unexpectedly included: Italy, with a poverty rate of 19.6% and a severe material deprivation rate of 11.2%, and Cyprus with respective rates at 14.5% and 10.7%.[67]

The *second* cluster consists of countries that tend to be characterized by high rates of severe material deprivation and poverty risk (8.7%-41% and 13%-22.3%, respectively). Eight out of the twelve new member states (Bulgaria, Romania, Estonia, Slovakia, Latvia, Lithuania, Hungary and Poland) are placed in this poverty and "*resource-poor*" cluster.[68]

The *third* cluster is comprised of a large number of heterogeneous countries, which perform below the EU average in most indicators. The main characteristic for these countries is that they have been severely hit by the financial crisis and are representatives of the so-called Mediterranean model (Greece, Portugal, Spain).[69] However, due to the low impact of social transfers in reducing poverty and similar threshold levels, Slovenia and Malta are more close to the Mediterranean countries, and are thus included in this cluster.[70] Czech Republic is also included, since it has a poverty threshold (€4471) closer to Portugal (€5046), and social transfers reduce the at-risk-of-poverty rate by 8 percentage points. This figure is similar to Spain and Malta and close to Portugal (7 percentage points).

The *fourth* cluster, with Denmark and Luxemburg, enjoys the best social situation, when compared to the rest of EU with all aspects taken into account (this is clearly seen by the level of the poverty threshold, the very low level of severe material deprivation and low percentage of people declaring ability to make ends meet with great difficulty).

The last column of Table 7-2 shows that only a few changes have occurred since 2008. Both the first (without Ireland) and the second group have largely remained the same although Czech Republic is included within this cluster in 2011. The third group clearly demonstrates that Ireland was seriously affected by the crisis, as in 2008 it formed a cluster with Luxemburg and Denmark, and had thus a better social situation when compared to 2011. Finally from the fourth group only the Czech Republic is omitted.

Table 7-2. Selected poverty and deprivation indicators 2011, and cluster groups 2011 and 2008

Country	At risk of poverty rate	Poverty before social transfers (pensions excluded)	Poverty threshold (€)	Severe material deprivation	People living in households with very low work intensity	Households making ends meet with great difficulty	Groups 2011	Groups 2008
"Good performers" – countries with above average values in all indicators								
Denmark	13	28.4	15837	2.6	11.4	4.2	4	4
Luxembourg	13.6	27.2	19523	1.2	5.8	2.7	4	4
Mediterranean countries and other low impact of social transfers reducing poverty risk countries (Malta, Czech Republic and Slovenia)								
Czech Republic	9.8	18	4471	6.1	6.6	8.7	3	2
Greece	21.4	24.8	6591	15.2	11.8	25.6	3	3
Spain	21.8	29.8	7509	3.9	12.2	10.1	3	3
Malta	15.4	22.9	6517	6.3	8.3	14.4	3	3
Portugal	18	25.4	5046	8.3	8.2	19.2	3	3
Slovenia	13.6	24.2	7199	6.1	7.6	9.3	3	3
"Resource poor" countries, with extremely high material deprivation or/and with above-average poverty risk								
Bulgaria	22.3	27.1	1741	41	11.0	27.8	2	2
Estonia	17.5	24.9	3359	8.7	9.9	8.5	2	2

Country	At risk of poverty rate	Poverty before social transfers (pensions excluded)	Poverty threshold (€)	Severe material deprivation	People living in households with very low work intensity	Households making ends meet with great difficulty	Groups 2011	Groups 2008
Latvia	19.3	27.3	2516	30.9	12.6	25.1	2	2
Lithuania	20	31.8	2403	18.5	12.3	11.2	2	2
Hungary	13.8	28.9	2721	23.1	12.1	26.1	2	2
Poland	17.7	24.1	3015	13	6.9	12.4	2	2
Romania	22.2	29.1	1270	29.4	6.7	20.8	2	2
Slovakia	13.0	19.5	3784	10.6	7.6	10.7	2	2
"Work-poor" or "better than average" group								
Belgium	15.3	27.8	12005	5.7	13.7	8.8	1	1
Germany	15.8	25.1	11426	5.3	11.1	3.1	1	1
Ireland	15.2	39.6	11836	7.8	24.1	14.7	1	4
France	14.0	24.7	11997	5.2	9.3	4.5	1	1
Italy	19.6	24.4	9583	11.2	10.4	17	1	1
Cyprus	14.5	23.3	10324	10.7	4.6	25.1	1	1
Netherlands	11.0	20.9	12186	2.5	8.7	3.3	1	1

Country	At risk of poverty rate	Poverty before social transfers (pensions excluded)	Poverty threshold (€)	Severe material deprivation	People living in households with very low work intensity	Households making ends meet with great difficulty	Groups 2011	Groups 2008
Austria	12.6	24.9	12791	3.9	8.0	5.4	1	1
Finland	13.7	27.4	13096	3.2	9.8	2.6	1	1
Sweden	14.0	27.9	13504	1.2	6.8	3.3	1	1
U.K.	16.2	30.5	10283	5.1	11.5	7.3	1	1

Thus, cluster analysis findings indicate that serious differences in terms of poverty, severe material deprivation and social exclusion among EU member states do exist. In the study, within the examined period and with the limitations of the selected indicators, no serious grouping differences were found in the countries in question. When the analysis results for 2008 and 2011 are comparatively reviewed, it is demonstrated that no serious changes actually occurred in these years.

One of the findings is that the Mediterranean countries (Greece, Spain, and Portugal) were always in a separate cluster. This can be explained partially by the fact that social transfers reduced only to a small degree the at-risk-of-poverty rate, and also had higher rates of individuals who suffered from severe material deprivation and remained as poverty risks after social transfers.

Another finding is that Ireland was seriously affected showing higher poverty rates; in addition, even though Czech Republic and Slovenia were closer to the Mediterranean countries, the majority of the new member states build a distinct cluster.

The analysis also shows that serious changes were not experienced in country clusters, although social policy and social inclusion strategies were actively implemented. Poverty, severe material deprivation and social exclusion—as a multidimensional process—continued to be the common problem of all EU member countries.

8. Main findings and conclusions

Although the at-risk-of-poverty rate seems to be relatively sensitive to the financial crisis in Greece, depicting an increase of 1.3 percentage points between 2010 and 2011, "inside" the poor population more significant and remarkable changes have been taking place. In sum, for the period 2008-2011 the following are observed:

- The crisis has an acute impact on the most disadvantaged members of society, as well as pushing increasing numbers of low and middle income earners into poverty and forcing them to seek the services of welfare agencies.
- The traditionally poor social groups (Third Country Nationals, the unemployed, low-educated individuals, people living in rented homes, households with more than three dependent children, single parents, households in scarcely populated areas, etc) are severely affected and show the highest rates of poverty and extreme poverty.

- For certain large social groups (the elderly, women, men), between 2008 and 2010, the risk of poverty remains close to the national mean and significantly lower than some years ago. However, the at-risk-of-poverty rate increased between 2010 and 2011.
- New groups of poor emerge, which, hadn't it been for the crisis, would have remained untouched: the working poor (mainly employees and part-time workers, as it becomes evident that employment is no longer a safety net against poverty), households with children and no employment, children (up to 17 years old), young people (18-24 years old), single households, households with two dependent children, homeowners.
- According to available data for the period 2010-2011, the at-risk-of-poverty rate anchored at a fixed moment in time (60% of the 2008 median income) shows a significant increase, reaching 22.9% in 2011 while in 2010 it stood to 18.0%. This fact is a strong indication of the deep impact of the crisis, since it concerns a more absolute rate rather than a relative one.
- In Greece, the persistent at-risk-of-poverty indicator for the period 2008-2010 follows an upward trend reaching 17.6% in 2010. It was second from the top (the highest risk is documented in Romania: 18.2%) and significantly higher than the EU-27 mean (9.7% in 2010).
- Children and elderly women constitute the predominant at-high-risk-of-persistent poverty groups. However, young people aged 18-24 also score very high.
- Material deprivation indicators, which in a way are closer to an absolute rather than a relative approach to poverty, are more "sensitive" to the economic crisis, since they show overall an increasing trend (rate of material deprivation), while in certain subcategories the increase is quite alarming.
- It is now evident that examining an individual's (or a household's) income level is not adequate in order to define poverty; it is rather necessary to also examine whether that individual (or household) is able to meet certain needs, like going annually for holiday for a week (in 2011, 87.2% of the poor stated they weren't able to do so), ability to keep home adequately warm (in 2011, 38.8% of the poor stated they were unable to do so) or affording to pay utility bills (in 2011, 41.3% of the poor stated they were unable to do so).

- At the same time, due to the crisis, a two-fold problem possibly emerges: (a) an inefficient welfare state and (b) the collapse of informal support networks, which constituted the prominent welfare model in the European South.
- In 2010, the European average in social protection spending was at 29.4% of the GDP, whereas Greece devoted 29.1% of the GDP to social policy. However, social interventions have reduced poverty by 10% on average in Europe from 25.7% to 16.4%, whereas in Greece poverty has been reduced only slightly from 23.8% to 20.1% (in 2010). The comparison with countries that provide targeted social policies—without spending a lot more—is disappointing for our welfare state. Sweden devotes 30.4% of its GDP to social policy (only 1.3% more than Greece), but succeeds in reducing its poor population by half—from 27.9% to 14.0% of the total population.

The future outlook for Greece is uncertain and with no policy for the creation of a just and effective welfare state, development cannot be achieved. There is a need for drastic improvement in the functioning of the labour market and the integration of more people into the labour market, supported by further progress in the welfare protection system. These measures might lead to a sustainable recovery, long-term growth and better jobs, while at the same time help to reduce poverty in Greece.

Notes

[1] The rate of growth was -6.9% in 2011, -3.5% in 2010 and –3.2% in 2009.

[2] The cuts in average wages were almost 30% between 2009 and 2011.

[3] 2011 is the last year covered by the EU-SILC, involving reference incomes of the previous year.

[4] The incomes of all household members and other household incomes are aggregated together, and total household disposable income is adjusted for differences in household size and composition by use of a modified OECD equivalence scale which assigns a value of 1 to the first adult in the household, 0.5 to additional members over the age of 14, and 0.3 to children under 14. By this procedure, in accordance with the Eurostat methodology, we construct the equivalised income. The poor are those with an income below 60% per cent of the median equivalised income.

[5] For example, the 2011 data refers to income (and employment) for 2010.

[6]Absolute poverty is commonly defined as the lack of material or financial resources necessary for survival or meeting basic needs. However, it is stated that–at least before the recession–absolute poverty had been eliminated in the EU countries. Therefore, most poverty indicators adopted by the European Union (EU)

and Eurostat (Statistical Office of the EU) are based on the concept of relative poverty, which is considered as a consequence of the distribution of income.

[7] According to Ringen (1988) and Halleröd (1995) income is merely an indirect measure of poverty, with an income threshold or poverty line used to identify the poor (relative income or monetary poverty approach); therefore, it is closely related to income distribution and transfer systems. The people concerned are conventionally defined as being at risk of poverty, since given their relative level of income they may not be able to enjoy the standard of living that most people in the country in question are able to.

[8] Originally proposed by Guio (2009), these indicators are now part of the EU set of commonly agreed-upon social indicators.

[9] At the EU –SILC, respondents are asked to clarify if they do not have or consume an item because: (a) they do not "need" it or (b) they "cannot afford" it. It is, therefore, possible to distinguish between "unenforced" and "enforced" hardship.The first five items define the "economic strain" dimension while the rest four items define the durables dimension.

[10] See: Atkinson and Marlier (2010: 136).

[11] Another indicator measures the intensity of deprivation, that is, the mean number of items (from 0 to 9) deprived by people (Eurostat 2012a).

[12] Council of the European Union, 2004: 8.

[13]Jenkins and van Kerm (2011: 1-2) argue that: "*The persistent at-risk-of-poverty rate measures the proportion of persons in a country who are currently income poor and who were income poor in at least two of the preceding three years. It has received much less attention than the at-risk-of-poverty rate, not least because longitudinal data spanning a four year period take longer to become available than cross-sectional data for a single year*".

[14] Those aged 0-59 living in households where the adults (aged 18-59) work less than 20% of their total work potential during the past year.

[15] People falling below 60% of the median equivalised disposable income are said to be "at risk of poverty". Most research studies on poverty also provide information for the *at-risk-of-poverty* rate at different thresholds (40%, 50% and 70% of the national median equivalised household income), as well as the median *at-risk-of-poverty* gap, the persistent *at-risk-of-poverty* rate, the *at-risk-of-poverty* rate anchored at a point in time (the share of the population whose income in year *t* is below a risk-of-poverty threshold calculated in the standard way for *t-3* and then up-rated for by inflation over three years) and groups exposed to the risk of poverty.

[16] Subjective poverty is the result of people's views, perceptions, preferences or feelings about their situation or well-being. A subjective method completes the picture by giving a measure of economic well-being to respondents themselves (Heikkilä, Moisio, Ritakallio, Bradshaw, Kuivalainen, Hellsten and Kajanoja, 2006).

[17] The near poor are those with income above (70%) the conventional poverty line (60%), while those with income at the 40% of the median equivalised income are the extreme poor.

[18] The persistent risk of poverty is defined, in the set of indicators used by the EU to monitor social inclusion, as "*having an equivalised disposable income below the at-risk-of-poverty threshold in the current year and in at least two of the preceding three years*". Thus, those whose income has fallen below the poverty threshold temporarily are distinguished from those whose income is consistently below this level, or at least in most years.
[19] The need for consolidation led the country to embark on a trilateral mechanism of financial support, comprising the EU, the IMF and the ECB.
[20] This is due to the fact that it concerns relative risk of poverty, which is estimated based on incomes from the previous year.
[21] Those "living in poverty" is the term introduced following a European Council meeting in Laeken in 2001. As part of the Laeken indicators, the poverty rates were calculated for both sexes, various age groups, the most frequent activity of the respondent, and household type.
[22] From 1994 to 2007, the at-risk-of-poverty rate, estimated by the same methodology, is relatively stable, ranging between 20% and 23% (fluctuating between 20% and 21% during the last 10 years). In any case, the at-risk-of-poverty rate in Greece is higher than in most of the EU-27 member countries.
[23] Mean household disposable income from 24,224.38€ in 2010 decreased to 21,590.07€ in 2011.
[24] The value of the Gini coefficient from 32.9 in 2010 increased to 33.6 in 2011.
[25]Typically, recessions reduce real income levels but the relative poverty rate need not rise if the poverty line (which is expressed as a fraction of average income) falls sufficiently.
[26] See: European Foundation for the Improvement of Living and Working Conditions, 2004: 17.
[27] More precisely, this group refers to citizens from non-EU-27 countries, having Third Country Nationals as the dominant group.
[28] The OECD forecasts that the number of single parents is likely to increase in the next few decades, which raises serious policy concerns regarding support for lone parents, especially in terms of their participation in the labour force (OECD, 2010).
[29] A high proportion of single parents are women.
[30] In 2011, the at-risk for two adults households with three or more dependent children was slightly below the national average (20.8%).
[31] ISCED 97: Pre-primary, primary and lower secondary education (levels 0-2).
[32] According to the Hellenic Statistical Authority (2010: 5), the classification is as follows: (a) High-density area: an area with more than 500 inhabitants per square kilometer and a population of, at least, 50,000 people (b) Medium-density area: an area with more than 100 inhabitants per square kilometer, which either has a total population of at least 50,000 people or is adjacent to a high-density area and (c) Scarcely populated area: an area which does not fall into either of the previous two categories.
[33] And those who are seeking entry into the labour market for the first time may find it increasingly difficult to obtain secure employment while low-educated and low-skilled workers are under constant threat of slipping into unemployment.

[34] And where the overall income of the household (including social transfers and after taxation) remains below the poverty line.
[35] The number of dependents in a household is decisive for in-work poverty. For example a household in which two adults work part time, may be at risk of poverty if there are three or more dependents.
[36] Eurostat defines the work intensity of a household as the overall degree of work activity of working age members in the household.
[37] In Greece, the traditional concept of welfare state was built around the norm that the average employee was a male whose earned wages were covering his domestic responsibilities. It meant that wages were supposed to be high enough to support also a wife and children. Paid wages were not "individual" but more of a "family wage". This system has been called a "wage-earner's welfare state" (see, e.g., Castles, 1985 and Beck, 1992).
[38] We think that not only the unemployed incur a higher risk of poverty, they also tend to represent a relatively higher proportion of overall poverty during the recession years.
[39] See, http://appsso.eurostat.ec.europa.eu/nui/setupModifyTableLayout.do [October 2013]
[40] Work intensity is defined as the number of months that all members of the household, who are in employment-active age, have worked during the income reference year, as a percentage of the total number of months they could theoretically have worked within the family. Individuals are classified in the work intensity categories, ranging from WI=0 (unemployed family) to WI=1 (full work intensity). The scale is as follows: Very low: 0 to 20% of the total work possibility; Low: 20% to 45% of the total work possibility; Medium: 45% to 55% of the total work possibility; High: 55% to 85% of the total work possibility; Very high: 85% of the total work possibility.
[41] Data refer to year 2011.
[42] We include in this category (although not demographic) also those with owned houses/dwellings.
[43] Data for all the groups refer to the period 2008-2011.
[44] 41.3% for the poor in 2011, compared to 18.4% for the non-poor.
[45] 22.2% for the poor in 2011, compared to 11.1% for the non-poor.
[46] 22.9% for the poor in 2011, compared to 7.7% for the non-poor.
[47] Pay their rent, mortgage or utility bills; keep their home adequately warm; face unexpected expenses; eat meat or protein regularly; go on a holiday.
[48] Note that the answers to the two questions: "ability to make ends meet" refers to the year of the survey, while the at-risk-of-poverty estimate considers income in the previous year(s).
[49] Which was 4320€ in 2008, 4598€ in 2009 and 4785€ in 2010 (per person). It represents about 67% of the amount corresponding to the conventional poverty line.
[50] On the contrary, in Finland 42% of the poor on the 60% of the poverty threshold are also poor according to the limit of 50% of the dividing line. In other words, 58% of the poor population has, according to the conventional definition, an equivalized income ranging between 50% and 60% of the equivalized income.

[51] See, http://appsso.eurostat.ec.europa.eu/nui/show.do?dataset=ilc_li11&lang=en [October 2013]
[52]Around 5,498€/ year.
[53] See, http://appsso.eurostat.ec.europa.eu/nui/show.do?dataset=ilc_li22b&lang=en [October 2013]
[54] It is a quasi-absolute measure of poverty, which offers information regarding improved living conditions stemming from economic development.
[55] See, http://appsso.eurostat.ec.europa.eu/nui/show.do?dataset=ilc_li22b&lang=en [October 2013]
[56]However, income mobility involves only a relatively small distance. Although a lot of people move up and down the income ladder over time, this mobility often involves moving to an adjacent step, i.e. not very far from the reference step.
[57]Persistent poverty indicators aim to reflect structural poverty situations; they, therefore, do not consider people as poor who have circumstantially or momentarily fallen into poverty.
[58] Available data for period 2008-2010.
[59] This conclusion is in accordance with other similar studies' findings (see Damioli, 2009).
[60] Normally, the two indices should have had the same values if, for example, all women above 65 were at the same time both poor and long-term poor. The fact that the percentage of long-term-poor-elderly women (23.6%) is larger than that for poor women (23.3%) is apparently due to some statistical error.
[61]See, http://epp.eurostat.ec.europa.eu/portal/page/portal/income_social_inclusion_living_conditions/data / database [October 2013].
[62] These three indicators are actually included in the composite poverty or social exclusion indicator.
[63] The actual level of income represented by the threshold differs substantially across member states. Accordingly, many individuals who are estimated to be at risk of poverty in a well-off country may have income well above the poverty threshold in a less wealthy one.
[64] This indicator examines the hypothetical non-existence of social transfers. Comparing this with the standard at-risk-of-poverty rate (after social transfers) shows that such transfers have an important redistributive effect that helps to reduce the number of people who are at risk of poverty (Eurostat, 2012: 3).
[65] A similar procedure was also applied by Lelkes and Zólyomi (2008) and Ada (2012).
[66] Finland, Austria, Netherlands and France are below but very close to the EU 27 value (10%).
[67] Naturally, the position of Cyprus must have undergone changes after the bailout. However, our data is up to year 2011.
[68] Slovenia, Malta and the Czech Republic perform better, with less poverty and less severe material deprivation and are placed in cluster 3, while Cyprus has been placed in the first cluster.
[69] The focus is on family although the state covers only specific social risks against which families cannot protect themselves. In general, this model is most family-

focused. These countries have a relatively low employment rate and relatively high poverty risk (Ferrera, 1996).

[70] In 2011, social transfers reduced the at-risk-of-poverty rate among the population of the EU-27 from 26.1 % before transfers to 16.9 % after transfers, thereby lifting almost 35 % of persons that would otherwise be at risk of poverty above the poverty threshold. In relative terms, the impact of social benefits was lowest in Greece, Bulgaria, Italy, Romania, Poland, Spain and Portugal (countries of groups 2 and 3) (Social Protection Committee, 2012).

References

Ada, A.A. (2012). 'The problem of social exclusion in the European Union: A study for Member States', *European Journal of Economics, Finance and Administrative Sciences* [Electronic] Issue 46, pp. 112-129, Available: http://www.europeanjournalofeconomics finance and administrative sciences.com/ejefas_issues.html [March 2012].

Atkinson A., B. and Marlier, E. (2010). *Income and living conditions in Europe*, Luxembourg: Publications Office of the European Union.

Balourdos, D. (2012). 'Poverty in Greece: Trends, challenges and policies' in Balourdos, D. and Petraki, M. (eds.) *New poverty and social exclusion: combating policies and establishment of a minimum guaranteed income*, Athens: Greek Parliament.

Beck, U. (1992). *Risk society: towards a new modernity*, London: Sage Publications.

Castles, F. (1985). *The working class and welfare: Reflections on the political development of the welfare state in Australia and New Zealand, 1890–1980*, Sydney: Allen and Unwin.

Council of the European Union, (2004). 'Joint report by the Commission and the Council on social inclusion', [Electronic], Available: http://ec.europa.eu/employment_social/soc-prot/soc-incl/final_joint_inclusion_report_2003_en.pdf [March 2004].

Crettaz, E. (2011). *Fighting working poverty in post-industrial economies. Causes, trade-offs and policy solutions,* Cheltenham, UK: Edward Elgar.

Damioli, G. (2010). 'How and Why the Dynamics of Poverty Differ across European Countries', paper presented at the *31st General Conference of The International Association for Research in Income and Wealth*, 22-28August, St. Gallen, Switzerland.

Desai, M. and Shah, A. (1988). 'An econometric approach to the measurement of poverty', *Oxford Economic Papers*, vol. 40, September, pp. 505-522.

Ferrera, M. (1996). ‘The southern model of welfare in social Europe’, *Journal of European Social Policy*, vol. 6, February, pp. 17-37.

EEC, (1985). ‘On specific community action to combat poverty (Council Decision of 19 December 1984) 85/8/EEC’, *Official Journal of the European Communities,* [Electronic] vol. 2, no 24, January, pp.24-25, Available: http://eur-lex.europa.eu/smartapi/cgi/sga_doc?smartapi!celexapi!prod!CELEXnumdoc&lg= EN&numdoc=31985D0008&model=guichett [1 January 1985].

European Foundation for the Improvement of Living and Working Conditions, (2004) *Working poor in the European Union, seminar report*, Available: http://www.eurofound.europa.eu/pubdocs/2004/127/en/1/ef04127en.pdf [July 2004].

European Commission, (2011). *Employment and social developments in Europe 2011,* Brussels: Directorate-General for Employment, Social Affairs and Inclusion.

—. (2012). *European economic forecast, European economy 1/2012,* Spring 2012, Brussels: Directorate-General for Economic and Financial Affairs.

Eurostat, (2012a). *Measuring material deprivation in the EU: Indicators for the whole population and child-specific indicators.* Eurostat Methodologies and Working papers, Luxembourg: Publications Office of the European Union.

—. (2012b). ‘At risk of poverty or social exclusion in the EU27’, *News release,* STAT/13/28, December 2012.

European Commission and Eurostat, (2010). *Income poverty and material deprivation in European countries*’, Luxembourg: Publications Office of the European Union.

—. (2011). ‘Older, more numerous and diverse Europeans’, *Demography Report*, Available: http://www.ec.europa.eu/social/BlobServlet?docId=6824& langId=en [March 2011].

European Commission, (2012) *Employment and social developments in Europe 2012*, Luxembourg: Publications Office of the European Union.

Goodman, A. and Myck, M. (2005). *Parental income and child outcomes: what can we learn from material deprivation?,* London: Institute for Fiscal Studies.

Guio, A. C. (2009) 'What can be learned from deprivation indicators in Europe?', *Eurostat methodologies and working paper*, [Electronic] Luxembourg: Eurostat, Available:

http://epp.eurostat.ec.europa.eu/cache/ITY_OFFPUB/KS-RA-09-007/EN/KS-RA-09-007-EN.PDF [08 June 2009].

—. (2005). *Material deprivation in the EU,* Statistics in Focus Series, Issue number 21/2005, Luxembourg: Eurostat.

Halleröd, B. (1995). 'The truly poor. Direct and indirect consensual measurement of poverty in Sweden', *Journal of European Social Policy*, vol. 5, no. 2, pp. 111–129.

Heikkilä, M., Moisio, P., Ritakallio,V-M., Bradshaw, J., Kuivalainen, S., Hellsten, K., Kajanoja, J. (2006). *Poverty policies, structures and outcomes in the EU 25. Report for the Fifth European Round Table on Poverty and Social Exclusion 16–17 October 2006,* Tampere, Helsinki: Stakes.

Hellenic Statistical Authority, (2011). *Statistics on income and living conditions 2010, Risk of poverty*, Piraeus: Press Release 2011.

—. (2012). *Statistics on income and living conditions 2011, risk of poverty*, Piraeus: Press Release 2012.

Jenkins, S. & Van Kerm, P. (2011). 'Patterns of persistent poverty: Evidence from EU-SILC', *ISER Working Paper Series*, [Electronic], nos. 2011-30 [November 2011].

Lelkes, O. and Zólyomi, E. (2008). *Poverty across Europe: The latest evidence using the EU-SILC Survey*, Centre for Social Welfare Policy and Research, Policy Brief 2008, Available: http://www.euro.centre.org/data/1226583242_93408.pdf [October 2008].

Mack, J. and Lansley, S. (1985). *Poor Britain*, London: Allen and Unwin.

Ministry of Labour, Social Security and Welfare, (2012). *Hellenic national social report 2012*, Athens: Ministry of Labour, Social Security and Welfare Publications.

Muffels, R. (1993). 'Deprivation standards and style of living indices', in Berghman, J. and Cantillion, B. (eds.) *The European face of social security,* Avebury: Aldershot.

Nolan, B. and Maitre, (2010). 'Protecting the vulnerable: Poverty and social exclusion in Ireland as the economic crisis emerged', *UCD Geary Institute discussion paper series.* [Electronic], available: http://www.ucd.ie/geary/static/publications/workingpapers/gearywp201023.pdf [22 April 2010].

Nolan,B. and Whelan, C. T. (1996). *Resources, deprivation and poverty*, Oxford and New York: Oxford University Press and Clarendon Press.

Quitini, G. (2010). *Greece 2010, Jobs for Youth Series*, Paris: OECD Publishing.

Ringen, S. (1988). 'Direct and indirect measurement of poverty', *Journal of Social Policy*, vol. 17, no. 3, pp. 351–365.

Social Protection Committee (2012) 'Third report on the social impact of the economic crisis and ongoing fiscal consolidation, 2011', Council of the European Union, Available: http://register.consilium.europa.eu/pdf/en/12/st05/st05858-ad01.en12.pdf [1 February 2012].

Townsend, P. (1979) *Poverty in the United Kingdom. A survey of household resources and standard of living,* Harmondsworth: Penguin Books.

Willitts, M. (2006). *Measuring child poverty using material deprivation: Possible approaches,* Department for Work and Pensions, Working Paper no 28, Leeds, Corporate Document Services.

CHAPTER EIGHT

THE IMPACT OF AUSTERITY MEASURES ON PEOPLE'S PERCEPTIONS OF SOCIAL AND POLITICAL INSTITUTIONS[1]

JOANNA TSIGANOU
NATIONAL CENTRE FOR SOCIAL RESEARCH

Abstract

The general frame of reference within which the main arguments are situated involves the impact of austerity measures on people's perceptions of social and political institutions on the one hand and the misleading —in my view—connection of certain "uncertainties" produced with the anomie theory debate. For the economy of the discussion, I will not specifically address the relevant theoretical issues involved but only when necessary. My arguments are concerned with documenting the empirical evidence across Europe. The measurements intended are indeed of vast importance, especially in the current debt crisis, since the quantitative data collected and properly processed may be used for the adoption of new public safety and criminal policy measures, or the introduction of new aspects in the exercise of social control. Therefore, my major point, in this respect, is that valid questions in measuring trust in society need further elaboration in order to lead to valid empirical data collection, especially when viewed in comparative perspective. Consequently, it is misleading to assume that it is possible to proceed to measure anxiety, insecurity and violence in general and abstract ways let alone to validate anomie theory in all of its subsequent versions.

Introduction

It is true that in an era of economic crisis—like the one we are witnessing at the moment on a global scale[2]—certain classical interpretations of citizens' behaviors and attitudes are making a dynamic comeback. Such is the case of anomie theory in explaining certain situations met occasionally or more permanently in contemporary societies. In the case of Greece, the present crisis as well as certain expressions of trust, anxiety, insecurity and violence in society are much too often connected in public rhetoric with explanations offered within the anomie theory domain (Tsiganou, 2011).

It is not my purpose to review here the whole field of anomie theory but to try to delineate certain aspects of its interpretative contribution to deciphering the impact of austerity upon the way people feel and perceive the established social and political institutions. Therefore, in the present paper I shall only refer to certain conceptual parameters that illuminate my discussion of the relevant field data of the Greek experience within the pan-European context.

As it is well-known, we use the term "anomie", literally, to describe a condition "without norms", but more usually, a state of society in which substantial disagreement exists over appropriate norms. Thus, some aspects of society are inadequately regulated, hence, anomie. Durkheim's appealing idea of anomie, when the division of labor in society has progressed faster than the moral basis for this division, reflects his belief that human happiness and social order depend on a high level of social regulation and on value consensus (Durkheim, 1952; Durkheim, 1964). Such an idea of psychological survival, however, in times of both economic boom and depression, leaves aside what happens in times of repression. This was amended by the Marxist radical concept of alienation which invoked a social structure that frustrates human needs. Further, in Merton's clarification, anomie changed from normlessness to norm conflict. Thus, unhappiness results because of the disjunction between different parts of the value structure of society between culturally prescribed goals (essentially high material achievements) and institutionalized, legitimate means for attaining them (Merton, 1957).

The basic question that arises, therefore, from the revival of anomie theory in public debate in Greece and its connection with the present economic crisis is whether it offers the necessary conceptual and interpretative tools to explain certain conditions of conflict in contemporary Greek society. After all, several theories, critiques, "revisionisms" and self-professed "orthodoxies" have given prominence to various elements of human behavior such as anxiety, confidence and trust, and/or "basic trust" versus "basic mistrust" (Giddens, 1984) and their role in holding society together. On the other hand, the essential role of the consensual aspects of law and morality for society's existence has been long ago appreciated, analyzed and discussed (Hart, 1984).

The empirical evidence

As Giddens has put it, security and danger, trust and risk, opportunity and danger—these polar, paradoxical features of modernity—permeate all aspects of daily life, once more reflecting an extraordinary interpolation of the local and the global (Giddens, 1990). Although contemporary debates in some western societies reveal an almost obsessive concern with questions of social order, there is very little agreement as to the foundations upon which such order rests or how it can best be secured. Some see it as depending upon widespread approval of mutually understood rules, while others consider that it is primarily maintained through the exercise of force—coercion.

At the same time, there is argument over the degree of order that is necessary or desirable, and, consequently, as to the significance of disputes: these can be viewed as pathological events, signs that something is "wrong in society" or as normal and inevitable features of social life. Indeed, societies differ widely as to the amount of friction and disorder which their members are able to tolerate. That is, societies differ widely as to the kinds of behavior which are approved or tolerated and hence also in the amount of tension and quarrelling that will be felt acceptable in terms of law and order (Roberts, 1979: Giddens 1984).

To assess our theoretical argument, we used data from the European Social Survey (ESS), a pan-European instrument of political sociology that runs throughout Europe for the last decade.[3] The data selected from the ESS pertained to trust in society (interpersonal trust), satisfaction with life and the economy, perceptions of the "other", trust in political institutions (democracy, parliament, law and the legal system), trust in the coercive institutions (the police) and sense of insecurity. A brief description of these and their measurement is given here, although the reader can access www.europeansocialsurvey.org for more analytical presentations of these variables.

The way ESS operationalises the concept of "trust" has indeed important subjective and structural connotations since it measures not only the people's confidence in others but also attitudes towards exploitation, helplessness or solidarity. In the ESS source questionnaire, "social trust" is measured in three distinct but intermingled ways: Initially, the aim is to measure social "distrust" rather than social "trust" since people are asked to decide on a ten-point scale, where *0* indicates absolute suspicion and *10,* absolute trust of most people in the society they live in. Secondly, the concept of exploitation as connected with trust and fairness is operationalised in a similar-to-the-above way. Thirdly, social trust is measured in terms of the contrast between self-interest and altruistic helpfulness.

More specifically, *trust in society* has been tapped by questioning the European, and in turn, the Greek public on whether "most people can be trusted or that (one) can't be too careful in dealing with people", where "being careful" means the need to be wary or suspicious. On a ten-point scale, the *zero* point meant that "you can't be too careful" and the *ten* point meant that "most people can be trusted".

Social trust has been importantly diminished in Europe and Greece alike during the past decade (Figures 8-1, 8-2). In fact, "trust in society" reflects not only social trust and social solidarity but also confidence in social networks

Figure 8-1. Trust in society, Europe 2002, 2005 and 2010

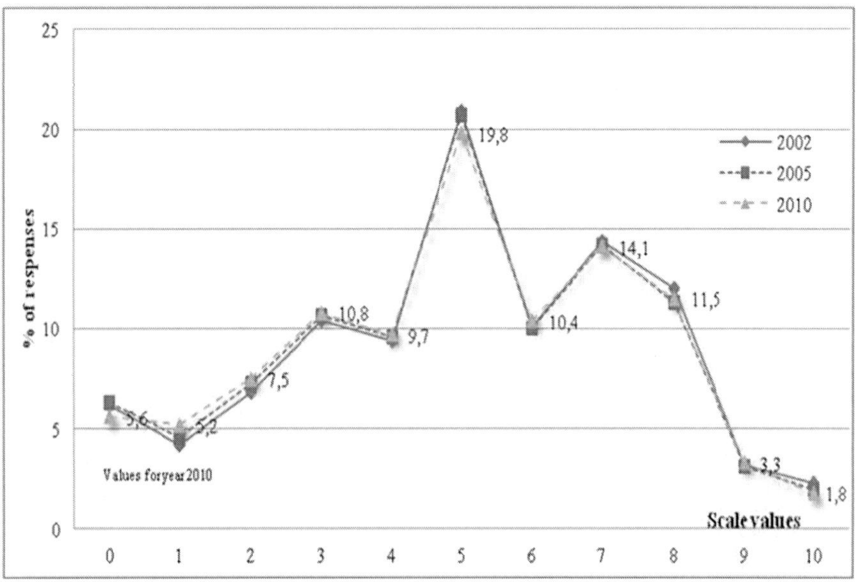

Source: European Social Survey (ESS), Round 1, 2002, Round 2, 2005, Round 4, 2010.

Figure 8-2. Trust in society, Greece 2002, 2005 and 2010

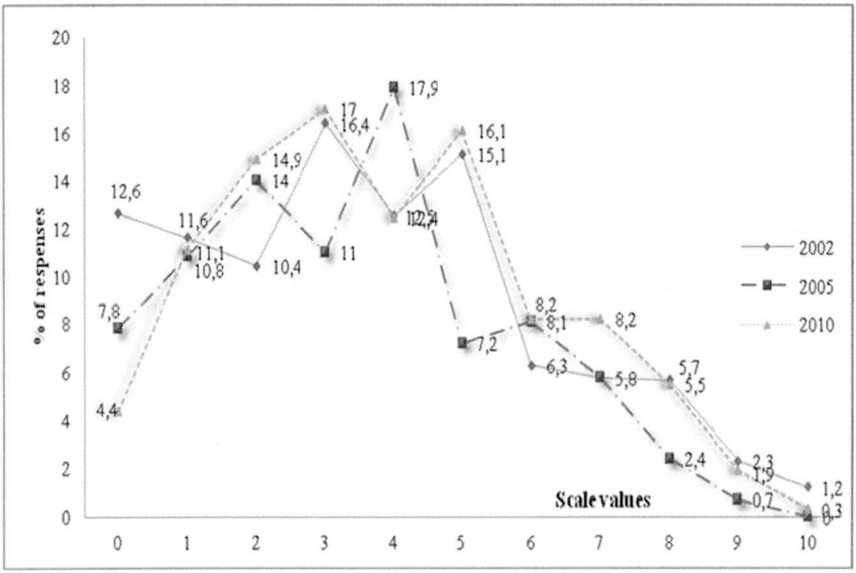

Source: European Social Survey (ESS), Round 1, 2002, Round 2, 2005, Round 4, 2010.

Taking up the next group of ESS concepts used in the present research—and that has to with *satisfaction with the economy, satisfaction with life and personal happiness*—it is necessary to note that there is a distinct way of measuring satisfaction with the economy and satisfaction with life, on the one hand, and the sense of personal happiness, on the other. Satisfaction with the economy and with life have been measured in a ten-point contentment scale by asking the questions: "how content are you with the present economic situation", and "how content are you with your life at present" with *zero* representing absolute discontent and *ten* representing total pleasure and contentment. There is also a complementary measurement included on "personal happiness" with one's life "*as a whole nowadays ... all things considered*" (italics added). The results for Europe and Greece are shown in the Figures 8-3—8-5.

The Mertonian high material achievements *vis a vis* the institutionalized, legitimate means of attaining them, under the present financial conditions of the Eurozone debt crisis, suffer too. The personal well-being in terms of satisfaction with life and of the function of economy seems severely traumatized. The same holds true for the case of personal sentiments of well-being, personal aspirations and happiness in both Greece and Europe. However, data for Greece by the end of the decade, and especially when the country was well under the debt crisis (2010-11), mark a dramatic low (Figures 8-3 – 8-5). It is important to note that results from all relevant ESS measurements mentioned above follow identical patterns.

The crisis was also expected to affect *tolerance toward the "other"*, either as a result of the perception of competition or as a result of scapegoating processes due to frustrations of the majority group's economic or life expectations. To measure tolerance toward the "other", one of the many ESS relevant variables pertaining to perception of foreigners, i.e., whether "the country is made a worse or a better place to live by people coming to live here from other countries" was used by the author. A ten-point scale was used, where *zero* represented "intolerance" and *ten*, tolerance toward the 'other'. Tolerance towards the "other" has also been importantly diminished (Figure 8-6). Thus, social attitudes also express sentiments of racism and xenophobia at an increasing rate. The cultural foundations of European civilization seem blurred.

Figure 8-3. Satisfaction with the economy, Greece and Europe 2002, 2005 and 2010

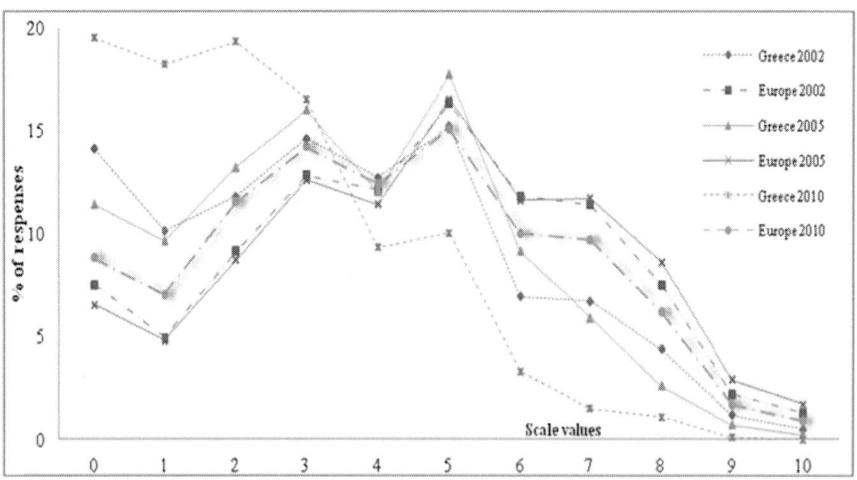

Source: European Social Survey (ESS), Round 1, 2002, Round 2, 2005, Round 4, 2010

Figure 8-4. Satisfaction with life, Greece and Europe 2002, 2005 and 2010

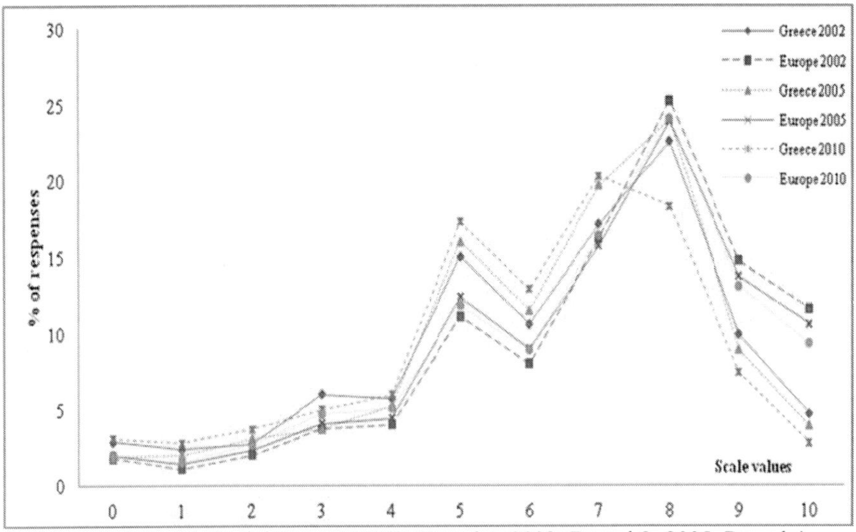

Source: European Social Survey (ESS), Round 1, 2002, Round 2, 2005, Round 4, 2010.

Trust in social and political institutions, which have been at the epicentre of controversy during the economic crisis, constitute the next important group of ESS variables. People were asked to mark, on a ten-point scale, "how much (they) *personally* (emphasis in the original) trust each of the following social and political institutions": Solidarity, the Parliament, the Legal System, the Police, Political Personnel and the European Parliament. Trust in institutions is measured comparatively in a sense, since matrix questions have been constructed to this end. The data (Figure 8-7 and Figures 8-8, 8-9, 8-10, 8-12 and 8-14) show that all political and social institutions seem to undergo a deterioration in the perception of European but mainly of Greek citizens. ESS data show that trust in important political institutions runs low in Greece, and there is evidence of a severe breach of confidence towards important social institutions and solidarity networks.

Figure 8-5. Satisfaction with life, Greece and Europe 2010

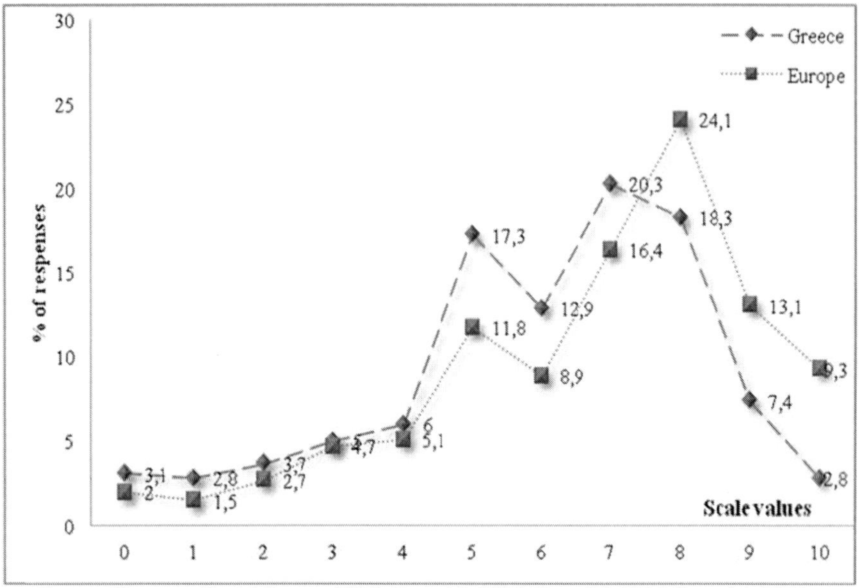

Source: European Social Survey (ESS), Round 1, 2002, Round 2, 2005, Round 4, 2010.

Figure 8-6.. Attitudes against foreigners, Greece 2002, 2005 and 2010

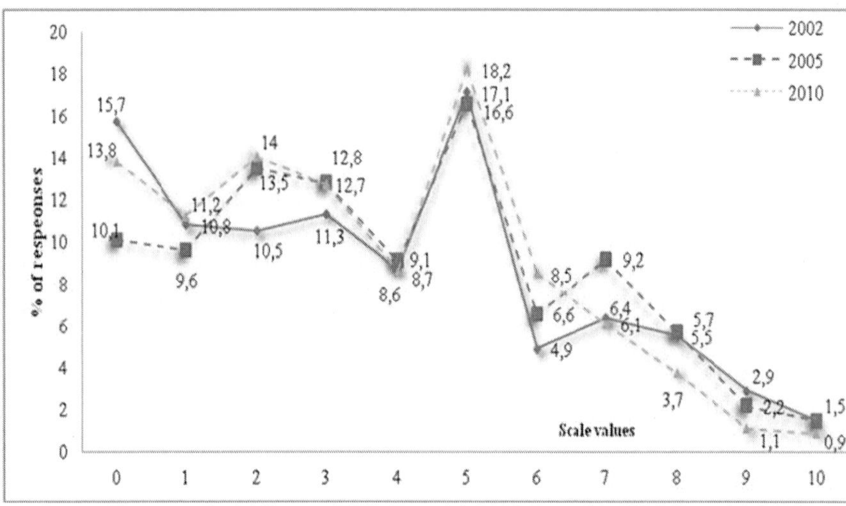

Source: European Social Survey (ESS), Round 1, 2002, Round 2, 2005, Round 4, 2010

Figure 8-7. Trust in Institutions, Greece 2010

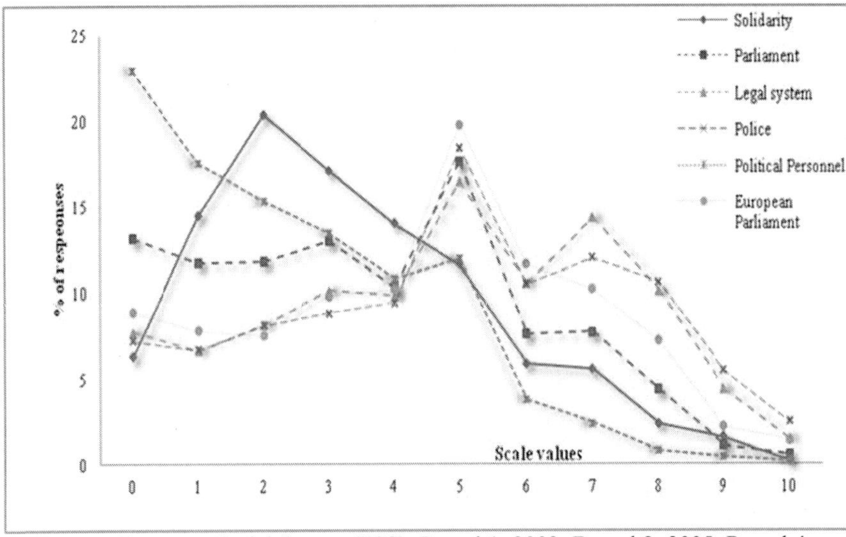

Source: European Social Survey (ESS), Round 1, 2002, Round 2, 2005, Round 4, 2010.

For Greece, said to be the "cradle of democracy" and the focus of austerity measures during the financial crisis, the assessment of how democracy operates was of vital importance. The satisfaction with the operation of democracy was measured, on a ten-point scale, by means of a direct question: "how satisfied are you with the operation of democracy", where *zero* reflects absolute dissatisfaction and/or discontent while the *ten* represents absolute satisfaction.

The operation of democracy seems vulnerable and the European citizens are dissatisfied with its function. Arguments have emerged with increasing pace, questioning its quality. By the end of the decade, people feel vulnerable to undemocratic rules and procedures. The present crisis, as the latest ESS data suggest, has exacerbated the situation alarmingly. Especially in Greece, with the initial implementation of the memorandum regulating the country's debt, the situation changed for the worse almost immediately (Figure 8-8).

Figure 8-8. Satisfaction with the operation of democracy, Greece and Europe 2002, 2005 and 2010

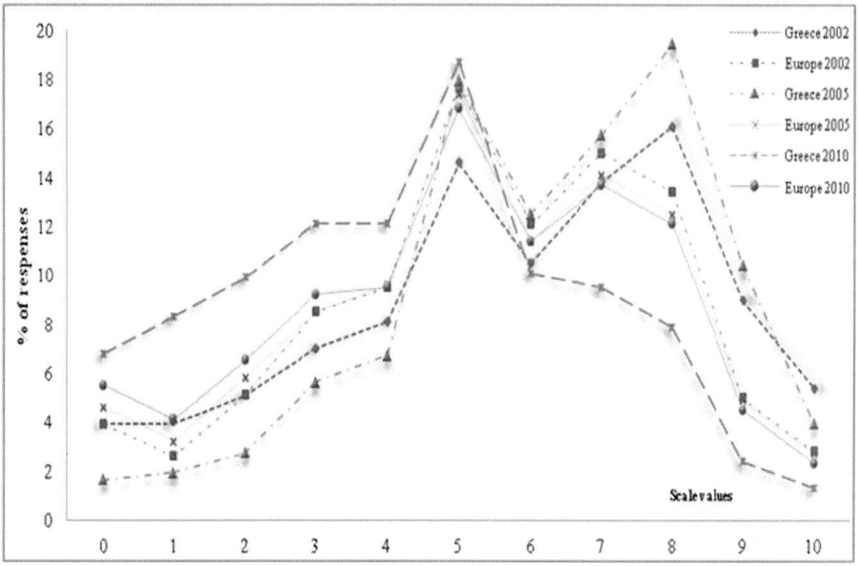

Source: European Social Survey (ESS), Round 1, 2002, Round 2, 2005, Round 4, 2010.

Special consideration was given by the author to the social and political institutions analyzed comparatively in Figure 8-7, in view of the significance of these institutions. It is important to note here that all measurements reflect people's attitudes, on a zero to ten scale, where the *zero* point indicates absolute distrust and the *ten* point, absolute trust (Figures 8-9 through 8-14). At the same time, trust in all the important social and public institutions like social solidarity, the parliament, the law, the legal system in general, the police and the European Parliament indicate a severe change to the worst in people's perceptions and attitudes towards state's law and order mechanisms as well as towards the political system and the political personnel. Trust in the role and function of the Greek Parliament runs in an historic low (Figure 8-9).

Figure 8-9 . Trust in Parliament, Greece 2002, 2005 and 2010

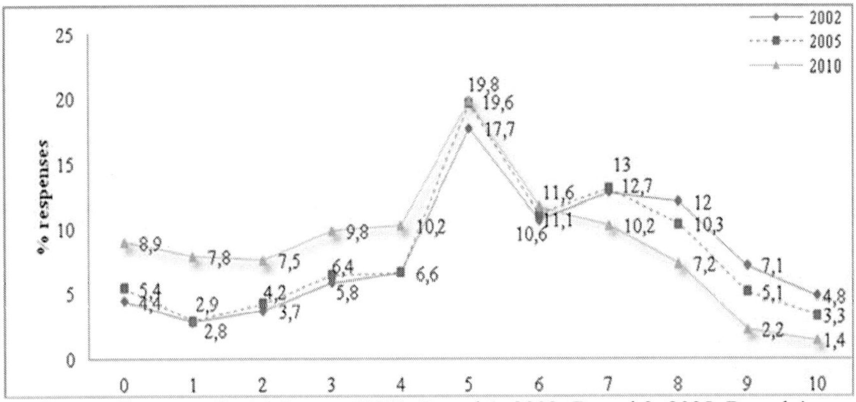

Source: European Social Survey (ESS), Round 1, 2002, Round 2, 2005, Round 4, 2010.

Figure 8-10. Trust in law and the legal system, Greece and Europe 2002, 2005 and 2010

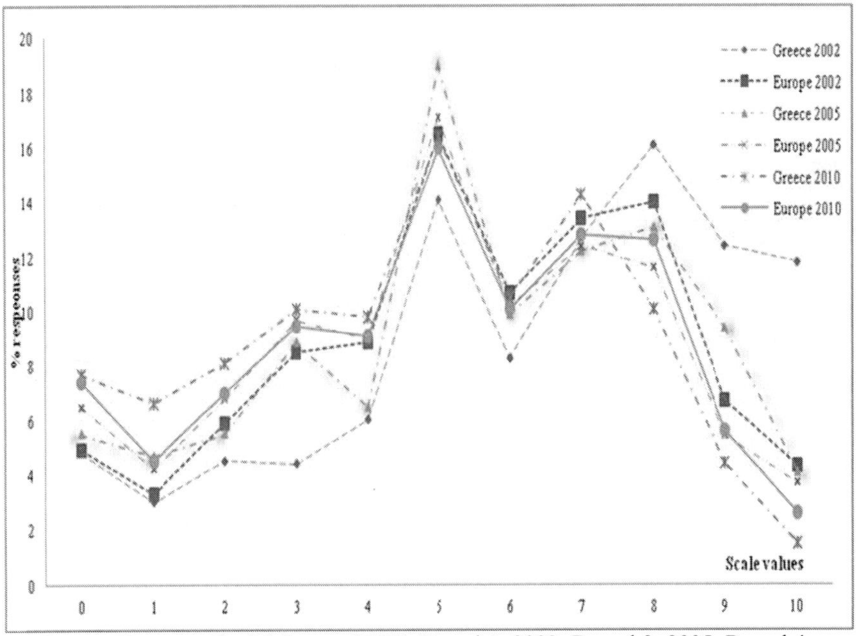

Source: European Social Survey (ESS), Round 1, 2002, Round 2, 2005, Round 4, 2010.

Figure 8-11. Trust in law and the legal system, Greece 2002, 2005 and 2010

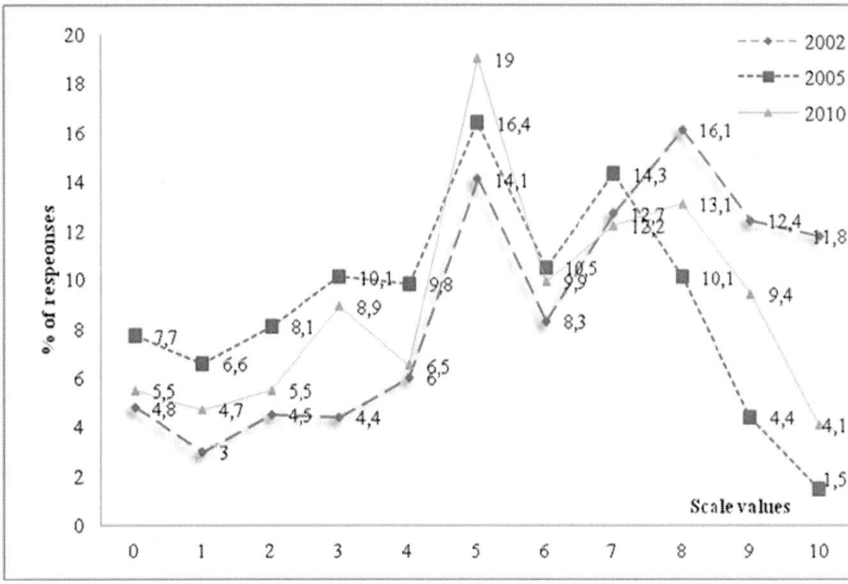

Source: European Social Survey (ESS), Round 1, 2002, Round 2, 2005, Round 4, 2010.

Respect and trust in laws and the legal system in general have also deteriorated all over Europe especially in Greece where the case has become more alarming with the implementation of the memorandum from 2010 onwards. Trust in justice has deteriorated further by the middle of 2011 as shown by the data of the 5th round of ESS (Figures 8-10, 8-11).

Trust in the political personnel, which includes the active politicians of the parties in Parliament has been gradually annihilated in both Greece and abroad at a pan-European level (Figure 8-12) as shown by ESS successive rounds data for the 1st decade of the 21st century.

The same holds true as regards the social stance towards mechanisms of coercion. Confidence in the Police, always running higher than confidence in law and order public institutions for the exercise of formal social control in Greece, has also been negatively affected (Figures 8-13, 8-14). ESS data also show that in Greece the situation has deteriorated further, if one considers comparatively the data provided from 2002 onwards in the successive ESS rounds until the present time.

Figure 8-12. Trust in political personnel, Greece and Europe 2002, 2005 and 2010

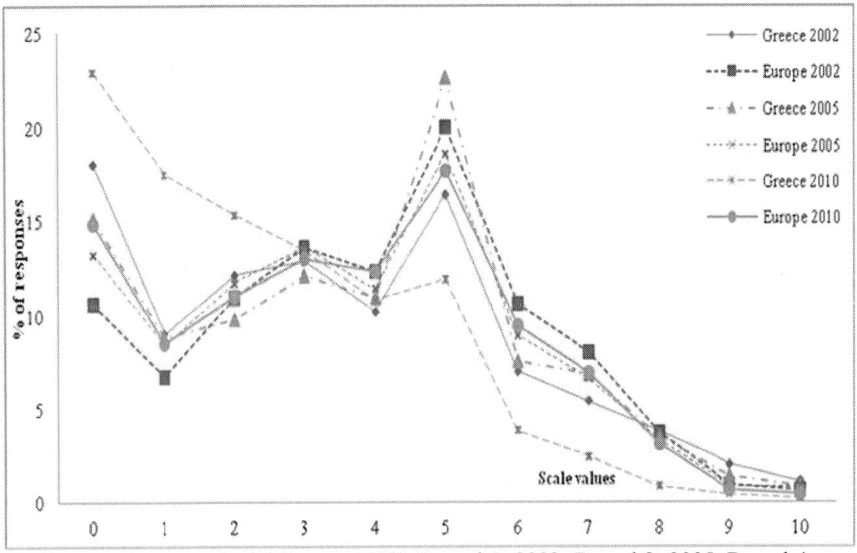

Source: European Social Survey (ESS), Round 1, 2002, Round 2, 2005, Round 4, 2010.

Figure 8-13. Trust in police, Greece and Europe 2002, 2005 and 2010

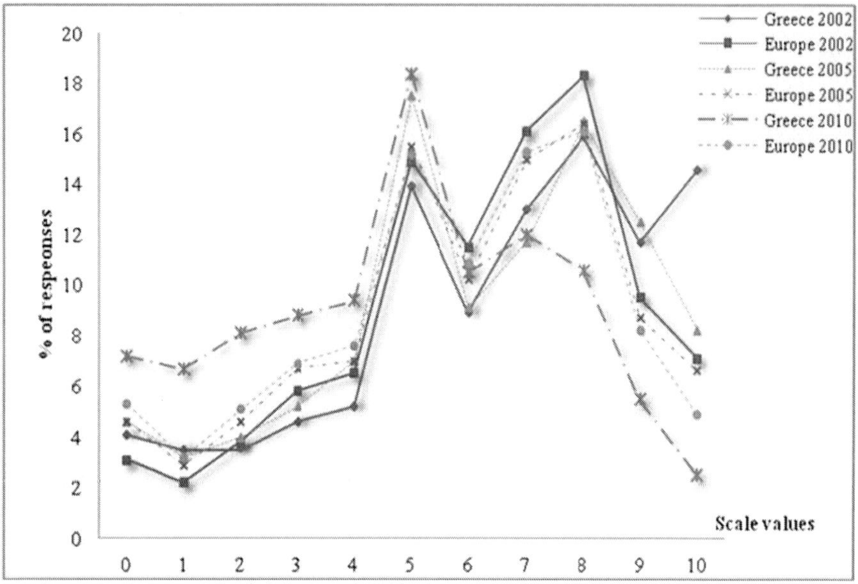

Source: European Social Survey (ESS), Round 1, 2002, Round 2, 2005, Round 4, 2010.

Figure 8-14. Trust in police, Greece 2002, 2005 and 2010

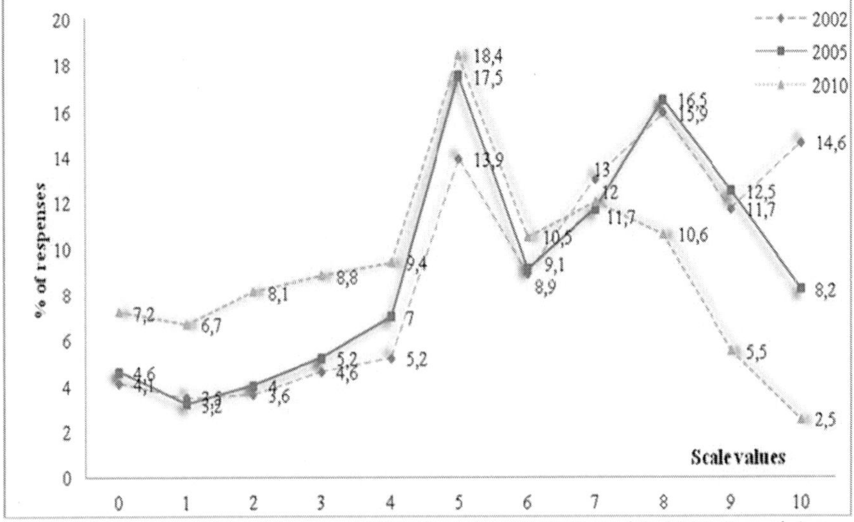

Source: European Social Survey (ESS), Round 1, 2002, Round 2, 2005, Round 4, 2010.

Another important issue that threatens social bonds and cohesion is the outcome reflected in the indices of safety and fear of crime. Despite the controversial arguments employed as to whether we have suitable tools at our disposal to measure these social parameters by means of a social survey alone—a quantitative operational instrument in fact—it is true that we can form an image and gain a wider understanding of the social dynamics produced in given social circumstances. Data are provided from the response to a common question in criminological research which has also been included in the ESS source questionnaire and asks the respondent whether he/she "feels safe or would feel safe walking alone in the local area or neighbourhood after dark". The quantitative survey data suggest that the debt crisis has not seriously, as yet, affected attitudes towards safety, fear of crime and violence in society apart from the case of terrorist acts (Figure 8-15).

Figure 8-15. Sense of Insecurity, Greece 2002, 2005 and 2010

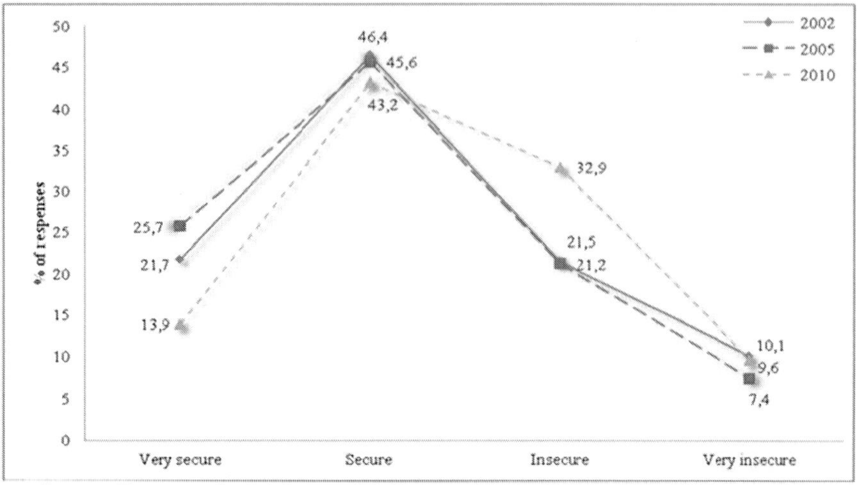

Source: European Social Survey (ESS), Round 1, 2002, Round 2, 2005, Round 4, 2010.

ESS data suggest that insecurity runs low all over Europe for the last decade. The same holds true for the fear of crime and fears associated with violence in society in general. However, there is a breach in our value system. Although people in Greece feel that they are not in danger to be victimised by a violent act they strongly believe that courts should impose more severe penalties. Such a stance may be dictated by the limitation of trust in justice and a confidence gap rather than derived from a feeling of increased insecurity. Although there is an increasing awareness about the volume of violent crime, the Greek public are far from feeling insecure and far from living in a fearful anxiety for violence. On the contrary, what more recent survey research data suggest[4] is that the economic crisis has affected the way people think about their participation in the local labour market, their future prospects of employment and the alarming percentages of unemployment, that is, their actual participation in the division of labour in society. Within the past decade, the primary concern of the Greek public, irrespective of their socio-demographic status, moved from fears associated to criminality and violence to insecurities associated with employment (economic insecurity). Such evidence suggests that Greece is witnessing serious facets of underdevelopment, once more, in its modern history.

Turning to the examination of the recorded increasing suicide rates during the past three years in Greece,[5] a period during which the country is undergoing the road of successive and abrupt austerity measures, there are two major issues that deserve attention: Firstly, with respect to the expert opinion on this matter, although the recorded suicide rates mark an unexpected increase during the past two years, corresponding systematic research evidence in Greece is lacking. Therefore, we are not in a position to evaluate Durkheim's conceptions of anomic suicide. Secondly, despite the increasing usage of anomie theory in public rhetoric, not once have the increasing suicide rates been associated with conceptions of anomie. On the contrary, media research has revealed that the concept of anomie has been associated with the current economic crisis in Greece with respect to law-breaking and more specifically with acts of (collective) violence, criminality and corruption (Tsiganou, 2011: Georgalis, 2012). It is mainly attributed to the malfunction of public institutions rather than the loosening of societal bonds. It is mainly conceived as being interwoven with the means and ways that power and authority are exercised in the country during the current crisis. Media research has shown that the notion underwent serious conceptual distortion although it is evident that its current use in Greece brings more to mind the Mertonian ideas rather than the Durkheimian original conceptions of anomie (Georgalis, 2012).

Furthermore, certain "uncertainties" are produced as a result of over-dependence on quantitative research data such as those involving the issue of violence in society. What I am actually suggesting is that the development of the quantitative investigation of violence in society, related fears and anxieties and the safety and insecurity questions, in certain cases may hamper our understanding instead of illuminating it. Most quantitative research questions on these issues have been identical in scope, rationale and phrasing with corresponding questions of crime and victimization surveys across the Western world since at least the end of the 1970s.[6]

The measurements intended are indeed of vast importance, since the quantitative data collected and properly processed, may be used for the formulation of new public safety and criminal policy measures, or the introduction of new aspects in the exercise of social control. Therefore, my major point in this respect is that these valid questions in measuring insecurity and/or fear of crime need further elaboration in order to lead to valid empirical data collection, especially when viewed in comparative perspective. Otherwise, the answers one might get through the content of the corresponding frequencies may seem unclear, blurred and confusing (Zarafonitou, 2002: Tsiganou, 2007).

One should also be cautious in order that various types of insecurities are not transformed to logical or non-logical fears. For example, in Greece, where violent offences are recorded as having occurred to a lesser degree than in other European countries, people appear to feel more insecure than the inhabitants of Britain, Holland, Spain and Portugal, with higher crime rates. Therefore, in order to obtain a more concrete knowledge of fears and insecurities, we should develop more cognitive operational tools. Otherwise, our picture will remain incomplete and "gray" with significant implications for the exercise of social and formal control policies.

Conclusions and Discussion

Undoubtedly, the Durkheimian notion of anomie has been one of the most influential and inspiring tools for understanding certain social realities. However, the "magic" of this theory has led to its abusive use in contemporary public debates in Greece which try to unravel the social consequences of the present debt crisis. The anomie theory is much too often seen as a holistic explanatory tool for current societal responses which are perceived as pathological or abnormal such as disobedience to norms or outbursts of violence. It is questionable, however, whether such interpretations may be empirically validated. In my understanding, one has to question such a paramount abuse of the theory in an era of intense inter-state and intra-state panoptical regulation of societal conflicts under the ideological rubric of a "New Societal Defence"; an ideology, which prominent as it was during the mid-war period, brought about the strengthening of social controls especially against criminals (Ancel, 1995).

As the data suggest, the main issue under consideration in an era of debt crisis is to what extent societal anomie and chaos prevail in given situations. It seems that as far as anomie theory is concerned what is at stake are the institutional foundations of the said societies. Research data do not support any argument that, in Greece, we live in a state of societal anarchy and chaos or in conditions of complete normlessness and social de-regulation. On the contrary, we are witnessing immense social regulation which leads to norm conflict and "legal explosion" (Barton, 1975, Habermas, 1976, Urger, 1976). Given the breach of confidence in leading state institutions of coercion, or formal control like the courts and the police, law and order institutions have entered an era of "legitimation crisis" (Habermas, 1976) which threatens the extent to which shared understandings are translated into explicit policies, or where the policies implemented are institutionally dictated rather than socially negotiated.

Although the imposed austerity has affected trust in social institutions and the capacity of Greece to invest in policies supporting social cohesion, Greek parliamentary democracy remains, on the whole, relatively stable and intact. Without being very optimistic, one may argue that confidence and trust in institutions can be restored if the State embarks upon policies alleviating poverty through, for example, the establishment of a "minimum guaranteed income" and/or combating unemployment and social exclusion through public spending and investments. Tolerance toward the "other" can be increased not only through an improvement of the economic situation, but also through the implementation of a more rational migration policy—on an EU level—that accomplishes a more successful regulation of the massive migrant waves into the country. Finally, trust and confidence in social and political institutions, as well as a sense of equity in the citizens, can be further restored if justice was also administered against politicians involved in scandals, and, if party politics were devoted more to the national cause rather than to party patriotism and survival.

Notes

[1] I am greatly indebted to prof. Petropoulos N. and my colleague Balourdos D. for their constructive reading of the original.

[2] The *Greek Review of Social Research*, Special Issue, "Greece in Crisis", Vol., A – B / 2011, no 134 – 135.

[3] The European Social Survey (ESS) runs across Europe for the past decade in successive "rounds". EKKE has been appointed as the responsible institution for undertaking and supervising the relevant survey research tasks in Greece. Presently, EKKE is preparing its 6th round. Greece participated in 4 of the previous successive surveys: the 1st round (2002-3), the 2nd round (2004-5), the 4th round (2008-9) and in the 5th round (2010-11).

[4]. Pilot EKKE's study on the "Consequences of the Debt Crisis", EKKE, 2012 (unpublished).

[5] "Greece of crisis and suicide", Available: http://www.prototheme.gr [25 October 2012].

[6] For those not familiar, for example, the question C5 of the ESS questionnaire reads as "Have you or a member of your family been a victim of a burglary or assault –physical assault in the last 5 years" while the C6 reads as follows: "How safe do you–or would you–feel walking alone in this area–respondent's local area or neighborhood–after dark?" .

References

Ancel, M. (1995). *New social defence,* Athens: Nomiki Vivliothiki.

Barton, J. H. (1975). 'Behind the legal explosion', *Stanford Law Review,* vol. 27, pp. 567-584.

Downes D. and Rock P. (2003). *Understanding deviance,* London: Oxford.

Durkheim, E. (1964) *The division of labour in society,* New York: Basic Books.

—. (1979). *Suicide,* London: Routledge & Kegan Paul.

Garofalo, J. (1981). 'The fear of crime: Causes and consequences', *The Journal of Criminal Law and Criminal Policy,* no 72, pp. 839-957.

Georgalis A. (2012). *Anomie and debt crisis: Content analysis of the media rhetoric in Greece 2009-2012*, unpublished M. Sc. Thesis, Panteion University.

Giddens, A. (1986). *The constitution of society*, U.S.A.: University of California Press.

—. (1990). *The consequences of modernity*, U.S.A.: Stanford University Press.

Habermas, J. (1976). *Legitimation crisis,* London: Heinemann.

Hart, H.L.A. (1984). *Law, liberty and morality*, U.K.: Oxford University Press.

Merton, R. (1957). *Social theory and social structure,* New York: Basic Books

Roberts, S. (1979). *Order and dispute*, London: Penguin.

Tsiganou, J. (2007). 'Data and methodological concerns regarding the investigations of the fear of crime', in Kafetzis P., Maloutas Th., and Tsiganou J. (eds), *Society, citizens and politics,* Athens: National Centre for Social Research.

—. (2011). 'Anomie and society: Scientific tools in crisis', *The Greek Review of Social Research*, Special Issue, vol. A-B/2011, no 134-135, pp. 257-270.

Urger, R. M. (1976). *Law in modern society:Toward a criticism of social theory,* New York: Free Press.

Zarafonitou, Ch. (2002). *The fear of crime,* Athens: Sakoulas.

CHAPTER NINE

CONTEMPORARY ECONOMIC-FINANCIAL CRISIS: POST– TRAUMATIC STRESS SYMPTOMS AND RELATED INDIVIDUAL AND SOCIAL REACTIONS

JOANNA DESPINA BERGIANNAKI
UNIVERSITY OF ATHENS,UNIVERSITY RESEARCH INSTITUTE OF MENTAL HEALTH (U.R.I.M.H)
AND STEFANOS DIMITRAKOPOULOS
UNIVERSITY OF ATHENS

Abstract

Since 2007 western civilization is experiencing a global financial crisis, considered as the worst since the Great Depression of the 1930s, leading to the European sovereign-debt crisis. This crisis affected seriously peoples' daily lives, due to the intolerable psychological burden associated with the consequences of: (a) the unemployment or fear of losing work (leading to increased stress levels, anxiety, feelings of frustration, disappointment and loss of self-esteem) (b) increased poverty (correlates with continuous insecurity, social withdrawal, violence, low educational levels, inadequate housing and malnutrition) (c) dramatic reduction of life quality level and (d) family crisis. All the above are evidence-based factors, each independently and altogether, causing stress in excessive and intolerable levels and inducing mental health disorders. According to the psychological trauma definition, the economic crisis itself should be regarded as a social disaster and as a traumatic event which provokes responses of negative feelings, intense fear, helplessness or sense of "horror". Since there is an increasing number of countries caught up in the whirl of the global financial crisis, this could justify the term of a contemporary «mental epidemic», relived and reinforced through optical and acoustic "information-pollution" via T.V. and other mass media which exacerbate insecurity and fear, induce confusion of the population, maintain the stress and increase the risk for the development of PTSD. Further, several of the classical symptoms of PTSD such as thoughts of/or suicidal emotions, feelings of desertion and loneliness, feelings of distrust and betrayal, and somatic complaints are, among others, also highly notable in the era of financial crisis. Finally, the present analysis makes some comments regarding the consequences of the global recession which has affected Greece more than other European countries. There are also references to the unemployment rate, the budget cuts in health and the health care system, the suicide rates and suicide attempts and the general increase of violence, homicide, theft rates and drug abuse, as well as to some factors that have made Greeks more resilient to the crisis.

Introduction

Since 2007, when global financial turmoil began, western civilization is experiencing historical years, as the *global financial crisis* is considered by many economists to be the worst financial crisis since the Great Depression of the 1930s (Reuters, 2009). It resulted in the threat of total collapse of large financial institutions, the bailout of banks by national governments and downturns in stock markets around the world. In many areas, the housing market also suffered, resulting in evictions, foreclosures and prolonged unemployment. The crisis played a significant role in the failure of key businesses, declines in consumer wealth and a downturn in economic activity leading to global recession and contributing to the European sovereign-debt crisis (Greenspan, 2010; Williams, 2012). The continuing development of the crisis has prompted fears of a global economic collapse, although there are now many cautiously optimistic forecasters in addition to some prominent sources who remain negative (Cho, 2009). It could be a realistic statement that nobody really knows, when and how it will end.

Economic recession, new risk groups and stress generation

The global economic crisis causes multiple upheavals in both individual and community functioning. People are affected in a daily, serious manner. For most affected people the contemporary «financial-economic crisis» exceeds the usual daily negative experiences. This intolerable psychological burden is related with several consequences originating from the economic recession.

1. Long-lasting unemployment

In a 2011 news story, *Business Week* reported, "More than 200 million people globally are out of work—a record high— as almost two-thirds of advanced economies and half of developing countries are experiencing a slowdown in employment growth (Hamilton, 2011). The life and personality of contemporary man are grounded on employment. Work is seen as a means of social and meaningful life and self-confidence. Therefore, those experiencing unemployment or fear of losing their job, face not only obvious practical issues but an equally important psychological "collapse". In a society with significant percentages of unemployment or fear to lose their work, people have been found with increased stress levels, anxiety, feelings of frustration, disappointment and loss of self-esteem. The long-term unemployment (population seeking work for more than 12 months, irrespectively of whether they are entering the workplace for the first time or been employed in the past) prolongs such symptoms. Most researchers agree that loss of employment increases the risk of mental disorders and their adverse effects on physical health. There is a greater rate of psychological problems amongst *unemployed* (34%) than *employed* (16%) persons (Karsten & Moser, 2009). Moreover, decreased health spending due to government financial policies, increased costs of treatment and reduced family income or insurance coverage affect use of health services and their quality. It's no surprise that unemployment is related with a rise in consumption of addictive substances, antisocial behavior, somatic diseases, development of anxiety disorders, subclinical or clinical depression and, finally, an increase in early death rates (Roelfs et al., 2011). In this study, investigators analyzed 40 years of data from 20 million people in 15 countries and found that being unemployed increases a person's risk of premature death by 63%. They also found that unemployment boosts men's risk of premature death much more than it does women's risk (78% vs. 37%) and that the risk of death is particularly high for people under 50.

2. Poverty

The economic slowdown and increased unemployment are accompanied by increased poverty. Poor become poorer and stressed become more stressed. There is a strong link between poverty and the stress that poverty generates (as revealed by, for example, cortisol levels). This link is important to break, because poverty-generated stress has been shown to produce many negative outcomes among children (e.g., lower school achievement) (Haskins, 2010). Continuous insecurity, social withdrawal, violence, low educational levels, inadequate housing and malnutrition, which are the correlates of poverty, are recognized as contributing to common mental disorders (Kuruvilla & Jakobs, 2007).

3. Dramatic reduction of "life-quality" level

The importance of a patient's quality of life is increasingly being recognized in all areas of medicine and health sciences as well as of sociology. Standard indicators of the quality of life include not only wealth and employment, but also the built environment, physical and mental health, education, leisure time and social belonging. The time of crisis brought new challenges to citizens. Many saw their standards of living deteriorating. This dramatic reduction of life quality level, given the fact that people predisposed to mental disorders can't adjust to the external stress, was linked with development or relapses of mental disorders (Angelmeyer et al., 2004), beginning or relapse of use/abuse of alcohol and/or narcotic drugs (Newmann, 2011) and the effect on the risk of suicide (Koivumaa-Honkanen, 2011). Many patients suffering from mental disorders require long-term management, which means that quality of life becomes an even more important consideration.

4. Consequences for family life

Generally, a family is thrust into a crisis, when two or more elements, contributing to a state of crisis, interact. These elements include: (1) experiencing a stress-producing situation (2) having difficulty coping (3) showing chronic difficulty meeting basic family responsibilities and (4) having no apparent sources of support. Families worry that one or both spouses may lose their job (especially the father of the household), and may not be able to meet the bills, pay their taxes on their home and property or give their children a decent education. These strains can cause some families to argue to the point of breaking the family unit apart, often ending in divorce or at least spousal abuse which in some cases is associated with development of aggressive or alienating behavior. Another interesting element, concerning a new family pattern, is that men become workless, stay at home and take care of household and children, while women work with low income. This may be a causative reason for role confusion between genders and inversion of traditional social behavior (Leinonen et al., 2003). The male's crowding out and devaluation is being referred to as an "andrectomy" and a kind of "postmodern social hermaphroditism".

5. Social consequences

In the early days of the crisis, there was willingness to boost social protection systems to prevent hardship, but this weakened as the priority shifted to reducing public deficits. It might also have been expected that the gap in income between the richest and the poorest would narrow during a recession, as the very wealthy lost out. In fact, however, there is increasing evidence of a widening gap between rich and poor. Much of the media focus in recent years has been on "the new poor" (Kaika, 2012). While it is undoubtedly true that many people who previously believed themselves to be secure are now falling into poverty, many of those who have been worst hit come from distinct vulnerable groups—in particular, people who have already experienced poverty before the crisis, young people, people who are educationally disadvantaged, migrants and ethnic minorities, older people, children and lone parents (Fryers et al, 2005). Thus, the gap widens, new vulnerable and exasperated social groups are being formed, confidence on former political values are under doubt, democracy is in danger, espousal of antisocial, violent, extremist and fascistic behavior become daily phenomena. Other social groups may have a more passive attitude, seeing a blind future with hopelessness and desperation, surrendered to an underproductive fatalism.

Economic crisis as a psychological traumatic event

All the above, concerning the contemporary economic-financial crisis's consequences, are evidence-based factors which, each independently and altogether, induce mental health disorders, causing stress in excessive and intolerable levels. A question frequently asked is if this type or kind of stress should be regarded as a psychological trauma and the economic crisis itself as a traumatic event? First of all, «a psychological trauma can be defined as a solitary, or enduring, or repeated experience, attestation, or involvement in an event, or situation that overwhelms the individual's ability to cope, or integrate the idea, the circumstance, and/or the emotions, either provoked or caused from it". The response includes negative feelings, intense fear, helplessness or sense of "horror". It's not the objective facts that determine whether an event is traumatic, but the subjective emotional experience of the event. The more frightened and helpless someone feels, the more likely he is to be traumatized.

It is common knowledge that traumatic events increase affective and anxiety disorders (Young et al., 1997; Quarantini et al., 2009). Moreover, one's mental health deterioration, because of his exposure to traumatic events and psychological trauma, makes him more vulnerable to various somatic diseases (Avdibegovic et al., 2010). Parallel to the depth and continuation of the economic crisis the level of stress rises, leading to aggravation of mental diseases. On the other hand, mental healthcare system services are severely degrading due to financial cuts because of the economic crisis. Mental health services are unprotected during a financial crisis much more than other health sectors (World Congress of World Federation for Mental Health, 2009). In other words, when healthcare medicine gets a cold, psychiatry gets pneumonia (Lieberman, 2012). Another indicator of the population's mental health deterioration is the Index of Emotional Health which includes 10 items (smiling or laughter, learning or doing something interesting, being treated with respect, enjoyment, happiness, worry, sadness, anger, stress and diagnosis of depression). The Index of Emotional Health is a measurement of negative feelings and increases in periods with economic recession. Furthermore, it correlates with increased mortality rates from various diseases and depression. The situation of continuous, chronic stress due to financial crisis predisposes to all kinds of mental disorders, mainly depression, the "burn-out" syndrome and anxiety disorders such as generalized anxiety disorder, unspecified anxiety disorder (McEwen, 2004; Chiba et al., 2012) and post traumatic stress disorder (Schiraldi, 2009).

All the above make us wonder if there is a new kind of PTSD which develops as a result of the economic crisis and, if so, which are its symptoms?

Significant events occur to a vast majority of people in the hotpot of the financial crisis. Events as economic disaster, job loss or constant insecurity about getting fired, financial fraud victimization, confiscation of property, prosecution by the tax department or banks, pressure or blackmails regarding debts, are being traumatically experienced. These traumatic events induce fear and horror with possible awakenings during the night, agonizing thoughts about early retirement, fear of an imminent danger of work loss, panic reaction induced by the decrease of income or, maybe, even terror at the thought of a forthcoming loss of house and property. In this way, acute or chronic fear seems to be the most considerable emotion for the development of PTSD. Specific symptoms of PTSD are related to an increased distress deriving from the financial crisis. The most common are difficulty to entrain and/or maintain sleep, irritability or outburst of rage, difficulty to maintain concentration and attention, hyperarousal and an easy-startle reaction. Surely, few people carry on living, sleeping, and acting normally as they become witnesses or victims of their financial and "end of well-being" tragedy. More specific symptoms matching the PTSD diagnosis (DSM-IV, 2000) according to DSM-IV-TR are:

- Re-experiencing the traumatic event: intrusive, upsetting memories of the event (e.g., intrusive memories of house confiscation or personal bank account crack), flashbacks (acting or feeling like the event is happening again), nightmares (either of the event or of other frightening things), feelings of intense distress when reminded of the trauma, intense physical reactions to reminders of the event (e.g., pounding heart, rapid breathing, nausea, muscle tension, sweating, when the phone rings and the bank asks for its money);
- Avoidance and emotional numbing: avoiding activities, places, thoughts, or feelings that remind you of the trauma (e.g., avoid listening to financial news);
- Inability to remember important aspects of the trauma;
- Loss of interest in activities and life in general;
- Feeling detached from others and emotionally numb;
- Sense of a limited future (no expectation of living a normal life span, getting married, having a career, raising kids, providing them with proper equipment and skills);
- Increased arousal: difficulty falling or staying asleep;
- Irritability or outbursts of anger (e.g., acts of violence against public entities);
- Difficulty concentrating;
- Hypervigilance (on constant "red alert", e.g., reminder of overdue loan payments, when the bell or the phone rings); and
- Feeling jumpy and easily startled.

Other common symptoms of PTSD are feelings of guilt, shame, self-blame, drugs/alcohol abuse, depression, disappointment, frustration, suicidal thoughts and emotions, feelings of desertion and loneliness, feelings of distrust and betrayal, somatic complaints such as headaches, gastrointestinal problems and chest pains (Kaplan and Sadock's, 2009). Moreover, PTSD correlates with high incidence of somatic diseases, particularly cardiovascular, neurological and gastrointestinal diseases. The increase of somatic diseases is highly notable in the era of financial crisis (Avdibegovic et al., 2010).

It needs to be highlighted that people didn't suddenly become sensitive, overwhelmed by stress, unable to cope with traumatic situations. It is repeated re-traumatization, lack of psychological anchor and every day increase of anxiety that makes them more vulnerable. There are four

Ds (Goulston, 2011) that make peoples' lives a living nightmare. These are elements of the economic crisis which increase "hyperarousal" and predispose to development of the PTSD:

1) **Debt**: Lenders' offensive practices, psychological pressure through phone calls aggravate the vulnerability of the economic victim.
2) **Dependence**: The individual feels like losing control, cannot afford to maintain himself or his family, feels frustrated, asks for help from others.
3) **Distrust**: When the individual depends on others, he becomes suspicious of his helpers' [benefactor's] intentions, especially in a financial status where everything seems fluid.
4) **Denial**: Denial of reality, of the problem's size. The individual is likely to develop "emotional numbness".

The prolongation of the financial crisis, unemployment and debt contributes to re-traumatization and reliving of the social disaster. This is further reinforced through optical and acoustic information via T.V. and other mass media. The amount of propounded information on the financial crisis is "toxic" (e.g., news in dramatic tones about stock-market failures, imminent, painful financial measures, cuts in salaries and wages). This "info–pollution" exacerbates insecurity and fear about tomorrow, induces confusion of the population, maintains the stress and increases the risk for the development of PTSD.

Is our world suffering from a PTSD due to the financial-economic crisis?

The financially traumatized victim watches news daily, speaks less and less with others, loses more and more his sense of humor, becomes irascible, frustrated and nervous, increases consumption of addictive substances (alcohol, tobacco, etc.), neglects his body and hygiene behavior (diet, exercise, self-care, relaxation, entertainment), disregards his usually normal sexual life. All the above could indicate that the person suffers from a PTSD resulting from the economic/financial crisis. Indeed, PTSD and PTSD-like symptoms are expected to become more and more common as reactions of people in countries with an economic recession. Since there is an increasing number of countries caught up in the whirl of the global financial crisis, this could justify the term of a contemporary *«mental epidemic»*.

Greece and the contemporary financial crisis

Greece has been for the past three years in the eye of the hurricane of global recession. Greece is affected more than other European countries by the financial turmoil. Fifteen years of consecutive growth in the Greek economy have reversed, and the nation has entered a long period of economic crisis with adverse effects on various aspects of daily life, including the mental health of its citizens. Indicative of the economic crisis in Greece is the rise of the unemployment rate from 6.6 % in 2008 to 16.6 % in 2011, while for the same years youth unemployment increased dramatically from 18.6 % to 40.1 % (Kentikelenis et al., 2011). Current recession has affected Health and the Health Care System in Greece, there were about 40% cuts in hospital budgets, understaffing and reported occasional shortages of medical supplies. Another impressive fact concerns an increase of people reporting that they do not go to the doctors or dentists despite feeling that it was necessary.

According to some researchers, suicides rose by 17% in 2009 from 2007, and unofficial 2010 data quoted in Parliament mention a 25% rise compared with 2009. The Minister of Health reported a 40% rise in the first half of 2011 compared with the same period in 2010. The national suicide helpline reported that 25% of callers faced financial difficulties in 2010, and reports in the media indicate that the inability to repay high levels of personal debt might be a key factor in the increase in suicides (Kentikelenis et al, 2011). Moreover, there was an increase of 36 % in suicidal attempts from 2009 to 2011. A significant higher proportion of respondents with an IPED (Index of Personal Economic Distress) score of more than 15 had attempted a suicide than respondents with a lower than 15 IPED score. Furthermore, a significantly higher proportion with a high IPED score had shown greater suicidal ideation than those with a lower IPED score. It seems that economic distress experienced by the population could be discerned in the increased rates of suicidality, meaning completed suicides, suicide attempts and suicidal ideation (Economou et al., 2012).

Violence has also gone up, homicide and theft rates nearly doubled between 2007 and 2009 (Kentikelenis et al, 2011).

As far as drug abuse is concerned, use of heroin rose by 20% in 2009. Budget cuts resulted in the loss of 1/3 of the country's street work programs. An authoritative report described accounts of deliberate self-infection by few individuals in order to obtain access to benefits of €700 per month and faster admission to drug substitution programs (Greek Documentation and Monitoring Centre for Drugs, 2011). These programs offer access to synthetic opioids and may have waiting lists of 3 years or more in urban areas (Economou, 2011; Economou, 2012).

A note of optimism in this modern Greek tragedy is the statistically marked reduction in alcohol consumption, drunken driving and cigarette smoking (Kentikelenis et al., 2011). The Greek nation is historically a multi-traumatized nation that has survived through civil wars, conquests, disasters, poverty and starvation. However, Greece has a worldwide known bright past as the birthplace of democracy, philosophy and the arts. Aside from that, the extended family continues to serve as a shock-absorber in contemporary Greek society. Both of these factors accord the Greeks a measure of resilience against the stresses of the economic crisis. Given this background, the authors are optimistic that the Greeks will once more surpass the crisis and its traumatic impacts on their health and will emerge as stronger on the national, community, family and individual levels.

References

Angelmeyer, A.J., Bernert, S., Bruffaerts, R. *et al.* (2004). 'Disability and quality of life impact of mental disorders in Europe: results from the European Study of the Epidemiology of Mental Disorders (ESEMeD) project', *Acta Psychiatrica Scandinavica,* vol. 109, no. 420, pp. 38-46

Avdibegovic, E, Delic A, Hadzibeganovic K *et al.* (2010). 'Somatic diseases in patients with posttraumatic stress disorder', *Medical Archives*, vol. 64, no. 3, pp. 154-157.

Chiba S, Numakawa, T., Ninomiya, M. *et al.* (2012). 'Chronic restraint stress causes anxiety- and depression-like behaviors, downregulates glucocorticoid receptor expression, and attenuates glutamate release induced by brain-derived neurotrophic factor in the prefrontal cortex.' *Progress in Neuro-Psychopharmacology and Biological Psychiatry*, vol. 39, no. 1, pp. 12-9.

Cho, D. and Appelbaum, B. (2009). 'Unfolding worldwide turmoil could reverse years of prosperity', *The Washington Post,* 8 March, p. A01.

Diagnostic and statistical manual of mental disorders (Revised 4th edition) (2000), Arlington, Va.: American Psychiatric Association.

Economou, M., Madianos, M., Peppou, L. *et al.* (2012). 'Suicidality and the economic crisis in Greece'. *Lancet,* vol. 380, no. 9839, 28 July, p 337.

Economou, M., Madianos, M., Theleritis, Ch. *et al.* (2011). 'Increased suicidality and economic crisis in Greece.' *Lancet,* vol 378, no. 9801, 22 October, p. 1459.

Fryers, T., Melzer, D., Jenkins, R. *et al.* (2005),.'The distribution of the common mental disorders: social inequalities in Europe', *Clinical Practice and Epidemiology in Mental Health*, 15 August, vol. 4, pp. 411-23.

Goulston, M. (2011) 'Does the World Have Financial PTSD?', Available: http://www.psychologytoday.com/blog/just-listen/201108/does-the-world-have-financial-ptsd [8 August 2011].

Greenspan, A. (2010). 'The crisis', *Brookings papers on economic activity,* Spring, 1 May, pp. 201-263.

Hamilton, S. (2011). World employment may not reach pre-crisis level for five years, *Business Week,* Available: http://www.businessweek.com/news/2011-10-31/world-employment-may-not-reach-pre-crisis-level-for-five-years.html [31 October, 2011].

Haskins R. (2010). 'The impact of early experience on childhood brain development', The Collaboration for Poverty Research (CPR), 13 April, Stanford University

Kaika M. (2012). 'The economic crisis seen from the everyday: Europe's noveau poor and the global affective implications of the 'local' debt crisis', *City: Analysis of urban trends, culture, theory, policy, action'*, vol. 16, no.4 , pp. 422-430

Kaplan and Sadock's Comprehensive textbook of psychiatry (2009), Sadock, B., Sadock V and Ruiz, P. (eds.) Wolters Kluwer Health, Philadelfphia, PA: Lippincoat William and Wilkins.

Kuruvilla, A. and Jacobs, K.S. (2007).. 'Poverty, social stress & mental health', *Indian Journal of Medical Research*, vol.126, no. 4, pp. 273-278.

Karsten, I.P and, Moser, K. (2009). 'Unemployment impairs mental health: Meta-analyses', *Journal of Vocational Behavior*, vol. 74, no. 3, June , pp. 264–282

Kentikelenis, A., Karanikolos, M, Papanicolas I et al. (2011). 'Health effects of financial crisis: omens of a Greek tragedy', *Lancet, v*ol. 378, no. 9801, 22 October, pp. 1457-1458

Koivumaa-Honkanen, H., Honkanen, R., Vinamaki, H. *et al.* (2001). 'Life satisfaction and suicide: A 20-year follow-up study', *American Journal of Psychiatry,* vol. 158, No 3, pp. *433-439.*

Leinonen, J.A., Solantaus, T.S. and Punamδki, R.L. (2003). 'Social support and the quality of parenting under economic pressure and workload in Finland: the role of family structure and parental gender'. *Journal of Family Psychology,* vol. 17, no. 3,, pp. 409–418.

Lieberman J.A. (2012). 'When healthcare gets a cold, psychiatry gets pneumonia'. Available: http://www.medscape.com/viewarticle/768259 [2 August 2012]

McEwen, B.S. (2004). 'Protection and damage from acute and chronic stress: Allostasis and allostatic overload and relevance to the pathophysiology of psychiatric disorders', *Annals of the New York Academy of Sciences,* Biobehavioral Stress Response: Protective and Damaging Effects. Vol. 1032, December, pp. 1–7

Newmann, R.G. (2011). 'The case for considering quality of life in addiction research and clinical practice', *Addiction Science and Clinical Practice,* vol. 6, no. 1, 1 July, pp. 44–55.

Quarantini, L.C., Netto, L.,Andrade-Nascimento, M. *et al.* (2009). 'Comorbid mood and anxiety disorders in victims of violence with posttraumatic stress disorder', *Revista Brasileira de Psiquiatria,* vol. 31, supplement 2, October, pp. 66-76.

Report of the ad hoc expert group of the Greek focal point on the outbreak of HIV/AIDS in Athens. (2011). Athens: Greek Documentation and Monitoring Centre for Drugs.

Roelfs, D.J., Shor, E., Davidson. K.W. and Schwartz, J.E. (2011). 'Losing life and livelihood: a systematic review and meta-analysis of unemployment and all-cause mortality', *Social Science and Medicine,* vol. 72. no. 6, pp. 840-854

Schiraldi, G.R. (2009). *The post-traumatic stress disorder sourcebook: A guide to healing, recovery, and Growth*, 2nd edition, New York: Mc Graw–Hill Education.

'Three top economists agree 2009 worst financial crisis since Great Depression; Risks increase if right steps are not taken', (2009). *Reuters*, 29 February, [Retrieved 30 September 2009 from Business Wire News database].

Williams, C.J. (2012). 'Euro crisis imperils recovering global economy, OECD warns', *Los Angeles Times*. 22 May.

Young, E.A., Abelson, J.L., Curtis, G.C. *et al.* (1997). 'Childhood adversity and vulnerability to mood and anxiety disorders', *Depression and Anxiety,* vol. 5, no. 2, pp. 66-72.

PART III.

MIGRATION, MIGRATION ATTITUDES AND RELIGION IN COUNTRIES UNDER AUSTERITY REGIMES

CHAPTER TEN

THE DETERMINATION OF THE SOCIAL INTEGRATION OF MIGRANTS WITHIN THE FRAMEWORK OF EMPLOYMENT POLICY: THE CASE OF GREECE IN TIMES OF CRISIS

NIKOLAOS NAGOPOULOS
UNIVERSITY OF AEGEAN
AND KONSTANTINOS RONTOS
UNIVERSITY OF AEGEAN

Abstract

This article attempts to explore the consequences brought about by the economic and social crisis in Greece with regard to the implementation of new migration policy measures, so as to promote a common framework for actions in the member states of the European Union. Specifically, the article analyzes issues in relation to migrant integration policies and the problems resulting from the worsening economic crisis that also affects the labour market, but also the spectacular increase in unemployment that damages social cohesion. Particular emphasis is placed on the inability to adopt a selective policy to attract migrants to employment in specific sectors and emerging jobs. This is evidenced by the fact that Greece is still considered a country attracting migrants with low qualifications, and, therefore, it does not seem to be currently able to adjust policies on migration in what today is promoted at European Union level as "selective migration".

Introduction

The social integration of migrants through the implementation of institutional and social policy measures constitutes a challenge, particularly in times of economic and social crisis. Within the Greek society which feels the impact of the current crisis intensely and at various levels, an institutional solution for integration issues and the social recognition of migrant rights face new conditions and difficult problems. One of the most important problems lies in the field of employment, since high unemployment rates cause huge problems in social cohesion. The situation is further aggravated by the fact that the existing migration policy in Greece is facing the following challenges: (a) the absence of a medium-long-term plan about migration and its consequences (b) large numbers of mixed migratory flows, with Greece being one of the main gates for irregular entrants into Europe (c) limited bilateral agreements with third countries to regulate migration for selected sectors and jobs and (d) the slow harmonization with the new European migration policy (selective migration).

Different national integration systems

Within the perspective of combating exclusion of migrants from Greek society and the labour market, in this article we focus on issues addressing social integration, legal residence within the EU, as well as equal opportunities and non-discriminatory access to labour markets. It should be pointed out that beyond the diverse national integration models[1] one of the issues relating to regional disparities in the European regional landscape is the fact that converging integration patterns impact upon apparent regional differentiations (Huysmans, 1995; Klos, 1998).

These are related to the geographical position of the affected regions that have to manage these policies and the volume of migrant flows (Heckmann, 1999; Niessen, 2000: 23; Koff. 2002; Alexander, 2003). New analyses have to be applied, with an emphasis placed on a more balanced methodology to collect and assess data from regional structures and departments, since integration policies require complex research approaches that will reach out to the primary sources themselves. In most EU member states there is a mismatch between labour market needs and incoming workforce skills supply, due to immigrants entering these countries as a potential workforce. In this article, an attempt is made to address this problem by designing a new European migration policy based on selective migration. Towards this objective there is mutual benefit, both for the member-state and the third-country nationals, who, on the basis of their skills and qualifications, can claim and make full use of their abilities in the posts they occupy. Furthermore, they display greater labour mobility and easily meet needs within a rational system of labour market supply and demand. Therefore, depending on their qualifications and skills, migrants have an opportunity to fully participate, engage and take part in the socio-economic, civic and cultural life of societies in which they reside.

Integration sectors of migrants

In principle, European Union policy on migrant inclusion involves areas and interventions that deepen the consolidation of social cohesion. At a research level, the notion of objective indicators (Koff, 2002) is readdressed, although the selection of basic segments of social inclusion presents limited variations among researchers. Attempting a synthesis of indicators that have been analysed in previous studies and reports (Koff, 2002; Vermeulen, 2004: 27-8; Baldwin and Edwards, 2005; Ager and Strang, 2008), the social inclusion of migrants in Greece will focus on the following issues:

a) Issues relating to the labour market, previously addressed in detail.
b) Supporting language-learning programmes for the host country language, providing psychological and social counseling, medical care, as well as resolving issues related to housing and temporary accommodation.
c) Access to all levels of education, regardless of parental status, is a key element of the inclusion process and integration. Moreover, success rates of migrant children (adjusted to their socio-economic class) are a key element during the inclusion progress assessment.
d) Addressing health issues and appropriate social care through adequately staffed social services facilitates the accession policies. In this respect, health and social services need to be improved, with the use of quality assurance systems over social protection patterns and the use of non-governmental structures with specialised staff (Nagopoulos and Sidira, 2006). Data relevant to the use of these services are incomplete and refer only to migrants that are recognised.
e) Housing is another crucial area for the assessment of migrants' inclusion into society at large. The key issues are: legal rights in relation to those of other citizens (including access to state-subsidized housing), discrimination in the housing rental market (such as refusal to rent or charge at a higher rent), urban segregation or formation of ethnic ghettos

and housing conditions (such as the number of persons per room, the space per person, quality housing including access to hot water, the existence of an internal toilet, etc). It should be noted that the importance and effect of immigration in the Greek housing market has not been adequately investigated.

f) Finally, socio-cultural parameters that relate to initiatives which serve to maintain cultural identity (homogeneity-heterogeneity, tolerance, assimilation) and the extroversion of social behaviour in relation to issues such as citizenship, respect for diversity and active participation in the social life of the host country. The broader cultural activities and participation of foreign communitics in Grcck social life, inclusive media (and coverage), the existence of foreign media services (press or television), multilingual press and journals, etc. In addition, the behavior of state authorities such as police behaviour in cases involving immigrants. Most of the relevant indicators require careful interpretation.

It should be noted that granting Greek nationality is an inclusion element, particularly for second generation migrants, following the reform of relevant legislation (on Citizenship) that primarily involved cases of Greek origin (Law 3838/2010)[2]

Moreover, drawing data relevant to administrative difficulties that migrants have had from their treatment by Greek authorities indicates that such data are incomplete and require a thorough quality assessment ahead of other considerations. Data quality assessment involves a consideration of the following:

a) The range of existing bureaucracy in resolving immigrant cases and the frequent impasse in problem solution;
b) The absence of reliable data in order to identify the particular characteristics and regional organization and the local practices regarding problem solution;
c) The effectiveness in implementing procedures relevant to social settings, adjustments and compatibilities of migrants, towards prevailing standards (formal or informal social control); and
d) Public safety, associated with extracted data regarding the mechanisms and procedures that lead to the deviation and migrant marginalization, as well as individual and collective victimization of migrants with relevant highlighted data.

All the above, including the lack of commitment to deliver necessary measures and institutional linkages, in order to promote and consolidate social cohesion, often lead to a restricted and fragmented range of interventions with a weakened set of targets. The aim is the amelioration of the socio-economic conditions, with an engagement of non-governmental and voluntary organizations, whilst if we exclude bilateral agreements (to be discussed further in the article), these interventions are not part of a compulsory integration process nor do they attempt to provide a bilateral response. On the other hand, as we shall observe, some of the procedures provided for smooth integration (such as adequacy of Greek language use and knowledge of history and culture) are prerequisites for third country immigrants in order to obtain long-term resident status.

In contrast to Greek legislation which can be considered quite advanced and thoroughly incorporates European principles on equality, diversity and inclusion, there are still difficulties in harmonising the implementation framework, especially in the direction of taking measures to face irregular immigration and expand initiatives of organised migration, through further agreements with third countries.

Consequently, social inclusion measures relate mostly to migrants already residing in Greece and only to a limited extent to potential immigrants, who, if relocated, may satisfy the prerequisites and conditions for social integration. Moreover, owing to the immediate need of Greece to solve issues of extensive irregular migration and to face difficulties in addressing migration problems, policies for immigrants who have not actively pursued nor enjoyed, on a regular basis, their inclusion and participation in Greek society and the labour market need to be further explored.

Migration and the labour market

The ongoing increase of migrant workers in member states specialized in highly-skilled jobs, as well as in those that require low-skilled qualifications, has created a necessity to regulate migratory flows in European space. Furthermore, in accordance with the strategy for "Europe 2020", priorities are set for effective management of migration and the encouragement of large numbers of migrants already residing within the EU to actively participate and integrate in the field of employment and member-state social space.

Within this context, a set of instruments is established, aiming to tackle matching skills and labour supply in a coordinated effort. In this respect, and in order to manage a long-term demand and supply of skills, an EU

Skills Panorama, a Europe-wide Vacancy Monitor and a European Job Mobility Bulletin have been launched. On the other hand, it is necessary to adopt measures to ensure accreditation of skills and qualifications acquired without discrimination during access to social and employment services. This has become especially a challenge at a time when EU and especially Greece are confronted with an unprecedented economic crisis.

As noted by the European Commission [SEC (2011) 620] there is an agreed-upon EU-wide method for evaluating the lack of specific skills/workforce in member states and of determining whether workers from third countries have the skills and qualifications to fill them. Not all member states have established systems that allow the authorities (or employers operating in their territory) to identify (future) skill shortages and/or how such shortages could be covered by immigrants with the suitable skills.

The mismatch between labour demand and skills supply that would favour a regulated mobility should first be identified in the current structure of occupations and developing sectors of the economy in member states, in order to assess the benefit obtained through implementation of the measure. It has to be stressed that regardless of the common necessity to urgently face these shortages across the EU, the nature and extent of skill shortages varies significantly among different member states.

In relation to this finding, and with regards to Greece, the mechanism to improve competitiveness of the labour market and to prevent shortages of highly-skilled professions is useful, primarily in maintaining a readiness for the country and the national economy to meet such needs in the future. It is particularly expected that a mechanism will be utilised in a period beyond the current crisis, aiming at eliminating regional inequalities and imbalances through appropriate preparatory actions, in order to satisfy future needs in highly-qualified jobs by employing foreign workers.

In any event and in accordance with Directive 2009/50/EC on the conditions of entry and residence of third country nationals for the purposes of highly-qualified employment (blue card), Greece, like other member-states, may retain the right to determine the volume of third country nationals admission, as they enter its territory in search of highly qualified employment. The proper management of migration policy is a national responsibility for Greece, especially when it largely results from the careful study of socio-economic data specifying concrete internal developments.

Within this context, the priorities of Greece with regard to the labour market, and the possibility to host a special category of migrants, are set. The absence of an immediate need and the current state of the national economy should not prevent the introduction of measures regulating migration policy, thus, allowing people who qualify for admission criteria to enjoy rights held by other resident citizens. A policy that strengthens legal and regulated migration favours legal residence and participation in society, as well as inclusion in the labour market. Meanwhile, it simultaneously acknowledges the mutual benefits that can accrue for both the host country and for the social integration of migrants.

The Greek crisis and irregular migration

Efforts to record shortages in human resources in the various sectors of the Greek economy, with a view to formulating and managing a sound Greek migration policy, should take into consideration:

a) The fact that irregular migration has now reached very high rates and that the priority of the State is to control this phenomenon;
b) The scarce data based on socio-economic surveys highlighting the existing needs in high or low-skilled professions; and
c) The need to create databases based on integrated information systems that will record migrants and their profiles, including their status and nature of employment,

On the other hand, as it is evident in the present document, the range of irregular migration is vast; nonetheless, it does not render migration a tool to combat labour demand. Indicatively, according to data from the United Nations High Commissioner for Refugees (UNHCR, 2011), Greece remains the main gate of entry for irregular incoming third country nationals (refugees and displaced persons) into the European Union. Over the last two years, 90% of the arrests for irregular entry in the E.U. were recorded in Greece. According to official data released by the Greek authorities (Police and Coast Guard), in 2012, there were 76,878 arrests of persons having irregularly entered or stayed in Greece (99,368 in 2011; 132,524 in 2010; 126,145 in 2009; 146,337 in 2008; 112,364 in 2007; 95,239 in 2006; and 66,351 in 2005). These numbers cannot accurately reflect the number of those entering irregularly each year since they include arrests which took place in the interior of the country and concern persons who entered the country in the past but do not include those who entered without being apprehended or arrested by the authorities (UNHCR, 2012).

We, therefore, observe that at this phase an important volume of irregularly entering migrants do not form part of a comprehensive policy aimed to attract migrants into Greece as a host country. Consequently, while the new European strategy of selective migration for highly-skilled workers is not favoured currently in Greece, the needs for skilled and low-skilled workers, largely, are not based on existing needs and a mobilisation of mass or individual invitations. Such needs are ultimately provided for through undeclared (unregistered) employment of irregular migrants.

In view of the economic crisis, the ongoing recession and high unemployment, there is no visible necessity for the workforce to be covered by third country nationals and neither is there a coordinated policy to attract such a labour force (Nagopoulos and Rontos, 2012)[3], as shown in the data presented in Table 10-1.

Table 10-1. Employed persons in Greece by groups of nationality, gender and level of skills, 2010

Skills level	Greeks			
	Male	Female	Total	% out of total
A. High-Skilled	880,988	663,272	1,544,260	38.80
B. Semi-Skilled	1,404,830	852,469	2,257,298	56.71
Γ. Low-Skilled	89,405	89,115	178,520	4.49
Total	2,375,222	1,604,856	3,980,078	100.00

Skills level	EU-15 Nationals			
	Male	Female	Total	% out of total
A. High-Skilled	2,238	1,857	4,094	34.99
B. Semi-Skilled	3,030	3,784	6,814	58.23
Γ. Low-Skilled	141	651	792	6.77
Total	5,408	6,292	11.700	100.00

Skills level	EU-10 Nationals*			
	Male	Female	Total	% out of total
A. High-Skilled	1,811	774	2,585	24.26
B. Semi-Skilled	3,286	2,608	5,893	55.31
Γ. Low-Skilled	519	1,657	2,176	20.42
Total	5,616	5,039	10,655	100.00

* [Czech Republic, Estonia, Cyprus, Latvia, Lithuania, Hungary, Malta, Latvia, Slovenia, Slovakia]

Skills level	EU-2 Nationals*			
	Male	Female	Total	% out of total
A. High-Skilled	632	1,119	1,752	3.36
B. Semi-Skilled	13,940	10,402	24,342	46.69
Γ. Low-Skilled	7,127	18,913	26,040	49.95
Total	21,700	30,434	52,134	100.00

* [Romania, Bulgaria]

Skills level	Third Country Nationals			
	Male	Female	Total	% out of total
A. High-Skilled	7,617	5,047	12,665	3.80
B. Semi-Skilled	154,103	37,301	191,405	57.36
Γ. Low-Skilled	56,839	72,774	129,613	38.84
Total	218,560	115,123	333,682	100.00

Source: Hellenic Statistical Authority, Labour Force Survey, 2010

Selective migration as a measure against the economic and social crisis

Moreover, what becomes apparent when introducing the measure of selective migration is that legalisation (and legitimacy) is secured through the employment status and, as a consequence, the notion of selectivity, as far as employment is concerned, is absolutely defined—apart from other reasons such as humanitarian, social protection and family reunification—by the attractivity of the foreign labour workforce in the form of controlled migration inflow. The existent residency status of many third country nationals (especially in Greece) with low-skilled specialization forces them to work (often undeclared) in occupations not particularly desirable to the natives.

Nowadays, during a period of severe economic crisis in Europe, the introduction of this measure becomes even more imminent, as it can help to deal more efficiently with problems relating to the structure of the economy and the productivity systems. By applying a controlled and rational matching system of qualifications with the job posts offered, many benefits can accrue such as the elimination of tax evasion and the reinforcement of the Social Security Funds as well as a personalized approach to legalization. It should also be noted that in relation to the halting of the mass arrivals of migrants from countries outside the E.U. (an issue which foreshadows the application of the measure of selective migration) there arises a need to sign bilateral conventions with third countries.

In this regard, states can combat irregular migration, facilitate legal and temporary or cyclic migration, as well as reinforce mutual growth between the host countries and the countries of origin. As such, the development of the countries of origin could constitute a means of regulation (therefore inhibition) of the migration pressures on the inhabitants of these areas. Certainly, this regulatory environment concerns the containment of a large mass of poorer citizens from the countries of origin, though not fully confirmed from O.E.C.D. Reports. In this way, it will become evident that mobility is an option for those persons that have a limited capacity to cope with the costs incurred for such an initiative; on the other hand, they will become aware of the fact that they possess some form of social and cultural capital which motivates them to take a decision and action to change their given living conditions.

Greece as a country for "low skilled" migrants

As far as Greece is concerned, we observe that targeted policies are absent, to the extent that they should link potential worker shortages in certain occupational categories, with workers invitations to highly-skilled third country nationals.

Greece remains a country attracting low-skilled migrants and the economic structure is such (f.i., SMEs form 97% of the national economy) that the need to attract highly-skilled workers from third countries (outside the E.U.) is limited, whilst such positions are covered by Community nationals (workers). On the other hand, it should be noted that a large number of migrants is engaged in micro- and small enterprises or is part of a household (domestic) staff. Within this employment context, cooperation between employer and employee is particularly firm and the relative conditions of cooperation are significantly different in comparison to enterprises larger in size. Furthermore, in a labour market mainly characterised by undeclared work it is particularly difficult to apply targeted actions or to trace (identify) and take advantage of the experience, knowledge and skills of migrants seeking work or already working in the country.

The job posts and professions assigned to low-skilled workers are still overrepresented by migrants, mainly those coming from non-E.U. countries in comparison to the limited figures of those migrants dealing with highly skilled occupations. This fact confirms the following:

a) Lack of targeted policies to attract migrants in registered occupational categories and to activate or put in use large-scale transnational cooperation agreements in this field, thus enabling the country to proceed further on current legislation allowing foreigners to enter the country legally and under certain criteria.

b) The surge of migration in Greece is in no case, nor to a limited extent, the result of a specified and targeted policy to strengthen certain occupations and sectors of economic and productive activity, with job posts that could be filled by a workforce from third countries.

c) The coverage of professional needs by migrants, in their vast majority a low-skilled workforce, confirms the fact that employment needs are dealt within a self-regulated economic activity within the labour market in professional occupations not covered by the indigenous workforce.

d) The coverage of low-skilled jobs by migrants reflects a preference by employers for cheap labour in areas of activity not attractive to the indigenous workforce, an issue that on the one hand does not confirm a competitive relationship with the indigenous workforce and, on the other hand, it raises a question over inspection (monitoring) and labour safety in certain sectors.

Policies, enforced and targeted towards high-skilled migrants are not confirmed by the current trends as shown by the tabulation analysis of the migrant workforce located within the country.

Finally, what the study of the current state of affairs demonstrates (and should become a concern in policy-making over migration in Greece) is that there is a migrant labour redundancy of low-skilled labour, relevant to the recent, large-scale and long-term economic crisis. Moreover, there is an obvious and drastic decline in the turnover of productive units and public works, where these occupational professions mostly apply. Migration policy should be carefully redesigned or reviewed in relation to the internal economic and structural characteristics that apply to Greece and a reservation should probably be kept in relation to measures not (currently) consistent with the internal needs and the current economic situation.

For example, the framework of active employment policy applied in Greece (Nagopoulos, 2005) should be extended to apply also to migrant workers. In view of all these, the benefits would be the improvement of internal needs planning, learning the language, ongoing training, entry in the labour market, social inclusion, cooperation with source countries and international organisations, taking into account any annual quota of immigrants from third countries. To a certain extent, the weight and emphasis on bilateral relations with countries of origin should be explored, in order to better manage legal migration (possibly limited, though not limited according to the high-skilled specialisation that appears not to be required) and to facilitate repatriation of those who wish to return to their country of origin. Measures necessary to reduce the irregular and sometimes uncontrolled migration (Triandafyllidou, 2005) should also be taken.

The emphasis in these measures—aiming to facilitate legitimation and mostly seasonal and circular migration as well as strengthen mutual cooperation between host countries and countries of origin—inevitably leads to a coordinated development assistance towards countries of origin, and also to benefits for these countries. For instance, the finding that many

African countries permanently lose over 50% of young graduates (Cogneau and Gubert, 2006; Kapsalis, 2009) should be duly considered. This trend is expected to be reinforced, since selective invitation of (skilled and educated) migrants into Europe, in conjunction with the difficulty to become absorbed in the national labour market of their homeland, will continue.

The role of the civil society

Parallel to the institutional acknowledgement and the provision of services by the host country, a critical role is assigned to citizens of the host country, Greece, with regards to a substantial, unimpeded and effective social integration of those people at different levels of social organisation. The reproduction of negative images and perceptions is perpetuated and often exaggerated, due to other reasons, mainly because of the inability of administrative mechanisms to monitor developments, regarding the phenomenon itself and the dimensions it takes, in a rational manner. A consequence of this development is the surfacing of dysfunctions and failures in the implementation of a political strategy and of the institutional framework on migration.

In addition, it becomes clear that institutional recognition and equal legal protection consist of a necessary, but not always sufficient, condition for addressing the issues of social inclusion of migrants in Greece, as two very significant preconditions should be satisfied. More specifically: (a) the successful institutional and social recognition of migrants, ensuring valid recording mechanisms and valuation of data, in order to dissolve any distortions or misunderstandings in relation to migration issues, effectively causing negative judgments by citizens (b) the ensuring of an institutional and legal protection that will facilitate the social recognition process, as it becomes assimilated by Greek citizens, and, if possible, would act as a deterrent towards the exclusion of migrants from society and the labour market.

On the basis of the above clarifications, a common goal for all parties involved in social inclusion issues should include an appropriate thorough study of all aspects of the migratory phenomenon, an evaluation and prioritisation of individual needs in order to use all available indicators and research data from primary and secondary sources for the benefit of the social inclusion of immigrants, to establish further the findings that will facilitate the planning and implementation of a migration policy. This would further assist actors at the regional level in order to confront difficult problems and activate civil society.

Going particularly towards this direction, it may be beneficial to use data that will result from the operation of the Councils for the Integration of Migrants, at a regional and local level, as instituted by Law 3852/2010—The "Kallikratis Programme" in Greece. According to article 78, paragraphs 1 and 2, all Municipalities will form a Council for the Integration of Migrants as a consultation body, aiming to reinforce the integration of immigrants in the local community. The Migrants' Council will be constituted and operate upon a decision of the Municipality Council. Members of the Municipality Council, representatives of migrant bodies, or representatives who are elected from the community of the migrants permanently residing in the Municipality, as well as representatives of social bodies for migrant-related activities within the Administrative Region may be selected. It is mandatory to designate third country nationals as Council members in the event that they have been elected as members of the Municipal Council. Participation in the above Councils for the Integration of Migrants is honorary and unpaid.

The work of the Councils for the Integration of Migrants involves (a) recording and exploring issues and problems faced by migrants residing permanently within the Municipal area, particularly as far as their integration and inclusion into the local community is concerned, their integration into the labour market and their relationship with public authorities or the municipal authority and (b) submitting proposals to the Municipal Council in order to develop a local action programme for the social integration of immigrants and tackle the problems they face, at large, especially through counseling services and awareness events as well as strengthening social cohesion within the local population.

Special research tools can be used, though it is most appropriate to act within an organised and coordinated framework with all actors involved. Monitoring the procedure of social and labour inclusion of migrants, in line with these instruments, facilitates the development of feasible action plans and ultimately policy-shaping and policy reform through data-updating and interpreting the complexities that accompany such ventures (Entzinger and Biezeveld, 2003).

Furthermore, comparative analysis shows deviations from a concerted, common European Union accession standard framework, for labour markets, social rights, social policy (Crul and Vermeulen, 2003; Baldwin-Edwards, 2004; Ager and Strang, 2008). For this reason, selected integration policy criteria and indicators used must take into account basic inclusion principles, as they emerge at the European Union level. Also, they should be accompanied by a careful analysis at the national, regional and local context of each country and Greece in particular. Thus, the utilisation of findings from social surveys and the usage of indicators for the inclusion process of migrants in an organised society and labour market focus on mapping a single social base and highlighting issues and problems faced by migrants in European space. A research applied with these standards facilitates both the smooth implementation of specific inclusion policies, on the basis of reliable and updated data, as well as strengthens social cohesion at both national and regional levels.

Conclusions

The development of the EU migration policy has been very advanced. The European Commission introduces a coordination process between the countries, in order to upgrade their levels of national policy. In the absence of a comprehensive European migration policy, it has become more than necessary for the EU to adopt common policies in order to accomplish effective management of migrants.

The EU should engage in further positive responsibility-sharing with countries that receive the largest influx of mixed irregular migration movements, compounded by conditions of economic and social crisis (the Greek case). To this end, a revision of the Dublin Regulation, providing for the examination of asylum claims by the first country of entry and, therefore, return of the asylum seeker to that country, if the person has departed to another EU Member State, is considered necessary. It should be noted though that the problem does not rest so much on the Dublin Regulation, which is applied to a specific category of people (asylum-seekers) but rather on the poor management of irregular migration that has been left unattended for several years and led to phenomena of protracted irregularity. Another approach to responsibility-sharing could be the activation of a "relocation-mechanism" within the Union, that could help alleviate pressure on countries that receive large numbers of migrants and asylum-seekers such as Greece.

A basic requirement for an effective common planning and implementation of social integration measures is the differentiation of the profiles and needs of persons collectively characterized as "migrants". And if it is assumed that member states explore and implement different models of social integration, it should be noted that these concern legal migrants, recognized refugees or other beneficiaries of international protection.

One of the basic arguments in the present article is that the social integration of migrants is a two-way active process of expectations, rights and obligations between the destination country and the migrants who live and work in the country. In other words, social integration refers to both the destination country and its organized social support services for the migrants, as well as to the migrants themselves vis-à-vis this new for them institutional and social reality in the destination country.

Consequently, the way a third-country national is accepted and registered defines significantly his/her future in the destination country, including his/her access to the labour market. It also defines the possibility to participate in the civil, social or economic life of the country through an institutional and social recognition or through the maintenance of legal status, if it already exists, for the protection of his/her rights.

All activities in relation to social integration in Greece should take into account the above. Such activities, because of the particular characteristics of migration in Greece, are scattered, cannot be comprehensive and focus on the improvement of socio-economic conditions with the participation of non-governmental and voluntary organizations.

Although Greek legislation is quite advanced, having incorporated European principles about equality, diversity and social integration, implementation remains problematic, mainly with regard to adopting measures for the management of irregular migration and exploring initiatives for the promotion of organized migration through new agreements with third countries.

As a result, social integration measures concern mostly migrants who find themselves already in Greece and not so much would-be migrants through bilateral agreements whose movement secures to a large extent the requirements for their social integration. This is due to the fact that Greece is in dire need to address the problems in relation to migration movements that have remained unregulated for many years but also to deal with the problems and difficulties associated with migrants who were not part of an integration procedure that could have facilitated their participation in the Greek society and labour market. At present, great numbers of migrants enter the country irregularly, without them forming part of a targeted policy for attracting migrants to Greece.

Notes

[1] For more information about different integration models in Europe, see Niessen, 2000; Koff, 2002; Alexander, 2003; Vermeulen, 2004; Baldwin-Edwards, 2005; Ager and Strang, 2008.

[2] The said Law permitted voting rights in local elections to second-generation immigrants (Art.14); introduced *jus soli* by granting automatically Greek citizenship to children born in Greece if at least one parent was also born in Greece (Art. 1); granted Greek citizenship to persons being born to immigrant parents that

have been living in Greece legally for five years as long as they have studied at a Greek school for at least six years (Art.1A). Law 3838/2010 was declared unconstitutional by the Council of State in November 2012, whereupon its implementation was suspended in view of future legislation.

[3] This Report is drafted within the actions of the Ministry of Interior, acting as the Greek National Contact Point for the European Migration Network (EMN) and within the subject area of: "Satisfying labour demand through migration in Greece".

References

Ager, A. and Strang A. (2008). 'Understanding integration: a conceptual framework', *Journal of Refugee Studies,* vol. 21, no.2, pp. 166-191.

Alexander, M. (2003). 'Local policies towards migrants as an expression of Host-Stranger relations: a proposed typology', *Journal of Ethnic and Migration Studies,* vol. 29, no.3, pp. 411–430.

Baldwin-Edwards, M. (2005). *Migration in the Middle East and Mediterranean, regional study prepared for the Global Commission on International Migration,* Geneva/Athens, Global Commission on International Migration (GCIM) and Mediterranean Migration Observatory.

—. (2004). 'Immigration, immigrants and socialisation in Southern Europe: Patterns, problems and contradistinctions', in Inglessi C., Lymberaki A., Vermeulen H. &. Wijngaarden G. J. V (eds.) *Immigration and integration in Northern versus Southern Europe,* Athens: Netherlands Institute in Athens, pp. 11-24.

Cogneau D. and Gubert F. (2006). *Les migrations et le developpement du sud,* Alternatives economiques, 253, pp. 78-81.

Crul, M. and Vermeulen, H. (2003). 'The second generation in Europe. Introduction to the special issue', *International Migration Review,* vol. 37, no. 4, pp. 965-986.

Entzinger, H. and Biezeveld R. (2003). *Benchmarking in immigrant integration,* Rotterdam, *ERCOMER*, Study carried out for the European Commission, DG Justice and Home Affairs. European Commission [SEC (2011), 620].

Heckmann, F. (1999). *Integration policies in Europe: National difference and/or convergence?,* EFNATIS Working Paper 28, efms, University of Bamberg.

Huysmans, Jef. (1995). 'Migrants as a security problem: Dangers of 'securitizing' societal issues', in Miles, R. and Thranhardt, D. (eds) *Migration and European integration. The dynamics of inclusion and exclusion,*. London: Pinter, pp. 53-72.

Καψάλης, Α. (2009). 'Το αξίωμα της επιλεκτικής μετανάστευσης ως απάντηση στις προκλήσεις του 21ου αιώνα', *Κοινωνική Συνοχή και Ανάπτυξη* , vol. 4, no. 1, pp.63-76.

Koff, H. (2002). 'Let's talk: Dialogue across disciplines on immigration and integration issues', *Working Paper 60*, Center for Comparative Immigration Studies, UCSD, Available: http://escholarship.org/uc/item/3kv4r9fg [02 October 2013].

Nagopoulos, N. and Rontos K. (2012). '*Satisfying labour demand through migration in Greece*', Report for the Framework of the European Migration Network.

Ναγόπουλος Ν. και Σιδηρά, Β. (2006). "Εθνικό θεματικό δίκτυο για τη διαχείριση της διαφορετικότητας. Έκθεση εμπειρογνωμόνων', Υπουργείο Απασχόλησης, Κ.Π Equal, Ευρωπαϊκή Επιτροπή.

Ναγόπουλος, Ν., (2005). *Μελέτη για τη σύσταση και λειτουργία Εθνικών και Ευρωπαϊκών Θεματικών Δικτύων στους τομείς της Απασχόλησης και Κοινωνικής Προστασίας*, Κ.Π Equal, Ευρωπαϊκή Επιτροπή.

Niessen, J. (2000). *Diversity and Cohesion: new challenges for the integration of immigrants and minorities*, Strasbourg: Council of Europe.

Τριανταφυλλίδου Α. (2005). *Ελληνική μεταναστευτική πολιτική: Προβλήματα και κατευθύνσεις*, Αθήνα: ΕΛΙΑΜΕΠ.

UNHCR Office in Greece (2011). *Η Κατάσταση των προσφύγων στην Ελλάδα: Διαπιστώσεις και προτάσεις της Ύπατης Αρμοστείας*, Available: www.unhcr.gr [02 October 2013].

Vermeulen, H. (2004). 'Models and modes of immigrant integration and where does Southern Europe fit?' in Inglessi C. et al. (eds.), *Immigration and integration in Northern versus Southern Europe, Athens*, Netherlands Institute in Athens, pp. 27-39.

CHAPTER ELEVEN

MIGRANT-RELATED ATTITUDES AMONG THE ETHNIC MAJORITY AND MIGRANT GROUP DURING PROSPEROUS AND RECESSIONARY TIMES: THE CASE OF GREECE

STEFANIA KALOGERAKI
UNIVERSITY OF CRETE

Abstract

The recent global financial crisis has cast its long shadow on the weak links in Eurozone's economy forcing highly indebted member states to adopt draconian austerity measures in order to improve their fiscal positions. Such measures were first implemented in Greece which has resorted to EZ and IMF bailout mechanisms to rescue its economy. The amalgamation of record unemployment rates, slashed salaries and increased poverty rates has multifaceted social impacts including among others, the escalation of anti-immigrant sentiments in the country. The main rationale of this article is to explore migrant-related attitudes in 2004 and 2010 representing two time periods of relatively prosperous and stringent macro- and micro-level economic conditions, respectively. Adopting a realistic group conflict theoretical framework and using data from the second (2004) and fifth (2010) round of the European Social Survey (ESS), Univariate 2-way (M) Anovas demonstrate that during the period of downward economic trends when the resources are scarcer and the macro- and micro-level actual competitive economic conditions heightened, the ethnic majority group is more inclined to greater levels of perceived ethnic threats and anti-immigrant sentiments. During recessionary times, ethnic threat perceptions not only gain momentum among the ethnic majority group but also the migrant one which is most vulnerable to the recession's detrimental impacts of unemployment, discrimination and poverty. The present study is a step toward further migrant-related research across Eurozone's indebted member states such as Portugal, Italy and Spain, sharing similar experiences of sizeable migrant groups and deteriorating macro- and micro-level economic conditions. Such studies deepen our insights and optimize our capacities to design effective policy initiatives that confront the potential inter-group ethnic clashes and social unrest between the ethnic majority and migrant groups as well as between the members of the latter during economic downswings.

Introduction

The recent global financial crisis, the greatest one since the Great Depression, has severely hit the Achilles Heel of the Eurozone's (EZ) economy including highly indebted member states. Greece has been probably most severely affected as it was the first member state which resorted to EZ and International Monetary Fund (IMF) bailout mechanisms under strict conditions including drastic curtailing of government spending. The Greek Government has implemented a draconian austerity model within compressed time frameworks including severe cuts in salaries, wages and pensions, reductions in social spending (for education, health and social security policies) as well as increased direct and indirect taxes which have undermined the lives of millions of Greek citizens (Malkoutzis, 2011).

The austerity of the Greek government's budgets led to an economic paralysis with disastrous socio-economic impacts. The unemployment rate hit a historic record in 2011 with 21%, whereas youth unemployment reached 45% (i.e., twice higher as two years ago) (European Commission, 2012). In 2010, the overall at-risk-of-poverty rate[1] for the total Greek population was much higher (27.7%) than the EU-27 average (23.4%) (European Commission, 2012). As the economic crisis worsens, Greeks experience an unprecedented socio-economic hardship that drives up suicide rates, depression syndromes, HIV infections, drug abuse, violence, homicide and theft rates (Economou et al., 2011; Kentikelenis et al., 2011; Madianos, et al., 2011).

In times of drastic austerity measures Greek society's social fabric has grown more frayed generating a mixture of fear and anger among Greek citizens which is directed to the most vulnerable social groups including, among others, immigrants (ENAR, 2011). The anger for the mismanagement of the economic vows, the accompanying high unemployment rates, low growth and painful reductions have re-enforced the anti-immigrant rhetoric propagating that immigrants are responsible for the ills of the Greek society (ENAR, 2011). As the head of United Nations High

Commissioner for Refugees (UNHCR) in Greece, Giorgos Tsarbopoulos[2], underlines:

> "The economic situation's created a climate where slogans and xenophobic rhetoric and easy solutions that are not solutions of course of 'kick them out, let's take the law into our own hands' can more easily be propagated in a population which faces problems regarding security and public order[sic]."

The rising tide of anti-minority sentiments has been partly expressed by the rise of the neo-fascist Golden Dawn which has grown from a fringe group to a nationwide political party winning almost 7% in the 2012 Greek elections and being responsible for an alarming number of attacks on immigrants (ENAR, 2011). Several non-governmental (NGO) and anti-racism organizations in Greece underline that the deteriorating socio-economic conditions have escalated the intolerance towards immigrants (especially undocumented ones), nationalism, xenophobic and racist sentiments, leading to inter-group conflicts and social unrest (Balourdos and Xrusakis, 2011; ENAR, 2011; Racist Violence Recording Network, 2012).

Research draws on a number of theories to explain anti-immigrant sentiments among which realistic group conflict theory is considered to be one of the most prominent ones. The theory underlines that hostile migrant-related attitudes arise when the competition between ethnic majority and minority group members over the same limited resources (i.e., jobs, material interests) heightens, provoking potential inter-ethnic clashes (Coser, 1956; Blalock, 1967; Sherif, 1967; Quillian, 1995). Under realistic group conflict theory's framework, the Greek debt crisis is likely to reinforce the inter-group competition leading to an upsurge in natives' threat perceptions and anti-immigrant sentiments.

However, during downward economic trends the competition over securing jobs and other rare economic resources not only intensifies between the ethnic majority and migrant group but also between the members of the latter. Immigrants occupy low-paid positions in sectors (e.g construction, manufacturing) which are vulnerable in economic downturns; hence, they are severely affected by unemployment and poverty (Fix et al., 2009; Papademetriou and Terrazas, 2009). Given that the recession's impact is hardest on the migrant employment sectors, immigrants' fears that other ethnic minority group members can become competitors in the diminishing labour market are likely to increase their own threat perceptions and intolerance to their counterparts leading to potential intra-group[3] tensions (Kalogeraki, 2012).

The main purpose of this study is to explore migrant-related attitudes and threat perceptions among the Greek ethnic majority and minority group members[4] in 2004 and 2010, representing two time periods of relatively prosperous and stringent economic conditions, respectively. Adopting a realistic group conflict theoretical framework, and using data from the second (2004) and fifth (2010) round of the European Social Survey (ESS), the study uncovers the escalation of ethnic threat perceptions and anti-immigrant sentiments in the Greek society and calls for further migrant-related research in indebted Southern European member states.

Theoretical background: Realistic group conflict theory

A wide range of scholars including sociologists, psychologists, economists, political scientists and historians has studied the origins of anti-immigrant sentiments. One of the most influential explanations is provided in realistic group conflict theory advocating that intolerance towards immigrants stems from the macro- and micro-level competition between ethnic majority and minority group members over finite resources (Coser, 1956; Blumer, 1958; Campbell, 1965; Blalock, 1967; Sherif and Sherif, 1979; Olzak, 1992; Quillian, 1995). Such resources include material interests (e.g., job positions, housing, resources of the welfare state) as well as issues associated with status, prestige and power. Proponents of the theory distinguish between actual and perceived competition as the former takes place on the societal level and the latter on the individual one (Blalock, 1967). Perceived competition is primarily shaped by the context of actual competitive conditions forming natives' perceived threats, which in turn induce specific attitudes towards immigrants (LeVine and Campbell, 1972). Under this framework, threat perceptions act as a crucial mediating link between actual and perceived competition and migrant-related sentiments (Bobo, 1988).

The inter-group actual competitive conditions are primarily defined by micro- and macro-level determinants. With respect to the former, individual level socio-economic attributes play a pivotal role in forming subjective threats, which in turn trigger migrant-related attitudes. More specifically, ethnic majority group members of lower social strata (i.e., economically underprivileged individuals, unemployed or individuals with lower educational attainment) are more vulnerable to the competition with ethnic minority group members as the former perceive that their group's status position, resources and prerogatives are threatened by immigrants holding similar positions (Olzak, 1992; O'Rourke and Sinnott, 2006; Malchow-Møller et al., 2008). Hence, socio-economically deprived natives perceive higher ethnic threats and are more susceptible to exclusionary views and anti-minority sentiments.

At the macro-level, actual competition is operationalized by specific contextual attributes such as the size of the migrant group and the prevailing economic conditions in the host country. With respect to the former, Blalock (1967: 187) argues that "Provided that minority competition underlies prejudice, there should be a positive association between minority percentage and discrimination". Anti-immigrant sentiments tend to be more pronounced in countries in which immigrants are heavily concentrated[5] as natives perceive that the increasing number of competitors heightens the struggle for societal and economic resources (Olzak, 1992; Quillian, 1995). In addition, a sizable migrant group entails higher threats to the cultural identity and homogeneity of the indigenous population (Semyonov, Raijman and Gorodzeisky, 2006).

Besides the size of the ethnic minority group, the economic climate in the host country plays a fundamental role in forming natives' level of threat perceptions and migrant-related sentiments. In stagnating economies (i.e., low GDP, high unemployment rates) the inter-group competition over jobs and other scarce economic resources becomes fiercer. Hence, ethnic majority group members perceive greater threats and are more inclined to anti-minority sentiments (Blalock, 1967). For instance, Kessler and Freeman (2005) show that the deteriorating economic conditions over the period 1993-2000 in EU-15 member states generated an increase in intolerance towards immigrants. Similarly, Wilkes, Guppy and Farris (2008) advocate that the negative economic climate in Canada during 1975-2000 created a hostile environment for ethnic minority group members. In line with realistic group conflict theory, empirical findings[6] indicate that stringent macro-level actual competitive economic conditions (in terms of low GDP and high unemployment rates), as well as sizeable minority groups, foster greater levels of ethnic threat perceptions and antipathy towards immigrants (Quillian, 1995; Lahav, 2004; Coenders, Gijsberts and Scheepers, 2004; Schneider, 2008; Semyonov, Raijman and Gorodzeisky, 2008).

Greece is selected as a case that satisfies the macro-level actual competitive conditions which escalate natives' threat perceptions and trigger anti-immigrant sentiments. More specifically, Greece belongs to the "Southern European model of immigration" including countries (i.e., Italy, Portugal and Spain) that in the early 1990s experienced a sizable migratory influx transforming them from emigration poles to host ones (King, 2000). The sharp increase of minority group size in a short period of time reinforced the perceptions that immigrants threaten the socio-economic and political order, as well as the cultural homogeneity and the Greek national identity. Such perceptions gradually transformed the Greek society from a tolerant and xenophilic country into one of the most xenophobic countries in Europe (Triandafyllidou and Mikrakis, 1995; Coenders, Lubbers and Scheepers, 2005; Meulman, 2009).

Although there are serious issues of data collection, collation and compilation of the Greek migration statistics, estimates that take into account undocumented (or illegal) immigrants indicate that the migrant population in the early years of the twenty-first century was more than one million accounting for more than 10% of the total population (Kasimis, 2012). The largest migrant group comes from Albania, accounting for about 60% of the total immigrant (legal and undocumented) population. In addition, immigrants come mostly from Bulgaria, Romania, Georgia, Ukraine and Pakistan, occupying primarily positions in the so called low-status "3D-jobs" (dirty, dangerous and demanding work) of traditional sectors of the Greek economy (such as construction, personal services, agriculture, tourism).

Aside from the sizable migrant group, since 2008 Greece has experienced an additional macro-level competitive condition that is likely to impact on natives' perceived threats and contribute to higher intolerance towards minority group members. In the context of the global financial crisis, Greece has been trapped into a vicious cycle of recession leading the country's economy into stagnation and threatening larger segments of the population with unemployment and poverty (Malkoutzis, 2011). Although at the beginning of 2000s Greece had high growth rates, mainly due to large-scale public works and construction associated with the Olympic Games of 2004, during the last four years the country has experienced one of the worst recessions in its recent history. Between the years under study, i.e., 2004 and 2010, the country's gross debt (as a percentage of the GDP) increased from 98.6% to 145% whereas the gross domestic product (GDP) declined from 4.4% to -4.5% (ELSTAT, 2011). The economic paralysis inevitably led to significant increases in unemployment rates, which arose from 10.5% in 2004 to 12.5% in 2010 (ELSTAT, 2011) and hit a historic record in 2011 with 21% (European Commission, 2012). The highest unemployment rates are reported for medium-skilled (20.1 % against 8.7 % in the EU-27) and low-skilled workers (14.6 % against 5.7 % in the EU-27) in sectors such as the construction, retail and tourism (European Commission, 2012). In addition, the share of persons declaring that they were having great difficulty in making ends meet escalated from 19% in 2007 to 24% in 2010 (European Commission, 2012).

However, in the context of the Greek debt crisis unemployment and poverty have not only threatened the indigenous population but have severely affected the migrant population. Although the highest unemployment rates are detected for medium-skilled and low-skilled workers, including both natives and immigrants of lower social strata (European Commission, 2012), the impact on the latter is hardest as the shrinking of the construction sector over the last four years has forced the largest group of immigrant workers to unemployment (Maroukis and Gemi, 2011). Hence, low-paid immigrants in traditional sectors of the Greek economy have been most profoundly exposed to poverty (ENAR, 2011). In 2009, for the first time in recent years, immigrants' unemployment rate surpassed the natives' one (OECD, 2011; Triandafyllidou and Maroufof, 2011). Between 2008 and 2010, the unemployment rate for Greek natives and citizens from other EU-27 countries increased by 3% and 4.6%, respectively, whereas for foreign citizens from countries outside EU-27 increased by 7.5%, i.e., from 7.2% to 14.7% (Karantinos and Manoudi, 2010). In addition, at the beginning of 2009 there has been a decrease in wages especially for undocumented immigrants as well as increased competition between legal and undocumented ones for low-skilled manual jobs (Triandafyllidou and Lazarescu, 2009).

Under such deteriorating economic conditions, ethnic minority group members face a two-fold competition, i.e., with natives of lower social strata as well as other immigrants. The intra-group competition is likely to escalate immigrants' fears that their counterparts threaten their jobs and wages leading to a potential escalation in threat perceptions and intolerance towards other minority group members (Zimmermann et al., 2007; Kalogeraki, 2012). During recessionary times, the competition over rare economic resources not only deepens, as realistic group ethnic theory proposes, between the ethnic majority and migrant group but also between the members of the latter leading to potential intra-group tensions, respectively. The main rationale of this research is to explore such arguments by investigating ethnic threat perceptions and migrant-related sentiments in the Greek ethnic majority and minority group during financially prosperous and recessionary times.

Data, measurement and methods

Data

The study explores migrant-related attitudes and ethnic threat perceptions among Greek ethnic majority and migrant group members using data from the second (2004) and fifth (2010) round of the European Social Survey (ESS). The ESS is a methodologically rigorous biennial study that charts the changing social attitudes and values within Europe. The study is carefully designed for optimal international comparability of the data using strict random sampling techniques (a minimum target response rate of 70%) and rigorous translation protocols in all participating countries.

The total sample sizes of the Greek datasets in the ESS2 (2004) and ESS5 (2010) rounds are n_{ESS2}=2406 and n_{ESS5}=2715, respectively. In the study, the concept of "immigrants" refers to foreign-born individuals, i.e., individuals whose parents and they themselves were born abroad, and not with the commonly applied definition of foreign-citizens. There are substantial differences in defining immigrants as foreign-born individuals and as foreign-citizens, since the former may acquire through naturalization the citizenship of the host country (Schneider, 2008). As in 2010 the Greek Government promoted a new law that allows easier access to Greek citizenship[7], immigrants are defined as foreign-born individuals in order to avoid inconsistencies in migrant group samples associated with differences in naturalization processes between the periods under study. In the ESS2 (2004) round, the Greek majority group accounts for 92.4% (n=2222) and the minority one for 7.6% (n=183) of the total sample size. In the ESS5 (2010) round the ethnic majority (n=2498) and migrant (n=217) group account for 92.0% and 8.0% of the total sample size, respectively.

Measurements

The ESS questionnaires include attitudinal items (e.g., attitudes towards immigration, trust in politics, social trust, religious involvement, media use, political participation, life satisfaction, human values) as well as various socio-demographic variables. From the core modules of the ESS2 (2004) and ESS5 (2010) questionnaires, common items measuring migrant-related attitudes, perceived ethnic threats and economic living conditions are selected. Migrant-related attitudes are assessed with three items asking respondents to what extent do they think that their country should allow individuals: (a) of the same race or ethnic group with the host country (b) of different race or ethnic group from the host country and (c) from poorer countries outside Europe to come and live in Greece. Respondents indicate their answers on four-point scales ranging from 1 (allow many) to 4 (allow none). As higher scores correspond to higher levels of migrant-opposition attitudes, the specific items assess ethnic majority and migrant groups' levels of anti-immigrant sentiments.

Ethnic threat perceptions are measured with three common items included in the two ESS rounds under study. The specific items assess respondents' threat perceptions associated with immigrants' impact on the economic ("Would you say it is generally bad or good for Greece's economy that people come to live here from other countries?"), cultural ("Would you say that Greece's cultural life is generally undermined or enriched by people coming to live here from other countries?") and general ("Is Greece made a worse or a better place to live by people coming to live here from other countries?") life of the Greek society. Respondents indicate their answers on scales from 0 to 10 with lower values corresponding to higher levels of economic, cultural and general ethnic perceived threats. The values of the specific items are inversed so that the higher scores indicate greater levels of the threat perceptions.

An additional common item from the ESS2 (2004) and ESS5 (2010) questionnaires is selected that assesses the respondents' subjective financial living conditions. The specific item asks respondents to describe their feelings about their household's income nowadays providing a 4-item scale (1=Living comfortably on present income, 2=Coping on present income, 3=Finding it difficult on present income, 4=Finding it very difficult on present income). The item is recoded into two broader categories (1=Living comfortably or coping on present income, 2= Finding it difficult or very difficult on present income) for analysis purposes.

Statistics

Univariate 2-way (M) Anovas are conducted to examine the effects of Greek ethnic majority and minority group members' micro-level financial living conditions in 2004 and 2010 on their migrant-related attitudes (towards immigrants of the same or different race from the host country and from poorer countries outside Europe) and their economic, cultural and general threat perceptions. The significant interaction effects are further investigated with post hoc analyses on simple main effects within each factor level using the Sidak adjustment for pairwise comparisons

(Tables 11-2 and 11-3). The effect sizes are determined with Eta-squared (η^2) indicating the proportion of the total variance that is attributed to the effects under study. Cohen's (1988) benchmarks are applied to characterize effect sizes of .01, .06 and .14 as small, moderate and large, respectively. In the analyses, the design weights provided with the ESS2 (2004) and ESS5 (2010) Greek datasets are applied to account for slightly different selection probabilities for individuals in different rounds. Statistically significant levels are reported for p values less than or equal to .05. The analyses are performed with SPSS 19.0.

Results

The Univariate 2-way (M) Anovas indicate that although the detected effect sizes (η^2) are small (i.e., less than .06) (Cohen, 1988), ethnic majority group members report significantly higher mean scores of migrant-opposition attitudes against immigrants of the same race/ethnic group with Greece (i.e., co-ethnics) in 2004 than in 2010 [$F(1,4386)=74.44$, $p\leq.001$, $\eta^2=.02$] (Table 11-1). On the contrary, natives perceive higher economic threats [$F(1,4352)=93.93$, $p\leq.001$, $\eta^2=.02$] and show greater intolerance towards immigrants of different ethnic group from the host country [$F(1,4391)=61.16$, $p\leq.001$, $\eta^2=.01$] and from poorer countries outside Europe [$F(1,4387)=85.87$, $p\leq.001$, $\eta^2=.02$] in 2010 than 2004. The significant main effects show that independently from natives' financial living conditions, cultural [$F(1,4339)=56.61$, $p\leq.001$, $\eta^2=.01$] and general ethnic threat perceptions [$F(1,4370)=57.61$, $p\leq.001$ $\eta^2=.01$] are significantly higher in 2010 than 2004.

The migrant-related attitudes of the majority group members against the migrant group members of the same or different ethnic group with the host country and from poorer countries outside Europe, as well as the perceived economic threats, are differentiated for more and less favourable financial living conditions both within and between the ESS rounds used in the study. With respect to the former, the post hoc analysis on simple main effects using Sidak-adjusted pairwise comparisons indicates that in 2004 intolerance towards co-ethnic immigrants is significantly higher among economically underprivileged natives than their counterparts living in more prosperous conditions (Table 11-2). In addition, both in 2004 and 2010 Greek natives living in less favourable economic conditions report higher mean scores of migrant-opposition against minority group members of different ethnic group from the host country or from poorer countries outside Europe than their counterparts living in more favourable conditions. Similar results are detected for financially deprived natives perceiving greater economic threats in both periods under study.

Table 11-1. Estimated marginal means of significant main effects in migrant-opposition attitudes and threat perceptions in ethnic majority group between 2004 and 2010

ESS2 & ESS5	Mean	SE	95% Confidence Interval	
			Lower Bound	Upper Bound
Migrant-opposition against immigrants of the same race/ethnic group with host country				
2004	2.74	.02	2.70	2.78
2010	2.48	.02	2.43	2.52
Migrant-opposition attitudes against immigrants of different race/ethnic group from host country				
2004	3.08	.01	3.05	3.11
2010	3.26	.01	3.23	3.29
Migrant-opposition attitudes against immigrants from poorer countries outside Europe				
2004	3.09	.01	3.07	3.13
2010	3.31	.01	3.28	3.34
Economic threat perceptions				
2004	6.34	.05	6.24	6.44
2010	7.04	.05	6.94	7.14
Cultural threat perceptions				
2004	6.48	.05	6.38	6.58
2010	6.99	.05	6.89	7.08
General threat perceptions				
2004	6.78	.04	6.68	6.87
2010	7.28	.04	7.19	7.37

Note: Data weighted by design weight to account for different selection probabilities of participants in the ESS2 (2004) and ESS5 (2010).

Table 11-2. Significant results of post hoc analyses on simple main effects in migrant-opposition attitudes and economic threat perceptions of ethnic majority group living in different subjective financial conditions in 2004 and 2010

ESS Round	Subjective financial conditions	Mean Difference[1]	SE	95% Confidence Interval	
				Lower Bound	Upper Bound
Migrant-opposition against immigrants of the same race/ethnic group with host country					
2004	**CSFC- DSFC**	-.26***	.04	-.34	-.18
Migrant-opposition attitudes against immigrants of different race/ethnic group from host country					
2004	**CSFC- DSFC**	-.28***	.03	-.35	-.22
2010	**CSFC- DSFC**	-.17***	.03	-.23	-.10
Migrant-opposition attitudes against immigrants from poorer countries outside Europe					
2004	**CSFC- DSFC**	-.25***	.03	-.31	-.19
2010	**CSFC- DSFC**	-.15***	.03	-.21	-.09
Economic threat perceptions					
2004	**CSFC- DSFC**	-.94***	.10	-1.14	-.74
2010	**CSFC- DSFC**	-.63***	.10	-.83	-.42

[1]"Mean difference" refers to the difference in the mean scores of migrant-opposition attitudes and economic threat perceptions between respondents living in comfortable subjective financial conditions (CSFC) and difficult subjective financial conditions (DSFC) in 2004 and 2010. The negative symbol implies that the mean score is higher among those living in difficult rather than comfortable subjective financial conditions in each period under study. Mean differences are calculated using the Sidak adjustment for pairwise comparisons.

*$p \leq .05$, **$p \leq .01$, ***$p \leq .001$, Data weighted by design weight.

Furthermore, the post hoc analysis between the periods under study indicates that more or less well-off ethnic majority group members show greater antipathy towards immigrants of different race from the Greek one and from poorer countries outside Europe as well as perceive greater economic threats in 2010 than in 2004 (Table 11-3). On the contrary, Greek natives living either in prosperous or stringent financial conditions report higher mean scores of migrant-opposition attitudes against co-ethnic immigrants in 2004 than in 2010.

Table 11-3. Significant results of post hoc analyses on simple main effects in migrant-opposition attitudes and economic threat perceptions of ethnic majority group living in different subjective financial conditions between 2004 and 2010

Subjective financial conditions	ESS Round 2 & 5	Mean Difference[1]	SE	95% Confidence Interval	
				Lower Bound	Upper Bound
Migrant-opposition against immigrants of the same race/ethnic group with host country					
CSFC	**2004-2010**	$.17^{***}$	.04	.08	.26
DSFC		$.36^{***}$	.04	.28	.44
Migrant-opposition attitudes against immigrants of different race/ethnic group from host country					
CSFC	**2004-2010**	$-.24^{***}$	.03	-.30	-.17
DSFC		$-.12^{***}$	.03	-.18	-.06
Migrant-opposition attitudes against immigrants from poorer countries outside Europe					
CSFC	**2004-2010**	$-.26^{***}$	.03	-.32	-.19
DSFC		$-.16^{***}$	.03	-.22	-.10
Economic threat perceptions					
CSFC	**2004-2010**	$-.85^{***}$	.11	-1.07	-.64
DSFC		$-.54^{***}$	.09	-.73	-.35

[1]"Mean difference" refers to the difference in the mean scores of migrant-opposition attitudes and economic threat perceptions between 2004 and 2010 for respondents living in comfortable (CSFC) and difficult (DSFC) subjective financial conditions. The negative symbol implies that the mean score is higher in 2010 than 2004 under each financial condition. Mean differences are calculated using the Sidak adjustment for pairwise comparisons.
$^{*}p\leq.05$, $^{**}p\leq.01$, $^{***}p\leq.001$. Data weighted by design weight.

The Univariate 2-way (M) Anovas for the minority group show that independently from subjective financial conditions immigrants report significantly higher mean scores of economic [$F(1,377)=9.58$, $p\leq.01$, $\eta^2=.02$] and cultural perceived threats [$F(1,374)=7.13$, $p\leq.01$, $\eta^2=.02$] in 2010 than in 2004, however the reported η^2 are considered to be low (Table 11-4). In addition, general threat perceptions [$F(1,380)=19.91$, $p\leq.001$, $\eta^2=.06$] are higher among immigrants in 2010 whereas the specific effect size is moderate one (Cohen, 1988). On the contrary, non-significant differences are detected in ethnic minority group's migrant-opposition attitudes between the two ESS rounds under study (data not shown).

Table 11-4. Estimated marginal means of significant main effects in migrant-opposition attitudes and threat perceptions in migrant group between 2004 and 2010

ESS2 & ESS5	Mean	SE	95% Confidence Interval	
			Lower Bound	Upper Bound
Economic threat perceptions				
2004	3.92	.20	3.52	4.31
2010	4.85	.22	4.41	5.29
Cultural threat perceptions				
2004	3.98	.18	3.63	4.32
2010	4.69	.19	4.30	5.08
General threat perceptions				
2004	4.43	.17	4.09	4.77
2010	5.58	.19	5.20	5.95

Note: Data weighted by design weight.

Summary and conclusions

Since 2008 Greece entered into a prolonged deep recession, the end of which is not yet visible. The economic woes have led the country into a financial instability as well as into a societal and political one with multifaceted impacts on the Greek society (Economou et al., 2011; Kentikelenis et al., 2011; Malkoutzis, 2011). The study uncovers one of the facets of the Greek debt crisis' consequences associated with the formation of a hostile environment for migrant group members.

In line with realistic group conflict theoretical framework, Greek natives' migrant-opposition attitudes against minority group members of non co-ethnic origins (i.e., immigrants of different race from the host country and from poorer countries outside Europe) are higher in the recessionary period of 2010 than the more prosperous 2004 (Table 11-1). Although, in each period under study economically underprivileged majority group members show greater migrant-related intolerance than their more affluent counterparts (Table 11-2), the increase in anti-minority sentiments between 2004 and 2010 takes place for natives of differentiated economic conditions (Table 11-3). Similarly, during the time of the economic downturn (2010), ethnic majority group members independently from subjective financial living conditions are inclined to perceive greater economic, cultural and general threats (i.e., immigrants make host country a worse place to live) than in the more prosperous period of 2004 (Table 11-1 and Table 11-3). Although the reported effect sizes (η^2) are low, the findings provide some preliminary evidence of natives' upsurge in perceived threats and anti-immigrant sentiments during the Greek debt crisis that can potentially lead to inter-group clashes and social strife in the Greek society.

Whilst natives during the period of downward economic trends show greater intolerance towards immigrants of different ethnic group from the Greek one and from poorer countries outside Europe, the inversed findings are detected for co-ethnic immigrants (Table 11-1 and Table 11-3). The lower level of migrant-opposition attitudes against co-ethnic minority group members in 2010 than 2004 is likely to be associated with the special provisions for immigrants of Greek descent, namely, ethnic Greek Albanians (Northern Epirotes) and co-ethnics from the former Soviet Republics (Pontic Greeks)[8]. These co-ethnic groups on the basis of their Greek ancestral ties were granted in 1990s and beginning of 2000s a favourable legal status to facilitate their social and labour market integration (Triandafyllidou and Veikou, 2002). The preferential treatment of Pontic Greeks and Northern Epirotes differentiated them from other migrant groups as the former have been considered members of the Greek society or as Konsta and Lazaridis (2010: 378) put it: as "one of us". The lower level of anti-minority sentiments towards co-ethnics in the recessionary period of 2010 might reflect their full integration and acceptance in the Greek society as individuals that do not threaten the country's diminishing resources.

In addition to these findings, the study provides some preliminary evidence on the relations formed between ethnic minority group members residing in Greece (Table 11-4). The analysis shows that in times of economic stagnation ethnic threat perceptions not only gain momentum, as realistic group conflict theory predicts, among the ethnic majority group but also among the migrant one. The members of the latter are most affected as typical sectors of migrant employment have been severely hit leading to a drastic increase in immigrants' unemployment and poverty rates (Karantinos and Manoudi, 2010; ENAR, 2011; Triandafyllidou and Maroufof, 2011). During a period of sharp recession, minority group members compete with economically underprivileged natives as well as with other immigrants to secure their jobs and their economic resources. Securing a job becomes a vital concern for minority group members as unemployment not only threatens their means of subsistence but also their legal status in the country which is intertwined with their employment status proven by their welfare contributions (ENAR, 2011). Although there are no significant differences in migrant-opposition attitudes between more and less prosperous times, immigrants' higher levels of all the threat perceptions under study in 2010 than in 2004 echo their fears of intense intra-group competition for scarce resources that can lead to potential tensions between ethnic minority group members.

Even though the study provides some evidence on the increase of anti-minority sentiments and perceived threats during the Greek debt crisis, there are a few limitations that need to be acknowledged. More specifically, the findings suffer from a lack of representative ethnic group samples of both legal and undocumented immigrants, which could shed more light on the relations formed between minority group members. In addition, the limited immigrants' sample sizes do not allow a further exploration of potential divergences and/or convergences in migrant-related sentiments and perceived threats between migrant groups of different ethnic backgrounds (e.g., Albanians vs. Pakistanis). Despite these limitations, the findings are a step toward further migrant-related research across indebted Southern European member states such as Portugal, Italy and Spain. These countries share similar experiences to Greece, i.e., sizeable migrant groups (King, 2000) as well as stringent actual economic competitive conditions due to the global economic crisis. Such studies deepen our insights and optimize our capacities to design effective policy initiatives that confront the potential inter-group ethnic clashes and social unrest between the ethnic majority and migrant group as well as between the members of the latter during economic downswings.

Notes

[1] According to Eurostat's definitions, the at-risk-of-poverty rate is the share of people with an equivalised disposable income (after social transfer) below the at-risk-of-poverty threshold, which is set at 60 % of the national median equivalised disposable income after social transfers. Available: http://epp.eurostat.ec.europa.eu/statistics_explained/index.php/Glossary:At-risk-of-poverty_rate [8 September 2012]

[2] Available: http://www.euronews.com/2012/06/01/racial-violence-on-the-rise-in-cash-strapped-greece/ [19 October 2012]

[3] In the literature, the term "intra-group" when it refers to immigrants it usually includes the members of an ethnically and culturally homogenous migrant group. However, in the present study the specific term is used more broadly to include immigrants of the same or different ethnic background (e.g., Albanians, Pakistanis)

Hence, intra-group relations (or tensions) refer to the relations among immigrants irrespectively from their ethnic or cultural background.
[4] In the present study the ethnic minority group includes first generation immigrants of the same or different ethnic background (see section Data for the operationalization of immigrants).
[5] In contrast to realistic group conflict theory's assumptions, other scholars suggest that sizable migrant groups increase the inter-group contact leading to potential friendships that can form positive migrant-related sentiments (Wagner et al., 2006).
[6] Despite the empirical evidence, the support to the realistic group-conflict theoretical framework is not unambiguous as some scholars have provided conflicting findings (see, for example, Sides & Citrin, 2007; Strabac & Listhaug, 2008).
[7] Law 3838/2010 lowered the requirement for naturalization from 10 to 7 years of legal residence in Greece, (ENAR, 2011) and, for the first time, gave the opportunity to children who were born in Greece, and whose parents were legal immigrants, to become Greek citizens (for more details, see Nagopoulos and Rontos, chapter 10, this volume).
[8] The special policy provisions were different for Pontic Greeks and Northern Epirotes. The former were granted Greek citizenship upon their arrival to Greece as well as generous social benefits (including accommodation, education, child support, unemployment, vocational training) (Triandafyllidou and Veikou, 2002). On the contrary, Northern Epirotes were conceded a favourable legal status (a kind of "quasi-citizenship") that in 2001 allowed them to have equal rights to Greeks in the labour market as well as in welfare and civil services. Since 2006 the Greek government has promoted the easier naturalization for Northern Epirotes.

References

Balourdos, D. and Xrusakis, M. (eds.) (2011). *Fighting against discriminations: Trends, challenges, policies,* Athens: Papazisi Publishing *(*in Greek*).*

Blalock, H. (1967). *Toward a theory of minority-group relations*, New York: Wiley and Sons.

Blumer, H. (1958). 'Race prejudice as a sense of group position', *The Pacific Sociological Review*, vol. 1, no.1, pp. 3-7.

Bobo, L. (1988). 'Group conflict, prejudice and the paradox of contemporary racial attitudes', in Katz, P. and Taylor, D. (eds.) *Eliminating Racism. Profiles in Controversy*, New York: Plenum Press, pp. 85-116.

Campbell, D. (1965). 'Ethnocentric and other altruistic motives', in Levine, D. (ed.) *Nebraska Symposium on Motivation,* Lincoln: University of Nebraska Press, pp. 283-311.

Coenders, M., Gijsberts, M. and Scheepers, P. (2004). 'Resistance to the presence of immigrants and refugees in 22 countries', in Gijsberts, M., Hagendoorn, L. and Scheepers, P. (eds), *Nationalism and exclusion of migrants: Cross-national comparisons*, Aldershot: Ashgate Publishing, pp.97-120.

Coenders, M., Lubbers, M. and Scheepers, P. (2005). *Majorities' attitudes towards minorities in Western and Eastern European societies: Results from the European Social Survey 2002-2003,* Vienna: European Monitoring Centre on Racism and Xenophobia (EUMC), Available: http://fra.europa.eu/fraWebsite/attachments/Report-4.pdf [9 October 2012].

Cohen, J. (1988). *Statistical power analysis for the behavioural sciences,* 2nd edition, New York: Academic Press.

Coser, L. (1956). *The function of social conflict,* Glencoe, Illinois: Free Press.

Economou, M., Madianos, M., Theleritis, C., Peppou, L. and Stefanis, C. (2011). 'Increased suicidality amid economic crisis in Greece', *The Lancet*, vol. 378, no. 9801, p. 1459.

ELSTAT, (2011). *The Greek economy,* Piraeus: Hellenic Statistical Authority, Available: http://www.statistics.gr/portal/page/portal/ESYE/BUCKET/General/greek_economy_23_9_2011.pdf [15 October 2012].

European Commission, (2012). *EU employment and social situation: Quarterly review,* Available: http://ec.europa.eu/social/ BlobServlet?docId=7548&langId=en [29 September 2012].

European Network Against Racism (ENAR), (2011). *ENAR Shadow Report 2010-2011: Racism and related discriminatory practices in Greece,* Report prepared by Shashati, A. & Greek Forum of Migrants, Brussels: ENAR, Available: http://cms.horus.be/files/99935/MediaArchive/publications/shadow%20report%202010-11/11.%20Greece.pdf [29 August 2012].

Fix, M., Papademetriou, D., Batalova, J., Terrazas, A., Yi-Ying Lin, S. and Mittelstadt, M. (2009). *Migration and the global recession: A report commissioned by the BBC World Service,* Washington, DC: Migration Policy Institute, Available: http://www.migrationpolicy.org/ pubs/MPI-BBCreport-Sept09.pdf [17 October 2012].

Kalogeraki, S. (2012). 'Migrant-related attitudes and perceived ethnic threats between in-groups and out-groups: The cases of Greece and Sweden', *Nordic Journal of Migration Research,* vol. 2, no.3, pp. 243-253.

Karantinos, D. and Manoudi, A. (2010). *Country report 2 2010: On employment, ethnicity and migrants: Greece,* Utrecht-Vienna: Network of Socio-economic Experts in the Anti-discrimination Field, Available: http://www.antigone.gr/en/library/files/selected_publications/greece/EKKE%20Report%20on%20DISCRIMINATION.pdf [23 September 2012].

Kasimis, Ch. (2012). *Country profiles. Greece: Illegal immigration in the midst of crisis,* Washington, DC: Migration Policy Institute, Available: http://www.migrationinformation.org/Profiles/display.cfm?ID=884 [18 October 2012].

Kentikelenis, A., Karanikolos, M., Papanikolas, I., Basu, S., McKee, M. and Stuckler, D. (2011). 'Health effects of financial crisis: Omens of a Greek tragedy', *The Lancet,* vol. 378, issue 9801, pp. 1457-1458.

Kessler, A. and Freeman, G. (2005). Public opinion in the EU on immigration from outside the community, *Journal of Common Market Studies,* vol. 43, no. 4, pp. 825-850.

King, R. (2000). 'Southern Europe in the changing global map of migration', in King, R., Lazaridis G. and Tsardanidis C. (eds.), *Eldorado or Fortress? Migration in Southern Europe*, London: Macmillan Press Ltd, pp. 3-26.

Konsta, A. and Lazaridis, G. (2010). 'Civic stratification 'plastic citizenship and plastic subjectivities' in Greek Immigration policy', *International Migration and Integration,* vol. 11, no. 4, pp. 365-382.

Lahav, G. (2004). *Immigration and politics in the New Europe. Reinventing borders,* Cambridge: University Press.

LeVine, R. and Campbell, D. (1972). *Ethnocentrism: Theories of group conflict, ethnic attitudes and group behaviour,* New York: Wiley and Sons.

Madianos, M., Economou, M., Alexiou, T. and Stefanis, C. (2011). 'Depression and economic hardship across Greece in 2008 and 2009: Two cross-sectional surveys nationwide', *Social Psychiatry Psychiatric Epidemiology,* vol. 46, no.10, pp. 943-952.

Malchow-Møller, N., Munch, J., Schroll, S. and Skaksen, J. (2008). 'Attitudes towards immigration: Perceived consequences and economic self-interest', *Economics Letters,* vol. 100, pp. 254-257.

Malkoutzis, N. (2011). *Greece: A year in crisis: Examining the social and political impact of an unprecedented austerity programme,* Berlin: Friedrich-Ebert-Stiftung, International Policy Analysis, Available: http://library.fes.de/pdf-files/id/ipa/08208.pdf [17 September 2012].

Maroukis, T. and Gemi, E. (2011). *Circular migration between Albania and Greece (METOIKOS Project)*, Robert Schuman Centre for Advanced Studies, San Domenico di Fiesole (FI): European University

Institute, Available: http://cadmus.eui.eu/bitstream/handle/1814/19717/METOIKOSCaseStudyGreeceAlbania.pdf?sequence=1 [3 November 2012].

Meuleman, B. (2009). *The influence of macro-sociological factors on attitudes toward immigration in Europe. A cross-cultural and contextual Approach,* Thesis Submitted in partial fulfilment of the Requirements of University of Leuven for the Degree of Doctor of Philosophy, Leuven: University of Leuven.

O'Rourke, K. and Sinnott, R. (2006). 'The determinants of individual attitudes towards immigration', *European Journal of Political Economy,* vol.22, no.4, pp. 838-861.

OECD, (2011). *International migration outlook 2011*, Paris: OECD Publishing.

Olzak, S. (1992). *The dynamics of ethnic competition and conflict,* Stanford: Stanford University Press.

Papademetriou, D. and Terrazas, A. (2009). *Immigrants and the current economic crisis*, Washington, D.C: Migration Policy Institute, Available: http://www.migrationpolicy.org/pubs/lmi_recessionJan09.pdf [7 October 2012].

Quillian, L. (1995). 'Prejudice as a response to perceived group threat: Population composition and anti-immigrant and racial prejudice in Europe', *American Sociological Review,* vol. 60, no.4, pp. 586-611.

Racist Violence Recording Network, (2012). *Pilot phase conclusions: 1.10.2011-31.12.2011*, Available: http://www.unhcr.gr/1againstracism/2012-annual-report-of-the-racist-violence-recording-network/ [5 November 2012].

Schneider, S. (2008). 'Anti-immigrant attitudes in Europe: Outgroup size and perceived ethnic threat', *European Sociological Review*, vol. 24, no. 1, pp. 53-67.

Semyonov, M., Raijman, R. and Gorodzeisky, A. (2008). 'Foreigners' impact on European societies. Public views and perceptions in a cross-national comparative perspective', *International Journal of Comparative Sociology*, vol. 49, no.1, pp. 5-29.

Semyonov, M., Raijman, R. and Gorodzeisky, A. (2006). 'The rise of anti-foreigner sentiment in European societies, 1988-2000', *American Sociological Review*, vol. 71, no. 3, pp. 426-449.

Sherif M. (1967). *Group conflict and co-operation. Their social psychology,* London: Routledge and Kegan Paul.

Sherif, M. and Sherif, C. (1979). 'Research on intergroup relations', in Austin, W. and Worchel, S. (eds.) *The Social psychology of intergroup relations,* Monterrey: Brooks/Cole, pp. 7-32.

Sides, J. and Citrin, J. (2007). 'European opinion about immigration: The role of identities, interests and information', *British Journal of Political Science,* vol. 37, no.3, pp. 477-504.

Strabac, Z. and Listhaug, O. (2008). 'Anti-Muslim prejudice in Europe: A multi-level analysis of survey data from 30 countries', *Social Science Research,* vol.37, no.1, pp. 268-286.

Triandafyllidou, A. and Maroufof, M. (2011). *Greece*, Report prepared for the SOPEMI Meeting 2011, Available: http://www.eliamep.gr/wp-content/uploads/2012/06/SOPEMI-Greece-report_2011.pdf [29 Sept 2012].

Triandafyllidou, A. and Mikrakis A. (1995). 'Greece: A ghost wanders through the capital', in Baumgartl, B. and Favell, A. (eds), *The New Xenophobia in Europe,* London: Kluwer International Law, pp. 165-179.

Triandafyllidou, A. and Lazarescu, D. (2009). *The impact of the recent global economic crisis on migration. Preliminary insights from the South Eastern borders of the EU (Greece)*, Robert Schuman Centre for Advanced Studies, San Domenico di Fiesole (FI): European University Institute, Available: http://cadmus.eui.eu/bitstream/handle/1814/12995/ CARIM_ASN_2009_40.pdf?sequence=1 [1 November 2012].

Triandafyllidou, A. and Veikou, M. (2002). 'The hierarchy of Greekness. Ethnic and national identity considerations in Greek immigration policy', *Ethnicities*, vol. 2, no.2, pp. 189-208.

Wagner, U., Christ, O., Pettigrew, T., Stellmacher, J. and Wolf, C. (2006). 'Prejudice and minority proportion: Contact instead of threat effects', *Social Psychology Quarterly*, vol. 69, no.4, pp. 380-390.

Wilkes, R., Guppy, N. and Farris, L. (2008). 'No thanks, we're full: Individual characteristics, national context, and changing attitudes toward immigration', *International Migration Review*, vol.42, no.2, pp. 302-329.

Zimmermann, K., Kahanec, M., Constant, A., DeVoretz, D., Gataullina, L. and Zaiceva, A. (2007). *Study on the social and labour market integration of ethnic minorities*, IZA Discussion Papers Series-Discussion Paper No 16, Bonn: Institute for the Study of Labor (IZA), Available: http://www.iza.org/en/webcontent/publications/reports/report_pdfs/iza_report_16.pdf [12 October 2012].

CHAPTER TWELVE

PERSONAL PERCEPTIONS AND POLITICAL AFFILIATION SHAPING IMMIGRATION ATTITUDES IN TIMES OF FISCAL AUSTERITY: THE CASE OF GREECE

KATERINA ILIOU
NATIONAL CENTRE FOR SOCIAL RESEARCH

Abstract

Contemporary academic interest, political discourse and everyday discussion about the debt crisis in the Eurozone associate economic recession with social unrest. European citizens experience a process of transformation of their lives as well as the European vision of multicultural coexistence. The financial downturn, however, threatens prosperity, social balance and political stability. Immigration has become a first-line matter in political discourse and the mass media. Aspects such as the economy, employment, welfare, security, social trust and political position are directly and/or indirectly affected by the immigrants' inflow. Greece constitutes the eastern border of the European Union and has received a disproportionately large population of immigrants. Therefore, the expanded flow of immigrants and the debt crisis compose in Greece a complex frame of imbalance with special impacts on the social level. The present work aims at examining the perceptions of the Greek population about immigration as depicted in European attitudes surveys (ESS and the Eurobarometer) before and after emergence and experience of the economic crisis. We focus on personal perceptions (social trust, institutional trust, subjective well-being, human values) and political views (political interest, electoral participation, political ideology, party allegiance) that form anti-immigrant attitudes[1].

Introduction

The Eurozone crisis and the current financial downturn jeopardize the European populations' prosperity. Especially in Greece, the debt crisis and the imposed measures for fiscal control cause social imbalance and political change.

Immigration is a pivotal issue in political discourse and the mass media. Increasing flows of immigrants combined with the debt crisis create in Greece a complex frame with special impacts on the social level and on intergroup relations. Empirical evidence has shown that "*increasing diversity is linked to reduced provision of public goods and that increasing migration stunts the growth of the welfare state*" (Pevnick, 2009: 146).

This research aims at examining the perceptions of the Greek population about immigration as depicted in European attitudes surveys. For this purpose, data bases such as the European Social Survey (ESS) and the Eurobarometer are used as sources for a time series analysis of public attitudes about immigration, before and after the emergence and experience of the economic crisis.

Realistic Group Conflict Theory (Sherif, 1966) sets the theoretical framework for our research. According to this theory, the dominant group may have negative predispositions for the minority groups that pose a threat to its social power. Negative attitudes toward outgroups essentially stem from the view that certain prerogatives of the ingroup are threatened by those groups (Meuleman et al., 2009: 354). Feeling of social threat may increase in times of economic crisis, since social and economic resources are limited (Krysan, 2000: 153)[2]. Scare resources (in labour market, housing and welfare benefits) cause more intensive competition, which in turn may lead members of the majority group (Greeks) to become more skeptical about immigrants. At present, minority ethnic groups and natives compete for limited economic resources. In addition, natives experience dramatic changes in group privileges or status, something that incites intergroup conflict. Therefore, immigrants are perceived with negative features: (a) as the cause of unemployment and (b) as the abusers of the welfare state of Western democracies which results in fewer state subsidies for natives (Rydgen, 2008: 746). Immigrant skepticism may reflect on attitudes that the majority group expresses for immigration policy and the collective impact of immigration. Although most studies find small economic impacts of immigration on native population (Card et al., 2012: 1), personal perceptions and the political preferences of the natives may affect formation of attitudes towards the outgroup. We focus on attitude change after the emergence of the economic crisis, driven by levels of perceived intergoup conflict (Meuleman et al., 2009: 354). For this reason, Realistic Group Conflict Theory can be a sufficient theoretical context for observing and understanding possible change in Greeks' attitudes toward immigrants, especially after years of economic constraint.

According to Realistic Group Theory, increasing perceived intergroup threat (fostered by the present economic crisis) should lead the dominant group to hold more negative attitudes toward the outgroup of immigrants. Therefore, we pose the following research questions: (1) How prominent is immigration compared to the economic situation for Greek population (2) How extensive are anti-immigrant attitudes in the Greek population (3) Do personal perceptions (such as social trust, institutional trust, subjective well-being and personal values) affect attitudes toward immigration policy and the economic and cultural impact of immigration (4) Do political aspects (such as political interest, electoral participation, political ideology, and party allegiance) affect citizens' attitudes toward immigration policy and immigration impact and (5) Which factors (personal perceptions and/or political views) contribute to the prediction of attitudes toward immigration?

All above issues will be tackled in a time-series perspective aiming at highlighting trends and attitudes that depict Greek people through time. Our main purpose is to detect differences before and after the economic crisis in order to locate important factors that form attitudes toward immigrants in times of poverty and fear of everyday life deterioration. This way, we hope to shed light on new factors or old ones that reemerge for future detailed research.

The problem that matters: Economic situation vs. immigration

In order to find out what are the main concerns of Greek people for their country we analyzed for the years 2003-2012 a relevant question in the Eurobarometer ("According to your opinion what are the main two problems that Greece is facing at this moment?")[3].

In 2009, the year when Europe is beginning to experience the effects of the economic crisis, the "immigration" issue becomes significantly more salient as a matter of concern (Figure 12-1). From then on, the Greek people are concerned more and more about the "economic situation" and "unemployment", while concern about "rising prices/inflation" tends to fall. It seems that, especially this year, when Greeks confront the economic crisis for the first time, the "economic situation" and "unemployment" obviously concern them more. However, a quadrupling of Greek citizens' concern for "immigration" to their country in 2009 reveals a negative reaction toward foreigners. Yet, the issue of "immigration" does not appear to occupy the collective consciousness of Greek people, in contrast to the issue of the "economic situation".

Figure 12-1. Main concerns at national level (2003-2012)

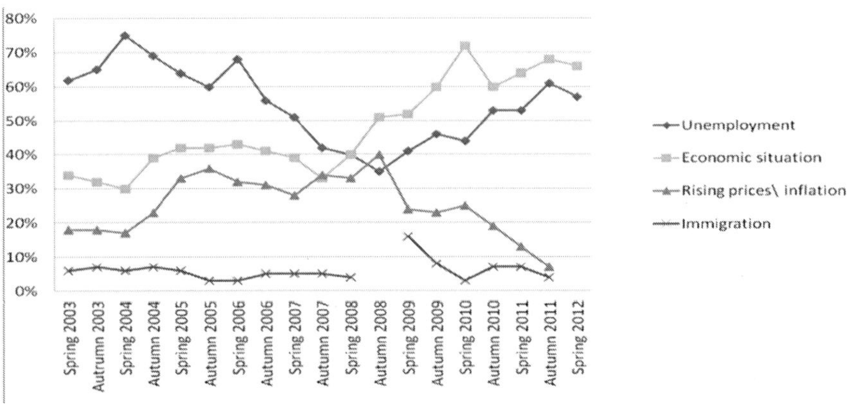

Although "immigration" appears to be a minor problem for Greeks through time, we examine the possibility that attitudes toward immigrants may change significantly after the economic crisis. In order to find out how extensive are Greeks' anti-immigrant attitudes, we use descriptive statistics (such as Means and Standard deviations) for three questions concerning Immigration Policy Attitudes in the European Social Survey (for the years 2002-2011)[4].

Through time, the Greeks express moderately negative attitudes (close to the scale mean) toward immigrants (Figure 12-2). In general, through time they are more negative toward immigrants "from poorer countries outside Europe" and for immigrants "of a different race or ethnic group". However, there is an increasing acceptance of immigrants "of the same race or ethnic group" through time. Nevertheless, analysis shows that Greek people express medium rejecting attitudes toward immigrants (close to the mean of the scale). Since the years of the economic crisis (2008/09) the negative attitudes toward immigration policy slightly rise, mostly against immigrants "from poorer countries outside Europe" and secondly against immigrants "of a different race or ethnic group".

Figure 12-2. Rejection of immigrants

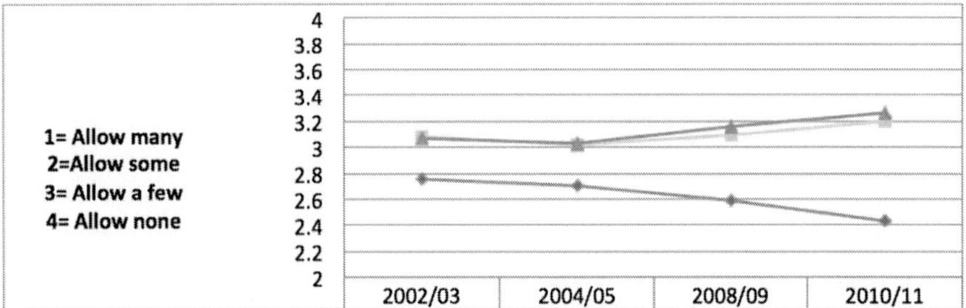

	2002/03	2004/05	2008/09	2010/11
Allow immigrants of same ethnic group	2.76	2.7	2.58	2.43
Allow immigrants of different ethnic group	3.08	3.02	3.09	3.2
Allow immigrants from poorer countries outside Europe	3.07	3.03	3.16	3.26

In addition, we use descriptive statistics (Means and Standard deviations) for three questions concerning attitudes about the immigration impact on the country in the European Social Survey (for the years 2002-2011)[5]. Although "immigration" appears to be a minor problem for Greeks through time, we examine the possibility that attitudes toward immigrants may change significantly after the economic crisis. In order to find out how extensive are Greeks' anti-immigrant attitudes we use descriptive statistics (such as Means and Standard deviations) for three questions concerning immigration policy attitudes in the European Social Survey (for the years 2002-2011)[6].

Greeks' attitudes toward immigrants appear to be rather negative over time (since answers are above the mean of the scale) (Figure 12-3). In general, Greek people perceive immigrants mostly as a collective threat for life in their country. At a second level, they perceive immigrants as a cultural threat and, finally, as an economic threat. Since the years of the economic crisis (2008/09) negative attitudes toward immigrants get worse. The belief that immigrants make Greece a "worse place to live" is more strongly supported and dominates Greek people's negative perceptions of immigrants. The perception of immigrants as a cultural and an economic threat is also reinforced. However, while until 2008/09 immigrants are mainly perceived as a cultural threat, after the emergence of the economic crisis they are mostly perceived as an economic threat and secondly as a cultural threat.

Figure 12-3. Negative attitudes toward immigrants

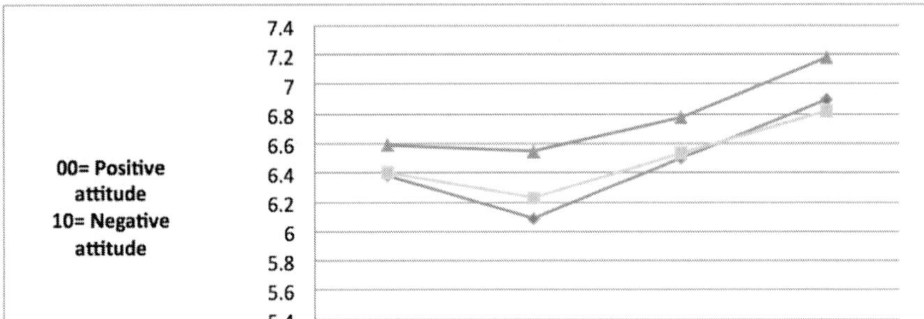

	2002/03	2004/05	2008/09	2010/11
Immigrants bad for the economy	6.38	6.09	6.5	6.9
Immigrants undermine cultural life	6.4	6.23	6.54	6.82
Immigrants make Greece a worse place to live	6.59	6.55	6.78	7.18

In conclusion, after the emergence of the economic crisis in the Eurozone, the "economic situation" and not "immigration" is the problem that matters for the Greek people. However, through time, Greeks appear rather skeptical about immigrants as far as attitudes toward immigration policy and impact of immigrants on the country are concerned. In agreement with the Greeks' main concern for the "economic situation", after the years of austerity (2008/09), the perception of foreigners as an economic threat takes priority over their perception as a cultural threat (in contrast to previous years). In a few words, the descriptive analyses demonstrate that the "economy matters" for Greeks during the years of economic resources restriction, since the economic situation plays an important role in Greeks' immigration attitudes.

These indications regarding reinforcement of anti-immigrant feelings lead to a need for further investigation about the factors that may be responsible for such a deterioration of interethnic attitudes.

Changes in personal aspects confound attitudes toward immigrants

In most studies, the theories about the dominant group's attitudes toward immigrants are tested using factors such as feelings for outgroup members, perceived threat, support or rejection of policies, etc. In our study we examine an additional set of different factors that may affect formation of Greeks' attitudes toward immigration policy and immigrants' impact. We focus on factors that may have significantly changed after 2008 due to the economic crisis. Also, it is worth stressing that our interest focuses on factors of an affective nature. Besides, affective factors determine in combination with cognitive factors the formation of attitudes. As Krysan (2000) notes, race-neutral factors may contribute to the formation of racial attitudes. Studies about exclusionist attitudes mostly focus on structural variables, economic interest, perceived threat, symbolic references (Fetzer, 2000; Scheepers et al., 2002; Dustmann & Preston, 2004; Sniderman et al., 2004; Semyonov et al., 2006; Sides and Citrin, 2007). Far fewer studies investigate the direct relationship between human values and attitudes (Davidof et al., 2008: 583). However, racial predispositions and basic values form individual preferences and attitudes toward immigration policy and immigrants (Sears & Funk, 1991: 13).

Important affective factors, likely to undergo change due to the loss of economic power by the dominant group, are "social trust", "institutional trust", "subjective well-being" and "human values". Specifically, "social trust" concerns the Greeks' perception of others being trustworthy and fair[7]. "Institutional trust" concerns the trust of dominant group members in various institutions[8]. "Subjective well-being" concerns a subjective perception of satisfaction with life and a feeling of happiness[9]. "Human values" concern a variety of ten values specified by Professor Shalom Schwartz for the European Social Survey[10] (Schwartz, 1992; Schwartz et al., 2001). As Davidof and et al. (2008: 584) point out: "*human values can be seen as abstract principles that underpin attitudes toward more specific objects, such as immigration*".

Descriptive analysis (Table 12-1) shows that "social trust" of the Greek population is slightly enhanced through time and even after the years of the economic crisis (2008/09). On the contrary, "institutional trust" and "subjective well-being" are declining through time and mostly after the years of the economic crisis. It appears that in times of economic downturn Greeks tend to reject the operation of institutions and express the feeling of depreciation of their lives. However, they appear to seek comfort through social contacts, since they trust others to a greater extent during the last years.

Table 12-1. Descriptive scale statistics for "social trust", "institutional trust", "subjective well-being"

	Round 1 (2002/03)		Round 2 (2004/05)		Round 4 (2008/09)		Round 5 (2010/11)	
	Mean	*SD*	Mean	SD	Mean	*SD*	Mean	*SD*
Social trust	3.44	2.012	3.63	1.957	3.64	1.949	3.73	1.940
Institutional trust	5.16	2.080	4.70	1.988	3.77	1.954	2.61	1.812
Subjective well-being	6.38	2.094	6.57	1.952	6.33	1.887	5.82	2.050

In order to test changes in human values we examine the frequency of endorsement by Greeks through time, focusing on the years before and after the economic crisis. According to the descriptive analysis (Figure 12-4) Greek people tend to consistently endorse "security[11]" and "benevolence[12]" more than any other value and "stimulation[13]" and "power[14]" less than any other value. After the years of the economic crisis, we do not observe significant changes in support or rejection of certain values. However, one important change emerges, since 2008/09, "universalism[15]" appears to be the most rejected value. In a few words, Greeks consistently through time endorse values that reflect support of stability, safety and protection of in-group members. At the same time, they reject values that reflect change and novelty, as well as social dominance. Since the emergence of the economic crisis, the endorsement and rejection of certain values do not appear to change, with the exception of the value of "universalism" that dramatically loses support after 2008/09. As a possible reaction to fiscal problems in Greece and the economic crisis in the Eurozone, Greeks tend to question the possibilities for protection of welfare worldwide. In this case, they tend to reject basic values of the European Union, such as tolerance and welfare protection.

Figure 12-4. Human values

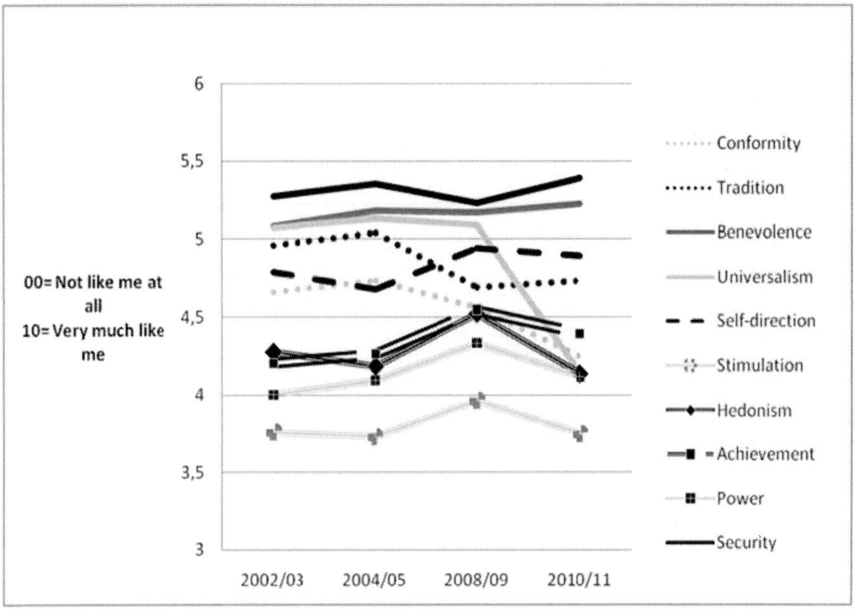

In order to further investigate if personal perceptions affect Greeks' attitudes toward immigration policy and the impact of immigration we ran Bivariate Correlations. Pearson indexes (r^2) of coherence are tested in time series for years before and after the economic crisis (2002-2011). We observe correlations between "social trust", "institutional trust", "subjective well-being" and "negative attitudes toward immigrants"[16] (Table 12-2). The correlation between "social trust" and "negative attitudes" is rather weak, but consistently inverse through time. The more that "social trust" increases the more negative attitudes toward immigrants decrease. No significant change is being observed after the onset of the economic crisis.

The correlation between "institutional trust" and "negative attitudes toward immigrants" is weak, but consistently negative through time. The less Greek people trust institutions, the more they hold negative attitudes toward immigrants. Also, the analysis shows that the correlation between "subjective well-being" and "negative attitudes toward immigrants" is weak, but consistent through time, even after the years of economic crisis. A perception of depreciation in personal well-being appears to be correlated to anti-immigrant attitudes.

Table 12-2. Correlations between "social trust", "institutional trust", "subjective well-being" and "negative attitudes toward immigrants" trough time

r^2	Social trust				Institutional trust				Subjective well-being			
Negative attitudes	**2002 /03**	**2004 /05**	**2008 /09**	**2010 /11**	**2002 /03**	**2004 /05**	**2008 /09**	**2010 /11**	**2002 /03**	**2004 /05**	**2008 /09**	**2010 /11**
Rejection of immigrants of same race	-0.12	-0.164	-0.059	-0.126	-0.098	-0.109	-0.51	-0.145		-0.044	-0.048	-0.115
Rejection of immigrants from different race	-0.222	-0.203	-0.137	-0.157	-0.165	-0.124	-0.071	-0.112	-0.14	-0.086	-0.105	-0.109
Rejection of immigrants from poorer countries	-0.213	-0.207	-0.121	-0.162	-0.146	-0.138	-0.047	-0.105	-0.125	-0.085	-0.112	-0.102
Negative impact on economy	-0.021	-0.263	-0.172	-0.2	-0.199	-0.2	-0.213	-0.234	-0.178	-0.132	-0.156	-0.153

r^2	Social trust				Institutional trust				Subjective well-being			
Negative impact on cultural life	-0.252	-0.261	-0.134	-0.228	-0.222	-0.183	-0.172	-0.213	-0.152	-0.115	-0.169	-0.17
Negative impact on country as place to live	-0.222	-0.279	-0.134	-0.205	-0.223	-0.209	-0.141	-0.235	-0.165	-0.131	-0.157	-0.16

In order to investigate if endorsement of certain human values affects the Greek's attitudes toward immigrants we ran Bivariate Correlations. Pearson indexes of coherence are tested in a time series for the years 2002-2011. Specifically, we explored the correlations between "conformity", "tradition", "benevolence", "universalism", "self-direction", "stimulation", "hedonism", "achievement", "power", "security" and "negative attitudes toward immigrants". A significant correlation is observed between "negative attitudes toward immigrants" and the following human values: "tradition[17]", "universalism" and "self-direction[18]". The analyses show that those who endorse "tradition" tend to express anti-immigrant attitudes consistently though time, while those who endorse "universlalism" and "self-direction" tend to express anti-immigrant attitudes to a lesser extent. These correlations do not appear to change significantly after the onset of the economic crisis.

Consequently, the descriptive analyses show slight differences in the personal perceptions of Greeks through time. After 2008/09, they tend to trust institutions less than previous years, and they express a feeling of depreciation of personal well-being. Nevertheless, the economic crisis appears to lead to a reinforcement of trust in others. As far as human values are concerned, it is worth stressing that after years of an economic downturn in the Eurozone, Greeks appear to reject "universalism" considerably more than during the times of European prosperity. It appears that Greek people, whose personal life conditions are perceived to be worse than the past, reduce their expectations from institutions and turn away from universal values for protection of all humans. At the same time, they turn for support to other people from their social environment.

Attempting to find out if personal perceptions that appear to change after the economic crisis may affect Greek people's attitudes toward immigrants, we ascertain that the effect of such factors does not differentiate them after the onset of the economic crisis. Therefore, personal aspects such as "social trust", "institutional trust", "subjective well-being"and endorsement of some specific "human values" appear consistently through time to contribute to formation of attitudes toward immigrants. The economic crisis does not change the relationship between these personal perceptions and Greeks' attitudes toward immigration policy and the impact of immigrants.

Political imbalance and immigration attitudes

Political attitudes affect formation of attitudes toward policies concerning immigrants. Many researchers focus on the role of intergroup affect in public opinion toward government policies in general and immigration policies in particular (Cottrell et al., 2010). In most cases, social scientists focus on support or rejection of practices that facilitate social integration of immigrants and stem from relevant immigration policies. In Greece, after 2008/09, the political landscape changes dramatically, reflecting the abrupt economic decline and fiscal crisis. Since then, the two largest political parties (PASOK and New Democracy), that alternated in the governing of Greece for the last thirty years, tend to lose support. What is more, radical right-wing parties appear to gain support and one such party obtains a high percentage of votes in 2012 elections. Van der Brug and al. (2000: 80) stress that recent studies demonstrate that even though voters of anti-immigrant parties tend to hold hostile attitudes toward foreigners, "*broader ideological concerns are more important determinants of their vote*" (Kitschelt, 1995; Tillie & Fennema, 1998).

Indications that political imbalance and reinforcement of radical right-wing parties may lead to social unrest and especially anti-immigrant attitudes is of great interest for further research. However, we do not focus directly on political preferences of Greek citizens, but rather on the indirect political factors that may affect their attitudes toward immigrants.

Specifically, we examine changes in political factors such as: "political interest", "electoral participation", "political ideology" and "party allegiance". "Political interest" concerns personal interest for politics in general[19]. "Electoral participation" concerns voting in elections for the national government[20]. "Political ideology" concerns self-placement on the left-right scale[21]. "Party allegiance" concerns personal preference for a specific political party[22].

Descriptive analysis aims at locating possible changes in political attitudes after the emergence of the economic crisis. It appears that "political interest" is steadily declining since 2004 and to a much more extent after the onset of the economic crisis (2008/09) (Figure 12-5).

What is more, since 2004/05 we witness a decline in the participation of Greek citizens in parliamentary elections (Figure 12-6). This decline is more intense after the emergence of the economic crisis. Time series results highlight a process of depoliticization that increasingly characterizes Greece and Western countries in general, and is growing rapidly in the recent years in parallel with the socio-economic crisis.

Figure 12-5. Political interest

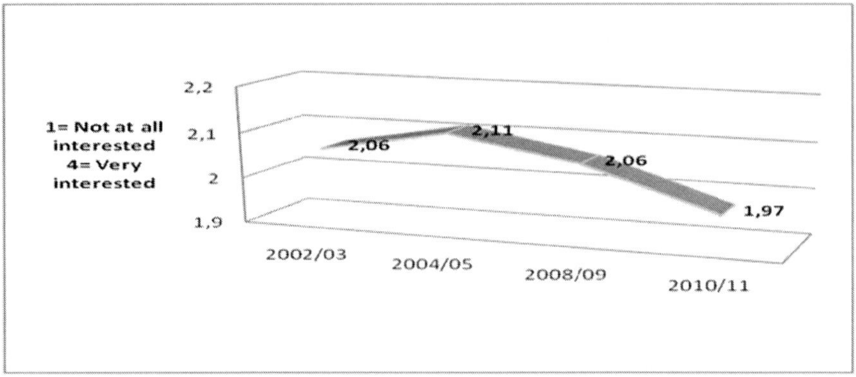

Figure 12-6. Electoral participation

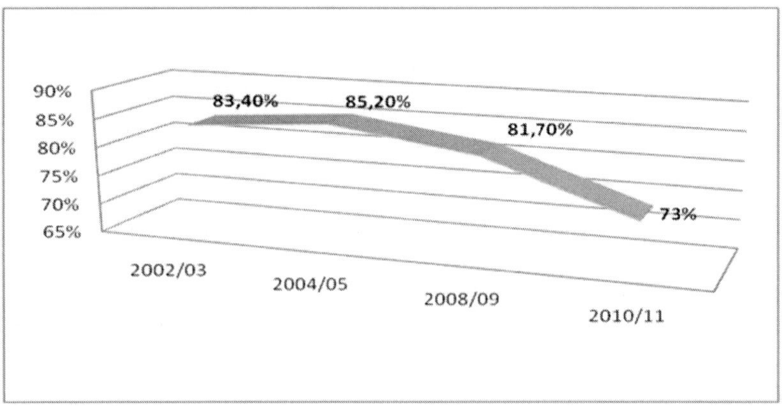

As far as "political ideology" and "party allegiance" are concerned, since 2004/05 a shift towards the center left is noted. This shift was also reflected in the parliamentary elections of 2008/09 onwards (Figure 12-7). Also, since the economic crisis (2008/09) we observe rapidly declining rates regarding allegiance, faith and loyalty of Greek voters in the two major parties (PASOK and New Democracy[23]) (Figure 12-8). In a few words, the economic crisis appears to change the political landscape in Greece. Citizens facing deterioration of living standards, unemployment and poverty risk react by rejecting the two major political parties that govern Greece for the last thirty years and seek political support from ideologies closer to the left.

Figure 12-7. Political ideology

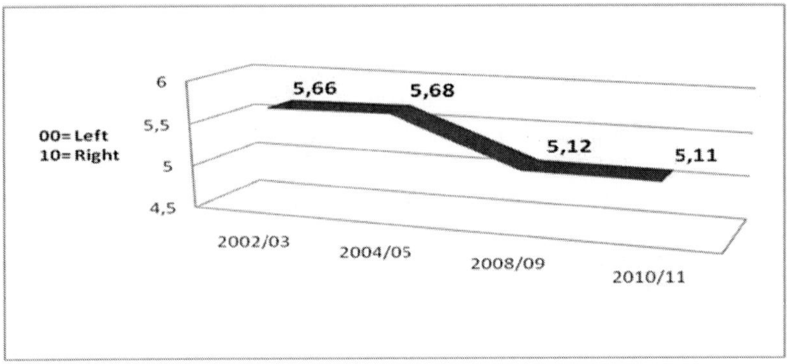

Figure 12-8. Party allegiance

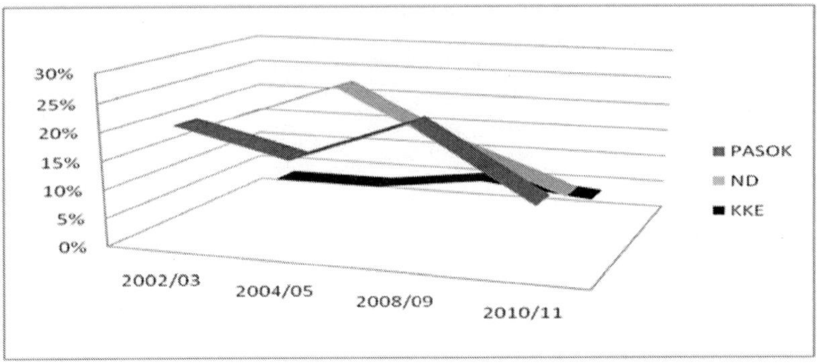

The changes in political attitudes of the Greek people could lead to changes in attitudes toward immigrants as well. In order to test this hypothesis we ran Bivariate Correlations between: "political interest", "electoral participation", "political ideology", "party allegiance" and "negative attitudes toward immigrants"[24]. Pearson indexes of coherence (r^2) are tested in time series for the years before and after the economic crisis (2002-2011) (Table 12-3).

Table 12-3: Pearson indexes between "political interest", "political ideology" and "negative attitudes toward immigrants"

r^2	Political interest				Political ideology			
Negative attitudes	**2002 /03**	**2004 /05**	**2008 /09**	**2010 /11**	**2002 /03**	**2004 /05**	**2008 /09**	**2010 /11**
Rejection of immigrants of same race	-0.129	-0.108	-0.113	-0.14	0.07	0.141	0.163	0.112
Rejection of immigrants from different race	-0.142	-0.104	-0.118	-0.137	0.119	0.194	0.176	0.189
Rejection of immigrants from poorer countries	-0.122	-0.085	-0.105	-0.137	0.119	0.205	0.208	0.212
Negative impact on economy	-0.13	-0.111	-0.159	-0.114	0.106	0.179	0.132	0.14
Negative impact on cultural life	-0.12	-0.076	-0.179	-0.121	0.11	0.173	0.179	0.142
Negative impact on country as place to live	-0.064	-0.093	-0.133	-0.095	0.087	0.157	0.106	0.108

According to the results, "electoral participation" and "party allegiance" do not consistently correlate with "negative attitudes toward immigrants" for the time 2002-2011. Therefore, we present correlations only between "political interest", "political ideology" and "negative attitudes toward immigrants" (Table 12-3). The correlation between "political interest" and "negative attitudes toward immigration" is inverse throughout the time series, i.e., as political interest declines the negative attitudes toward immigrants are strengthened. The correlation between "political ideology" and "negative attitudes toward immigrants" is consistently positive for the years 2002-2011; espousal of conservative ideologies is associated with anti-immigrant attitudes. According to previous results (Figure 12-5), a decline of interest in politics may be accompanied by a rise in "negative attitudes toward immigrants". On the contrary, since support of the Greeks for the left ideology is increasing during the last years, the "negative attitudes toward immigrants" may decrease.

Testing a model for prediction of immigration attitudes

In order to test which factors consistently through time contribute to the prediction of Greeks' attitudes toward immigration policy and socio-economic impact of immigrants we ran Stepwise Linear Regression. The analysis was repeated for each year of field research (2002-2011). We tested the following model:

Figure 12-9. Anti-immigrant attitudes model

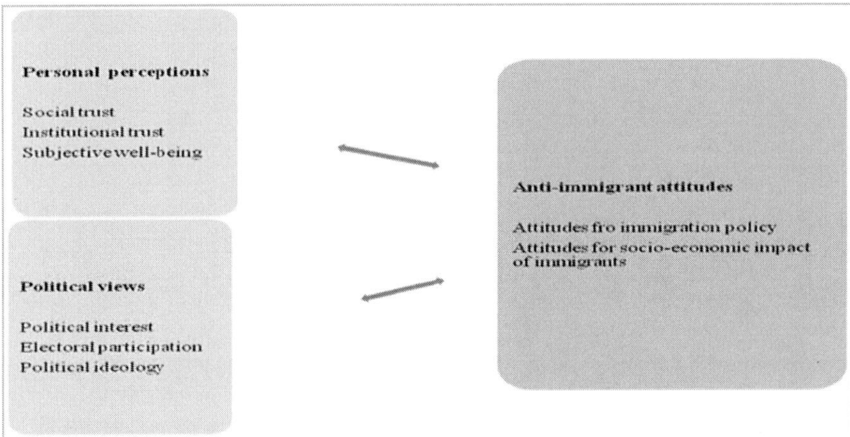

In general, no model was found in the time-series analysis able to interpret factors that consistently form Greeks' attitudes toward immigrants. For different years of field research, "anti-immigrant attitudes" appear to be affected either by the "personal perceptions" or by the "political views" of Greeks. Since no model is verified though time (for the years 2002-2011), the question remains and points to a new direction for future research about factors that form attitudes toward immigrants before and after the economic crisis.

Summary and conclusions

Summarizing the results of our research it is worth pointing that:

The economic crisis is the dominant problem that concerns the Greek population and not immigration. However, in 2008/09 the anti-immigrant attitudes are strengthened. Besides, since then, Greeks tend slightly to support more strict immigration policies and perceive foreigners as an economic threat, while during the previous period perception of immigrants as a cultural threat was dominant. It appears that the economic crisis is the major concern for Greeks, and in agreement with this aspect, immigrants represent an economic threat. In this case, according to Realistic Group Conflict Theory, rejection of the out-group by the dominant group is possible. Consequently, the economic crisis may intensify intergroup conflict.

We tested intergroup conflict theory by focusing on changes in political views and personal perceptions after the onset of the economic crisis. Restriction of resources that might lead to intergroup conflict is verified by the Greeks' personal perceptions. After 2008/09, members of the dominant group tend to trust institutions less than before, express feelings of deterioration of personal well-being, as well as rejection of the value of "universalism". Besides, "political interest" and "electoral participation" of Greeks decrease after 2008/09, pointing to a loss of interest for gaining social power through politics. The significant withdrawal of interest of the dominant group for political control leads unavoidably to restriction of political power and relevant socio-political resources. In this case, immigrants may play the role of the scapegoat and absorb rejection for a real economic threat (in addition to other factors stemming from fiscal austerity). Statistical analysis (Bivariate correlations and Regression analyses), however, point out that the economic crisis does not change relations between personal perceptions, political views and attitudes toward immigrants. What is more, factors concerning personal perceptions and political views do not appear to predict attitudes toward immigrants though time.

Our research highlights that there are interesting indications for a deterioration of intergroup relations after the economic crisis. Since 2008/09, when the economic crisis emerged in the Eurozone, Greece has been the center of international interest because of immense economic deprivation, social unrest, and political uncertainty. The majority of Greek people are in danger of unemployment, deprivation of economic resources, strict deterioration of living conditions, and an upsurge of psychological burdens, which constitute "realistic threats"[25] (Durrheim et al., 2011). Such conditions may unavoidably lead to social conflict and enmity for outgroups such as immigrants. We stress that the personal perceptions of Greeks in international research depict a deterioration of personal and collective life conditions, while their political views reflect lack of faith in the political system for overcoming the economic crisis. Negative beliefs and values concerning foreigners may be used for justification of negative attitudes toward them. Besides, "*fear and threat are easily communicated and create powerful social norms that can be used to justify bigotry, discrimination, and racism*" (Stangor et al., 2003: 275). Therefore, it is important to examine values and feelings as factors designating racial attitudes and interethnic relations. Our research continues the existing discourse on anti-immigrant attitudes, which focuses on factors such as educational level, economic interest, human values, perceived threat, voting behavior, economic context and size of immigrant population (Meuleman et al., 2009).

The present article, therefore, may contribute to the debate regarding the causes and responses to intergroup conflict in times of socio-economic crisis. Jakcman (1994) stresses that intergroup conflict may be used by the dominant group as an immediate way to preserve anti-racial policy attitudes. She notes that "*racial policy attitudes are not an outgrowth of personal prejudice, but a product of institutions and inequalities in our society—an ideology derived to defend the dominant's group interests*"[26]. The fact that Greeks appear to express a deprivation of socio-economic resources may abet competition for restricted resources and social conflicts with immigrants. However, the fact that the members of the dominant group reject political resources as a means for gaining social power puts contemporary political and social fields at risk of degradation. Future research should focus on factors depicting the dominant group's efforts for gaining social power and preserving personal and collective social status. In a few words, taking social unrest and intergroup conflict for granted (as long as economic restriction exists), we should try to find out what will replace political power as a means for gaining social power. Scientists from different fields already have pointed out that majorities might turn to more reactionary ways to confront the economic deprivation and to inhibit the minorities' claims for equal rights and opportunities, an alternative that does injustice to Greek history and to conceptions of modern democratic societies.

Notes

[1] We thank Angelo Tramountanis (political scientist) for helpful comments on determination of political views for this article.

[2] Krysan (2000, p.153) points out that perceived threat is not an objective assessment but "is connected to perceptions of incompatible interests and fraternal deprivation".

[3] "According to your opinion what are the main two problems that Greece is facing at this moment? – Unemployment, Crime, Economic situation, Razing price, Inflation, Health and care system, Immigration, Terrorism, Pensions, Taxation, The educational system, Housing, Protection of the environment, Public transport, Defense/Foreign affairs, Other, Don't know." (Standard Eurobarometer 59, 60.1, 61, 62, 63.4, 64, 65, 66, 67, 68, 69, 71, 72, 73, 74, 75, 76).

[4] "To what extent do you think the country should allow people of the same race or ethnic group as most people to come to live here? / How about people of a different race or ethnic group from most people? / How about people from poorer countries outside Europe? – Allow many to come and live here/Allow some/Allow a few/Allow none /Don't know" (ESS, Round 1, 2, 4, 5).

[5] "Would you say it is generally bad or good for country's economy that people come to live here from other countries?/Would you say that the country's cultural life is generally undermined or enriched by people coming to live here from other countries?/Is the country made a worse or a better place to live by people coming to live here from other countries?" (ESS, Round 1, 2, 4, 5).

[6] "To what extent do you think the country should allow people of the same race or ethnic group as most people to come to live here? / How about people of a different race or ethnic group from most people?/How about people from poorer countries outside Europe?" (ESS, Round 1, 2, 4, 5).

[7] Data derived from the following questions: "Would you say that most people can be trusted, or that you can't be too careful in dealing with people? / Do you think that most people would try to take advantage of you if they got the chance, or would they try to be fair?" Code values vary from 00 = You can't be too careful/Most people would try to take advantage of me to 10 = Most people can be trusted/Most people would try to be fair" (European Social Survey, Round 1, 2, 4, 5). We calculated mean of answers to relevant questions for "Social trust" repeatedly for each Round.

[8] Data derived from one question: "How much you personally trust each of these institutions?—The country's parliament/The legal system/The police/Politicians/ Political parties/The European Parliament/The United Nations" (European Social

Survey, Round 1, 2, 4, 5). We calculated mean of answers to the relevant question repeatedly for each Round.

[9] Data derived from the following questions: "All things considered how satisfied are you with your life as a whole nowadays/Taking all things together, how happy would you say you are?" Code values are: "00=Extremely dissatisfied/Extremely unhappy, 10=Extremely satisfied/Extremely happy" (European Social Survey, Round 1, 2, 4, 5). We calculated mean of answers to relevant question repeatedly for each Round.

[10] In detail these values are specified as follows: Conformity, Tradition, Benevolence, Universalism, Self-Direction, Stimulation, Hedonism, Achievement, Power, Security.

[11] Meaning "safety, harmony, and stability of society, of relations, and of self" as defined in the European Social Survey Education Net (ESS EduNet), (http://essedunet.nsd.uib.no/cms/topics/1/1/1.html).

[12] Meaning "preserving and enhancing the welfare of those with whom one is in frequent personal contact (the in-group)" as defined in the European Social Survey Education Net (ESS EduNet) (http://essedunet.nsd.uib.no/cms/ topics/1/1/1.html).

[13] Meaning "excitement, novelty, and challenge in life" as defined in the European Social Survey Education Net (ESS EduNet) (http://essedunet.nsd.uib.no/cms/topics/1/1/1.html).

[14] Meaning "social status and prestige, control or dominance over people and resources" as defined in European Social Survey Education Net (ESS EduNet) (http://essedunet.nsd.uib.no/cms/topics/1/1/1.html).

[15] Meaning "understanding, appreciation, tolerance, and protection for the welfare of all people and for nature" as defined in European Social Survey Education Net (ESS EduNet) (http://essedunet.nsd.uib.no/cms/ topics/1/1/1.html).

[16] "Negative attitudes toward immigrants" concern attitudes toward immigration policy (rejection of immigrants of same race, rejection of immigrants from different race, rejection of immigrants from poorer countries) and attitudes for impact of immigrants (negative impact for economy, negative impact for cultural life, negative impact for country to live).

[17] Meaning "Respect, commitment, and acceptance of the customs and ideas that traditional culture or religion provide the self" as defined in the European Social Survey Education Net (ESS EduNet) (http://essedunet.nsd.uib.no/cms/topics/1/1/1.html).

[18] Meaning "Independent thought and action; choosing, creating, exploring" as defined in the European Social Survey Education Net (ESS EduNet) (http://essedunet.nsd.uib.no/ cms/topics/1/1/1.html).

[19] Data derived from one question: "How interested would you say you are in politics?" Code values vary from 1=Not at all interested to 4=Very interested" (answers recoded) (European Social Survey, Round 1, 2, 4, 5). We calculated the mean of the answers to the relevant question repeatedly for each Round.

[20] Data derived from one question: "Some people don't vote nowadays for one reason or another. Did you vote in the last national election?" Code values are: "Yes/No/Not eligible to vote" (European Social Survey, Round 1, 2, 4, 5). We

calculated the mean of the answers to the relevant question repeatedly for each Round.

[21] Data derived from one question: "In politics people sometimes talk of "left" and "right". Where would you place yourself on this scale, where 0 means the left and 10 means the right?" (European Social Survey, Round 1, 2, 4, 5). We calculated mean of answers to relevant question repeatedly for each Round.

[22] Data derived from one question: "Which political party you feel closer to than all other parties?" (European Social Survey, Round 1, 2, 4, 5). We calculated mean of answers to relevant question repeatedly for each Round.

[23] PASOK (Panhellenic Socialist Movement) is the social democratic party and New Democracy (ND) is the main centre-right political party.

[24] "Negative attitudes toward immigrants" concern negative attitudes toward immigration policy and negative attitudes regarding the impact of immigrants on Greece.

[25] "Realistic threats centre on conflicts over collective possessions and rights which can mostly be defined in material terms (e.g., competition for jobs, housing, access to social services, political power, etc.") (Durrheim et al. 2011: 32).

[26] As cited by Krysan (2000:151).

References

Card, D., Dustmann, Ch., Preston, I. (2012). *Immigration, wages, and compositional amenities*. Norface Migration, Discussion Paper No. 2012-13.

Cottrell, C., Richards, D.A.R., Nichols, A.L. (2010). 'Predicting policy attitudes from general prejudice versus specific intergroup emotions', *Journal of Experimental Social Psychology*, vol. 46, pp. 247-254.

Davidof, E., Meuleman, B, Billiet, J, Schmidt, P. (2008). 'Values and support for immigration: a cross-country comparison', *European Sociological Review*, vol. 24, no.5, pp. 583-599.

Durrheim, K., Dixon, J, Tredoux, C., Eaton, L, Quayle, M, Clack, B. (2011). 'Predicting support for racial transformation policies: Intergroup threat, racial prejudice, sense of group entitlement and strength of identification', *European Journal of Social Psychology*, vol. 41, no.1, pp. 23-41.

Dustmann, C. and Preston, I. (2004). *Racial and economic factors in attitudes to immigration*, London: CreAM.

Fetzer, J.S. (2000). 'Economic self-interest or cultural marginality? Anti-immigration sentiment and nativist political movements in France, Germany and the USA', *Journal of Ethnic and Migration Studies*, vol. 26, no.1, pp. 5-23.

Jakcman, M.R. (1994). *The velvet glove: Paternalism and conflict in gender, class, and race relations*, Berkeley: University of California Press.

Kitschelt, H. (1995). *The radical right in western Europe. A comparative analysis*, Ann Arbor, MI: University of Michigan Press.

Krysan, M. (2000). 'Prejudice, politics, and public opinion: Understanding the sources of racial policy attitudes', *Annual Review of Sociology*, vol. 26, pp. 135-168.

Meuleman, B., Davidof, E., Billiet, J. (2009). 'Changing attitudes toward immigration in Europe, 2002-2007: A dynamic group conflict theory approach', *Social Science Research*, vol. 38, no.2, pp. 352-365.

Pevnick, R. (2009). 'Social trust and the ethics of immigration policy', *The Journal of Political Philosophy*, vol. 17, no.2, pp. 146-167.

Rydgen, J. (2008). 'Immigration sceptics, xenophobes or racists? Radical right-wing voting in six West European countries', *European Journal of Political Research*, vol. 47, no. 6, pp. 737-765.

Scheepers, P., Gijsberts, M. and Coenders, M. (2002). 'Ethnic exclusion in European countries. Public opposition to civil rights for legal migrants as a response to perceived ethnic threat', *European Sociological Review*, vol. 18, no. 1, pp. 17-34.

Schwartz, S.H, (1992). 'Universals in the content and structure of values: theoretical advances and empirical tests in 20 countries', in Zanna, P. (ed.), *Advances in Experimental Social Psychology*, vol.25, San Diego: Academic Press, pp. 1-65.

Schwartz, S.H, Melech, G., Lehmann, A., Burgess, S., Harris, M., Owens, V. (2001). 'Extending the cross-cultural validity of the theory of basic human values with a different method of measurement', *Journal of Cross-Cultural Psychology*, vol. 32, no. 5, pp. 519-542.

Sears, D.O., Funk C.L. (1991). 'The Role of self-interest in social and political attitudes', *Advances in Experimental Social Psychology*, vol. 24, pp. 1-91

Semyonov, M., Raijma, R., and Gorodzeisky, A. (2006). 'The rise of anti-foreigner sentiment in European societies, 1988-2000', *American Sociological Review*, vol. 71, no. 3, pp. 426-449.

Sherif, M. (1966). *Group conflict and cooperation*, London: Routledge & Kegan Paul.

Sides, J. and Citrin, J. (2007). 'European opinion about immigration: the role of identities, interests and information', *British Journal of Political Science*, vol. 37, no. 3, pp. 477-504.

Sniderman, P.M., Hagendoorn, L., and Prior, M. (2004). 'Predisposing factors and situational triggers: exclusionary reactions to immigrant minorities', *American Political Science Review*, vol. 98, pp. 35-49.

Stangor, Ch., Leavy, S.P. (2003). 'Intergroup beliefs: Investigations from the social side', *Advances in Experimental Social Psychology*, vol. 38, pp. 243-281.

Tillie, J. & Fennema, M. (1998). 'A rational choice for the extreme right', *Acta Politica*, vol. 33, pp. 223-249.

Van der Brug, W., Fennema, M., Tillie, J. (2000). 'Anti-immigrant parties in Europe: Ideological or protest vote?', *European Journal of Political Research*, vol. 37, no.1, pp. 77-102.

CHAPTER THIRTEEN

RELIGIOSITY, TRUST AND TOLERANCE IN TIMES OF RECESSION: THE CASES OF SPAIN AND GREECE

THEONI STATHOPOULOU
NATIONAL CENTRE FOR SOCIAL RESEARCH
AND ANASTASIA KOSTAKI
ATHENS UNIVERSITY OF ECONOMICS AND BUSINESS

Abstract

In this chapter, we focus on the implications of the Eurozone debt crisis for social cohesion by analyzing the varying levels of trust and tolerance in two South European countries mostly affected by austerity measures. Spain and Greece are used as case studies in order to examine the factors affecting interpersonal trust, trust in institutions and tolerance for diverse others as well as tolerance for political extremes. Based on data drawn from the European Social Survey for the years 2009 and 2011, our analysis showed a significant decrease of institutional trust in both countries followed by an increase in interpersonal trust. Tolerance towards immigrants, especially those from poorer countries decreased mainly in Greece. In the case of Greece, religiosity has a negative impact on tolerance and social trust. Education was found to be the strongest predictor of trust and tolerance.

Introduction

The current recession in the Eurozone has triggered a lot of public and academic debate on the character of the crisis, its causes and its particular effects on the economy, society and politics. More conspicuous from a sociological point of view are the implications of the crisis for social cohesion. Economic uncertainty, austerity measures and unemployment have led large segments of the population in the countries mostly hit by the crisis to the brink of social exclusion and poverty. Thus solidarity, trust in others, and tolerance of difference are seriously threatened by the scarcity of material resources.

In particular, the problem of tolerance has attracted scholarly attention long before the emergence of the crisis due to the diversity-challenges imposed by immigration, legal and illegal, in Europe. Old and new host countries have to deal with integration policies, naturalization and asylum procedures, second-generation immigrants. The fast-growing literature on the impact of ethnic diversity on native populations[1] either in terms of plurality (Triandafyllidou, 2011) or in terms of the existing social capital (i.e the generalized trust in society and its institutions) (Hooghe et al., 2008; Gesthuizen, van der Meer and Scheepers, 2009; Kesler and Bloemraad, 2010; Kesler and Demireva, 2011; Savelkul, Gesthuizen and Sheepers, 2011; Sturgis et al., 2011) is centered along the lines of the two-fold schema: trust and tolerance. Moreover, stemming from Allport's seminal work on prejudice (1962) much of the existing literature pays attention to religious involvement as a predictor of intolerance (Gibson, 1992a, 1992b; Laythe et al., 2002; Burdette et al., 2005)

Indeed, acceptance of diverse others sets tolerance as a precondition, and tolerance requires in turn a minimum element of trust. Belief in other's trustworthiness can be derived by internalized norms and values during the early childhood, the socializing process and learning from participation in social life. The kind of conviction such a belief implies is sometimes interconnected to religion as a system of values affecting moral consciousness, social commitment and collective solidarity, thus generating a specific relationship between "faith and trust"[2] (Stathopoulou, 2010). Faith as expressed through religious beliefs and practices shares in this respect the same value domain with trust but on the contrary has a different orientation as "the first pertains to an individual universe and the latter leads to the public space, the sphere of *civitas*" (Stathopoulou, 2010:194), the sphere of institutions.

The link between social trust and trust in institutions or political trust, lies at the core of social capital research and theory. In a recent publication, Newton and Zmerli (2011) have summed up the divergent approaches on the issue, distinguishing between three types of association: a compatible one, which accepts the intertwined relationship of social and institutional trust, an incompatible one that does not affirm the positive interrelation [3] and a conditional one according to which social and institutional trust "may be positively associated in some cases but not necessarily in most or all cases" (Newton and Zmerli, 2011: 175). The influence of individual-level factors such as education and interest in politics is evident in the case of the incompatible type of association.

The individual-centered theories consider trust as a personality trait formed, as noted above, in early life, persistent and resistant to external events (Mishler and Rose, 2001; Uslaner, 2002) or culturally defined through civic participation in various sorts of organizations (Putnam, 1995). In opposition, institutional theories focus on the effective functioning of institutions, political and non-political, as the generator of trust [4] (Delhey and Newton, 2005; Norris and Davis, 2007).

Most of these perspectives examine to a varying degree the role of religion in explaining and forming social and institutional trust (Daniels and von der Ruhr, 2010). As put by Koenig (2008: 453): "Individual religiosity and congregational life sometimes, but not always, enhance social capital. And the sort of social capital generated by religion sometimes bridges the boundaries of ethnicity, status and class, while in other cases it bonds communities precisely along such boundaries".

Several of the empirical approaches in the existing literature scrutinize the relation of religious involvement and trust across different confessional frames. In this respect, an analysis of the EVS data (1999-2000) (van Oorshot, Arts and Gelissen, 2006) has shown that Catholics have less trust in institutions than Protestants and more trust in national than supra-national institutions (Nelsen and Guth, 2003). Adequate analyses on a country level frequently cut across denominational lines revealing patterns of association among different measures of religiosity and levels of trust (Stromsnes, 2008; Lehmann, 2008; Stathopoulou, 2010; Stathopoulou, 2011). The co-existence of opposing trends, secular and religious, is apparent specifically in the European setting denoting a fluid picture of religious identification, belief and practice where religious revival goes hand in hand with religious decline. Most conspicuous among related research addressing this issue are the contributions of Halman and Draulans (2006), Miklos Tomka (Tomka, 2006; Tomka and Yurash, 2006; ReÏvay and Tomka, 2007) and Yves Lambert (2004) who have shown that there is not a clear cut picture of religiosity in Europe. People who proclaim themselves as indifferent to religious dogma show a significant frequency of church-attendance or praying. Additionally, people who are strongly opposed to the church as an institution appear to be advocating the necessity of church in social life[5] (Davie, 2007; Voas, 2009).

What lies behind this state of affairs is the notion of secularization and its relation to modernity. Almost three decades after the secularization thesis presented by Peter Berger (1967) in the *Sacred Canopy* the same author argued: "the world today with some exceptions [...] is as furiously religious as it ever was, and in some places more so than ever" (Berger, 1999: 2). In between this period of time, many changes have challenged the established view that religiosity was incompatible with modernity. To mention but a few, the fall of socialist regimes, growing immigrant flows, and European enlargement were some of them. In an attempt to explain religious vitality and religious pluralism, rational choice theorists (Finke and Stark, 2003) have argued that competition between religious institutions has offered new options for believers-"clients" in an ever-growing religious "market". This line of thought is very close to the privatization of religion (Casanova, 1994) and the various types of secularization (i.e., societal, organizational, individual) indicated by Dobbelaere (2002). Religiosity, according to these approaches, is a personal matter of taste and selection mainly within the context of western Christendom that presupposes a certain view of modernizing and secularizing paths.[6] Eastern developments in this respect call for other methodological approaches of the religious phenomenon, able to address the specificities of secularization in a different setting (Tomka, 2006; Flere, 2008; Morozov, 2008; Brechon, 2009).

Spain and Greece as case studies

In order to examine the relationship of religiosity, trust, and tolerance in the context of economic recession, we have chosen two countries which are particularly affected by the debt crisis[7]. Spain and Greece share some common features as regards their political trajectories, religious profile and immigration patterns.

First, they have both experienced civil war and dictatorship, Spain before the 2nd World War (1936-1939), Greece soon after (1946-1949). Dictatorship in Greece had a short duration (1967-1974) compared to that of Franco's in Spain but left the same negative imprint in social and political life. These experiences have to a certain extent shaped the political culture in the two countries, defining the levels of political cynicism and political participation. Second, though Spain is a pronounced Catholic country, it has undergone through various stages of secularization[8]. Greece's religious homogeneity has remained intact until the '90s when immigration challenged established identities. In this respect, Greece has much more in common with Ireland or Poland in terms of secularity. The two countries also share the same characteristics as regards the visibility of the established church[9] and the diffusion of religion in everyday life. The latter are demonstrated in the statistical figures on religiosity; according to ESS data, Greek respondents scored very high in 2002 when 23.5% declared to be very religious, while only 9% declared the same in 2011.

Moreover, the religious composition is similar in both countries. In Spain, Roman Catholics are between 93% and 94%, while in Greece the percentage of the Orthodox population is between 93.3% and 93.8%.[10] The share of Muslims is almost the same in both countries (2,3% in Greece[11], 2,8% in Spain. Catholicism in Spain, as Orthodoxy in Greece, is intertwined with national identity. As Triandafyllidou notes (2011: 17): "Spain has strong centrifugal tendencies due to regional nationalisms [and] the nation is contested by minority nationalisms".

Third, Greece and Spain are among the new host countries of immigrants in Europe, thus sharing the same immigration policy concerns. Although the financial crisis has decreased the number of immigrant arrivals in both countries by 4% in Greece and by 8% in Spain between 2009 and 2010 (OECD, 2012), the two countries face quite similar challenges as regards border control, asylum permits and citizenship rights, as well as integration and assimilation policies.

A concluding remark should be made in reference to the context or the climate under which the ESS survey was conducted in both countries. The fieldwork period was characterized by significant changes in the countries examined. In Greece, the 2009 National Elections have resulted in a change of government, the ruling conservative party was defeated by the socialist party. In Spain the victory of socialist Zapatero in 2008 quickly proved to be fragile under the pressure of austerity measures he was obliged to take, a fact evident in the outcomes of the 2009 European Parliament elections where the pro-socialist votes were reduced alarmingly. The signing of the first Memorandum by the Greek government in May 2010 launched a period of turbulent times in the political and social realm. Repeated mass protests, some of which ended in violence, in the capital of Greece, and a sharp rise of the far-right wing have added an extra negative potential to economic insecurity. As expected, emergency cuts to wages and pensions, public investment and civil service salaries triggered severe protest in both countries [12].

Data and methods

The data used in our analysis are drawn from the 4th (2008-2009) and 5th (2010-2011) round of the ESS datasets. In order to analyse the relation between religiosity, trust and tolerance, we have chosen three sets of variables from the ESS questionnaire as measurements of the concepts in question. As regards religiosity, it should be noted that ESS questions do not focus on the actual content of religious beliefs (i.e., belief in God, belief in hell, sin, etc.), but they aim at documenting their existence. ESS uses the term religiosity as a multi-dimensional concept, with three indicators. In our analysis we used the following sets:

A. Religiosity: self-defined religiosity ("how religious are you") tapped by an 11-point scale which ranges between 0 (not at all religious) and 10 (very religious), frequency of church attendance and frequency of praying, ranging, apart from holy days, from 1 (every day) to 7 (never).

B. Trust: Interpersonal [social] trust and trust in institutions: the former was measured by three items[13] and the latter by a question on national and supra-national institutions;[14] both were rated on an 11-point scale (0=no trust at all, 10=complete trust). Interest in politics (scored on a 4-item scale) is also included as a measure closely linked to institutional trust.

C. Tolerance: To analyze tolerance we have used three measures:

    1. Attitudes towards immigrants as an out-group and immigration as a social phenomenon. Tolerance towards immigrants as an out-group is tapped by three questions on how many people "from same race", "different race" and "from poorer countries" should be allowed to come and live in the country (1=allow many, 4=allow none). The first two questions measure respondents' attitudes on the basis of ethnic origin whereas the latter indicates the perceived threat to the country's labour market. Immigration as a social phenomenon, affecting the country's general situation (making the country a worse or better place to live") or the country's economic and cultural life (making them worse or better) is measured on an 11-point scale, where 10 represents the more positive impact.

    2. Attitudes towards homosexuals. Tolerance toward homosexuals was tapped by one question ("Gay men and lesbians should be free to live their own life as they wish") and response was measured using a 5-point scale (1=agree strongly, 5=disagree strongly), whereby the high score indicates negative attitudes toward homosexuals.

3. Political tolerance, indicated here as tolerance for political extremes, is a much debated issue in political science literature (Sullivan, et al., 1979; Gibson 1992a, 1992b). Political tolerance was tapped by one question ("To what extent you agree or disagree with the following statement: "Political parties that wish to overthrow democracy should be banned") and response was measured on a five-point scale (1=agree strongly, 5=disagree strongly), with higher score indicating tolerance toward political extremes.

D. Feeling about household's income[15] and having paid work as appeared in respondent's main activity during last seven days[16] were also used in the analysis as measures of the impact of recession on the individual level.

Socio-demographic variables (age, gender, educational level, and level of urbanization) were added to the set of independent variables as classical control variables.

For the purpose of our analysis, we utilized multiple linear regression and binary logistic modeling. *Multiple regression models* were fitted, considering as *dependent variables* the mean scores of the three questions of the questionnaire referring to trust in others *("Interpersonal [social] trust*"), the mean scores of the seven variables indicating trust in institutions *("Trust in Institutions")*, and the mean scores of the three questions referring to tolerance towards immigrants (*"intolerance towards immigrants")*. As *independent variables* we considered two *quantitative covariates*, i.e., the scores in the question "how religious are you" (*Self-defined religiosity)* and age, as well as a set of dummy variables for *gender* where male=1 and female=0; *education level* represented in two dummy variables, the first of them taking the value of one when the education level was less than upper secondary and zero else, and the second one being equal to one when the educational level was upper secondary, zero else (thus for education level, more than upper secondary both these two variables take the value zero); two *dummy variables* related to *church attendance*, the first one (*Church attendance I)* being 1 if the individual attends religious services at least once a month and zero else, and the second one (*Church attendance II*) being 1 if the individual attends religious services less than once a month and zero else (thus, if both these variables equal zero, the individual never attends religious services); and two *dummy variables* related to *frequency of praying*, the one of them (*Frequency of praying I)* being one if the individual prays at least once a week and zero else, and the other one (*Frequency of praying II*) being one if the individual prays less often than once a week and zero else (thus, if both of them are zero, then the individual never prays); as well as four *binary variables* each of them being one if the individual has the characteristic and zero else. These characteristics were the following: *Interest in politics*, *feeling comfortable with present household's income*, *living in a big city*, and having paid work, all of them being one if the individual responds positively, zero else.

In turn, *binary logistic regression models* were fitted, considering as *dependent variables* a number of binary ones related to: *Intolerance towards homosexuals*, taking the value one if the individual is against homosexuals ("intolerant") and zero else; *intolerance towards political extremes,* being one if the individual agrees that political parties that wish to overthrow democracy should be banned ("intolerant") and zero else; and *tolerance toward immigrants* measured by the answers to the questions regarding immigrants: "Allow immigrants of the same race/ethnic group as majority", "Allow immigrants of different race/ethnic group from majority" and "Allow immigrants from poorer countries outside Europe", being one if the individual responds positively (i.e, shows tolerance) and zero else. As *independent variables* in these models, we considered *age* and *self-defined religiosity* measured by the scores on the question "how religious are you" as covariates and *gender*, *interest in politics*, *feeling comfortable with present household's income*, *living in a big city* and *having paid work* as binary variables; all of the latter being one if the individual responds positively and zero else. Moreover we used in the analysis three ordinal variables on three levels each, *education* (less than upper secondary, upper secondary, and more than upper secondary), *church attendance* (at least once a month, less than once a month, never), and *frequency of praying* (at least once a week, less than once a week, and never). All the models were fitted to the overall data set of both waves, for each country, while "*Round*" was also incorporated in the set of explanatory variables as a binary indicator variable taking the value of one if the case belonged to Round 5 and zero if the case belonged to Round 4. A summary description of the variables in both the multiple and the logistic regression models is provided in Table13-1.

Table 13-1. Summary description of the variables in the models

Multiple regression modeling	**Independent variables**
Dependent variables	**Covariates**
Interpersonal trust Trust in Institutions Tolerance towards immigration	Age Self -defined religiosity
	Dummy variables (1:yes, 0:no)
	Male gender Less than upper secondary educational level Upper secondary educational level Church attendance I: at least once a month Church attendance II: less than once a month Frequency of praying I: at least once a week Frequency of praying II: less than once a week Interest in politics Feeling about household's income Living in a big city Having paid work ESS Round 5
Binary logistic regression modeling	Independent variables
Dependent variables (1:yes, 0:no)	**Covariates**
Intolerance towards homosexuals Intolerance towards political extremes Tolerance towards immigrants from same race Tolerance towards immigrants from different race	Age Self-defined religiosity **Dummy variables (1:yes, 0:no)**

Tolerance towards immigrants from poorer countries	Male gender Interest in politics Feeling well about household's income Living in a big city Having paid work ESS Round 5
	Ordinal variables (three levels)
	Educational level (0 =<upper secondary, 1=upper secondary and 2=>upper secondary) Church attendance (1-3, with 1 = highest frequency) Frequency of praying (1-3, with 1 = highest frequency)

Findings

Social and institutional trust

According to the parameter estimates of the regression model, shown in Table 13-2, despite the feeling of insecurity, economic recession and its impact on the surveyed population, *interpersonal[social] trust* has increased in both countries between the two ESS rounds. One would expect that the decrease of material resources and scarcity of jobs would lead people to be more suspicious. The finding opposes the pattern of very low scores of Greeks as regards social trust. A possible explanation is that the crisis is conceived as an emergency situation awakening the reflexes of an "ambivalent" solidarity as some researchers argue (Panagiotopoulou and Papliakou, 2007: 251). This kind of solidarity is evident in times of natural disasters or major national events. [17] Portes (1998) has also pointed out to solidarity in times of crisis as one of the causes of social capital. Low levels of trust in Greece are related to political indifference and political cynicism mostly apparent in late 80s (Kafetzis, 2011). Political party competition, social class conflict, Europeanization and the influence of mass media are variables that have a significant influence on the formation and the kind of social capital in Greece (Sotiropoulos, 2007).

The increase of social trust in Spain during the period discussed (2008-2011) is also in opposition to the picture of a stable lack of trust "transmitted from one generation to another virtually intact" (Torcal and Montero, 1998, p.17).

Moreover, the results for both countries (see Table 13-2) indicate that education remains one of the strongest predictors of trust (Allum et al., 2010); less educated people in both Spain and Greece have less trust in others. Interest in politics and the feeling of coping with present income have a positive contribution in both cases. In the case of Greece, age and having paid work have both a significantly negative impact on interpersonal [social] trust, while living in a big city has a significantly positive impact on social trust. However, the contribution of the latter three independent variables is not statistically significant in the case of Spain. The relation between self-defined religiosity and social trust is negative in the case of Greece, in contrast to Spain—a result that conforms with previous empirical findings[18] (Billiet and Meuleman, 2008).

Table 13-2. Multiple linear regression modeling with the dependent variable: Social trust

	Greece			Spain		
Independent variables	β	Se(β)	p-value	β	se(β)	p-value
Gender	.011	.059	.850	-.082	.049	.094
Age	-.009	.002	.000	-.002	.001	.143
Self-defined religiosity	-.045	.015	.002	.038	.012	.002
Church attendance I	-.061	.163	.707	-.035	.085	.681
Church attendance II	-.112	.152	.463	.028	.065	.668
Frequency of praying I	-.096	.148	.516	-.121	.087	.167
Frequency of praying II	.052	.143	.716	.026	.073	.718
Less than upper secondary educational level	-.282	.083	.001	-.226	.061	.000
Upper secondary educational level	-.095	.075	.205	-.313	.074	.000
Interest in politics	.178	.064	.005	.270	.055	.000
Feeling about household's income	.518	.059	.000	.427	.058	.000
Living in a big city	.240	.058	.000	.043	.058	.456
Having paid work	-.222	.061	.000	-.185	.149	.216
Round	.180	.058	.002	.103	.048	.031
Intercept	4.250	.181	.000	4.710	.101	.000

Our analysis for both countries examined indicates a symmetrical pattern of positive contribution of the following variables as regards *institutional trust*: Self-defined religiosity, church-attendance, interest in politics and living comfortably or coping with the present income (Table 13-3). The more religious the respondents declare and the more frequent church-goers (at least once a month) they are, the more they trust institutions in both countries. The urbanization level has a positive effect only in the case of Greece. As one would expect due to the persistent recession, trust in institutions has significantly decreased for both countries between the two rounds. Age shows a reverse influence: older people in Spain have lower levels of trust in institutions, whereas the opposite holds for Greece.

Table 13-3. Multiple linear regression modeling with the dependent variable: Trust in institutions

Independent variables	Greece			Spain		
	B	se(β)	p-value	β	se(β)	p-value
Gender	.032	.060	.586	-.104	.060	.083
Age	.004	.002	.051	-.006	.002	.001
Self-defined religiosity	.050	.015	.001	.112	.015	.000
Church attendance I	.426	.166	.010	.217	.106	.041
Church attendance II	.165	.155	.285	.104	.080	.194
Frequency of praying I	.217	.151	.150	-.166	.107	.123
Frequency of praying II	.229	.145	.116	.054	.089	.546
Less than upper secondary educational level	-.004	.084	.959	.009	.072	.897
Upper secondary educational level	-.004	.074	.961	.036	.087	.683
Interest in politics	.596	.064	.000	.425	.066	.000
Feeling about household's income	.239	.059	.000	.372	.073	.000
Living in a big city	.241	.058	.000	-.071	.071	.319
Having paid work	-.188	.061	.002	.056	.180	.758
Round	-1.146	.059	.000	-.358	.059	.000
Intercept	2.504	.181	.000	3.994	.125	.000

In addition, being in paid employment is not a positive predictor for institutional trust in Greece. Given the growing uncertainty associated with the pervasive crisis, this finding might be interpreted as a reaction to institutional instability, which is reinforced by changes in the state's functions and infrastructures and by its withdrawal from traditional roles such as a guarantor of fundamental constitutional rights.

Tolerance

As previously discussed, Spain and Greece face similar challenges posed by their status as immigrant host countries. The recent economic crisis in both countries has further exacerbated the effects of illegal immigration and the competition for shrinking employment opportunities in the labour market. Table 13-4 below shows the estimated values of the regression coefficients for tolerance towards immigration as a phenomenon affecting the country's economy and culture.

Age and low education have a negative impact, while interest in politics has a positive impact on tolerance towards immigration for both countries. Males show higher tolerance than females in Spain. High ranking in self-defined religiosity, frequent church attendance, high frequency of praying and lower education have a negative impact on tolerance towards immigrants in the case of Greece. Interest in politics has a positive impact on tolerance toward immigration in both countries; coping on present income and living in a big city have a positive impact on tolerance towards immigration for Greece, but their contributions are insignificant for Spain. Tolerance towards immigration, as a phenomenon affecting the quality of life in the country and its economy and culture has significantly decreased in Greece between 2009 and 2011. No significant difference is observed between the two rounds for Spain.

Since the question of tolerance is of great importance in times of crisis, due to scarcity of resources as discussed above, we have used two additional measures, besides tolerance towards immigration and immigrants, in order to expand our analysis to facets of tolerance less affected by circumstantial conditions. For this purpose, we explore intolerance towards gays and lesbians and political intolerance defined here as intolerance towards political extremes.

Table 13-4. Multiple linear regression modeling with the dependent variable: tolerance towards immigration

Independent variables	Greece β	Greece se(β)	Greece p-value	Spain B	Spain se(β)	Spain p-value
Gender	-.056	.065	.386	.215	.064	.001
Age	-.006	.002	.002	-.010	.002	.000
Self-defined religiosity	-.091	.016	.000	.007	.016	.652
Church attendance I	-.483	.178	.007	-.070	.110	.526
Church attendance II	-.531	.167	.001	-.145	.085	.087
Frequency of praying I	-.331	.163	.043	.171	.114	.132
Frequency of praying II	-.079	.158	.615	-.088	.094	.347
Less than upper secondary educational level	-.271	.091	.003	-.889	.078	.000
Upper secondary educational level	-.299	.082	.000	-.148	.095	.117
Interest in politics	.332	.070	.000	.349	.071	.000
Feeling about household's income	.228	.065	.000	.130	.075	.085
Living in a big city	.170	.063	.007	.117	.075	.120
Having paid work	.009	.067	.892	.009	.191	.961
Round	-.317	.064	.000	.064	.062	.302
Intercept	4.866	.200	.000	5.932	.130	.000

Table 13-5. Binary logistic regression modeling with the dependent variable: Intolerance towards homosexuals

	Greece				Spain			
Independent variables	β	se(β)	p-value	odds ratio	β	Se(β)	p-value	odds ratio
Gender	.446	.088	.000	1.562	.881	.133	.000	2.413
Age	.017	.003	.000	1.018	.031	.004	.000	1.031
Self-defined religiosity	.076	.022	.001	1.079	.257	.032	.000	1.293
Church attendance			.078				.621	
Frequent	-.029	.251	.908	.972	.152	.205	.460	1.164
Less frequent	-.239	.240	.319	.787	.008	.189	.966	1.008
Praying			.112				.360	
Frequent	.127	.244	.602	1.135	.160	.232	.491	1.173
Less frequent	-.111	.242	.647	.895	-.088	.217	.684	.916
Educational level			.000				.024	
Less than upper secondary	1.022	.140	.000	2.779	.506	.199	.011	1.659
Upper Secondary	.603	.136	.000	1.828	.179	.261	.493	1.196
Interest in politics	-.110	.095	.246	.896	-.506	.161	.002	.603
Feeling about household's income	-.261	.090	.004	.770	-.395	.136	.004	.674
Living in a big city	-.022	.086	.798	.978	-.136	.156	.383	.873
Having paid work	.140	.093	.133	1.150	.363	.418	.384	1.438
Round	.852	.092	.000	2.345	-.145	.124	.245	.865
Intercept	-4.124	.309	.000	.016	-5.882	.333	.000	.003

As observed in Table 13-5, the most significant variables as regards tolerance towards homosexuals for both countries examined are gender, age, self-defined religiosity, educational level and feeling comfortable or coping with the household's income. Men in particular are roughly 50% more likely to be intolerant towards homosexuality in comparison to women in Greece and roughly two and a half times more likely than women in Spain. Higher educational level significantly decreases the odds of being intolerant towards homosexuality especially in Greece; the more educated the more tolerant they are. People with lower than upper secondary educational level are almost 2.8 times more intolerant towards homosexuals than people with higher than upper secondary education level in Greece and 1.7 in Spain, while people with upper secondary education level are 1.8 times more intolerant than the higher educated in Greece and 1.2 times in Spain. Differences in tolerance between the two countries are more striking for low educated Greeks. In Greece, one is roughly 2.4 times more likely to be intolerant towards homosexuals in 2011 than two years earlier, a finding that supports the view that the current crisis has left its imprint even on cultural norms and values. Increased conformity and conservatism, as regards acceptance of homosexuality, is not a characteristic of the Spanish case; in Spain, no significant change is observed between the two rounds.

Political tolerance in the literature is mainly addressed as tolerance towards specific groups (Stouffer, 1955; Sullivan, et al., 1979), usually ethnic minorities, and not as tolerance towards political parties, as is the case of the ESS question. Nevertheless, the analytical tools remain the same. The data in Table 13-6 confirm that education remains the most important predictor of tolerance[19]. Paradoxically, especially in the case of Greece, but even in the case of Spain, though to a lesser degree, lower levels of education are associated with higher levels of intolerance for the parties that wish to overthrow democracy. This finding needs further investigation, especially as regards the comprehension of the question by respondents.

Table 13-6. Binary logistic regression modeling with the dependent variable: Intolerance for political extremes

Independent variables	Greece				Spain			
	B	se(β)	p-value	odds ratio	β	se(β)	p-value	Odds ratio
Gender	-.051	.070	.471	.951	.128	.080	.110	1.136
Age	.001	.002	.769	1.001	.009	.002	.000	1.009
Self-defined religiosity	.021	.017	.230	1.021	-.042	.020	.035	.959
Church attendance			.008				.640	
Frequent	.340	.190	.073	1.405	-.090	.136	.505	.914
Less frequent	.096	.176	.585	1.101	-.099	.107	.351	.905
Praying			.183				.092	
Frequent	-.153	.172	.376	.858	.041	.141	.773	1.041
Less frequent	.000	.166	.999	1.000	.224	.120	.063	1.251
Educational level			.000				.003	
Less than upper secondary	.467	.097	.000	1.594	-.315	.102	.002	.730
Upper Secondary	.324	.086	.000	1.382	-.049	.126	.697	.952
Interest in politics	-.226	.074	.002	.797	.298	.094	.002	1.347
Feeling about household's income	.222	.070	.002	1.248	.223	.090	.013	1.250
Living in a big city	-.095	.068	.160	.909	.160	.098	.103	1.174
Having paid work	.067	.072	.355	1.069	.142	.255	.578	1.153
Round	-.062	.069	.367	.940	.193	.078	.013	1.213
Intercept	.332	.208	.110	1.394	.843	.163	.000	2.323

Though religious involvement is a strong predictor of intolerance as regards homosexuality, it does not equally affect attitudes towards political extremes. In Spain, for every additional year of age, the odds of being intolerant towards political extremes increases by 6%. As indicated by Rother and Medrano (2006: 169) younger cohorts are more tolerant in Spain due "to the socializing impact of Franco's dictatorship on the older generations". Feeling comfortable with the present income increases the odds of intolerance towards political extremes by 25% in both countries. No significant differences in the levels of tolerance towards political extremes are observed between the two rounds in Greece, while in Spain intolerance towards political extremes increases with time.

In the Tables 13-7, 13-8, and 13-9 tolerance towards three groups of immigrants is examined for those from the same race, a different race and those coming from poorer countries, respectively. Here again, higher education level and interest in politics increase the odds of being tolerant toward "Immigrants of same race" in the two countries. Tolerance towards same-race immigrants decreases by age in Spain, a result that could be interpreted in the context of regional diversities and internal nationalist rivalries in the country. The odds of being tolerant towards immigrants of the same race decrease by 33% between Round 4 and Round 5 in Greece, while they increase by 32% in Spain.

Table 13-7. Binary logistic regression modeling with the dependent variable: Tolerance towards immigrants of same race

	Greece				Spain			
Independent variables	β	se(β)	p-value	odds ratio	β	se(β)	p-value	odds ratio
Gender	.017	.086	.843	1.017	-.013	.099	.897	.987
Age	-.003	.003	.277	.997	-.009	.003	.001	.991
Self-defined religiosity	-.032	.021	.134	.969	-.026	.024	.280	.975
Church attendance			.396				.127	
Frequent	-.145	.249	.561	.865	.317	.166	.056	1.373
Less frequent	-.014	.236	.953	.986	.074	.131	.571	1.077
Praying			.860				.284	
Frequent	.021	.229	.926	1.021	.015	.172	.932	1.015
Less frequent	.073	.225	.744	1.076	.190	.148	.199	1.210
Educational level			.001				.000	
Less than upper secondary	-.481	.128	.000	.618	-.750	.140	.000	.472
Upper Secondary	-.380	.119	.001	.684	.024	.190	.899	1.024
Interest in politics	.273	.095	.004	1.314	.551	.127	.000	1.735
Feeling about household's income	-.006	.085	.945	.994	.237	.107	.026	1.268
Living in a big city	.345	.084	.000	1.412	.106	.121	.383	1.112
Having paid work	-.083	.088	.348	.921	.093	.343	.785	1.098
Round	-.394	.086	.000	.675	.229	.097	.018	1.257
Intercept	2.361	.283	.000	10.604	2.329	.207	.000	10.272

The picture is not very different as regards tolerance towards immigrants of a different race (Table 13-8). Age, educational level and interest in politics are associated with tolerance in both countries. The younger, the more educated and the more interested in politics are more tolerant towards immigrants of a different race, in both countries. Interest in politics increases the odds of being tolerant for immigrants of different race by 23% and 47% in Greece and Spain, respectively. In 2011, Greeks are by far less tolerant towards immigrants compared to 2009, a result that is also related with the rise of the far-right during the same period. On the contrary no significant difference is observed between the two rounds for Spain.

As shown in Table 13-9, for both countries, age has a negative impact on tolerance towards immigrants from poorer countries, while high levels of self-defined religiosity are significantly negatively related to tolerance towards immigrants from poorer countries in the case of Greece, but insignificantly related in the case of Spain. Higher education and interest in politics have a positive impact for both countries. Once again only Greece appears less tolerant in 2011 (Round 5), whereas no significant difference is observed between the two rounds in Spain.

Table 13-8. Binary logistic regression modeling with dependent variable: Tolerance towards immigrants of different race

	Greece				Spain			
Independent variables	β	se(β)	p-value	odds ratio	β	se(β)	p-value	odds ratio
Gender	.066	.069	.338	1.068	-.017	.095	.861	.984
Age	-.011	.002	.000	.989	-.009	.003	.000	.991
Self-defined religiosity	-.088	.017	.000	.916	-.036	.023	.119	.965
Church attendance			.454				.219	
Frequent	-.042	.201	.834	.959	.196	.159	.219	1.217
Less frequent	-.128	.191	.504	.880	-.033	.125	.794	.968
Praying			.051				.407	
Frequent	-.152	.185	.412	.859	.157	.164	.339	1.170
Less frequent	.051	.182	.778	1.053	.186	.140	.182	1.205
Educational level			.000				.000	
Less than upper secondary	-.581	.098	.000	.560	-.769	.132	.000	.463
Upper Secondary	-.324	.091	.000	.724	.033	.179	.855	1.033
Interest in politics	.206	.074	.006	1.228	.387	.116	.001	1.472
Feeling about household's income	.114	.068	.094	1.121	.187	.103	.068	1.206
Living in a big city	.121	.067	.070	1.128	.120	.116	.301	1.127
Having paid work	.004	.071	.953	1.004	-.089	.307	.772	.915
Round	-.527	.068	.000	.591	.060	.091	.510	1.062
Intercept	2.293	.233	.000	9.907	2.417	.199	.000	11.210

Table 13-9. Binary logistic regression modeling with the dependent variable: Tolerance towards immigrants from poorer countries

Independent variables	Greece				Spain			
	β	se(β)	p-value	odds ratio	β	se(β)	p-value	odds ratio
Gender	.034	.067	.616	1.034	-.014	.096	.883	.986
Age	-.007	.002	.000	.993	-.009	.003	.000	.991
Self-defined religiosity	-.065	.017	.000	.937	-.013	.023	.568	.987
Church attendance			.172				.234	
Frequent	-.248	.194	.201	.780	.272	.160	.089	1.313
Less frequent	-.315	.184	.087	.730	.138	.126	.275	1.148
Praying			.012				.795	
Frequent	-.094	.174	.589	.910	.048	.167	.773	1.049
Less frequent	.145	.170	.394	1.156	.093	.141	.511	1.098
Educational level			.000				.000	
Less than upper secondary	-.678	.095	.000	.508	-.837	.135	.000	.433
Upper Secondary	-.345	.088	.000	.708	.023	.184	.900	1.023
Interest in politics	.193	.072	.007	1.212	.460	.119	.000	1.585
Feeling about household's income	.103	.066	.120	1.109	.235	.103	.022	1.265
Living in a big city	.024	.065	.708	1.024	.083	.117	.479	1.086
Having paid work	-.009	.068	.901	.991	.201	.343	.558	1.222
Round	-.391	.066	.000	.676	.082	.092	.372	1.086
Intercept	.034	.067	.616	1.034	2.315	.200	.000	10.130

Conclusion

Having recession as the starting point of our research questions, we have tried to investigate its impact on trust and tolerance and also examine the effect of religiosity on both measures. Our hypothesis is that recession acts as a multiplier upon existing problems, thus calling for a redefinition of established convictions and patterns of thought. The two countries selected for our analysis were at different stages of the debt crisis, during the period discussed (2009-2011) besides the fact that the crisis in Spain was basically restricted to the banks and Spain never signed memorandums.

Our analysis indicated that the crisis has actually reduced the levels of trust and tolerance mainly in Grcccc. Morc spccifically, tolerance towards immigration as a phenomenon, as well as towards immigrants from poorer countries and immigrants of the same race, has changed during the two rounds. Greeks become less tolerant under the pressure of austerity policies. This finding is quite alarming if it is combined with the rise of far-right party, and anti-immigration acts observed in Greece during the period under discussion.

Trust in institutions has significantly declined in both countries while trust in others has shown a significant positive change. Though generally tolerance towards homosexuals is not period-bound, the results for Greece show a significant increase of intolerance between 2009 and 2011—a finding that signals a shift towards conformity. Religiosity has a slightly negative impact on accepting immigrants in both countries. Age does not have a consistent influence on tolerance nor does gender, while he opposite holds for education and interest in politics.

Educational level remains the most influential factor for trust and tolerance. Differences across the three educational levels analyzed in our models are more striking in the case of Greece; low educated people are generally less tolerant and less trusting with the exception of tolerance towards political extremes where the less educated are for their banning. In Spain, less and more than upper secondary educated people seem to have nearly the same attitudes on the concepts measured.

Urbanization level, has a more profound impact in the case of Greece, not in Spain. Different patterns of societal development between the two countries may account for this result as well as the interplay of rural and urban elements in the context of the transformation of Greek rural communities. The same can be said for religiosity either as belief (self-defined religiosity) or practice (praying and church attendance); its influence is more visible in the case of Greece. Religiosity seems to have a slightly negative impact on attitudes towards immigration as a phenomenon affecting the country's culture and economy thus reducing the levels of tolerance toward immigrants. During the period under examination, it seems that religion reinforces the exclusionist attributes of a closed system, which sets same race, ethnicity and identity as a prerequisite for participation in social and political life. It thus generates a kind of social capital which is centered along bonding ingroup similarities rather than bridging diversities Our observations, finally, reinforce concerns about the quality of democracy in countries mostly affected by recession. Deprivation seems to lead to a resurgence of old dichotomies, between "us" and "them", rather than creating new forms of solidarity.

Notes

[1] See EUDO citizenship observatory in http://www.eudo-citizenship.eu
[2] A similar parallelism is found in Welch et al. (2004) "Trust in God and Trust in Man".
[3] As put by Newton (1999) socially trusting people are not necessarily politically trusting, and vice versa.
[4] It is beyond the purpose of this paper to discuss other equally important theories of social capital like Bourdieu's, who has brought class and social inequalities to the forefront of theoretical analysis.
[5] A phenomenon labeled by Davie (2007) as vicarious religion.
[6] For a most recent account see Fokas 2012.
[7] In Spain, Ireland and Greece, unemployment rates for youth almost doubled, reaching more than 40 per cent in the case of Spain and reversing all of the earlier positive trends experienced over the 2000s. (Global employment trends. International Labour Office 2012:48)
[8] Perez-Agote (2009:189) indicates three waves of secularization spanning from the 19th century to the present day. The third wave began in the '90s when the majority of young people lost contact with the Catholic church and religion.
[9] Until 2005, when the scandals were revealed, the levels of trust in the institution of the church were high (Lyberaki and Paraskevopoulos 2002)
[10] The range in figures refers to round 4 and round 5 ESS data.
[11] The rate has decreased (from 2.3% to 1.6%) in Greece, as people from more variant religious backgrounds were interviewed in round 5
[12] The movement of Indignados or 15-M relevant to the protesters in Syntagma square in Greece.
[13] The question wording is as follows: [Would you say that] "most people can be trusted, or you can't be too careful", "most people would try to take advantage of you if they got the chance, or would they try to be fair", "most of the time people try to be helpful or they are mostly looking out for themselves".
[14] The question refers to the following institutions: Country's parliament, legal system, police, politicians, political parties, European Parliament and United Nations.

[15] The value codes to the question "how do you feel about your household's income nowadays" are: 1= Living comfortably on present income, 2= Coping on present income, 3=Finding it difficult on present income, 4=Finding it very difficult on present income.
[16] The other categories included in the question are: in education, unemployed and actively looking for a job, unemployed but not actively looking for a job, permanently sick or disabled , retired, in community or military service, doing housework, looking after children or other persons.
[17] Olympic Games in Athens in 2004 was such an event.
[18] In an analysis of ESS round 2 data (2004) by Billiet and Meuleman (2008: 17), while in less than half of European countries there was a weak but positive relation between religious involvement and social trust, in Greece the relation was negative.
[19] Though criticized by some researchers as time-bound. See Sullivan et al., 1979, p.792.

References

Allport, G. W. (1962). 'Prejudice: Is it societal or personal?', *Journal of Social Issues*, vol. 18, pp. 120–134.

Allum, N., Patulny, R, Read, S & Sturgis P. (2010). 'Re-evaluating the links between social trust, institutional trust and civic association'. In: Stillwell, J, Norman, P, Thomas, C, and Surridge, P (eds.) *Spatial and Social Disparities. Understanding Population Trends and Processes,* Springer, vol. 2, pp. 199-215.

Berger, P. (ed.), (1967). *The sacred canopy. Elements of a sociological theory of religion*, New York. Doubleday.

Berger P. (1999). *The Secularization of the world: Resurgent religion and world politics*, Grand Rapids, Mich.: Eerdmans.

Billiet, J & Meuleman, B. (2008). 'Religious diversity in Europe and its relation to social attitudes and value orientations', CeSO – K.U. Leuven. 3mc proceedings.

Bréchon, P. (2009). 'La mesure de l'appartenance et de la non-appartenance confessionnelle dans les grandes enquêtes européennes'. *Social Compass*, vol. 56, pp. 163-178.

Burdette, A.M., Ellison, C.G., and Hill, T.D. (2005). 'Conservative Protestantism and tolerance toward homosexuals: An examination of potential mechanisms', *Sociological Inquiry*, vol. 75, no. 2, May 2005, pp. 177–196.

Casanova, J. (1994). *Public religions in the modern world*, Chicago: Chicago University Press.

Daniels, J. and von der Ruhr, M. (2010) 'Trust in others: Does religion matter?', *Review of Social Economy*, vol. 68, no. 2, pp.163-186.

Davie, G. (2007). 'Vicarious religion: A methodological challenge', in Ammerman, N. (ed.) *Everyday religion: Observing modern religious lives,* New York: Oxford University Press, pp. 21-36.

Delhey, J. andNewton, K. (2005). 'Predicting cross-national levels of social trust: Global pattern or Nordic Exceptionalism?', *European Sociological Review*, vol.21, no.4, pp. 311-327.

Dobbelaere, K. (2002). *Secularization: An Analysis at three levels,* Brussels: P.I.E -Peter Lang.

EUDO Citizenship Observatory, Available: http://www.eudo-citizenship.eu [15 July 2013].

Flere, S. (2008). 'Questioning the need for a special methodology for the study of Eastern Orthodoxy', *Social Compass* 2008, vol. 55, no.1, pp. 84-100.

Fokas, E. (2012). ''Eastern' Orthodoxy and 'Western' secularisation in contemporary Europe (with Special Reference to the Case of Greece)', *Religion, State and Society*, vol. 40, nos. 3-4, pp. 395-414.

Gesthuizen, M, van der Meer, T. and Scheepers, P. (2009). 'Ethnic diversity and social capital in Europe: Tests of Putnam's thesis in European Countries', *Scandinavian Political Studies*, vol. 32, no. 2, pp. 121-142.

Gibson, J.L. (1992a). 'Alternative measures of political tolerance: must tolerance be 'least-liked?'', *American Journal of Political Science*, vol.36, no 2, pp. 560-577.

—. (1992b). 'The political consequences of intolerance: cultural conformity and political freedom', *The American Political Science Review*. vol. 86, no. 2, pp. 338-356.

Halman, L. and Draulans V. (2006). 'How secular is Europe?', *British Journal of Sociology*, vol.57, no. 2, pp. 263–88.

Hooghe, M., Reeskens, T., Stolle, D. & Trappers, A. (2009). 'Ethnic diversity and generalized trust in Europe : A cross-national multilevel study', *Comparative Political Studies*, vol. 42, no. 2, pp. 198-223.

International Labour Office. (2012). Global employment trends.

Kafetzis, P. (2011). 'Political indifference and social cynicism'. in Papliakou, V, Stathopoulou, Th and Stratoudaki, H (eds.) *Institutions-Values-Practices. Interpretations of the ESS findings (2008-2009),* Athens, EKKE. (in Greek).

Kesler, C. and Bloemraad, I. (2010). 'Does immigration erode social capital? The conditional effects of immigration-generated diversity on trust, membership, and participation across 19 countries, 1981–2000', *Canadian Journal of Political Science* , vol. 43, no.2, pp. 319–347.

Kesler, C. and Demireva, N. (2011). *Social cohesion and host country nationality among immigrants in Western Europe. Naturalisation: a passport for the better integration of immigrants*? OECD.

Koenig, M. (2008). 'Introduction'. Special issue on religion and social capital, *Social Compass,* vol. 55, no.4, pp. 451–456.

Lambert, Y. (2004). 'A turning point in religious evolution in Europe', *Journal of Contemporary Religion,* vol. 19, no.1, pp. 29–45.

Laythe, B., Finkel, D.G., Bringle, R.D. and Kirkpatrick, L.A. (2002). 'Religious fundamentalism as a predictor of prejudice: a two-component model', *Journal for the Scientific Study of Religion,* vol. 41, no.4, pp. 623–635.

Lehmann, D. (2008). 'L'économie miraculeuse de la religion: essai sur le capital social', *Social Compass,* vol. 55, no.4, pp. 457-477.

Lyberaki, A. and Paraskevopoulos, C. (2002). 'Social capital measurement in Greece'. Paper presented at OECD-ONS International Conference on Social Capital Measurement, 25–27 September, London.

Mishler, W. and Rose, R. (2001). 'What are the origins of political trust? Testing institutional and cultural theories in post-communist societies', *Comparative Political Studies,* vol. 34, no.1, pp. 30–62.

Morozov, A. (2008). 'The Fourth secularisation', *Religion, State and Society*, vol. 36, no.1, pp. 33-38.

Nelsen, B, & Guth, J. (2003). 'Religion and youth support for the European Union', *Journal of CMS,* vol. 1, no. 1, pp. 89–112.

Norris, P. and Davis, J. (2007). 'A Continental divide? Social capital in the US and Europe', in R. Jowell, C. Roberts, R. Fitzgerald and G. Eva (eds) *Measuring attitudes cross-nationally: Lessons from the European Social Survey*, London: Sage, pp. 239–64.

Newton, K. (1999). 'Social and political trust in established Democracies'. in Norris, P. (ed.) *Critical citizens. Global support for democratic government,* Oxford: Oxford University Press.

Newton, K and Zmerli, S (2011). 'Three forms of trust and their association', *European Political Science Review*, vol. 3, no. 2, pp. 169-200.

OECD (2012). International Migration Outlook.

Panagiotopoulou, R. and Papliakou, V. (2007). 'Facets of formation of social capital in Greece', in Kafetzis, P, Maloutas, T. and Tsiganou, J. (eds.) *Politics, society, citizens: The European Social Survey – ESS.* Athens, EKKE, pp. 219–69 (in Greek).

Pérez-Agote, A. (2009). 'Les trois vagues de la sécularisation des consciences en Espagne', *Social Compass*, vol. 56, no.2, pp. 189-201.

Portes, A. (1998). 'Social Capital: Its origins and applications in modern sociology', *Annual Sociology*, vol. 24, pp. 1-24.

Putnam, R. D. (2000). *Bowling alone: the collapse and revival of American community*, New York, London: Simon & Schuster.

Révay, E. & Miklós, T. (eds.), (2007). *Church and religious life in post-communist societies*, Budapest-Piliscsaba: Loisir.

Savelkul, M., Gesthuizen, M. and Scheepers, P. (2011). 'Explaining relationships between ethnic diversity and informal social capital across European countries and regions: Tests of constrict, conflict and contact theory', *Social Science Research,* Elsevier, vol. 40, no. 4, pp. 1091-1107.

Sotiropoulos, D. (2007). 'Social Capital in Greece in comparative perspective: A brief theoretical analysis and empirical documentation on the basis of the European Social Survey', in Kafetzis, P, Maloutas, T and Tsiganou, J, (eds.) *Politics, society, citizens: The European Social Survey – ESS*, Athens: EKKE, pp. 271-291 (in Greek).

Stathopoulou, Th. (2010). 'Faith and Trust: tracking patterns of religious and civic commitment in Greece and Europe. an empirical approach', in Roudometof, V. and Makrides, V. (eds.) *Orthodox Christianity in 21st century Greece. The role of religion in culture, Ethnicity and Politics*, London, Ashgate, pp.193-217.

—. (2011). 'Religious beliefs and practices in the European landscape', in Papliakou, V, Stathopoulou, Th. and Stratoudaki, H. (eds.) *Institutions-values-practices. Interpretations of the ESS findings (2008-2009),* Athens: EKKE, pp. 122-141 (in Greek).

Strømsnes, K. (2008). 'The Importance of church attendance and membership of religious voluntary organizations for the formation of social capital', *Social Compass,* vol. 55, no. 4, pp. 478-496.

Sturgis P., Brunton-Smith, I., Read, S. and Allum N. (2011). 'Does ethnic diversity erode trust? Putnam's 'hunkering down' thesis reconsidered', *British Journal of Political Science*, Cambridge: Cambridge University Press, vol. 41, no.1, pp. 57-82.

Sullivan, J. L., Piereson, J. and Marcus, G. E. (1979). 'An alternative conceptualization of political tolerance: Illusory increases 1950s-1970s', *The American Political Science Review*, vol. 73, no.3, pp.781-794.

Tomka, M. (2006). 'Is Conventional sociology of religion able to deal with differences between Eastern and Western European developments?', *Social Compass,* vol. 53, no. 2, pp. 251–65.

Tomka, M. and Yurash, A. (eds), (2006). *Challenges of religious plurality for Eastern and Central Europe,* Lviv, Ukraine: Taras Soroka.

Torcal, M. and Montero, J. R. (1998). *Facets of social capital in new democracies. The formation and consequences of social capital in Spain*. Working Paper 259, The Helen Kellog Institute for International Studies.

Triandafyllidou, A. (2011). *Addressing cultural, ethnic and religious diversity challenges in Europe. A comparative overview of 15 European countries,* European University Institute.

Voas, D. (2009). 'The rise and fall of fuzzy fidelity in Europe', *European Sociological Review*, vol. 25, no.2, pp. 155- 168.

Uslaner, E. M. (2002). *The moral foundations of trust*, Cambridge: Cambridge University Press.

van Oorshot, W., Wil, A. and Gelissen, J. (2006). 'Social capital in Europe: measurement and social and regional distribution of a multifaceted phenomenon', *Acta Sociologica,*vol. 49, no. 2, pp. 149–67.

Welch, M.R., Sikkink, D., Sartain, E. and Bond, C. (2004). 'Trust in god and trust in man: The ambivalent role of religion in shaping dimensions of social trust', *Journal for the Scientific Study of Religion,* vol. 43, no. 3, pp. 317-344.

PART IV.

MASS PROTESTS AND POLITICAL IMPACTS, WITH SPECIAL FOCUS ON THE SPANISH AND GREEK INDIGNADOS

CHAPTER FOURTEEN

SYNCHRONIZING IDENTITIES: CRAFTING THE SPACE OF MOBILIZATION IN THE SPANISH 15M

IGNACIA PERUGORRÍA
RUTGERS UNIVERSITY
AND BENJAMÍN TEJERINA
UNIVERSITY OF THE BASQUE COUNTRY

Abstract

The present chapter seeks to analyze the mobilizations that took place in Spain as a result of the multi-dimensional crisis unleashed in 2008. We study the "15M movement", or that of the Spanish *indignados*, by focusing on three analytical axes: the cognitive, emotional and relational processes feeding the construction of a social movement identity. First, we refer to the diagnostic, prognostic and motivational framing tasks performed by 15M participants to define the problematic situation and attribute blame, to articulate a solution to the problem and devise strategies to achieve that end, and to motivate participants to sustain their engagement and remedy the situation. Second, we concentrate on the emotions that were "mobilized" by social movement organizations linked to the 15M (e.g., outrage or indignation) and those emotions that emerged spontaneously during the "encounters" that took place in the public space: joy, efficacy and empowerment. Finally, we address the relational aspects entailed in the process of identity construction, that is, the activation and de-activation of both "real" and "imaginary" ties between 15M members and previous and/or current political and social collectives within the "progressive camp". In following this triple objective, our study describes the process of identity-synchronization that has allowed people with no previous political participation and with different, and oftentimes opposing, politico-ideological trajectories to feel part of the movement. Our data comes from in-depth interviews and focus groups with key activists, ethnographic observations in camps and assemblies in Bilbao and Madrid during the summer of 2011, and visual materials displayed in webpages and facebook accounts associated to the 15M.

Introduction

The global scenario of social mobilization is rapidly mutating. Periods of relative calmness and stability are being abruptly altered by moments of social effervescence that seem to be marking a point of fracture with previous decades. The year 2011 was particularly fruitful in the visualization of a series of "mobilizations of the indignant" that spread like wildfire around the world. Many observers have reported on these unprecedented global protests. They have portrayed citizens who articulate new kinds of alienation in a now globalized world dominated by finance capital, who declare feeling marginalized, if not scapegoated, and who reject the increasing disparities between the rich and the poor, the declining mobility of most, the exclusion and expulsion of many, and governments and politicians who are indifferent at best, duplicitous at worst, and, in any event, blatantly closed to popular concerns.

Given its multiple sources and diverse manifestations, the task of assessing and diagnosing the recent cycle of protest is especially arduous. The realities of countries in Northern Africa or the Middle East show relevant nuances among themselves, and also profound differences with the state of affairs in Western countries. However, two broad mobilizational "threads" can be analytically distinguished within the cycle. First, we have those mobilizations that have mainly demanded political reforms to initiate or deepen ongoing processes of democratization in countries such as Tunisia, Egypt, Morocco, Libya and Syria, among others. Second, there are the massive demonstrations of discontent regarding the erosion of the Welfare State and the political mismanagement of the socio-economic crisis in Southern Europe and also in the United States. Among the latter are the 15M mobilizations in Spain, the *Indignate-vous* protests in France, Italy and Greece, Occupy Wall Street, and other mobilizations spearheaded by young people and students in England, Belgium and Israel.

However different these mobilizations may be in terms of the grievances they express and the demands they present, we contend they are both temporally and internally connected. On the one hand, these mobilizations are a result of the increasing social inequalities that have been either triggered or deepened by de-industrialization processes, structural adjustment policies, and an uneven process of globalization that has created great wealth but has concentrated it in the hands of a small minority. Although they have been portrayed as "purely political" mobilizations (i.e., primarily concerned with the democratization of dictatorial political regimes), the Arab Spring uprisings have also been rooted in the particular impact neoliberalism has had on their respective societies.[1] On the other hand, the influence of collective action repertoires of movements upon each other, the international borrowing of slogans, the replication of organizational arrangements, the salience of the internet/social media, and the centrality of public space as the contested terrain for counter-hegemonic protest, have characterized most of these mobilizations.

Among them, however, the Spanish case is particularly significant. Since May 15, 2011, the "15M movement", as it came to be known for its inception date, or that of the Spanish *indignados*, as its participants were trivially labeled by the mass media, has served as beacon for mobilizations in Europe, the Mediterranean area, and the United States. Transmitted through the most recent information and communication technologies both by passersby, individual participants and, in a more systematic and strategic manner, by its World Extension Teams (WET), 15M mottoes, activities and organizational traits were quickly broadcast to the world. The WET commission of Acampadasol [the 15M camp in the Puerta del Sol Square, Madrid] was in fact set up during the first days of the movement with the explicit objective of disseminating and coordinating the *indignados* movement at the international level.

The inspirational character of 15M alone would encourage social movement scholars to pay special attention to its study. If we, however, zoom in in order to analyze the movement´s characteristics and peculiarities, and if we zoom out in order to encompass the changes that occurred in the Spanish political arena during the last few decades, we find elements that give an additional patina of scientific attractiveness to this movement. In this article we analyze the 15M by focusing on three axes: the cognitive, emotional and relational processes feeding the construction of a social movement identity. First, we concentrate on the diagnostic, prognostic and motivational framing tasks performed by 15M participants to define the problematic situation and attribute blame, articulate a solution to the problem, devise strategies to achieve that end, motivate participants to sustain their engagement and remedy the situation. Second, we concentrate on the emotions that were "mobilized" by social movement organizations linked to the 15M (e.g., outrage or indignation), and those emotions that emerged spontaneously during the "encounters" that took place in the public space: joy, efficacy and feelings of empowerment. Finally, we address the relational aspects entailed in the process of identity construction, that is, the activation and de-activation of both "real" and "imaginary" ties between 15M members and previous and/or current political and social collectives within the "progressive camp". In following this triple objective, our study will describe the process of identity-synchronization that has allowed people with no previous political participation and with different, and oftentimes opposing, politico-ideological trajectories to feel part of the movement. Before delving into the analysis of the 15M, we offer a description of the socio-historical context, and the cycle of protest within which it emerged. Data comes from in-depth interviews and focus groups with key activists, ethnographic observations in camps and assemblies in Bilbao and Madrid during the summer of 2011, as well as webpages and facebook accounts associated to the 15M[1].

Context of emergence of the 15M movement: Multi-dimensional crisis and the cycle of protest

By 2007, the Spanish community was blossoming: it had a public account surplus of more than 2 percent of the GDP, and the economy was growing by 3.5 percent. Just one year later, the surplus had become deficit, growth had fallen to less than 1 percent, and the Spanish economy was officially entering recession. Although the economic decline was related to a worldwide financial crisis, it also responded to clearly identifiable domestic facts: the bursting of a decade-long real estate bubble and the implosion of the associated lending market. Following the lead of other developed countries, the Spanish government rapidly created a 99 billion-euro bail-out fund and began to rescue vulnerable banks. In addition, it urged the merger of savings banks that had lent heavily during the property boom; in less than one year the number of savings banks was cut down to 17 from 45. Moreover, in an attempt to weather the socio-economic impacts of the financial storm, the government adopted an economic stimulus plan. The pack included an 8 billion-euro investment in infrastructure, the extension of jobless subsidies to the long-term unemployed, and a 2,500-euro "Baby Check" for each newborn child.

Despite these measures, the recession ravaged most Spaniards, with a particularly severe impact on the young. Unemployment rates soared to more than 40 percent for 20- to 24-year-olds—about twice the already alarming national average and the highest for younger populations in the European Union. Those with jobs were, however, not much better off; despite having one or more university degrees, many of them were caught in a system of temporary contracts, and poorly paid, low-status jobs completely unrelated to what they were trained for. As such, the Spanish youth was forced to resign to a key trait of adulthood; in late 2011, almost 70 percent of the 18- to 29-year-olds still lived with their parents. This delayed independence was, in addition, putting further pressure on tight family budgets and overburdened support networks.

After initially denying that the Spanish economy was in trouble, in May 2010 president Zapatero announced a slew of adjustment policies. The pack included wage cuts for civil servants, the end of the "Baby Check", and the freezing of pension increases. As talks about Greece's potential economic bailout began to intensify, attention turned on Spain amid worries over its public deficit (60 percent of its GDP). As a result, the government continued to pass austerity measures, combining them with a considerable rise in the Value Added Tax. In addition, a labor market reform was approved in September: Presented as a necessary means towards reducing joblessness, the reform actually made it easier and cheaper for employers to hire and fire workers. In late September, trade unions called for the first general strike in a decade to protest against the measure; despite the bleak state of affairs, the mobilization's impact was almost negligible. In January 2011, the government passed a pension reform raising the retirement age from 65 to 67 thus hindering the "repleneshing" of labor posts. This time, surprisingly, the unions were on board.

In March 2011, university students called for a general strike. Thousands of students marched throughout the country in protest against the unemployment rate, labor precariousness, the rise in tuition fees, the Bologna Plan, and budget cuts in education. A few days later, the platform "Youth Without Future" (*Juventud Sin Futuro*) organized a demonstration against the economic crisis and the bipartisan "PPSOE partitocracy". The slogan was: "Homeless, jobless, pensionless, fearless" (*Sin casa, sin curro, sin pensión, sin miedo*) (see Figure 14-1). The long-standing repudiation of the government's socio-economic and educational policies was soon to be combined with a novel factor: the rage triggered by a measure that intended to suffocate the "free culture" of the internet. In early February 2011, the internet-based initiative "#donotvoteforthem" (*#nolesvotes*) called for a withdrawal of votes from the political parties that had approved the so-called Sinde Law in the upcoming municipal and regional elections. This "antipiracy" bill aimed at shutting down previously legal websites that enabled the free download of music and film.

Figure 14-1. Photograph showing the Youth Without Future demonstration slogan: "Homeless, Jobless, Pensionless, Fearless"

Note 1: The t-shirt worn by the man depicted in this photograph shows the slogan of the demonstration called by Youth Without Future on April 6, 2011: "Youth Without Future. Homeless, Jobless, Pensionless, Fearless". The photograph was taken in Sol Square (Madrid) during the first week of the Acampada by Samuel Sánchez; it appeared in the front page of the newspaper El País on May 20, 2011. In the back of the picture, a placard reads "#spanishrevolution YES WE CAMP!" Photo source: Manifestación Democracia Real Ya © Ediciones El Pais,S.L./ Samuel Sánchez, 20 May 2011.

Spain's internally restless groups, however, did not "act" alone; it was boosted by a chain of international events, in which youth was the *avant garde*. Among them were the Arab Spring mobilizations for political reforms and civil liberties, Iceland's "silent revolution" against neoliberal adjustment policies, and the mobilizations of the Portuguese "Generation in Trouble" or "Desperate Generation" (*Geração à Rasca*), The disclosure of WikiLeaks documents showing Spanish government officials to be less than forthright, and Stéphane Hessel's book, *Indignez-vous* ("*Time for Outrage*!"), also contributed to inflaming Spanish passions. Seemingly, there was not a single or final straw breaking the camel's back. This conjuncture of uncoordinated domestic and international events worked in a synergic fashion, prompting a collective outburst of indignation. In this combustible context, the call issued by the digital platform "Real Democracy Now" (DRY, *Democracia Real Ya*) to take to the streets was "just" the spark that ignited the *indignados* mobilizations.

Using twitter and facebook, DRY called "the unemployed, the poorly paid, the subcontractors, the precarious, the young people..." to take to the Spanish streets on May 15, the week prior to the regional and municipal elections. The protest was called under the motto "we are not commodities in the hands of politicians and bankers" (see Figure 14-2). Despite being silenced by the corporate media channels, hundreds of thousands of people took to the streets in fifty Spanish cities; small supporting demonstrations were also organised in Dublin, Amsterdam, Istanbul, Bologna, Paris, London and Lisbon. In harmony with the slogan "they don't represent us" (*no nos representan*), the demonstrations were characterized by the absence of flags and political or trade union acronyms.

Figure 14-2. Photograph taken during the "Real Democracy Now!" Demonstration on May 15, 2011

Note: The placard reads: "Real Democracy Now! We are not commodities in the hands of politicians and bankers. Source: Manifestacions Democracia Real Ya / © Ediciones El Pais, S. L./Uly Martin, 15 May 2011.

Triggered by the political and police mismanagement of the 15M mobilization, in the following evenings the calling for "Real Democracy Now" quickly gave way to an "Occupy the Square" (*Toma la plaza*) movement. Despite the explicit restrictions made by the electoral bodies and the constant threat of evictions, the *acampadas* held the squares in several Spanish cities until mid-July; these occupations constituted the movement's most evident act of civil disobedience. Campers rapidly equipped themselves with organizing committees, thematic working groups and assemblies. The committees dealt with the day-to-day functioning of the *acampadas*; they concentrated on issues such as cleaning, infrastructure, infirmary, nutrition, respect, action (performances and civil disobedience activities), expansion (art and placard-painting) and communication. The working groups, instead, focused on themes such as the economy, sustainability, short-term and long-term politics, international liasons, etc.

Finally, the *acampadas* held their own assemblies, as well as general assemblies for non-camping participants. When the camps could no longer be held in mid-June, they gave rise and passed the torch to decentralised assemblies in small towns and villages, and neighbourhoods within large cities. This movement towards "the local" was characterized by a steep decrease in the overall number of participants and, paradoxically, it was accompanied by an internationalization of the protest. The "15M Movement", as it came to be known, or that of the Spanish *indignados,* as its participants were trivially labeled by the mass media, was rapidly emulated in towns and cities all over the globe. On October 15, 2011, more than 1,000 cities in 82 countries took to the streets and squares in a global non-violent protest guided by the motto "united for global change".

Despite these massive popular mobilizations, Mariano Rajoy's right-wing People's Party (PP, *Partido Popular*) won a landslide victory in both the May (municipal and regional) and November (general) 2011 elections. As voters punished the outgoing center-left Socialist government (*Partido Socialista Obrero Español)* for the worst economic crisis in generations and the European Union's highest jobless rate, Rajoy declared that the public deficit for 2011 would come in at 8 percent of GDP, and that the government would be forced to pass new austerity measures. On December 30, the President announced a cut in the following year's public spending by 8.9 billion euros.

The cognitive dimension: Superhero against injustices

Previous studies (Freidin and Perugorría, 2007) have pointed at the difficulties involved in forging collective identities amidst social movements composed of "publics" (Mische, 2005), that is, of interstitial activist forums where participants build relations and pursue joint actions through the equalization and synchronization of multiple identities[2]. Figure 14-3 [A and B] shows a conceptual map of *Acampada Sol* elaborated by the hacker and 15M member Marga Padilla. Emanating from what the author has called "an individual contribution to the movement based on her specific know-how", the map turned into an interactive and collective "product" after it was posted in various webpages, and 15M members circulated it in different digital networks and even posted it in the *Puerta del Sol* camp. In a matter of weeks, the map received hundreds of comments expressing praise, making suggestions, and posing critiques that were incorporated by Marga in three ensuing versions. Although the map is intended to "depict" Sol's *acampada*, we use it to delve into the process of collective identity construction that is taking place within the 15M. As Padilla puts it, "this conceptual map (...) is only a help to depict what cannot be represented. It is a humble, unfinished map, precarious at its core. And needed all the same..."[3]

As mentioned earlier, the 15M demonstration was the spark that ignited the *acampadas* and ensuing mobilizations. Although "DRY is decoupled from the *acampada*", according to Padilla's conceptual map "there is continuity in the message". The placards designed by DRY for the May 15 march (see Figure 14-4) help us understand what that message was about: political corruption, capitalist greed, vital (not only work) precariousness, and special "treats" awarded by the Spanish government to banks and big fortunes while "common people" suffer adjustment measures and the curtailment of their social rights. This diagnostic framing exemplifies what Gamson (1995) calls an "injustice frame", that is, an interpretive scheme that characterizes the actions of an authority system as unjust and legitimates disobedience against it (Snow et al., 1997). As stated in the 15M manifesto "How to Cook a Non-Violent Revolution": "We don't understand why we need to pay the bills of a crisis whose authors continue to enjoy record benefits. We are fed up of injustices". In the words of a 15M member, "The 15M has turned into a collective superhero that goes wherever there is an injustice" (Interview to Zulo). This framing of injustice provided a common language in which activists from different movements, and persons with no previous political participation, could communicate and find common ground.

Figure 14-3A. Conceptual Map of *Acampada Sol* (3rd version), elaborated by Marga Padilla (Continued in Figure 14-3B)

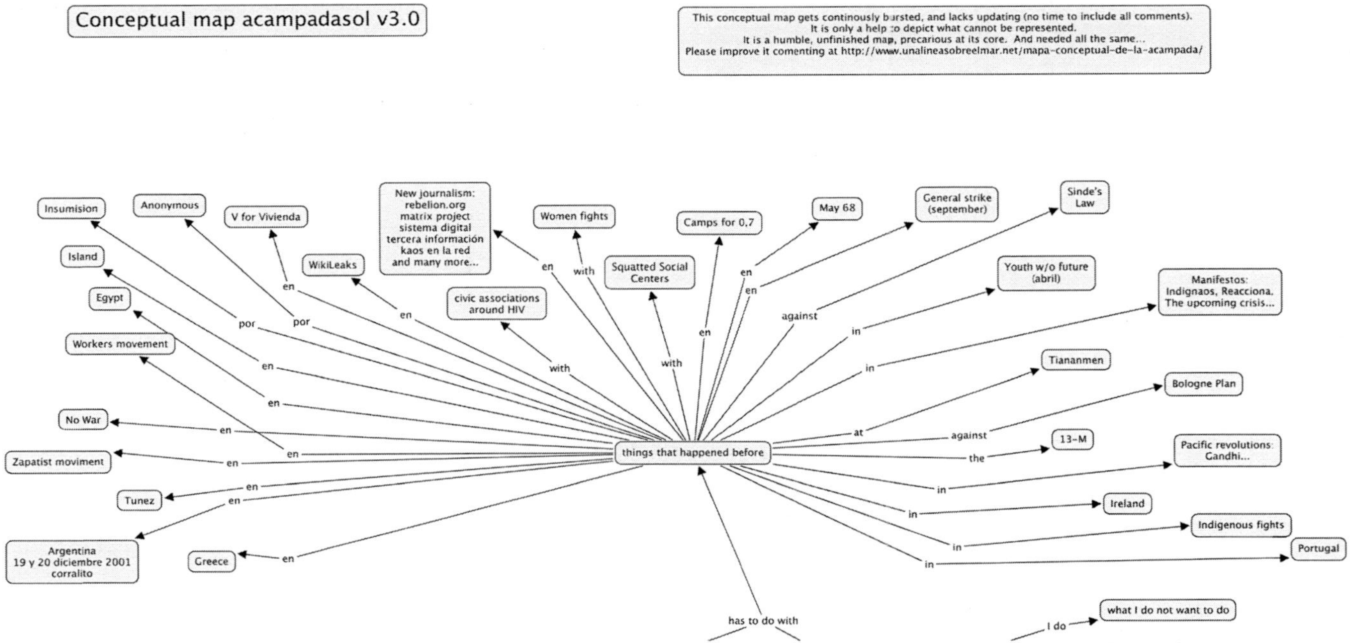

Note: Figure 14-3A shows the upper part of Padilla's conceptual map and Figure 14-3B its lower part. The map has been split in two halves to facilitate its reading. Text in larger fonts (e.g., "Collective", "Disembodied", "Global") has been inserted by the authors as part of the analytic process and does not appear in the original version of Padilla's map. For more details, see endnote 3. The whole Spanish version of the map is available at this website: http://www.unalineasobreelmar.net/mapa-conceptual-de-la-acampada/.

Figure 14-3B. Conceptual Map of *Acampada Sol* (3rd version), elaborated by Marga Padilla (Continued from Figure 14-3A)

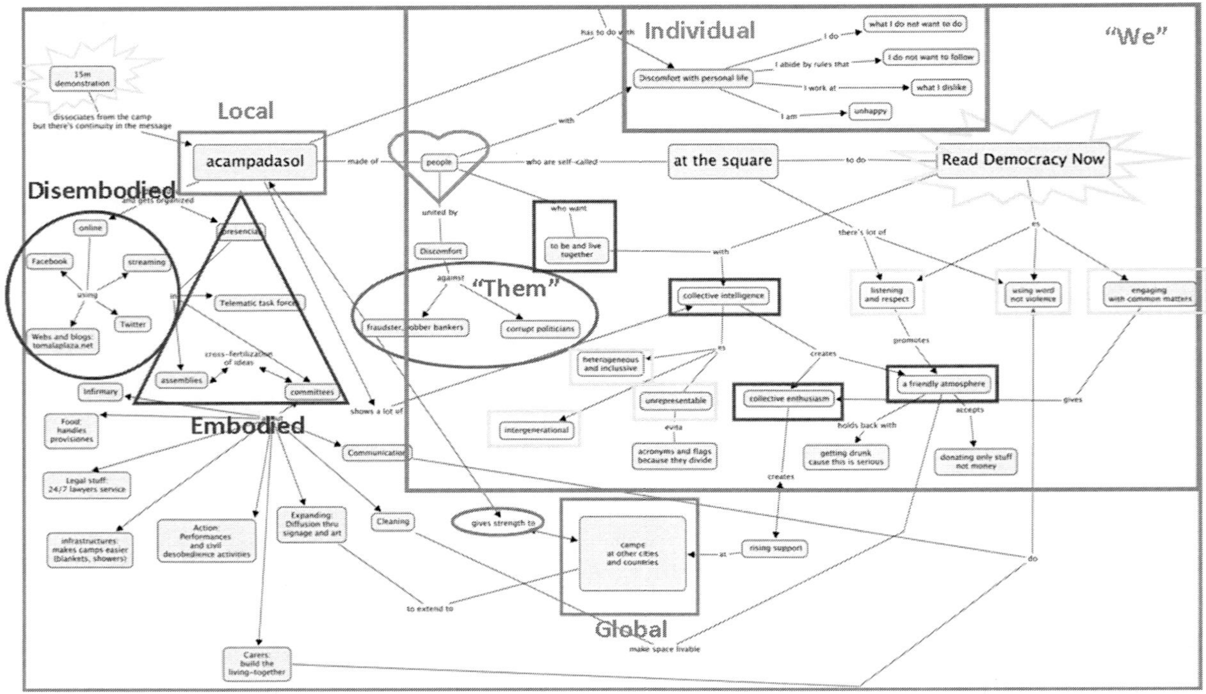

Figure 14-4. Real Democracy Now! Placards for the May 15, 2011 demonstration

Because company benefits are now the cause of layoffs.

Because the current electoral law benefits big parties, those that are indicted in more than 700 corruption trials.

Because when you no longer have a job, your parents no longer have a pension, the price of mortgages goes up, and they take away your home, you will still be owing money to the bank.

Because you will not have a pension unless you have 35 years of continued work.

Because the minimum salary of a congressman is 3,996 euros.

Because almost 50% of the Spanish young are un-employed.

Because you pay taxes, and "big fortunes" fly their money to tax havens.

Because while they trim your social rights banks get public (state) subsidies.

Because the 5 largest Spanish banks obtained benefits for 14K million euros in 2010.

Because our politicians rule for the markets, and not for the citizens.

Because we are not commodities in the hands of politicians and bankers.

However, the 15M did not "just" emerge to denounce this injustice, or to accomplish a "cathartic" mission. Social movements spring up to alleviate or alter situations that activists identify as problematic; their direct action therefore depends on the identification of the sources of the problem, and relies on boundary and adversarial framing (Benford & Snow, 2000: 616). Marga Padilla's conceptual map allows us to reconstruct the identity work through which 15M participants have crafted a "we", and a "them" (Gamson, 1995; Aminzade & McAdam, 2001; Diani, 2003). The "them" has included those antagonists identified as responsible for the situation of injustice: mainly thieving and swindling bankers (*banqueros estafadores y ladrones*) and corrupt politicians. 15M members are "united by their discontent" against these actors; these are the "enemies" against whom their collective action has been directed:

> "We can vote, but we don't have a voice, and we are frustrated by the politicians' lack of will to develop mechanisms of direct participation in decision-making processes. Mechanisms that would put an end to corruption and to the lack of transparency in politics and public institutions, and that would place the citizen before the markets and other private interests" (15M manifesto: "How to Cook a Non-Violent Revolution").

The emotional dimension: Indignant, but also joyful and empowered

Having diagnosed the problematic situation and identified the sources of and those responsible for the injustice, DRY encouraged "persons" to put an end to cynicism and apathy. It called Spaniards to feel, and to act; as Figure 14-5 shows, its slogans read "take the street" (*toma la calle*), and "be outraged!" (*Indígnate*!). Borrowing from Stephane Hessel's viral manuscript, DRY utilized the emotion of outrage, or indignation, as a stepping stone for the construction of the movement's collective identity. The formation of a collective actor not only involves cognitive agreements and negotiations—such as those entailed in the diagnostic framing tasks mentioned above—but also demands affective or emotional investments. Passion and emotions, as much as ideology and interests, push people to mobilize and act together (Goodwin, Jasper and Polletta, 2001: 6).

Figure 14-5. Real Democracy Now! placards for the May 15, 2011 demonstration

Note: The placard reads: "Take the street. May 15, 2011. www.democraciarealya.es. Be outraged!".

Several 15M members concur with Zygmunt Bauman's controversial statement: "The 15M is an emotional movement" (Interview to Javier de la Cueva). However, in their view, emotions and cognition are not mutually exclusive, but mutually invigorating:

> "A friend of mine said during the first days of the *acampada*: 'There is no cynicism here. Everybody believes in what she is doing'. [...] Maybe that's what Zigmunt Bauman meant when he said the 15M was, above all, emotion. [...] We are alive, and we are together! There is a change of atmosphere [*clima*], and that has a very strong emotional intensity. And

> you can sense that in the bodies, in the faces... But I wouldn't say that it is just an emotional movement and that there is no thinking involved. There is thought in emotions, and we are thinking a lot." (Interview to Amador Fernández-Savater).

"The 15M is an emotional movement", but despite the media's trivial *indignados* label, outrage was not the sole emotion pushing the 15M forward. Once the uprising was in motion, and people were taking the streets and occupying squares, indignation would be replaced, or at least complemented, by collective enthusiasm and joy. As a 15M member put it, "The feeling during the 15M demonstration was of happiness" (Interview to Leila Nachawati). Or, "[the 15M] is a cry coming from a society that is tired, fed up. It's been a cry, but a smiling one" (Interview to Julio Albarrán). Once they were in action, 15M members also felt empowered:

> "[With the 15M] we have moved from powerlessness to power, from isolation and competition to being together, to discovering the other as an accomplice and no longer as an obstacle, from cynicism to 'we can change things' and we can be protagonists of that change. That generates a very strong emotion." (Interview to Amador Fernández-Savater).

The relational dimension: Identity construction and synchronization

But, who are the 15M members after all? Or, more specifically, how do 15M members perceive and "present" themselves? As mentioned above, the boundary framing performed by 15M participants has identified both a "them" against whom collective action has been directed, but also a "we" bound by bonds of trust and affection. We argue that this "we" has been synthesized in the term "persons"; "persons"—not people—are at the heart of the process of collective identity construction being conducted within the 15M.

Most 15M members do not portray themselves as activists or militants. In their viewpoint, these terms are associated to an "old way of doing politics" (*la vieja política*) based on ideological or partisan affiliations; 15M members reject these "acronyms and flags, because they divide" (Interview to Miguel Arana). In turn, they think of themselves as members of a community of "persons"; they thus encouraged the development of individual messages and personalized placards. The centrality of the term "person" can also be observed in the banners utilized during the October 14, 2011 world demonstration for global change (see Figure 14-6), and appreciated in this interviewee's portrayal of the 15M:

> "A movement whose protagonists were not militants, that doesn't have a codified vocabulary of protest, that was very inclusive, that wasn't just talking about the Left, that didn't speak about revolution in a classical sense [...], that tries to have everybody, anybody, do politics... Some militant friends used to tell me 'they are talking about 'persons,' and that is not a political concept. I, on the contrary, saw the power associated to talking about persons: we are all persons, and talking about persons and persons' problems we can be together, and start talking." (Interview to Amador Fernández-Savater).

Figure 14-6. Banners utilized in the "Occupy" demonstrations that took place all over the world on October 15, 2011

Note: The placard on the left reads: "October 15. Stop the cuts. Rescue persons now!!! United for global change. Take the street. 6 P.M.. Address". The placard on the right reads: "October 15. #Worldrevolution. An ethical revolution, a change of course, is needed. This system treats human beings as numbers and not as persons. Together we can change it".

As with injustice frames, talking about "persons" allowed both people with no previous political participation and with different militant trajectories to feel part of a same collective. This term, "persons", "synchronized" (Mische, 2005) different and probably opposing political ideologies; it also blurred other potentially alienating axes of dissent: gender, class, religious and national identities, among others. The "we are the 99 percent" slogan issued by Occupy Wall Street activists and immediately apropriated by the 15M, synthesized this principle of "inclusiveness" in a brilliant fashion. So did the "united by common sense" (*unidos por el sentido común)* motto that could be seen in banners all across Spain:

> "We are bringing up the fact that we are the 99 percent, that what unites us are problems and ways of thinking that are common to many people, in a very transversal way. [...] All these things can be common to many different people, people who do not have a clear identity. We need to start thinking over the basis of common problems, in lieu of identities. [... 15M's]. Inclusiveness has to do with this: it is a movement that is based on problems, and not on identities. We want to begin with concrete problems, not with ideologies. We will arrive to that, or not, eventually. Concrete problems having to do with real life, with everybody's life; this way the movement will become real, will have to do with the lives we lead and not with eruditions about the world that do not bear any relation to practices, to life." (Interview to Amador Fernández-Savater).

Having "problems", instead of "ideologies" or "identities", as a point of departure marked a path of "inclusiveness" for the 15M since its inception. But these "transversal" problems weren't limited to the "crisis train", and weren't just collective; they also had individual manifestations, and both levels seem to be intertwined in the perspective of 15M members. According to Marga Padilla's map, the "we" is integrated by persons who feel "discomfort with their personal lives" for "doing what they don't want to do, abiding by rules they don't want to follow, and working at jobs they dislike". As we will show below, collective involvement has provided a mitigation to this individual distress for 15M members.

At the collective level, in turn, the "we" is associated with traditional social movements (e.g., labor organizations), new social movements (e.g., feminism, indigenous movements, squatter movements) and, using an interviewee's terminology, "social movements of diverse kinds that are not movements" (e.g., "V de Vivienda", "Anonymous", "#donotvoteforthem", "Youth without Future"). The "we" can also be observed in "events" (e.g., May '68 and Argentina 2001) and even books or manifestos (e.g., *Indignez-vous!, Reacciona*). Moreover, the "things that happened before"—section of Padilla's conceptual map—can be interpreted as a social movement genealogy composed of both international and domestic progenitors, of remote, more recent and even contemporary ancestry.[3] The real and "imaginary" ties, linking the 15M to these actors with what could be called the "progressive field", refer to the relational dimension of identity construction processes (Melucci, 1995). This genealogy can be thought of, too, as a "narrative of becoming" (Polletta, 1998).

The relational dimension: Politics of the encounter

As we mentioned above, collective involvement in the 15M has provided a mitigation to people's individual distress. According to Padilla's conceptual map, *Acampada Sol* is "made of people who want to be and live together" to combat their discomfort with their personal lives. In the words of an interviewee, "With 15M we have recovered that part of a "person who is willing to share", a part we had long forgotten" (Interview to Carolina García). In a previous section, we showed that "sharing" or "being together" gave 15M participants a sense of empowerment, efficacy, and joy. This "encounter" (Merrifield, 2011) has motivated participants to get involved in the 15M, and to sustain their engagement even in times of declining activity. This "encounter" is also at the core of the prognostic framing performed by 15M members (Freidin & Perugorría, 2007); it is seen as a first step in the bumpy and sinuous road towards finding a solution to the multi-dimensional crisis (Benford & Snow, 2000:617).

15M members do not "just" want to be together; this is not a "play date". They see themselves as "self-convened" persons that "occupy the square" "to do real democracy now". As Padilla's map shows, democracy is associated to "using words, not violence", and to a "friendly atmosphere" promoted by the act of "listening and respect". It is also tied to "engaging with common matters", with problems that affect society as a whole. Real democracy is achieved with "collective intelligence", described as "heterogeneous and inclusive", "inter-generational" and "unrepresentable" —that is, avoiding "acronyms and flags because they divide". As mentioned before, one of the outcomes of this from-the-bottom-up democratic praxis is collective enthusiasm. So is "growing support" in other cities and countries, which in turn, "gives strength to" *Acampada Sol*.

As can be observed in Padilla's map, real democracy is accomplished (or "done") in two different ways: "by actual presence" in *acampadas,* assemblies, thematic working groups and committees, and in a "disembodied" and deterritorialized fashion through the use of online media. The 15M manifesto "How to Cook a Non-Violent Revolution" (2011) explicitly alludes to this double embeddedness of collective action:

> "We recovered and utilize the public space: we occupied the squares and the streets of our cities to meet and work in a collective, open and visible way. We inform and invite every citizen to participate. We debate about problems, look for solutions and organize actions and mobilizations. Our digital networks and tools are open: all the information is available on the Internet, in the streets and in the squares."

The 15M "encounter" thus combines online activism with more "traditional" forms of militancy. On the one hand, it embraces the digital-age sociability, where "everybody is getting together" in social media, and where groups can "operate with a multi-national's scope and a birthday party's informality" (Shirky, 2008), and can "organize without organizations" in order to "change the world without taking power" (Holloway, 2002). This form of activism is inspired by the idea that grassroots organizing no longer needs an organizer, a mediator; it follows the "do-it-yourself-with-others" spirit. On the other, the 15M is based on traditional repertoires: *acampadas*, assemblies and demonstrations are characterized by the physicality of bodies being present in a spatial meeting place (Gladwell, 2010). 15M members create group commonality through face-to-face, "strong-tie" offline activism, but also through online "weak-tie" association. Their "territorialized" way of doing politics from-the-bottom-up through the (re-)occupation of the public space and their "disembodied" political praxis mediated by the possibilities and constraints offered by the internet and online social networks seem to be complementary, and not contradictory or mutually exclusive. The two flanks strengthen one another; adding speed, a new dimension (Merrifield, 2011). We contend that this mutual reinforcement is facilitated by the structural affinity of their methods: assemblies and online networks are both characterized by direct participation, horizontality, and open deliberation.

Conclusions

The 15M movement counts on different organizational precursors in the process of social mobilization (Youth Without Future) and in the articulation of forms of online (#donotvoteforthem) or hybrid (online-offline) protests (Malestar.org). As we have pointed out, the movement has its immediate origin in the profound discontent regarding the erosion of the Welfare State, and the political mismanagement of the socio-economic crisis. The plural composition of the *indignados* reflects the rejection of the most negative consequences of the process of globalization: the increased levels of social inequality and the precariousness of the life conditions of broad social sectors, especially, but not exclusively, the young. In addition, the 15M movement transfers to the public sphere a long-term discontent with the functioning of the Spanish democracy and persistent demands for deeper democratization and transparency in the administration of public affairs. In the perception of 15M members, this situation and this authority system are defined as "unjust", and it is precisely this "injustice frame" which has legitimated their disobedience.

Several members have agreed with the statement that the 15M is an emotional movement. The emotion of outrage, or indignation, constituted a central stepping stone for the construction of a collective identity in the beginnings of the movement. However, once the uprising was in motion, indignation was overflown by collective enthusiasm and joy derived from the experience of being together. As one interviewee put it, "[the 15M] is a cry coming from a society that is tired, fed up. It's been a cry, but a smiling one".

Although 15M members have tried to build on "common problems" in lieu of available "identities", they have nonetheless performed prognostic, diagnostic and motivational framing tasks that have begun to craft and shape their own, novel collective identity. Their boundary and adversarial framing has demarcated a "them" against which collective action has been directed: mainly thieving and swindler bankers and corrupt politicians. It has also forged a "we", composed of "persons"—not people, not militants—united by their "discomfort" towards these actors, but also towards the labels and methods coming from "old-time politics" (*la vieja política).* Talking about "persons" allowed both people with no previous political participation and with different militant trajectories to feel part of the 15M; it "synchronized" different and probably opposing political ideologies and blurred other potentially alienating axes of dissent.

15M members have also crafted a narrative of becoming; that "we" has a present and a future, but also has a traceable past. This narrative draws on the relational dimension of identity construction processes, and is depicted as a social movement genealogy tying the 15M to both international and domestic "progenitors". The ties—real and imaginary—composing this "family tree" link the movement to recent and also far-removed struggles, traditional and new social movements, and even "social movements that are not movements"—to use an interviewee's expression—that belong to what might be denominated the "progressive field". In addition, 15M members have invested their narrative of becoming with an individual dimension. 15M members are "persons" who used to feel a discomfort with their individual lives, and who now want to "be and live together" in a friendly atmosphere. The "progressive" genealogy crafted by 15M members could eventually enter in conflict with the all-synchronizing portrayal of the 15M as a "social movement of persons".

"Being together", "sharing" has allowed them to universalize their personal experiences, understandings and emotions, and has given them a sense of joy, empowerment, and efficacy. It is thus at the core of the prognostic framing performed by 15M members, and of the motivation drawing them to get involved and sustain their participation. This "politics of the encounter" has been facilitated and boosted by a mutually-reinforcing offline, "strong-tie" activism and online, "weak-tie" association, both based on an open, horizontal and participatory philosophy. In the words of Merrifield (2011), squares and digital media have provided a scenario for an illicit rendezvous of human bonding and solidarity, a material, virtual, and emotional topography in which something disrupts and intervenes in the previous social paralysis. But 15M members do not "just" want to be together; they gather to do, to do "real democracy". Real democracy is interpreted, and enacted, as an engagement in "common matters", an involvement thought of as inclusive, non-violent and necessarily direct or "unrepresentable". In their "encounters", 15M members materialize, and experience, what until then seemed an utopia.

Notes

[1] The interviews to Julio Albarrán, Miguel Arana, Javier de la Cueva, Amador Fernández-Savater, Carolina García, Leila Nachawati and Zulo were conducted by Stéphane M. Grueso, Patricia Horrillo and Pablo Soto during 2011 and 2012 for the project 15M.cc, available in http://15M.cc. Textual and graphic materials are available in the following websites: http://takethesquare.net/;
http://tomalaplaza.net/; http://madrid.tomalaplaza.net/;
http://acampadabcn.wordpress.com/; and http://15october.net/

[2] We use "collective identity" and "social movement identity" as exchangeable terms; the latter is defined as "the collective identity based on shared membership in a movement" (Polletta and Jaspers, 2001:289).

[3] A translation of this conceptual map from Spanish into English was made by 15M members themselves. Although this translation is at times incomplete or ambiguous, we have decided to keep the primary document untouched and to offer a complementary or alternative translation. If we read Padilla's conceptual map (Figure 14-3A) clockwise, the "Things that happened before" are: "in Greece; in Argentina on December 19 and 20 of 2001 [social upheavals triggered by the socio-economic crisis, restriction of cash withdrawals, and devaluation of bank savings]; in Tunisia; in the Zapatist movement; in No War [Anti-Iraq War movement]; in the workers movement; in Egypt; in Iceland; by Insumisión [anti-militarist social movement that encouraged the refusal to do military service in Spain]; by Anonymous; in V for Vivienda [pro-worthy housing and anti-foreclosure movement in Spain]; in Wikileaks; with the civic associations [working] around HIV; in New Journalism: Rebellion.org, Matrix Project, Sistema Digital, Tercera Información, Kaos en la Red and many more; with women fights; with Squatted Social Centers; in Camps for 0.7; in May 1968; in General strike [Spain, September 2010]; against Sinde's Law; in Youth without Future [Spain, April 2011]; in Manifestos: Indignaos, Reacciona, The upcoming crisis; at Tiananmen [Square]; against the Bologna Plan; the 13-M [11-M attacks in Madrid,

Spain]; in pacific revolutions: Ghandi…; in Ireland; in indigenous fights, and in Portugal".

In Figure 14-3A, the word "bursted" stands for "overflown"; the word "en" should be replaced by "in"; the word "por" should be replaced by the word "by". In Figure 14-3B, "discomfort" stands for "discontent" (*malestar*); the word "es" should be replaced by "is"; the word "evita" should be replaced by "avoids"; "living together" stands for "cohabitation"; "signage" stands for "sign/placard/banner-making". The word "Read" should be replaced by "Real".

References

Aminzade, R. and McAdam, D. (2001). 'Emotions and contentious politics', in Aminzade, R., Goldstone, J., McAdam, D., Perry, E., Sewell, W., Tarrow, S. and Tilly, Ch. (eds.), *Silence and voice in the study of contentious politics*, Cambridge: Cambridge University Press.

Anderson, B. (2006). *Imagined communities*. London: Verso.

Benford, R. and Snow, D. (2000). Framing processes and social movements: An overview and assessment. *Annual Review of Sociology*, vol. 26, pp. 611-639.

Calle, Á. (2005). *Nuevos movimientos globales. Hacia la radicalidad democrática*. Madrid: Editorial Popular.

Diani, M. (2003). 'Networks and social movements: A research programme', in Diani, M. and McAdam, D. (eds.) *Social movements and networks: Relational approaches to collective action,* New York: Oxford University Press.

Freidin, B. and Perugorría, I. (2007). 'Un enfoque multi-narrativo para el estudio del movimiento asambleario en Argentina', in Sautu, R. (ed.) *Práctica de la investigación cuantitativa y cualitativa. Articulación entre la teoría, los métodos y las técnicas,* Buenos Aires: Ediciones Lumiére, pp. 209-246.

Gamson, W. A. (1995). 'Constructing social protest', in Johnston, H. and Klandermans, B. (eds.) *Social movements and culture*. Minneapolis: University of Minnesota Press.

Gladwell, M. (2010). 'Why the revolution will not be tweeted', *New Yorker*, 4 October, pp. 1-5.

Goodwin, J., Jasper, J. and Polletta, F. (2001). 'Why emotions matter', in Goodwin, J., Jasper, J. and Polletta, F. (eds.) *Passionate politics. emotions and social movements,* Chicago: The University of Chicago Press, pp. 1-27.

Holloway, J. (2002). *Change the world without taking power: The meaning of revolution today,* London: Pluto Press.

Melucci, A. (1995). 'The process of collective identity', in Johnston, H. and Klandermans, B. (eds.) *Social movements and culture,* Minneapolis: University of Minnesota Press.

—. (1996). *Challenging codes. Collective action in the information age*, Cambridge: Cambridge University Press.

Merrifield, A. (2011). 'Crowd politics, or, 'Here comes everybuddy''. *New Left Review*, vol. 71, pp. 103-114.

Mische, A. (2005). 'Partisan performance: stylistic enactment and suppression in contentious publics', Paper presented at the Annual Meeting of the American Sociological Association, 13-16 August, .Philadelphia (U.S.A.),

Movimiento 15M, 'Manifesto "Cómo cocinar una revolución no violenta"', ('How to Cook a Non-Violent Revolution'), Available: http://takethesquare.net/es/2011/08/18/como-cocinar-una-revolucion-no-violenta/ [20 January 2012.

Padilla, Marga, 'Conceptual map acampadasol v3.0', Available: http://www.15m.cc/2011/09/metodologia-de-trabajo.html [20 January 2012].

Polletta, F. (1998). ''It was like a fever...' Narrative and identity in social protest', *Social Problems*, vol. 45, no. 2, pp. 137-159.

Polletta, F. & Jaspers, J. (2001). 'Collective identity in contentious politics', *Annual Review of Sociology*, vol. 27, pp. 283-305.

Shirky, C. (2008). *Here comes everybody. The power of organizing without organizations*, New York: Penguin Books.

Snow, D., Burke Rochford, E., Worden, S. and Benford, R. (1997). 'Frame alignment processes, micromobilization, and movement participation', in McAdam, D. & Snow, D. (eds.) *Social movements: Reading on their emergence, mobilization, and dynamics*, Los Angeles: Roxbury Press.

Tarrow, S. (1997). *Power in movement*. Cambridge: Cambridge University Press.

CHAPTER FIFTEEN

POLITICAL DISAFFECTION OR CRISIS OF THE IDEOLOGICAL LEFT? POLITICAL EFFECTS OF THE DEBT CRISIS IN SPAIN[1]

ALBERTO COTILLO
UNIVERSIDAD DE LA CORUÑA, SPAIN

Abstract

Different polls of public opinion carried out in Spain in the past years reveal a growth in political disaffection clearly related to an increasingly negative assessment of the Spanish economic situation. The usual interpretation of these results suggests so much a civil withdrawal from institutionalized politics as an increasing concern regarding the answers that institutionalized politics can offer to settle the negative implications of the debt crisis. The diffusion and popularization of diverse political initiatives that are beyond the reach of political parties and pre-existing social movements, such as the "15-M movement", can be understood just as an example of this withdrawal. Far from this usual interpretation, this chapter supports the idea that political disaffection cannot be understood either as a withdrawal from institutionalized politics or as a questioning of representative democracy and, therefore, the foundations of the Spanish political system. In addition, it cannot be understood as a concern regarding the answers the institutional politics can offer in order to respond to the challenges that the debt crisis raises. Rather, political disaffection in Spain must be understood as a response to the crisis of ideas among the parties and organizations of the ideological, institutionalized left. More than a public test of political disaffection, the results of public opinion polls must be understood as a reflection of the ideological crisis of the institutionalized left concerning answers to the challenges of the debt crisis.

Introduction: Theoretical and methodological considerations

The debt crisis' consequences have shaken Southern European societies and they are seen as a menace to global economy. Those who are suffering their marked outcomes are looking for a way out in political institutions. In representative democracies, political institutions are seen in away as responsible for the solutions to the debt crisis. It's not strange to find that lengthening of that crisis has increased citizens' pressure on democratic institutions. The delay in finding solutions to the debt crisis' consequences results in an increase in discontent with the performance of democratic representative institutions. Such a discontent can clearly be seen in such collective expressions as general strikes, mass demonstrations, social protest movements and the increase in political disaffection in general. For many citizens, political performance has stopped being part of the solution and is starting to become part of the problem itself.

Discontent with political answers to the economic crisis' consequences and political authorities' performance has been covered under the umbrella term of *political disaffection*. The recent increase in political disaffection has been a usual concern in western democracies. In particular, this concern has spread enormously as a consequence of the increase in discontent with political answers to the debt crisis. So, it's not strange to find the statement that a political disaffection process has taken place in Spain in recent years.

One of the most usual ways that sociological research has focused on the gap between citizens and democratic representative institutions has been centred on the concept of political disaffection, primarily thanks to the significant work of Di Palma (1970). In its canonical definition, disaffection is related to a subjective feeling, but some authors have broadened this term to refer to an attitudinal syndrome defined by:

> "…a certain estrangement or detachment from politics and the public sphere, as well as a critical evaluation of their core political institutions, their representatives, and the democratic political process. This attitudinal attribute is characterized by a number of specific symptoms, including a sense of personal inefficacy, cynicism and distrust, lack of confidence in representative institutions and/or the representatives elected, the belief that political elites do not care about the welfare of their citizens, and a general sense of estrangement from both politics and the political processes." (Torcal and Montero, 2006: 5).

Several sets of factors have been used to explain the increase in political disaffection levels. One kind of explanation has emphasized the role of cultural factors in the increase of disaffection levels. An example of this kind of cultural explanation revolves around the well-known term of social capital. This term emphasizes certain social organization features as trust, norms, and networks (Torcal and Montero, 2006). To social capital theory, political disaffection is a reflection of social trust decline, as this decline essentially depends on the disaffection process.

Instead of social capital theory explanations of political disaffection in terms of a lack of social trust, Newton (2001) argues that there is no such thing as general trust, but rather different kinds of trust which are expressed by different types of people for different reasons. In addition, he argues that political disaffection does not arise out of social disaffection, nor can it be explained in terms of social capital. For instance, membership in voluntary organizations seems to have a rather weak association with social trust, and barely any relationship with political trust (Newton, 2006: 82). At the national level, there is a general tendency for countries with high levels of social capital to have well-developed democratic systems, but the direct link between social capital and political disaffection can be broken by political factors, especially by poor government performance.

Instead of cultural explanations, a rational explanation model has been developed to emphasize that the increase in political disaffection depends on citizens' judgments about institutional performance, political corruption and macro-economic conditions. A usual instance of this explanation is focused on the gap that sometimes exists between citizens' performance expectations of a political realm and the frustration they feel when those hopes have not been fulfilled (Pharr and Putnam. 2000; Magalhaes, 2006).

This study constitutes an attempt to overcome the limitations of both kinds of explanation by recognizing the relevance of ideological factors in shaping citizens' judgments about political institutional performance. Cultural explanations appropriately stress the role of values, norms, and rules. Rational explanations adequately emphasize the role of the political and economic context in which those judgments are made. The concept of ideology gives contextual load to values and makes sense of citizens' judgments.

According to Newton and Norris (2000), ideological scale self-positioning is an essential variable in mediating the effect of politics on individuals' institutional confidence (cited in Torcal, 2006). In that sense, Segatti (2006) points that a:

> "...severe disaffection is a syndrome with the potential to become endemic across the ideological spectrum. While in some years it may affect voters

with certain ideological positions more than others, in other years it can spread to respondents with different ideological leanings."

However, other studies on political disaffection that focused on the analysis of the relationship between citizens' ideological self-positioning and their disaffection level come to a very discouraging conclusion. Several studies have shown that ideology does not have any effect on disaffection (Torcal, 2003; Torcal, 2006) or that it has a lesser impact and constitutes a secondary factor, clearly behind several others more relevant. For Offe (2006:34), arguing from a De Tocqueville perspective, patterns of political behaviour and attitudes are not so much constituted by individual properties (such as education, income and wealth), individuals' values and ideological orientations, "political culture" or structural background conditions, but by the institutional contexts in which citizens are embedded.

Contrary to the discouraging results that the sociological literature on political disaffection has been producing, this study tries to show that ideology has to fulfil a more relevant role than has been previously acknowledged. In particular, this study supports the idea that the inability to appreciate the real role that ideology has played in the explanation of political disaffection levels is due to certain limitations in most of the research in this field.

As a first limitation, the research has usually understood political disaffection in static terms rather than as a time process. Just from a time point of view, it can be appreciated that there is not a disaffection process without a previous political affection process. For this reason, this paper is dealing with the study of the political disaffection process that has taken place in Spain in the past decade, from 2002 to 2012. All throughout this period, economic conditions have varied considerably, from an economic expansion phase to a lasting recession over the past few years. There were also two changes in the governing political parties: the substitution of *Partido Popular* (conservative, PP henceforth) by *Partido Socialista Obrero Español* (socialist, PSOE henceforth) in 2004 and the replacement of PSOE by PP in 2011. Therefore, a cross-classification of the two variables produces four different political and economic situations as it is shown in Table 15-1.

The second limitation of the research on political disaffection has been the lack of a set of commonly accepted indicators and a clear definition of their different dimensions. This is a question more social than technical.

Table 15-1. Different scenes in economic and political context in Spain, 2002-2012

		Political situation (party in government)	
		Conservative	Socialist
Economic situation	Expansion	2002 to 2004 (March)	2004 (March) to 2008 (March)
	Recession	2011 (November) to the present	2008 (March) to 2011 (November)

The main difficulty that arises from this limitation is that the research on political disaffection adopts a different set of indicators, which makes difficult the task of comparing their outcomes and can even lead to outcomes clearly irreconcilable between them.

The same concept of political disaffection is clearly related to other terms such as discontent or disenchantment (Offe, 2006). However, such an attitude syndrome has a specific nature that can be distinguished from other terms. In this work, it is proposed that political disaffection makes reference to three aspects that are usually related to one another but that constitute clearly different dimensions. First of all, it refers to an estrangement from politics, the feeling that politics is something apart from citizens, too complicated to understand, where nothing can be done, either because of their own limitations or because of a lack of communication and control devices in the relationship between citizens and politicians. This first sense constitutes the central core of the concept of *political disaffection*, as it can be seen in Table 15-2. The specific indicators used to depict this first dimension are internal (called *complexity* by Listhaug, 2006) and external inefficacy, particularism (also called *political cynicism* by Bynner and Ashford, 1994) and the citizens' perceived lack of influence on politicians.

Political disaffection also makes reference to two other aspects or dimensions. The first one is related to the loss of confidence in representative political institutions, from here on referred to as *institutional disaffection*. This kind of disaffection is clearly different from the first because it refers to the projection of citizens' own feeling of political disaffection on institutions, but it can be independent from it and can be an answer, for instance, to the assessments about economic and political system performance.

Table 15-2. Indicators of political disaffection

Indicator	Item / Question	Answer (disaffection codes)
Political disaffection		
Internal inefficacy	"In general, politics seems so complicated that people like me cannot understand what is happening."[2]	Agree or strongly agree
External inefficacy	"Politicians do not care much about what people like me think."[3]	Agree or strongly agree
Particularism	"Politicians only look after their own interest, it doesn't matter who is in power."[4]	Agree or strongly agree
No influence	"People like me have no say over what the government does."[5]	Agree or strongly agree
Institutional disaffection		
Lack of confidence in government	"Would you be so kind to tell me how much confidence do you have in government?"[6]	None or 0-1
Lack of confidence in Parliament	"Would you be so kind to tell me how much confidence do you have in Parliament?"[7]	None or 0-1
Lack of confidence in political parties	"Would you be so kind to tell me how much confidence do you have in political parties?"[8]	None or 0-1
Political disengagement		
Lack of interest in politics	"How much interest do you have in politics?"[9]	None
Lack of political information	"Apart from the news, do you hear or see other programs about politics on radio or tv?"[10]	Never
Lack of satisfaction with democracy	"In general, how much satisfied are you with the way democracy works in Spain?"[11]	Not at all or 0-1

Lack of confidence in representative institutions sometimes is related to a general dissatisfaction towards democratic system performance, but sometimes not. Although dissatisfaction with the way democracy works can be one of the indicators of loss of confidence in a representative system, it can also constitute an independent indicator. Lack of interest in politics is another indicator of this distrust (also called *political apathy* by Bynner and Ashford, 1994). This distrust can be expressed by a lack of information about the political system. All these indicators will comprise for our study a set of indicators for the third dimension of political disaffection under the umbrella term of *political disengagement*.

Finally, the third usual limitation in some of the empirical studies on political disaffection is an unfortunate choice of analysis units and data analysis techniques. Many of the studies on political disaffection have been done on the individual level of analysis, and they have focused on the disaffected citizen (Evans and Letki, 2006). However, the main problems stem from the choice of the technique of data analysis, especially some variants of linear regression analysis. To a large extent, the obtained outcomes and conclusions depend on that analysis technique. Sometimes, it is not clear if they meet the parametric assumptions, such as normality and linearity, that are necessary for a correct interpretation of outcomes.

Instead of taking for granted that parametric assumptions are fulfilled, I have confirmed that this assumption does not hold for many of the disaffection indicators. For this reason, I have opted to apply a binary logistic regression analysis. The ultimate aim of this choice was to establish the effect of self-positioning on the left and far left of the ideological scale on any of the ten political disaffection indicators under consideration.

Logistic regression analysis is especially useful in assessing the role of ideology in political disaffection variations over the past decade in Spain. In particular, the aim of this study is to establish if the citizens' positioning on the ideological left is related to different levels of political disaffection. For that, it is firstly necessary to deal with the descriptive analysis of the changes in several political disaffection indicators and, secondly, to determine if the citizens positioned on the ideological left show different paths in the evolution of political disaffection than those from other positions.

The most abundant and continuous data on political disaffection in Spain over the past decade come from the *Centro de Investigaciones Sociológicas* ("Sociological Research Centre", henceforth CIS). In order to achieve that ultimate aim, I will rely on several surveys that CIS has carried out over the past decade in which were included some of the political disaffection indicators used in the present research. Unfortunately, although CIS included a number of the relevant questions, this has not been done in a systematic way. CIS has included most of the questions on political disaffection in many surveys on political attitudes over the past decade, but only on two occasions, March 2002 and January 2006, it included all the items. In spite of that, I prefer to include all the data on political disaffection that can be found in CIS surveys, even though they do not seem to be uncontested.

The point I would like to make, in this study of Spanish political attitudes, is that what has usually been understood as the political disaffection process being a by-product of the debt crisis has rather been a political crisis that is mainly due to a clear divorce between the institutional and ideological left. By *institutional* left I refer to political parties, unions and associations that place themselves on the ideological left. By *ideological* left I refer to citizens who place themselves on the left side of the ideological scale (1 to 4, in a 10-point scale of ideological self-positioning). After a period of increase in political affection of those citizens in the ideological left towards representative institutions following the PSOE electoral victory in March 2004, the current economic crisis has marked the end of that affection process.

Consequently, a first hypothesis of this study is that the political disaffection process in Spain over the past decade has been a much more complex process than is commonly assumed, considerably varying across dimensions. In particular, if it is supposed that the loss in political affection is due, first of all, to the divorce between institutional (mainly government, parties and trade unions) and ideological (citizens' self-placement) left, then it could be expected that different dimensions of political disaffection would show a different evolution. So, the main variation in disaffection levels would be produced by institutional disaffection rather than by other dimensions. In other words, this study supposes that a true crisis of confidence in democratic representative institutions has occurred in Spain in the past few years instead of just an increase in political disaffection.

This crisis of confidence contrasts with the previous affection process and the especial interest in politics among those on the left of the ideological scale. As a second hypothesis, I would like to pose that those self-positioned on the left would show more positive attitudes to politics than those on other positions of the ideological scale and that these attitudes were starting to change due to the recent crisis of confidence. Consequently, it is supposed that the political affection process has given place to higher levels in political competence among those self-positioned in the ideological left and that these levels have tended to diminish, to a certain extent, as a result of the loss of confidence in representative institutions.

Finally, as a third hypothesis, this study proposes that self-positioning on the ideological left is related to observed variations in the evolution of political disaffection indicators in Spain during the past decade. To put it another way, this study hypothesizes that self-positioning on the ideological left and far left (points 3 and 4 on a ten-point scale for the center-left and points 1 and 2 for the far left) is more related to those political disaffection indicators which have been more subject to change during the past decade. In that way, the variations in political disaffection indicators can be attributed, to a certain extent, to belonging to a particular set of positions in the ideological self-positioning scale.

If the three previous hypotheses are confirmed, then it cannot be asserted that political disaffection is a one-dimensional proccss where ideology is worthless. Moreover, it has to be admitted that ideology has played an important role in the evolution of political disaffection in Spain in recent years. Finally. instead of talking about an increase in political disaffection it would be more appropriate to talk about the end of the affection that the ideological left showed to representative institutions during the middle years of the past decade. In case of confirmation, the process would be better understood as a true crisis in the institutional left rather than a general process of disaffection.

Disaffection? What disaffection?

One of the main difficulties from a lack of a unique and synthetic measure of political disaffection is that it is hard to establish its magnitude at any time. Usually, the increase in political disaffection in Spain in recent years is exemplified by the fact that politicians are considered as the third of citizens' concern, just after the economic situation and the alarming unemployment rates (CIS). However, it seems very reductionist to limit the disaffection problem to a perception of politicians as a part of the problem and not as part of the solution.

A more adequate measure of the increase in citizens' concern about the role that politics plays in the solution of problems posed by the economic crisis is related to the percentage of those who consider the economic situation as very bad to the percentage of those who think exactly the same about the political situation. As it is shown in Figure 15-1, there has been a considerable increase in citizens' concern about the economic situation. A decade ago, in a period of economic expansion, less than five per cent of Spaniards considered that economic situation was very bad. In the July 2012 survey, the percentage of those who thought the same was around fifty per cent, ten times more than before. But the move from a minority perception about the seriousness of economic situation to a majority judgement about it did not happen at a constant rhythm. The perception of the seriousness of the situation has increased at a constant way just from the first months of 2008, and it has remained in high levels since then.

The more relevant outcome is that the concern about the political situation has increased dramatically in past years as much as has increased the concern about the economic situation. In fact, the concern about the political situation has increased in parallel to the economic situation with a year gap. Only in 2003 and 2007, the years just before the two national elections, the political situation was considered worse than the economic situation. Certainly, these particular concerns about the political situation were temporary as it is shown by the fact that it rapidly dropped after each new electoral process (2004, 2008, and 2011).

It seems to be proved that concern about the political situation has tended to move in parallel to concern about economic situation with a year gap. However, can it be said that this relationship does mean an increase in disaffection? The answer to this question depends critically on the set of disaffection indicators that is used. If the analysis is centred around the set of indicators that has been assumed to constitute the central core of the political disaffection concept, then the answer has to be rather negative. Political disaffection (first dimension) has not undergone important variations in the past decade, and in 2011 it was on very similar levels to those in 2002. The internal consistency of the four disaffection indicators reveals that they have tended to change very slightly and in a similar way during the past decade, as it can be seen in Figure 15-2.

It can be stated that there was a limited process of political disaffection from 2008 and that this process is related to the increase in concern about the economic and political situation. But the most important outcome is that the levels of disaffection in 2011, a time when there was a dreadful perception about the economic and political situation, were very similar to those found in 2002, a time when there was economic expansion in Spain. Thus, it makes sense to talk about political disaffection, something that can be stated only in relation to a previous process of political affection. The fact that the "internal" and "external inefficacy", "particularism" and "no influence" levels increase since 2008 is only due to the previous drop in them from 2004 to 2007.

As a consequence, political disaffection levels measured by the first set of indicators seem quite independent from the perception about the economic situation and they only seem to depend on the perception about the political situation to the extent that they previously had entailed a political affection process. But, can the same conclusion be reached in relation to *institutional disaffection* indicators? It seems quite clear that the answer is a negative one. In fact, institutional disaffection has undergone a notable increase from 2008, in clear relation to the rise in citizens' concern about the economic and political situation (see Figure 15-3).

The concern about the economic and political situation seems to have affected every democratic representative institution to a similar extent. In general, the increase in institutional disaffection has affected trust in government more than any other. However, lack of confidence in Parliament and political parties has also been increasing since 2008. Although there is a great spread in different measures of the same indicator for every year, the rapid loss of confidence in main democratic representative institutions seems to be a very solid tendency.

Figure 15-1. Evolution of negative assessment of the economic and political situation of Spain

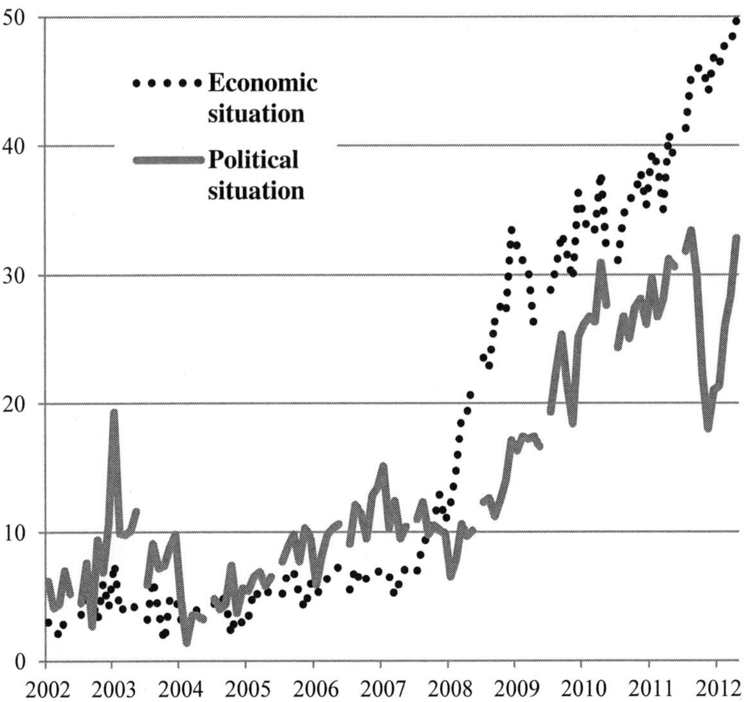

Source: CIS. Negative assessment = very bad. Values in %.

Figure 15-2. Indicators of political disaffection in Spain, 2002-11

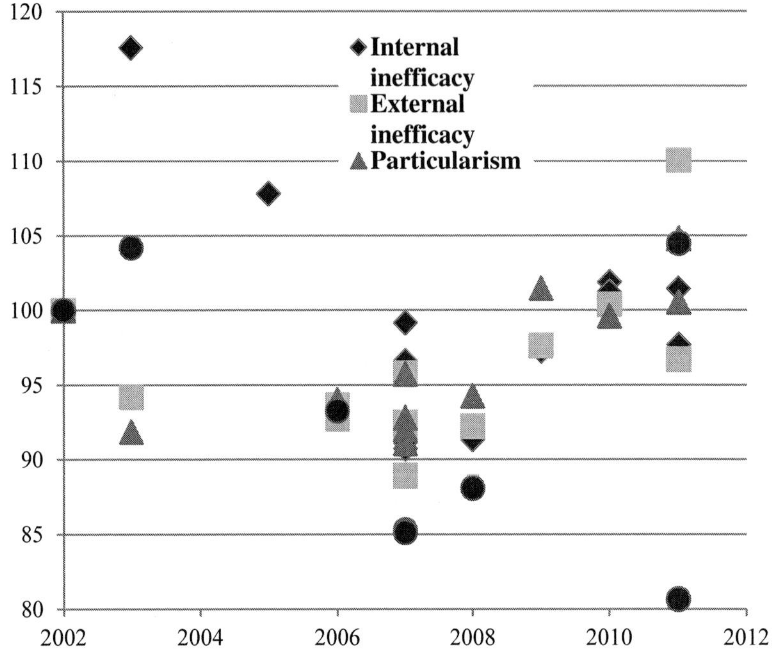

Source: CIS. Base: 2002=100. The presence of several points in the same year means the indicators have been measured several times during this year.

This conclusion allows us to assert that there has taken place a process of a real crisis of confidence in representative institutions in Spain during the past years rather than a process of political disaffection. However, has that confidence crisis affected citizens' *satisfaction with democracy*? According to CIS, it seems that the answer to that question is that the confidence crisis has affected it to a certain extent. The rise in concern about the economic and political situation and the parallel increase in the lack of confidence in representative institutions have affected satisfaction with democracy. In fact, the lack of satisfaction with the way democracy works in Spain has been increasing since 2008 to a very notable extent (see Figure 15-4).

In spite of the relevance of this outcome, it has to be emphasized that the proportion of citizens completely dissatisfied with the way democracy works in Spain runs in very low magnitudes (less than five percent). The recent increase in the lack of satisfaction barely has exceeded the threshold of ten percent. This still entails high levels of support for democracy. Therefore, the dramatic increase in lack of satisfaction with the way democracy works in Spain in the past four years seems to be correlated to the confidence crisis in representative institutions.

Figure 15-3. Indicators of institutional disaffection in Spain, 2002-11

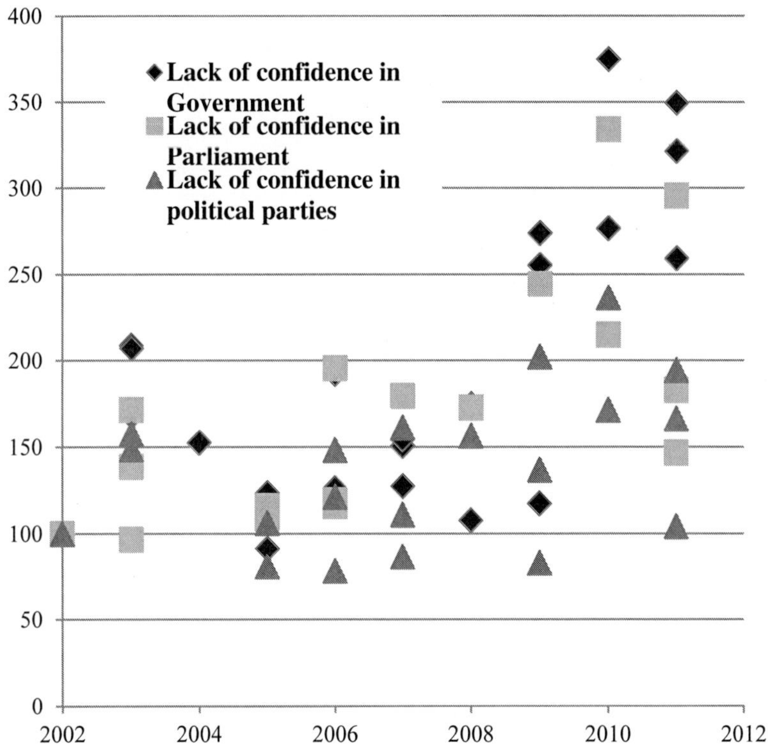

Source: CIS. Base: 2002=100. The presence of several points in the same year means the indicators have been measured several times during this year.

On the contrary, the incidence of concern about the economic and political situation has seemed to be non-existent in relation to the *interest in politics and the attention to political information*. Both of these indicators of disaffection have not undergone any notable change during the past decade in Spain. If both are taken to be indicators of *political disengagement*, then the conclusion seems to be solid: the institutional confidence crisis does not depend on the concern about politics. In other words, the fact that most of the citizens don't trust the democratic representative institutions does not mean necessarily disengagement from politics. In so far as disengagement is taken to be one dimension of political disaffection, then it must be concluded that political disaffection can be independent from the rise in institutional lack of confidence.

Figure 15-4. Indicators of political disengagement in Spain, 2002-11

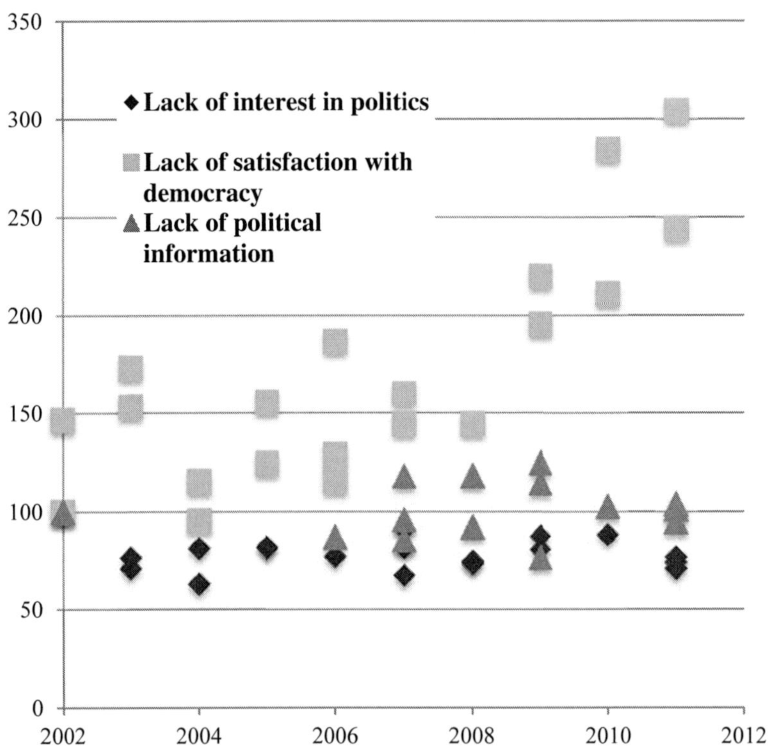

Source: CIS. Base: 2002=100. The presence of several points in the same year means the indicators have been measured several times during this year.

In short, there is a narrow relationship between negative assessments of the seriousness of the economic situation and the increase in the concern about the political situation. But this relationship is only translated in a very limited way to an increase in political disaffection. The rise in concern about the economic and political situation is clearly correlated to the rise in mistrust in representative institutions. An increase in the negative assessments about the economic and political situation runs in parallel to an increase in the lack of confidence both in government and Parliament and, to a lesser extent, to political parties. The confidence crisis is translated, in turn, into a relevant increase in the lack of satisfaction with the way democracy works (see Table 15-3).

Therefore, the concern about the economic and political situation, the institutional crisis of confidence, and the increase in lack of satisfaction with democracy seem to be tendencies that have been running in parallel in Spain in the past decade. The temporary sequence seems to confirm the idea that the concern about the economic situation increases dissatisfaction with the political situation with a year gap, and this in turn is translated to a crisis of confidence in representative institutions that question the citizens' firm support to the way democracy works.

But these are not the elements that traditionally have been used to define and measure political disaffection. As it is conceived, political disaffection seems relatively impervious to any particular economic situation and to any answers that politics can give to that situation. The worsening in the citizens' assessments about the situation is only adequately correlated to a slight increase in political particularism, that is, to the idea that politicians only look after their own interest. To a lesser extent, it is also inversely correlated to the idea that citizens do not have a say over what the government does, apart from voting.

The increase of mistrust in democratic representative institutions is not related to a great extent to any of the political disaffection indicators or, to put it another way, institutional disaffection seems to be independent from political disaffection. So, political disaffection indicators seem to be scarcely related to institutional disaffection indicators, apart from external inefficacy, that is, the idea that politicians do not care much about what people think. Neither does it seem to be correlated enough to satisfaction with democracy.

In spite of showing a limited relation to other disaffection dimensions, political disaffection indicators have an internal consistency as is shown by the fact that they are relatively well intercorrelated. Nevertheless, the number of cases is so small that this conclusion must be taken carefully. Almost the same can be said about political disengagement indicators as well as the lack of interest in politics and the lack of political information. These two variables seem to be quite independent from any other institutional and political disaffection indicators and even from any support to the democratic system.

Table 15-3. Spearman's ρ correlations between some indicators of political disaffection in Spain, 2002-12

	Economic situation	Political situation	Internal inefficacy	External inefficacy	Particu-larism	No influence	Lack of confid. in gov/ment	Lack of confid. in Parl/ment	Lack of confid. in pol. parties	Lack of political Interest	Lack of polit/cal inform/tion
Political situation	.883**										
	(114)										
Internal inefficacy	-.046	-.231									
	(15)	(15)									
External inefficacy	.335	.360	.609*								
	(13)	(13)	(11)								
Particularism	.636*	.529	.391	.727**							
	(12)	(12)	(11)	(12)							
No influence	-.381	-.419	.976**	.536	.393						
	(8)	(8)	(8)	(7)	(7)						
Lack of conf. in	.655**	.684**	.115	.571	.536	.200					
Government	(23)	(23)	(10)	(8)	(7)	(4)					
Lack of confid. in	.620**	.709**	-.048	.700	.200	-.500	.801**				
Parliament	(17)	(17)	(8)	(5)	(4)	(3)	(16)				
Lack of confid. in	.579**	.558*	.218	.650	.619	-.200	.881**	.845**			
pol. parties	(20)	(20)	(11)	(9)	(8)	(4)	(19)	(15)			

	Economic situation	Political situation	Internal inefficacy	External inefficacy	Particu-larism	No influence	Lack of confid. in gov/ment	Lack of confid. in Parl/ment	Lack of confid. in pol. parties	Lack of political Interest	Lack of polit/cal inform/tion
Lack of interest in politics	-.106 (19)	-.058 (19)	.350 (12)	.048 (8)	.286 (8)	.036 (7)	-.303 (13)	.151 (9)	-.011 (12)		
Lack of political information	.125 (14)	.178 (14)	.183 (9)	.429 (8)	.119 (8)	.179 (7)	-.371 (6)	-.500 (3)	-.257 (6)	.030 (10)	
Lack of satisfact. with democracy	.741** (25)	.754** (25)	.505 (10)	.417 (9)	.381 (8)	.800 (4)	.644** (20)	.521 (13)	.570** (18)	-.374 (14)	-.314 (6)

Source: CIS. ** Correlation is significant at the 0.01 level (2-tailed). * Correlation is significant at the 0.05 level (2-tailed) (N in brackets).

The left and far left in the disaffection universe

The so-called process of political disaffection in Spain in the past years has not been evident. If the political disaffection definition that has been established in sociological literature during the past decades is taken into account, it must be concluded that only in a very limited way there has been a *"subjective feeling of powerlessness and cynicism... with no questioning of the political regime"* (DiPalma, 1970). This conclusion openly contrasts with the rapidly advancing loss of confidence in main democratic representative institutions. Political disaffection has been no more than a crisis of confidence in democratic representative institutions. They are now in question as a consequence of the debt crisis, but not politics as a whole.

This study tries to show that the crisis of institutional confidence is due, first of all, to a prior increase in confidence and a later disenchantment in those citizens self-positioned on the left of the ideological scale. While the moderate ideological left is supposed to have different orientations to politics than those on the ideological far left, it is necessary to distinguish between the two groups of citizens. The fact that someone is self-positioned on the far left of the ideological scale may be related to a greater or lesser degree of political or institutional disaffection or could even imply a smaller interest in political news.

During the past decade, the main political disaffection indicators have been hardly modified. They have not changed in a sizeable way even in those self-positioned on the ideological left. In fact, political disaffection indicators hardly distinguish those on the left from the others, although it is true that citizens from the ideological left seem a little bit less disaffected. So, citizens self-positioned on the left and far left consider themselves more competent to understand politics and have a more positive idea about politicians than the others, as it can be seen in Figure 15-5. This is very clear from the fact that the average scoring of those citizens self-positioned on the left in particularism and internal inefficacy indicators has been kept under the scoring of the others during the past decade.

The most important outcome is that the levels of political disaffection of those citizens self-positioned on the left have varied in a very limited degree during the past decade. There is a slight tendency to reduce disaffection in external inefficacy and particularism, but the internal inefficacy and no influence indicator levels have tended to be unchanged after minor increases. On the contrary, the belief that politicians do not care much about what people think and that they only look after their own interest distinguishes nowadays a little bit more the other citizens from those self-positioned on the ideological left. However, this hardly changes the fact that those on the ideological left consider themselves as more competent in politics and as more influential over what the government does than the others.

Those self-positioned on more extreme positions on the left of the ideological scale hardly differ from citizens on the left, as a whole, in their general orientation towards the political field and their political disaffection during the past decade. So, those on the far left are as different from the others in their political disaffection as those on the left as a whole. The main difference between those on far left and the others is that they do not think as much that politics is so complicated that people cannot understand what is happening. Nevertheless, this indicator distinguishes them less now than before 2008, as it can be seen in Figure 15-6. During the past decade, there is a tendency that those on far left feel slightly less disaffected than the others. However, there is a relevant increase in the levels of political disaffection among those on far left in every single indicator from 2007 on. So, in recent years the levels of political disaffection of those on the far left are very similar to those of other citizens.

In short, it seems that the recent trends regarding the indicators of political disaffection have not had a significant impact on the traditional feelings of political competence among those in the ideological left. What can be validated is a certain tendency among those self-positioned in the far left to show levels of political disaffection similar to other citizens in 2011. The relative permanence of the patterns of political disaffection during the past decade openly contrasts with the sudden changes in institutional disaffection. Institutional disaffection has grown remarkably in the past years, and it is also the best set of indicators to distinguish those on the ideological left from other citizens. It is really in this aspect where it can be said that disaffection is clearly related to ideological self-placement.

Figure 15-5. Indicators of political disaffection and left self-placement in Spain, 2002-11

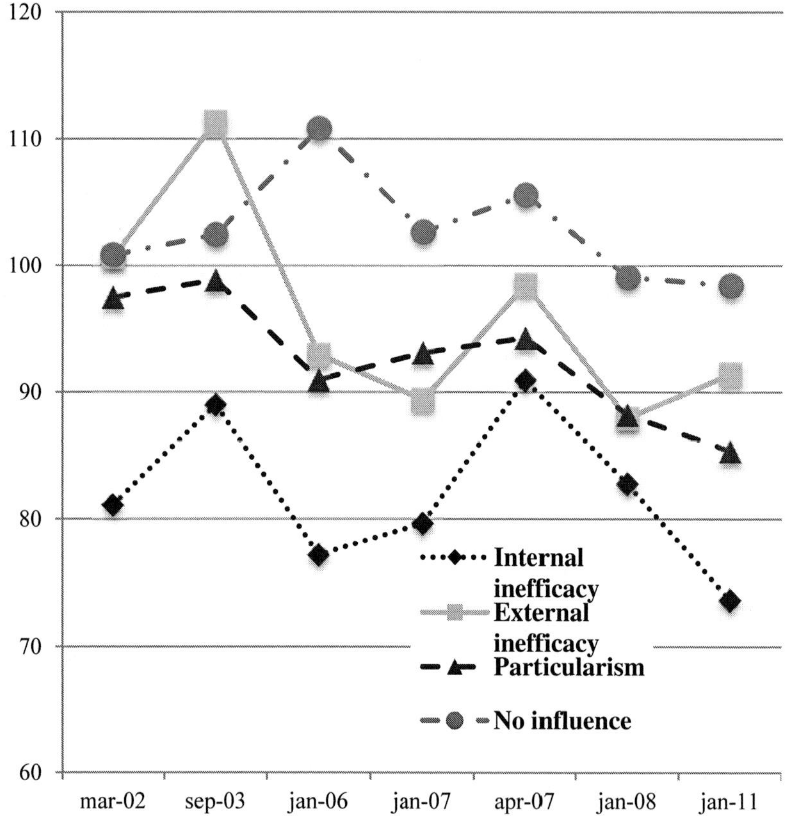

Source: CIS. Surveys 2450, 2535, 2632, 2672, 2700, 2749, and 2860. Base: other = 100.

Figure 15-6. Indicators of political disaffection and far left self-placement in Spain 2002-11

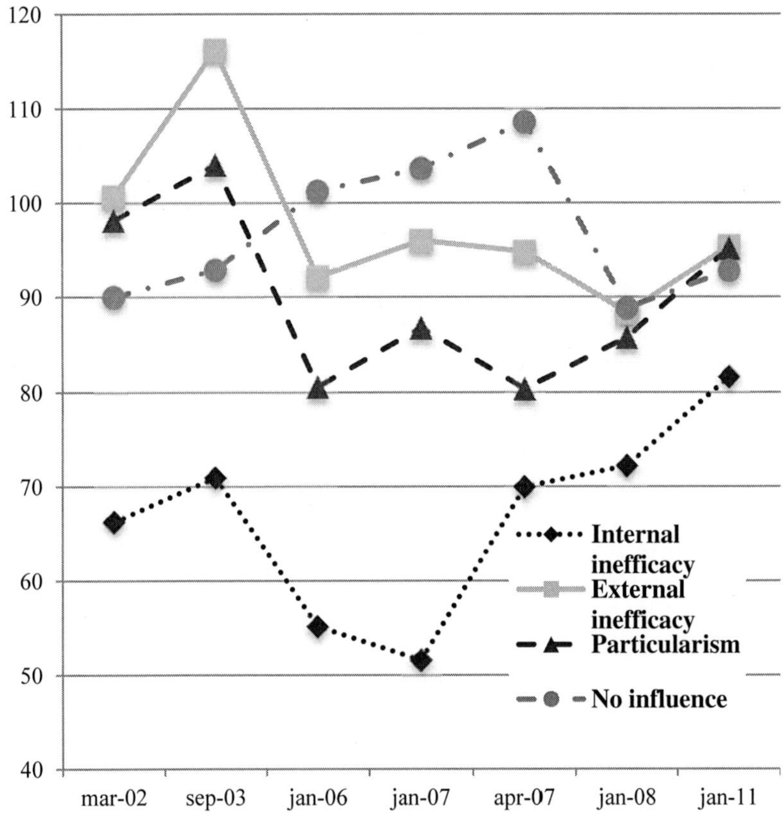

Source: CIS. Surveys 2450, 2535, 2632, 2672, 2700, 2749, and 2860. Base: other = 100.

Institutional disaffection, as well as political disaffection as a whole, can only be understood in relation to a previous process of political affection. That affection process can be easily checked in Figure 15-7. In 2003, institutional disaffection among those citizens self-positioned on the ideological left was much higher than among the others, and it was particularly high in relation to the lack of confidence in government. In 2006, the situation was fully reversed as citizens on the left showed a greater confidence than other citizens in all of the three representative institutions. This is a process of true political affection that implies increasing institutional confidence among the citizens self-positioned in the ideological left.

From 2005, the confidence in representative institutions is much higher among the ideologically left citizens than among the others,. The lack of confidence among those self-positioned on the left was very notable before that date in view of the fact that there was an ideologically divergent party in government. From 2006 to 2009 every single indicator of institutional disaffection clearly distinguishes those on the left from the rest. Those on the ideological left are more confident in democratic representative institutions than the other citizens. Therefore, it can be validated that different levels of confidence in representative institutions depend upon which political party is in government and that institutional disaffection has a strong partisan component.

The partisan component is also evident in Figure 15-8, that juxtaposes different indicators of institutional disaffection and far left self-placement in Spain during the past decade. The evolution of institutional disaffection of those self-positioned on far left has been very similar to that of the left as a whole. The main difference between both sets of citizens is that those on the far left have been as suspicious of Parliament and political parties as the others (including the center-left). That partisan component can clearly be seen in the low levels of disaffection toward government shown among those on the ideological far left from 2006. In fact, trust in government is the disaffection indicator that has distinguished more those on the far left from other citizens. At present, they show more or less the same disaffection toward any of the three considered institutions and in a very similar way to other citizens.

It seems like the *political disengagement* indicators distinguish in a better way those self-positioned on the ideological left from the others. In general, they are less disengaged from politics than the rest, as it can be seen in Figure 15-9. Their lack of interest in politics, their lack of political information, and their lack of satisfaction with democracy have always remained clearly below the levels shown by the rest of the citizens. In particular, those on the ideological left felt especially satisfied with the way democracy works in comparison with other citizens, although it is true that this indicator has been subjected to notable ups and downs during the past decade. Satisfaction with the way democracy works also seems to have a clear partisan component considering that it is especially intense during the socialist government's early years.

Figure 15-7. Indicators of institutional disaffection and left self-placement in Spain, 2002-11

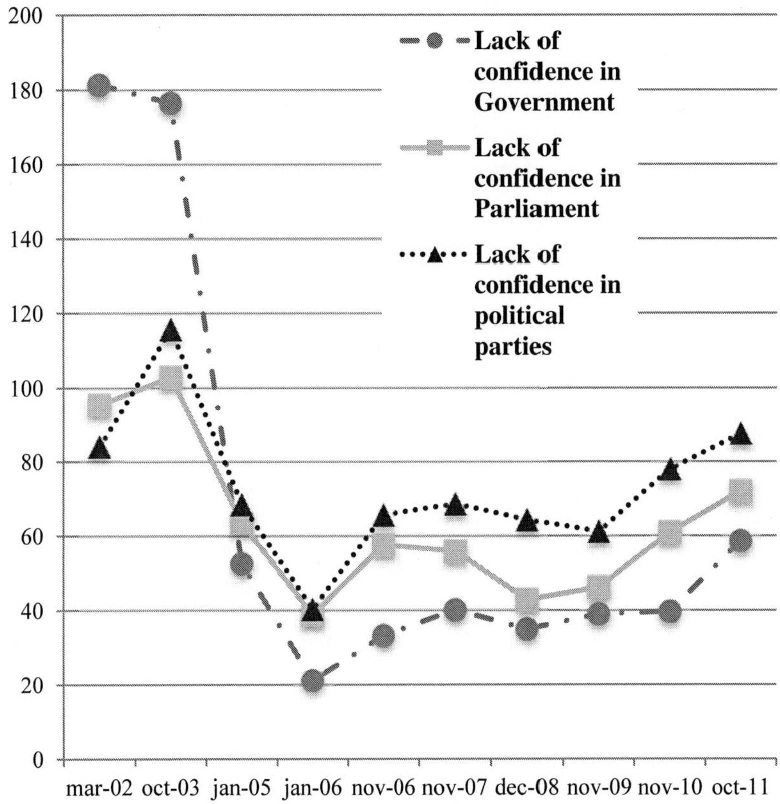

Source: CIS. Surveys 2450, 2540, 2588, 2632, 2663, 2741, 2777, 2823, 2853, and 2914. Base: other = 100.

Figure 15-8. Indicators of institutional disaffection and far left self-placement in Spain 2002-11

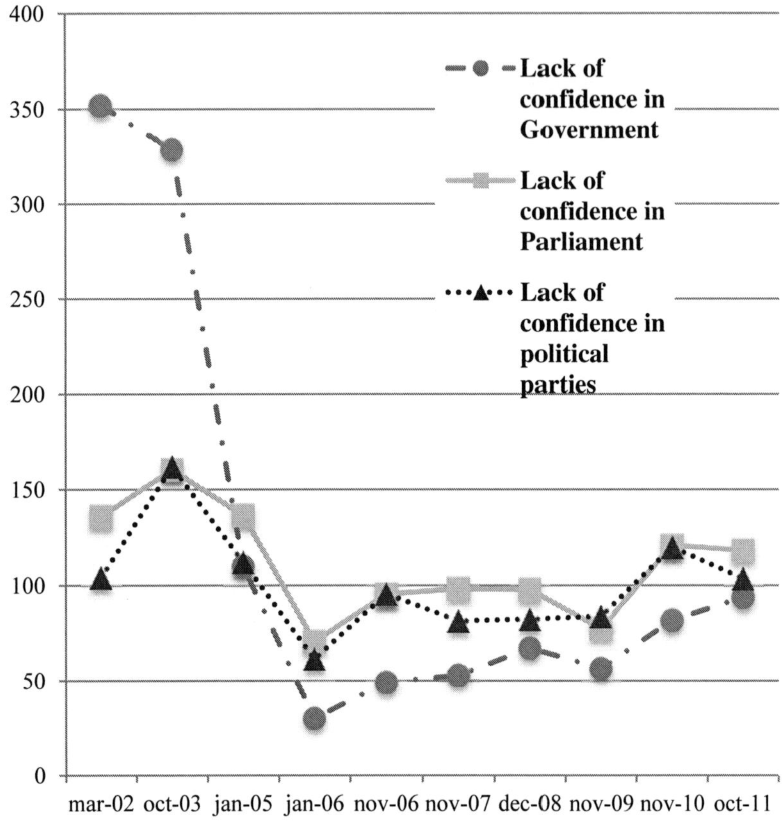

Source: CIS. Surveys 2450, 2540, 2588, 2632, 2663, 2741, 2777, 2823, 2853, and 2914. Base: other = 100.

Political engagement of the ideological left also seems to be more intensive in the far left. They show a bigger interest in politics, and they have more frequent political information than the rest of the citizens, as it happens in the left as a whole. However, political disengagement indicators are those that best distinguish between those on the ideological far left and those on the left as a whole, as can be seen in Figure 15-10. The main difference between them is based on the far left's lower level of satisfaction with democracy. The level of satisfaction of those on the far left is currently as different from that of the other citizens as it was in 2002, with an ideologically-divergent government. The disaffection pattern among those on the ideological far left shows a solid engagement in politics and an increase in dissatisfaction with democracy after a short period of political affection to the democratic system at the same time.

Even though this descriptive analysis gives clear enough hints on the way that the ideological left self-placement is related to different patterns of political disaffection, it is necessary to delimit the explanatory power of every single indicator of political disaffection considered here. For that reason, three successive logistic regression analyses were carried out in order to achieve that goal. These analyses have taken as independent variables all the single political disaffection indicators and the ideological self-placement as the dependent variable. In a first analysis, the dependent variable has been dichotomized giving the 1 value to those on the ideological left (points 4 or less), so left includes those self-positioned from 0 to 4 in the ideological scale. In a second analysis, the value 1 was assigned to those on the ideological far left (points 2 or less), so far left includes those self-positioned from 0 to 2 in the ideological scale. In both of these analyses the value 0 was assigned to the rest of the interviewees.

Unfortunately, not every indicator of political disaffection considered here was assessed in all of the relevant surveys. However, we can count on three surveys that used all of the indicators. Fortunately, these surveys were conducted in different economic and political periods: 2002, 2006, and 2011 (see Table 15-1).

As the logistic regression analysis reveals (Table 15-4), in March 2002 the best predictors of ideological positioning on the left were those indicators relating to trust in government and lack of interest in politics, both of them with a negative sign. The ideological left was distinguished by its especial lack of confidence in the conservative government from that period and its stronger interest in politics. Also statistically significant are its lower confidence in political parties and its greater access to political information. However, the other logistic regression coefficients are so low that none of them supposes a relationship that could be extrapolated to the Spanish population as a whole. Thus, in 2002 political disaffection among those from the ideological left shows two unique features. Firstly, their bigger lack of confidence in the conservative government and their greater trust in political parties clearly show a partisan component. Secondly, they are not different from the others in relation to their political disaffection or their satisfaction with the way democracy works. In general terms, the logistic function correctly classifies only 69.5 percent of the interviewees while a random classification correctly classifies 62.8 percent. As such, indicators of political disaffection as a whole are only slightly better predictors of ideological left self-positioning than chance, although there were significant differences in relation to confidence in government and interest in politics.

Figure 15-9. Indicators of political disengagement and left self-placement in Spain, 2002-11

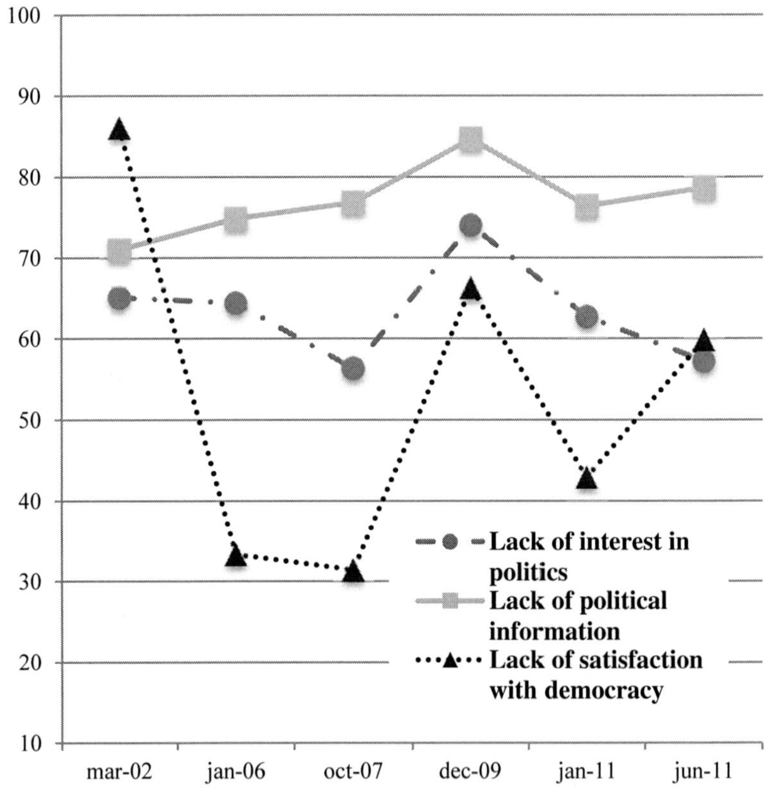

Source: CIS. Surveys 2450, 2632, 2736, 2826, 2860, and 2905). Base: other = 100.

Figure 15-10. Indicators of political disengagement and far left self-placement in Spain, 2002-11

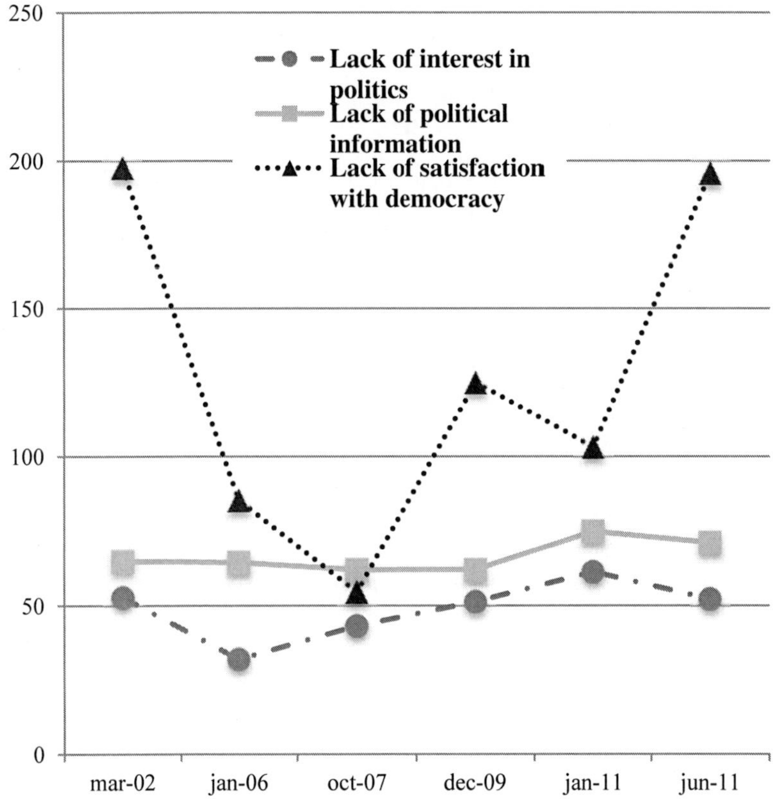

Source: CIS. Surveys, 2450, 2632, 2736, 2826, 2860, and 2905). Base: other = 100.

The poor predictive power of the indicators of political disaffection and the significant explanation of the indicators of institutional disaffection are even bigger when the far left self-positioning is taken into account. The lack of confidence in government, the interest in politics and a slightly greater confidence in political parties are the only indicators that distinguish significantly those on the far left from the others. A lesser satisfaction with democracy is the only relevant difference between them and those on the ideological left as a whole. But, once again, indicators of political disaffection such as internal and external inefficacy, particularism and no influence on politics do not distinguish at all those self-positioned on ideological far left from the other citizens. The predictive power of the logistic function was very small—with a percentage of cases correctly predicted of 87.4—and only slightly better than the random one. In addition, the value of the Nagelkerke's R^2 coefficient is quite low (less than 0.2) in both logistic functions.

Consequently, in 2002 the self-positioning in the ideological left just implies a lesser confidence in government and a bigger interest in politics than the self-placement on any other ideological position, while there was no difference in relation to the political disaffection indicators. In January 2006 that outcome was different to a certain extent. Confidence in government was still the most relevant variable to distinguish those on the left from the rest, but in the opposite direction. The ideological left felt much more confidence in government than any other position. In addition, self-positioning on the left implies disaffection patterns a bit different from the rest of the interviewees. In particular, they had a lesser sense of internal inefficacy, since they thought to a lesser degree that politics were so complicated that people cannot understand what was happening, and they also had a slightly stronger feeling of political influence.

The same differentiation pattern can be seen as well in those interviewees self-positioned on the far left. They showed a greater confidence in government and a lesser trust in Parliament, apart from a stronger interest in politics than the others. In the same way, they showed a political disaffection significantly different from the rest of the interviewees in all of the four disaffection indicators considered here. The ideological far left exhibited lesser political disaffection in relation to their internal inefficacy, particularism and lack of political influence than others. This means that they trusted more than the rest their own political knowledge, they considered to a greater extent that politicians only looked after their own interest, and they believed more than other citizens that they had a major influence over what the government did. In this way, the disaffected nature that has been attributed to those people self-positioned on far left of the ideological scale does not appear in Spain in 2006. On the contrary, in that year, the ideological far left showed a stronger political affection than other ideological placements and even a greater satisfaction with the way democracy worked (see Figure 15-10).

It can be said that the main outcome in comparing 2002 and 2006 surveys is the increase in political affection among the ideological left at that time. They move from a previous mistrust in government to a greater confidence in it and from a previous trust in Parliament to a significantly greater suspicion. In addition, this process of political affection did not only influence institutional disaffection indicators; it was also accompanied by some change in political disaffection feelings in relation to internal and external efficacy, particularism and political influence. Nevertheless, the predictive power of both logistic functions is quite limited. The percentage of cases correctly predicted is hardly different from a random function and Nagelkerke's R^2 coefficients are low.

The outcomes from the January 2011 survey are very similar to those from 2002. Those self-positioned on the ideological left showed a greater confidence in government but a lesser trust in political parties. They also exhibited statistically significant differences in relation to their greater interest in politics and their stronger feeling of influence over what the government did. However, they lost part of their feeling of affection in relation to the indicators of internal political inefficacy and particularism. At present, there are no statistically significant differences between the ideological left and those holding other ideological positions in seeing politics as a complicated matter or considering that politicians only look after their own particular interest.

The same conclusion can be deduced from the analysis of the answers of those self-positioned on the ideological far left. They also showed a stronger confidence in government but to a lesser extent than others in the more moderate left-wing. In addition, they showed a bigger trust in political parties but not to the same extent as those on the ideological left as a whole. The more relevant outcome was that the political affection they showed in 2006 had almost completely disappeared in 2011. In relation to the political disaffection indicators such as internal and external inefficacy, particularism, and lack of political influence and in relation to the political disengagement indicators, almost nothing distinguishes those on the far left from the others. This outcome explains the fact that the explanatory power of the logistic functions is quite poor as it is shown by the low value of Nagelkerke's coefficient.

Table 15-4. Logistic regression on predictors of left and far left ideological self-placement in Spain, 2002-2011

Survey	2450 (March 2002)				2632 (January 2006)				2860 (January 2011)			
Predictors	Left		Far left		Left		Far left		Left		Far left	
	B	Sig.	B	Sig.	B	Sig.	B	Sig.	B	Sig.	B	Sig.
Political disaffection												
Internal inefficacy	-.107	.216	-.208	.101	-.184	.000	-.181	.001	-.093	.088	-.063	.376
External inefficacy	.096	.421	.310	.074	.087	.091	.132	.043	-.004	.961	.013	.889
Particularism	.018	.883	-.090	.593	-.034	.485	-.157	.007	-.101	.148	.098	.275
No influence	.184	.054	.032	.808	-.090	.035	-.106	.047	-.144	.018	-.093	.228
Institutional disaffection												
Lack of confidence in government	.395	.000	.341	.000	-.456	.000	-.346	.000	-.309	.000	-.189	.000
Lack of confidence in Parliament	-.051	.079	-.046	.250	.159	.000	.153	.000	---	---	---	---
Lack of confidence in political parties	-.150	.000	-.095	.018	.018	.552	.027	.489	.191	.000	.108	.004

Survey	2450 (March 2002)				2632 (January 2006)				2860 (January 2011)			
Predictors	Left		Far left		Left		Far left		Left		Far left	
	B	Sig.	B	Sig.	B	Sig.	B	Sig.	B	Sig.	B	Sig.
Political disengagement												
Lack of interest in politics	-.376	.000	-.376	.000	-.366	.000	-.565	.000	-.188	.000	-.246	.000
Lack of political information	-.071	.023	-.068	.127	-.060	.080	.042	.342	-.009	.802	-.034	.451
Lack of satisfaction with democracy	-.025	.702	.217	.017	-.014	.577	.034	.293	-.032	.136	.039	.168
Constant	-.284	.333	-2.360	.000	3.099	.000	1.250	.000	2.208	.000	-.350	.357
Nagelkerke's R^2	.189		.152		.263		.175		.138		.054	
Percentage correctly predicted	69.5		87.4		70.0		84.6		66.7		84.5	
(N)	(3158)		(3158)		(2506)		(2506)		(2114)		(2114)	

Source: CIS.

Note: The coefficients represent non-standardized betas (B) and significance (Sig.) in binary logistic regression analysis models predicting ideological self-placement. *Left* includes those self-positioned from 0 to 4 in the ideological scale. *Far left* includes those self-positioned from 0 to 2 in the ideological scale. Dependent variable encoding: 1 = left or far left, 0 = other. Minus signs on B coefficients mean less disaffected than the other.

In short, the political disaffection pattern among those in the ideological left in 2011 was very similar to that found in 2002, though in a very different economic situation. The main disparity between both surveys has to do with institutional disaffection patterns in the same way that the main difference between both periods is based on the diverse political and ideological orientation of the party in government. Political disaffection in Spain has a strong partisan component, so political considerations mediate different disaffection patterns. To a great degree, economic considerations, such as the assessment of the impact of the debt crisis on citizens' political attitudes, seem to be quite disconnected from political affection and disaffection processes. In the Spanish case, during the past decade, they almost exclusively have experienced an institutional affection and disaffection process and not a political disaffection process as a whole. If we keep in mind this conclusion, we can understand the real role ideology has played in that process. To a great extent, the ideological left, as a whole, has shown a different level of confidence in socialist governments than in conservative governments, regardless of economic considerations.

Conclusion

Political disaffection patterns seem to be relatively impervious to the assessment of a particular economic situation in Spain during the past decade. These patterns result from a clearly partisan component, so the change of the party in government becomes the main variable to keep in mind in order to understand changes in institutional disaffection. In this sense, ideological self-placement seems to be a more promising variable in order to explain political disaffection patterns than simply to pay attention to the evolution of the assessments about the economic and political situation. The majority of negative assessments about the economic and political situation have only produced an institutional confidence crisis, but not an increase in political disaffection. This crisis of confidence has, of course, affected citizens from very different ideological orientations, but it has also altered the relationship between different ideological self-placements. Thus, ideology is clearly associated to the partisan component that has affected political disaffection in Spain during the past decade.

These conclusions are relevant to the sociological literature in the study of political disaffection processes in Spain and in the comprehension of political disaffection in general. First, the usual idea consists in understanding political disaffection as an attitudinal syndrome that implies an estrangement, as well as a detachment, from politics with a consistent increase in the lack of confidence in democratic representative institutions

(Di Palma, 1970; Torcal and Montero, 2006). However, the recent Spanish example forces us to reconsider the idea of political disaffection as a uniform process whereby changes in any indicator automatically imply changes in the others. On the contrary, different dimensions of disaffection can show and, in fact, they do show different patterns of evolution that entail different conclusions about disaffection processes. The increase in institutional mistrust that has occurred in Spain since 2008 has not been accompanied by any noticeable change in other indicators such as internal inefficacy or lack of interest in politics.

Second, political disaffection has usually been connected with relatively sudden changes such as a timely increase in discontent related to a negative perception of a specific public authority's performance. Accordingly, it has been said that discontent has an easily reversible nature and does not affect the democratic ideals (Montero, Gunther and Torcal, 1998; Torcal, 2003; Gunther and Montero, 2006). However, the Spanish example is better understood as a confidence crisis and a process that is separated from a hypothetical increase in political disaffection. A crisis of confidence does not necessarily have a stable nature and depends on particular situations. Of course, a confidence crisis can be reversible, although it is not easy for any institution to recover the confidence that has been lost. But political disaffection seems to have a more stable nature and it is only slightly modified by a more or less timely increase in political affection.

Third, assessments of the economic situation seem to be related to institutional confidence, although they are not closely related to any relevant change in political disaffection levels. As a consequence, the usual idea that economic situation assessments have no impact on the estimation of democratic system performance seems to be wrong (Montero et al. 1997a; 1997b; Nye et al. 1997; Montero and Torcal, 2006). The institutional confidence crisis is rather clearly related to the assessment of the democratic system performance. This is highlighted by the fact that the recent increase in discontent with the economic and political situation is noticeably related to a drop in the satisfaction with the way democracy works in Spain (see Table 15-3).

Fourth, a hasty appraisal of the role of ideology in political affection and disaffection processes has led some researchers to conclude that ideology is not related to institutional disaffection (Torcal, 2003; 2006; Offe, 2006). However, some of that research exhibits limitations which underestimate the role that ideological self-positioning plays in the increase or decrease of institutional disaffection. This study has shown that the role of ideology in this matter depends on an essential distinction between the usual indicators of political disaffection, such as internal and external inefficacy, particularism and lack of political influence, on the one hand, and the indicators of institutional disaffection, such as lack of confidence in representative democratic institutions, on the other. Even though ideological self-positioning is relatively independent from political disaffection, it is not from the indicators of institutional disaffection. Ideology plays a very important role in relation to the evolution of these indicators. In this way, the Spanish example during the past decade highlights the fact that the confidence crisis is related to a particular attitudinal base: ideological self-placement. Specifically, the ideological left self-positioning is related to an increase in institutional affection in the early years of the socialist government (from 2004 to 2008) and is also related to the preservation of their different assessment regarding political representative institutions under very different economic situations.

Fifth, the limited but relevant role that ideology has played in the crisis of institutional confidence, which has been taken place in Spain in the past years, results from the purely partisan nature associated with confidence in the main democratic representative institutions and in the government in particular. This conclusion is openly contrary to the usual assumption in the sociological literature that institutional disaffection is independent from the ideological positioning and that it is equally distributed among different categories of citizens. In this way, Torcal (2003: 35) concludes that contrary to recent findings (Newton and Norris, 1999), ideology does not have any effect on institutional confidence. Once again, this depends on whether or not one distinguishes between political and institutional disaffection. It seems to be true that partisan proclivity is to a certain extent independent from political disaffection. But in the Spanish example, it also seems quite clear that the increase in political affection among those self-positioned on the ideological left from 2004 to 2008 is related to changes in the party governing the country.

The partisan component of the institutional disaffection and the stated relationship between ideological self-positioning and institutional confidence lead us to conclude that ideology has played a relevant role in the process usually known as political disaffection. The process has been limited to a crisis of confidence in democratic institutions in Spain during the past decade. Such an institutional disaffection process must be understood mainly as a growing divorce between the ideological and the institutional left. In this sense, what has been wrongly called a process of political disaffection in Spain in the past years must be understood to a large extent as a response to the crisis of ideas among the parties and organizations of the institutional left. This means that political disaffection in Spain in the past decade must be better understood as a reflection of the ideological crisis of the institutionalized left concerning answers to the challenges of the present debt crisis.

Notes

[1] I would like to thank Dr. Nicholas Petropoulos and Dra. Laura Román for their kind interest and devotion in revising the original text and improving it with their aluable comments.

[2] Source: CIS surveys 2450, 2535, 2632, 2671, 2700, 2736, 2741, 2749, 2826, 2829, 2849, 2853, 2860, 2914, and 2920.

[3] Source: CIS surveys 2450, 2535, 2632, 2663, 2671, 2700, 2701, 2736, 2749, 2826, 2853, 2860, and 2920.

[4] Source: CIS surveys 2450, 2535, 2632, 2671, 2700, 2701, 2736, 2749, 2826, 2853, 2860, and 2920.

[5] Source: CIS surveys 2450, 2535, 2632, 2671, 2700, 2749, and 2914.

[6] Source: CIS surveys 2450, 2476, 2479, 2540, 2571, 2588, 2620, 2632, 2657, 2663, 2701, 2736, 2741, 2778, 2777, 2790, 2823, 2826, 2849, 2853, 2860, 2861, and 2914.

[7] Source: CIS surveys 2450, 2476, 2479, 2540, 2588, 2620, 2632, 2657, 2663, 2741, 2777, 2823, 2849, 2853, 2861, 2914, and 2920.

[8] Source: CIS surveys 2450, 2476, 2540, 2588, 2620, 2632, 2657, 2663, 2701, 2736, 2741, 2777, 2790, 2823, 2826, 2849, 2853, 2860, 2914, and 2920.

[9] Source: CIS surveys 2450, 2535, 2540, 2571, 2575, 2588, 2620, 2632, 2671, 2736, 2741, 2749, 2760, 2823, 2826, 2849, 2860, 2905, and 2914.

[10] Source: CIS surveys 2450, 2632, 2671, 2700, 2736, 2749, 2760, 2798, 2826, 2829, 2834, 2860, 2905, and 2914.

[11] Source: CIS surveys 2450, 2471, 2476, 2535, 2540, 2562, 2571, 2588, 2620, 2632, 2641, 2657, 2663, 2701, 2736, 2741, 2777, 2778, 2790, 2823, 2826, 2849, 2853, 2860, and 2905.

References

Bynner, J. and Ashford, S. (1994). ‘Politics and participation: Some antecedents of young people’s attitudes to the political system and political activity’, *European Journal of Social Psychology,* vol. 24, pp. 223-236.

Di Palma, G. (1970). *Apathy and participation. Mass politics in Western societies,* New York: The Free Press.

Evans, G. and Letki, N. (2006). ‘Understanding the relationship between social capital and political disaffection in the new post-communist democracies’, in Torcal, M. and, Montero J.R. (eds.) *Political disaffection in contemporary democracies. Social capital, institutions, and politics*, Routledge Research in Comparative Politics, London: Routledge, pp. 130-154.

Gunther, R.P. and Montero, J.R. (2006). 'The multidimensionality of political support for new democracies. Conceptual redefinition and empirical refinement', in Torcal, M. and Montero, J.R. (eds.) *Political disaffection in contemporary democracies. Social capital, institutions, and politics,* Routledge Research in Comparative Politics, London: Routledge, pp. 46-78.

Listhaug, O. (2006). 'Political disaffection and political performance. Norway, 1957-2001', in Torcal, M. and Montero, J.R. (eds.) *Political disaffection in contemporary democracies. Social capital, institutions, and politics*, Routledge Research in Comparative Politics, London: Routledge, pp. 215-243.

Magalhaes, P.C. (2006). 'Confidence in Parliaments. Performance, representation, and accountability', in Torcal, M. and Montero, J.R. (eds.) *Political disaffection in contemporary democracies. Social capital, institutions, and politics,* Routledge Research in Comparative Politics, London: Routledge, pp. 190-214.

Montero, J.R. *et al.* (1997a). *Democracy in Spain: Legitimacy, discontent, and disaffection,* Madrid: Instituto Juan March, Working Paper 100.

Montero, J.R. (1997b). 'Democracy in Spain: Legitimacy, discontent, and dissatisfaction'. *Studies in Comparative International Development,* vol. 32, no. 3, pp. 124-160.

Montero, J.R., Gunther, R. and Torcal, M. (1998). 'Actitudes hacia la democracia en España: legitimidad, descontento y desafección'. *Revista Española de Investigaciones Sociológicas,* vol. 83, pp. 9-49.

Montero, J.R., Torcal, M. (2006). 'Some basic conclusions about political disaffection in contemporary democracies', in Torcal, M. and Montero, J.R. (eds.) *Political disaffection in contemporary democracies. Social capital, institutions, and politics*, Routledge Research in Comparative Politics, London: Routledge, pp. 335-342.

Newton, K. (2001). 'Social trust and political disaffection: Social capital and democracy'. Paper prepared for the EURESCO conference on Social Capital, Interdisciplinary Perspectives, Exeter, Available: http://www.vanderveld.nl/teaching/2005-2006%20RM%20MVA/2001%20-%20Newton.pdf [21 May 2012].

—. (2006). 'Institutional confidence and social trust', in Torcal, M. and Montero, J.R. (eds.) *Political disaffection in contemporary democracies. Social capital, institutions, and politics*. Routledge Research in Comparative Politics, London: Routledge. pp. 81-100.

Newton, K., Norris, P. (1999). 'Confidence in public institutions: Faith, culture or performance?'. Harvard University, Available: http://www.hks.harvard.edu/fs/pnorris/Acrobat/NEWTON.PDF [21 May 2012].

Nye, J. S. (1997). 'Introduction: The decline of confidence in government', in Nye, J.S., Zelikow, P.D. and King, D.C. (eds.) *Why people don't trust government*, Cambridge: Harvard University Press, pp. 1-18.

Offe. C. (2006). 'Political disaffection as an outcome of institutional practices?', in Torcal, M. and Montero, J.R. (eds.) *Political disaffection in contemporary democracies. Social capital, institutions, and politics,* Routledge Research in Comparative Politics, London: Routledge, pp. 23-45.

Pharr, S.J. and Putnam, R.D. (2000). *Disaffected democracies. What's troubling the trilateral countries*, Princeton: Princeton University Press.

Segatti, P. (2006). 'Italy, forty years of political disaffection. A longitudinal exploration', in Torcal, M. and Montero, J.R (eds.) *Political disaffection in contemporary democracies. Social capital, institutions, and politics*, Routledge Research in Comparative Politics, London: Routledge, pp. 244-275.

Torcal, M. (2003). 'Political disaffection and democratization history in new democracies'. The Helen Kellogg Institute for International Studies Working Paper 308, Available: http://kellogg.nd.edu/publications/workingpapers/WPS/308.pdf [21 May 2012].

—. (2006). 'Desafección institucional e historia democrática en las nuevas democracias'. *Revista SAAP,* vol. 2, no. 3, pp. 591-634, Available: http://www.saap.org.ar/esp/docs-revista/revista/pdf/2-3/Torcal.pdf [21 May 2012].

Torcal, M., Montero, J.R. (2006). 'Political disaffection in comparative perspective', in Torcal, M. and Montero, J.R. (eds.) *Political disaffection in contemporary democracies. Social capital, institutions, and politics,* Routledge Research in Comparative Politics, London: Routledge, pp. 3-19.

CHAPTER SIXTEEN

A SOCIOPOLITICAL PROFILE AND THE POLITICAL IMPACT OF THE GREEK *INDIGNADOS*: AN EXPLORATORY STUDY

NICHOLAS P. PETROPOULOS
FORMERLY OF THE PEDAGOGICAL INSTITUTE OF GREECE

Abstract

Following the integration of Greece in the tripartite bailout (EU, ECB and IMF) in the spring of 2010 and the implementation of the austerity program in order to meet the demands of its debtors (e.g., cuts in wages and social security benefits, raising of taxes, reform of public administration), there took place both organized and less organized protests by various groups impacted by the austerity program. One of these collective reactions was the "movement" of the Greek indignados, that was mobilized in the spring of 2011 and became essentially defunct at the end of July 2011. The author uses a variety of qualitative, quantitative and unobtrusive methods to determine the ideology and sociopolitical profile of the Greek indignados, including participant observation, content analysis of slogans, graffiti, general assembly resolutions and social surveys. Special attention was given to the analysis of the "ideology" and the orientation to violence—non-violence dimension. In turn, the analysis tackles the question as to whether the indignados constitute a social movement in the classical sense and accounts for it using the theoretical framework of "*relative deprivation*". Finally, the study discusses the short- and long-term impacts, e.g., reshuffling of the government in power, the challenging of the two-party system and the emergence of new parties on the entire political spectrum.

Introduction

In the case of Greece, where collective phenomena (mass protests, demonstrations, etc.) had been an almost daily phenomenon, following the fall of the dictatorship in 1974, it is difficult to demarcate the onset of the "movement" of the indignados (*aganaktismenous*).[1] More specifically, there was a mass protest demonstration on 5/5/2010 in Athens against the announced austerity measures contained in the first bailout Memorandum of Understanding (MoU-I) between the troika (EU, IMF, ECB) and Greece. The demonstration was organized by trade unions (General Confederation of Greek Workers, Federation of Public Employees, Pan-Labour Front of the Communist Party). Following a confrontation between the "Units for the Restoration of Order" (MAT) and the extra-parliamentary groups, Molotov cocktails were thrown into the Marfin Egnantia Bank and three bank employees lost their lives. Extra-parliamentary groups were suspected, but up to now none has been apprehended and brought to justice. Although this was the first major mass protest against the austerity measures, I shall concentrate on mass protests that took place in Greece *after* the 15 May 2011 mass demonstrations of the Spanish indignados, in *Puerta del Sol* of Madrid, who reportedly challenged the Greeks to "wake up".

It did not take long for the Greeks to mobilize, given the implementation of the austerity measures and thanks to the social networks available to them by the new technologies. The first mass demonstration of the Greek indignados (GIs)—that constitutes also the formal commencement of the GI movement—took place on 25 May 2011. Police estimated the demonstrators' force at about 8,000 (Athens), while the relevant facebook page had recorded 52,000 followers. The mass demonstrations included a march to the Parliament building in Athens and a general assembly following the march and the rallies. There followed an escalation of mass protest demonstrations and mass assemblies in Constitution Square (CS), with an estimated force of 50,000 demonstrators on 31/05/2011, about 200,000 during the pan-European protest day (5/06/2011), about an equal number the day of a 24-hour general strike (15/06/2011) called by trade unions (which the GIs also endorsed) and between 20,000 and 50,000 during the two-day general strike (28-29/06/2011) to protest the voting of the Medium Term Economic Program (MTEP) or Memorandum of Understanding II (MoU-II). A number of these demonstrations (15/06 and 28-29/6) were accompanied by violent confrontations between the MAT and demonstrators or between demonstrators of various ideological persuasions. Mass demonstrations, with general assemblies, were also organized, though on a smaller scale, in the squares of other capital cities (e.g., Thessaloniki, Patras, Volos, Irakleion, Chania, Ioannina, Larisa, Tripolis, Kerkyra, Rhodes) of the Greek provinces. Following the voting of the MTEP, the number of indignados steadily diminished. By 29 July 2011, the number of indignados in Athens itself, both in the "upper' and the "lower" part of Constitution Square, amounted to less than 100 people and never reached the number of people during the height of the movement (5 June 2011). The reduction of numbers has been attributed to various reasons including, among others, the advent of vacation time, resignation attendant to the shock of the austerity programs, police suppression, the intervention of provocateurs, infiltration by various interest groups, the decentralization of the movement and the displacement of the locus of protests to the universities and neighborhoods.

Figure 16-1. The Greek indignados at Constitution Square, and in front of the Parliament building, demonstrating against the austerity memorandums (29 May 2011)

Source: Syntagma Square Protest/©Nikos Pilos/29 May 2011

In analyzing the Greek indignado*s*, the author concentrates on the demonstrations in Athens Constitution Square, because of accessibility and because these were the object of more systematic participant observation. I participated in at least 30 of the 45 CS rallies of the indignados. Except for the days of the key demonstrations (see above), when I participated from the start of the rallies (12-13:00 or 18:00-19:00), my participant observation took place between 22:00 and 01:00 hours. First, I spent about one-half to one hour in the "upper" part of CS, where I "recorded" mostly songs and slogans, but also observed social behaviour and other events. Afterwards, I descended to the "lower" part of CS, where the General Assemblies (GAs) and "peoples' consultations"[2] were being held and where the encampments were also located. In all cases, I took photos of people, banners and graffiti. Photos of damages due to violent confrontations were also taken usually the day following the confrontations, since the lack of protective equipment (e.g., gas masks) rendered my on-site presence prohibitive. In addition to photos, I collected leaflets distributed usually by various extra-parliamentary groups. Finally, I also made occasional interventions during the GAs in the "lower" part of CS, mainly in the direction of reducing polarization between "them" and "us". However, aside from my own participant observation, the study also relies on newspapers, website sources, as well as on relevant surveys, to give a more representative sociopolitical profile of the Greek indignados.

Ecological, ideological and tactical orientation of the Greek indignados— Location, banners, graffiti and orientation to non-violent and violent tactics

The social ecology of the Constitutional Square GIs

It is necessary to distinguish between the "upper" and the "lower" parts of Constitution Square. The "upper" part includes the Parliament building, the tomb of the Unknown Soldier, the hourly ceremonial change of the Presidential Guard wearing the uniform of the evzones[3], and a segment of the main street (Amalias) in front of the Parliament building. Besides the rallies of the GIs, the "upper" part hosted stalls by the "300 Greeks" who were collecting signatures for a referendum against the "Memorandum of Understanding", a stall by Orthodox priest activists and a platform for speeches and bands. On a usual evening rally, the indignados converged first on the "upper" part of CS, where they demonstrated (with banners, slogans, songs) against the government and the members of Parliament (MPs) for about 2-3 hours and about 9 pm an undetermined number of indignados descended to the "lower" part of CS for the General Assembly[4] and other activities. Besides the GA, the lower part hosted the Secretariat and the various working and thematic groups; the role of the former was mainly logistical and tactical, while the role of the latter was to propose and organize "peoples' consultations", using specialists, on issues relevant to the debt crisis, and to promote the application

Figure 16-2. A General Assembly—an example of direct democracy—organized by the Greek indignados in the lower part of Constitution Square

Source: Syntagma Square Indignant Citizens/©Eurokinissi Photo Press Agency/ Tatiana Bolari/9 June 2011

of "direct democracy". In addition, the "lower" part of CS hosted the projection of films (e.g., on "debtocracy"), a first-aid station staffed by volunteer doctors, skype connections with other indignados movements (e.g., Spanish), a lunch-supper section with food contributed by restaurants sympathetic to the indignados, an encampment with about 40 tents, a slogan suggestion box, and posters listing needed equipment and services. Several sources (Tzavella, 2011; Boubouka 2011; Charalambous, 2011; Rocamadur, 2011: 4-5) indicate, and I observed that myself, that the "upper" and "lower" parts of CS hosted two different political subcultures: the more "conservative", ethnocentric, right-wing and super-patriotic indignados demonstrated and remained in the "upper" part of CS, while the more "progressive", "leftist" and "anarchist" ones congregated in the "lower" part of CS to take part in a General Assembly, the so-called parallel Parliament. During late hours (after 11pm), the lower part was conducting a General Assembly and the upper part had cordoned off the area and played soccer on Amalias street, in front of the Parliament. Despite efforts on the part of the organizers to minimize the polarization between the "upper" and "lower" part of CS, by insisting that "we all have a common target", one could observe heightened tension during the GAs when indignados from the "upper" part of CS made interventions during the GAs, especially on issues relating to the integration of non-documented migrants.

Political claims and platform

Generally, the GI movement claimed to have no political or party affiliation. In their collective documents and resolutions, they acknowledged their divergent ideological origins, which they purportedly put aside for the sake of a more transcendent goal: to get rid of a government which brought the Memorandums, the troika of EU, ECB and IMF, a new occupation of the country and the austerity program which subverted their individual, political and social rights. They also felt that the government no longer had the legitimacy to "make decisions for them without them". There were no party or trade union banners since the Greek trade unions were associated with political parties, and the distribution of partisan literature was forbidden following a decision by the General Assembly[5]. Their anti-party stand was stated specifically in at least two of their resolutions[6] (See 13/06/2011 and 14/06/2911); in the first case, they voted to abolish the parties, while in the second they voted down a proposal not to abolish the political parties but to make them function more democratically. This anti-party stand was also reflected in social surveys of the GIs. In one of these (Georgiadou *et al.,* 2012), only about 5% felt that "the political parties were necessary for the operation of democracy", 27% said "the political parties are all the same", 29% said "the governing parties have become estranged from the people and the smaller ones represent better the people", while 39% said that the parties "only care for themselves and they deceive the people". In another social survey (Chiotis, 2011a), the majority of the CS indignados were against the evolution of the GI movement into a political party (49% against, 44% for and 7% gave no reply or did not know). In practice, the indignados' strongest aversion was to the two parties (Panhellenic Socialist Movement and New Democracy) that had alternated in the government of the country during the 37 years after the fall of the dictatorship in 1974 and less to the minority parties, inside or outside the Parliament[7].

On the other hand, movements against authoritarian regimes, for immigrant groups or domestic organizations against racism, were welcome[8]. The more "established" extra-parliamentary groups (e.g., the Marxist-Leninist Greek Communist Party, the Greek Communist Marxist Leninist Party, the Trotskyite "Workers Revolutionary Party", the organization of the Communist Internationalists of Greece, the *Kontra*/Insurrection Magazine, ANTARSYA[9] and "*Xekinima*"—the Socialist Internationalist Organization), several "emergent" groups (e.g., the "I Won't Pay Movement", "300 Hellenes", ENA-the "United-Resolved Ones" "the Committee for a Debt Review"), as well as the "anarchist" groups, also had access to the podium of the GAs and distributed their literature as long as it conformed with the "non-partisan" spirit of the GI movement. The resolutions of the GAs actually voted on were inclusive and non-partisan but were nonetheless in a "progressive" political direction.

Yet, despite the overall non-partisan orientation of the Greek indignados, there are charges that the "Alliance of the Radical Left" (SYRIZA) played a decisive role in the mobilization, the organization and coordination of the GI movement. Moreover, the fact that most of the specialists who participated in the "peoples' consultations" were either sympathizers and/or members of SYRIZA; the fact that the Committee for a Review of the Debt that had been a creation of SYRIZA and was allowed to have a stall in the "lower" square in order to collect signatures for setting up an International Review Committee, also point to the primary role of SYRIZA in the indignados movement.[10] Nonetheless, SYRIZA, while not dissociating itself from the goals of the GIs, denied charges that it was dominating the movement, or that it was providing it with the equipment, and insisted on safeguarding its "autonomous" character. In any case, the crucial questions have to do with the social causes of the collective response and whether or not the political parties have harvested the short- and long-term political benefits from the indignados movement (see section on impacts).

Of all the parliamentary political parties, the SYRIZA party was the one that embraced the GIs, both inside and outside of the Parliament. It has been common practice for SYRIZA to take advantage of all mass movements, that have "anti-Memorandum platforms", to increase its recruitment, and to recover the percentages lost during the 2008 urban riots as a result of its ambivalent position toward the hooded extra-parliamentary youths who took advantage of a just cause to burn the city[11]. The small opposition right-wing party—the Popular Orthodox Union (LAOS)—showed a tolerance toward the indignados and even proposed that the Parliament invite a delegation of them, possibly to approach the constituency of the "upper" part of the CS. The Communist Party of Greece (KKE), on the other hand, saw the GI movement as an unorganized protest reaction isolated from the workers' movement. At the same time, it escalated its own demonstrations and occupations of ministerial offices as a counterbalancing response. The two governing parties, being the main targets of the GIs for mis-government during the past 37 years, could only have ambivalent attitudes toward them. The press representative of the New Democracy (ND) party said "they are monitoring with interest the movement; the most interesting thing is that it is not under anybody's tutelage and it should remain that way" (Papoulia, 2011:24). The government of the Panhellenic Socialist movement (PASOK) and many of its MPs (most of whom were victims of mocking), while speaking in Parliament, recognized the indignados' democratic right to protest; however, they condemned the mocking of MPs and many of them suspected that some of these attacks were organized by members of the SYRIZA party (Stefanis, 2011). The Vice President of the George Papandreou government (E. Venizelos, now President of PASOK) said that "out in the squares there are pure-hearted citizens who are indignant and insecure, and to them we extend an invitation for an open dialogue", The PM himself, the most hated and caricatured, after the Vice President Pangalos, in a reply to the President of SYRIZA (Alexis Tsipras) who talked about agents provocateurs said: "Out there in the squares they are protesting, some because they have been aggrieved [by the austerity program] and others because they have lost their privileges", but "it is absolutely crucial that none of them lives the impacts of a [fiscal] breakdown" (Rova and Kountouris, 2011)

Slogans, banners and graffiti of the Greek indignados

These can constitute significant "unobtrusive measures" not only for political platforms but also for the level of emotional involvement in the Greek indignados movement. For the slogans, I relied exclusively on my "recordings" in the "upper" part of CS, while for the banners and graffiti I relied on visual materials both from the "upper" and the "lower" parts of the CS. With regard to the slogans, they can only be illustrative, to demonstrate the range in types, rather than exhaustive since I was not able to cover the entire mass event nor was I able to record all the slogans. Moreover, it's possible that the time of collection may impact on the content of the slogans.

Slogans, Hymns and Songs

Between 30/5/20ll and 19/06/2011, I observed 11 rallies in the *upper* part of CS, between 10:30 and 11:30 pm, and recorded 188 slogans (some overlap). Five were discarded because they were incomplete, the target was not clear and they made no sense. Table 16-1 shows the distribution of the 183 slogans, in descending order of frequency, without subjection to censorship. The left column shows the Greek slogans in Latin characters, to preserve their rhyme, while the right column shows the English translation. Among the 106 most recurrent ones (>4 references) are those that: satirize Vice-President Th. Pangalos for his account of the crisis during its breakout;[12] compare the current crisis (deprivation) to the 1967 dictatorship; express patriotism and a Spartan determination; call the MPs thieves (accompanied by the derogatory palm gesture);[13] attack the establishment journalists/media for their support of the "Memorandum" (accompanied by laser beams aimed against them at King George and the Grand Bretagne hotels); reflect discontent against the IMF; call for the burning of the Parliament; demand the ousting of the MoUs; challenge the politicians to live with 500€; invoke the Greek national anthem; express the GIs' resolve not to pay for a debt for which they do not feel responsible; revive a slogan of the conservatives in the early 1990s against the then socialist government (following the Koskota bank scandal); call for throwing the politicians into the "deep" Piraeus Port; and invoke the Argentine economic crisis (1999-2002), the December 2001 violent protests in *Plaza de Mayo*, the resignation of President Fernado de la Rua, his alleged fleeing from the country in a helicopter,[14] warning at the same time the Greek government that the same fate awaits them. There follow 77 other slogans, with lower frequencies (<5), which have as targets the politicians, the governments since 1974, the current government, the PM, the current opposition and the journalists, as well as a number which reflect concern about the course of the indignados movement. These specimens reflect not only the current concerns of the GIs, within their historical and international contexts, but also reveal a lot with regard to their heterogeneous political composition.

Table 16-1. Selected slogans of the Greek indignados in the "upper" Constitution Square (30.05.2011 - 19.06.2011)

Greek Slogans in Latin characters	Translated slogans	F
"Einai chontros, einai chontros, einai tis poutanas gios, troei troei poly, ton lene thodori" (7) & "Ante gamisou Pangale"(8).	"He is obese, he is obese, he is a son of a bitch, he eats, eats a lot, they call him Theodore" (7) & "Screw you Pangale" (8).	15
"Psomi, paideia, eleftheria, i junta den teliose to '73",	"Bread, education, freedom, the junta didn't finish in '73".	12
"Hellas, Hellas, i tan i epi tas".	"Hellas, Hellas, come back with your shield either victorious or dead on it".	11
"Kleftes, kleftes, kleftes" [the moutza follows].	"Thieves, thieves, thieves" [Derogatory hand gesture with palm open].	10
"Kai aaah kai oooh, gamo to DouNouTou".	"And aaah and oooh, fuck the IMF".	7
"Alites, roufianoi, dimosiografoi".	"Bums, informers, journalists".	7
"Na kaei, no kaei, to bourdelo i Vouli".	"Let it burn, let it burn, the Parliament-bordello".	6
"Eeeh..., Oooh..., Parte to Mnimonio kai figete apo do, oust".	"Eeeh... Oooh..., take the Memorandum and get out of here, *Ust"*.	6
"Edo, Edo, Kathe mera edo, elate seis na zisete me 500 euro",	"Here, here, everyday here, you're welcome to live with 500 euro".	6
[Tragoudontas ton ethniko ymno kathe fora pou alazei i Proedriki Froura (evzones)].	[Singing of the Greek National Anthem every time the Presidential Guard (Evzones) changes shifts].	6
"Den tha plirosoume pote, den tha plirosoume pote, pote".	"We shall never pay, we shall never pay, never, never".	5
"To Limani tou Pirea einai poly vathi, rixtous/ton sti thalassa [na pnigoyn] na kanoume giorti".	"The Port of Piraeus is very deep, throw them/him in the sea [to drown] & make a holiday of it".	5
"Mia nichta magiki san tin Argentini, na doume sto elikoptero pios tha protobi".	"A magical night, like in Argentine, let's see who will be the first to board the helicopter".	5
"Aera, aera, na figei i cholera. Theloume prothypourgo kai ohi kamariera".	"Air, air for cholera [the government] to go way. We want a PM, not a chambermaid".	5
"Georgaki, allaxe kariera, sti Nea Yorki psahnoune gia poutana/kainourgia kamariera".	"Georgaki [pet name for George], change career, in New York they are looking for a whore/new chambermaid".	4

Greek Slogans in Latin characters	Translated slogans	F
"Den ta fagame mazi, poustides politikoi".	"We did not eat it [the taxes , the posts, etc.] together, fags politicians".	4
"Naah, naah malakes [prodotes] naah" [akolouthei klasiki chironomia].	"Here, here, fucking idiots [traitors] here" [accompanied by hand gesture to genital zone].	4
"Olga Tremi, p… poulimeni; Pretenteri i 'Anatropi' den einai giorti; tha peste san ton Kosta ton Kenteri, Pretenteri, Pretenteri; p… Tremi, p… Pretenteri".	"Olga Tremi, w... sold to [vested interests] ; Pretenteri, "Overthrow" [TV talk show] is not a holiday. Pretenteri, Pretenteri, you willl have the fate of Kostas Kenteris; w… Tremi, f… Pretenteri".	4
"Lae polema, sou pinoune to aima".	"People fight, they are sucking your blood".	3
"Koufales, koufales [poutanes, poutanes], erchonte oi kremales".	"Fags, fags, the scaffolds are coming"	3
11 slogans with a frequency of 2		22
33 slogans with a frequency of 1		33
Total		**183**

A more qualitative classification of all 183 slogans (Figure 16-3) revealed that over 100 of them (N=118, 65%) had as a *target the "politicians*" (either collectively or individually); 28 (15.3%) revolved around *"political corruption"* (e.g., calling the MPs thieves, charging them with misuse of public funds); 27 (14.8%) concentrated on *attacks against the IMF, the MoU, the pay cuts* (e.g., "screw the IMF, out with the MoU; "can you live with 500€"; "we don't owe, we won't pay"); 15 (8.2%) involved *satirical/sexual attacks on VP* Theodore Pangalos (e.g., "he's obese"; "he eats a lot", "screw him"); 15 (8.2%) were concerned with *derogatory, racist, sexual references* to the PM George Papandreou" (e.g., denying his Greekness, doubting the legitimacy of his birth, calling upon him "to fill a vacancy in NY as a chambermaid"); 14 (7.7%) were pre-occupied with the *punishment of the politicians* (e.g., "the gallows, execution, prison awaits you"); 11 (6%) targeted the *establishment journalists* (e.g., calling them informers, bitches, fags, etc); 10 (5.5%) centered about *religion* (e.g., reference to masons-politicians, the presence of the priests, and the "citizens card"); 27 (14,8%) reflected *social racism* (e.g., saying "the Greeks are born, not made", suggesting that politicians were born out of wedlock, calling politicians fags/American bastards, labelling journalists as whores/fags and satirizing the obesity of government officials); 21 (11.5%) were concerned with *ethnic symbols* and were chauvinistic in nature (e.g., shouting "Hellas", singing the national anthem, asserting that "Greeks are born not made" and inviting "all Greeks to raise their hands"); 33 (18.8%) made reference to *historical-cultural figures/events, current events and/or popular culture* (e.g., Leonidas, Spartans, Goudi, WW II occupation, the 1967 Greek dictatorship, the Argentine bankruptcy, the 2008 December events, songs against the dictatorship, the Stros-Kan affair, popular songs); and finally, 18 (10.2%) were preoccupied with *the course of the indignados movement* at home and abroad (e.g,. come back victorious or dead on your shield, people keep up the struggle, have a peoples' assembly in Parliament, assert that the priests are here, all the Mediterranean to become a square for indignados). The percentages exceed 100% (N=183) due to the multi-thematic classification of the slogans.

Figure 16-3. Selected slogans of the Greek indignados in the "upper" Constitution Square (30.05.2011 - 19.06.2011)

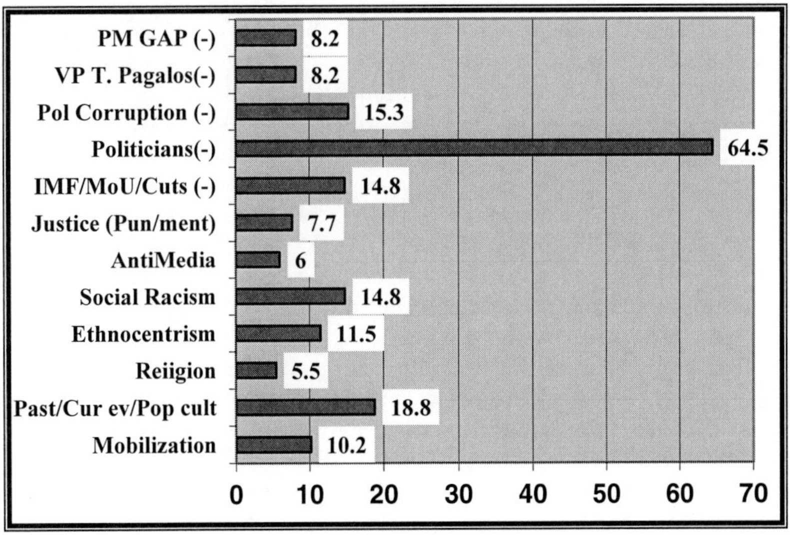

A note on the use of "obscenities" and sexual language on the oral and gestural level. I don't think the use of obscenities in the slogans is a matter of sexual deprivation and substitution in a Freudian sense. Secondly, this sort of language may have been facilitated in a crowd (anonymous) situation, especially at night, and by the fact that the slogans were mainly on the oral level of communication.[15] Third, they also may reflect the *machismo* of organized hooligans who had invaded the GI movement (Gourgouris, 2011;2). The fact that a group of indignados wrapped in Greek flags had cordoned off the Amalias Street in front of the Parliament and played soccer justifies this interpretation. On the other hand, as an integral part of the "revolutionary lingo", it may be an effective mechanism to express indignation and to humiliate the opponents (the politicians). These points need further investigation on an individual interview level. In addition, there is a need to employ field-team observation techniques to record their universality, the range and intensity of the slogans in a mass situation.

Banners, placards, paintings and posters (BAPPPs)

The banners, posters and placards can be another indicator of the profile and goals of the GIs. The author took hundreds of pictures of GI events and mass rallies, that included banners, placards and posters of various sizes, ranging from small posters stuck on tree trunks to large banners more than 10 meters long hung between electricity poles, during the period the GIs were in action (25/05/2011–30/07/2011). Some of the photos included more than one BAPPP; those readable were counted as separate posters.[16] The BAPPPs were situated in the environs of Constitution Square, *both in the "upper" and the "lower" segments of CS.*[17] Moreover, the focus was on those "permanently" fixed on electricity posts, on trees, structures, etc. rather than on those in marching situations. Thus, an attempt was made to avoid photographing posters and banners from the marches (general strikes) of 15 and 28-29 June 2011 since these were organized by the established trade unions, toward which the GIs had an ambivalent attitude. Nonetheless, the author does not maintain that this survey is an exhaustive study of the banners, placards and posters of the Greek indignados.

The analysis of the 178 BAPPPs and their classification was not an easy task. Each of these documents was treated as a single unit; an attempt was made to base the content analysis on the predominant concern (theme), though there were several BAPPPs which were composite; however, a dominant theme was extracted and each was classified only in one content category. Therefore, the percentages cumulate to 100%.

The results (Figure 16-4) show the predominance (21.3%) of *negative content against the troika* (IMF, MoU, EU and the MTEP)[18] (e.g., "we don't owe, we won't pay"; "the crisis was designed by the murderers of IMF", "down with the MoU, referendum now"; "no to world government, national independence"; "we support CS, won't leave until the government, troika and the debt go"); this category also included several paintings/posters with a negative depiction[19] of the USA, the IMF,

Chancellor Angela Merkel, the PM George Papandreou, Antonis Samaras and George Karatzaferis.

Figure 16-4. Selected banners, posters, and placards of the Greek indignados—the "upper" and "lower" sections of Constitution Square, 25/05/2011-30/07/2011 (N=178)

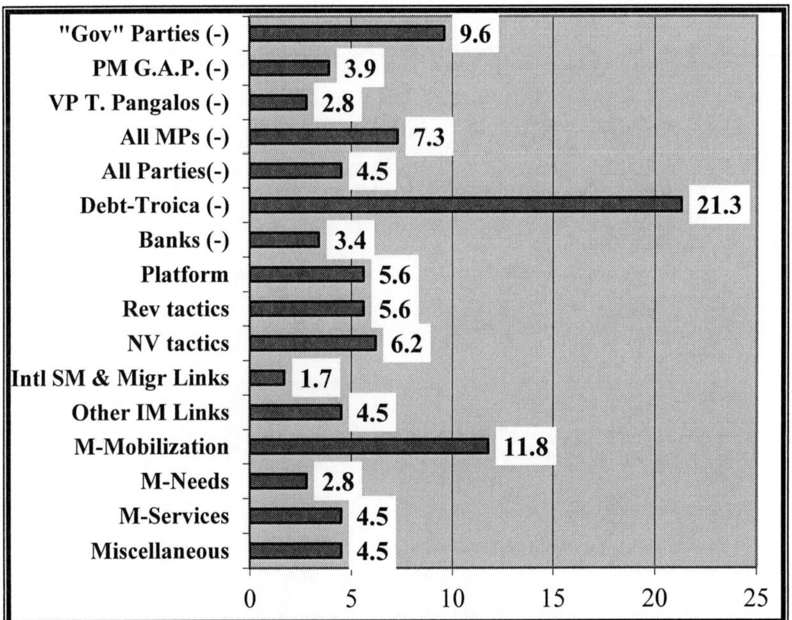

Key: PM G.A.P. Prime Minister George Andreas Papandreou, VP=Vice President, NV=Non-violent, M=Movement, SM=Social Movement.

To the predominant category, one could also add the first three categories (16.2%) targeting (1) *the Prime Minister* (e.g., two posters, one saying "Jefry [*sic*] go home, the USA" and the other saying "George Papandreou: School for Cycling"; a painting depicting George Papandreou crushing wagon trains that correspond to Greece, workers and trade unions and at the bottom the five political parties in Parliament receiving state funding (Figure 16-5); an ad for a PM who, among other assets, has a command of the Greek language and is a Greek citizen" (2) the Vice President *Th. Pangalos* (e.g., a painting/poster showing Pangalos devouring dollars and euro and calling him a traitor for surrendering Ocalan to the Turks; another BAPPP addressed to him and saying "wretched fascist Pangale, you threaten us with violence, with dismissal and unemployment"; and a poster showing Pangalos defecating and a man behind him with a broom and a dustpan that is accompanied by the legend, "control Pangalos' statements, don't leave him without a leash") and (3) the *"governing parties"* (e.g., a poster saying "down with the Junta"; another poster depicting collaboration between CIA and the two ministers of the Ministry of the Citizen Protection (Papoutsis and Chrysochoidis) being hanged in CS, alleging that they were responsible for the death of the four Marfin workers; a poster showing the emblem [sun] of PASOK with the party name distorted to read "BATSOK" meaning the party of cops *[batsos]* and suppression, and a poster-painting depicting VP E. Venizelos (new Minister of Finance) as the new *germanotsolias* ("germano-evzones") of PASOK etc).[20] If the latter three categories are added to the one that dominates the posters, then we could say that 37,5% of the BAPPPs reflect an anti-government (anti-PASOK) orientation.

Figure 16-5. Examples of painting and banner with the paining satirizing PM George Papandreou and the five political parties with Parliamentary representation (left) and the banner showing solidarity to the Spanish indignados

Source: Author's photo archive (29 May 2011 and 2 June 2011).

A total of 11.8% of the BAPPPs had either all or almost all MPs and Parliamentary parties or party leaders as a target for negative evaluation. A sample of representative content in these two categories includes the following: "down with the junta of the rich, forward with the workers, the quislings stay back"[21]; "we are for direct democracy, above all parties"; "we don't belong to any party"; neither right nor left, just humanity"; "380 BC, 300 heroes and one traitor, 21st century. 300 traitors MPs"; "popular mandate, you vote for MoU, you will win Goudi"[22]; "you're not an MP[*Vouleutis*] you are an opportunist [*Voleutis*] and if you have a modicum of conscience leave before it's too late"; "opportunists [*lamogia*] of Parliament, wherever you go we shall find you"; and a painting showing the heads of five political leaders [Papandreou, Samaras, Papariga, Tsipras and Karatzaferis…] in a mortar pounded with a pestle and with a legend that says, "The Greek people, permanent general strike, now the pestle, no to the underlings of the world dictatorship". Although as said above, the General Assembly of the GIs had taken a collective decision against parties—especially against the governing parties—the anti-party stand was not so evident, at least in the banners, the placards and the posters.

The overwhelming majority of the remaining BAPPPs (42.7%) had as an object the movement's mobilization, platforms, tactics, links, needs, and services.

Movement mobilization constituted the most common category and included BAPPPs with a variety of content, including exhortations to wake up (e.g., "*et vous combien de temps allez-vous dormir*?"); tactical/ideological considerations (e.g., "resistance, self-organizing, solidarity, social revolution for a world of freedom and equality"; "we don't negotiate our ideals, we broaden [*plateiazoume*][23] our solidarity, all together"); announcements of movement actions (e.g., the "2nd Pan-European rendezvous on 5/06/11, the "encirclement" of the Parliament on 28-29/06/11, the holding of peoples' assemblies in CS and Athens neighbourhoods, general strikes); expressions of solidarity (e.g., a letter-poster from a grandmother in the remote island of Ikaria urging the GIs not to retreat; BAPPPs saying "the people are here and struggle for Democracy" and "Greece is not for sale, Crete is here"); and communication resources (e.g., websites, radio stations).

The category *platform* included usually ideological positions and lists of demands (e.g., "PIGS program: nationalization of banks, abolition of all rights to inheritance, fixed salaries of 30,000€ regardless of worker qualifications"; "Democracy and capitalism are contradictory concepts"; "the greatest violence is release from a job and unemployment"; and "*para todos todo*").

Tactics included both "*violent-revolutionary*" and *non-violent* approaches to social change. The former included such texts as "Greece on sale, Tel. 1821";[24] "when the struggle becomes a necessity, revolution becomes a way of life"; "revolt against the looting of our lives by IMF, the state and capital"; quoting article 120 of the Greek Constitution, stating that "the protection of the Constitution is up to the patriotism of the Greeks" and mandating the Greeks to "resist by any means against whomever attempts to dissolve it by force";[25] and "29/06/11, now *Intifada* in Greece". *Non-violent* tactics included both social and personal transformation approaches. Examples of such BAPPPs texts include: "indifference finished, direct democracy", "permanent strike, out with IMF/EU"; signature-collection [petition] for a referendum regarding MoU; a demand for a peoples' constitutional assembly; "if you want to change the world, change yourself" and "God, why have you forgotten us, come down, we need You now more than ever".

A significant aim of the movement was making *connections with other like movements*; this was especially part of the subculture in the lower part of CS. Thus, the GIs made links with other indignados movements, especially the Spanish ones (Figure 16-5), as reflected in these foreign language BAPPPs: "*Los pueblos unidos, jamas seran venidos*! *Hellas, Spain Portugal*"; "*Are you 'PIGS' like us? Join us. It's your fight, too, dude*"; "*Hasta, la Victoria siempre*" with a photo of Che Guevara; and "*A forca do povo, unido jamais sera vencido*". Aside from the links with the international indignados movements, the GIs also gave their support to other international and domestic movements (causes) like the "Arab Spring" and the domestic migrants' movements: "no attack on Libya, close Suda base [in Crete], victory for the Arab revolution"; "Sunday School for migrants, equal rights for all, legalize migrants, asylum to the refugees"; and "the migrants are the earth's damned, but in the world of the bosses, we are all foreigners".

Two other categories that refer to the indignados movement are those pertaining to the GIs' *needs and services*. In regard to *services*, one poster listed the operation of 17 working groups, while separate posters announced the presence of a First Aid Station, task groups for meals, a group for the environment (clean up), a group for maintaining calmness, legal support, Yoga lessons and alternative communities. Given these services—and the lack of own resources—the posting of *needs* was unavoidable. Therefore, 5 posters called for donations of foods, refreshments, medical specialties, electronic equipment and volunteers for various task groups.[26] In a sense, the GIs succeeded in establishing a semi-permanent autonomous community with Constitution Square as the seat.

Finally, two content categories included the BAPPPs that targeted the *banks* (3.4%) and "*miscellaneous*" (4.5%) objects. Posters having the *banks* as targets included content such as the following: "Thieves, black marketeers, bankers"; "No homes in the hands of bankers"; "Pigs are the banks and not the people";[27] and if "the 151 (parliamentary majority) decide for us, we can decide for ourselves by withdrawing our money from the banks". With respect to the "*miscellaneous*" BAPPPs texts, these included a variety of targets. Examples include: "I hope nothing, I believe nothing, I am Greek"; "history is breaking down, the present is in a state of flux";[28] "Greek people demand "Bring back the Parthenon Marbles'"; and a poster with a list of journalists by name, medium and station with the title: "Bums, informers, journalists".[29]

The GIs and graffiti

The author has been to many countries, but nowhere has he seen such extensive graffiti as in Greece. Exception may be the protest graffiti in Northern Island, which, however, is aesthetically complete. While graffiti is a most unobtrusive measure of collective phenomena, it's usually hard to determine its maternity and age. In Athens, there are usually spurts of graffiti by hooligans following football matches and by demonstrators or anarchists after collective protests. Two main streets in downtown Athens, Stadiou and University Avenues, are the most stepped on streets, since they connect Omonia with CS, where is located the Greek Parliament—the "symbol of power". Protests usually start from Omonia Square, march on Stadiou Avenue to Syntagma and return from University Avenue. The graffiti on these two streets besides providing employment to Municipal workers, can also be a barometer of the demonstrators' platform and intentions My own 70 specimens cover the time period, 31/05/2011-0/07/2011, and the overwhelming number of them were located in the vicinity of Constitution Square (imprinted on the sidewalks, on the streets, on monuments, on benches and the entrance to the metro), while a small number were located in University Avenue and were photographed following the 28-29 June mass demonstrations of the GIs and the TUs against the Medium Term Economic Program.

Figure 16-6. An example of graffiti on the sidewalk in front of the Parliament building, in the upper part of Constitution Square, using traffic symbolism (top) and the traditional open palm gesture *moutza* (bottom) to express disapproval against party leaders, prime ministers, government officials and politicians[*]

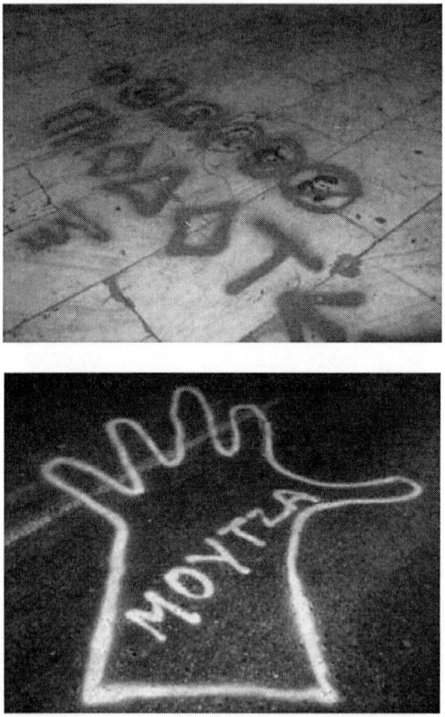

Source: Author's photo archives: Top: 7 June 2011. Bottom; 10 June 2011.
[*]The figures inscribed in the sidewalk are [from left to right] A. Chipras, G. Papandreou, A. Papariga, K. Karamanlis, Th. Pangalos and G. Karatzaferis). The word "traitors' is written under the six figures.

An analysis of the graffiti reveals some continuities and discontinuities with that of the slogans and the BAPPPs, though the categories are not exactly comparable (Figure 16-7). Thus, there was some continuity: first, with regard to *a negative evaluation* of (a) *t*he *governing party* (e.g., "leave with helicopter now or in a hearse later"; "death to the PASOKERS"; "fuck PASOK"; "down with the junta") (b) the *post-1974 governments* (e.g., "1967-2011, the junta ends tonight"; "the people will hang the new quislings"[30]; "thieves, Goudi is waiting for you") and (c) *all*

Parliamentary parties (e.g., "rebel, all the politicians betrayed us"; an imprint of government officials and party leaders on the CS sidewalk accompanied by label 'traitors"; a *moutza* with arrows pointing toward Parliament)[31]; and second, with regard to a *positive perception of international movements and migrants* (e.g., "Greeks and migrants, workers united"). However, discontinuity can be observed in most of the other dimensions. Thus, the troika becomes a less common target (e.g., "organ donors, give your balls to IMF"; "kill WTO and IMF"; "out with the globalization of exploitation, taxes and loans") while a negative targeting of the then PM George Papandreou, the banks and the state apparatus becomes more marked. In addition, there is increased support for violent revolutionary interventions as well as approval of urban terrorist groups.

Figure 16-7. Graffiti in Constitution Square and University Avenue, 31/05 – 30/07/2011 (N=70)

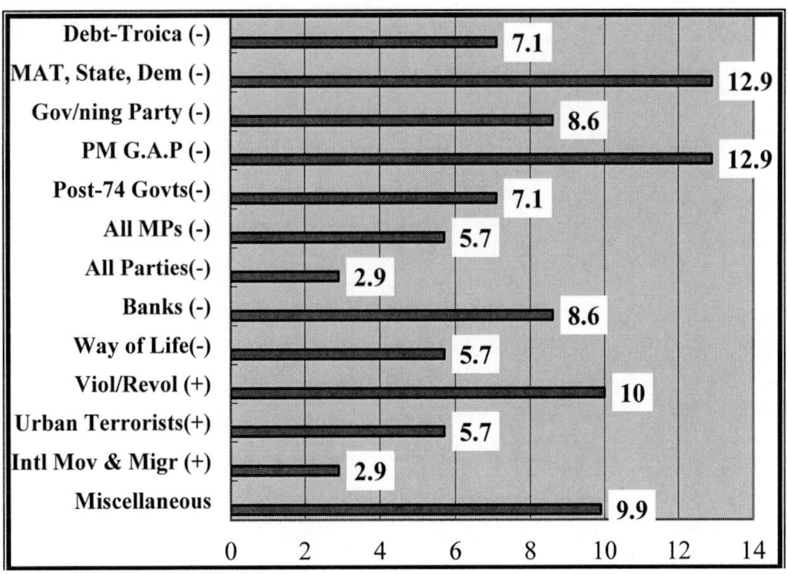

The then *PM George Papandreou* became a popular target for graffiti authors. Examples include a photo of GAP inscribed in the sidewalk in front of CS, with a superimposed "prohibition sign" (circle and diagonal line in red) and with the legend "come, banana"; a similar photo accompanied by the word "wanted"; an inscription on the entrance to the subway at CS saying "fag Jeffrey, resign"; and another one on the wall of a preserved building on University avenue saying: "goodbye G.A.P.". The above graffiti implies that the PM has converted Greece into a "banana republic"; at the same time it recycles the conspiracy theory about the PM's American background and reflects racist attitudes— attitudes usually expressed by right-wing groups.

A significant number of graffiti reflected negative relationships with the established order and *the social control mechanism*s—the MAT (e.g., "fuck progress, free everyone"; "cops, pigs, murderers"; "fuck your democracy"; "love or power"; "MAT to the KAT[32]. The graffiti coincided with charges in the press, by demonstrators and political parties on the left, of unprovoked police brutality and/or the infiltration of the movement by agents provocateurs during the June 15 and June 28-29 protest demonstrations. It is noteworthy that 5 of the 9 graffiti in this category had the mark of anarchists (A within a circle).

The *banks and the bankers* were another favourite target. Almost all of the graffiti was written on the banks themselves (Bank of Greece, Agricultural Bank, Eurobank, Alpha Bank, etc.) either on the closed metal shutters or on the building façade. Examples of texts include; "burn me, you can"; "thieves-bankers, you are sucking our blood"; "whore, Babylonia"[33] and "the enemy is in the banks and the ministries". A number of banks (especially ATMs) suffered damages following violent confrontations during the GI mass demonstrations, though they were small in magnitude compared to the December 2008 demonstrations, and one could not attribute them with certainty to the GIs themselves.

In close proximity to the banks on University Avenue and inscribed on store fronts were located a number of graffiti that satirized or lamented the lost "*way of life*" of the Greeks. Examples include "consumption is over"; "shopping is finished" and "live your Greece in myth"—the latter being a satiric version of a tourist slogan ("live your myth in Greece).

Worth distinguishing were also two categories that had to do with *revolutionary and/or violent approaches* to structural changes. The first of these, "*violence/revolution*", included both violent and non-violent tactics and strategies. Text examples include: "revolution now, along with love-making" (*erotas)*", "peoples to arms!"[34].; "now with the new measures, think again and throw some stones"; "class rebellion and not patriotic indignation". The second category, "*urban terrorism*" was an endorsement of urban terrorist organizations and individuals imprisoned, killed in confrontation with the police or under trial for participation in terrorist organizations. Examples of texts include: "'honour to the 'Revolutionary Struggle', the 'Nuclei of Fire', and '17N'"; "honour to Lambros Fountas";

and "hands off Nikitopoulos, Stathopoulos and Kortesi". Again, it is noteworthy that 7 of the 11 cases of graffiti in these two categories were accompanied by the symbol of the anarchists which attests to the infiltration of the indignados by anarchist groups at least with regard to graffiti which as said is a sector not easily subject to control by the GIs' Committees.

The GI movement and violence

The meaning of violence is relative. The slogans, the posters and the graffiti can constitute violence if they incite violence against persons or property. When the graffiti, "fire to the banks", leads to actual burning of the banks (with human victims as we saw in the case of Marfin), then it's violence. However, there is also the notion of structural violence (e.g., poverty, police brutality) that may also cause disease and death. Although structural violence is of vital importance, the concept of "violence" in the present text refers to overt physical violence against persons and property. Were the GIs violent in this restricted sense? Analysing the resolutions of the General Assemblies in the "lower" part of CS from 25/05/2011 to 30/07/2011 when the encampments were removed by the municipal authorities, the formal position of the GIs was one of a non-violent protest (See GA resolutions 2/06/11, 11/06/11, 14/06/11, 18/06/11, 27/06/11), though these decisions were usually preceded by heated debates given the heterogeneous composition and the presence of anarchists and extra-parliamentary groups among the GIs. Thus, all the mass demonstrations of the GIs between 25/05/11 and 15/06/11, including the Pan-European one on 5/06/11 (which in the author's opinion was the most massive of all during the summer of 2011) were non-violent. Mass violent confrontations occurred during the 24-hour general strike called by the trade unions and the GIs on 15/06/2011 and during the 48-hour strike (28-29/06/2011) called again by trade unions and the GIs to block the voting on the Medium Term Economic Program.[35] Undoubtedly, the attendant violence, that was started either by provocateurs (Gougouris, 2011: 4) or extra-parliamentary groups, changed the composition and reduced the size of subsequent GI demonstrations. Following these violent confrontations, the General Assembly of the GIs condemned violence whatever its source, though it adopted a more flexible position regarding the use of violence by demonstrators for defensive purposes. It also took a stand against a sit-in demonstration, fearing the indignados would become sitting ducks in the case of violent confrontations not their doing. Nonetheless, they endorsed protest rallies outside the courts and the Ministry of Citizen Protection to support those arrested, not making any distinctions between "GIs", "anarchists" or the members of "extra-parliamentary" groups.

Figure 16-8. Examples of human injuries and property damage following the 29 June 2011 mass protests of Greek indignados against the austerity memorandums

Photo sources: Left: ID:10115962/©ANA-MPA/Saitas P./29 June 2011. Right: Author's photo archive (30 June 2011).

Another form of violence that needs some special attention is the individual targeting and mocking of supporters of the austerity programs (MPs, journalists, spouses of MPs, etc), often accompanied by insulting hand gestures (e.g *moutza*), the hurling of epithets, the throwing of yogurt, eggs, wild oranges, bottled water and rocks, as well as the aiming of laser beams at the eyes of their opponents. In one of his interventions during a General Assembly, the author as a participant had cautioned against the polarization with regard to the MPs and the journalists, because it could "legitimize" violence against these individuals and their families (see note 29). On this point, the General Assembly showed "contradictory" behaviour. In one of its decisions (2/06/11), it rejected a proposal to encircle (cordon off) the private houses of MPs who were in favour of the Medium Term Economic Program (MoU-II). In a subsequent decision (5/07/2011), the GA rejected a proposal "to condemn the individual targeting of MPs from all parties", implying that it was OK to mock the MPs of the parties who had voted for the MTEP.[36] In two other relevant decisions (1/07/2011, 5/07/2011), that are not necessarily contradictory with the general stand on violence, since the target is the source of the "suppression", the GA supported the proposal for protest demonstrations outside of the private houses of the Minister of Citizen Protection and the Chief of Police. During the period under study, there took place systematic harassment and several attacks against MPs, especially of the governing party, but also an attack against an MP of the Greek Communist Party and a journalist (Stefanis, 2011; Hasapopoulos, 2011a, 2011b; Margomenos, 2011; Apergis, 2011; Kemanetzi, 2011).[37] The general atmosphere—and not only that cultivated by the GIs—led many MPs of the governing party to restrict their public appearances, essentially putting themselves under "house arrest".

The social, demographic and political profile of GIs: Evidence from social surveys

There have not been many systematic studies yet of the GIs. With regard to their *age-gender-urban* distribution, a national survey by Public Issue (SKAI Radio Station, 2011), that was conducted in the period 7-10 June 2011, observed an even *gender* distribution, with slightly more women (51%) than men (49%), reporting that they had taken part in rallies in the country's squares. Apparently, there is no relationship since it coincides with the gender distribution in the population. The same survey showed a Gaussian distribution with regard to *age,* with almost 50% of the interviewed indignados in the age categories 35-54. Finally, with respect to *residence*, 77% of them came from urban places, 9% from semi-urban and 15% from rural areas. About 38% came from the capital area, which is about the proportion of the Athens population in the national population.

On the level of *education*, the above Public Issue survey showed that 42% of the participants in Greek squares demonstrations had higher education, 50% had secondary education and 8% had elementary education. In a semi-structured interview study of 79 Greek indignados from Constitution Square in Athens[38] (Georgiadou *et al.*, 2012; Kollia, 2012), conducted during May-June 2011, the research team noted that 6% had elementary education, 26% had lower/higher secondary education, 60% had higher education and 8% had graduate school education. According to 2009 OECD educational statistics, the percentage of Greeks (25-64 years old) with higher education (includes graduate school) was about 25%. Though the ages may not be exactly comparable, as the surveys sample adults 18 years-old and above, both the social survey and the interview study at CS suggest that the GIs were over-represented among the higher education categories.

With regard to *economic and income* status, two national surveys (Public Issue and Kapa Research) contain some relevant data. The data used in these two studies are more or less indirect indicators of economic status, and include employment status, "income performance" and "household status". The *Public Issue* study (7-10 June 2011) used the "*employment and the income performance*" measures. It showed that 54% of those who took part in public square demonstrations to be employed, 15% to be unemployed and 31% to be outside the labour force. No doubt, the latter, besides housewives, may also include large numbers of students. With regard to "income performance", 2% said they "live comfortably", 22% that they "make ends meet", 38% they have "difficulty" and another 38% that they "have a great difficulty making it". Finally, the *comparative social survey* of Kapa Research (Chiotis, 2011a: 26-27), that was carried out 14-15 June 2011 and that compared the CS indignados (N=643) with the general national population (N=1208) on "household status", revealed the following: 84% of the CS indignados and 67% of the general population reported that "the current status of their household does not permit them to make plans", while 13% of the former and 30% of the latter said that "the current status of their household allows them to make plans".[39] Although in both populations the overwhelming majority cannot make plans, the situation is much more pessimistic for the Constitutional Square indignados than the general population.

Ideological and political characteristics. In this case, relevant data were available from the Public Issue (7-10 June 2011) national social survey of GIs and the CS interview study. The Public Issue survey used both subjective (ideological self-placement) and objective (vote in 2009 elections) indicators, while the Georgeadou *et al.* (2012) CS study used only a "self-placement" measure. The voting behaviour shows (Figure 16-9) that the distribution of party affiliation in the national sample of indignados was almost comparable to their strength in Parliament except for SYRIZA and LAOS, where the former occupies a higher rank than LAOS in the sample of indignados. It also shows a large percentage (12%) who had not voted (young students) and a larger percentage yet with undetermined affiliation (30%) that could be translated into alienation from the established political parties. In any case, the vote data show an ideological diversity among those who had reported participation in the public squares' protests, *with the highest percentage being voters of the governing party (PASOK).*

Figure 16-9. Vote of the GIs in the 2009 national Parliamentary Elections (Public Issue Survey, 7-10 June 2011)

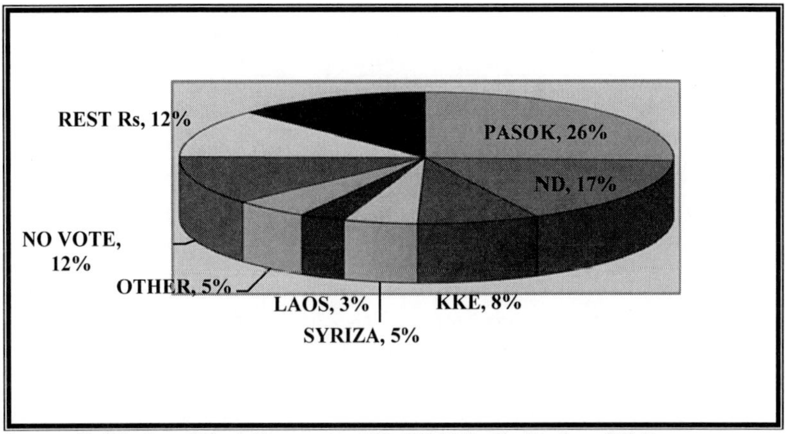

Source: Public Issue Flash Barometer 159 (SKAI Radio Station, 2011).
KEY: PASOK=Panhellenic Socialist Movement, ND=New Democracy, KKE=Communist Party of Greece, SYRIZA=Alliance of the Radical Left, LAOS= Peoples' Popular Union.

Focusing on the *self-placement* criterion, the data (Table 16-2) show a more even ideological distribution of GIs in the Public Issue national survey than in the Constitution Square interview study, though the data of the national survey are slightly skewed to the left of the spectrum. In the CS interview study, the distribution is more markedly skewed toward the left. While this may in part be due to the use of fewer categories in the interview study, there is no doubt that the social conditions in Athens (e.g., seat of the government, anarchist bases, tradition of demonstrations) may have also contributed to the skewed distribution. A lot may also depend upon the sample distribution in the "upper" and "lower" CS, as well as on the fact that the General Assemblies held in the "lower" CS were under the control of left-oriented participants. Both of these hypotheses need to be further explored. Nonetheless, both studies show that more than 40% find the traditional ideological spectrum irrelevant. This shows high alienation from the traditional parties, that also matches the indignados' aversion to political parties and their commitment not to evolve into a political party.

Table 16-2. Self-placement of Greek indignados on the ideological spectrum

Study Agency	Left	Centre/ Left	Centre	Centre/ Right	Right	None
Public Issue (June 2011)	17%	10%	10%	6%	10%	41%
Georgiadou et al (2012)	36,8%	14,7%	------------	1,5%	4,4%	42,6%

Sources: Public Issue Flash Barometer 159 (SKAI Radio Station, 2011) and "The square was full of indignants"… (Kollia, 2011:39).

Lastly, in view of the fact that the MoUs of austerity played a significant role in the mobilisation of the Greek indignados, it would be instructive to refer to the *comparative attitudes of the general population (public opinion) and the CS indignados with regard to the European Union and the Medium Term Economic Program (MoU II)***.** The KAPA Research comparative survey (Chiotis, 2011a: 26-27) provides the relevant data. To the statement "The fact that Greece belongs to the European Union", 80% of the general population and 45% of the CS sample replied that it constituted a "positive/perhaps positive" event; conversely, a higher percentage of the CS indignados (48%) than the general population (16%) replied that it constituted a "negative/or perhaps negative" event. Furthermore, a higher percentage of the CS indignados (84%) would prefer the MTEP (MoU-II) to be voted down by the Parliament and proceed immediately to national elections than the national population for whom the corresponding percentage was 48%; on the other hand, a higher percentage of the general population (35%) wanted the MTEP to be approved in order to secure the next instalment than the CS indignados for whom the corresponding proportion was only 3,7%. Two years of austerity programs have made the indignados question the advantages of belonging to the EU and the legitimacy of the current government.

A Theoretical note on the emergence of the Greek indignados "movement"

Before attempting an explanation of the GI mass protest, I would like to come back to the question raised in the introduction: Did the GIs constitute an autonomous "social movement". In the literature, a social movement is a structured and organized form of collective behaviour with specific goals. It has an ideology, a platform, and a leadership structure.

Reference was made in the introduction to the diversity of political orientation among the indignados, the presence of political subcultures, and the problems the General Assembly had in deciding on a "*common declaration*", that would state specifically not only what they were against but also what they were for, beyond "direct democracy" that is more procedure than purpose. Although in practice a "progressive" platform was emerging with regard to values, e.g., justice, equality, dignity, freedom, solidarity, and with regard to condemnation of racist interventions, this *emergent platform* was never adopted formally by the GA as a whole and as a resolution. Also, a *leadership structure* was not evident, though admittedly leadership can be collective, rotational, and underground in case of fronts. Nonetheless, there are indications (Livitsanos, 2011: 4; Kehagia, 2011: 22) that SYRIZA and "extra-parliamentary" groups played a significant leadership role in organizing and coordinating the indignados. This, as well as the use of only first names during the GA and the short-life of the GIs, makes one suspect that the Greek indignados was a front that provided an opportunity to the above groups for recruitment. If it was a front, then it was part of another movement. If it was not a front, then it was merely an "unstructured collective behaviour" [expressive] phenomenon rather than a "social movement". In any case, labelling it a front or an "expressive" social movement does not mean that the masses themselves were not genuinely indignant or that the mass phenomenon does not convey a vital message for the governors of society (Exadaktylos, 2011:3; Gourgouris, 2011;5). On the other hand, perhaps it is premature to judge such movements as one Stanford sociologist suggests (Soule, 2011: 33).[40] Moreover, with the new technologies, perhaps the classical forms of leadership should not be a necessary criterion for modern movements.[41] It remains to be seen whether the GI mass phenomenon will crystallize into an autonomous social movement, on the level of civil society if not as an institutionalized political party, or be coopted by various established political parties depending upon their spatial distribution in CS or pass into history as an "expressive" form of mass phenomenon.

Whatever the long-term outcome, this mass phenomenon needs explanation. Theoretically, various frameworks (e.g., Neil Smelser's *value-added* theory of collective behaviour phenomena, Durkheim-Merton's theory of *social anomie*, Davies' *theory of revolutions*) could be invoked to account for the indignados phenomenon. Although the first two frameworks could be relevant, the author believes that Davies' theory of revolutions provides a more relevant and parsimonious account for the emergence of the Greek indignados. For Davies, the experience of *relative deprivation* plays a crucial role. The argument is that following the fall of the dictatorship in 1974 and the assumption of power by the Socialist Government (Andreas Papandreou) in 1981, a new middle class came into existence (Daskalopoulou, 2011)[42]. All the governments since then, whether "socialist" or "conservative", supported the emergence and consolidation of this new middle class. The citizens had access not only to the basics but also to amenities. Loans or EU subsidies of all types were available to them (for farms, houses, cars, consumption and vacations, etc.). Their children had more chances than ever for higher education, either at home or abroad, more access to education for personal progress and enlightenment (e.g., languages, music, dance, ballet) and more chances for landing a job at home following graduation. Then, after 2008, came the debt crisis, the austerity measures, the recession, the unemployment, business failures, the lack of access to credit and the threat of house seizures by banks. In short, there followed a "proletarianization", if not "impoverization", of the Greek middle classes (Rocamadur, 2011: 1). These actual conditions caused a sudden reversal of rising expectations and life styles and created a strong "relative deprivation" among the new middle classes, both in relationship to the past and to privileged groups in Greek society who often accumulated illegal wealth with impunity[43] but also in relationship to their future expectations.[44] Mobilization and the Greek indignados movement were a natural sequel. The composition of the Greek indignados (education, 2009 voting, etc.), both in the national samples and especially in the Constitutional Square sample, constitute empirical proof for the relative deprivation theory. This sequence of events and the composition of the indignados, however, were not apparently sufficient for the Greek indignados to crystallize into a genuine autonomous and viable social movement, at least not until the present writing. On the other hand, it does not mean that they have had no impact on the Greek political system.

The short- and medium-term political impacts of the Greek indignados

At the end of September 2011, an article appeared in a progressive newspaper (Karatziou, 2011:37)[45], with the title, "Where have the indignados gone?", especially at a time when the government was taking the most unpopular and oppressive measures. The journalist invokes the opinion of Greek and foreign social scientists (Serafeim Seferiadis, Alexander Afouxenidis and Naomi Klein) who attribute the decline of the movement to police suppression, the shock and numbness attendant to the harsh neoliberal policies, as well as to the inability of the movement itself

Figure 16-12. The Greek indignados encampment in full action (top) and on the day following its dismantling by municipal authorities (bottom)

Photo sources: Top: Author's photo archive (29 June 2011). Bottom: Author's photo archive (30 July 2011).

to develop a more homogeneous orientation and constitute an alternative radical political solution. According to the same journalist, the then website of the indignados (real-democracy) announced that for the moment they are "keeping silent" until they [Greeks] "wake up and hit the squares again…" Though there is no doubt that the heterogeneous composition and ideology were a critical factor in their "disappearance", other answers to the journalist's question are also possible. Firstly, some of them, heeding the calling of the General Assembly, may have decentralized to the beaches, the neighbourhoods (Xenaki, 2011: 34)[46], the work places or the universities, implementing somewhat the Spanish indignados model of action (European Revolution, 2012:4). Secondly, some of them were eventually co-opted by the established TUs or parties which they could not persuade to join them. Thirdly, the established parties that used the indignados as a front may have achieved their goals for broadening their base and recalled their supporters to the fold to work for the upcoming elections. Finally, it is possible that the indignados felt they had accomplished their goals—had made their point—not only within the Greek society but also abroad (Fakatselis, 2011; 31; Bastea, 2011a: 30, 2011b: 39; Psychari, 2011a: 32-33; 2011b: 36; Vasilopoulou, 2011: 27) and, therefore, it was logical for them to suspend their activities or to hibernate and wait for a more opportune time in the future.

This section explores both *the short and medium political impacts* of the GI "movement" using as criteria the results of public opinion surveys, Parliamentary voting on MoUs, government reshuffles, party realignments, the turnout at the first anniversary rally, general election results and current website status.

GI Impact on public opinion

First, let us look at the survey results and the impact the GIs had on public opinion. Two national surveys had relevant results. The *first* was conducted the week 10-17/06/2011 using a sample of 2131 individuals. Among other things, the survey observed that 70% of the respondents had "very positive" or "probably positive" attitudes toward the movement of the "indignant citizens" (Panas, 2011).[47] The *second* was conducted during the period 7-10/06/2011 (SKAI Radio Station, 2011), using a sample of 819 respondents in the general population, of which 35% had taken part in demonstrations of indignados in various squares. When asked to assess the "outcome/impact" of the squares' protests, 52% felt that they would "bring results", 36% said that they would not "bring any results" and 12% expressed no opinion. Thus, the public's attitudes were overwhelmingly positive, and a majority of the population thought that they would have an impact on the political system.

GI aims and parliamentary outcomes

The immediate aims of the GI mobilization were: (1) to persuade the MPs to vote against the MTEP (MoU-II) that was being voted on in Parliament on 28-29 June 2011 and (2) to force the George Papandreou government to resign. On the *first aim*, despite the ongoing street battles outside the Parliament between demonstrators and the MAT, the MTEP program was voted on by the majority party (153 votes) and an MP of the ND conservative party who had become independent (Varinou, 2011:3). One of the PASOK MPs voted against the program for reasons of "conscience" and was summarily expelled from the party.[48] The conservative LAOS party and one of the ND MPs, who had voted for

MoU-I, did not vote for MoU-II. Although, the Memorandum block was weakened, the MoU-II became law. On the *second aim*, the Papandreou government survived and the PM did not leave the country on a helicopter as the indignados had erroneously expected. Undoubtedly, and for the moment, the failure to accomplish their two immediate goals constituted a double defeat for the Greek indignados.

Along the same lines, on 20 October 2011, amidst mass protests organized by the trade unions and the indignados outside the Parliament, as well as amidst violent confrontations between members of PAME, the followers of the "I Won't Pay Movement" and the hooded "extra-parliamentary groups" (Marnellos, 2011:19; Morou, 2011:20; Dama, 2011:21)[49], the Papandreou government passed a "multi-faceted legislative bill" pertaining to taxes, retirement, a uniform salary system for the civil servants and collective bargaining. The new reform law was a pre-requisite of MoU-II (MTEP) for disbursement of the next instalment and was voted, as a whole, by 154 MPs of the governing party. During the voting by article, the PASOK government lost one deputy (an historical figure) who voted against the article that restricted collective bargaining. Another PASOK MP—also an historical member of the party who had voted for the law both as whole and all the articles—declared that "this was the last time" she would give her vote to such legislation. The cracks in the governing party can be seen as mini-victories for the indignados.

Resignation of PM George Papandreou–Formation of a "new government"

The indignados were calling for the resignation of the government, the abolition of parties and the adoption of "direct democracy" on all levels of government. Protest groups around the country not only continued to mock systematically the governing party MPs, they also began mocking the country's symbols such as the President of the Republic during public appearances (parades) as well as during the national holidays that commemorated the Greek people's resistance against the Ottoman and German occupations (Vasiliadou, 2011: 39). In addition, the opposition, especially the minority party of SYRIZA, taking advantage of the declining popularity of the Papandreou government in the Gallup polls and the PASOK party defections, questioned the legitimacy of the government and demanded that it resign and proclaim elections. Within this climate, PM Papandreou, during a meeting at Cannes with President Sarkozy and Chancellor Merkel, proposed that a referendum on the euro be held in Greece before the end of the year (2011). This reportedly upset not only his hosts and biggest loaners abroad but also created friction among officials of the governing party who were afraid that the climate in Greece against the MoUs (and the austerity programs) may lead to a result against both the euro *and* the European Union. There were also reactions from the official opposition and the smaller conservative parties, to the effect that the country's credibility was undermined. In short, the PM was forced to take back his proposal for a referendum, and following pressures from his own party apparatus and his parliamentary group, *he agreed to resign after receiving a "vote of confidence"* that would at least give him the mandate to form a new government with the participation of other parties. Although George Papandreou did not leave the country in a helicopter, as the Greek indignados wished, there is no doubt that their movement was a contributing factor in the multi-factor equation of the PM's resignation.

After receiving the vote of confidence (5/11/2011), George Papandreou (PASOK) proceeded to the formation of a coalition government, with the two other conservative parties (ND and LAOS) and with a technocrat Prime Minister (Loucas Papadimos) acceptable to the three parties. The ministries were not distributed proportionately—especially in case of the ND party; most of the ministers (36) were from PASOK, 6 from ND and 4 from LAOS. In this way, the centre-right ND party could avoid equal responsibility and the political costs, in case of failure of the new "coalition" government. The mandate of the new government was restricted to overseeing the "haircutting" of the debt, the signing of a new "loan contract" with the EU, the IMF and the ECB (the notorious troika) and the holding of national elections as soon as possible.

GIs and impact on the public's vote-intentions

As was said in the introduction, the parties held different attitudes toward the GIs, with the Alliance of the Radical Left (SYRIZA) being more favourably disposed toward them. One wonders if the GI "movement" impacted on the public's vote intentions. Relevant data are taken from two survey agencies which, however, cover slightly different periods. In addition, the first survey presents the "unspecified" votes, while the second redistributes them to the parties based on past voting in actual elections. The data of the first survey (Figure 16-10) show an absolute reduction of votes for the governing party (PASOK) and a more significant reduction among those with an unspecified vote preference. Absolute gains are noted for all the opposition parties (ND, KKE, LAOS, SYRIZA and "other" parties) but especially the conservative (centre-right) New Democracy party. Nonetheless, the base survey (7 July), when the mass phase of the GI movement was almost over, may not be the best measurement to test the impact of the movement on vote intentions.

Figure 16-10. Survey of vote intentions of Greek population, July and October 2011

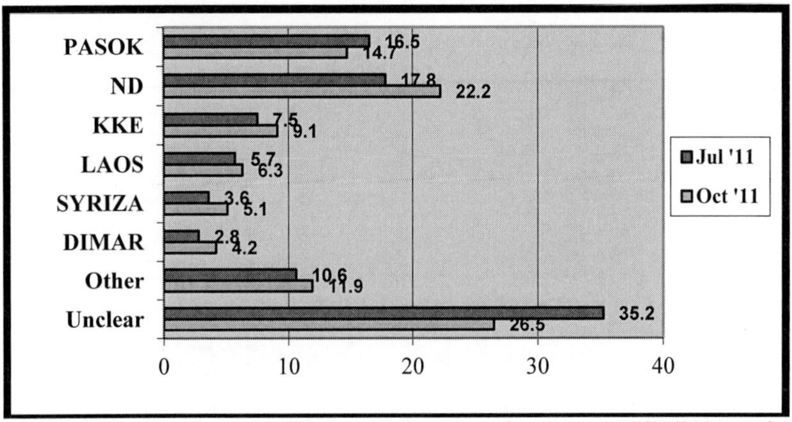

Source; Telephone Interview/Electronic Questionnaire Survey, 7/07/2011 and 27/10/2011, KAPA Research surveys (Karakousis, 2011:17; Chiotis, 2011b:15).
KEY: PASOK=Panhellenic Socialist Movement, ND=New Democracy, KKE=Communist Party of Greece, LAOS=Peoples' Popular Union, SYRIZA= Alliance of the Radical Left, DIMAR=Democratic Left.

The data of the second survey (Figure 16-11) are a more crucial test since almost the entire mass phase of the GI movement intervenes; moreover, the survey measures the public's view of the *influence of the parties* by redistributing the unspecified votes to the parties. These data show absolute reduction of influence in both the governing (PASOK) and the official opposition (ND) parties (7.5% and 2.5%, respectively); stability of influence for the Communist party (KKE), the Ecology Greens and the Democratic Alliance (DISYM); a slight increase (0.5) in the small right-wing party of LAOS; and more substantial increases for the two left-oriented parties—SYRIZA (5.5%) and DIMAR (4.5%). The data suggest that the intensive critique by the GIs of the two-party system may have impacted on public opinion and that most benefits were accrued to the two left-leaning parties, the moderate Democratic Left and the Alliance of the Radical Left (SYRIZA) party. Thus, SYRIZA's policy toward the indignados has paid off, though no doubt other factors may have also impacted on SYRIZA's gains.

Figure 16-11. Survey of the Greek public's opinion about the influence of political parties, June and November 2011

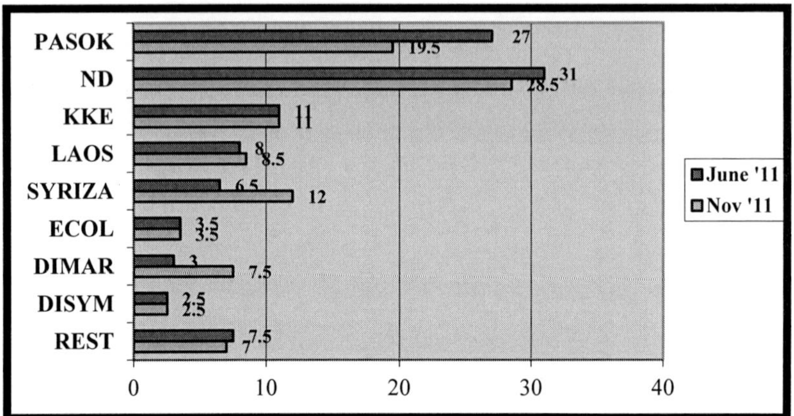

Source: Telephone Interview/Electronic Questionnaire survey, 1-7/06/2011 and 7-10/11/2011 Public Issue surveys (I. Mavris, 2011a:10, 2011b: 8).
Key: PASOK=Panhellenic Socialist Movement, ND=New Democracy, KKE=Communist Party of Greece, LAOS= Peoples' Popular Union, SYRIZA= Alliance of the Radical Left, ECOL=Ecologists, DIMAR = Democratic Left, DISYM=Democratic Alliance.

2012 national election outcomes

Although the mandate of the Papadimos government was to terminate at the end of February 2012 or the latest March 2012, the haircutting process of Greek bonds (PSI) and the new loan contract with troika took longer than expected. National elections were thus set for 6 May 2012.

More than 25 parties took part in the 6 May elections. Except for the two established parliamentary parties (PASOK and ND), the smaller parliamentary parties (the Communist Party, LAOS and SYRIZA) and the far-right non-parliamentary Golden Dawn (*Chrysi Avgi*) party, in the elections also took part the Democratic Left (DIMAR, a more moderate offshoot of SYRIZA), the Independent Hellenes (ANEL, a more conservative offshoot of the ND party), and several other small parties, among which were some with a strong presence in the CS indignados demonstrations (e.g., ANTARSYA, "*Den Plirono*" and *OHI* parties).[50]

In the *first round* of the elections (6/05/12), out of an electorate of 9,949,491, 65.10% voted, 34.9% abstained, and 2.36% of the votes were invalid. The outcomes (Table 16-3) show upsets, as the governing socialist party fell to the third position, the centre-right ND party occupied the first position, the Alliance for the Radical Left (SYRIZA) climbed to the second position, the conservative Independent Hellenes (ANEL) obtained a substantial percentage, the small right-wing party of LAOS failed to enter the Parliament, and the far-right Golden Dawn party entered the Parliament without any problem. Two of the smaller parties that had an active presence in the CS demonstrations, the "I Won't Pay" and ANTARSYA parties, received 0.88% (55,675) and 1.19% (75,428) of the votes, respectively, and won no seats. The data suggest that the votes previously given to the ND and the LAOS parties were redistributed to the "Independent Hellenes" and the "Golden Dawn" party which came into power exploiting the issue of non-documented immigration and crime [which for them were interwoven], while the PASOK votes were redistributed to the Alliance of the Radical Left (SYRIZA) and the Democratic Left (DIMAR). Nonetheless, none of the parties obtained a parliamentary majority, and the attempts of the first three parties to form a government were fruitless, though mathematically a coalition government could have been formed either by the first three parties (201 seats) or by the first (ND), the third (PASOK) and the seventh (DIMAR) parties (168 seats).[51] Genuine ideological divisions, especially with regard to the Memorandums and the austerity programs, as well as the usual political games, militated against the formation of a government; the three parties used the mandate as a propaganda platform for the second round of elections scheduled for 17/06/2012.

Table 16-3. The May and June 2012 Greek national elections (as percentage of valid votes cast)

	ND	SYRIZA	PASOK	ANEL	KKE	GD	DIMAR	REST
6.05.12	18.85	16.78	13.18	10.61	8.48	6.97	6.11	19.02
	108*	52	41	33	26	21	19	0
17.06.12	29.66	26.89	12.28	7.51	4.50	6.92	6.26	5.98
	129*	71	33	20	12	18	17	0

* Seats in Parliament

Key: ND = New Democracy, SYRIZA=Alliance of the Radical Left, PASOK=Panhellenic Socialist Movement, ANEL = Independent Hellenes, KKE=Communist Party of Greece, GD= Golden Dawn, DIMAR = Democratic Left.

In the *second round* (17/06/12), out of an electorate of 9,952,570 voters, 62,47% voted, 37.53% abstained, and 0.99% of the votes were invalid. Fewer independent parties and more coalitions took part in the repeat elections. The results of the repeat elections showed a polarization of votes between the two first parties, the conservative New Democracy party and the Alliance of the Radical Left party. The ND took votes from PASOK, the Independent Hellenes (ANEL) and from the "Rest", while SYRIZA took votes from PASOK, the "Rest" and the Greek Communist Party which from 5th place in the initial elections fell to the 7th place in the repeat elections. DIMAR also took votes from PASOK. The two parties, the "I Won't Pay" and "ANTARSYA", that had a marked presence in the CS demonstrations, lost some of their strength, with the former obtaining 0.39% (23,274) and the second 0.33% (20,391) of the votes; the lost votes of ANTARSYA were most likely gained by SYRIZA, which came close to winning the elections, while the lost votes of the "I Won't Pay" party were more likely redistributed to SYRIZA, ANEL and Golden Dawn.

Divergence of opinion among the constituents (*synistoses*) of SYRIZA during the campaign, the fact that SYRIZA had characterized the insistence on the euro as a "fetishism" and, most importantly, its controversial platform to repeal the MoUs with the troika created insecurity in the voters (especially with regard to the bank deposits) and led them to vote the New Democracy party. This notwithstanding, the skyrocketing of SYRIZA from 4.5% to 26.89% and from the last in parliamentary seats in 2009 to the second in the 2012, was indeed an unprecedented feat, that must be attributed not only to the unprecedented crisis but also to the populist platform and the personal qualities (e.g., communication style, youthfulness, novice in politics) of the party's leader—Alexis Tsipras.

The data suggest that the GI movement had an impact upon the electoral outcome, despite their "apolitical ideology". I have a hunch that they either abstained from voting due to their negative stance toward the party system or that the "lower" CS indignados voted for either SYRIZA, DIMAR or ANTARSYA and the "upper" CS indignados for the Independent Hellenes (ANEL) and the Golden Dawn (GD) parties. Nonetheless, the author's hunch can constitute a working hypothesis; it remains to be documented, using national samples, the method of personal interviews, and a retrospective measuring of the interviewees' participation in the GI movement. An especially interesting research question would be the vote of PASOK voters who had "participated" in the indignados demonstrations.

Electoral behaviour is not the only indicator for assessing the impact of the GI movement. Although, on the level of macro-politics, the GIs founded no political party, consistent with their aversion to political parties, there is no doubt that the GI movement was a catalyst in: (1) the splitting/shrinking of the two establishment parties that had alternated in power for the last 37 years (2) the genesis and/or strengthening of smaller political parties and (3) opening the way for coalition governments—that allow for a broader participation in the national decision-making process and the re-inforcement of a culture of compromise in Greek politics. This is a significant structural change in Greek society whose long-term impact awaits further scientific assessment.

The first anniversary of the Greek indignados and some conclusions

The author went to Constitution Square on the first anniversary to determine if the call by the GIs for a demonstration on the anniversary date (25.05.12, Wednesday, 6 PM) had any impact and to assess further the viability and continuity of the GI movement. He monitored the event for about 6 hours, until midnight. When he arrived there (about 6 to 7pm), there was no crowd formation, either in the upper or the lower part of CS. Traffic in the *upper part of CS* had been stopped and rerouted. Songs by a left-wing protest singer (V. Papaconstantinou), referring to the feats of the 1821 revolutionary heroes, Kolokotronis and Makrigiannis, were blasting out loud, but there were few indignados to hear them. A small group of super-patriots (5-6) in the upper part of the CS had spread out the Greek flag with the words "*molon lave*" on it (reference to the Leonidas's answer—"come and take them"—to Xerxes ultimatum to surrender their weapons at Thermopylae). Besides this group, a group of 40-50 "indignant motorcyclists" had paraded and parked their cycles on Amalias Street in front of the Parliament building.

On the *lower part of CS*, an anarchist lying on the ground was writing anti-fascist graffiti on the ground, the place where the GA was to take place, and where a microphone was set up. Few banners and posters were present, except for those of the Motorcyclists, the Micky Theodorakis Movement *Spitha* (Spark), an environmentalist group and the anarchists. Two or three demonstrators in the lower part of CS were distributing leaflets, on behalf of the "Coordinating Team of the Movements" (SOK). One of these pamphlets was the call for the 1st anniversary rally, endorsed by 18 groups constituting the coordinating team;[52] the other was an "announcement-resolution" of the 18 SOK groups that made a review of the various land-mark demonstrations against the "memorandums of dependence and barbarity" and also pointed to the critical role of the anniversary rally for the upcoming 17 June elections: "*to promote the election of those forces that would take the country out of the impasse and contribute to its renascence*". The fact that these were not accompanied by the stamp of the "General Assembly of the Constitution Square GIs" surprised the author, and he wondered if there had been some kind of transformation into a more institutionalized form of action. Representatives of the 18 groups then took the microphone in the lower part, for an intervention. An intervention was also made by a Spanish delegation from Catalonia. This was followed by a General Assembly of about 100 indignados; microphone was accessible to anyone without the lot system that was used a year ago when about 2000 indignados took part. Nonetheless, very few took the microphone despite repeated calls. The rally ended with songs by radical bands as was the tradition during the 2011 GI mobilization.

The anniversary constituted a replica of the 2011 movement on a small scale. At most, about 250-300 people, both in the "upper" and "lower' part of CS, took part in the anniversary rally. No comparison with last year's mass demonstrations of the GIs. What intervened? First, one cannot exclude the impact of suppression and violence, regardless of the instigator, that accompanied the previous years' protest and deterred broad participation. A second interpretation is that they were disillusioned by the lack of more immediate, concrete and effective outcomes in the GI movement. A third, but related, interpretation is that the initial organizers/activists saw no future in an ideologically heterogeneous movement; the "contradictory dynamics" of the "upper" and "lower" Syntagma subcultures may have impacted adversely on the GI movement (Rocamadur, 2011: 7-8). Along the same lines, the "openness" of the 2011 GI movement led the organizers to provide refuge to marginal groups (e.g., drug addicts, beggars, pickpockets) who availed themselves of the amenities (e.g., free meals) but could not contribute "to the shaping of public space" (Gourgouris, 2011: 4) A fourth interpretation has to do with "infiltration into its ranks of organized social interest groups" (Exadactylos, 2011;1) as the GI movement grew —interests that came into contradiction with its anti-party orientation. Once these interest groups [parties] accomplished their goal of forcing national elections and increasing recruitment (see survey and 6 May election outcomes), they saw no reason for continuing. These interpretations suggest that most of the indignados finally opted to work within the Parliamentary representative system and that the slogan "direct democracy" was in part a populist slogan used to attack the two established parties (PASOK and ND) that had alternated in power during the last 37 years and at the same time had abused the system of parliamentary representation. Nonetheless, as said above, the GIs played a catalytic role in the displacement of the established parties and the formation of coalition governments, which is a step in the direction of "direct democracy". Finally, all of the above interpretations should be taken as working hypotheses, in need of further documentation by political sociologists, both on the level of micro- and macro-politics.

A final note on the indignados' website

The principal website of the Greek indignados (www.real-democracy.gr) was operational on the first anniversary and at the time of the first writing of this article (9/2012). At the time of the final writing, the above site was no longer operational as an autonomous website. An internet search revealed the presence of a blog (http://realdemocracygr.wordpress.com) that was designed on a "a free worldpresss.com template" which occasionally featured ads. The blog was organized by "members of the multimedia team of Constitution Square", though no names were listed. It functioned under the name of "Mind the Cam-Citizens' Media", and one could also find them in the facebook and the twitter social media. Their stated purpose was to host audiovisual material produced by the team during the GI movement and also to update AV materials from recent mobilizations in Greece. Their ultimate hope, aside from becoming autonomous (and "clean" from ads), was to become a "ring in the chain of information... from the people to the people". In other words, to promote "grass roots journalism". Although on 9/12 the blog had active links with an original indignados site on direct democracy (http://amesi-dimokratia .org), a more recent exploration (29/06/2013) gave the answer: "parked for renewal or expired". Nonetheless, it remains to be seen if the goal "real democracy" has replaced the goal of "direct democracy".[53]

In any case, the blog website also had provisions for the coverage of various current mobilizations (e.g., the local community's reactions against the exploitation of gold resources in northern Greece, protests against the privatization of water resources and the closure of the public radio-television stations by the government), peoples' conferences in the Attica region, the rest of Greece and abroad, as well as for expressions of international solidarity for the crisis-ridden Greek peoples.

The website efforts of the "multimedia team" reflect, in general, a continuity with the cultural tradition of the "lower" section of Constitution Square. Whether or not the new website initiative can provide an impetus for the revival of the 2011 GI movement, given the intervening resignation and political cooptation, remains a question. Perhaps, a lot may depend on whether the recent signs of macroeconomic stabilization can be translated into immediate relief measures for the benefit of the victims of the austerity programs. On the other hand, the revival of the GI phenomenon, as an ecological whole (i.e., in both its "upper" and "lower" CS dimensions), may be counter-indicated as a goal. The new website can indeed play a crucial role in the chain of information for the mobilization of citizens for humanitarian causes, as long as it remains faithful to the General Assembly's resolution for non-violent approaches to social and cultural change.

Overall summary and conclusions

The study used both participant observation and secondary quantitative sources to shed light on the composition and the ideological stigma of the Greek indignados (GIs). More specifically, through participant observation he photographed samples of slogans, banners, posters, placards and graffiti, which in turn he analyzed using various levels of content analysis. The quantitative data relied on national public surveys, interview studies of the indignados, surveys of vote intentions and the actual election results, in order to determine the short- and long-term social impacts of the Greek indignados.

The participant observation and the qualitative analysis revealed that the GIs were an ideologically heterogeneous mass. In fact, one could talk about two "political subcultures", ecologically identified, with the "superpatriots" dominating the "upper" part of Constitution Square and the more "progressive" indignados, the "lower" part of CS. The only thing that united them was their stand *against* the troika (IMF, EU, ECB) and the politicians, and especially against the governing party that was managing the bailout program. The quantitative data also revealed an heterogeneous political composition, with proportional participation (according to 2009 election results) from all parties, including a high proportion of disillusioned voters from the governing party. Finally, the data revealed participation by all ages (Gaussian distribution), both sexes, the more educated, the more urbanized, and those worse hit by the economic cuts.

While several theoretical approaches can contribute to our understanding of the phenomenon of the Greek indignados, the author invoked Davies' theory of revolutions and the concept of *relative deprivation* as the most plausible and parsimonious explanatory framework. The substantial improvement in the standard of living of Greek people during the last 40 years following the fall of the junta (1974) and the emergence of a middle class—to which the EU policies contributed—were abruptly interrupted by the bailout austerity measures and a recession which led to the proletarianization of the middle classes and upset both past experiences and future levels of expectation. These conditions, in conjunction with the higher level of education among indignados and a general consciousness of inequitable distribution of the tax burdens, set the conditions for mobilization, though they alone were not sufficient for the viability of an autonomous social movement.

Examining the status of the GIs a year after their mobilization (first anniversary)—and after the intervention of two national elections—the author noted that the GIs had essentially closed their cycle, before becoming a genuine social movement with a leadership structure and a common ideological platform.[54] This was documented by the low turn-out during the first anniversary and on subsequent calls for anti-MoU demonstrations. How can one account for the eclipse of the GI phenomenon? Several interpretations were invoked, including, among others, the initial ideological diversity, the presence of two diametrically opposite political subcultures, an openness that allowed the infiltration by various interest groups, the resignation due to state suppression and a frustration of short-term goals, decentralization of action in the districts and work places, and cooptation by the established political party system facilitated by emergence of new political parties. However, some mass phenomena can also undergo an eclipse due to total or partial success. Although their basic goal, "direct democracy" (or "real democracy"), was not exactly achieved, the author believes that the GIs contributed to the eventual resignation of the PM, the speeding up of the election process, the breakdown of the two established parties (ND and PASOK), the strengthening of small parties on the left (SYRIZA and DIMAR) and the right (the conservative Independent Hellenes and the neo-fascist Golden Dawn). The breakdown of the two established parties, the multiplicity of parties in Parliament after the 2012 elections and the failure to obtain parliamentary majority by any party led to the formation of a coalition government, which essentially broadens representation in the political system and promotes a culture of compromise. Further changes on the political system may accrue with the upcoming constitutional revisions, that could render more feasible the realization of "direct democracy" given the new technologies.

The attribution of the political impacts to the GIs should not be exaggerated; in assessing the impacts, the author has consistently used the word "contributed" and not "caused". Finding the "causes" of any phenomenon is a complex issue. The relative contribution of the GIs to the political system changes should be assessed concomitantly by multi-factorial studies taking into account other relevant sources of political changes, including the pressures by the troika. These studies should be done both on a micro- and macro-sociological level. Micro-sociological studies, that use national samples and personal interviews, could be conducted in order to determine the impact of GI participation on 2012 election behaviour and party realignments. Naturally, these should include voting behaviour in both the 2009 and 2012 elections, level of participation in the intervening GI movement, as well as data on other factors that may impact on 2012 voting behaviour. On the other hand, macro-sociological studies, that focus on the impact of the indignados on political-system changes, can be done using comparative studies and involving nations that were confronted with debt problems and austerity programs. These studies should not restrict themselves to European countries under bailout regimes nor to characteristics of the debt (e.g., size, debtor/creditor factors, debt conditions) as factors in mass protest but also include countries in somewhat comparable situations and other altrnative relevant factors (e.g., general culture, political culture, presence of civil society) in order to increase the size of samples and make a more comprehensive assessment of the impact of protest movements on the political system.

Regardless of the level of analysis, the study of collective behaviour phenomena, as an "independent" variable, requires collective methodologies. The collection of data by one trained participant observer is not sufficient; the samples (e.g., slogans, posters, graffiti) are necessarily accidental and the findings constitute working hypotheses for future studies. A research team and a number of trained interviewers, depending upon the magnitude of the mass event, are a prerequisite. In addition, the research team needs to be furnished with all the modern digital technologies, as well as the latest safety ware in case mass protests get out of hand. Data should include both observations and brief (one page) interviews of participants. Moreover, there should be a division of labour, with other research workers doing the interviews, and others recording the observations (note-keeping, photographing, video-scoping and audio recording). The research workers should be deployed, following contingency scenarios constructed by the research investigators and the research workers, so as to represent the entire geographical area (core, periphery, sectors, natural separations, etc.) occupied by the protesters or all the participating groups in case the demonstration is organized separately along partisan lines. From these more objective and representative studies, one could better document the more micro-sociological studies based on interviews but also develop collective indices of the mass phenomenon that could be used in macro-sociological studies of political systems.

Notes

[1] We shall use the Spanish term, indignados, instead of the Greek word, for comparative reasons and to honour Stéphane Hessel (2010) whose short book was one of the sources of inspiration for Spanish and other comparable international movements (Gialketsi, 2011: 18). In regard to the word "movement", it should be used with quotes; it is used in the text without quotes for the sake of economy. Later on, the author shall discuss whether or not the GI "collective phenomenon" fits the category of a social movement.

[2] Specialists on EU, the Eurozone crisis and direct democracy, were invited to speak, after a proposal by the "thematic group" and approval by the General Assembly.

[3] The men's skirt (*foustanella*) is said to have 400 folds, one for every year of Ottoman occupation. It has become a national symbol that honors the heroes of the 1821 Independence Revolution.

[4] The General Assembly put to a discussion various items proposed either by the "working groups" or the "thematic groups". The Coordinator of the GA was selected by rotation (or by lot), interventions were based on the lot system (indignados picked numbers from a box that circulated)—a procedure reportedly used in ancient Athenian democracy (*eclisia tou dimou*); they could speak for 1 ½ minutes (Gourgouris, 2011: 2). If there was time, a second or third round of speakers was selected by lot. Communication among the members of the coordination committee and between the speakers and the audience were on a first-name basis. At the end, the GA made a decision by hand raising. If there was a clear majority, there was no counting. Among the decisions, there were several resolutions with regard to programs, ideological identity, support of other protests and tactics (including the content of banners, slogans, etc.). It remains an empirical question the extent to which these resolutions were implemented. In any case, one of the criticisms of the General Assembly was that it had become "a factory for resolutions", while others complained that the time allotted for discussion before the voting was not adequate.

[5] Although there was a heated debate about an anti-racist banner because it was associated with a particular group, with leftist or anarchist orientations, the banner remained, testifying to the presence of a more progressive "subculture" in the "lower" part of CS.

[6] All the resolutions and decisions of the CS General Assembly can now be accessed at the http://realdemocracygr.wordpress.com which has temporarily replaced the original website (www.real-democracy.gr)

[7] In a relevant article (Maratzidis, 2011), the author, Prof. of the University of Macedonia, claims that this derives from the Marxist-Leninist stance against "bourgeois democracy" and recognizes how the failure of representative democracies to prevent the economic crisis fed the current anti-parliamentarianism but sees risks for democracy in the demand to abolish the parties and suggests ways for revitalizing the parliamentary system (e.g. more referendums). Along the same lines, Greek sociologist, G. Siakantaris (2011) sees dangers (bonapartist movements) in the notion of "direct democracy" and the abolition of

"intermediaries" (representatives), especially if the wrong "charismatic" leader exploits the situation, and he suggests the dissociation of parties from vested business and trade-unionist interests.

[8] Thus, the podium was open not only to indignados from other countries (e.g. Spain, US) but also to all organizations promoting the Palestinian cause ("Freedom Flotilla"), to speakers who had taken part in the "Arab Spring' demonstrations, as well as to Syrian immigrant/refugee groups protesting the Ashad regime.

[9] "The Anti-Capitalistic Left Cooperation for the Overthrow" of the capitalist system. A militant leftist party established during the last 6 years; it has taken part in several local and national elections, but gets a very low percentage of votes. In the 2010 local elections, it elected a councilor in the Municipality of Athens.

[10] Here, I might refer to the rejection by the General Assembly of a proposal for inviting a professor from the Economic University of Athens, who had done a survey on the Greek indignados, to speak to the GA. The proposal was rejected after someone from the audience said that "he was PASOK". My argument that his findings are positive with regard to the indignado*s* and that his ideology does not affect his research were not convincing to the Assembly.

[11] Survey polls had given 16%-18% to SYRIZA, but after the riots, the rates for SYRIZA fell again to 5% levels.

[12] When the debt crisis broke out (after winter 2010) and the mass reactions to the austerity measures had begun, the VP in a TV panel said that "we all ate it [the money, the taxes, the posts] together". While VP Pangalos had the "clientelistic" state in mind, the leveling of responsibility evoked angry reactions. In addition, the VP was often very blunt in his political interventions, often resorting to the use of foul language (e.g. when he called public employees "lazy-bones" [*koprites*—literally dogs "doing their business"]). These, plus his body type, made the VP a favorite target for caricaturing, satire and revenge.

[13] The *moutza is* an insulting hand gesture which involves the opening of one or both palms and projecting it/them toward the person (s) who made a mess out of things (See Figure 16-6.) Theoretically, it can also be directed toward the self, suggesting the person acknowledges his foolishness and mistakes.

[14] According to a documentary on the Argentine crisis ("New Folders", Sky TV, 2/4/2013) this was a myth. The President often used the helicopter for going to his home. In fact, the next morning the President went to his office to meet a foreign official.

[15] The Le Bon notion of contagion may have been present, though it was not a universal phenomenon since some of the crowd participants did not partake of the obscene sloganeering and gesturing.

[16] Many of the banners were in the front line, facing the Parliament and were not accessible to the camera. Also, in the case of multiple BAPPPs, problems of overlapping, demonstrator congestion, and the wind factor complicated the process of photographing. In some cases, zooming into the photograph increased the legibility of BAPPPs.

[17] Though a Task Group had been set up to approve slogans, banners, etc., the author doubts whether all the slogans, banners and posters etc. were reviewed by this task group.

[18] The Medium Term Economic Program (MTEP), characterized as Memorandum II, was to be voted by Parliament on 28-29 June 2012. The frustration of this vote was the main goal of the GIs.
[19] E.g. paintings/posters showing: (a) the PM leaving the country on a plane on whose wings are written USA/IMF (b) Chancellor Merkel, the IMF officials and the three Greek political party leaders (George Papandreou, Antonis Samaras and George Karatzaferis) with a Hitler moustache and (c) a boy urinating on the MoU —a variation of a 1975 poster (boy urinating in the crown) used in the referendum campaign against the monarchy.
[20] The principal target in this category was the PASOK governing party, though there were also few posters against the two major parties that governed Greece after 1974 (e.g. "Neither PASOK, Nor New Democracy, direct popular rule") but also against parties that supported the 2009-2011 PASOK government (e.g. poster with the photos and names of the 173 MPs from PASOK, LAOS and Democratic Alliance who voted for the first MoU). *Germanotsolias* was a Greek collaborator of the Germans during the Nazi occupation of Greece.
[21] Allusion to the "Greek" government-collaborators during the WWII German occupation.
[22]Goudi was the place in Athens, where 6 Greek government and military officials were executed for treason following the 1922 Asian Minor campaign disaster.
[23] Double entendre. "Plateia" in Greek means square; plateiazo (verb) means broadening a discussion to a point of irrelevance. Here, however, *plateiazoume* is used literally to mean "expand solidarity".
[24] Formal date for the breakout of the revolution of Independence from the Ottomans.
[25] Wanting to avert dictatorships, the Greek Parliament embodied this provision in the new 1975 Constitution. However, one may wonder whether this article can be applied against governments—the outcome of democratic elections.
[26] The poster for the donation of food was accompanied with the following saying: "a hungry bear does not dance".
[27] A reaction to the characterization of SE Europe countries (+Ireland) with debt problems as "PIIGS"
[28] The last two posters are adaptations of texts from Greek literature and philosophy, the first from the inscription on Kazantzakis' tomb ("I hope for nothing. I fear nothing. I am free") and the second, from Heraklitus ("everything is in a state of flux").
[29] One of the journalists on the list, Mr. Tassos Telloglou, of SKY RADIO/TV station, was the victim of an attack. While walking downtown during the 15 June demonstration, he was hit on the head from the back and knocked unconscious (Telloglou, 2011). An eye-witness to the attack said the attacker was shouting the slogan "Hellas, Hellas" which suggests that he came from the "upper" part of CS. Undoubtedly, the general climate (slogans and posters) against the journalists contributed to the attack. During the General Assembly, the author cautioned against polarization and the targeting of individuals, citing the attack on Mr. Telloglou as a consequence. He even said that Mr. Telloglou was one of the "muckraking" journalists. A member of the General Assembly urged the author to

look more into the station owner's past ecological record as a tanker owner. Nonetheless, the author wonders if the station owner's past record justifies the attack on one of the workers of the station?

[30] The current economic dominance of Germany in the E.U. system facilitated the use of WWII terminology and stirred up traumatic memories associated with the German occupation and the Civil War in the 1940s.

[31] The negative attitudes toward all parties conforms with the "non-partisan" orientation of the indignados, voted during the General Assembly. It is possible that these were the work of anarchists, who infiltrated the indignados movement and who, in principle, are against "parliamentary democracy". However, they could also be the work of extremist extra-parliamentary groups, especially on the far-right pole of the political spectrum.

[32] An Orthopaedic Hospital in Athens.

[33] Written on the front walls of the Central Bank of Greece.

[34] Located on a bench next to the Secretariat of the General Assembly of the indignados.

[35] Following the 15/06 confrontations between the MAT security forces and anarchists/extra-parliamentary groups (or between anarchists and right-wing demonstrators), 25 demonstrators were detained, 16 were arrested and 25 men of the security forces were wounded. The security forces used tear gas, clubs and flash grenades to disperse the crowds, while the anarchists used marble chiseled from the square and nearby hotel steps as well as Molotov cocktails (Souliotis, 2011). There was substantial damage to public property, to hotels and banks. The episodes of violence escalated during the two-day General Strike and the voting of the MOU in the Parliament. During the two days, 28-29/06/201, there were 31 arrests of demonstrators, 60 demonstrators were detained, 70 security men were wounded, and over 700 demonstrators/citizens visited the improvised medical centers in CS and the CS subway entrance. Of these, 99 visited the hospitals with respiratory problems, burns and wounds inflicted by the security forces. There were extensive damages (from partial to total) to banks, stores, hotels, post-offices, kiosks, bus stops and sidewalks (Nesfige et al., 2011; Morou, 2011; Argyrakis *et al.,* 2011; Liliopoulo,. 2011).

[36] An interview study of the Greek indignados of CS conducted by Georgiadou *et al.* (Kolia, 2012*),* during the Spring-Summer mobilizations, showed that 61.4% of the sample was either in favour of mocking the MPs or would tolerate it if done by others, while 38.6% were against this kind of protest. On the other hand, the overwhelming majority (76%) were against the use of violence as a means for political action and 24% were either for it or would tolerate it when engaged in by others.

[37] One of these sources (Hasapopoulos, 2011b) reports attacks against 97 MPs, without specifying political affiliation. Nonetheless, most of the attacks targeted the MPs of the governing party.

[38] The interview data were collected during the period May–June 2011 and covered the entire breadth of CS in order to guarantee representation (Kollia, 2012: 38-39).

[39] For a report of the methodology and results of the study, see article by Chiotis (2011a: 26-27).

[40] In replying to criticism that the "Occupy Wall Street" or the "99%" protests were unorganized, leaderless collective behaviour, Sarah Soule said that "no movement in the U.S. (including the Civil Rights Movement) or in other countries had become crystallized in just four weeks" (Soule, 2011: 33) .

[41] Psycharis (2012: 36) makes a rreference to the 69 year-old Canadian Cale Lans, who is said to have inspired the "Occupy Wall Street" movement as a response to the "credit money dictatorship" and in an interview reportedly said that when we have the "social networks", we do not need leaders.

[42] See Dina Daskalopoulou, "Requiem for the Middle Class: The Rise and Fall of a Dream following the Fall of the Dictatorship in 1974", *Epsilon Magazine*, 6/11/2011, pp.33-42. The author of the article bases her analysis on interviews with Greek social scientists. She also makes a reference to Aristotle and the importance of the middle class for democracy and political stability.

[43] Among 182 countries—and where rank 1 equals least corruption—Greece occupied the 80th rank in the perception of corruption, while almost all the EU countries were in the first 25 ranks (Transparency International-Greece, 2011).

[44] See also Cohen (2011:26) and Seferiadis (2011:26) for the rising unemployment among western youth, their relative deprivation in comparison to the parent generation, the greater opportunities for employment in the BRIC countries, the role of the corrupt politicians in a parliamentary system, etc.

[45] The paper, *Eleftherotypia*, had been closed as a result of the economic crisis but resumed circulation in the beginning of 2013.

[46] Like the Spanish indignados who changed their mobilization targets and their slogans from "Occupy the Squares" (*Toma La Plaza*) to "occupy the neighbourhoods" (*Toma los Barrios*)

[47] Incidentally, Prof. Panas was the Professor who was proposed to present his results to the General Assembly but the proposal was voted down when a group unknown to the author vetoed it because he "was PASOK".

[48] This is not the first dropout from the PASOK which after the 2009 elections started out with a clear majority of 160 MPs. Cumulatively, and since the voting of MoU-I (May 2010), George Papandreou, as President of the party, had expelled from the PASOK parliamentary group and the party 6 of his MPs; at the same time, one of these became independent and remained in Parliament, while two others resigned and were replaced by the party candidate next in number of votes in the 2009 elections. Most of the expulsions and resignations took place *before* the emergence of the indignados, mainly as a protest against the passing of MoU-I legislation.

[49] Some trade unions, political parties, and anarchist groups objected to members of PAME (militant Trade Union which leans to the Communist Party) for assuming the role of the Security Forces by occupying the space in front of Parliament and prevented extra-parliamentary groups and demonstrators of the "I Won't Pay Movement" from invading the Parliament building. Many of PAME youths were not wearing helmets and were easy targets for the rock and Molotov throwing by extra-parliamentary groups and hooded youths. Injuries were inevitable. When the author asked a member of the Security Forces why they do not intervene to prevent the bloodshed, he revealed to him that *"PAME told them*

not to intervene" (Marnellos, 2011:19; Morou, 2011:20; Dama, 2011:21). I myself wondered "who governs this country?'. Later on, in the day, PAME withdrew from the Parliament grounds and the Security Forces took over, continuing the confrontations with the extra-parliamentary groups. According to journalistic reports (Routsoni, 2011:22), there were 74 injured persons transferred to the hospital, 79 temporary detentions, 12 arrests and extensive property damage once again.

[50] ANTARSYA ("Anti-capitalist Cooperation of the Left for the Overthrow"). The acronym means "rebellion", a movement that started before the GI movement but had a strong vociferous presence in the GI movement. OHI ("NO") was a coalition of EPAM (United All Peoples' Front). DEN PLIRONO is the "I Won't Pay" movement—a movement that had started before the GI movement and was very active in the indignados movement at CS. The author had a confrontation with the last one in the entrance to the subway. A small group of them had blocked the ticket invalidation machines and were allowing passengers to pass without paying. I insisted on invalidating my ticket. They grabbed me by the arm and urged me to pass through without invalidating. I refused. Then two young men and a middle-aged men threatened me with beating me up and pushed me toward the exit. Not wanting to cause an episode, I withdrew to CS and returned later when they had finished their symbolic protest (ethnomethodology has its limits!). I should mention that before this group descended to the subway to block the machines, they circulated among the thousands of indignados above the CS trying to recruit demonstrators for their impending action. There was no response on the part of the other indignados

[51] The large difference in number of seats between the first and the second party is due to the fact that the Greek election law gives a bonus of 50 seats to the first party in order to facilitate the formation of a government. A long standing demand of the left has been the adoption of a "simple proportional" system, but the two established parties that have alternated in power since 1974 have blocked it. At this point, it might be instructive to note that one of the recurrent demands of some indignados who made interventions at CS was the reduction of the number of deputes from 300 to 200, for reasons of economy in a period of crisis. A number of MPs have adopted this proposal.

[52] The 18 groups were; EN.A. (United and Resolved), EPAM (Unified Popular Front), KAP Spitha (Movement of Independent Citizens-Spark), 300 Hellenes, Peoples' Movement, Laconic Conduct (reference to ancient Sparta), Hellenic Vision, Militant Hellenes, Union of Greeks, Greek Youtubers, the Greek Flame-Piraeus, Alexandros Thalassinos, Pan-Hellenic Citizens' Chariot, Independent Greek Movements, the Coordinating Team Calling for the Demonstration, the Indignant Motorcyclists, the Lawyers' Renewed Intervention and the Indignant Resolved Greeks.

[53] Although the *idea* of "direct democracy" was born in Greece, the community segmentation in Skouries, Chalkidiki, over the Gold-mine investment (environment vs. jobs) raises serious questions as to what should constitute "the constituency" for the application of "direct democracy". The author wonders if a local community alone can decide on issues pertaining to the exploitation of rare

natural resources vital for the national security of "nation states"—especially when a country is in a state of economic recession and when all precautions have been taken for the protection of the local community?

[54] Exception constitutes a "new website", that contains the history and adopts the platform of the "lower' part of CS, though the author has some reservations whether this cyberspace can re-mobilize the GIs, in view of the cooptation and other inhibiting processes.

References

Apergis, G. (2011). 'Yogurt attack against Liana Kanelli', *Eleftheros Typos*, 30 June, p. 17.

Argyrakis, Th. et al., (2011). 'The square bled' [MATose i plateia], *Eleftheros Typos*, 30 June, p. 15.

Bastea, N. (2011a), 'The epidemic of indignation spreads to the USA', *Ta Nea*, 6 October, p. 30.

—. (2011b). 'We are at the point where the future begins' [interview of Saskia Sassen], *Ta Nea*, 31 October, p. 39.

Boubouka, A. (2011). 'The upper and lower Constitution Square', *Eleftherotypia*, 5 June, p. 17.

Charalambous, D. (2011). 'Upper and lower Constitution Square', *To Vima*, 5 June, p. 22

Chiotis, V. (2011a). 'The public square wants a permanent movement", *To Vima*, 19 June, pp. 26-27.

—. (2011b). 'They say 'no' to the 'haircut' and the party leaders', *To Vima*, 30 October, pp. 14-15.

Cohen, R. (2011). 'We entered the age of indignation', *To Vima*, 27 August, p. 26.

Dama, G. (2011). 'Hand to hand combat in front of the Parliament', *Eleftherotypia*, 21 October, p. 21.

Daskalopoulou, D. (2011). 'Requiem for the middle class: The rise and fall of a dream following the fall of the dictatorship in 1974', *Epsilon Magazine*, 11 June, pp.33-42.

Davies, J.C. (1962). 'Toward a theory of revolutions', *American Sociological Review*, vol. 27, no. 1, February pp. 5-19.

European Revolution (2011). 'Reflections on 2011: From indignados to occupywhere, a year of protest in Europe', Available: http://takethesquare.net/2012/01/03/from-indignados-to-occupywhere-reflections-on-year-of-struggle-in-europe/ [13 August 2012].

Fakatselis, A. (2011). 'The indignants of Wall Street', *Eleftherotypia*, 25 September, p. 31.

Georgiadou, V., Kafe, A. & Pierides, C. (2012). 'Anti-party, anti-parliamentary or anti-democratic social movements of the 'outraged' citizens in Greece', 22nd World Congress of the International Political Science Association, Madrid, 8–12 July Madrid, Spain.

Exadaktylos, T., 'Whither the indignados of Athens?'. Available; http://blogs.lse.ac.uk/greeceatlse/2011/07/12/whither-the-indignados-of-athens/ [17 May 2012].

Gialketsi, Th. (2011). 'I am indignant, therefore…I am rebelling', *Eleftherotypia*, 5 June, p.18.

Gourgouris, S. (2011). "Indignant politics in Athens – Democracy out of rage', *The Greek Left Review,* 17 July 2011. Available; http://www.thenewsignificance.com/2011/07/18/by-stathis-gourgouris-indignant-politics-in-athens-%e2%80%93-democracy-out-of-rage/ [13 August 2012].

Hasapopoulos, N. (2011a). 'We can't take anymore the yogurt-throwing', *To Vima*, 12 June, p. 19.

—. (2011b). 'It was a shock for me, the worse form of fascism', *To Vima,* 10 July, p. 12.

Hessel, St. (2010). *Indignez-vous!* [Αγανακτήστε!], Indigène Editions [October].

Karakousis, A. (2011). 'The Greek society at the extremes', *To Vima*, 10 July, pp. 16-17.

Karatziou, D. (2011). 'Where have all the indignados gone', *Eleftherotypia*, 25 September, p. 37.

Kemanetzi, S. et al., (2011). 'Twelve hours that shook the center of Athens', *Ethnos,* 30 June, pp. 20-21.

Kehagia, V. (2011). 'Invasion in the squares; SYN opens a political umbrella for the "indignados"', *Ta Nea*, 11-12 June, p. 22.

Kollia, E. (2012). 'The square was full of indignants', *To Vima*, 22 July, pp. 38-39.

Liliopoulou, M. (2011). 'The subway station at Constitution Square converted to a hospital', *Ethnos,* 30 June, pp. 22-23.

Livitsanos, P, (2011). 'The Greek 'indignados' and global research', *The International Journal of Inclusive Democracy,* vol. 7, nos. 2/3, Summer/Autumn 2011, pp. 1-5.

Maratzidis, N. (2011). 'The anti-Parliamentarianism of the squares', *To Vima,* 26 June, p. 20.

Margomenou, M. (2011). 'Password: Don't draw their attention', *Kathimerini,* 19 June, p. 12.

Marnellos, G. (2011). 'Elsewhere the MAT [Units for the Restoration of Order], elsewhere the blood', *Elefherotypia*, 21 October, p. 19.

Mavris, I. (2011a). 'Change of scene, ND in front', *Kathimerini*, 12 June, p. 10.
—. (2011b). 'The impacts of the government reshuffle', *Kathimerini,* 13 November, p. 8.
Morou, A. (2011a). "Along with a blood tax", *Eleftherotypia*, 30 June, p. 11.
—. (2011b). 'Constitutional Square, a wasteland', *Eleftherotypia*, 21 October, p. 20.
Mouzakis, Y. (2012). 'The prodigal Greek: The chronicle of a struggle', Available: http://theprodigalgreek.wordpress.com/2012/01/18/the-chronicle -of-a-struggle, 18 January [4 February 2014].
Nesfige, L. et al., (2011). 'Scenes of violence and destruction', *Ta Nea,* 29 June, pp. 14-15.
Panas, E. (2011). 'Research on the movement of indignant citizens in Greece', Executive Summary, Athens: Economic University of Athens, Department of Statistics.
Papoulia, F. (2011). 'They 'drove crazy' even the political analysts', *Eleftherotypia*, 29 May, p. 24.
Psychari, E. (2011a). 'We are the 99% of America', *To Vima*, 16 October, p. 32.
—. (2011b), 'Why Do We Need Leaders?', *To Vima*, 13 November, p. 36.
Rocamadur, (2011). 'The 'indignados' movement in Greece', Available: http://www.blaumachen.gr/2011/11/the-%E2%80%98indignados% E2%80%99-movement-in-greece/ [July 2011].
Rova, K. and Kountouris, S. (2011). 'War scenes with wild confrontations in Athens', *Ethnos*, 30 June, p. 19.
Routsoni, D. (2011). 'The last demonstration of Dimitris was a declaration for life', *Eleftherotypia,* 21 October, p. 22).
Seferiadis, S.I. (2011). "They are revolting to win their lives", *To Vima* 27/ August, p. 26.
SKAI Radio Station, (2011). 'The indignant citizens movement', Flash Barometer No. 159, National social survey conducted from 7 to 10 June by Public Issue, Available; http://www.publicissue.gr/1785/plateies/ [25 August 2012].
Siakantaris, G. (2011). 'Society without policy", *Ta Nea*, 19 July, p. 7.
Soule, S. (2011). 'They are neither headless, nor hippies', *To Vima*, 18 October, p. 33.
Souliotis, I. and Giannarou, L. (2011). 'The center of Athens, a battleground', *Kathimerini*, 16 June, p. 5.
Stefanis, P. (2011). 'War over the spontaneous ambush', *Ta Nea*, 4-5 June, p. 21.

'Tasos Teloglou was the target of an attack', *Kathimerini* (16 June 2011), p. 7.

Teloglou, T. (2011). 'The sweater with the number '9'', *Kathimerini*, 19 June, p. 12.

Theodoropoulos, D. (2011). 'We aren't going to the square, we're staying at the square', *Vimagazino*, 12 June, p. 22.

The Universal Solidarity Blogspot (2011). Available: http://universalsolidarity.blogspot.gr/search/label/29-30%2F7%2F2011, 30 July [4 February 2014].

Varinou, E. (2011). '154 plus Elsa inside, teargas and clubs outside', *Eleftherotypia*, 30 June, p. 3.

Vasiliadou, N. (2011). 'They don't respect us, we do not respect them", *Eleftherotypia*, 6 November, p. 39.

Vasilopoulou, K. (2011). 'Occupy Europe', *Eleftherotypia*, 23 October, p. 27.

Xenaki, K. (2012). 'Indignation as a European disease: The Spaniards left the squares and took to the neighbourhoods', *Ta Nea*, 22 July, p. 34.

PART V.

INSTITUTIONAL CAPACITY BUILDING AND FISCAL RESILIENCE FOR DEBT-CRISIS PREVENTION

CHAPTER SEVENTEEN

THE EUROZONE CRISIS: SOCIAL FACTORS AND IMPACTS, EMERGENT SOCIALITY AND COMMUNITY EMPLOYMENT CAPACITY BUILDING

GEORGE ODYSSEAS TSOBANOGLOU
UNIVERSITY OF THE AEGEAN

Abstract

This chapter addresses firstly the issue and impacts of the current socio-economic crisis in Greece and secondly the role of *assembling sociality* and *social economy* as a remedy to this calamity by building institutions for employment capacity. Two institutional areas drew our attention in this research as areas where social participation is crucial. One area represents the not-for-profit social economy which provides an alternative basis for worker and consumer participation in governance to that provided by commercial for-profit enterprises. The other refers to emerging forms of worker-citizen cooperation associated with social movements such as the "basic income" or "living wage" campaigns, community organising to provide mutual-aid groups, and citizens' actions in response to conditions of exclusion and austerity. Assembling sociality issues have become pivotal for the emergence of social economy actions essential for community employment capacity building. They allow for the new informational social economy to develop in the social reproduction spheres such as health, education, tourism, culture and the environment. In Europe, policies such as flexicurity have eroded solidarity relations leading to new situations of social crisis. Considering Greece in this environment, the chapter makes reference to its idiosyncratic labour-market institutions. The lack of public interest policy measures at the local level to protect the citizenry is hindering the emergence of comprehensive social economy measures to combat poverty and unemployment in Greece. Basic anti-poverty measures and a general social security (healthcare) system are not in place as such spending is not considered productive but "inflationary".

Therefore, such a responsibility is being surrendered to church-cum-community-based voluntary activities while taxation for "solidarity" actions is being used in a non-representational manner due partly to a lack of sociological indicators.

Introduction

This chapter addresses the theme of the social impact of the crisis in an EU member-state, Greece, in light of the idiosyncrasies of the country's labour institutions. Social innovations in social policy and practice have the potential to enhance work-related capacities in particular by promoting new forms of economic and political participation beyond both the state and the market. The focus here is on the issue of *assembling sociality* and the *social economy* as local institution employment capacity building and relates it to the current crisis in the EU and Greece in particular. Two institutional areas require our attention as areas where social participation is crucial:

- Social enterprises, including mutuals and cooperatives, which provide an alternative basis for worker and customer participation in socio-economic governance to those offered by commercial enterprises (companies limited by share-capital and other joint-stock companies) or governmental organisations and
- Emerging forms of worker-citizen cooperation associated with social movements such as the "basic income" and anti-poverty campaigns, community organising to provide mutual-aid groups, and citizens' actions in response to conditions of exclusion and austerity.

A deeper understanding of relationships in these fields will certainly improve information available for such policies focusing on the problem of job formation for new quality jobs at a time of economic crisis. To this end, one needs to pay attention to the idiosyncrasies of the very same policy-making process as it relates to the informational base of labour-market institutions and to their capacities to communicate and appropriate knowledge from sociological practice in policies and institutions.

The *employment capacity-building approach* provides a critically useful tool for evaluating innovations in employment and labour-market policies in Europe. As part of the Europe 2020 Strategy (Commission, 2010a; Commission, 2010b; Commission, 2010c; Commission, 2010d), innovation in employment policy is directed to the goals of a better functioning labour market, dynamic job creation and a more highly skilled workforce to match new jobs with new skills. In this context, the concept of "capacity building" provides a framework both for understanding the conditions for effective participation of individuals in the labour market and for assessing employment outcomes according to a social assemblage that empowers the community.

Participation as empowerment at work includes ways to minimise the costs of external control central to work motivation and hence to efficiency in productive activity. In the context of social and employment policy in the industrialised economies and democracies of the EU, emphasis has been placed on the relevance of social justice (Ferreras, 2007), active participation in decision-making (Bonvin, 2008a; Bonvin, 2008b), active citizenship (Hvinden and Johansson, 2007), a lifelong learning and career development perspective (Lambert and Vero, 2012) in addressing the issue of intrinsic work motivation.

Thus, in the framework of the capacity building and empowerment approach, the emphasis on incentives and competences, which is often found within employment policy, is counterbalanced by an equal attention on the empowerment of workers to act in the face of the uncertainties which characterise, seemingly by definition, flexible labour markets (Supiot, 2011).

Labour-market capacities can be understood as the ability of individuals to draw their work-life perspectives and professional development via participatory work which is socially and individually valuable. Capacities, however, in order to be valued and workable, need to be embedded in the relevant institutions. Institutions are an expression of social practice and of basic knowledge that is tacit and codified within a community, regional or national cultural experience. Institutions have historical, topographical and organisationally-based normative dimensions which act as regulatory parameters based on local forms of power dynamics, rules and sanctions.

Institutions are socially and communally constrained reflexive mechanisms that dictate outcomes. Institutional reflexivity can be conceived in a variety of ways, depending on whether the case refers to top-down or bottom-up approaches. The bottom-up approach places particular emphasis on the idea of institutional reflexivity, thereby stressing the role of learning and knowledge embeddedness in providing the substantive content of the capacity-building process.

The issue for a European employment and labour-market policy is above all a problem regarding the generation of a learning process which will permit the formation of those institutional rules and practices which best promote workers' capabilities in a sustainable way. Context and experience seem to define the form and content of work organisation and the institutions embedded in a national territory. National institutions in their interaction with their supranational counterparts need to be receptive to new forms of knowledge and practice as they emerge at different levels.

Social institutions are multi-level structures interacting among themselves and the markets, that is, the labour market, enterprises and the socio-political institutions with their supports as partners at local, national and European level.

Part I. Greek institutional crisis, issues and impacts

Austerity in Greece: "The IMF didn't know but should have known"

According to the Hellenic Statistical Authority, during the third trimester of 2012 the Greek Gross Domestic Product (GDP) fell by an annual rate of 7.2%, while during the first trimester it fell by 6.7% and the second by 6.3 %. Cumulatively, and since the crisis "began" in 2008, the Greek GDP fell by nearly 20% and is estimated to reach 25% by the end of 2013. During the same period, the country's public dept increased from 106.1% to 142.8% its GDP (Figure 17-1). At the end of 2013, the corresponding figure will skyrocket to 195%. The Annual Official Commission report for labour and the social situation released on 8 January 2013 states that during the period 2008-2011 Greek households lost 17% of the real dispensable income which compares with Spain's 8% and Ireland's 5%. Greece also has the highest rate of long-term unemployment (49.6% of the total), as well as youth unemployment (66 % for second quarter of 2013), while it has the highest percentage of households without anyone in employment resulting in a dramatic situation in the labour market according to the EC-EU Employment Commissioner. The Commissioner is supporting the measures that reduce the non-wage cost of labour for Greece (i.e., social security contributions or the lowering of taxation in order to allow for labour employment). In September 2012, the general unemployment was 27% with the highest being women's unemployment at 30.1% (Nikas, 2013). In 2011, single-parent families in poverty were 43.2% of the total, up from 33.4% in 2010, according to the Hellenic Statistics Authority (Nikas, 2013).

Figure 17-1: Greek debt in comparison to the Eurozone average

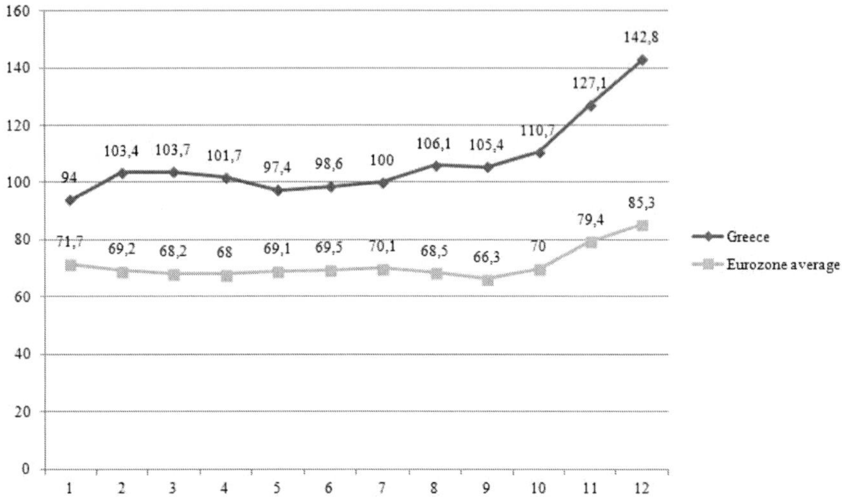

Source: Eurostat 1999-2010.

The casualties, which the IMF is now calling accidental, include the reduction of the Greek public sector salaries by 25-50%, with similar cuts in the private sector, while the minimum wage has been reduced by up to 50% and pensions cut by 25-50%. Moreover, to meet its obligations to the troika the government imposed a new property tax for all taxpayers including those under the poverty line (3.4 million in 2011). The State Electricity Company is using private contractors to cut-off the electricity supply to those not able to pay the imposed new property tax—attached along with the municipal taxes and the tax for Public TV to the electricity bill. Approximately 30,000 households a month are experiencing this rather unusual for a European Country measure. A 48% increase in the price of heating oil (apparently to control the black market due to the price difference between heating oil and motor oil) has made heating oil more expensive than high-performance diesel leading to an 80% drop in purchases of heating oil. Burning wood, in order to heat their homes, has caused a 400% increase in air pollution in large cities such as Athens and Thessaloniki multiplying health dangers and regressing to situations reminiscent of the thirties in big European cities.

While suicides have increased dramatically, by at least 50%, the real disruption has been on the health care system in its entirety, where public funding has been slashed by over 30%. The government has not reimbursed pharmacies for prescriptions, leading to strikes by the pharmacists and forcing patients to pay in cash, which virtually denies pensioners, the unemployed and most employed persons the heart, cancer and other expensive drugs they need. In many cases, international pharmaceutical companies have stopped selling to Greece. And despite a hiring freeze over the least three years, the Second Memorandum demands another 10% reduction in the number of doctors.

The International Monetary Fund has issued a report acknowledging the severity of the policies that the "troika" (EU, ECB and IMF) has imposed on Greece, Portugal, Ireland, Spain, Italy, and saying that "we had no idea what it would lead to". The Greek population is dying or migrating. The death rate, for Greece, increased from 10.4 per thousand in 2008 to 10.8 per thousand in 2012, while the birth rate decreased by 15%, from 118,302 in 2008 to 100,980 in 2012 (Smith, 2013). The next census is expected to show reduction of life expectancy. The Irish population is emigrating en masse. Spaniards and Portuguese are likewise leaving, scavenging in trash bins, their death rates have jumped up and their birth rates fallen while public self-immolations, like those in Greece, have also started in Spain. Underlying the gravity of the situation, a top official in Portugal's Ministry of Health, issued a call on the 28 December, 2012 for Portuguese citizens not to fall ill, because it would contribute to the bankruptcy of the National Health Care System!

The IMF's chief economist Olivier Blanchard, along with Fund economist Daniel Leigh, have issued a report saying that the Fund formulated, demanded, and imposed this harsh austerity on Greece in error, without understanding what its results would be. *The Washington Post*, in its 4 January 2013 issue called it "a *mea culpa* submerged in a deep pool of calculus and regression analysis".

In working out the first bailout package in 2010, the IMF economists thought Greece could "cut deeply into government spending and pretty quickly bounce back to economic growth and rising employment". Instead, 30 months later, the economy is contracting at an 8% annual rate while public debt has ballooned to 195% of GDP (2013).

It is commonly declared by economists and politicians, both in Greece and abroad, that the Greek citizens do not pay taxes. However, in Greece, revenue as a percentage of the GDP is higher than in the USA, Japan and Spain. What is the issue in the Greek case is the balance between taxes imposed on wage labour, on capital and consumption. In Greece, there is a difference between the nominal tax, the effective tax paid by natural (citizens) and legal persons (business) and the collected tax received by the Revenue Department. This is the reason why in the past three years, during the most devastating economic crisis since the World War II triple Occupation and its sequel—the Civil War, taxation legislation has changed over 10 times. It still needs a stable taxation system that would be able to organise all the parts involved and be able to define rights and responsibilities.

One issue of interest to us here regards the rate of tax wedge on labour in Greece. Tax wedge pertains to the difference between the total wage cost in a business and the net payment to the employee. The net payment as result of the above is inflated due to the higher general taxation which leads to undeclared work and unemployment.

In 2008, Greece had the highest tax wedge on labour in the Eurozone, well above Sweden, France and Belgium. The high taxation of employed labour leads to a higher unemployment level. In the Eurozone, the tax wedge between the total wage cost and the net wage cost is high and is associated with service delivery in a welfare system. In the Greek case, the high tax wedge on wage labour is not related to service delivery. This detail is the problem. Different outcomes are due to the appropriated tax revenue which is diverted elsewhere, not necessarily due to a corrupt bureaucracy which is a popular assertion, but due to its disappearance from the common good, leaving, as usually, state bureaucracy empty handed with little to distribute in the manner of benefits. This non-return of taxation as a general redistribution for general benefits like, for instance, social security for all (health for all and unemployment security associated with training), leads to a legitimatization crisis. Thus, taxation is not sustainable as it is not connected with the social reproduction of labour. Such a system is also leading us to witness in practice the incapacity of the formal economy system in Greece to measure real inflation and the chasm between the nominal and the effective economies. This diversion of labour taxation to other routes and destinations is anti-social and rather a "private" mechanism bearing the properties of the patronage system as it, quite paradoxically, does not allow, for the market institutions to emerge. National taxes as political rents have been diverted to national defence expenditure without much accountability as those and other funds are being siphoned off and under the table to discrete places for hoarding (not productive accumulation) or into interest-bearing bank accounts and real estate both domestically and abroad. The high labour tax that does not go into the development of social protection, i.e., unemployment insurance, day care services for children, a health system for families and training facilities for labour, is an obvious cause for the dramatic labour situation in Greece.

As a common result of the above, the built-environment infrastructure is parcelised mirroring the extremely divided political power fiefs or domains that constitute the political power system. These political controls are in a perpetual conflict for resources in an informal world of private work. Such resources are usually of the tax/rent type rather than founded upon a continuous work process based on labour security and local productive systems. The human agency dimension both in production and consumption at the local level is the key focus here. Although community sustainability requires building permanent physical social health, education, culture and caring services for its livelihood, the source of such resources is mystified and is exteriorised. The Greek communities are poor as they have a sizeable underground economy while lacking community mechanisms to enhance capacity building, to form capital goods and clusters. The high direct and indirect taxation on labour and consumption becomes exacerbated by the lack of social protection and the lack of controls over essential resources be it those of labour, in the manner of services controlled by them, or those of the physical environment such as transport services, including ports, buses and local commuter trains as well as production and distribution services such as energy and water provision. Even parks and local taxes are being managed by others than the municipal authorities themselves.

As national taxation is not associated with representation (for social welfare redistribution) but goes to returns for pensions, the imposed austerity measures, due to the high borrowing of the private banks in Greece and the associated high interest rates, have led to a serious humanitarian crisis.

The IMF's chief, Christine Lagarde, demands new "adjustment packages" and new, brutally regressive taxes at every stage, while infamously chiding the Greeks for not paying their taxes. The so-called memoranda created mass but high-skilled (especially professional) emigration from Greece and destroyed labour rights under the euphemism of productivity and competitiveness but in reality to pay un-payable debts. They have caused the deaths of unknown thousands and threaten the lives of millions in a country of 11 million people.

In the Tables 17-1 and 17-2, we can see the changes in unemployment rates in Greece as the crisis takes its hold, according to age, gender and level of education. Between the 3rd and the 4th year, after Greece had signed the bailout agreement and the austerity program had started, the gross unemployment rate climbed by 5%. Figure 17-2 shows the categories of the unemployed and their status for the 1st trimester of 2011. One can see the very small percentage of those in training; a detail which is probably the Achilles' heel or the devil in the detail of the Greek failure to address the employment situation.

Table 17-1. Unemployment by age group and gender for the 1st trimester of 2012 and 2013

Age	1st Semester					
	2012			2013		
	Male	Female	Total	Male	Female	Total
Total	**19.7**	**26.5**	**22.6**	**24.7**	**31.0**	**27.4**
15-24	46.1	60.4	52.7	54.9	66.3	60.0
25-29	33.3	38.7	35.7	39.2	43.7	41.2
30-44	18.1	25.4	21.3	22.9	30.1	26.1
45-64	13.9	17.0	15.1	18.4	21.5	19.7
65+	2.4	4.8	3.2	8.6	5.1	7.5

Source: Hellenic Statistical Authority, Research on Labour Power 2012, 2013, 1st Trimester

Table 17-2. Unemployment according to gender and educational level for the 1st trimester of 2012 and 2013

Educational level	1st Semester					
	2012			2013		
	Male	Female	Total	Male	Female	Total
Total	**19.7**	**26.5**	**22.6**	**24.7**	**31.0**	**27.4**
Postgraduate	11.7	12.4	12.0	13.3	18.0	15.3
Undergraduate	11.9	19.3	15.7	14.6	20.4	17.6
Technical education	20.9	29.3	25.0	23.7	36.4	29.9
Higher secondary education	20.9	30.5	24.7	26.1	35.4	29.8
Secondary education	21.4	32.7	25.2	31.1	37.5	33.4
Elementary education	22.4	23.1	22.7	28.6	26.9	27.9
Partial elementary education	35.1	29.2	33.1	37.8	20.1	32.2
No education	35.4	32.5	34.3	39.0	47.6	42.9

Source: Hellenic Statistical Authority, Research on Labour Power 2012, 2013, 1st Semester

Figure 17-2: Analysis of recorded unemployment 1st Trimester 2011

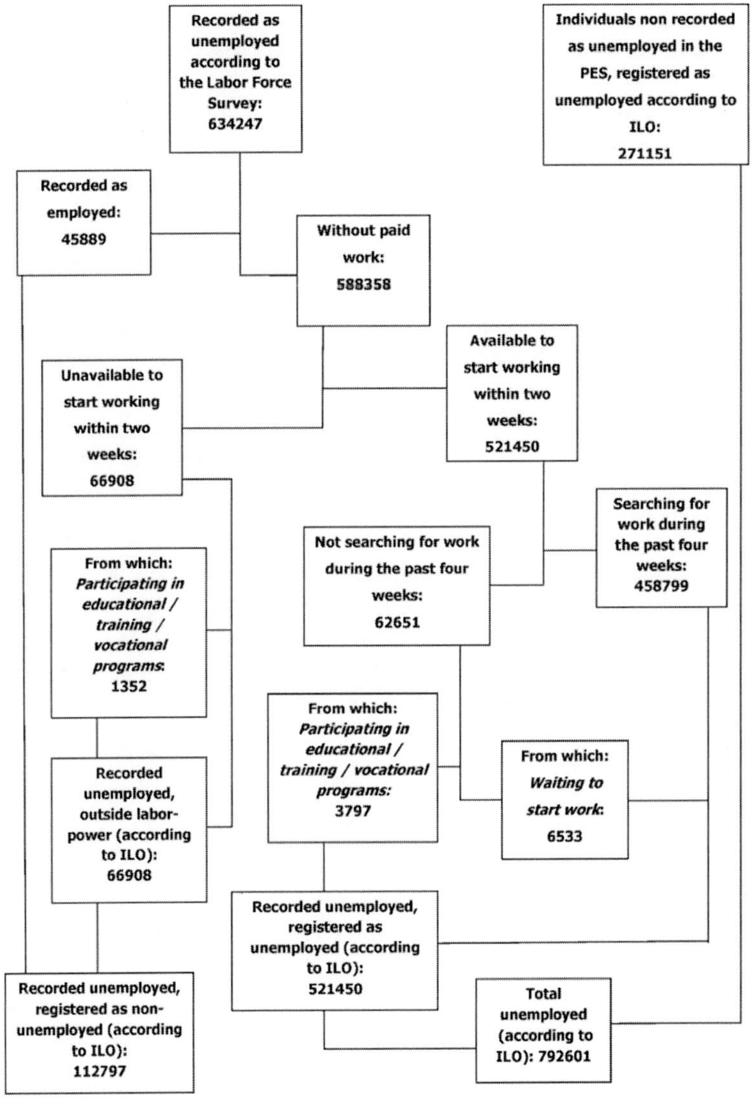

Source: Hellenic Statistical Authority, Research on Labour Power, 2011.

Part II. Social economy and assembling sociality

The idea of assembling sociality as an organising principle of labour-market institutions

Alongside "capacity building", the concept of "assembling sociality" is a central directive in this analysis. The idea of "sociality" implies a form of interdependence between individuals which arises from the common exposure to risk and the shared participation in organisations and agencies in order to cope with that risk (Supiot, 2011). This may facilitate the emergence of institutions which balance or reconcile the demands of flexibility and security (flexicurity) in the work process. There are several ideas implicit in the concept of assembling sociality. At its most elemental form, sociality implies social capacity in an integrated fashion.

Sociological concepts, such as "assembling sociality", stem from notions of a shared obligation on the part of individual actors in a productive or reproductive labour process activity (e.g., consumption) to contribute to a redress of the impacts of a common risk, such as illness, unemployment or old age, which are confronting all members of the community at some point in time. Similarly, in the context of social insurance systems where Occupational Health and Safety and Unemployment Insurance become institutionalised in order to handle risk at work, including transport to work (e.g., in Germany among others in the EU), there is a need for a commitment on the part of employers and wage earners to be regulated by the assembling sociality steered by the *general and public interest*. This way, social partners exposed to labour-market risks are to make contributions (defined within the social wage contributions) to sickness, unemployment and retirement funds. The inclusion and enforcement of these provisions, by such institutions of the labour market as unemployment insurance and a general wage relationship, has been the result of social struggles. Their constitution is based on a system of social relations between labour and capital that were an integral part of the New (State) Deal formulated by President Roosevelt in the 1930s (Tsobanoglou, 2012c).

The concept of sociality bonding and group responsibility

The principle of equality in the labour process generates the principle of redistribution to homogenise the value chain in action in order to have a valuable labour process. Those at risk need to be included in the system of labour security in order to obtain equal strength in the value chain that the employment security system maintains. The strength of the labour (chain) relation is equal to the strength of its weakest link. So redistribution of resources (knowledge, information, material supports as benefits, care and health services) constitute an organizational requirement essential for the survival of the national socio-economic process of labour. Everybody must be contributing "*for all and for ever*" in the working community of the region. Emergency periods—such as those that the Eurozone countries are currently experiencing—indicate the urgency of the matter and the necessity for a unified response to the crisis as realised by socially responsible regimes organised in a tripartite (state, labour and business) organisational form.

The Charter of Fundamental Rights of the European Union represents such an umbrella institution promoting the *Federation of Europe*. In this highly contemporary manifestation, social rights take the form of claims to resources or as rights to take part in forms of procedural or institutionalized interactions such as those arising out of collective bargaining (Browne et al., 2004). The idea of sociality in action provides an institutional underpinning for the idea of capacities, understood as substantive labour-market ways and means (Sen, 1999; Salais and Villeneuve, 2004; Rogowski et al., 2012).

However, one of the consequences of labour-market flexibilisation over the past three decades—intensified during the current debt crisis—has been the fracturing of the traditional institutions of sociality and solidarity. Where once it would have been plausible to present the "social risks" of unemployment, sickness, old age and… "childhood" (in the Greek case) as affecting, potentially, all wage earners and their dependents, and hence the vast majority of both economically active and inactive members of society (Baldwin, 1990), nowadays this view of social risks has become more difficult to maintain as a result of the more varied work experiences of different social categories and their different levels of exposure to risk environments (e.g. note the unemployment rates in Greece and Spain nearing 30% while in the other South European states such as Italy staying at 12%) (Esping-Andersen, 1999).

The deregulation or flexibilisation of labour has hard to define in a uniform manner across the EU labour systems as they differ substantially and at times, as in Greece, organisationally in their national institutions. The Greek environment was characterised by high informality and extreme fragmentation in the labour security domain while it acquired (and still has) the characteristics of an ironclad politically-administered system of labour apartheid between the public and the private employment sectors (Tsobanoglou, 2012). The flexibility issue in Greece increased the informality of labour and the size of labour imports (often clandestine labour abetted by the Dublin II Agreement and the border status of the country, among other things) while very little has been achieved in the organisation of the "national" labour "market" by the Public Employment Authority which is responsible only for the "private labour market". As a result of this national idiosyncrasy, the Greek employment scene is radically divided in a way that defines privilege and separate social development. The political worlds of favouritism and clientelism define the Organisation for the Employment of the Labour Force (OAED)—the Greek version of the Public Employment Service—since the organisation is incapable of providing nationally the two basic poles for the supply and demand of labour, or in constructing the most important infrastructure for a labour market, namely, the National Catalogue of Professions. Of course, this last basic administrative infrastructure can only be realised if the labour and employment situation become operationally unified and based on skills and professions for all the citizens. As it is now, OAED is responsible only for qualifications in the so-called private labour market without any jurisdiction over public enterprises (DEKO) such as the Railways or Local Government Authorities. This divided, along legal lines, national system (public and private) lacks also a general and unified foundation for a qualification system within its employment structure that is nationally monitored as in other EU states, i.e., the National System of Vocational Qualifications in the UK for instance.

The current upside down situation in Greek employment reflects a general drive towards the integration of the numerous pension funds, but it still lacks focus as long as the general labour conditions are registered and identified on the basis of qualifications and across the country. The drive for mainstreaming of the life course that has been introduced as a remedy for a system of inefficiency has led to declining shares of the population participating in formal employment while it allowed many others to migrate to neighbouring countries with competitive taxation environments.

Flexibilisation also led to the displacement of general risk to private risk for categories of workers excluded due to reproduction costs and to the special needs difficult to mainstream as services (Kalleberg, 2009). The continuous drive for the mainstreaming of services is a dramatic consequence of the drive to minimise service costs; however, many forms of general solidarity undergo a minimisation in the scope of sociality institutions as segmentation at work, firm-level collective bargaining and individual agreements between the firm and the worker replace collective bargaining between employers and trade union representatives on the national level. National social security schemes are broken up in favour of industry or firm-level agreements, with further devolution to the level of individual insurance devices such as individualised savings plans or pension schemes (Deakin and Wilkinson, 2005: chs. 3, 4).

Sociality as solidarity has also being put on reserve by the response to the sovereign debt crisis at the EU and member state level. The dismantling of collective bargaining (sector level) and its replacement by firm-level bargaining, while dramatically lowering the value of social security benefits, have been among the measures required by the memoranda of understanding agreed between the EU, the IMF and the Eurozone states (Greece, Ireland and Portugal) with Spain and possibly Italy or states in the Eurozone Plus group (such as Latvia) also being at risk of entering into such an agreement.

At the EU level, the steps taken to enhance macroeconomic and budgetary surveillance (the "six pack" of regulations adopted in the spring of 2011, the Euro Plus Pact of March 2011, and the fiscal compact agreed in December 2011) envisage the monitoring of member states' labour-market policies, undertaken through an "open coordination" type methodology, with a view to preventing imbalances caused by (among other things) divergences in unit labour costs within the Eurozone and Eurozone Plus group (Barnard, 2012).

The evolution of "open coordination" methods of governance, both in the context of the Employment Strategy which began in the late 1990s and more generally in the area of social policy and other policy areas to which they were later extended, has to be reviewed as the issue of general government and its interaction with national and territorial needs to be understood also in terms of the big divide between the North and the South in Europe.

The promise of the Open Method of Coordination (OMC) against Poverty, as the Lisbon Process (2000) has been alternatively recognised, was that it would allow member states to retain autonomy over key policy decisions in the economic and social sphere, while also generating a learning process that would allow the Union as a whole to benefit from the diversity of experience which existed at the national level. This learning process was expected to bring about convergence in the achievement of shared policy goals.

Although there is evidence of learning having taken place across the member states in a number of social policy areas, particularly on work-life balance issues, the labour-market and employment policies of the member states were not realigned according to a common model such as, for instance, of "flexicurity" (Commission, 2007). And while flexicurity continues to be a crucial element of the Employment Guidelines and of the

European Employment Strategy as a whole, and while integrated flexicurity policies were identified as having a key role in the achievement of the 75% employment rate target set by the Europe 2020 Strategy (Commission 2010a; Commission, 2010b; Commission, 2010c), it is easy to understand how the dramatically divergent labour security systems—as the one dominant in Greece with its different political make-up (weak transparency in transactions and general exchanges, the dramatic informational asymmetries, and political divisions in the labour market that lock the private and "public" domains in a hierarchical manner)—constitute obstacles to social realignment. The lack of organic socio-economic links between these sectors, regulated by the two-party nomenclatures in dominance since 1974, resulted in extreme flexibilisation of employment in the private sector and the displacement of formal labour by informal and foreign labour under substandard conditions. A manifestation of this is the hermetic seal between the two key sectors of domestic labour—the precarious private and largely informal labour domain with weak health and social security benefits based on the employers' controls of labour security (Tsobanoglou, 2012a; 2012b) and the secure public wage relations determined usually by political, non-professional considerations. In short, the skill basis of the work system is inadequate as general qualifications are not defined let alone assessed and controlled. Flexicurity has a meaning in Northern Europe where the social homogenisation of labour is advanced and the challenge of globalisation requires cost cutting and mainstreaming of services out of the general welfare system. This new knowledge development (flexicurity) articulated the state's ability to develop new forms of social control based on new forms of work organisation. Poverty became a field of study and labour organisation and its conditions for social reproduction started to build up as new relations between state and civil society began to take shape. The scientific concept of society and indeed of labour became strategic points of study and development as the state organisation started to develop an administration for care for citizens and not only for the parties' members chosen by the patrons. General laws emerged and social rights for employment became the new state way to control and regulate society (Tsobanoglou, 2012c). Former political controls excluded from employment those not politically correct defining thus "unemployment" as a category of exclusion without any wage form. Semantically, unemployment nowadays in Greece reflects the lack of social benefits and supports. Only one in ten receives unemployment benefits in the country. As they lack training or benefits, food aid stamps, shelter provision, health benefits from the official system, they are seeking supports from the Church (meals), shelter from next of kin, and sporadic underground jobs since formally there is no organisation for such provision aside from local government initiatives such as social groceries and pharmacies. Institutionally, Greece lacks an anti-poverty agency, volunteer work is not organised in a standard form and the third sector (e.g, non-profit work) is not recognised and organised on the basis of the principles of social economy. Over 3.4 million Greeks in 2011 fell under the poverty line according to the Greek Statistics, with income less than 5,951 euro (Nikas, 2013). Hellenic Statistics counted 1,109,658 unemployed in 2011 of which OAED had as registered unemployed only 782.000. As of June 2012, those who are entitled to unemployment benefits are only 188,000. For those who receive the benefit it lasts for a year; and if it can be extended for another year, it will cost 1.6 billion euro. The others remained unprotected. The labour market has been “freed” from any regulation. Since its complete “liberalisation”, compensations were severely cut so dismissals were easier for employers (from 2% the limit went to 5%); the basic wage was reduced as well, once the daily wage and private company-level agreements with the employees were enforced. As a result, the labour market in Greece has been literally dismantled, so the lowering of the cost of work (via wage and benefits, pensions) has been due to the lowering of the wage alone. In Spain, according to the European Commission, the lowering of the wage cost has been due to productivity gains (Nikas, 2013). This lowering of the wage cost did not lead to an increase in employment or the lowering of consumer prices in the Greek case.

Questions therefore remain over the effectiveness of Open Coordination Methods in realising flexicurity issues for the crisis-ridden Southern European States like Greece. Shortcomings in OMC processes have been attributed to defects in the relevant procedures and instruments, including the definition and design of indicators (Zeitlin, 2005). The selection of a given set of indicators may frame the normative background of the political decision-making process at the national government level (Salais, 2006a; Salais, 2006b). The efforts of member states to meet targets for employment outcomes have been mediated through performance indicators some of which are crudely expressed and open to manipulation.

The current crisis, therefore, is as much a crisis of the forms of European governance, including the Open Method of Coordination, as it is a crisis of economic and financial management for the Union and the member states. The question to be addressed in the context of employment and labour-market policy is whether new forms of association can emerge from the circumstances of the crisis.

New forms of sociality representing innovative responses to the fragmentation of collective action have been promoted by the institutions of the social economy and the development of *general interest* services at the local level. The erosion of old forms of community brought with it significant changes which demand the emergence of new forms of participation at local level and utilizing new forms of enterprises such as the social enterprises (Noya, 2009a; Noya, 2009b).

However, such enterprises, if they are clustered in a region, can themselves determine the social welfare distribution to cover labour security. The distribution of socio-economic opportunities and social benefits depends on the national definitions and the politics of democratic service delivery in place. Local sustainability depends on the stability of the basic services provided on a non-market basis but skilled-based and evaluated by standards of social governance. In some member states, including some in the Eurozone (Greece), basic social services are privately delivered as personal services (for those who can afford them) while philanthropy and the Church cover the rest. Local government receives less than 5% of the tax revenue of natural persons while local municipal taxes are being collected by the Public Electricity Corporation S.A.

In this way, local government does not have the financial tax basis to develop employment at the local level while the capacity for work for all social categories, and not just for the most marginalised or excluded ones who are the ones most immediately affected, is undermined. The de-fragmentation process of social community survival (risk-pooling) structures, the essential objective of the OMC for the European South, was halted and suspended by the monetarist tsunami that has been going on in the country during the last four consecutive years. Basic understanding of the specifics of the Greek labour situation, where there is lack of national social security and a minimal basic income policy, defines a situation that is remote even from its Mediterranean counterparts. While the public sector has been secure in terms of employment and pensions, the low salaries for the middle and lower administration levels, as well as the high hidden costs of parallel state-health and education systems, made a second job a necessity for the majority of civil service employees. Parallel jobs outside the formal work system constitute an important cause for the delay in the transition from school to work. The public labour security system in Greece ended up, till this crisis, being considered as a "general" social security system covering social labour costs and maintaining a stable salaried employment security for a privileged political stratum alone while denying such basic social security rights for the rest of the private and largely unprotected sector. This sector has been characterized by under-employment and substandard work, inclusive of large immigrant populations. The dominant practices in this sector have led people to bargaining for the attainment of basic services such as child, health, and elderly care. The Greek entry into the EU witnessed the growth of Public Enterprises of Common Good (DEKO) which represented the basic business for the provision of General Interest Facilities (non-profit welfare communal services) and constituted an organisational innovation for the public economy of Greece. However, many of such enterprises collapsed financially as local community private investments (supports) were not allowed to emerge in an over centralised state system—leading successive governments to start the process of privatising in order to address the debt crisis.

Reconstructing institutions of solidarity, including at workplace level at a time when they are under threat poses an acute version of the "collective action" problem (Poteete et al., 2010): how to bring about the conditions under which participation in cooperative self-help measures becomes possible.

The appearance of new forms of social enterprises (social exchange economies that are based upon communal and cooperative work, proximity services for youth, children, elders) is a sign that responses to the fragmentation of existing mechanisms of collective action are occurring (Laville, 2011). Social enterprises challenge the identification of the economy with the self-regulating market and of the firm with the shareholder-owned or investor-oriented business enterprise. Social enterprise is based on a pluralistic view of the economy, founded on reciprocity between the contribution of inputs by different stakeholders and on their participation in firm-level governance (Cook et al., 2002).

In the political sphere, social enterprises challenge the subordination of public policy to a market-testing or market-correcting logic, while also stressing the role of civil society and deliberative democracy as counterweights to a hierarchical conception of public discourse revolving around the institutions of representative democracy.

By promoting a multiplicity of voices, these forms of enterprise can contribute to an enlargement of the informational bases of a "just economy" (Sen, 1993). In particular, they have the capacity to contribute to the integration of vulnerable and disadvantaged workers into the labour market and to their empowerment as economic and social actors (Noya, 2008a).

In addition, new forms of solidarity are emerging at grassroots level through the self-organising activities of workers, consumers, and citizens more generally. Examples include basic income and anti-poverty campaigns, the activities of self-organising community groups, the movement without middlemen, eco-social community groups based upon alternative economic organisation and citizen action in response to the imposition of austerity measures.

These emerging forms of social response to the crisis involve alliances of new cooperation types such as those between producers and customers and between workers and employers in many cases defined by local traditions and anxiety over protection of the home territory. These alliances define local market interests enhanced through the communication revolution by land (rail transport), by air travel and e-communication. Tourism and the emergence of local pools of knowledge allowed many new issues to be solved locally and new markets to be captured both in tourism and international trade. Cooperative adjustment and participation allowed the recomposition of work solidarity to take place particularly where national or local government was keen in seeing the advantages of cooperation for the local economy. Thus, a recomposition of private enterprise led to its organisation as employee-owned cooperative enterprise as were traditionally the agricultural cooperatives everywhere in Europe. What has been the characteristic of such schemes was the need to aggregate private resources as cooperatives in order to provide for the community its basic resources and a productive basis.

The emergent forms operate not on the basis of mandated participation supported by legal or even contractual relations, but through various kinds of voluntary action which in reality rests on basic self-interest and local social capital initially represented by faith-based communal leaders. Thus, they represent an expression of local agencies as they interact together in a deliberative process of engagement and dialogue between themselves and eventually the outside world.

These initiatives might run up against legal constraints on autonomous collective action of the kind needed to sustain such norms by the central state authority for instance. The key issue here pertains to whether public policy can adjust to allow new forms of sociality to emerge and develop. Once these productive labour forms emerge and sustain themselves, as they develop associated institutions in the work value chain, i.e., production and product design, distribution of products, local financial credit, logistics and transport facilities and educational institutions, social integration gets a new dynamic. Once workers own the enterprise and develop their own managers, a division of labour develops associated with a mixed-ownership system that is able to develop the region as well as both inward (local) and outward markets. These local production systems and regional autonomy develop local taxation and associated social insurance as well as collective bargaining mechanisms across the various private producers. The Trento Cooperative Society and the Mondragon Cooperatives represent such examples in Europe (Tsobanoglou, 2007).

As these new forms of sociality and cooperation emerge at a decentralised level, as the result of the initiatives of particular actors, the issue for policy is to see how knowledge is embedded in the value-chain process both at member-state and the EU level. Thus, the importance of the reflexivity of institutional legal and regulatory institutions at different levels in this social cooperation is a critical question for research and for policy in the context of the current crisis.

Information based on forms of political governance

At the level of the state, the capacity of governmental bureaucracies organised along hierarchical and top-down lines to deliver effective employment policy results has been called into question particularly in its weakness to understand territoriality and sociality. This has been manifested in the growing experimentation around the idea of local public-private partnerships and in strategic alliances between state and market agencies. The fragmentation of the state and the accountability of the myriad of hybrid public-private forms is a real point to be considered. These developments pose the question of what kind of public governance structures are best equipped to engender knowledge around the issue of labour-market regulation and to give expression to the idea of capacity formation as part of the basic work security rights of individuals in the employment context. The answer to this question is especially crucial at a time when Greece and other countries in the Eurozone are confronted with a humanitarian crisis.

The levels of regulation which involve the tripartite system of civil administration, enterprises and labour are inter-connected organisationally and form the basis for capacity building. In line with a capacity-building approach, the critical question for policy is how to analyse the channels of communication (social, economic, political or mixed) between them, so that local level information can be routed through the institutions of the market and the enterprise to those of the state.

Political institutions must be sustainable if they are to operate effectively and regulate the labour-market processes and outcomes in such ways as to promote substantive labour-market reproductive relations. An institutional focus that is compatible with the capacity-building approach is one that focuses on forms of public action located within established decision-making processes in territories locally and socially integrated in networks of businesses and labour (Storper and Salais, 1997; Clark et al., 2010).

Information based on labour-market forms

At the level of the labour market, information takes place via processes of knowledge generation and transfer which are inherent in the act of exchange. However, exchange relations depend for their operation on a prior established normative environment, which is expressed in tacit norms and conventions and in more formal rule-based structures such as those provided by the legal system. In this regard, the formation and expansion of socio-legal mediation is a strategic indicator of mature development of this process. The conventions which shape the practice of employment are constantly evolving in response to new manifestations of work organisation due to policy changes resulting from information modalities affecting globalisation and local economies. Long-standing institutional mechanisms, such as those of multi-employer collective bargaining, are responding to the need to promote active participation on the part of workers. New forms of labour contracting, such as those associated with the practice of "*groupements d'employeurs*", are giving new expression to the organisation of work involving security and flexibility (Zimmermann, 2011a; Zimmermann, 2011b). The *basic income institution and campaigns for a living wage* reflect an attempt to redefine the concept of the wage as a basis for the equitable allocation of risk between workers and employers, who are also consumers and taxpayers (Citizens UK, 2011). Consumption at community level becomes a strategic institution whose conceptual understanding gives us a clue as to the basis for the sustainability of productive work. Production cannot be thought without consumption. Here, the role of government and local institutions is of strategic importance as there is a need for the regulation of this relationship embedded in a new sociality assembly (social economy).

Enterprise-based forms of information

At the level of the enterprise, the internal structure and boundaries of it are continuously mutating as a consequence of the need to realign corporate governance with the demands of a knowledge-based economy (Commission 2010a; Commission, 2010b; Commission, 2010c; Commission, 2011). Alternatives to shareholder control, on the one hand, and government ownership, on the other, are emerging, or in some cases, being revived

(Defourny, 2001; Laville, 2011a; EMS Network, 2012; Social Europe, 2012). These initiatives reflect the priority given to direct worker and customer participation in firm-level governance (Noya, 2009a; Defourny and Nyssens, 2010).

In this context, mutuals and cooperatives are being presented as forms of an increasingly social enterprise which allow for the building of internal, firm-level capabilities, based around complementarities between the human, physical and virtual assets of businesses (Cook et al., 2002). The nature also of shareholder influence, is changing in response to concerns over the responsiveness of institutional investment processes to the inter-generational issues of affecting communities such as those of pensioners and savers. This is the context in which a serious debate is developing in most countries about the increasingly important role of the socially-responsible investment initiatives (Dembinski et al., 2003).

Advancing knowledge of Greek employment issues beyond the state of the art

The capacity-building approach, based on an institutionalist understanding of the economy and society, and the consideration of an integrated and interdisciplinary approach, which will meet the methodological requirements of general social science, economics, political science and sociology, allows us to go beyond considerations of current employment policy concepts (e.g. labour activation policies, flexicurity, part-time unemployment and social investment) as remedies to the crisis (Morel et al., 2011).

From a historical perspective, the public benefit-based social economy formed the backbone of the Greek public sphere albeit under the form of foundations (Zappeion, Averoff-Tositsa, Niarchos, Onnasis, Panagia Soumela etc) and today represents an invaluable resource for social development and community cohesion (Tsobanoglou, 2007). But it was not recognized sufficiently by the administration and the political system until today (Law, 2011). Broader scientific issues and known weaknesses of public administration in the country, even now, hold the precious resources of social economy in a scandalous disuse. The dominant change in the bankrupt pattern will come from the articulation of the inherent societal dynamism of social science professionals who need to be empowered in order to organize this largely informal economic community action in Greece.

Legal overregulation, the fragmented and divided labour market, the lack of registered socio-economic forms, and the related weakness of the tax-assessment system seem to give the clue as to why informal socio-economic activity becomes so pervasive leading to the appearance of profit and non-profit operations, while non-profit operations are forced to be taxed as if they were profit organisations (SOS Doctors, Cooperative Hotels of Naousa, etc.)

There is a peculiar tax-control immunity for the social economy in Greece as a result of the friction of the public and the private sectors, with state agencies often supporting the private and not the public interest. The tragic fate of the vast majority of rural cooperatives and food processing factories and agencies, such as the Agricultural Export Agency (AGREX), the Central Storage Facilities for Coops (KYDEP) and three Food Processing Coops (SYNEL, SEBATH, SEPEK), which were financially monitored by the former Agricultural Bank, are cases in point. The administration of this general agro-industrial system did not manage to use productively the over 100 billion euro transferred under the agricultural development fund program of the EU in a manner that would establish their firm basis into the national and/or local food chains. The cooperative value chain did not establish itself in the urban markets and the exports despite the high volume of agricultural produce. The lack of skills in the rural sector and the inability to organise the commercialisation of these products was also hindered by the numerous "clientelist" employment appointments provided for the cooperatives. This overstaffing was positively linked with the economic subsidies provided through dominant political channels. The mass influx of migrants created also a competitive pressure for cooperatives having to compete with private businesses while the emergent division of labour did not allow the mainstreaming of production and the development of the productive value chain with the inclusion of marketing. Most of these enterprises failed because the subsidies did not allow for the business organisation to emerge due the state's control and the role played by the EU subsidisation of agricultural markets. For decades, thousands of tons of agricultural produce, such as oranges and peaches, were weighed and buried while supervised by agronomists in order to maintain prices. At the same time, the weak application of agricultural chemistry in the product development process did not allow at the time for the transformation of these products into by-products to service all seasons and the dynamic tourist industry. Agricultural cooperatives, without state clientelist intervention, with the necessary training in organization and marketing skills, and a facilitating state/EU agricultural policy, could transform the economic landscape of the country in many ways.

Conclusion: Greece in the EU and the issue of assembling sociality as local institution capacity building

It is important to relate the issue of assembling sociality as local institution employment capacity building to the current crisis in the EU and Greece in particular. Social enterprises, including mutuals and cooperatives, which provide an alternative basis for worker and customer participation in economic governance to that offered by commercial enterprises (companies limited by share-capital and other joint-stock companies) or by governmental organisations, are key responses to conditions of austerity and poverty. Emerging forms of worker-citizen solidarity, associated with social movements such as "basic income" campaigns, community organising to provide mutual-aid groups and consumer protection actions, also constitute key responses.

The idea of support to those in need is based on the basic capacity to recognise and constitute evidence of ability to contribute. Constituting such evidence is a basic task of government as citizenship systems are based on information regarding employment income activity that is regionally based. The task of government, as expressed in the capacity to form the social foundations of its organisation, is indissolubly linked with the mutuality inherent in the democratic conception of national citizenship and expressed through the duality of skilled employment and taxation with representation. Citizen's taxation should be directed towards their community delivery service supports (Germany, Canada, Scandinavia, Belgium, Netherlands etc). This represents the basic requirement for social trust that builds social capital essential for the provision of general services. These services define basic social reproductive institutions at local level (health, knowledge diffusion, care, mobility, environmental and cultural sites) which are quality-assured on the basis of usage and controls that also generate general revenues. The improved social environment in a locality can stimulate interest in a region as it chooses to enhance its educational and cultural facilities, environmental services for local, regional, national or international citizens. Taxation systems are generally formulated on such regionally-based employment knowledge. Of course, employment and its qualifications are both integrated characteristics that form an objective basis for employment accounting systems. These are essential requirements for the reproduction of the system as it directly informs long-standing mechanisms of risk-failure–management under a social welfare state. Collective bargaining and social insurance schemes are essential elements of these institutions. Health insurance for all (Occupational Health and Safety and general health for children, pensioners and the unemployed) and general provisions for the unemployed, such as welfare and training, are essential labour supports that keep the labour market functioning. Current manifestations of this system stress the continuity of supports as practical knowledge outcomes under life-long learning provisions.

A deeper understanding of these areas is to inform policies aimed at promoting job creation and fostering high-quality employment at a time of economic crisis. The nature of the policy-making process, in particular as it relates to social knowledge, the informational base of labour-market capacities, and the embedding of lessons from practice in policies and institutions need to be examined individually in each case.

The *community employment capacity-building approach* provides a critically useful tool for evaluating innovations in employment and labour-market policies in Europe. Social capacity at the community level allows for market-based knowledge in articulation with enterprise-based information to be mediated by the public to form sociality assemblies for a social economy. This leads to the realization that assembling sociality issues are to become pivotal for the emergence of social economy actions, essential for community employment capacity building. They allow for the new information basis for social economy to develop in the new extended reproduction spheres of health, education, tourism, culture and the environment. One key vehicle for this is the social enterprise (Borzaga and Defourny, 2001; Noya, 2009a).

In Europe, policies such as flexicurity during the past years have eroded assembling-sociality relations subsequently leading to an intensification of the social crisis. Greece has been one such crisis-ridden weak link in the Eurozone system partly due to its differing structure obtained in the labour-market institutions. These differences, when the crisis hit the country, created, under the troika panoply, a dramatic situation leading to a near Depression. The lack of public interest policy measures at the local level to protect the citizenry is also hindering the emergence of comprehensive social economy measures to combat poverty and unemployment. Social needs expenditure is considered by official economists as "inflationary" resulting in the near surrendering of much civic welfare responsibility to church-cum-community-based voluntary agencies to help while the state uses "solidarity" taxation in a non-representational manner leading to the rise of political "protest" forms. While there have been sporadic communal initiatives in the direction of social economy, that which would really address the current problems is a coherent, inclusive and participatory government/EU policy for youth, women, the unemployed, the immigrants, the handicapped and all citizens who are in an especially vulnerable situation.

References

Baldwin, P. (1990). *The politics of social solidarity: Class bases of the European welfare state 1875-1975,* Cambridge: CUP.

Barnard, C. (2012). 'The financial crisis and the Euro Plus Pact: A labour lawyer's perspective', *Industrial Law Journal*, 41, pp. 98-114.

Barnard, C. and Deakin, S. (2012). 'Social policy and labour market regulation' in S. Weatherill et al. (eds.) *Oxford Handbook of European Union Law,* Oxford: OUP.

Bonvin, J. M. (2008a). 'Capacités et démocratie', *Raisons pratiques*, n° 19, Paris: EHESS, 237-61.

Bonvin, J. M. (2008b). 'Activation policies, new modes of governance and the issue of responsibility', *Social Policy and Society*, May, pp. 367-77.

Borzaga, C. & Defourny, J. (eds.) (2001). *The emergence of social enterprise,* London: Routledge.

Browne, J., Deakin, S. and Wilkinson, F. (2005). 'Capabilities, social rights and European market integration', in R. Salais and R. Villeneuve (eds.) *Towards a European politics of capabilities?,* Cambridge: CUP.

Citizens UK (2011). *Living wage campaign*, Available: http://www.citizensuk.org/campaigns/living-wagecampaign/ [25 March 2013]

Clark, G., Huxley, J. & Mountford, D., (2010), *Organizing local economic development: The role of developing agencies and companies,* Paris: OECD.

Commission (2007). *Towards common principles of flexicurity: More and better jobs through flexibility and security.* Communication from the Commission to the European Parliament, the Council, the European and Economic and Social Committee and the Committee of the Regions, COM(2007) 359 final, 27 June 2007, Brussels.

Commission (2010a). *Europe 2020: A strategy for smart, sustainable and inclusive growth,* COM (2010) 2020 final.

—. (2010b). *Europe 2020 Flagship initiative innovative union*, COM (2010) 546 final.

—. (2010c). *An agenda for new skills and jobs: A European contribution towards full employment*, COM (2010) 682 final.

—. (2010d). *The European platform against poverty and social Exclusion: A European framework for social and territorial cohesion*, COM (2010) 758 final.

Cook, J., Deakin, S. and Hughes, A. (2002). 'Mutuality and corporate governance: the evolution of UK building societies following deregulation', *Journal of Corporate Law Studies,* vol. 2, pp. 110-138.

Deakin, S. and Wilkinson, F. (2005). *The law of the labour market: Industrialization, employment, and legal evolution,* Oxford: OUP.

Defourny, J. (2001). 'From third sector to social enterprise', in C. Borzaga and J. Defourny (eds.) *The emergence of social enterprise,* London: Routledge, pp. 1-28

Defourny, J. and Nyssens, M. (2010). 'Conceptions of social enterprise and social entrepreneurship in Europe and the United States: convergences and divergences, *Journal of Social Entrepreneurship*, vol., 1, no. 1, pp. 32-53.

Dembinski, P., Bonvin, J.M. et al. (2003). 'Ethical foundations of socially responsible investment', *Journal of Business Ethics*, vol. 48, no. 2, pp 203-13.

Esping-Andersen, G. (1999). *Social foundations of post-industrial economies,* Oxford: OUP.

Eurostat Annual Statistics 1999, 2000, 2001, 2002, 2003, 2004, 2005, 2006, 2007, 2008, 2009, 2010, Luxemburg.

Ferreras, I. (2007). *Critique politique du travail. Travailler à l'heure de la société des services,* Paris: Presses de Sciences Po.

Heidenreich, M. and Zeitlin, J. (2009). *Changing European employment and welfare regimes: The influence of the open method of coordination on national reforms,* London: Routledge.

Hellenic Statistical Authority, Research on Labour Power (2010, 2011), 3rd Trimester.

Hvinden, B. and Johansson, H. (2007). *Citizenship in Nordic welfare states,* London: Routledge.

Kalleberg, A. (2009). 'Precarious work, insecure workers: employment relations in transition', *American Sociological Review*, 74, pp. 1-22.

Lambert, M. and Vero, J. (2013). 'The capability to aspire for continuing training in France: The role of the environment shaped by corporate training policy,. *International Journal of Manpower,* vol. 34, no. 4, pp. 305-325

Laville, J. L. (2011a). *Agir à gauche: L'économie sociale et solidaire,* Paris: DDB.

—. (2011b). 'What is the third sector? From the non-profit sector to the social and solidarity economy. Theoretical debate and European reality', *EMES Working Papers*: 11 (01).

Mangan, J. (2000). *Workers without traditional employment: An international study of non-standard work,* Cheltenham: Elgar.

Morel, N., Palier, B., and Palme, J. (2011). *Towards a social investment welfare state? Ideas, policies and Challenges,* Bristol: Policy Press.

Nikas, S. (2013). 'Under poverty condition over 3.4 m citizens in 2011', *Kathimerini,* 9 January, p. 17.

Noya, A. (ed.) (2009a). *The changing nature of the social enterprises,* Paris: OECD.

Noya, A., Clarence, E. and Graig, G., (eds.) (2009b), *Community capacity building: Creating a better future Together,* Paris: OECD.

Poteete, A., Janssen, M. and Ostrom, E. (2010). *Working together: Collective action. the commons, and multiple methods in practice,* Princeton, N.J.: Princeton University Press.

Rogowski, R. Salais R., and Whiteside N. (eds) (2011). *Transforming European employment policy: Labour market transitions and the promotion of capability,* Cheltenham: Elgar.

Salais, R. (2006a). 'Reforming the European Social Model and the politics of indicators: from the unemployment rate to the employment rate in the European Employment Strategy', in M. Jepsen and A. Serrano (eds.) *Unwrapping the European social model,* Bristol: Policy Press, pp. 1-38.

Salais, R. and Villeneuve, R. (eds.) (2004). *Towards a European politics of capabilities?,* Cambridge: CUP.

Salais, R. (2006b). 'On the correct (and incorrect) use of indicators in public action', *Comparative Labour Law & Policy Journal,* vol. 27, pp. 237-256.

Sen, A. (1976). 'Rational fools: a critique of the behavioural foundations of economic theory', *Philosophyand Public Affairs*, vol. 6, pp. 317-344.

—. (1999). *Development as freedom*, New York: Alfred Knopf.

—. (1993). 'Positional objectivity', *Philosophy and Public Affairs*, vol. 22, pp. 83–135.

—. (2009). *The idea of justice,* Cambridge, MA: Harvard UP.

Smith, H. (2013). 'Greece's birth rate falls as austerity measures hit health care', *The Guardian,* Available: http://www.theguardian.com/world/2013/sep/18/greece-birthrate-austerity-measures-healthcare [18 September 2013].

Storper, M. and Salais, R., (1997). *Worlds of production: The action frameworks of the economy,* Cambridge: Harvard University Press.

Supiot, A. (2011). *L'esprit de philadelphie. La justice sociale face au marché total,* Paris: Seuil.

Tsobanoglou, G. O. (ed.) (2007). *Social development and communal cohesion: Sociological approaches,* Athens: Papazisi.

Tsobanoglou, G. O. (ed.) (2012a). 'Barriers to Social Economy Empowerment in Greece', *Onati Socio-Legal Series*, 2, ISSN: 2079-5971.

Tsobanoglou, G. O. (ed.) (2012b). *The politics of participation and empowerment: Current issues and practices*. Hidelsheim: Verlag fur Gesellschaftsarchitektur.

Tsobanoglou, G. O. (2012c). 'Controls at Work, Democracy and Communication: A view from Greece', in Tsobanoglou, G. O. (ed.) *The politics of participation and empowerment: Current issues and practices*, Hidelsheim: Verlag fur Gesellschaftsarchitektur.

Vero, J., Bonvin, J.M., Lambert, M. and Moachon, E. (2012). 'Decoding the European dynamic job security indicator through the lens of the capability approach. A comparison of the United Kingdom and Sweden', *Transfer*, 2012/1, pp. 55-67.

Vero, J. (2011). 'Responsabilité des entreprises et capacité des salariés à se former', in *Education Permanente*, Special issue on *Responsabilité Sociale des Entreprises et Formation*, vol. 188, no.3, pp. 79-88.

Zeitlin, J. (2005). 'Social Europe and experimental governance: Towards a new constitutional compromise?', in de Búrca G. (ed.) *EU Law and the Welfare State,* Oxford: OUP.

Zimmermann, B. (2011a). *Ce que travailler veut dire. Une sociologie des capacités et des parcours Professionne,* Paris: Economica.

—. (2011b). ''Making employees' pathways more secure: A critical examination of the company's responsibility', in R. Rogowski, R. Salais and N. Whiteside (eds.) *Transforming European Employment Policy: Labour Market Transitions and the Promotion of Capability.* Cheltenham: Elgar, pp.117-137.

CHAPTER EIGHTEEN

FACETS OF GREEK SOCIAL CITIZENSHIP IN TIMES OF CRISIS: NORDIC AND SOUTHERN WELFARE INSTITUTIONS IN COMPARATIVE PERSPECTIVE

CHRISTOS KANELLOPOULOS
UNIVERSITY OF ATHENS
AND SOTIRIA LIAKAKI
INDEPENDENT RESEARCHER

Abstract

This contribution attempts the elaboration of a conceptual approach for citizenship by focusing especially on its "full" version, which is further explored by referring to the Scandinavian citizenship model. Drawing on various theoretical tools, our conception of citizenship highlights its *relational* character, emphasizing the *internal* and *external* factors affecting its institution and corresponding policies. Institutional constraints and opportunities, the crucial importance of *trust* and the "leveling" effect of the Eurozone's financial crisis constitute useful elements for an in-depth analysis of social citizenship's transformations and the institutional and "social traps" that take shape. The *social* element in citizenship is put under examination in the case of the current Greek crisis. Will this crisis and the imposed austerity measures succeed in initiating the much debated "change" in the Greek political economy? As we will demonstrate, with reference to the Scandinavian example and citizenship model, the outcome of the "Memorandum" policies does not offer a fertile ground for reinforcing the equal distribution of social resources and preventing the creation or reproduction of "social traps" and policy gaps. Political channeling through clientelistic corporatism has not only blocked "encompassing" reforms in the past, but it has also opened the way for a legitimization rhetoric of austerity as "moral reprimanding", accentuating the weak policy outcomes in a context of economic recession and political turmoil.

Citizenship: a malleable concept for rigorous use

In the ongoing research on democracy and citizenship, we come across the "return of the citizen" (Kymlicka and Norman, 1994), the importance of rights and their expansion in order to overcome the "citizenship gap" produced by the process of globalization (Brysk, 2002; Brysk and Shafir, 2004a; 2004b and 2004c) and the necessity to look at new dimensions or modes of citizenship, that will allow citizens to influence the policy making on a local, regional, national, and international (for example European) level (Faist, 2000; Shafir, 2004; Brysk and Shafir, 2004b; Brysk and Shafir, 2004c: 209-210; Seidman, 2004; Kivisto and Faist, 2007: 139-140).

In the relevant literature, citizenship is described as manifesting shortcomings and "gaps"[1] that define its concept. Such an approach helps us to understand citizenship not only as a "process" (Thériault, 1999: 6, 8, 9, 12, 13), but also as an "instituted" one (Somers, 1993: 587, 589, 611). Margaret R. Somers, building on Karl Polanyi, explains how the "instituted process" conceptualization views citizenship as:

> "[…] a set of institutionally embedded social practices [...] contingent upon and constituted by networks of relationships and political idioms that stress membership and universal rights and duties in a national community […] citizenship rights are only *one* (italics in the original) potential outcome of a configuration of national membership rules […] normatized and transmitted via national laws and institutions […] Whether or not these rules are converted into actual universal rights depends fully on the local contexts—the social and political place—in which they are activated." (Somers, 1993: 589).

However, the limitations of citizenship are further reinforced by modern processes. According to Alison Brysk and Gershon Shafir, the rights usually offered with citizenship undergo a "deflation" because of the pressures due to the effects of globalization[2] (Brysk and Shafir, 2004b: 6-7). Pressures that can have a remarkable impact especially on the content of rights guaranteed by citizenship (Shafir, 2004; Lipschutz, 2004; Sassen, 2004; Brysk and Shafir, 2004b; Brysk and Shafir, 2004c: 209-210; Seidman, 2004; Kivisto and Faist, 2007: 139-140).

More precisely, ongoing changes cannot anymore be controlled by citizens whose representation of interests seemingly depends on the image and economic strength of the state to which they belong (Brysk and Shafir, 2004b: 6-7). We witness, for example, how "economic nationalism" (Tilly, 2007), a strong and distinct feature in the German case, collides with the need for Eurozone mechanisms and flexible tools with solidarity integrated in their structure.

Nevertheless, taking into account how "globalization creates a citizenship gap, but also furthers the import and spread of the rights that potentially may close the gap" (Brysk and Shafir, 2004b: 6), this process contributes to the transformation of the "political opportunity structure"[3] and the emergence of new challenges for thinking about participation and rights. In short, quoting Brysk and Shafir (2004b: 7), "[…] globalization also creates new opportunities and multiple venues in which to claim rights in other states and global institutions".

Thus, we argue that the "antinomies of citizenship" (Balibar, 2010a: 11) may be conceived and understood, through the aforementioned developments, in terms of citizenship's *relational*[4] modus operandi.

More precisely, the *complex interrelation* of institutions, actions and societal norms[5], induces friction and generates stress points that underline not only the importance of a "citizenship constellation"[6] approach, but also the necessity to look for all *versions and types* of citizenship models, seeking the traces of their "historicity"[7].

There, "the tensions at the core of citizenship" (Purvis and Hunt, 1999: 457) reemerge as an "instituted process"[8] conferring to citizenship its *malleable* character. It is exactly this trait that makes citizenship swing like a pendulum: from the perspective of, following John Hoffman, a "momentum concept […] that has a potential for freedom and equality, but whose progress is infinite, and therefore can never be realized" (Hoffman, 2004: 187), to where a strict form of—, borrowing Balibar's term—"anti-citoyenneté" (Balibar, 1997: 374) is established.

In our analysis, we equally draw on Peter Kivisto and Thomas Faist (2007), who, when discussing citizenship's formation and progress, discern four "discourses", which are "inclusion", "erosion", "withdrawal" and "expansion" (Kivisto and Faist, 2007: 6) with the first three having to do "[…] with developments that have occurred within the modern nation-state" (Kivisto and Faist, 2007: 130), i.e., "internal factors shaping citizenship regimes" (Kivisto and Faist, 2007: 131).

Welfare institutions are closely related to the second thematic category, the "erosion" of social rights (Kivisto and Faist, 2007: 8-10, 49-74, 134-136), one of "[…] the three discourses concerned with internal factors contributing to the form and content of citizenship […]" (Kivisto and

Faist, 2007: 131). Nevertheless, social rights are no longer a *purely national* matter.

> "The erosion of rights—particularly social rights—that has been the hallmark of neoliberalism must be seen in terms of deindustrialization and the global restructuring of capitalism. Labor unions are discovering this fact [...] unions have come to recognize that their futures are tied to the unionization of workers in the nations of the South and to the promotion of decent wages and living standards for workers in those developing economies." (Kivisto and Faist, 2007: 139-140).

Peter Kivisto and Thomas Faist insist on the interplay between forces inside and outside[9] the nation-state: particular and historically-specific political and social parameters, defined as "[...] the internal dynamics of particular nations [...]" (Kivisto and Faist, 2007: 139), interact with globalization's influence on the content of rights (Kivisto and Faist, 2007: 138-140)[10], introducing "[...] a new era wherein the nation-state will no longer be the sole arbiter in defining the meaning of citizenship" (Kivisto and Faist, 2007: 140).

In this light, from now on, inspired by Kivisto and Faist's analysis and drawing on their terminology, we will use the terms *internal* and *external* (*vis-à-vis* the nation-state) when we describe the factors affecting citizenship's institution. In the pages that follow, we will focus on the *social* dimension of citizenship, which not only maintains a causal relationship with the existing form of welfare regime, but is equally influenced, as described above, by *internal* and *external* factors *vis-à-vis* the nation-state: governmental decisions, specific economic, political and social conjunctures, pressures from global financial forces, a state's position in the international relations, its exchange rates and state of finances, etc.

In line with the aforementioned analysis, our argument holds that if the design of a citizenship model promotes the "ideal of 'full citizenship'" (Goul Andersen and Hoff, 2001: 251)[11], it may prove to be a decisive factor for securing rights even when a severe global economic and financial crisis occurs. According to Goul Andersen and Hoff (2001: 263, note 3):

> "In welfare state theory, welfare state regimes and specific policies are often evaluated from a citizenship perspective: In particular on the basis of the social *rights* (italics in the original) they provide (treating receivers as equal and autonomous citizens), and on the basis of their ability to provide for 'full participation' in all spheres of social life in accordance with the ways and standards of life in that society."

This last point will be the guiding line for our analysis. Our aim is to delineate how the case of Greece, where the welfare state is under extreme pressure from harsh austerity measures and a severely depressed economy, sheds light on the dangers of a "shredded" citizenship and the subsequent long-term consequences of a possible corrosion of the social fabric. Particular *internal* and *external* factors affecting the Greek welfare state, with the role of clientelist political channeling and Eurozone's architecture as the most crucial among them, may derail any attempt for a more *just* distribution of social resources, neutralizing all efforts to mitigate the crisis' repercussions on the most vulnerable.

From institutions to trust and back again: equality as part of a "citizenship deal"

Employing an approach inspired by "historical institutionalism"[12], we turn our attention to the concept of "path dependence"[13]. A path dependence, however, that, as it has been suggested, may not only be "institutional" but also "ideational"[14]. Our argument implies that choices and decisions pertaining to citizenship models create such a *dual* path dependence, upon which social policies, that may serve as a "litmus test"[15] for the quality of welfare provision, are enacted.

In this context, citizenship's multiple *path-related* ideational, institutional and societal *constants*, persisting traits and characteristics deriving from the aforementioned *dual path dependence*, do not and cannot remain unchanged. They succumb to the powerful effect of the human condition, or borrowing the words of Doug McAdam, Sidney Tarrow and Charles Tilly (2004: 22), to the "relational persuasion", which understands "[…] social interaction, social ties, communication, and conversation not merely as expressions of structure, rationality, consciousness, or culture but as active sites of creation and change" (McAdam, Tarrow and Tilly, 2004: 22).

However, these *ever-changing constants* should not be understood as a *contradictio in terminis*, but as a key ingredient of a process where, in the words of Mark Blyth (2011: 99), "[…] ideas and environment […] combine to produce outcomes that no one expects". Ideas that even though work through "cognitive locking" (Blyth, 2011: 99)[16], directing "[…] people to ignore certain types of policy solutions […]" (Béland and Cox, 2011: 14), they also act "[…] as both the medium and media of stability and change" (Blyth, 2011: 99). As Sheri Berman explains:

> "In practice, of course, […] structure and agency work together to shape ideologies, and therefore, a true understanding of their origins and development must take both into account." (Berman, 2011: 123).

For once more we turn to Somers, who approaches citizenship as an "instituted process", whose examination should take into account:

> "[…] networks of memberships and relationality. Thus, the abstractions of state and capitalism, citizenship, and social class can be replaced with the concept of contingent patterns of relationships and social practices grounded in time and space." (Somers, 1993: 611).

Building on Somers' arguments, we may fully comprehend citizenship's functioning and development as a *time-sensitive*[17] and *space-circumscribed* process. Our conceptualization of citizenship through public policies draws equally on the approach of Rothstein and Uslaner (2005), who, when discussing "equality of opportunity", utilize:

> "[…] a narrow definition that focuses on the establishment of *public policies* (italics in the original) that are intended to create equal conditions for citizens regardless of their income, ethnic/religious background, sex, and race in areas such as health care, education, and social security and legal protection ('equality before the law'). Thus, central to our conceptualization of 'equality of opportunity' is not whether there is 'equality of opportunity' in general but whether the state does (or does not) promote equality of opportunity." (Rothstein and Uslaner, 2005: 42, note 7).

In this context, the importance of the "administrative element" is paramount for achieving the desired outcome through policies promoting "equality of opportunity". The process of administrative change should therefore be taken into consideration when analyzing the parameters affecting social citizenship's institution. In other words, welfare and administration meet, with various results. Stella Ladi, analyzing the process of administrative reform in Greece perceives "the international economic crisis as a critical juncture" (Ladi, 2012: 13), pointing out "[…] that the exogenous pressure is high" (Ladi, 2012: 16).

Therefore, the aforementioned *internal* and *external* factors *vis-à-vis* the nation-state affecting social citizenship's institution, should also be examined with regard to the "genetics" of a specific system's character, in this case the social and political functioning, but also the administrative traits of the Greek social citizenship model. We can understand, in this light, how the "internal" and "external" factors acquire a new meaning and role in defining citizenship's institution and corresponding policies.

In our analysis, based on diverse theoretical approaches and arguments, we will describe how, through the policies imposed on Greece by the troika, the attempted process of institutional reforms, i.e., structural, fiscal and administrative (Memorandum, 2012), was, for the most part, initiated by *forces outside the nation-state*, which threw into disarray the previous welfare-related *status-quo* that maintained up to this point the Greek social citizenship's *deal*. However, the table was already set from the "inside": the model of Greek "particularistic" social citizenship, which we will trace in the pages that follow, had paved the way for making the impact of austerity measures worse. More precisely, in the case of Greece, the *complex interrelation of internal and external factors* formulating citizenship's institution, before and after the crisis, resulted in deeply affecting Greek citizenship's social dimension.

Most importantly, with the first austerity Memorandum imposed upon Greece, an *original path* was forged inside the European Union, as more Memorandums in other South European countries followed, a path that was nevertheless compatible with the—deeply rooted in the Eurozone mechanisms—ideology of "ordoliberalism" (Featherstone, 2012; Kanellopoulos and Liakaki, 2012).

Ordoliberalism, a German version of neoliberalism (Ptak, 2009), in stark contrast to both Keynesianism and monetarism, rejects fiscal *and* monetary stimulus in the face of a depressed economy. It focuses on internal devaluation/deflationary policies and liquidationism. On the other hand, ordoliberalism fits with the corporatist institutions of the "coordinated" social market economy of Germany as opposed to the Anglo-American "liberal" model of capitalism.

In addition, our focus on citizenship sheds light on the element of "trust", which is of crucial importance for the enhancement of social cohesion and the prevention of "social traps" (Rothstein, 2005). In the words of Kumlin and Rothstein:

> "The empirical analysis, based on Swedish survey data, suggests that the specific design of welfare-state policies matters for the production of social capital. Contacts with universal welfare-state institutions tend to increase social trust, whereas experiences with needs-testing social programs undermine it. The policy implication is that governments, by designing welfare-state institutions, can invest in social capital." (Kumlin and Rothstein, 2005: 339).

In this light, this contribution's point of departure and also reference point with our chosen citizenship example, Scandinavian citizenship, will be as follows: our argument implies that the "collective deal", encapsulated inside each social citizenship model, has a lot to do with the welfare policy architecture and how citizenship rights developed over time[18]. Peter Kivisto and Thomas Faist (2007: 135), referring to T. H. Marshall's theory of citizenship, explain that the "historic compromise" through welfare state institutions between capitalism's inequalities and citizenship's claim for equality, became endangered by neoliberal policies. However, they insist that the welfare state's retrenchment was different in each country "[…] depending on how expansive and institutionally embedded the welfare state was in the first place", with Scandinavian states serving as the *par excellence* example of resilience and sustainability (Kivisto and Faist, 2007: 135).

According to Thomas Janoski's definition (cited in Kivisto and Faist, 2007: 50): *"Citizenship is passive and active membership of individuals in a nation-state with certain universalistic rights and obligations at a specified level of equality*" (italics in the original). It is exactly this "specified level of equality", or we could argue of *inequality*, that introduces the question of how a society arrives at a specific *status quo*. Charles Tilly's elaboration of "categorical inequality" is revealing on the matter, with Tilly delineating two principal "causal mechanisms", which are "exploitation"[19] and "opportunity hoarding"[20], that play a crucial role in solidifying this kind of inequality (Tilly, 1998: 10). This approach brings back in, once again, the concept of "full citizenship" and its relevance for citizenship models and equal opportunities:

> "[…] the ideal of 'full citizenship' or the 'Scandinavian citizenship' is based not only on formal civil, political and social rights but also on the idea that everyone has resources enough, and feel (sic) confident enough to take advantage of these possibilities, and that citizenship is therefore both 'participatory and egalitarian'." (Goul Andersen and Hoff, 2001: 261).

Focusing on the institutional and ideational aspects of a "full citizenship" version, as a foundation for the corresponding welfare regime, we use the Scandinavian paradigm as a benchmark for highlighting concepts, notions and policy practices that open the way for reflection on the Greek social citizenship modalities under duress.

Nordic universalistic vs. Southern particularistic welfare institutions

A perspective of citizenship, especially Nordic citizenship, can illuminate social policy in a way that is revealing of the fundamental weaknesses of the welfare state in Greece: its failings, its shortcomings and its contradictions.

The faulty structure of the Greek welfare state results in low quality of services, inadequate coverage of social risks and social problems and a huge waste of resources that makes welfare policies fiscally precarious[21]. Still, the most important consequence rests in the inequality and injustices established and reproduced by Greek welfare institutions. In the words of Matsaganis (2012: 413) and Ferrera (1996: 21):

> "On the eve of the crisis, the Greek system of social protection fitted perfectly the celebrated characterization of the Southern European model of welfare as a combination of serious gaps in the social safety net and 'unparalleled peaks of generosity reserved for the protected core of the labour market'."

Groups of individuals at the same income level and sharing the same needs, enjoy totally different levels of social protection and welfare benefits depending on their having employment and on their occupational status. People who do not work or work undeclared have restricted access to public healthcare. Employment in public enterprises, the government or the private sector entails very different welfare benefits for individuals and their families. Working as an independent contractor—although regularly hired by a single employer—also matters since it is followed by reduced pension benefits. In all, access to healthcare, family allowances and pension insurance varies according to occupation; there are those insured at a so-called "noble"[22] pension and health insurance fund attached to special occupational categories, e.g. public utilities employees, public banks employees, engineers, lawyers, doctors, and those insured at a regular one destined for the general public as is the case with the self-employed or the wage-earners of the private sector. Even after a series of reform programs aimed at integration of social security providers and a severe downsize in coverage and benefits, unequal access remains. Often enough new rules exempt older generations and apply to the young and the newly insured. In other words:

> "Rationing resources—scarcer now than ever before—by political influence rather than by need for social protection has reaffirmed itself as the guiding principle behind the exercising of social policy in Greece." (Matsaganis, 2012: 417).

Inequality in benefits and coverage is coupled by a blatant inequality in what citizens contribute to the Welfare State. Due to massive tax evasion, contribution to tax revenue varies widely, depending on the working status: per capita tax revenue from wage earners vastly overshadows those from self-employed or businessmen. On the other hand, certain occupational funds (e.g., for journalists, lawyers, utility employees, chemists, engineers) are funded from the general public through a number of special transaction charges in advertising, publishing, construction works, imports, real estate contracts, alcohol or cement production.

Furthermore, an horizontal redistribution takes place where the private sector wage-earners finance through the income tax system "noble" occupational categories for benefits that employees and workers themselves cannot enjoy: For example, a doctor's or an engineer's pension is significantly larger than that of an employee with the same years of work and the same level of contributions (Tinios, 2005; Matsaganis, 2012;).

Inequality and injustices have deep corrosive effects on the functioning of institutions in Greece and on any attempt to reform them. As Bo Rothstein (2005) has shown, unjust institutions result in citizens perceiving themselves as "fools of the system" thus eroding trust both in institutions and in each other.

How does the study of citizenship in the Nordic countries contribute to a better comprehension and interpretation of the Greek welfare state? Through the main attribute of Nordic citizenship: *the principle of universalism* that defines access to social services, benefits, participation in the labour market, etc. (Esping-Andersen, 1990; 1999).

In the Nordic case, social rights to universal health care, family benefits, early childhood education services or childcare, care for the disabled or needy elders, to a protection against poverty or unemployment, depend solely on citizenship. In Greece either the right itself or the level and quality of benefits that accompany it, depend on having employment, on the *kind* of employment and the *type* of social security one might have.

The efficiency of the Scandinavian welfare states stems from this universal character of social rights. They protect against fluctuations in working life, as well as encourage risk taking; they shelter workers, especially low-skilled workers, from the instability and precariousness inherent in the services industry or the contemporary flexible forms of manufacturing. They facilitate change of employment, retraining and continuing education[23]. It is certainly easier to raise children, especially for single-parent families or parents with precarious employment.

We already knew that Nordic welfare states facilitated access to the labour market and to a decent life for women and the poor. What they successfully managed to do in the 1990s and the early 2000s has been to extend this protection to groups that in contemporary societies face a high risk of marginalization: unskilled or low-skilled precarious workers, single-parent families (Huber and Stephens, 2001; Bonoli and Armingeon, 2006; Hausermann and Palier, 2006).

Again, universalism of rights and its attachment to citizenship, a unique characteristic of the welfare state in the Nordic countries, has a considerable effect in both access to rights and welfare outcomes.

Concerning access, a series of social rights are detached from work, and in most cases, income. This prevents the establishment of a more or less insiders-outsiders pattern of welfare policies to be found in continental Europe and especially the South, which reproduces a corresponding segregation of the labour market: Traditional occupations and types of employment, that in more propitious times for the labour movement and redistribution policies managed to attain a higher level of social benefits, coexist with types of employment encountered in services and post-Fordist/flexible industrial production (mainly in outsourcing), where workers are deprived of union or labour law protection and social rights[24].

Moreover, Nordic universalism affects results: the level and quality of services is such that they contribute more than anywhere else in Europe to minimizing the exclusion of vulnerable individuals. Apart from providing for a secure, highly trained, thus productive workforce, Scandinavian countries achieve an extremely high employment rate for the general population and women especially. All these provide for an enlarged tax base, assuring financial sustainability.

In addition, there is a somewhat "collateral" effect that differentiates Nordic countries from those with liberal or continental/Christian democratic welfare states: It has to do with the political and electoral consequences:

A) Limiting the practice of "means testing", for access to benefits and a high level of services that satisfy middle class standards, prevents a separation between citizens who pay for welfare policies (middle and higher incomes) and those who enjoy them (lower incomes): a case that takes place in countries with liberal/means-tested welfare states. In the United States and Britain, a political reaction to redistributing policies is encountered usually in one form or another of "a refusal to pay for the undeserving poor".

B) In continental welfare states, especially in the European South, the favorable status of certain social and professional categories and the attachment of social rights to the type of employment discriminate between workers and hamper the inclusive/encompassing mobilization for the defense or extension of welfare policies. Relative actions tend to be politically and electorally fragmented: Since a spreading of benefits is unattainable, privileged groups react desperately to cutbacks but fail to mobilize support from other groups. Retrenched and isolated, these privileged interest groups can be easily manipulated by political parties or the media.

As we claimed above, the essential difference of Scandinavian social citizenship from the Southern and especially Greek citizenship is not to be found in size, in the quantitative level of benefits or the extent of risks and problems covered. That kind of difference is to be expected given the divergence of fiscal capabilities between North and South in Europe. That is not to say that size does not matter, since a high level of benefits and services acquires a qualitative aspect when it assures an equality of participation.

However, in our analysis we do insist on the welfare policy *architecture*, the institutional design. It is there that the essential difference is to be found. The keys to understand it are the principle of universality and the citizenship perspective. Therefore, we claim that it is not the budget but the institutional structure of the Greek welfare state that:

1. Prevents the extension of coverage to vulnerable groups, particularly new social risk groups;
2. Undermines its fiscal/financial sustainability; and
3. Complicates and obstructs political and electoral advocacy for social policies and for their reform in a universalistic direction.

For example, the elimination of pensions for "unmarried orphaned daughters" (of public servants) or of premature retirement for mothers of minors could have allowed for funding of childcare services and family benefits for young parents or single parent families, thus contributing to the *demographic*—and therefore financial—sustainability of the Social Security system.

Thus, the absence of universality in the Greek welfare state remains rather extreme, although under reform. There is a Tower of Babel built around the pension system, welfare structures, benefits and allowances that is the reflection of a fragmented interest organization and representation (Sotiropoulos, 2003; Lavdas, 2005; Matsaganis, 2007). To explain that, we have to look back at the historical structure of Greek society and economy: small and fragmented rural property, weak industrialization, small scale industrial production and—by European standards—unparalleled numbers of self-employed in the bloated service sector[25]. Furthermore, it was the product of government policies, especially after the Civil War, trying to contain and control the development of any kind of independent collective action.

Of course, this welfare Babel is not just a source of enormous waste of resources or inefficiency. It is mainly a source of inequality, mistrust, tensions between social classes and groups that require—that generate the need for—constant intervention by the party system to mitigate those tensions with ever new particularistic arrangements that merely complicate even further the maze.

Concerning the fragmented interest representation, let us emphasize that although there is enough media talk of powerful labour unions that block reforms in Greece, what is relatively understated is the fact that organized labour remains almost nonexistent in the private sector of the economy. Interest representation is limited in publicly controlled enterprises or privatized former public enterprises where indeed a dual working regime (reproducing the dual Greek labour market) survives between "old" and "new" workers, exactly because the extension of old privileges was incompatible with the privatized company's profitability.

Citizenship stands as nothing less than an antagonist, a rival to Greek society's familialism reproduced by clientelism and corruption. Lack of trust in deficient and infirm state institutions and the privatization of those institutions by networks of patronage and corruption actually reinforce familialistic and clientelistic allegiances. It's a paradox, a "social trap" that takes shape when what serves at the individual level as a rather rational behavior becomes socially destructive when generalized at a collective level[26].

Thus, in the Greek case, access to goods or services often depends on having certain particularistic qualities: your connections, your place of birth[27], your occupation. History of social policy in Greece stands out as the allocation of benefits through a clientelistic and particularistic bargaining between the party system and certain occupational categories and patronage networks—a process which resulted in a kind of "particularistic" social citizenship.

Speaking in Mancur Olson's terms, in Greece there is a stark absence of encompassing institutions (Olson, 1982: 77-98). It certainly has to do with the specific path to democratization and modernization followed in Greece, a process that prevented an independent civil society mobilization and the creation of encompassing collectivities as was the case in Northern Europe and the Scandinavian countries.

Encompassing collective action and institutions tend to represent large social groups, for example *all* wage-earners or farmers, instead of particular occupations or narrow social or local interests. They give rise to universal demands and to allocation of benefits with non-excludable qualities, i.e., public goods and services instead of retirement benefits for a particular occupational group or generous farm subsidies for a particular region. In other words, encompassing institutions and collectivities, that have to take into account the interests of large parts of the society or even the public interest, constitute the corresponding agency mechanism of full citizenship; it is the collective action mechanism of full citizenship institutions—a vehicle of claims that leads to public policies directed to universal needs.

What is austerity "represented to be"? From structural reforms to "self-defeating" policies

If *par excellence* welfare-related public policies are those which "make and break"[28] social capital (Kumlin and Rothstein, 2005: 339), the comparison between the Scandinavian and the Greek citizenship models does not allow for much optimism in the midst of the ongoing crisis.

Several studies underline the low-trust character of Greek society and the corresponding negative outcomes (Jones et al, 2008; Poupos, 2010; Papliakou, Stathopoulou and Stratoudaki, 2011). As Lars Torpe (2003: 27) indicates in an article on Danish social capital, "[…] the welfare state facilitates the production of social capital, partly by supporting civil society infrastructure, partly by the very structure of its institutions". Taking also into account how certain public policies, like the educational one, reflect on social capital enhancement, as in Finland (Poupos, 2010: 268), it is very disturbing that early childhood education and care (ECEC), an important policy domain which may work as "investment" in the future human potential (Esping-Andersen, 2002), is pushed to the margins in the crisis-ridden Greece.

The example of early childhood education and care policy highlights the prevailing conditions in the field of social services in Greece. This policy, commonly heralded as one of the policy cornerstones for fighting poverty and social inequalities (OECD, 2001; OECD, 2006; Plantenga and Remery, 2009; European Commission, 2011; OECD, 2012) and which may be seen as a "litmus test"[29] for the choices a state makes in terms of public policies, appears in Greece to be in an *enduring* crisis, even before the austerity and depression period. A variety of factors (Petrogiannis, 2010) indicated in a relevant analysis concerning Greek early childhood education and care contributes to a dim environment for combating inequality from an early age in Greece.

On the contrary, in Sweden, a country with *institutional depth*, the aforementioned policy confirms the importance of trust as a result of policies in favor of *rights*, even when doubts are expressed; in an excerpt from a study on pre-school policy in Sweden (Martin-Korpi, 2007), we read:

> "Child Care Guarantee incorporated in New Act (1995) […] The new legislation on child care which entered into force […] Most of what was laid down in the law were principles that were already familiar, but the formulation 'provide places without unreasonable delay' was completely new […] The legislation put great demands on the municipalities, particularly as thousands of parents in each municipality would be acutely aware of their rights […] But the legislation actually worked, despite the many reservations on the part of the Swedish Association of Local Authorities […] A new generation of Swedish parents with small children no longer regard child care as a privilege, but as a right." (Martin-Korpi, 2007: 56-58).

On the other hand, "despite some improvements recorded […] in the last decade in the field of early childhood care and education in Greece, there is still a substantive lack of services in these areas" (Petrogiannis, 2010: 136), with children of vulnerable social groups becoming those who may lose the most, considering how the ECEC policy:

> "[…] supports children, not only in their future education but also in their integration into society, generating well-being, and contributing to their employability when they become adults […] is also particularly beneficial for the disadvantaged, including those from migrant and low-income backgrounds. It can help to lift children out of poverty and family dysfunction […]" (European Commission, 2011: 1).

Reaching our conclusions, what can we conclude about Greek social citizenship in times of crisis, through the prism of citizenship's "full" version, as well as the *internal* and *external* factors forging Greek citizenship's pattern?

A first conclusion, related to the architecture of the Greek welfare regime, is that for the first time, weaknesses and malfunctions operating *inside* the Greek social citizenship are no longer acceptable or invisible. The crisis' effects on trust, social capital and solidarity, following cuts in public spending and welfare services, complicate an already challenging situation. A declining welfare state and disintegrating social policies (Matsaganis, 2011 and 2012; Petmesidou, 2011; Venieris, 2011), lead to a point where inequality and poverty are significantly increased, taking into account "[…] that the Greek welfare state is simply unfit in its current form to help vulnerable groups cope with the emergency" (Matsaganis, 2011: 509).

So far, the Greek state was not characterized by a strong sense of *welfare state-"channelled"* solidarity[30], with little or no conception of measures and practices in service of strengthening the pubic appreciation of the state's institutions. Nevertheless, since "just institutions matter" (Rothstein, 1998), special attention should be given to "the principle of impartiality" embedded in governmental institutions (Teorell and Rothstein, 2008), which may prove indispensable in times of pressure in order to avert individualistic or free-riding behaviors that further disintegrate the social fabric[31].

Drawing on recent analyses of how the structural reforms actually take place, as well as the effects of the crisis and austerity on the Greek welfare state (Petmesidou, 2011; Venieris, 2011; Matsaganis, 2011 and 2012; Ladi, 2012; Varoufakis, 2012), it seems that there is a lot to be said about the importance of "path dependence" and administrative traditions under extreme financial duress and social pressure. Our point being that these reforms, even when necessary, are communicated, designed and implemented in such a way that undermines even more the already fragile trust in the state's institutions and welfare services. As Stella Ladi (2012: 28) remarks:

> "[…] Greece is still not moving towards an administrative paradigm shift and what we observe is mainly policy experimentation and cost-cutting changes."

At this point, we should also note how crucial can be the role of a "welfare elite"[32], as the one established in France during the Third and Fourth Republic (Martin, 2010: 46-47): a welfare elite as an integral part of a broader administrative elite of civil servants combining excellent scientific and administrative competence in their domain and dedicated to the ideal of a regulatory and reformist state. However, in the Greek case there seems to be a "missing link", at least regarding the administration's capacity to design and implement public policies. High ranking civil servants never formed an administrative elite as they lacked prestige, independence from political patronage and policy influence (Sotiropoulos, 2001: 37-38). As Alivizatos (2013: 100-101) observes:

> "[…] Greece, in contrast to what happens in other countries, for example France during the Fourth Republic or Italy today, lacks a sufficient and professionally organized public administration, which could ensure the

> smooth progress of the country for a long time, especially in periods of crisis."

A "professionally organized" administration which, we may add, would not only provide a strong organizational and *esprit de corps* support to policy-designing but would also assure institutional stability of social services, limiting irrational costs and implementation difficulties.

Furthermore, following Dimitris A. Sotiropoulos, reference should be made to the important "implementation gap" related to gender policies in Southern European countries, in other words the chasm observed between the formal legal framework and the reality of policies' implementation. In addition, Sotiropoulos points out that there are two main principles underpinning the welfare state's performance in Southern Europe. The first promotes the traditional role of women regarded as receivers preferably of financial support by the male members of the family rather than institutional help by the state. The second principle relies on the role of the family, and more precisely its female members, as the main structure for providing care for its dependents (Sotiropoulos, 2007: 93, 95-96).

In a sense, we could argue that Greece, "une société bloquée"[33] according to Kevin Featherstone (2005: 223, 226) and now under severe austerity, deteriorates even more, as persisting pressures requiring an impossibly fast restructuring of welfare services delegitimize reform attempts and contribute to a highly contentious social environment:

> "The failure to protect low incomes (coupled with the widespread feeling that other injustices, such as tax evasion at top incomes, remained endemic) has dealt a blow to the acceptability of austerity policies. This, in turn, has fuelled protests against the cuts, and raised serious doubts about the feasibility of reconciling the expectations of markets abroad with the requirements of democracy at home." (Matsaganis, 2012: 416).

As a result, the Greek social citizenship model described above, which we have defined as "particularistic" social citizenship, tends to be replaced through the proposed reforms by one designed for failure from the outset, even though it is presented as more fair and efficient. According to Manos Matsaganis, the crisis reestablishes the importance of supporting the welfare state's institutions, a task that not only should come to the fore as "an emergency agenda" but has also to resist "temptations" to resort to the usual practice of selective and impractical means-tested benefit increases (Matsaganis, 2011: 509-510).

In addition, any attempt to redirect Greek welfare institutions to a "full citizenship" path must overcome the adversity of a low-trust society plagued by corruption and partial institutions. In the words of Rothstein and Uslaner:

> "Since social trust is a measure of how people evaluate the moral fabric in their society, there is little reason to believe that countries with low social trust will establish universal social programs precisely because such programs must be based on a general political understanding that the various groups in society share a common fate. Countries with an initial level of high inequality and with dishonest government are less likely to establish universal social programs." (Rothstein and Uslaner, 2005: 43).

Building upon our study on Scandinavian social citizenship and welfare regime *vis-à-vis* the Greek ones, we arrive at the following observations regarding the effects of the crisis on the design and functioning of Greek social citizenship:

1. A real shift to a more equitable distribution of rights and duties among different social groups does not occur, especially with regard to taxation and effectiveness of public administration.
2. Reducing the quality of public services pushes people towards the private sector, but taking into account the recessionary economic environment such a solution is out of reach for a great number of people who feel trapped between austerity and their own declining economic status[34].
3. Proposals are made by the troika of creditors for a welfare state that is not universal with encompassing institutions, but targets specific vulnerable social groups in need, without the important provision of high-quality public and social services for all, middle class included.
4. Attempted reforms in the social care sector during the crisis appear unfair and unjust, adding burden on those who have no privileged access to social resources through political channels (Matsaganis, 2012: 416-417).

Another conclusion that we may draw, in the case of Greek social citizenship, is that we notice a shift in favor of the *external* factors affecting citizenship's institution. Firstly, we may trace these "external" factors shaping Greek social citizenship by taking into account what kind of pressure is put on the *administrative* as well as on the *fiscal* aspect of welfare services. As Ladi points out with regard to the public administration's attempted reform:

> "[…] the importance of the exogenous factors in the reform process allows us to argue that this is the most coercive phase of Greece's Europeanization since its entry in the EC." (Ladi, 2012: 28).

In addition, when examining "external" factors, we should also consider the crucial role of dominating ideas on austerity and perceptions of fiscal discipline in the Eurozone area. Ideas carried by certain conservative elites placed in key European institutions, having an extremely tight grip on the way policies concerning employment, rights, and social cohesion are realized as such (Kanellopoulos and Liakaki, 2012).

In his work Jal Mehta discusses the role of ideas "as problem definitions", examining, among others, the question "what determines which problem definitions prevail?" (Mehta, 2011: 32, 35). In this light, in order to understand the "logic" behind the justification of austerity, our analysis draws on Mehta's arguments, as well as on Carol Bacchi's (2012) approach "What's the Problem Represented to be?"[35]. Thus, we argue that the crisis, whose explanation and definition are determined by the aforementioned elites, is presented as *fiscal irresponsibility* and tied in a *quid pro quo* logic to structural reforms accompanied by austerity measures: a perception not allowing for encompassing or just welfare institutions and creating a path which—from a "full citizenship" perspective—is far from generous. As Southern European countries are going through one of the worst crisis in their history, they and their citizens are vilified as the "ungrateful", "weak links" of European integration. EU's institutional impediments thus create a highly unfavorable environment for "full citizenship" as a policy objective.

Moreover, the aforementioned policy ideas remind us once more how the *social* and *economic* aspects of citizenship may be obscured under an incomplete understanding of their functioning and possible repercussions, which in turn redirects us to Rainer Bauböck's (2010) "citizenship constellation" approach. What do we gain from such an analysis? In this case, valuable information on how citizenship regimes are interrelated, especially regarding access to different kinds of rights in the European context (Bauböck, 2010: 848-850). The critique of the inadequacies pertaining to "social Europe" comes to mind (Moschonas, 2009c), when the subject of European citizenship emerges, for reasons that should be examined in the broader context of institutional "traps" and "constraints" (Moschonas, 2002: 262-263) deriving from EU's "paradox"-ridden architecture (Ferrand, 2009) and multiple "asymmetries" (Moschonas, 2009a; Cramme, 2011).

The crisis' effects, an unprecedented depression of 25% of the Greek GDP and extremely high unemployment[36], are combined with implementation gaps[37] and a divisive discourse (often linked with the ideological repertoire of the far-right), in the context of Yanis Varoufakis' (2013a) "self-defeating austerian (sic) terms"; all these overshadow how neoliberal, and, more precisely, ordoliberal policies were "locked" inside Eurozone's monetary structure (Moschonas, 2009b; Featherstone, 2012; Kanellopoulos and Liakaki, 2012).

Furthermore, depression and unemployment can delegitimize, through facilitating an insidious shift of public discourse to an extreme-right direction, if not democracy itself, at least any attempt to modernize public services, by opening the way for welfare anxieties to divide and rule a population hit hard by the policies of austerity.

The ongoing crisis emerges as a catalyst accentuating the formation of "social traps" and their repercussions. Instead of enhancing civic responsibility, the proposed economic measures turn out to be a "public policy disaster"[38]: a situation in which the use of "toxic myths" mobilizes stereotypes and generalizations about the work ethic of South and North Europeans (Varoufakis, 2011b).

However, there is a flip side to all these stereotypes condemning Southern populations: the menace of unemployment, which can destroy not only the very pillars of a nation's economy but also the prospects and potential of "full citizenship":

> "Basically, employment should be seen as a means—maybe indispensable but still as a means—to ensure full citizenship, on the one hand, and economic sustainability on the other." (Goul Andersen and Halvorsen, 2002: 3).

Growing unemployment does not allow for *complete* citizens, as "full citizenship" is becoming gradually nonexistent in a welfare state burdened by past inefficiencies and which may soon prove to be unsustainable:

> "The current crisis [...] has caught the Greek welfare state poorly equipped to cope with its social consequences. [...] policy responses [...] (with the partial exception of pension reform) failed to redress the system's traditional imbalances and to strengthen social safety nets. As a result, the provision of social benefits and services left many victims of the crisis with little or no support, exactly when the need for social protection was greater than ever." (Matsaganis, 2012: 416).

This vicious spiral is created in the most part by austerity, which, according to Varoufakis (2013b) "during a debt-deflation-banking crisis is utterly self-defeating". This austerity contributes to a never-ending crisis, perpetuated by repeated harsh measures, endangering social cohesion in the crisis-ridden countries.

The structural adjustments pursued through the Memorandums, albeit some of them important per se, fail to deal with the institutional shortcomings and failures of both the Eurozone's architecture and EU's inadequate actions for subduing the crisis.

Quoting Étienne Balibar, it is about "politics hiding its name", and "[…] to the extent that it exists, the discussion is deeply biased, because essential determinations are hidden or dismissed" (Balibar, 2010b)—a discussion mobilizing generalizations that, as mentioned above, may turn against European cohesion. In the words of Varoufakis (2011a):

> "Thus the dominant story in Europe today is that […] the southern grasshoppers are knocking on the northern ants' doors […] The ants, understandably, are coy and will only respond if the grasshoppers promise to change their ways. In short, the stocks that the ants accumulated […] are being endangered by hungry, careless grasshoppers who resist changing their profligate ways. The problem (for those seeking to understand a Crisis) with attractive allegories is that the latter can be as much of a help as a hindrance […] when we assume that all the ants are in the north and all the grasshoppers in the south, the remedies we introduce are toxic."

Through the negative international representation and image of Greece as a *nation "resisting" modernization*, citizens of richer EU member countries cannot but feel strongly *exploited*, as "the fools of the (European) system", making it almost impossible to trust EU, seen as the "nanny state" for the "undeserving" populations of the Southern European countries:

> "Aesop was sounding the alarm bell against both the grasshopper's spendthrift ways and the ant's extreme parsimony. Today there is another wrinkle that needs to be added to his moral: That, when the ants and the grasshoppers are distributed across the division separating surplus from deficit nations within a badly designed monetary union, the stage is set for a depression that sets all against all in a vicious spiral from which only losers can emerge." (Varoufakis, 2011a).

In other words, the current financial crisis sets up the *ultimate "social trap"* not only for Greek citizens but also for citizens of other Eurozone countries.

Conclusion

In our analysis, we tried to discern, through a comparison with Scandinavian welfare institutions, the dominant traits of the Greek social citizenship before and after the crisis.

Our study permitted us to detect a shift towards factors *outside the nation-state*—mainly European Union forces—affecting Greek social citizenship during the crisis. At the same time, it is becoming increasingly difficult to sustain the consolidated in previous decades "particularistic" form of social resources' distribution lying at the center of Greek citizenship, so that various social groups begin to mobilize and create new claims in a highly contentious context. In the case of the Greek welfare state, "internal" factors resulted in a certain model of "opportunity hoarding"[39] that was institutionalized in the *citizenship deal* before the austerity programs and which now unravels, as the crisis undermines the material conditions of particular groups' aforementioned social bargaining.

Furthermore, based on our analysis above, we could argue that the EU, "solidarity rhetoric" aside, forms a negative environment where the need for reforms acquires a punitive logic which, accompanied by an austerity-driven depression, leads to a triple negative result: (1) impossibility of effective implementation of structural adjustments that adds itself to the already existing policy problems (2) de-legitimatization of austerity and reforms with reinforcement of the insiders-outsiders situation facilitating the emergence of highly negative aspects of social behavior and (3) perpetuation of insidious "myths" reproducing contempt for South European populations.

As a result, austerity measures, by preparing the ground for the *ultimate social trap*, challenge trust in institutions and further undermine social solidarity. Taking into consideration that "[…] in an economically unsustainable welfare state it makes little sense to discuss citizenship at all" (Goul Andersen and Halvorsen, 2002: 12), a most fearful prospect arises along with the menace of depression and unemployment: the reduction of Greek social citizenship to a limited form of a "shredded" relic, where it will not be possible even to address the issue of a sustainable welfare state.

In line with our previous argumentation, the policy recommendations that this paper could propose fall in two categories. First, there is a short-term crisis management to be done by shedding ordoliberal policies and adopting a mix of Keynesian and monetarist interventions similar to those employed in the USA or Japan: liquidity injections, massive public investment and a reflation policy in the Northern Eurozone economies that will restore growth in the South.

Then, there is a longer-term reform program that, apart from the transformation of the Eurozone institutions that cannot preoccupy us here, entails a redesigning of the welfare institutions of the South European countries that will move them closer to northern standards. A detachment of welfare rights from employment and their reattachment to citizenship is imperative. It will not only extend equal coverage to marginalized groups but it will also build trust in state institutions, a lack often cited by international organizations as contributing to the "failures" of Southern European governments.

Furthermore, universal welfare coverage, funded mostly by the national budget and not by payroll contributions, will alleviate employment costs by reducing the disincentives for the hire of low-skill and young workers. In addition, and since deep and prolonged austerity forces a protracted inactivity that depreciates and erodes human and material capital, a universal safety net with family benefits and minimum income guarantees decreases the social risks from the business restructurings and skill adjustments that Southern economies will have to go through the coming years to restore their productivity.

Notes

[1] For a rigorous analysis of citizenship's limitations and perspectives, see Balibar (1992; 2010a), Bauböck (1992), Dimoulis (2001: 157-209) and Magnette (2001). For the term "citizenship gap" and its relation to globalization, see Brysk (2002: 10-14) and Brysk and Shafir (2004a; 2004b: 6 and 2004c: 210).

[2] As Brysk and Shafir (2004b: 6) write: "The first characteristic manifestation of the citizenship gap is the growing number of residents in increasing numbers of states who are *noncitizens* (or ambiguous citizens), whose lives are subject to global markets and mobility without secure membership in a national community." [italics in the original]. Brysk and Shafir, in the same page, also point out: "But formal, *legal citizens* are also at risk from the deflation of citizenship rights by global influences [...] The lives of more and more legal citizens depend on distant decisions over which they cannot exert effective political influence." [italics in the original].

[3] For "political opportunity structure" see Tilly and Tarrow (2008: 105-110).

[4] For the definition of the term "relational" vis-à-vis citizenship, we draw on how the "relational" concept is used in Somers (1993) and McAdam, Tarrow and Tilly (2004: 22-24). We also build on Christopoulos' analysis (2012: 25) where he refers

to Foucault's theory of power relations. We also refer to Miaille (2001) for an analysis of citizenship through the prism of Poulantzas' relational theory of power.

[5] Our argument here is also inspired by Margaret R. Somers (1993: 589, 608, 610), as well as by Dimitris Christopoulos' analysis (2012: 25, 43, 273-274) where he explains how citizenship's institution encompasses practices (especially administrative ones), ideas, norms, histories, political strategies, class struggles, decisions, policies and ideologies.

[6] The concept of "citizenship constellation" belongs to Rainer Bauböck who writes (2010: 848): "What I suggest calling a 'citizenship constellation' is a structure in which individuals are simultaneously linked to several such political entities, so that their legal rights and duties are determined not only by one political authority, but by several". Bauböck, when studying citizenship and migration introduces "[…] a perspective that goes beyond the dominant framework without replacing it. For both comparative and normative purposes, we need to study the citizenship traditions, laws and policies of states not merely separately, but rather as part of intertwined citizenship constellations" (Bauböck, 2010: 848).

[7] For "historicity", in relation to citizenship, see Sassen (2004: 191) and Christopoulos (2012: 25-26).

[8] For "instituted process", in relation to citizenship, see Somers (1993: 587, 589, 611).

[9] Kivisto and Faist (2007: 110) mention, for example, the role of "[…] internal and external forces contributing to a profound shift in the way states and publics view dual citizenship […]".

[10] Kivisto and Faist (2007: 139) note the role of "global factors" when they point out that "[…] it is clear to us that the factors shaping inclusion—the debates over multiculturalism, erosion, and withdrawal—are all increasingly being influenced by global factors."

[11] We base our argument on Goul Andersen and Hoff's (2001) work, where they write that "the concept of citizenship also serves to point out what are the major challenges to the ideal of 'full citizenship'—that is, equal access of citizens to participate in all areas of social and political life" (Goul Andersen and Hoff, 2001: 251). For the concept of "full citizenship", see Goul Andersen and Hoff (2001), especially pp. 1-3, 10, 15, 20, 80, 135, 188, 251, 257, 259, 261 and 263.

[12] For an analysis of "historical institutionalism", see Hall and Taylor (1996).

[13] For "path dependence", see Pierson (2000).

[14] For the existence of these two types of path dependence, "institutional" and "ideational", see Hay (2011: 68-69): "Further differentiating it from new institutionalist orthodoxy, constructivist institutionalists emphasize not only institutional path-dependence but also ideational path-dependence. In other words, it is not just institutions but the very ideas on which they are predicated and which inform their design and development that exert constraints on political autonomy." Moreover, according to Mehta (2011: 30): "Scholars interested in ideas have adapted historical institutionalists' emphasis on path dependence to encompass the 'path dependence of an idea,' […]". See also the extract from Blyth's work (2001: 4) included in note 16 of this chapter.

[15] For the idea of policies as "litmus test", in relation to the quality of government, we draw upon the following question raised in an article on governmental quality by Helliwell and Huang (2008: 595): "If a government's goodness is to be defined by the nature and consequences of its policies, which policies and which results should be used as litmus tests?"
[16] For the concept of "cognitive locking", see Blyth (2011: 99) where he refers to Berman (2011) as well as to his own earlier work (Blyth, 2001). In his 2001 article, Blyth writes: "Whereas historical institutionalists have hitherto understood policy continuity in the face of environmental changes as a function of the path dependence of institutions, what is suggested here is that if path dependency occurs, it may also be a function of cognitive locking and is thus an *ideational* rather than an institutional phenomenon." (Blyth, 2001: 4) [italics in the original].
[17] On this point, see also Jensen and Pfau-Effinger (2005: 6) who stress the importance of examining citizenship's changes "[…] in relation to the historical and social conditions in which they are produced at a given moment in time".
[18] For how citizenship rights developed over time, we refer to Marshall and Bottomore (1992).
[19] "[…] which operates when powerful, connected people command resources from which they draw significantly increased returns by coordinating the effort of outsiders whom they exclude from the full value added by that effort" (Tilly, 1998: 10).
[20] "[…] which operates when members of a categorically bounded network acquire access to a resource that is valuable, renewable, subject to monopoly, supportive of network activities, and enhanced by the network' s modus operandi" (Tilly, 1998: 10).
[21] For a detailed analysis of the Greek welfare state and its evolution, see Matsaganis (2012), Ferrera (1996), Katrougalos and Lazaridis (2003), Petmesidou and Mossialos (2006). See Matsaganis (2012: 411-413) for an emphasis on the differential effects of the crisis on occupational groups and Ferrera (2005) for a historical overview of Southern European welfare states.
[22] Noble, i.e., rich in funds, usually from direct or indirect state subsidies.
[23] Greece, in comparison, presents serious difficulties and risks involved in changing between social security funds or moving to another employment since an entitlement to severance pay or special retirement benefits etc. is attached to a certain employment position.
[24] In 2011, the percentage of uninsured workers was 30%. See European industrial relations observatory:
http://www.eurofound.europa.eu/eiro/2012/02/articles/gr1202039i.htm
[25] In 2011, salaried work in Greece amounted to around 63% of total employed work force, one of the lowest rates in Europe. See European industrial relations observatory online,
http://www.eurofound.europa.eu/eiro/country/greece_2.htm (cited 30/12/2012)
[26] According to Rothstein (2005: 12): "The *social trap* may be considered an 'umbrella term' for a number of strategic situations in which social actors find themselves, in which the central element is that their behavior is determined by their assessments of the future action of others […] Conclusion: Efficient

cooperation for common purposes can come about only if *people trust that most other people will also choose to cooperate.* Lacking that trust, the social trap will slam inexorably shut. That is, we end up in a state of affairs that is worse for everyone, even though everyone realizes that they would profit by *choosing to cooperate.*" [italics in the original].

[27] Certain localities or regions in Greece have stronger clientelist networks than others.

[28] We refer here to Kumlin and Rothstein's (2005) article's title "Making and breaking social capital. The impact of welfare-state institutions".

[29] See note 15 of this chapter.

[30] For a typology of different forms of solidarity in relation to the welfare state, see Entzinger (2007: 121-124).

[31] According to Matsaganis (2011: 510): "Strengthening the social safety net cannot be a question of cash benefits alone. The expansion of child care, the restoration of the 'home help' […], the reform of the public employment service, the revival of publicly provided healthcare, and the opening of state schools to all children, including those of undocumented migrants (which, to its credit, the government has guaranteed), are all essential to the task".

[32] The term is found in Martin (2010: 46) as "élite du Welfare".

[33] Featherstone defines "une société bloquée" as "a political setting of stalemate between contending veto points" (2005: 226).

[34] As Matsaganis (2011: 510) points out: "[…] policy failures in health or education have placed a heavy burden on family budgets through higher private spending, while failing to soften the impact of the crisis is likely to prove costlier still in terms of social unrest and rising crime."

[35] As Bacchi (2012: 21) explains: "The '*WPR*' approach is a resource, or tool, intended to facilitate critical interrogation of public policies. It starts from the premise that what one proposes to do about something reveals what one thinks is problematic (needs to change). Following this thinking, policies and policy proposals contain *implicit* representations of what is considered to be the 'problem' ('problem representations')." [italics in the original].

Bacchi (2012: 22) also notes that "in this account policy is not the government's best effort to *solve* 'problems'; rather, policies *produce* 'problems' with particular meanings that affect what gets done or not done, and how people live their lives […] Instead, the aim is to understand policy better than policy makers by probing the unexamined assumptions and deep-seated conceptual logics within implicit problem representations." [italics in the original].

[36] Recent figures place unemployment percentage at 27,4% (Hellenic Statistical Authority, 2013).

[37] According to Stella Ladi (2012: 28): "[…] the pace of the reforms is slow, delays are observed, and an implementation gap can be noticed."

[38] Characterization inspired by the title of Gray and Hart's (1998) book *Public policy disasters in Western Europe.*

[39] For "opportunity hoarding", see note 20 of this chapter.

References

Alivizatos, N. K. (2013). *What democracy for Greece after the crisis? For the restoration of words and their meaning*, Athens: Polis (in Greek).

Bacchi, C. (2012). 'Introducing the 'What's the Problem Represented to be?' approach', in Bletsas, A. and Beasley, C. (eds.) *Engaging with Carol Bacchi: Strategic interventions and exchanges*, Adelaide: University of Adelaide Press, pp. 21-24.

Balibar, É. (1992). *Les frontières de la démocratie*, Paris: Découverte.

—. (1997). *La crainte des masses: Politique et philosophie avant et après Marx*, Paris: Galilée, pp. 371-380.

—. (2010a). *La proposition de l'égaliberté: Essais politiques 1989-2009*, Paris: Presses Universitaires de France, pp. 11-52.

—. (2010b). 'Europe: final crisis? Some theses', *Theory & Event*, vol. 13, no. 2. Available: http://muse.jhu.edu/journals/theory_and_event/v013/13.2.balibar.html [20 December 2012]

Bauböck, R. (1992). *Immigration and the boundaries of citizenship*, Coventry: University of Warwick, Centre for Research in Ethnic Relations.

—. (2010). 'Studying citizenship constellations', *Journal of Ethnic and Migration Studies*, vol. 36, no. 5, pp. 847-859.

Béland, D. and Cox, R. H. (2011). 'Introduction: Ideas and politics', in Béland, D. and Cox, R. H. (eds.) *Ideas and politics in social science research*, Oxford: Oxford University Press, pp. 3-20.

Berman, S. (2011). 'Ideology, history, and politics', in Béland, D. and Cox, R. H. (eds.) *Ideas and politics in social science research*, Oxford: Oxford University Press, pp. 105-126.

Blyth, M. (2001). 'The transformation of the Swedish model: Economic ideas, distributional conflict and institutional change', *World Politics*, vol. 54, no.1, pp. 1-26.

—. (2011). 'Ideas, uncertainty, and evolution', in Béland, D. and Cox, R. H. (eds.) *Ideas and politics in social science research*, Oxford: Oxford University Press, pp. 83-101.

Bonoli, G. and Armingeon, K. (eds.) (2006). *The politics of post-industrial welfare states: Adapting post-war social policies to new social risks*, London: Routledge.

Brysk, A. (2002). 'Introduction: Transnational threats and opportunities', in Brysk, A. (ed.) *Globalization and human rights*, Berkeley: University of California Press, pp. 1-16.

Brysk, A. and Shafir, G. (eds.) (2004a). *People out of place: Globalization, human rights and the citizenship gap*, New York: Routledge.

Brysk, A. and Shafir, G. (2004b). 'Introduction: Globalization and the citizenship gap', in Brysk, A. and Shafir, G. (eds.) *People out of place: Globalization, human rights and the citizenship gap*, New York: Routledge, pp. 3-9.

—. (2004c). 'Conclusion: Globalizing citizenship', in Brysk, A. and Shafir, G. (eds.) *People out of place: Globalization, human rights and the citizenship gap*, New York: Routledge, pp. 209-215.

Christopoulos, D. (2012). *Who is Greek citizen? Nationality regime from the creation of the Greek state till the dawn of the 21st century*, Athens: Vivliorama (in Greek).

Cramme, O. (2011). 'The changing space for EU politics. Democracy and ideology in times of crisis', *Policy Network*, Available: http://www.policy-network.net/ publications_detail.aspx?ID=4066 [10 October 2012]

Dimoulis, D. (2001). *The law of politics. Studies in constitutional theory and interpretation*, Athens: Ellinika Grammata (in Greek).

Entzinger, H. (2007). 'Open borders and the welfare state', in Pécoud, A. and de Guchteneire, P. (eds.) *Migration without borders: Essays on the free movement of people*, New York/Paris: Berghahn/Unesco, pp. 119-134.

Esping-Andersen, G. (1990). *The three worlds of welfare capitalism*, London: Polity Press.

—. (1999). *Social foundations of post-industrial economies*, Oxford: Oxford University Press.

—. (2002). 'A child-centered social investment strategy', in Esping-Andersen, G. Gallie, D., Hemerijck, A. and Myles, J. (eds) *Why we need a new welfare state*, Oxford: Oxford University Press, pp. 26-67.

European Commission (2011). *Early childhood education and care: Providing all our children with the best start for the world of tomorrow*, Communication from the Commission, COM(2011) 66 final, Available: http://ec.europa.eu/education/school-education/doc/childhoodcom_en.pdf [10 September 2013]

Faist, T. (2000). 'Social citizenship in the European Union: Residual post-national, and nested membership?', *Institut für Interkulturelle und Internationale Studien-Arbeitspapier*, no. 17.

Featherstone, K. (2005). 'Introduction: 'Modernisation' and the structural constraints of Greek politics', *West European Politics*, vol. 28, no. 2, pp. 223–241.

—. (2012). 'Le choc de la nouvelle? Maastricht, déjà vu and EMU reform', *LEQS Paper*, no. 52, Available: http://www.lse.ac.uk/europeanInstitute/LEQS/LEQSPaper52.pdf [10 August 2013]

Ferrand, O. (2009). 'L'Europe d'aujourd'hui se dresse contre l'Europe de demain', *Libération*, 2 June, Available: http://www.liberation.fr/politiques/0101570782-l-europe-d-aujourd-hui-se-dresse-contre-l-europe-de-demain [20 December 2012]

Ferrera, M. (1996). 'The 'Southern model' of welfare in social Europe', *Journal of European Social Policy*, vol. 6, no. 1, pp. 17-37.

—. (2005). 'Welfare states and social safety nets in Southern Europe. An introduction', in Ferrera, M. (ed.) *Welfare state reform in Southern Europe*, London: Routledge, pp. 1-23.

Goul Andersen, J. and Halvorsen, K. (2002). 'Changing labour markets, unemployment and unemployment policies in a citizenship perspective', in Goul Andersen, J., Clasen, J., van Oorschot, W. and Halvorsen, K. (eds.) *Europe's new state of welfare: Unemployment, employment policies and citizenship*, Bristol: Policy Press, pp. 1-19.

Goul Andersen, J. and Hoff, J. (2001). *Democracy and citizenship in Scandinavia*, New York: Palgrave.

Gray, P. and Hart, P. (1998). *Public policy disasters in Western Europe*, London: Routledge.

Hall, P. A. and Taylor, R. C. R. (1996). 'Political science and the three new institutionalisms', *Political Studies*, vol. 44, no. 5, pp. 936-957.

Hausermann, S. and Palier, B. (2006). 'The politics of employment-friendly welfare reforms in post-industrial economies', *Socio-Economic Review*, vol. 6, no. 3, pp. 559-586.

Hay, C. (2011). 'Ideas and the construction of interests', in Béland, D. and Cox, R. H. (eds.) *Ideas and politics in social science research*, Oxford: Oxford University Press, pp. 65-82.

Hellenic Statistical Authority (2013). Press release. Labour force survey – 1st Quarter 2013, Available: http://www.statistics.gr/portal/page/portal/ESYE/BUCKET/A0101/PressReleases/ A0101_SJO01_DT_QQ_01_2013_01_F_EN.pdf [10 July 2013]

Helliwell, J. F. and Huang, H. (2008). 'How's your government? International evidence linking good government and well-being', *British Journal of Political Science*, vol. 38, no. 4, pp. 595-619.

Hoffman, J. (2004). *Citizenship beyond the state*, London: Sage.

Huber, E. and Stephens, J. D. (2001). *Development and crisis of the welfare state: Parties and policies in global markets*, Chicago: The University of Chicago Press.

Jensen, P.H. and Pfau-Effinger, B. (2005). '"Active" citizenship: The new face of welfare', in Goul Andersen, J., Guillemard, A.-M., Jensen, P. H. and Pfau-Effinger, B. (eds.) *The changing face of welfare: Consequences and outcomes from a citizenship perspective*, Bristol: The Policy Press – University of Bristol, pp. 1-14.

Jones, N., Malesios C., Iosifides, T. and Sophoulis, C. M. (2008). 'Social capital in Greece: Measurement and comparative perspectives', *South European Society and Politics*, *13*, vol. 13, no. 2, pp. 175-193.

Kanellopoulos, C. and Liakaki, S. (2012). 'Euro and the socialists', *Synchrona Themata (Current Affairs)*, no. 117, pp. 11-21 (in Greek).

Katrougalos, G. and Lazaridis, G. (eds.) (2003). *Southern European welfare states. Problems, challenges and prospects*, Basingstoke: Palgrave Macmillan.

Kivisto, P. and Faist, T. (2007). *Citizenship: Discourse, theory, and transnational prospects*, Malden (MA): Blackwell.

Kumlin, S. and Rothstein, B. (2005). 'Making and breaking social capital. The impact of welfare-state institutions', *Comparative Political Studies,* vol. 38, no. 4, pp. 339-365.

Kymlicka, W. and Norman, W. (1994). 'Return of the citizen: A survey of recent work on citizenship theory', *Ethics*, vol. 104, no. 2, pp. 352-381.

Ladi, S. (2012). 'The Eurozone crisis and austerity politics: A trigger for administrative reform in Greece?' *GreeSE Papers,* no. 57, London School of Economics and Political Science, Hellenic Observatory, London, UK, Available:
http://eprints.lse.ac.uk/43383/1/GreeSE%20No57.pdf [10 August 2013]

Lavdas, K. (2005). 'Interest groups in disjointed corporatism: Social dialogue in Greece and European 'competitive corporatism'', *West European Politics*, vol. 28, no. 2, pp. 297-316.

Lipschutz, R. D. (2004). 'Constituting political community: Globalization, citizenship, and human rights', in Brysk, A. and Shafir, G. (eds.) *People out of place: Globalization, human rights and the citizenship gap*, New York: Routledge, pp. 29-51.

Magnette, P. (2001). *La citoyenneté: Une histoire de l'idée de participation civique*, Bruxelles: Bruylant.

Marshall ,T. H. and Bottomore, T. (1992). *Citizenship and Social Class*, London: Pluto Press.

Martin, C. (2010). 'Les politiques de la famille', in Borraz, O. and Guiraudon, V. (eds.) *Politiques Publiques. 2, Changer la société*, Paris: les Presses de Sciences Po, pp. 31-55.

Martin-Korpi, B. (2007). *The politics of pre-school – Intentions and decisions underlying the emergence and growth of the Swedish pre-school* (3d edition, first printing – translated into English by B. R. Turner), Stockholm: The Ministry of Education and Research (Sweden), Available: http://www.government.se/content/1/c6/09/10/62/322638cd.pdf [10 October 2012].

Matsaganis, M. (2007). 'Union structures and pension outcomes in Greece', *British Journal of Industrial Relations*, vol. 45, no. 3, pp. 537-555.

—. (2011). 'The welfare state and the crisis: The case of Greece', *Journal of European Social Policy*, vol. 21, no. 5, pp. 501-512.

—. (2012). 'Social policy in hard times: The case of Greece', *Critical Social Policy*, vol. 32, no. 3, pp. 406-421.

McAdam, D. Tarrow, S. and Tilly, C. (2004). *Dynamics of contention*, Cambridge: Cambridge University Press.

Mehta, J. (2011). 'The varied roles of ideas in politics: From 'whether' to 'how'', in Béland, D. and Cox, R. H. (eds.) *Ideas and politics in social science research*, Oxford: Oxford University Press, pp. 23-46.

Memorandum of Understanding on Specific Economic Policy Conditionality (2012). Hellenic Republic, Ministry of Finance, 13 March, Available: http://www.minfin.gr/content-api/f/binaryChannel/minfin/datastore/d1/d9/7c/d1d97cb60bad8706a2cabbf83e5ae9fb7f3ab369/application/pdf/MOU+_+MEFP+13+march+2012%5B1%5D.pdf [10 October 2013]

Miaille, M. (2001). 'Citizenship in contemporary France: Substantial transformation?', in Rigos, A. and Tsoukalas, K. (eds) *Politics today. Nicos Poulantzas and the actuality of his work,* Athens: Themelio and Hellenic Political Science Association, pp. 58-86 (in Greek).

Moschonas, G. (2002). *In the name of social democracy. The great transformation, 1945 to the present* (translated into English by Gregory Elliott), London: Verso.

—. (2009a). 'When institutions matter: The EU and the identity of social democracy', *Renewal,* vol. 17, no. 2, pp. 11-20.

—. (2009b). 'Social democracy and Left in Europe', Interviewed by Ioannis Balambanidis for *Kyriakatiki Avgi*, 29 November, Available: http://archive.avgi.gr/ArticleActionshow.action?articleID=508461 [26 October 2013] (in Greek).

—. (2009c). 'The big lie. The aim and myth of social Europe', *Ta Nea online*, 10 July. Available: http://www.tanea.gr/ellada/article/?aid=4525930 [26 October 2012] (in Greek).

OECD (2001). *Starting strong. Early childhood education and care*, Paris: OECD Publications.

—. (2006). *Starting strong II: Early childhood education and care*, Paris: OECD Publications.

—. (2012). *Starting strong III - A quality toolbox for early childhood education and care*, Paris: OECD Publications.

Olson, M. (1982). *The rise and decline of nations: Economic growth, stagflation, and social rigidities*, New Haven: Yale University Press.

Papliakou, V. Stathopoulou, T. and Stratoudaki, H. (eds.) (2011). *Institutions – Values – Practices. Interpretations of the ESS key findings (2008-2009)*, Athens: National Centre for Social Research (in Greek).

Petmesidou, M. (2011). 'Is the IMF-EU 'rescue plan' dealing a blow to the Greek welfare state?', *Poverty Brief 4. CROP Brief Series,* Available: http://www.crop.org/viewfile.aspx?id=225 [10 June 2013]

Petmesidou, M. and Mossialos, E. (eds.) (2006). *Social policy developments in Greece*, Aldershot: Ashgate.

Petrogiannis, K. (2010). 'Early childhood care and education in Greece: Some facts on research and policy', *International Journal of Early Childhood*, vol. 42, no. 2, pp. 131-139.

Pierson, P. (2000). 'Increasing returns, path dependence, and the study of politics', *The American Political Science Review*, vol. 94, no. 2, pp. 251-267.

Plantenga, J. and Remery, C. (2009). *The provision of childcare services: A comparative review of 30 European countries*, Luxembourg: Office for Official Publications of the European Communities, Available: ec.europa.eu/social/BlobServlet?docId=2803&langId=en [10 October 2012]

Poupos, E. (2010). *Social capital in Greece*, Athens: KEPE, Series Reports, no. 61 (in Greek).

Ptak, R. (2009). 'Neoliberalism in Germany: Revisiting the ordoliberal foundations of the social market economy', in Mirowski, P. and Plehwe, D. (eds.) *The road from Mont Pèlerin: The making of the neoliberal thought collective*, Cambridge, Mass.: Harvard University Press, pp. 98-138.

Purvis, T. and Hunt, A. (1999). 'Identity versus citizenship: Transformations in the discourses and practices of citizenship', *Social & Legal Studies,* vol. 8, no. 4, pp. 457-482.

Rothstein, B. (1998). *Just institutions matter: The moral and political logic of the universal welfare state*, Cambridge: Cambridge University Press.

—. (2005). *Social traps and the problem of trust*, Cambridge: Cambridge University Press.

Rothstein, B. and Uslaner, E. M. (2005). 'All for all. Equality, corruption, and social trust', *World Politics*, vol. 58, no. 1, pp. 41–72.

Sassen, S. (2004). 'The repositioning of citizenship', in Brysk A. and Shafir, G. (eds.) *People out of place: Globalization, human rights and the citizenship gap*, New York: Routledge, pp. 191-208.

Seidman, G. W. (2004). 'Deflated citizenship: labor rights in a global era', in Brysk A. and Shafir, G. (eds.) *People out of place: Globalization, human rights and the citizenship gap*, New York: Routledge, pp. 109-129.

Shafir, G. (2004). 'Citizenship and human rights in an era of globalization', in Brysk A. and Shafir, G. (eds.) *People out of place: Globalization, human rights and the citizenship gap*, New York: Routledge, pp. 11-25.

Somers, M. R. (1993). 'Citizenship and the place of the public sphere: Law, community, and political culture in the transition to democracy', *American Sociological Review*, vol. 58, no. 5, pp. 587-620.

Sotiropoulos, D. A. (2001). *The summit of the clientelist state*, Athens: Potamos (in Greek).

—. (2003). 'Facets of Babylon: Interpretations of postwar welfare state development in Greece', in Venieris D. and Papatheodorou C. (eds.) *Social Policy in Greece. Challenges and Prospects*, Athens: Ellinika Grammata, pp. 89-131 (in Greek).

—. (2007). *State and reform in contemporary Southern Europe: Greece – Spain – Italy –Portugal*, Athens: Potamos (in Greek).

Teorell, J. and Rothstein, B. (2008). 'What is quality of government: A theory of impartial institutions', *Governance: An International Journal of Policy, Administration, and Institutions*, vol. 21, no. 2, pp. 165-190.

Thériault, J.-Y. (1999). 'Présentation: la citoyenneté: entre normativité et factualité', *Sociologie et sociétés*, vol. 31, no. 2, pp. 5–13.

Tilly, C. (1998). *Durable inequality*, Berkeley, Calif.: University of California Press.

Tilly, C. and Tarrow, S. (2008). *Politique(s) du conflit : de la grève à la révolution* (translated into French by Rachel Bouyssou), Paris: Presses de Sciences Po.

Tilly, R. (2007). 'The European Union 50 years on: Some comments on its early history', in Welfens, P. J. J., Tilly, R. and Heise, M. (eds.) *50 years of EU economic dynamics. Integration, financial markets and* innovations, Berlin: Springer, pp. 11-23.

Tinios, P. (2005). 'Pension reform in Greece: 'Reform by installments' – A blocked process', *West European Politics*, vol. 28, no. 2, pp. 402-419.

Torpe, L. (2003). 'Social capital in Denmark: A deviant case?', *Scandinavian Political Studies*, vol. 26, no. 1, pp. 27-48.

Varoufakis, Y. (2011a). 'NEVER BAILED OUT: Europe's ants and grasshoppers revisited', *yanisvaroufakis.eu*, 15 December, Available: http://yanisvaroufakis.eu/2011/12/15/never-bailed-out-europes-ants-and-grasshoppers-revisited/ [10 June 2013]

—. (2011b). 'Grasshoppers and ants', *Protagon.gr*, 16 December, Available:http://www.protagon.gr/?i=protagon.el.8emata&id=11081 [10 June 2013] (in Greek).

—. (2012). 'Prerequisites for hope', *Protagon.gr*, 10 May, Available: http://www.protagon.gr/?i=protagon.el.8emata&id=15079 [10 June 2013] (in Greek).

—. (2013a). 'Is Europe loosening up austerity's iron clasp?', *yanisvaroufakis.eu*, 29 May, Available: http://yanisvaroufakis.eu/2013/05/29/is-europe-loosening-up-austeritys-iron-clasp/ [2 July 2013]

—. (2013b). 'Q&A on Greece, Portugal and Ireland – June 25th 2013', *yanisvaroufakis.eu*, 25 June, Available: http://yanisvaroufakis.eu/2013/06/25/qa-on-greece-portugal-and-ireland-june-25th-2013/ [2 July 2013]

Venieris, D. (2011). 'Economic crisis and social policy deregulation: The new 'Greece Minor disaster' 2010-2011', *The Greek Review of Social Research*, no. 134-135, A΄- B΄, pp. 101-131 (in Greek).

CHAPTER NINETEEN

THE PROTECTION OF THE BANKING SYSTEM AS A CRITICAL SOCIETAL INFRASTRUCTURE[1]

ANTTI SILVAST
UNIVERSITY OF HELSINKI

Abstract

Over the last six years, I have been engaged in research regarding the protection of critical societal infrastructures with a particular interest in electricity systems. This exploratory article inquires into the following question: how has banking been understood as an infrastructural system and what are the practices for its protection like? As is well-known, banking affects investments to critical infrastructures like roads and energy, and many infrastructure companies compete in the free markets which makes them generally vulnerable to financial crises. However, a different issue is that banking itself has been deemed as one of society's vital or critical infrastructures in many countries over the last few decades. Also, in 2005 the EU designated finance as a critical infrastructure sector, although this sector was not incorporated in the EU's 2008 Critical Infrastructure Protection directive. The present article looks at definitions of banking as a critical infrastructure and explores the ways in which the banking system can be protected from crises such as the current debt crisis. The key source materials are the well-developed infrastructure protection practices in Finland supplemented by international documents from the EU and critical infrastructure protection handbooks.

Introduction

During the past decades, several social scientists have inquired into large infrastructure systems and their social and technical interrelated features (see Van Der Vleuten, 2004). Recent studies have sought to know, for example, how networked infrastructures like electricity and telecommunications figure in urban and public policies (Graham and

Marvin, 2001), in governance of national security (Collier and Lakoff, 2008; Kristensen, 2008), in broader processes of "modernization" in societies (Edwards, 2003), and in day-to-day work and practices (Star, 1999). The vantage point of this article is to consider banking as a vital and ubiquitous societal infrastructure, depending on how infrastructures have been outlined by social science discussions. My particular interest is in financial crises and their framing as an infrastructural security threat and a problem. Specifically, I focus on anticipated "breakdowns" (Star, 1999) of banking infrastructures and on how these disruptions have been framed as a threat to societal security and as a crisis to be mitigated by national security experts (Collier and Lakoff, 2008; Kristensen, 2008).

Based on recent discussions, banking affects large societal infrastructures on several levels from investments to on-going operations. For instance, *Connecting Europe Facility*, a 50 billion Euros investment instrument for trans-European infrastructures, generated commentary about how the "on-going crisis … hampers, for example, bank lending for infrastructure investment" (European Commission, 2012a). At the same time, an increasing number of infrastructure providers such as electricity generation companies compete in free markets (Graham and Marvin, 2001) and are thus in general affected by financial crises. On the other hand, as Paul N. Edwards and his colleagues (2009: 365) have noted—and evoking images of the American Recovery and Reinvestment Act of 2009—infrastructures are not merely vulnerable to the current crises, but also one possible means of recovering from them: "infrastructure projects dominate economic stimulus proposals; repairs to ageing bridges and roads compete intensively with investments in renewable energy sources and electronic medical records". Hence, according to these arguments, the banking sector and the infrastructure industries are inherently interdependent and create specific conditions of possibility for each other.

In this article, my focus shall be on a specific aspect of this interdependence: I explore how banking as such has assumed a position as society's critical infrastructure. Over the past decades, experts in national security have produced a variety of materials to be utilized in such an analysis. As many scholars have argued (Dunn and Wigert, 2004, 2006; Collier and Lakoff, 2008; Kristensen, 2008; Brunner and Suter, 2009), contemporary national security discourse designates various kinds of "infrastructures" (see below) as increasingly "critical" to the modern society, economy, and polity. According to this security discourse, modern nation states are highly vulnerable to breakdowns of their infrastructures, whose functioning should be protected against different security threats from natural disasters to major technological breakdowns (Collier and Lakoff, 2008).

The lists of critically important or vital national infrastructures typically include technical networks and goods like telecommunications, internet, energy, electricity, transportation, food supply, and water supply along with more abstract provisions like governmental functions and emergency and rescue services (Brunner and Suter, 2009: 529). At the same time, many governments and international bodies have also defined banking and finance as one of their critical infrastructures. In 2003, all 14 countries of a policy survey—ranging from U.S. to Denmark, France, New Zealand, Sweden, and others—viewed banking and finance as a critical infrastructure sector (Dunn and Wigert, 2004: 345). Two years later, the number of such countries had risen to 20 (Dunn and Wigert, 2006: 388-389) and in 2008, they totalled 24 (Brunner and Suter, 2009: 530-531). The European Commission (2005) also proposed the financial sector as a European critical infrastructure in its *Green Paper on a European Programme for Critical Infrastructure Protection;* payment services, payment structures, and government financial assignment were denoted as parts of this critical sector (*ibid*: 24). However, the sector was not incorporated in the 2008 Critical Infrastructure Protection directive, where only energy and transport appear as European critical infrastructures (European Council, 2008: ANNEX I).

While the current global economic crisis broke in 2008, many of these governmental and international security measures preceded the crisis. Already in the early to mid-2000s, banking and finance were seen as critical infrastructures that should have been protected from threats against their functioning. Hence, it would be interesting to know whether national security experts anticipated financial crises as part of their infrastructural security discourse and practice and how they expected to manage such crises if they occurred. Starting from these considerations, my article poses the following questions:

1. What is a critical societal infrastructure according to national security experts?
2. How can banking and finance be characterized as a critical infrastructure?
3. Were financial crises anticipated by the national measures that protect banking and finance, how were the effects of such crises to be mitigated, and how were banking and finance to bounce back from a crisis?

The remainder of this article explores these questions by focusing in one national context, the security of Finnish national infrastructures. The choice of this setting is motivated by several reasons. First, the protection of vital societal infrastructures from various emergencies (with historical stress on military threats) is a well-developed security practice in Finland with long traditions and close co-operation among public policy makers, authorities, and companies (Seppinen, 1996). According to a former manager of the National Emergency Supply Agency in Finland, this emergency planning through voluntary contracts can even be named as the "Finnish Model" of infrastructure protection (Purhonen, 2006). The existence of established practices and models then suggests that materials are readily available regarding the protection of banking as one key infrastructure. Second, related to international fiscal infrastructures and threats, the country's economy is often perceived as utterly reliant on foreign trade and the success of Finnish businesses in international markets (e.g., SFVS, 2006; EK, 2013). Finland then could posit a useful case study of the mitigation of the effects of international financial crises in public policies. Third, I have already studied Finnish infrastructure protection practices elsewhere though focusing on the electricity infrastructure (Silvast, 2013) and will draw partly from the same materials and research methods. The article also supplements the Finnish materials with policy papers from other countries and the EU.

The structure of the remaining article is as follows. The next section details the empirical materials and introduces the research method. The results of the analysis are presented in the following section. The final section concludes by discussing the results and considering possibilities for further research.

1. Research focus: National strategies and enactments of infrastructures

One common type of knowledge pertaining to the vulnerabilities of large infrastructures stems from applied technical studies such as systems analysis and simulations of the propagation of infrastructure component errors (Dobson et al., 2007), or analyses about the behaviour of interconnected infrastructures and the characteristics of their failures (Rinaldi, Peerenboom and Kelly, 2001). In studies such as these, the interest typically concerns identifying, quantifying, and then mitigating system-level vulnerabilities to threats (Dunn, 2006: 48). Terminology, while often defined in much technical detail, rarely figures as a research topic in its own right. Yet, according to a number of social science researchers, a key to infrastructural security is more qualitative and found specifically in security practice and *discourse* (Dunn, 2006: 52; Kristensen, 2008; Collier and Lakoff, 2008), i.e., concrete instances of language in the context of their use (Blommaert and Bulcaen, 2000: 448-449). The argument here has been that concepts such as infrastructures, systems, criticality, resilience, crises, vulnerabilities, and threats are not given but have to be enacted to become effective, which then generates "certain conditions of possibility for what security is ... and what security strategies can and cannot be applied" (Kristensen, 2008: 66). This in turn suggests that security policy documents are an important research object to generate new knowledge also about banking infrastructures and their resilience.

Based on these arguments, the article takes its material from security texts, and specifically, a recent Finnish national security strategy published in 2003, 2006, and 2010. The stated origins of the strategy can be found in a heightened awareness of "structural changes in society", "internationalization", and "threats associated with international developments" in the early 2000s (Finnish Security and Defence Policy Report, 2004: 145). To consider such wide-ranging issues, the Security and Defence Committee of the Finnish Ministry of Defence began to reimagine a question that had been afloat for almost a century in Finnish economic defence planning (Seppinen, 1996; see also Collier and Lakoff, 2008): namely, what are those vital provisions without which the Finnish society would not function and how can these provisions be protected against various security threats?

The national strategy that addressed this question was promptly produced in the early 2000s, originally named *The Strategy for Securing the Functions Vital to Society* (SFVS) (2003, 2006) and then *Security Strategy for Society* (SSS) (2010). According to its official designation, the general objective of the document is threefold: to uphold "national sovereignty, the security of society, and the livelihood of the population in all security situations" (SFVS, 2006: 1). To these ends all of the published strategies comprise four related goals. First, the vital functions strategy lists and defines what Finnish society's "vital functions" are. Second, it characterizes the threats against these functions by describing a number of qualitative "threat scenarios" of events that may endanger the functions. Third, the strategy assigns tasks to ministries, and to a lesser extent, to other authorities, businesses, and civil society actors, with the purpose of mitigating the impacts of the hypothetical threats. And finally, it proposes crisis exercises, monitoring, schedules, and new focus areas to implement its considerations.

The specific format of the strategy is a Finnish government resolution. This means that the strategy contains "guidelines" and "instructions" to the elected government that are a sort of a "position paper" and a "preparatory" decision. While resolutions bind the elected government, they do not contain concrete policy decisions and have no direct legal effects (Finnish Government, 2013). Nonetheless, all of these characteristics make the strategy a promising source for examining the protection of banking infrastructures in Finland. Less binding and more loosely structured than a parliamentary decision or a legal text, the strategies provide interesting material to study the expectations that Finnish security experts had at the time of their writing about vitally important infrastructures, the most relevant threats, and the resilience of these infrastructural provisions.

A topic specific to the questions in this article, the functioning of the economy, has been a designated vital function since the strategy's first version in 2003. This is not surprising from a historical vantage point: finance has been identified as a "basic" Finnish societal infrastructure necessary for "national independence" since 1984 (Seppinen, 1996: 100). Indeed, already the earliest Finnish government consideration for economic defence preparedness from 1929 aspired to provide "the arrangement of monetary and credit conditions" during collective emergencies (*ibid*: 21). In the light of my interest in security practices that directly preceded the current financial crises, I will however mainly focus on the strategy from 2006. To my knowledge, this was also the first strategy to appear in English and is online in its own public web page as is the case with the 2010 version (SFVS, 2006; SSS, 2010).

Methodologically, my analysis is loosely based on the sociology of the markets and Science and Technology Studies and their recent considerations on economic agency. In particular, it follows those discussions where the concrete performing of economic actions through market discourse and other practices or tools is the main research object, focusing especially on how people pose problems with the economy, offer solutions to these problems, and attribute meaning to their solutions (e.g., Chiapello and Fairclough, 2002; Boltanski and Chiapello, 2005). Drawing from recent Science and Technology Studies on markets, specific attention can be given to how banking is "enacted" as a critical infrastructure within security texts that problematize the functioning of the economy, with a view to the different interacting "actors" and events that constitute and affect the economic infrastructure in different situations (Latour, 2005: 54-55; MacKenzie, 2009: 20). Figuring as actors or "actants", these artifacts relevant to an infrastructure can take various characteristics: they can appear as subjects that do something, as objects that are attained, as helpers or opponents of an action, as motivations to do something, or as generic objectives or results of an action (Greimas, 1983). According to previous research, infrastructures are assemblages of various systems, peoples, institutions, and equipment on different levels (Edwards, 2003), and the interrelations of these actors tend to become more visible in breakdowns (Star, 1999: 382). The method of analysis proposed above then provides a promising vantage point to analyse banking as an infrastructure and its "infrastructural" failures.

2. The "economy" and threats to its functioning

Defining an infrastructure

To experts in national security, an important initial step of characterizing infrastructures is definitional. That is to say, before the relevant risks can be understood and mitigated, it is of interest to know what constitutes a critical infrastructure in a specific context (e.g., Rinaldi, Peerenboom and Kelly, 2001; Edwards, 2003). Let me begin by quoting three definitions of a [critical] infrastructure, from the United States, the European Union (European Council) and Finland:

> "The framework of interdependent networks and systems comprising identifiable industries, institutions (including people and procedures), and distribution capabilities that provide a reliable flow of products and services essential to the defense and economic security of the United States, the smooth functioning of government at all levels, and society as a whole." (DHS, 2009: 110).

> "An asset, system or part thereof located in Member States which is essential for the maintenance of vital societal functions, health, safety, security, economic or social well-being of people, and the disruption or destruction of which would have a significant impact in a Member State as a result of the failure to maintain those functions." (European Council, 2008: Article 2(a)).

> "The technical structures and organizations which are necessary to provide a livelihood for the population and for the functioning of society." (SFVS, 2006: 16).

The definitions and their emphases are clearly different. For instance, the US definition views the flow of products and services as "critical", while the EU and Finnish definitions designate infrastructure systems themselves as "critical". And whereas the US definition mentions "society as a whole", it lacks consideration of well-being and livelihood, visible in the other definitions. Finally, in the US and Finnish cases, organizations and institutions are defined as part of an infrastructure, but they are not directly referred to in the EU's definition. Nonetheless, in one way or the other, all three texts designate infrastructures as those vital provisions without which the society "as a whole" could not operate (Edwards, 2003: 187). The slight terminological differences indicate that the understanding of such "infrastructures"—albeit not necessarily uniform as I will discuss —may be somewhat more extensive in the Finnish and European policy discussions than the US case.

When looking for a definition of banking and finance as an infrastructure in the Finnish strategies for securing society's vital functions, one notes a peculiarity. The strategies actually refer to the *functioning of the economy*, which is merged in the same section with another function. In 2003, the aggregated provision was called "functioning of the economy and the society" (YETTS, 2003: 22), while since 2006, it has become "functioning of the economy and infrastructure" (SFVS, 2006: 16; SSS, 2010: 36).

If the Finnish strategies literally were programmes of critical infrastructure protection like the US and EU documents referred to above, the definitions would be circular. The 2003 definition would designate the "society" as one of "society's critical infrastructures" and the one from 2006 and 2010 the "infrastructures" as a "critical infrastructure". But this is not altogether the case here. Rather, neither of the strategies is specifically just about infrastructures. As the names of the 2003 and 2006 versions indicate, they are policy programmes about *vital functions.* These vital functions are characterized as "*measures vital to the functioning of the society. Securing the functions vital to society helps maintain national sovereignty, security in society as well as the livelihood of the population*" (SFVS, 2006: 67.)

Tangible provisions like energy networks and water supply, and services like banking and finance, appear in the strategies as elements of vital functions. Yet, they are present as "measures" to attain "vitality" of the society, national sovereignty, societal security and the population's livelihood. To some degree, all of the term definitions of an infrastructure, quoted above, refer to similar broad societal and national objectives. But the Finnish strategy makes this reference more explicit by not choosing the term infrastructure and by talking about more abstract vital societal functions.

Economy as a vital societal function

The 2006 Finnish strategy uses the following definition for the *functioning of the economy* as a *vital function*: "*The functioning of the economy refers to the economic exchange which meets the population's and the business community's basic needs and supports a sufficiently healthy state economy*" (SFVS, 2006: 16).

This economic exchange should contribute to four key goals, also supported by public authorities according to the document (SFVS, 2006: 16). These goals are "economic growth", "employment", "price stability" and "the fair distribution of earnings" (*ibid*). Such are the generic objectives of a functioning economic exchange system, a kind of a "promise" held in this context by the free competitive markets as well as public agencies (Boltanski and Chiapello, 2005: 21).

Thc strategy next specifies which actors and institutions attain these goals. However, finding them from the document is not altogether simple. This is because, as mentioned above, the functioning of *the economy* is considered as the same vital function as the functioning of *infrastructure,* and the difference between the two functions is not always clear. But I suggest that the document's definition of a functioning economy includes at least the following elements (SFVS, 2006: 16-18):

1. The underlying "hardware" of the economy, including money supply, payment systems, and financial systems and services;
2. A functioning public economy comprising efficient budgeting, the funding of key societal institutions, the borrowing of the central government, a surplus state economy, and tax collection;
3. The stability of prices, which is attained by monetary policy, particularly by the European Systems of Central Banks (ESCB), but also nationally in some particular security situations;
4. Financial mechanisms of social security, including the population's insurance coverage and the payment of pensions and other social security compensations;
5. A competent labour force;
6. Research functions and a "first-rate education system" (SFVS, 2006: 16); and
7. Companies "indispensable to the national economy" (*ibid*: 18), and including those responsible for the provision of basic infrastructures, critical goods and services, the production, research and development of high-technology products and defence consumables.

Ranging from tangible technological hardware to the public economy, stable prices, social insurance and social security, labour and nationally important organizational sectors, these elements are obviously diverse.

They also make it clear that "breakdowns" of banking and finance systems could have wide implications or even predispose society to unusual disasters in some cases. If banking and finance are tightly coupled with the above elements, then their disruptions can easily be spread from one sphere to the other—as the current banking and debt crises have perhaps already demonstrated in many countries, especially in countries like Ireland and Spain where the crisis started with the banks and then spread to other systems.

However, there is also a notable omission in the list: foreign trade is not operationalized as a part of a functioning of the economy. Indeed, trade does not appear in the elements even if the strategy notes its importance in several ways elsewhere: for example, "import and export" is "vital ... to the functioning of the business community" (SFVS, 2006: 14) and "Finland is completely dependent on foreign trade in all security conditions" (*ibid*: 52). The effects of such dependence were apparent just a few years later: when the Gross Domestic Product in the euro area fell by more than four percent in 2009, the Finnish national economy followed cue and contracted by eight percent compared to the previous year (Official Statistics of Finland, 2010; Patomäki, 2012: 71). The Confederation of Finnish Industries, a leading lobby of the business community, is now confronting the problem of how "Finland's export success took a downturn especially after the financial crisis" while it is also clear to them that "Finland is dependent on international markets and on businesses that succeed in them and are internationally competitive. Many Finnish businesses are highly internationalized and the world's leading players in their fields" (EK, 2013).

Yet, in the 2006 Finnish strategy, foreign trade appears as a part of another vital though "non-economic" function—*international activity*. This placement and many of the strategy's expressions indicate a tension that has been increasingly relevant in international political economies since the late 20th century (see Patomäki, 2012: 53): the security of a sovereign state has an ambivalent role in open international markets, as the protection of national security could initiate market protectionism.

The safeguarding of the national economy

The document notes the tension between international markets and national security when assigning tasks to secure Finland's foreign trade. First of all:

> "regulating foreign trade is a part of the European Community's common trade policy, in which the Member States exercise joint jurisdiction ...

> Finland's membership in the European Monetary Union (EMU) entails that problems relating to monetary and foreign exchange policies must be primarily solved through the EMU's common procedures." (SFVS, 2006: 27-28).

So, matters of international markets ought to be managed by common procedures among market players. Nonetheless, according to the strategy (SFVS, 2006: 27), national security interests in human health, animal health, plant health, and military supplies can also function as exceptions to this arrangement and motivate import and export restrictions or restrictions to the movement of labour and capital. It seems that in these cases—and the document also invokes the Treaty of the European Union as a justification for this—national security can override considerations of the international market players and their financial exchanges.

A similar shift of objectives is visible in monetary policy considerations, already referred to above. As a member of the Eurozone since 1999, Finland in principle follows the common market's monetary policy and joint measures. These common measures, the document from 2006 stressed, may also be implemented in "serious financial crises and emergency conditions" (SFVS, 2006: 16)—a formulation that did not foresee Finnish policy makers' many criticisms of the Eurozone crisis measures like bailouts (BBC, 2012).

However, the strategy continues by stating that "national arrangements also have significance" (SFVS, 2006: 16). What security strategies could the Finnish document commit itself to beyond European monetary and foreign exchange policies? As it turns out, it can at least regard technical problems caused by a failing finance system, mitigate such failures, and minimize the effects on other vital national functions. Many proposals for increasing fiscal security in the 2006 strategy are therefore inherently operational. For instance, the proposals relate to co-operation among interdependent actors, such as insurance companies and banks, since the safeguarding of finance is seen as essential to the functioning of insurance (SFVS, 2006: 35-36). They also consider technical back-up systems and the payment systems' information security and how these can be maintained in collaboration among different actors (*ibid*: 35). Further attention is given to disaster situations not necessarily due to financial crises, considering how a functioning economy—for example, the collection of taxes and state budgeting—can be managed during what is called "emergency conditions" (*ibid*: 16). Such conditions include military threats like armed attacks, violations of territorial integrity, and international military crises, but also threats to vital infrastructures like energy shortages and any other events that can be understood as a "catastrophe", where the "authorities cannot control the situation with regular [ordinary] powers" (Emergency Powers Act, 2003).

At the same time, there is a short passage that anticipates the internationalization of the financial sector and looming international economic crises. Accordingly, as financial markets become more international and technologically complicated, these transformations should be taken into account when making societal preparedness arrangements (SFVS, 2006: 35). The strategy's imaginative threat scenarios, located in an Appendix of the strategy documents, are the place in which such considerations are elaborated.

Economic crisis as a societal disturbance

One of the key four sections of the Finnish strategies on vital functions is called *threat scenarios*. These are hypothetical, what-if accounts of potential catastrophes that threaten Finnish society's vital functions. The scenarios do not provide quantitative or even semi-quantitative accounts of these catastrophes and their probability or damages (cf. Collier, 2008). Rather, they comprise more qualitative descriptions of threats that are imminent as well as their potential impacts.

In 2003, when the strategy contained ten threat scenarios altogether, the fifth of them was called "economic threats". These threats were primarily against Finnish and European economic growth and included national and international depressions as well as market protectionism, an ageing workforce, risks from the information industries and disruptions of imports such as energy and food (YETTS, 2003: Appendix 2, 5-7). In 2006, among nine scenarios, the third had become "a serious disturbance in the functioning of the economy". The vital functions strategy was reviewed in 2009, where a significant update was required: a response should be crafted to the then newly perceived economic crisis and global fiscal interdependencies and vulnerabilities (Gaia Consulting, 2009: 19). The 2010 strategy raised two different financial threat scenarios: "serious disturbances in the financial and payment systems" and "disruptions in the availability of public funding".

Nonetheless, the 2006 scenario directly preceded the current crises and will be my main concern. The scenario begins by noting that while accidents, terrorist attacks, and "minor environmental accidents" cause notable economic damage at both the individual and the local level and the actual state of war damages national economies, in some cases, the economy itself can become a threat to the society and its vital functions.

The key to economic risks is economic integration. According to the threat scenario, economic integration increases the efficiency and the output of the world economy. However, the same integration leads to interdependency which in turn makes national economies "more vulnerable to various economic crises breaking out in different parts of the world" (SFVS, 2006: 51). Similar unintended effects figure in technological networking of the world economy: namely, networking increases stability but also spreads risks and disturbances (*ibid*).

If interconnected national economies are vulnerable to financial crises that occur in different parts of the world, as the document stresses, then there is a logical solution: the relevant risks could be regulated internationally. The European banking union, an initiative of the European Council meeting on 28-29 June 2012, offers a useful example of this idea. Founded to "restore confidence in banks and the euro, and as part of a longer-term vision for economic and fiscal integration" (European Commission, 2012b), the banking union has suggested several new crisis management measures such as EU-wide rules for banking activities in general and the prevention of banking failures in particular, a single regulator to oversee banking in the EU, and standard European arrangements to protect deposits and prevent panic withdrawals in the eventuality of failing banks. When implemented or even merely raised in a discourse, such measures could doubtless raise confidence in the functioning of an international banking system as the European Commission suggests.

However, such is not the route taken by the 2006 Finnish strategy. Instead, the document views risks and threats as an integral part of the world economy. Moreover, it characterizes—and perhaps, in effect, normalizes—the occurrence of economic crises by placing them in the context of the "business cycle":

> "Business cycles characterise economic development even in normal conditions. Underlying factors often include changes in the demand or production conditions of commodities, which can seriously impact the economic growth prospects of different countries. The consequences of these phenomena are almost immediately witnessed in the world economy through foreign trade or on the financial market. When aggravated, various structural imbalances in the world economy may result in a serious recession." (SFVS, 2006: 51).

While such an outcome—a serious recession—does not threaten society's vital functions directly, the resulting political imbalance may do so according to the strategy (SFVS, 2006: 51). However, later on, it also notes the impacts that economic crises have on the state's ability to gain revenue, on national infrastructures, and on economic activities at large (*ibid*). These impacts are in line with the broad operationalization of the functioning of the economy, described in previous sections.

At the same time, while the 2006 strategy managed to anticipate an economic crisis and even many of its general effects, it did not associate a crisis with the European markets. Instead, several other triggers of an economic crisis were raised, including a "United States massive trade deficit" (SFVS, 2006: 51), the internationalization of Finnish banks and insurance companies, technical and operational problems with banking and insurance, the uncertainties of the information technology industry, the increasingly networked and international logistic systems, animal-plant epidemics and interruptions of energy imports.

The Eurozone, in turn, was viewed as a means of risk mitigation: "Finland's memberships in the EU, as well as the European System of Central Banks (ESCB), have increased economic growth and the stability of the financial market" (SFVS, 2006: 51). This account precedes the current crises, but it is important to stress that a similar rationale has not become less important in more recent discussions. For example in June 2013, the Finnish Minister for European Affairs and Foreign Trade, Alexander Stubb (2013), stated how "the euro has brought the Finnish economy unprecedented stability. Due to recent improvements [EU-wide policy coordination, new European legislation, and the banking union], the Eurozone has even better conditions for facing crises in the future." His claims were promptly contested (Niskakangas, 2013; Patomäki, 2013), and a brief remark in the 2003 vital functions strategy, but not in the subsequent versions, should also be invoked for comparison: "a financial crisis of the Finnish state and companies operating in Finland may only emerge as part of a broader European financial crisis" (YETTS, 2003: Appendix 2, 6).

Nonetheless, the line of thinking in the 2006 strategy is more straightforward than the last proposition suggests. The Eurozone increases stability, while other "foreign" world markets contribute to efficiency at the expense of increasing risks. In summary, then, there may be more than one kind of an international market that affects the stability of the economy as a vital societal infrastructure according to the present analysis.

A final notable omission pertaining to the 2006 Finnish strategy should be mentioned. Even if it is a strategy about society's vital functions, and by implication about national sovereignty, the livelihood of the population, and public security, there are few details about what happens should the Finnish banking system fail: what kinds of disasters could this failure pose and how would banking and its users bounce back from such a disruption?

Unlike the European banking union, the Finnish strategy, for example, does not raise depositors' panic withdrawals as an issue or try to mitigate such collective panics. At the same time, Finnish banks had already confronted issues during the severe recession of the early 1990s when banks could not make loans and several companies went bankrupt as an effect (Patomäki, 2012: 57). Yet, such serious disruptions to businesses are not considered in the context of a financial crisis in the 2006 document—reflecting a lack of institutional learning.

Also, the notion of resilience—increasingly popular in international disaster discourses since the mid-2000s and designating a vital capacity of a system, community, or society to adapt to and survive an external shock (Manyena, 2006: 446)—is not mentioned in the 2006 Finnish strategy. While the 2010 edition does raise this concept, it is viewed as "psychological resilience to crisis", which is a matter of education, parenting, religion, and culture, but not as resilience of the financial system (SSS, 2010: 51-52). Financial matters are then mostly excluded from everyday life, its disasters and resilience. The rationale for such a generic perspective is only partly made explicit; accordingly, the strategies are about threats that "fall between" the security of an individual and global insecurities, and such in-between threats mostly concern the state, the society, and the population at large (SFVS, 2006: 9). Yet, that such separate societal scales from "micro" to "macro" exist as entities is not self-evident as many social scientists have said (e.g., Pollock & Williams, 2009: 103; Patomäki, 2012: 36). The 2006 strategy also raises this argument, namely, that the said levels are "interdependent" and have "no clear boundary" between them (SFVS, 2006: 9), but then it arguably draws these same boundaries by considering only specific kinds of disasters rather than others in the context of protecting the banking infrastructure.

All in all, the strategy from 2006 and also the other versions are not very well-vested in terminology about disaster, crisis, or resilience to a financial crisis. The strategies outline scenarios that threaten the society as a whole, and find intricate interdependencies between various vital infrastructures or functions, but this work remains relatively hypothetical rather than dealing with concrete damages, their perception, and post-disaster recovery. The ways in which banking and financial crises affect individuals' lives and how exactly they could cause public distress fall outside the scope of the strategies and are not considered in any depth.

3. Discussion and conclusions

This exploratory article studied the protection of the banking system as a critical societal infrastructure. It focused on a particular Finnish policy practice: government resolutions that concern society's vital functions and their protection against security threats. In these resolutions, the functioning of the economy has been deemed Finnish society's vital function since 2003 and economic crises were anticipated as a major threat scenario in 2003, as well as 2006, immediately preceding the current global crisis.

The article was based on a textual analysis of the 2006 strategy and a less structured reading of the other versions and international policy documents. Based on this rather exploratory analysis, the notion of a critical infrastructure may still provide a relevant starting point to consider banking and its resilience. In particular, terminology has been developed by many different countries and bodies creating opportunities for comparisons. According to this article, Finnish policies are not limited to considering banking, finance, or even just infrastructures, but consider the whole economy and its functioning as a *vital societal function*. From such an extensive premise, the economy relates to concrete material technologies and systems as well as social security, companies, public policies (e.g., taxation, budgeting), price stability, labour and other components, all of which are tightly coupled to the stability of finance and banking. The current banking and debt crises have already made such interconnections and their effects are visible in many countries.

At the same time, while the national security texts invoked in the present analysis displayed rich definitions and even anticipated economic crises and some of their effects on a broad scale, the crises' triggers were not foreseen in as much depth. Applying a qualitative, scenario-based approach to national security, the strategy gave prominence to threats against economy that were topical in the mid-2000s, from animal epidemics to energy import disruptions. The technical aspects of finance—for example, the dependence of banking and insurance on electronic computer networks—were also given relative consideration. Meanwhile, the possibility of a European crisis was largely left unaccounted in the document. In fact, on the contrary, the European market was seen as an economic and efficient means of stabilizing financial systems, a view still held in some prominent Finnish public discussions.

The level of abstraction in the security documents places yet other important bounds for their analysis. Their stated level concerns the society, the state, and the population as a whole, and only a few specific details are given about the experiencing of a failing banking system. Social crises and disasters like panic withdrawals, lack of access to bank loans, major bankruptcies, public insecurity or public protesting are hinted at in the strategies, but their detailing would provide further insights into the failure of banking as a critical societal infrastructure. Discussing such matters in more depth then requires different materials than those invoked in the present article.

Finally, the method used in this article poses some limitations that should be acknowledged when considering the results. Overall, I have provided merely a close-up of an emblematic document on a broader field of policy practices. The methodological focus has been on security policy as a discourse, and therefore, I have paid more attention to the articulation of financial risk than to its measurement: that is to say, to those statistics, price estimations, computer simulations, and other measurements and calculations that could be crucial for invoking economic issues as threats or crises to begin with. However, the materials I deployed are visibly short on numbers, making it difficult to explore the quantitative aspects of fiscal risks in the present article. Indeed, other scholarship on risks might suggest that these security documents invoke financial crises as an "incalculable" risk precisely because of the difficulties in foreseeing their exact probabilities and damages, requiring different rational risk assessment methods (see Collier, 2008).

A second point requiring further study concerns historical contextualization. My focus has been on contemporary policies and their discourse; at the same time, the ways in which finance and banking emerged as a security problem and a vital societal infrastructure in Finland have not been considered in this article and would warrant further attention (Collier and Lakoff, 2008). Such considerations could, for example, look further into the military and civil protection of credit and monetary arrangements and the problematic of these protections during pivotal events (Seppinen, 1996), such as World Wars, energy crises, or the detachment of currencies from the gold standard. All in all, many governments have identified the criticality of banking and finance as a societal infrastructure during the past decades and beyond. This article indicates that the documents produced by their initiatives and the rich problematic within these documents would offer promising materials for future studies.

Notes

[1] An earlier version of this article was presented at the European Sociological Association's Disaster, Conflict and Social Crisis Research Network (DCSCRN) Interim Conference: 'The Debt Crisis in the Eurozone (EZ): Social Impacts", Mytilene, Greece, 13-14 September 2012. I acknowledge all the suggestions of the participants and am especially grateful to Dr. Nicholas Petropoulos for his comments and suggestions. I also acknowledge with thanks the comments of Vincent Ialenti.

References

Abele-Wigert, I. and Dunn, M. (2004). *International CIIP handbook 2004: An inventory and analysis of protection policies of fourteen country,* Zürich: ETH, Swiss Federal Institute of Technology.

Abele-Wigert, I. and Dunn, M. (2006). *International CIIP handbook 2006: An inventory of 20 national and 6 international critical information infrastructure protection policies,* Zürich: ETH, Swiss Federal Institute of Technology.

BBC (2012). Finland threatens eurozone bailout plans, 2 July 2012, Available: http://www.bbc.co.uk/news/world-europe-18675496 [20 September 2013].

Blommaert, J. and Bulcaert, C. (2000). 'Critical discourse analysis', *Annual Review of Anthropology,* vol. 29, pp. 447-466.

Boltanski, L. and Chiapello, E. (2005). *The new spirit of capitalism,* London—New York: Verso (French original 1999).

Brunner, E. and Suter, M. (2008). *International CIIP handbook 2008/2009: An inventory of 25 national and 7 international critical information infrastructure protection policies,* Zürich: ETH, Swiss Federal Institute of Technology.

Chiapello, E. and Fairclough, N. (2002). 'Understanding new management ideology: A transdisciplinary contribution from critical discourse analysis and new sociology of capitalism', *Discourse & Society*, vol. 13, no. 2, pp. 185-208.

Collier, S. (2008). 'Enacting catastrophe: Preparedness, insurance, budgetary rationalization', *Economy and Society*, vol. 37, no. 2, pp. 224-250.

Collier, S. and Lakoff, A. (2008). 'The vulnerability of vital systems: How critical infrastructures became a security problem', in Dunn Cavelty, M. and Kristensen, K. S. (eds) *Securing 'the homeland': Critical infrastructure, risk and (in)security,* London: Routledge, pp. 17-39.

DHS (U.S. Department of Homeland Security) (2009). National

infrastructure protection plan: Partnering to enhance protection and resiliency, Available: http://www.dhs.gov/national-infrastructure-protection-plan [20 September 2013]

Dobson, I., Carreras, B., Lynch, V. and Newman, D. (2007). 'Complex systems analysis of series of blackouts: Cascading failure, critical points, and self-organization', *Chaos*, vol. 17, no. 2.

Dunn, M. (2006). 'Understanding critical information infrastructures: An elusive quest', in Dunn, M. & Mauer, V. (eds.) *International CIIP handbook 2006, Vol. II: Analyzing issues, challenges and prospects*, Zürich: Center for Security Studies, pp. 27-54.

Edwards, P. (2003). 'Infrastructure and modernity: Force, time and social organization in the history of sociotechnical systems", in Misa, T., Brey, P. and Freeberg, A. (ed.) *Modernity and technology,* Cambridge, Massachusetts: MIT Press, pp. 185-225.

Edwards, P., Bowker, G., Jackson, S. and Williams, R. (2009). 'Introduction: An agenda for infrastructure studies', *Journal of the Association for Information Systems*, vol. 10, no. 5, pp. 364-374.

EK (Confederation of Finnish Industries) (2013) *Suomi maailmantaloudessa* ('Finland in the world economy'), Avail-able: http://www.ek.fi/ek/fi/yritysten_kv_toiminta/yritykset_maailmantaloudessa/suomi_maailman taloudessa.php [20 September 2013]

Emergency Powers Act (2003). 1080/1991, amendments up to 696/2003 included. Unofficial translation by the Ministry of Justice, Finland, Available:
http://www.finlex.fi/en/laki/kaannokset/1991/en19911080.pdf
[22 October 2013]

European Commission (2005). *Green paper on a European programme for critical infrastructure protection*, COM(2005) 576 final.

—. (2012a). *"Connecting Europe"—business leaders and policy-makers strongly support the Commission's 50 billion plan for strategic infrastructure investment in transport, energy and internet*, Press release, Available: http://europa.eu/rapid/press-release_IP-12-1046_en.htm [20 September 2013].

—. (2012b). *A banking union for Europe*, Available:
http://ec.europa.eu/news/eu_explained/120626_en.htm [20 September 2013].

European Council (2008). *On the identification and designation of European critical infrastructures and the assessment of the need to improve their protection,* Directive 2008/114/EC.

Finnish Government (2013). *Periaatepäätös* ("Resolution"), Available:
http://valtioneuvosto.fi/toiminta/ periaatepaatokset/lisatietoa/fi.jsp [20

September 2013].

Finnish Security and Defence Policy Report (2004). Prime Ministers' Office: Publications 18/2004, Available: http://www.defmin.fi/files/311/2574 [20 September 2013].

Gaia Consulting (2009). YETT-strategian arviointi ('Evaluation of the YETT strategy'), written by T. Raivio, H. Lonka, and J. Lunabba, Helsinki: Gaia Consulting.

Graham, S. and Marvin, S. (2001). *Splintering urbanism: Networked infrastructures, technological mobilities and the urban condition,* London: Routledge.

Greimas, A. J. (1983). *Structural semantics: An attempt at a method,* Lincoln—London: University of Nebraska Press (French original 1966).

Kristensen, K. S. (2008). 'The absolute protection of our citizens: Critical infrastructure protection and the practice of security', in Dunn Cavelty, M. and Kristensen, K. S. (ed.) *Securing 'the homeland': Critical infrastructure, risk and (in)security*, London: Routledge, pp. 63-83.

MacKenzie, D. (2009). 'Ten precepts for the social studies of finance', in MacKenzie, D. (ed.) *Material markets: How economic agents are constructed,* Oxford: Oxford University Press, pp. 8-36.

Manyena, S. B. (2006). 'The concept of resilience revisited', *Disasters*, vol. 30, no. 4, pp. 433–450.

Niskakangas, H. (2013). 'Ministeri Stubb ei tunne euroalueen tila' ('Minister Stubb does not know the state of the Eurozone'), *Helsingin Sanomat*, Opinion, 28 June 2013, p. B8.

Official Statistics of Finland (2010). Quarterly national accounts [e-publication]. ISSN=1797-9765. 4th quarter 2009, Gross domestic product contracted by 7.8 per cent last year. Helsinki: Statistics Finland. Available: http://tilastokeskus.fi/til/ntp/2009/04/ntp_2009_04_2010-03-01_kat_001_en.html [22 October 2013]

Patomäki, H. (2012). *Eurokriisin anatomia: Mitä globalisaation jälkeen?* ('The anatomy of the euro crisis: What follows globalization?'), Helsinki: Into.

—. (2013). 'Euron myötä on ajauduttu kurimuksen partaalle' ('The euro has led us to an edge of the maelstrom'), *Helsingin Sanomat*, Opinion, 28 June 2013, p. B8.

Pollock, N. and Williams, R. (2009). *Software and organisations: The biography of the enterprise-wide system or how SAP conquered the world,* London: Routledge.

Purhonen, M. (2006). 'Toimintaympäristön muutoksista huolimatta energia-alan huoltovarmuus on edelleen hyvä' ('In spite of the shifting working environment, the security of supply of the energy sector is still good'), in *Voimatalouspooli 50 vuotta* ('Power Economy Pool 50 Years'), Helsinki: Puolustustaloudellinen suunnittelukunta (Finnish Economic Defence Planning Authority) and Voimatalouspooli (Power Economy Pool), pp. 6-7.

Rinaldi, S., Peerenboom, J. and Kelly, T. (2001). 'Identifying, understanding, and analyzing critical infrastructure interdependencies', *IEEE Control Systems*, vol. 21, no. 6, pp. 11-25.

Seppinen, I. (1996). *Ahdinkoajan varalle: Taloudellinen puolustusneuvosto ja puolustustaloudellinen suunnittelukunta huoltovarmuuden kehittäjänä 1929-1955-1995* ('For times of distress: The Economic Defence Council and the Economic Defence Planning Authority as developers of security of provision 1929-1955-1995"), Helsinki: Puolustustaloudellinen suunnittelukunta (Finnish Economic Defence Planning Authority Authority).

SFVS (The Strategy for Securing the Functions Vital to Society) (2006). Finnish government resolution 23 November 2006, authored by the Security and Defence Committee of the Finnish Ministry of Defence and published by Finnish Ministry of Defence, Available: http://www.defmin.fi/files/858/06_12_12_YETTS__in_english.pdf [20 September 2013].

Silvast, A. (2013). *Anticipating interruptions: Security and risk in a liberalized electricity infrastructure*, Doctoral thesis, University of Helsinki, Department of Social Research, Sociology, Helsinki: Helsinki University Print Unigrafia.

SSS (Security Strategy for Society) (2010). Finnish government resolution 16 December 2010, authored by the Security and Defence Committee of the Finnish Ministry of Defence and published by Finnish Ministry of Defence, Available: http://www.yett.fi/en/materials/doc_download/26-security-strategy-for-society [20 September 2013].

Star, S. L. (1999). 'The ethnography of infrastructure', *American Behavioral Scientist* vol. 43, no. 3, pp. 377-391.

Stubb, A. (2013). 'Ilman euroa Suomen asema olisi paljon huonompi' ('Without euro, the position of Finland would be much worse'), *Helsingin Sanomat*, Guest Editorial, 26 June, p. A5.

Van Der Vleuten, E. (2004). 'Infrastructures and societal change: A view from the large technical systems field', *Technology Analysis & Strategic Management*, vol. 16, no. 3, pp. 395-414.

YETTS (Yhteiskunnan elintärkeiden toimintojen turvaamisen strategia) (2003). ('The strategy for securing the functions vital to society'), Finnish government resolution 27 November 2003, authored by the Security and Defence Committee of the Finnish Ministry of Defence and published by Finnish Ministry of Defence, Available: http://www.mpkl.fi/mpkl/mpklweb.nsf/0/B97732D883A27941C225733E00576D8B/$FILE/YhtkunnanToimintTurvStrategia.pdf [20 September 2013].

CHAPTER TWENTY

INFO-COMMUNICATION GLOBALIZATION AND DIGITAL TAX PAYMENTS CULTURE: THE GREEK CRISIS AND THE GLOBAL INFO-CASH

GEORGE K. GANTZIAS
UNIVERSITY OF THE AEGEAN

Abstract

The internet has radically changed how cultural organizations, political parties, banks and tax systems interact with their citizens/customers and manage their everyday operations systems. Digital transactions have changed how tax systems operate and governments function in the recent cultural and economic crisis. Mobile contactless payments together with plastic credit and debit cards are the main drivers to develop the digital payments culture in our everyday transactions. Both mobile phones, as "digital wallets", and cloud-computing networks have changed how businesses operate, banking systems function and people live. Digital tax payments culture together with the domination of digital technologies in a free-market economy transform how the tax system processes information payments and how mobile money operates as a transparent, accountable and reliable system of payments in our everyday life. This chapter examines digital transactions culture and mobile payments in info-communication globalization. It defines the Info-communication Landscape, digital payments culture and the multicultural payment model "Code of Digital Transactions" (CO.D.TRA.). It analyses the role of bitcoin and cyberlaundering and defines info-communication globalization during a cultural and economic crisis. It describes the Greek crisis and introduces the CO.D.TRA and the digital form of the "Global Info-Cash" (GIC). Finally, it proposes the "Digital Tax Payments Culture" (D.T.P.C) as a three-pronged action programme to introduce the multicultural payment model CO.D.TRA and the digital form of money (GIC) as a practical way for countries such as Greece, Spain, Italy, Portugal, Cyprus and France to emerge from the crisis.

Introduction: Digital payments culture in info-communication globalization

Digital technologies have reshaped how humanity communicates and how people make transactions in a global free-market society. The internet is "changing everything" in our traditional cultural, social, political and economic systems. The info-communication industry together with the Info-Com PC technologies, mobile phones, digital banking services and digital tax payments systems have radically reformed the traditional tax and banking systems (Gantzias, 1998; Gantzias, 2001). Technological options should be translated into social political and economic realities in South European countries. Most European countries have been living with plastic credit cards and other payment systems. Mobile contactless payments, together with plastic credit and debit cards, are the main drivers to develop the digital payments culture in our everyday transactions. Banking institutions have started to modernize their traditional systems by digitalizing their services and creating cloud-computing applications. Both mobile phones, as "digital wallets", and cloud-computing networks have changed how businesses operate, banking systems function and people live. Digital tax payments culture together with the domination of digital technologies in a free-market economy transform how the tax system processes information payments and how mobile money operates as a transparent, accountable and reliable system of payments in our everyday life.

Mobile payments are part of our everyday life. Mobile money derives from a 50-year conjuring of a value chain in the act of payment: creating new payment systems to foster "efficiencies" and generate revenue through transaction fees in the info-communication landscape. Citizens, working in the "payments info-communication landscape" use that phrase to refer to a new world of retail digital payment systems—everything from credit cards based on magnetic stripe technology, to radio-frequency ID chips used to store value and/or access a remote account, to mobile phones used in various ways, i.e., carriers of money, airtime minutes, text messages and other things that can be transferred from mobile-to-mobile as a form of currency, to mobile point-of-sale terminals reverse-engineered to serve as a channel for banking and financial services. No company or a country can afford to ignore the new phenomenon of digital money, the Global Info-Cash (GIC). Every transaction and tax system needs to "go digital" in the info-communication globalization. Digital content about citizens has been exploding. More than 90% of digital content has been created in the last three years. According to "The Info-Communication Landscape, CO.D.TRA and the GIC" research report, "by 2020 there will be more than 5 billion internet users globally, and the internet economy will have reached $7 trillion in the G-20 countries".

The internet is becoming interactive and participatory in the recent crisis. IBM predicts that one trillion devices will be connected to the internet by 2015. The internet has radically changed how cultural organizations, political parties, banks and tax systems interact with their citizens/customers and manage their everyday operations systems. Digital transactions have changed how tax systems operate and governments function in recent cultural and economic crisis. National tax systems need to develop a "smart" digital regulatory mechanism and a digital payments culture, i.e., the "Digital Tax Payments Culture" (D.T.P.C). Within this context, the D.T.P.C is more than just a "smart" regulatory mechanism of paying taxes and making transactions: the idea is that by using the "Code of Digital Transactions" (CO.D.TRA) and the "Global Info-Cash" (GIC), everyone has the opportunity to develop a digital payments culture such as D.T.P.C that empowers citizens/consumers to trust their tax payment and banking systems and make mobile payments at anytime and anywhere. Therefore, the emergence of a multicultural payment model such as CO.D.TRA and the production of the digital form of money such as GIC together with a digital payment culture such as D.T.P.C are likely to create new opportunities in countries such as Greece, Spain, Italy, Portugal, Cyprus and France to fully digitalize their tax- payments systems and make their regulatory mechanisms more reliable, accountable and transparent in a global free-market economy.

This chapter examines digital transactions culture and mobile payments in info-communication globalization. It outlines the digital transformation of banking systems and financial services. It defines the Info-communication Landscape, digital payments culture and the multicultural payment model CO.D.TRA. It analyses the role of bitcoin and cyberlaundering and defines info-communication globalization at times of a cultural and economic crisis. It introduces Info-Communication Regulatory Culture (ICRC) and describes the Greek crisis. It analyses the CO.D.TRA and the digital form of GIC in cultural and economic crisis. Finally, it proposes the "Digital Tax Payments Culture" (D.T.P.C) as a three-pronged action programme to introduce the multicultural payment model CO.D.TRA and the digital form of money GIC as a practical way for countries such as Greece, Spain, Italy, Portugal, Cyprus and France to emerge from the crisis.

Digital payments culture and mobile phones as "digital wallets": Payments in the info-communication landscape

The *Net-generation's* digital payments culture is here. We live in a global info-communication landscape where mobile devices and mobile payments have exponentially increased in free-market economies. According to "The Info-Communication Landscape, CO.D.TRA and the GIC" research report:

> "The Info-communication Landscape (ICL) is the type of digital space which consists of the digital technology payment systems, cloud-computing services, the multifunctional info-communication devises (all type of mobile phones, computers, tablet PC, etc.) and broadband networks in which all national economic, cultural and political systems become open, transparent and accountable to info-communication regulation mechanisms, and all national-states systems needed to behave according to the logic of multicultural public interest principles both globally and locally."

According to the above report, the future is mobile in the info-communication landscape. ICL is the global digital space where multifunctional Info-Com PCs (i.e., phones, tablets, latops, mobile phones, etc.) are used as "digital wallets". Ericsson predicts that more than 50 billion multifunctional devices (i.e., phones, tablets, laptops, and smart meters) will be connected to the web by 2020[1]. Within this context, card networks are also making investments in innovative firms to keep an eye on potentially disruptive technologies. Visa owns part of Square, which struck a deal with Starbucks to make its mobile-payment service available to 7,000 of the coffee chain's outlets in America. Visa had also invested in Monitise, a mobile-banking specialist. American Express, for its part, has set up a $100m digital-commerce fund, one of whose investments is in iZettle; a Square-like firm based in Sweden, for example, is a "digital wallet" that holds multiple payment cards in a virtual repository (see Figure 20.1). Instead of providing their personal details and card numbers to pay for services and products online, customers just enter a username and a password (*The Economist*, 2012).

Figure 20-1. Global digital payments

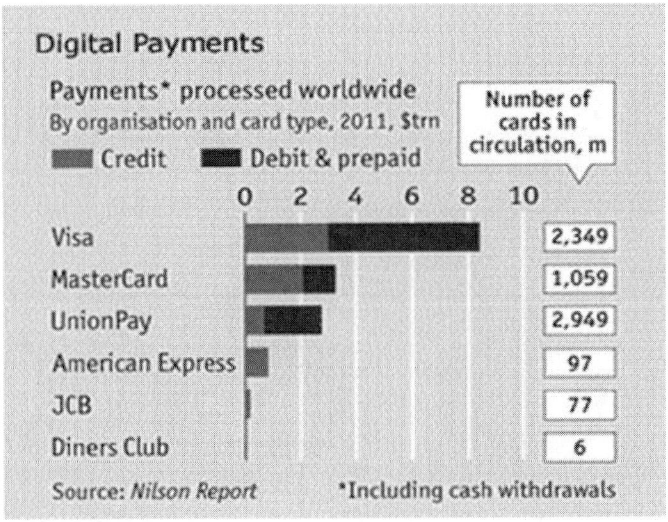

Source: Nilson Report.

The internet together with the domination of digital payments systems has become a vital economic force and a driver of growth in developed and developing countries (see Figure 20-2).

Moreover, according to the *Economist* (2013), non-cash payments are very important factors in a free-market economy:

> "About 280 billion non-cash payments were made in 2010, 7% more than in 2009. The rich world accounts for 80% of these. But the *World Payments Report* estimates that robust growth in emerging markets could have pushed the number of transactions above 300 billion in 2011 (see Figure 20.3). Cards account for 56% of non-cash payments; more than one in three payments are made with a debit card (increasingly chosen over cash for small amounts) in Brazil and USA. As the use of cheques falls, electronic and mobile payments could grow annually by 20% and 53% respectively between 2009 and 2013."

Figure 20-2. Internet in 21st Century: Developed and developing countries

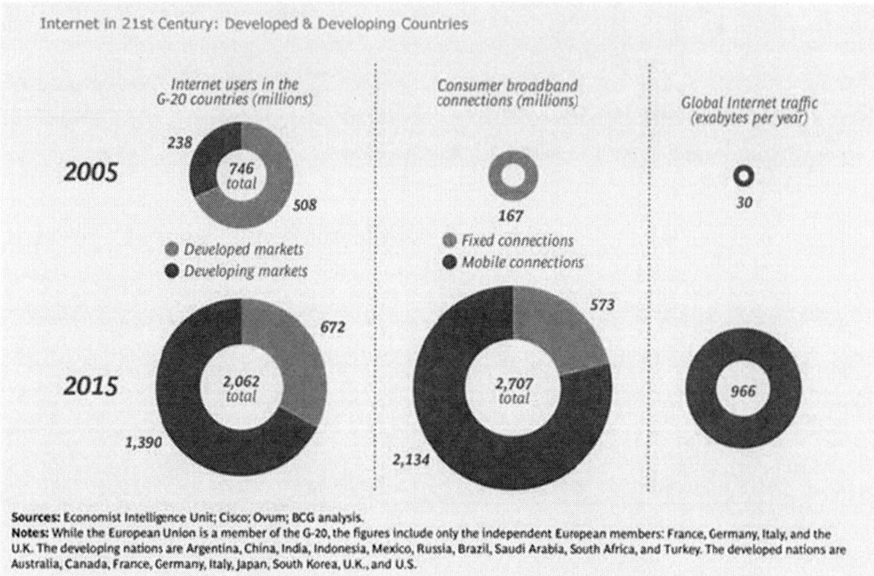

Sources: Economic Intelligence Unit, Cisco, Ovum, BCG analysis.

Benson and Loftesness (2010) pointed out that "advances in mobile technology and the worldwide spread of the mobile phone have encouraged industry participants to add functionality to devices in order to increase "average revenue per unit" (ARPU). New functionalities place higher bandwidth demands on networks and thus enhancing potential for enhanced revenue and the interest of the GSMA in mobile money. Mobile funds transfer is attractive to mobile providers in developing world markets where many people—even non-subscribers—have access to a mobile phone but limited access to banking and financial services". According to "the Info-Communication Landscape, CO.D.TRA and the GIC' research report":

> "Credit-card companies and banks have long collected 'purchasing data' about customer's habits. In digital payments culture, the 'purchasing data' is being put to incredible new uses with the assistance of inexpensive computer memory, powerful processors, smart algorithms, intelligence software, and math that borrows from basic statistics. 'Purchasing data' is about more than just information about customer's habits: the idea is that we can develop a multicultural payment system such as CO.D.TRA which

is subject to customers' needs and multicultural public interest principles in the global free-market economy."

Figure 20-3. Digital Transactions: Global non-cash payments

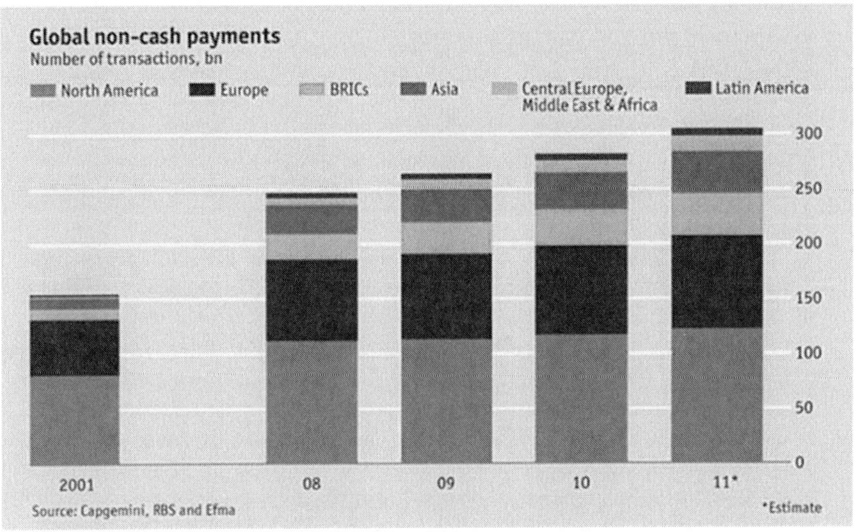

Source: Capgemini, RBS and Efma.

Mobile payments, with mobile phones and "purchasing data" changed traditional payment models (i.e., paper-money payments models) in the global free-market economy. Within this context, mobile payments and mobile financial services (MFS), as the "wave of the future", are creating multicultural payment models such as CO.D.TRA and are introducing the digital form of money such as GIC. In countries such as Greece, Cyprus and Spain, the serious problems of traditional banking infrastructures, the bureaucratic management systems and the lack of paper money to support economic development, growth and investment lead us to suggest that digital phones as "mobile wallets" and CO.D.TRA. are a practical way to emerge from the crisis. Within this context, mobile networks will be an effective way to offer basic electronic payments to consumers by making all payments transparent, reliable and accountable (Gantzias, 2012; Gantzias, 2013)[2].

The digital form of money has penetrated all countries and sectors of the economy. Mobile phones have already been used as digital wallets in some countries. A striking example is Afghanistan, where in 2001 the penetration of mobile phones climbed from 0% to 30% of the population.

As a result, more than 95% of Afghans, not having bank accounts, conduct their daily financial transactions digitally via mobile phones. In Kenya, a company developed software for transferring money via mobile phone (i.e., M-PESA) (Gantzias, 2010; Mavros, 2011; Gantzias, 2013). The report, *"Connected Agriculture"*, concludes that 80 % of the potential 100 billion euro uplift in emerging market farmers' incomes will be derived partly from the growth of mobile money transfer systems, such as Vodafone M-PESA, which provide farmers with the ability to exchange, save and borrow small amounts of capital as well as take out short-term insurance policies. According to the same report, mobile communications can help to meet the challenge of equipping an estimated 9.2 billion around the globe by 2050[3]

In Sweden and Denmark, most daily transactions of consumers/citizens are digital, and tax services are digitally connected with the cash registers of most companies. In Northern European countries, digital transactions are a routine. Within this context, Sweden has reduced public spending as a proportion of GDP from 67% in 1993 to 49% in 2013. As a result of the digital transaction culture, Sweden cut the corporate-tax rate from 26.3% in 1993 to 22% within 2013. Its public debt fell from 70 % of GDP in 1993 to 37% in 2010, and its budget moved from an 11 % deficit to a surplus of 0.3 % over the same period. This allowed a country with a small open economy to recover quickly from the financial storm of 2007-08. The most important factor that contributed to changing economic performance was the domination of digital technology in payment systems of the Northern European countries (*The Economist,* 2013: 3). Therefore, the domination of mobile payments together with the introduction of the "Digital Tax Payment Culture" (D.T.P.C) and the development of a multicultural payment model like CO.D.TRA are likely to help South European countries such as Greece, Cyprus, Spain, Portugal, Italy and France to emerge from the crisis.

CO.D.TRA to bitcoin in the digital revolution: Cyberlaundering and info-communication regulation mechanisms

The domination of digital technology has contributed significantly to creative destruction in our capitalistic systems. The Harvard economist Joseph Schumpeter defines "creative destruction" as the ability of the capitalist system to adapt to changes in new technologies and markets. The pressures are both domestic and global, as international trade increases and digital technology is placing digital transactions in a free-market economy

(McKnight et al 2001; Gantzias 2005a; Gantzias 2013: 92; www.info cash.gr). Digital technology has affected all sectors of our lives:

- Production sector—digitization of production process of turning raw material into a product that is sold;
- Trade sector—digitization of trade products and services, i.e., financial sector;
- Communication sector—digitization of information, education and entertainment, i.e., cultural industries, creative industries, info-communication industry;
- Everyday economic activities, i.e., cloud-banking services, digital payments, credit cards payment by using mobile phone "tools" and applications; and
- Government bureaucratic systems—electronic tax payments.

The digital revolution is the driving force behind the domination of digital transactions and digital culture in a global free-market economy. The internet has become an ingrained feature of our everyday life, reflecting multicultural characteristics as well as political, economic and social influences specific to individual countries in the info-communication globalization (Castells 2009; Gantzias 2012; Gantzias 2013; www.globalinfocash.com). According to Info-Communication Globalization, Participatory Freedom and the Global Info-Cash (GIC) research report:

> "Info-communication globalization is the type of globalization which is defined by the participatory internet, the global culture, digital transactions, the net generation, the info-communication landscape and info-communication regulative mechanisms and multicultural public interest principles in which all economic, cultural and political systems become open, transparent and accountable in free-market economies."

In info-communication globalization, people want safe digital transactions, trustworthy banking services and a reliable digital payment system. But global regulation of digital transactions is never a popular idea. Emerging technologies, including cloud-computing banking services, will "revolutionize" the digital money process and make it significantly easy for regulators to introduce multicultural public interest principles into a global free-market economy. Certainly, the revolution of digital money and cloud-computing banking services, together with the introduction of transparent, reliable and accountable multicultural payment models such as CO.D.TRA. and regulative mechanisms for producing digital money such as GIC will challenge seriously "cyberlaundering" which is encouraged by the recent introduction of the bitcoin as a global virtual currency in a global free-market economy. Bitcoin is an experimental digital currency created, managed and transferred ("spent"), via a Peer-to-Peer (P2P) info-communication network, over the info-communication landscape via internet users running a specialized computer programme. A bitcoin is a string of numbers generated by a powerful computer network system and is normally stored in computers without any transparent, reliable and accountable global regulatory official mechanism. The Bitcoin can be used as a payment system by any retailer who accepts bitcoins as a reliable payment system (or transferred to any individual running a bitcoin computer programme). As a payment system, the bitcoin, is not regulated by any government or commercial organization and, as such, there is no local or global official regulative mechanism to support each bitcoin. According to the digital payments culture manifesto, the bitcoin will encourage the money laundering process and make it easier for launderers to turn illegally obtained money into clean, untraceable funds.

Nowadays, most mobile phone owners are using cloud-computing services, or email on their phones, to download financial information or a banking application. Cloud-computing services are shaping a transparent and reliable ICL so that customers/citizens can have access to cloud financial services and to facilities such as vast financial data storage and infinite computing capacity. In that respect, if ICL remains an open info-communication public sphere, customers/citizens will be given many more choices and much more info-communication power to access financial services in ways previously impossible or even unimaginable (Beck, 2000; Webster 2005; Gantzias, 2005b; Lametti, 2012: 195-196; Gantzias 2012; Gantzias 2013). The survival of cloud-computing banking services in recent cultural and economic crisis depends on the bank's ability to convince customers to bank online by:

- Restoring customers trust and engagement;
- Developing secure cloud-banking information services;
- Introducing secure services for digital transactions in their info-communication landscape; and
- Implementing the multicultural payment model "Code of Digital Transaction"(CO.D.TRA) in order to introduce the digital form of money, i.e., GIC in global free-market economy.

The CO.D.TRA and the GIG are the driving forces for the introduction of the digital payments culture to the banking system in order to enhance their digital trustworthiness in the eyes of their customers. Cloud-computing banking services, in terms of time, provide a continuous communication and digital payments between banks and their customers, i.e., 24 hours a day and 7 days a week transaction services irrespective of bank holidays, thus avoiding queuing during rush hours and losing valuable time. At the same time, the fact that cloud-computing banking services can provide more specialized transactions services by encouraging and facilitating the active participation of customers who could easily make payments by using cloud-computing banking application programmes as a trustworthy payment system in the info-communication landscape. Digital transactions culture becomes a reality for monetary systems and financial transactions, involving many actors—banks, investors, traders, entrepreneurs, non-governmental organizations, governmental departments, software providers and political parties. This raises obvious questions for the role of digital transactions culture in a free-market economy. As info-communication globalization gets more complex and chaotic, regular citizens/users/ consumers are gaining access to digital banking services, entertainment, information and education anywhere and at any time (Negroponte, 1995; Castells, 1996; Gantzias, 1998; Gantzias, 2005b; Castells, 2009; Gantzias 2012; Gantzias, www.codtra.com). Digital transactions culture makes an important contribution to national economic development and has become more critical with increased global competition, mobile payments, banking cloud-computing services and the info-communication industry[4]. Effective digital transactions culture in a free-market economy is likely to reduce tax evasion significantly, create new digitally-generated jobs and firms, increase overall private sector investment and contribute to the digitization of bureaucratic systems. Digital technologies can also give rise to better diagnostic assessment of economic assets and create transparent and reliable tax systems in info-communication globalization (Tapscott, 1996; Gantzias, 2001; Lametti, 2012: 207-218; Gantzias, 2013).

According to Bosworth-Davies, "it would require a counsel of perfection to require banks and financial institutions to institute a regulative regime which would ensure that the phenomenon of money laundering became extinct forever from commercial life" (1994: 56). The banking industry is strongly associated with high levels of trust related to security and privacy issues in the physical environment. However, this association has been seriously damaged by the recent cultural and economic crisis (Mavros, 2012a; Marvos, 2012b; Mavros, 2013; Gantzias, 2013). The aim of introducing a multicultural payment system CO.D.TRA is not to prevent every instance of tax evasion or laundering from occurring but rather to create a "payment info-communication landscape" as global digital space, making it increasingly difficult for tax evasion and laundering to exist both globally and locally. Within this context, the CO.D.TRA is a multicultural regulation payment model of how digital payment systems in the info-communication landscape will support transparent, reliable and accountable systems for developing a global regulative mechanism in the global free-market economy. The debate about a global regulative mechanism for introducing CO.D.TRA and producing the GIC is about values, not facts. According to this view, when people disagree about a rule that would protect transparency in digital payment systems or increase freedom of choices in using different mobile payment systems, it is because of what they value most, not because they disagree upon evidence. In some of the biggest issues, values and predispositions do play a critical role. At the same time, it is easy to overstate the point. For example, most people's values do not lead to a clear judgment as to whether a regulative mechanism in a global free-market economy is required. Values alone cannot serve as a guide to reduce the level of tax evasion in South European countries. To evaluate how to reduce the level of tax evasion, factual evidence is indispensable. When the evidence is clear, it will often lead people with different values to the same conclusion. If the introduction of the multicultural payment model CO.D.TRA, with the production of GIC, reduces the level of tax evasion and costs very little, people are likely to support it regardless of their party identification; on the other hand, if the bitcoin will produce few benefits, increase insecurity and impose heavy costs, people are unlikely to favor it regardless of their idea about "cyberlaundering". Within this context, "Info-Communication Regulation Culture" (ICRC) should be introduced in order that citizens will be able to make free choices in a free-market economy without relying heavily on intuition, anecdotes, dogmas and impressions. Therefore, a new global tax payment regulation mechanism should be subject to transparency, reliability and accountability of global rules and introduce global multicultural public interest principles for digital transactions by forming the multicultural payment model CO.D.TRA and creating a global digital form of money in the real economy, i.e., the GIC.

The CO.D.TRA (Code of Digital Transaction)—a dynamic payment model

A powerful payment model for changing customer behavior through the use of web and social connectivity is the CO.D.TRA, which is digitally transforming traditional payment systems in free-market economies.

Recently, digital payments are gradually emerging in our everyday life. On 26 February 2013, Neelie Kroes, Vice-President of the European Commission responsible for the Digital Agenda, made the following point:

> "A range of services using standardized technology, widely available in mobile phones like near-field communication (NFC)—supported by proven security solutions and easy billing. Not to build new walled gardens, but as a platform for choice and convenience, at less cost. Member States support our broadband targets; and many of them actively call for a Single Digital Market. Our proposals will help deliver both of those goals…we are now approaching the mid-point of the digital agenda. It's a chance to take all the knowledge and experience gathered in the last 3 years–and use it, focus it on what must be delivered…our target of universal "basic broadband" coverage, by the end of 2013...tomorrow's world is a connected world: no policy-maker, and no industry player, should be making plans on any other basis."

To make use of these opportunities, European governments may need to digitally transform the European economy by introducing new digital models such as CO.D.TRA to effectively manage all European digital transactions in a free-market economy. This includes fostering digital skills of the labour pool as well as improving digital productivity of infrastructure and the attractiveness of the info-communication landscape which is likely to provide better quality of life in our society. It can also involve explicit efforts to introduce digital payment systems and to replace the physical form of money (i.e., paper money) by the digital form of money (i.e., Global Info-Cash) in a global free-market economy (Gantzias 2005a; Castells, 2009; Gantzias, 2013; Gantzias, www.codtra.com). According to Info-Communication Globalization, Participatory Freedom and the Global Info-Cash (GIC) research report:

> "The difference between the physical form of money and the digital form of money in an economic crisis is enormous because a hand-to-hand transaction could be opaque, and thus deprive the state of valuable resources for payment of salaries and pensions, spending on health and education and investments in development projects. Conversely, a digital transaction is unavoidably recorded and thus taxed. Therefore, the digital form of money is likely to reform the way in which we communicate, make transactions and conduct business in info-communication globalization."

Within this context, digital payment models such as the CO.D.TRA are important for producing, managing and transmitting the digital form of money (i.e., the GIC) as a multicultural good (product and service) in a free-market economy. According to Info-Communication Globalization, Participatory Freedom and the Global Info-Cash (GIC) research report:

> "The CO.D.TRA is a multicultural payment model which produces, manages and transmits the digital form of money, i.e., the GIC as unique, authenticated tokens (unique encrypted numbers) for various digital and physical transactions both locally and globally. This type of dynamic multicultural system of payment (i.e., CO.D.TRA) seeks to emulate the functionality of a global ecosystem of the regular physical form of money in monetary free-market economy. In particular, the most important functions of the CO.D.TRA. as a dynamic multicultural payment ecosystem, are the following: (a) authenticate the citizen's use of reliable encryptions system (b) store and transfer value both globally and locally (c) secure the payment process and (d) create specific digital rights transactions which are subject to public interest principles." (Gantzias, 2013: 90, www.codtra.com).

Moreover, according to the above research report: "the comparative advantages of having and using the Code of Digital Transactions (CO.D.TRA) as a tool for introducing the Global Info-Cash (GIC) in a global free-market economy include:

- improved alignment of goals and strategies for digitization between different public sector players and civic/private partners;
- pace and certainty of the response to digital investors and developers;
- scale of the digital development that is simultaneously feasible within the info-communication globalization;
- the quality and conclusiveness of on-line negotiations over how risks and costs will be shared between digitalized public and private entities;
- the availability of a digital mechanism to capture the digital value and digital benefits of global and local investments and developments;
- the unlocking of digital assets;
- increased transactions flexibility, and global profitability, in real and digital transactions markets;
- developing an info-communication platform to introduce the code of digital transactions in property, labour and investment in a free-market economy,
- wider efforts to foster digital transactions in entrepreneurship; and

- better co-ordination, generally, leading to use of the code of digital transactions against real/physical transactions in a real market economy".

Potential inter-banking co-operation and global regulation are aimed to provide greater opportunities for sharing financial content among the banking institutions by using cloud-computing services and the CO.D.TRA. According to the "Info-Communication Landscape, CO.D. TRA and the Global Info-Cash (GIC)" research report:

> "All banking institutions (Investment and Credit Banks) face the necessity of achieving the digital transformation of their management and administrative systems by introducing a dynamic payment management model such as the 'Code of Digital Transactions' (CO.D.TRA). This dynamic payment model is likely to empower bankers to be flexible, accountable and reliable by effectively managing financial transactions both locally and globally."

A practical way for Greece to emerge from the crisis: D.T.P.C, CO.D.TRA. and GIC

In December 2013, the Greek economy was still in recession with an unemployment of 27.8% compared to 21.4% in December 2011, while public sector salaries were cut, taxes were going up, shops and businesses were closing down, and Greek banks were trying to merge in order to survive in info-communication globalization. Digital technology was the main factor for increasing unemployment in the public and private sectors in Southern European countries. For example, in Greece, the emergence of the digital broadcasting systems, together with the domination of digital technologies in all banking services, is likely to lead to an increase of unemployment not only in the traditional public-service television organizations (as the recent closing down of the Greek Public Broadcasting Service ERT, with an estimated loss of more than 2000 jobs); but also in the banking sector, a lot of people will be losing their jobs due to the digitization of banking, broadcasting and telecommunication organizations in global free-market economies. Within this context, mobile payments are likely to prove increasingly popular, over time, especially among younger European consumers who often seem to be surgically spliced to their handsets. The Juniper Research report estimates that the volume of mobile payments made worldwide will almost quadruple over the next five years, reaching over $ 1.3 trillion annually. This will represent just 4% of global transactions[5].

The reform which has taken place in established banking institutions, markets, regulations and legislations is important in order for Greek society to emerge from the crisis. It is incumbent upon financial institutions to keep pace with the time. Within this framework, the payment management model CO.D.TRA is a practical way for Greece to produce, store and transmit digital money (i.e., the Global Info-cash) in order to emerge from the crisis. The crisis in Greece is not only economic but also cultural. Digital technology is challenging the existing global free-market structures by making a reality of the digital transactions both locally and globally. According to Keith Pilbeam (2010), "The credit crunch is a step towards the reduction in the volume of funds available for loans and credit in the economy"; together with the global economic and cultural crisis, Greek austerity measures and the emergency "haircut" imposed on the deposits of the Cyprus's banking system are associated with the monetary chaos (especially in the US and Europe) in a global free-market economy. In that respect, the economic crisis in most EU member-states such as Greece did not happen by accident; rather, it commenced with the launching of the European Monetary Union (EMU) in 1999 with the creation of euro as the global competitor to the dollar (Gantzias, 2012) but without a regulatory mechanism for taking seriously into account the economic, political, cultural and social differences of the EU member states. However, the economic crisis is not only Greek or European but also global (see Figure 20.4)

The global economic crisis is a reality. In the first decade of the twenty-first century, the global credit crisis, together with the Greek, Spanish and Italian financial crisis, marked the start of the visible part of the crisis in the European monetary system. According to Brendan Brown (2010), "Right at the start the monetary union, and indeed even half-year before its formal start (from mid- to end-1998) the founding members of the European Central Bank (ECB) took a series of ill-fated decisions regarding the design of the monetary policy framework". According to The Info-Communication Globalisation, Participatory Freedom and the Global Info-Cash (GIC) research project, "the Greek crisis would have not been so serious if the guiding monetary principle in the Treaty (the monetary clause) would have included not only the goal of monetary stability alongside the aim of price level stability in the long- run but also a set of clear public interest principles for monetary union and a 'regulatory mechanism' for the single currency (i.e., euro)".

Figure 20-4. Global economic crisis: The world in the red—State debt per capita and as percentage of GDP (2011)

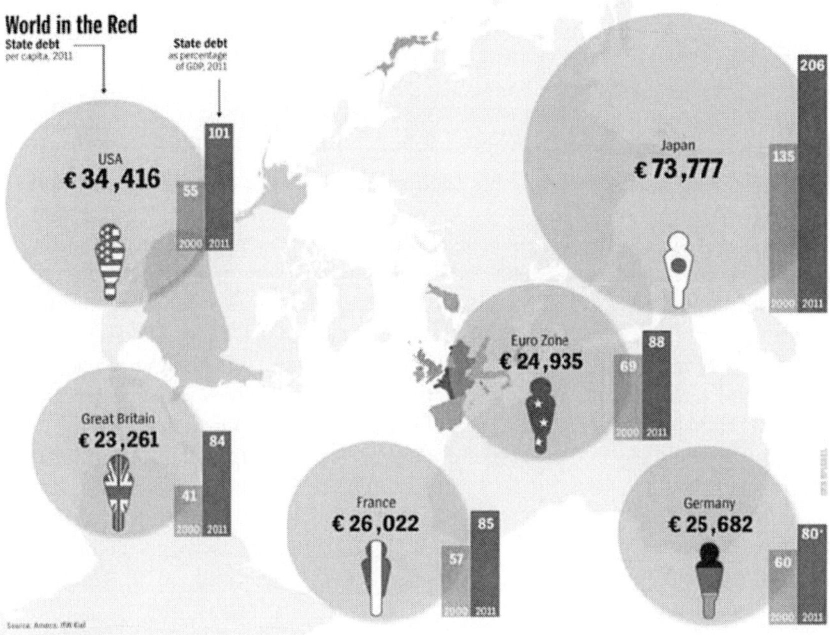

Source: Ameco, IfW, Kiel.

Moreover, according to the above research "the monetary policy was mainly a policy for establishing the euro as a single unit for making easer the transactions in EU markets and not as a cultural asset for achieving political and economic convergence of the EU members". In that respect, the idea of a European citizen-member as a consumer or a business investor in European and global markets, although supported by the advantage of equal participation in the monetary system of a single European market economy, in fact, it could not be implemented successfully without being supported by backup systems, which have the authority to monitor, regulate and manage effectively and, at the right time, the single currency's cultural, political and social characteristics (Gantzias, 2012). As already said, the recent crisis in Greece is not only economic but also has cultural, political and social ramifications.

According to the first president of the ECB, Wim Duisenberg: "The euro is much more than just currency. It is a symbol of European integration in every sense of the word" (Manolopulos, 2011: 46). In 1st

January 2002, Romano Prodi claimed on the CNN: "The euro is not economic at all. It is a completely political step…the historic significance of the euro is to construct a bi-polar economy in the world. The two poles are the dollar and the euro. That is the political meaning of the single European currency. It is a step beyond which there will be others. The euro is just an antipasto" (Manolopulos, 2011: 33). Moreover, Manolopoulos (2011: 55) pointed out "that the time when Greece joined the euro, the total public debt was above the "maximum" of 60 per cent of the GDP, but the EU had watered down this requirement through Article 104c which simply required that the debt be in the process of falling and that it should "approach the reference value (60%) at a satisfactory pace". The European leaders, of that time, focused on spending more energy on meeting the single currency targets (i.e., monetary union, participation of Greece in the European elite club, etc.) rather than formulating a clear set of public interest principles and a regulatory mechanism for achieving actual cultural, political and economic convergence. Nowadays, history repeats itself, and the European leaders are focused on spending more energy in meeting the targets to save the "euro" and the collapsing European monetary system, rather than seriously exploring other possible solutions to the recent crisis, such as the introduction of a multicultural digital payment model, CO.D.TRA (Code of Digital Transactions) and the digital form of money i.e., the Global Info-Cash (GIC) (Gantzias, 2010; Mavros, 2011; Gantzias, 2012)[6].

Nowadays, European leaders and banking managers need to become aware of how citizens/people make transactions and express their fears for the cultural and economic crisis. According to "Info-Communication Globalization, Participatory Freedom and the Global Info-Cash (GIC)" research project: "Greek citizens/people are very disappointed with the existing banking system and they want to see an authentic relationship between 'speaking and being heard, input and output, touching the lever and watching the wheel turn". According to the above research report, "Greek citizens/users/customers do not want merely to be asked their opinions so that bankers can claim that they have asked them; Greek citizens/users/consumers do want to be asked and heard by the bankers when they are making decisions which are affecting seriously the quality of their everyday life". According to "Info-Communication Landscape, CO.D.TRA (Code of Digital Transaction) and the Global Info-Cash (GIC)" research report (Gantzias, www.codtra.com): "the emergence of a net-generation digital transactions culture and the introduction of CO.D.TRA as the multicultural payment model in a global free-market economy are likely to help Greek citizens/users/customers to:

- be accountable for their debt responsibilities;
- understand the serious role of the public interest in the banking decision-making process;
- have digital access to appropriate financial sources;
- be well informed about their financial and humans rights in the financial info-communication public sphere;
- set up an appropriate digital mechanism for structuring and displaying the banking decision-making process;
- articulate their ideas about the future of banking transactions, the credit card transactions and the Mobile phone as a "digital wallet" for everyday transactions; and
- protect their basic transactions rights such as participatory freedom in the global free-market economy, digital access to financial information, validity of transparency in all financial services, etc".

Google, PayPal, Visa, Master, Diners and leading mobile phone operators are moving into the digital transaction free-market economy. PayPal is in negotiations with retails to get them to accept payments from its mobile internet services in store. AT&T, Version, and T-Mobile in the USA are seriously considering investing more than 90 billion dollars in building their own info-communication mobile payment platform (Gantzias, 2013). The Pew Internet Project and Elon University's Imagining Internet Center pointed out that by 2020 most people will have embraced and fully adopted the use of smart-devices swiping for purchases they make, nearly eliminating the need for cash in a global free-market economy (Aaron and Rainer, 2012, www.pewInternet.org). The Payments Council Report, which oversees payments strategy in the UK, has pointed out that using the physical form of money could be a minority activity by 2050[7]. Within this context, the three trends, that is, the Info-Communication Content, the Info-Communication Services and the info-Communication Customers Behavior together with the multifunctional info-communication PC (i.e., tables, smart mobile phones, etc.) are likely to lead to digitization not only of the tax and financial systems but also of payment transactions at a time of cultural and economic crisis (see Figure 20-5)

Figure 20-5. Digitization process of the tax and financial payments system

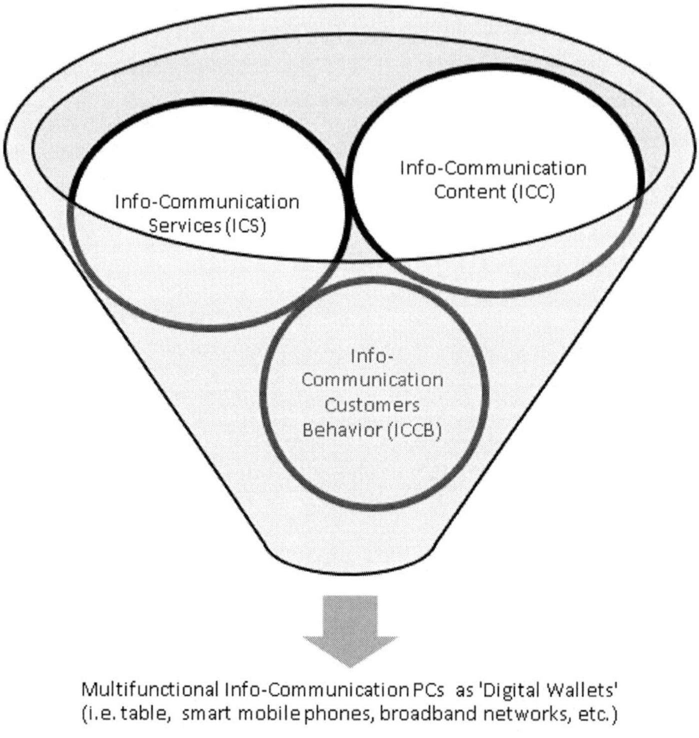

Source: Info-Communication Landscape, CO.D.TRA and the GIC.

Figure 20-5 shows the digitization process of tax and financial payment systems by using multifunction info-communication PCs as "digital wallets" to access tax and financial data in the info-communication landscape. According to the "Info-Communication Landscape, CO.D.TRA. and the GIC" research project, "Digital tax payments culture emerges as a result of the third and fourth generation mobile phones, digital transactions, payments using mobile phones, cloud-computing financial services, etc. Within that context, the digital transactions culture in the info-communication landscape consists of the following:

- "Info-Communication Content (ICC). Digital content such as the financial data will be dispersed across the info-communication landscape, i.e., in houses, outsourcing vendors, cloud-computing providers, third-parties and will be under the control of far more owners, thus securing a transparent and fair competition between investment banks and credit bank institutions, business and info-communication network platforms, and among global business markets. The CO.D.TRA will set up basic public interest principles and regulation platforms for transparency, reliability, accountability and anonymity in digital transactions.

- Info-Communication Services (ICS). The disaggregation of a bank's business process flow, applications and network infrastructure is likely to improve distribution of services by improving business agility, including faster and lower-cost geographical expansions, and introducing mobile payments and social media networks. CO.D.TRA will set up info-communication networks which will enable banks to consider sourcing discrete business processes as info-communication services from third-parties by being subject to global regulation and multicultural public interest principles.
- Info-Communication Customers Behavior (ICCB). Banking cloud-computing services are placing banks in the info-communication landscape. Digital transactions and digital banking are a reality in our everyday life which enables banks to track and analyze everything from keystrokes to customer's behavior. This brings opportunities for introducing CO.D.TRA in order to develop more sophisticated global regulatory mechanisms and to digitally monitor all transactions in an environment of info-communication globalization." (Gantzias, 2013: 93 www.codtra.com).

In the case of Greece, the inability of politicians to understand the digital payments culture, coupled with an unwillingness on the part of Greeks to institute reliable regulative mechanisms in public and private sectors, has been the main reason for the austerity measures and the increased unemployment in the Greek free-market economy. Therefore, we recommend the D.T.P.C, together with the CO.D.TRA, the GIC and the ICRM, as a crucial practical and feasible measure that would help Greece emerge from the crisis.

Conclusion: The Digital Tax Payments Culture Programme as a way to emerge from the global cultural and economic crisis

Mobile phones and digital transactions are very widespread in Greece, and there is no turning back. Web, social media and mobile payments are remaking daily life for Greek people—from how they work to how they pay. In the wake of this digital revolution, the Greek people have new expectations as to how to interact with each other and from product and service providers. Digital transactions and, in particular, the CO.D.TRA payment model are likely to transform Greek people into empowered consumers who want seamless and secure digital transaction experiences tuned expressly to their needs. But are the Greeks ready? Do they have the right infrastructure in place? How can they adapt to the info-communication landscape? Who regulates the regulator, both globally and locally, in info-Communication globalization?

In the case of Greece, the existing political and economic culture needs to be digitally reformed due to the domination of digital payments in our everyday life. According to the "Info-Communication Globalization, Participatory Freedom, and the GIC" research project, this chapter recommends the D.T.P.C for developing "smart" three-action programmes to introduce the multicultural payment model, i.e., the "Code of Digital Transactions" (CO.D.TRA) and create the global digital currency, i.e., the Global Info-Cash (GIC) in a free-market economy. Within this context, the "Digital Tax Payments Culture" (D.T.P.C.) is working as a global dynamic mechanism for introducing digital payment culture, global regulations and multicultural public-interest principles in order to mitigate the impacts of the cultural and economic crisis (Figure 20-6).

The DTPC global regulative mechanism (Figure 20-6) is a way to create a transparent, reliable, accountable and secure digital payment system in the info-communication landscape both locally and globally. Local regulation mechanisms and public interest principles, to control tax revenues and financial transactions, have always been a very complex issue in all countries around the world. Nowadays, the lack of a common global regulatory mechanism to collect taxes, to control free-market prices and to supervise financial transactions are among the main reasons for austerity measures in Greece and the emergency "haircut" that was imposed on deposits accounts in Cyprus. Therefore, a vital corrective to the above problems would be the D.T.P.C. which consists of the following three-pronged action programme:

Figure 20.6. The Digital Tax Payments Culture (D.T.P.C.) as a global regulative mechanism

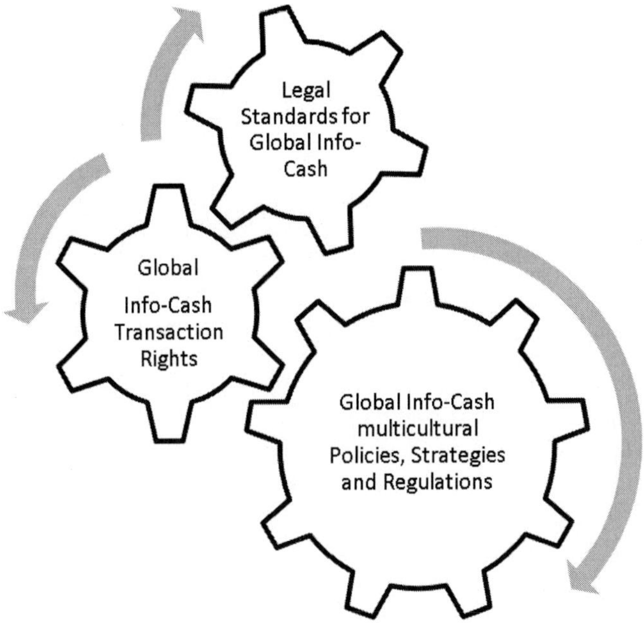

Source: Info-Communication Globalization, Participatory Freedom, and the GIC.

- "Legal Standards for Global Info-Cash" (LSGIC). This action programme aims to create a globally compatible legislative framework in which all interested parties agree to use the digital form of money (i.e., the Global Info-Cash) for multicultural digital goods (products and services). The LSGIC could create a regulatory mechanism both globally and locally in order that irresponsible behavior in the info-communication landscape will be penalised by criminal and economical sanctions.
- "Global Info-Cash Transaction Rights" (GICRT). This action programme aims to create a network of hierarchical regulative mechanisms for managing money as multicultural digital goods (products and services). The production of the Global info-Cash as multicultural digital services should be subject to a specific multicultural set of public interest principles. Digital transaction rights in which all interested parties know where to ask for

support for their problems and where to complain at the local, national, regional and global levels.

- "Global Info-Cash multicultural Policies, Strategies and Regulations" (GINCPLR). This action programme aims to develop a globally compatible framework of multicultural policies, strategies and regulations for switching to the digital form of money both globally and locally. These types of multicultural policies, strategies and regulations are likely to be subject to transparency, accountability, reliability, global public interest principles, participatory freedom and democracy, local and global collective will." (Gantzias, www.codtra.com).

To conclude, we are convinced that if countries like Greece, Cyprus, Spain, Italy, Portugal and France were to introduce the D.T.P.C as a global mechanism and digital payments culture, along with locally-focused and globally-ranged public interest principles, they could cut spending, collect taxes, improve services and products, reduce their debt, be transparent and accountable for their policy making. In short, they would make a big step toward the mitigation and/or prevention of the cultural and economic crises.

Notes

[1] For more information about mobile devices, internet users and mobile payments, research projects, see www.accenture.com and www.internetworldstats.com and www.globalinfocash.com.

[2] For more information, see www.codtra.com, www.globalinfocash.com, www.infocash.gr and www.gantzias.gr

[3] For Research Reports in the Net generation and mobile payments culture, see the following websites www.accenture.com, www.globalinfocash.com and www.codtra.com, respectively.

[4] For more information about the Info-Communication Industry, see the Info-Com PC and digital markets in George Gantzias (1998). *The Info-communication industry: Digital markets*, Global Services, Zenon Publishers; London.

[5] See The Mobile Payments Strategies Briefing 2012-2017, Juniper Research Report, Available: http://www.juniperresearch.com/reports.php?id=446 [15 August 2012].

[6] For more information: www.codtra.com and TV Programme 1+ENA, ERT 3, BitCoin and CO.D.TRA, Gantzias interview, http://www.youtube.com/watch?v=rscaxI1adYI [13 April 2013].

[7] BBC web site: http://www.bbc.co.uk/news/technology-12287009 [27 July 2011].

References

Aaron S and Lee R (2012). 'The future of money: Smartphones swiping in mobile age', Pew Research Center's Internet and American Life Projects', Washington, D. C., Available: www.pewInternet.org [21 May 2012].

Accenture Report, 'Enterprise mobility management services', (n.d.) Available: www.accenture.com [15 August 2012].

—. 'Mobility: Services overview' (n.d.), Available: www.accenture.com [15 August 2012]

BBC (2011). 'Orange customers of everything everywhere get mobile payments', (n.d.) http://www.bbc.co.uk/news/technology-12287009 [27 July 2011].

Beck, U. (2000). *What is globalisation?* Cambridge: Polity press, pp. 17-77.

Benson, C. and Loftesness, S. (2010). *Payments systems in the US: A guide for the payments professional*, Santa Clara, CA: Glenbrook Partners.

Bhabha, H.K. (1994). *The Location of Culture*. London: Routledge.

Bosworth-Davies, R. (1994). 'CJA 1993: Money laundering', *Company Lawyer*, 15, pp. 56–58.

Camdessus, M. (1998). 'Money laundering: The importance of international countermeasures. An address to the FATF at the plenary meeting of the financial action task force on money laundering', Available: http://www.imf.org/external/np/speeches/1998/021098.htm [19 August 2012].

Castells, M. (2009). *Communication power,* New York: Oxford University Press.

—. (1996). *'The Rise of the Network Society'*. Oxford: Blackwell

'Connected Agriculture: The role of mobile in driving efficiency and sustainability in the food and agriculture value chain', Available: http://www.vodafone.com/content/dam/vodafone/sustainability/ 2011/pdf/connected_agriculture.pdf [25 August 2012]

Dicker, P. (2007). 'Economic globalization: corporations', in Ritzer, G. (ed.) *The Blackwell companion to globalization*. Oxford; Blackwell, pp 291–306.

Forrester Research, (2010). 'How US financial services firms should approach interacting with consumers on social web sites', October. Available: http://www.forrester.com/How+US+Financial+Firms+Should

+Approach+Interacting+With+Consumers+On+Social+Web+Sites/full text/-/E-RES57845 [27 August 2012].

Gantzias, G. (1998). *The Info-communication industry: Digital markets, global services*, London: Zeno Publishers.

—. (2000). 'Communication systems in the 21st century: Reform and public interest" in Gantzias, G. and Kamaras, D. (eds.) *Digital communication, new media and the Greek information society: Convergence, e-commerce and portals,* London: Zenon Publishers, pp. 11-56.

—. (2001). *The dynamics of regulation, global control, local resistance: Cultural management and policy*, Adldershot, England: Ashgate, pp. 1-49.

—. (2005a). 'Cultural policy and regulation in the info-communication industry' in Vernikos, N, et.al. (eds.) *Cultural Industries*, Athens; Kritiki, pp. 277-333.

—. (2005b). '*Info-Communication Culture: Diversity, Power and Media', Cultural Technology and Policy Journal*, vol. 1, pp.1-5, Available: http://www.eklogesonline.com/ctpj/en/articles.asp?state=articles [20 August 2012].

—. (2010). 'The crisis is an opportunity to Greece: from euro to info-cash', *Kosmos of Ependitis, Economic Newspaper*, 15 May, p 20.

—. (2012). 'Info-communication globalization and the global info-cash (GIC): A practical way for greece to emerge from crisis' in Liargovas, P. (ed.) *Greece: Economic, political and social issues*, Washington D.C., USA: Nova Publishers, pp. 221-235.

Gantzias, G. K. (2013). 'The Greek crisis & CO.D.TRA (Code of Digital Transactions): Mobile payments and the global info-cash" in Carayannis, E. and Korres, G. (eds.) *European socio-economic integration: challenges, opportunities and lessons learned*, New York: Springer, pp.85-95.

Gantzias G. *The Info-Communication Globalization, Participatory Freedom and the Global Info-Cash (GIC)* (Research Report, forthcoming, www.codtra.com)

—. *The Info-Communication Landscape, CO.D.TRA (Code of Digital Transactions) and the Global Info-Cash (GIC)* (Research Reports, forthcoming, www.codtra.com)

Internet World Stats, Available: http://www.internetworldstats.com [13 January 2013].

Kroes, N. (2013).'Smashing barriers and thinking big', Speech by the Vice-President of the European Commission responsible for the Digital Agenda, SPEECH/13/159, 26 February, Available:

http://europa.eu/rapid/press-release_SPEECH-13-159_en.htm [26 March 2013].

Lametti, D. (2012). 'The cloud: Boundless digital potential or enclosure 3.0?', *Virginia Journal of Law & Technology*, vol. 17, no. 3, pp. 192-242.

Littlechild S (2000). *Privatization, competition and regulation.* London: IEA,.

Livingstone S. (eds) *Handbook of new media social shaping and consequences of ICTs*, London: Sage, pp. 22-34.

Manolopoulos J. (2011), *Greece's 'ODIOUS' debt*, London: Anthems Press.

Mavros, G. (2011). 'Digital money will save us!', *Imerisia Economic Newspaper*, Social Issues, 12-13 March 2011, pp. 38–39, Available: http://www.imerisia.gr/article.asp?catid=12333andsubid=2andpubid=102955157# [25 January 2013].

McKnight, L. W. et al (2001). *Creative destruction.* Cambridge: MIT Press.

Negroponte, N. (1995). *Being Digital,* London: Hodder and Stroughton.

Pilbeam, K. (2010), *Finance and financial markets,* 3rd edition, Palgrave MacMillan, pp. 457-481

Tapscott, D.(1996). *The digital economy: Promise and peril in an age of networked intelligence*, New York: McGraw-Hill.

Terranova T. (2004). *Network culture: politics for the information age*, London: Pluto Press, pp. 39-75.

The Economist (2012), 'Credit-card companies war of the virtual wallets', 17 November, Available: http://www.economist.com/news/finance-and-economics/21566644-visa-mastercard-and-other-big-payment-networks-need-not-be-victims-shift?zid=291&ah=906e69ad01d2ee51960100b7fa502595 [25 May 2013].

The Economist (2013). 'The nordic countries', Special Report, 2 February, pp. 3-16.

Webster, F. (2002). 'The information society revisited, in Lievrouw, A. and Livingstone, S. (eds.) *Handbook of new media social shaping and consequences of ICTs*. London: Sage, pp. 22-34.

—. (2005). 'Making sense of the information age: Sociology and cultural studies', *Cultural Technology and Policy Journal,* vol. 1, pp. 49-66. Available: http://www.eklogesonline.com/ctpj/en/articles.asp?state=articles [13 August 2012].

Xuequan, M. (2013). 'Cyprus president says he was confronted with *faits accomplis* at Eurogroup meeting', Available: www.english.news.cn [17 March 2013].

CONCLUSIONS AND RECOMMENDATIONS

CHAPTER TWENTY-ONE

CONCLUSIONS AND RECOMMENDATIONS

NICHOLAS P. PETROPOULOS
FORMERLY OF THE PEDAGOGICAL INSTITUTE OF GREECE
AND GEORGE O. TSOBANOGLOU
UNIVERSITY OF THE AEGEAN

The social scientists and the historians of the future will determine whether the crisis that the world, the Eurozone and, especially, the peripheral countries of the Eurozone, are now confronting is of the same magnitude as the 1929 Great Depression. The purpose of this Chapter is to highlight some of the principal conclusions and recommendations of the contributors, without getting into the theoretical, methodological and statistical details. This may require a grouping of contributors that does not necessarily follow the table of contents. First, we shall start with the contributors' main conclusions and focus on the "social impacts" of the crisis on society (unemployment, poverty, social welfare, social and institutional trust, personal/social reactions, migration and attitudes, political disaffection and mobilization). In this case, we are fortunate that many of the authors use time-series analysis and, therefore, we are in a better position to assess the impact of the debt crisis. In turn, we shall discuss some macro-intergroup processes (migration, regional fragmentation and emergent conflicts) that may exacerbate the debt crisis as well as the macro-political and economic processes said to have caused the current debt crisis and the accompanying austerity policies. Finally, the authors will discuss overall "crisis-management" and propose solutions and policy recommendations drawn from the contributions to the present volume.

Social and political impacts of the Eurozone debt crisis

Social welfare, unemployment and poverty. A number of contributors (Balourdos, Tsobanoglou, Kanellopoulos & Liakaki) deal with these impacts. Poverty and employment in Greece have undergone both quantitative and qualitative changes following the economic crisis. According to Dionyssis Balourdos who uses a composite index of poverty (income and material deprivation), the poverty and "persistent poverty" rates have gone up; the condition of the traditional poor has worsened: the groups at-risk-of-poverty have increased; we have new types of poverty, especially from the middle classes, and employment no longer provides a safety net for those "lucky" to have a job (see also Stathopoulou and Kostaki).

Without doubt, the changes in the Greek poverty profile are due to several factors aptly dealt with by George Tsobanoglou. These include, among others, numerous business lockouts, high rates of unemployment, displacement of collective bargaining to the individual business level, coverage of only a small fraction of the unemployed by unemployment benefits, the flexibilisation of labour policies and an unprecedented 25% fall in the GDP during the last four years. And all of this, in order to meet the austerity criteria of the bailout system for fiscal stabilization.

The social welfare system itself is threatened by the high unemployment rate and an active/inactive population ratio of about 1:1 when the viable ratio is 3:1. Moreover, the long-term demographic indicators are pessimistic (See Balourdos and Tsobanoglou). Finally, despite the reformist intentions of the "bailout" creditors, the welfare reform proposals become de-legitimized due to the austerity program imposed by the troika, as well as to the deficiencies in the traditional "social insurance" model that will be spelled out below (see Kanellopoulos & Liakaki).

Social trust, institutional trust and sense of security. From a Bourdieuian perspective, these parameters generally fall within the "social capital" domain (See Chtouris & Miller, Chapt. 4). Tsiganou, Stathopoulou and Kostaki have especially dealt with the impact of the crisis on these parameters. Theoni Stathopoulou and Anastsia Kostaki, who study these issues in two crisis-ridden countries—Greece and Spain—observed decreases of "trust in institutions" in 2011 (Round 5 of ESS) as compared to 2009 (Round 4), but increases of social [interpersonal] trust during the same period for both countries. Moreover, they observed, among other things, that a "feeling of being able to cope with household income" was positively associated with both kinds of trust in both countries, whereas "having paid work" impacted negatively on both kinds of trust but only in Greece—reflecting perhaps the greater intensity of the crisis and job insecurity. Using a longer time perspective (2002-2010, 3 rounds), Joanna Tsiganou noted no clear-cut trend with regard to social trust, suggesting that in some cases the social networks were strengthened while in others they were weakened during the crisis. However, with regard to "trust in social and political institutions"—especially toward political personnel—there were clear-cut reductions in trust overtime, that were more marked in Greece than in the EU-27, reflecting no doubt the poor management of the crisis on the part of the political personnel. In addition, Tsiganou observed a shift in the content of "social insecurity", from a fear of crime to a fear and anxiety associated with the employment dimension. The level of trust, as part of "social capital" has an impact on a person's condition and relations, but also mediates the acceptance of reforms in social welfare (see Kanellopoulos & Liakaki) and constitutes a crucial factor that impacts on economic/monetary capital development (wee Chtouris & Miller).

Post-traumatic stress disorder and other stress reactions. The concept of Post Traumatic Stress Disorder (PTSD) has been customarily a phenomenon studied in the context of "natural", "technological" and "humanitarian" (e.g., wars) mass emergencies and disasters. Joanna Bergiannaki and Stefanos Dimitrakopoulos apply the concept/process to the current economic and financial crisis that has struck mainly the Southern European countries. Situations like business closures, sudden unemployment, inability to meet installment payments, unprecedented pressures from creditors, the subversion of life plans and the overnight fall in the quality of life, etc. are hypothesized to create the conditions for the development of PTSD and other personal disorders (e.g., depression). Nonetheless, Bergiannaki and Dimitrakopoulos end with an optimistic note, identifying certain conditions in Greek society (e.g., history, family) that may provide a measure of resilience, allowing the transcendence of the crisis. Undoubtedly, the application of PTSD to the "economic-financial" crisis needs further exploration and specification of conditions that have led some to express stress-disorder symptoms and others to develop growth-types of responses and reactions.

Migration perceptions and attitudes. Classical theories of intergroup relations—either those inspired by intensified economic competition at times of recession (e.g., "realistic group conflict" theory) or those inspired by the authoritarian personality studies of the Frankfurt school—predict increased, direct or displaced ("scapegoat"), hostility during an economic crisis. The impact of the debt crisis has been systematically investigated by Greek social researchers, especially its impact on attitudes toward migrants. Using various concepts of tolerance toward migrants/the "other" (e.g., perceptions of threat, impact of migration on life, culture and the economy) as well as a number of ESS rounds (2009-2011, 2002-2010, etc.), they observed that the attitudes toward migrants of a different "race" or from the "poorer" countries became negative over time (Tsiganou, Kalogeraki, Iliou, and Stathopoulou & Kostaki). In one of these cases

(Stathopoulou & Kostaki), using a cross-country approach, the attitudes were more negative in Greece but not in Spain. The Editors believe that this is understandable in view of the fact that Greece entered the bailout system much earlier than Spain; in addition, Greece signed a series of "Memoranda of Understanding" with the troika and was long before Spain under the austerity regime and reform program. In another study, by Stefania Kalogeraki, the increasing negative attitudes and perceptions over the period under study were observed both for the native "majority" (Greeks) and the migrant ("minority") groups; the latter primarily because of the increasing competition among migrants due to the recession (especially in the construction industry). A related finding is the observation of greater hostility toward homosexuals in 2011 than 2009 (Stathopoulou & Kostaki). This observation, according to the Editors, seems to confirm the Frankfurt School. Whether the above outcomes are the result of the intensified competition due to the recession or an outcome of psychodynamic processes or to both of these processes or even to other factors, it remains to be further investigated, using different tools. Undoubtedly, the empowerment of the fascist-racist Golden Dawn, after its election in the municipal and national government since 2010, the conceptions of racial-cultural continuity and homogeneity among many Greeks and the successive governments' indecision regarding the management of attacks against immigrants during the past few years, in connection with the crisis, may have exacerbated the situation.

Political impacts: the indignados and political disaffection. Alienation from the established political system was a common sequel of the economic crisis in most of the affected countries, though in varying levels of magnitude. Dennis Smith, employing a sociological typology of coping tactics and response strategies following the "humiliation" attendant to the bailout program, as well as relying on a review of Irish and Greek geo-political history in the last 200 years, observed that the Greek response to "humiliation" was more rejecting and aggressive against the troika and the governments who implemented its imperatives than was the case of the Irish response that was more "escapist" and acceptant in nature. However, he notes that the "… complaining in the media about the failings of national politicians in the so-called PIIGS countries, especially in Greece, has drawn attention away from the origins of the present crisis" that actually "lie in the neglectful and sometimes fraudulent behaviour of bankers and allied professions in and around the finance industry". According to Smith, the historical experiences of the two countries since the 1920s and up to the 1970s were crucial in accounting for the differential response to the troika humiliation.

Three other authors (Perugorria &Tejerina, Petropoulos)—using ethnographic, qualitative, and/or quantitative methods—studied more in-depth the *indignados* "movements" in Spain and Greece. Following a political-economic account of the emergence of 15M and a multidimensional analysis of its dynamic properties ("cognitive", "emotional" and "relational"), Ignacía Perugorria and Benjamín Tejerina describe how the Spanish *acampadas* (of *Puerta del sol*) eventually "synchronized" their identities, allowing people with no previous political participation or even with divergent "political trajectories" to form a "community of persons", putting aside old divisive political culture categories. Nonetheless, the authors noted that as the movement decentralized to towns and neighborhoods, it experienced a "steep decrease" in participants that was paradoxically followed by internationalization ("Occupy Wall Street", "99%", etc.). In the case of the Greek indignados (*aganaktismenoi),* Nikos Petropoulos noted a phenomenological convergence of identity, projecting a platform against all parties; however, the author also observed the presence of two political subcultures—an ethnocentric right-wing and a progressive left-wing one—on the "upper" and "lower" Constitutional (*Syntagma)* Square, respectively. Though the Greek indignados "movement" adopted non-violence, it was nonetheless aggressive and vindictive, as revealed by an analysis of slogans, banners and graffiti, confirming Smith's perceptive analysis regarding the differential response strategies. The Greek indignados (GIs) had higher levels of education, reported more difficulties in making ends meet (compared to non-indignados) and a high percentage of them came from the two established parties (according to 2009 elections). The author has some doubts if the indignados, as a whole, can constitute a spontaneous collective phenomenon since he suspects that the "movement" may have functioned as a front—especially for new left parties; he also doubts if they constitute a "social movement" in the classical sense, with a common political platform and a leadership structure. In any case, it managed to recruit thousands of people affected by the austerity programs. The author accounts for the mobilization using "relative deprivation" theory, especially of the middle classes (See also Smith on Greece following the fall of the junta as well as Dionyssis Balourdos for the new poverty groups). Consistent with their *modus operandi,* the Greek indignados did not evolve into a "political party" (formalization phase of a social movement); they became vulnerable to factionalism and to cooptation, as well as the "success" of decentralization and internationalization à la *acampadas.* Nonetheless, the author believes that they contributed to (1) the breakdown of the two parties that governed Greece for the past 35 years (2) the emergence and/strengthening of political parties on the right ("Independent Hellenes", "Golden Dawn") and on the left (SYRIZA, DIMAR and ANTARSYA) depending upon the space they occupied in CS and, finally (3) to the necessity to form coalition governments.

Alberto Cotillo looks at the Spanish indignados as a "withdrawal", as an alienation from and a "disaffection" with the establishment politics of the conservatives and socialists. We might also extend this observation to the Greek indignados. In any case, using national survey statistics, a multi-dimensional analysis of "disaffection and a time-series analysis (2002-2012), Cotillo observes that it was "disaffection with institutions" (e.g., parliament, governments, political parties, operation of democracy)—and not personal "political disaffection" (e.g., perceptions of inefficacy) or "political disengagement" (e.g., information, participation)—that went along with the increasing negative perceptions of the "economic and the political situations" (especially after 2008) and could lie behind general political disaffection. Looking at the levels of disaffection, for the center-left and the far-left (according to self-placement), and taking into account the ideology of the governments that governed Spain during the years under study, Cotillo concludes that it was not the debt crisis per se that led to "political disaffection" (alienation), but the management of the debt crisis by the institutionalized left and the disillusionment with the organized left following an "affection" with the organized left in the previous years.

Closing the discussion on the social impacts, the Editors would like to point out that a number of researchers used a time-series analysis and collected their last data either in 2010 or 2011. The economic crisis had been well on its way in Greece, Ireland and Portugal—formally at least—since 2008, with the failure of Lehman Brothers. Later on, the debt crisis broke out in Spain, Italy and Cyprus. We would hope that the authors of this volume, as well as other social scientists, would conduct an assessment of social impacts when these countries have "returned to the open market", or more substantively, when their levels of unemployment reach EZ averages. Comparative studies by social scientists, both in the historical and cultural sense, which take into account the magnitude of the crisis in various countries would constitute a significant value-added contribution to policy-makers.

Social, economic and political factors causing, exacerbating or mitigating the Eurozone debt crisis

Factors and processes complicating or exacerbating solutions to the debt crisis. Four of the volumes' authors (Gräbener, Nagopoulos & Rontos and Vobruba) dealt with subjects that are not necessarily direct impacts of the crisis but could complicate its solution. Josua Gräbener suggests that the implementation of the ESF educational training program for workers by the Labour-Capital Joint Management Commissions (the FPIs), the emphasis that employers put on the training for special instead of general skills, as well as a reluctance of employers to participate in EU-public programs for fear of changing their agenda, may reinforce regional [North-South] fragmentation in Italy and the reproduction of regional inequalities. On their part, Nikos Nagopoulos and Kostas Rontos point out how the high volume of irregular (non-documented) migration to Greece distorts the rational working-out of the labour market and the implementation of EU policies for the attraction of a more specialized workforce; furthermore, they note how non-documented migration into Greece, together with the ongoing crisis, obstructs the full integration of all migrants while at the same time reinforcing xenophobic behavior. In this regard, and using Chtouris and Miller's ' "Total Social Value Stock", this does not allow a full exploitation of all the social factors that could contribute to economic development. Finally, GeorgVobruba, arguing basically from a Dahrendorfian conflict perspective, demonstrates how the adoption of the common currency (EMU) has led to a transformation from conflicts between classes or nations to conflicts among peoples (or interest groups) across Eurozone members—complicating the resolution of the economic crisis in the debt-ridden countries while at the same time making the countries of the Eurozone [and perhaps not only] more vulnerable to exploitation of the situation by populist groups. The new constellation of conflicts could make or break the EU, depending upon certain factors (See below).

Capacity and resilience building. Five of the contributors (Tsobanolgou, Kanellopoulos & Liakaki, Silvast and Gantzias) to this volume dealt more than the others with alternative forms of social organization (Part V).

George Tsobanoglou, aside from an analysis of the unemployment and GDP situation (referred to above) and a critique of the IMF that we shall discuss below, points out how the Greek government policies (e.g., tax system not allowing for a sustainable productive labour, private-public labour hierarchization, clientelistic practices, lack of marketing skills), the organization of Greek labour and agricultural institutions, the EU policies (e.g., Open Method of Coordination, common agricultural policy) and the troika austerity packages (e.g., mainstreaming reforms such as raising retirement age and the "monetarist tsunami") have discouraged the development/survival of sociality assembly/social economy and have not brought the expected outcomes for the Greek labour-market. He is encouraged by the new forms of "sociality assembly" such as the campaigns for a living wage, the exchange economy and the movements without middlemen" that have cropped up mainly as a result of the crisis. He recommends the further development of these forms of sociality assembly and social economy, and, more specifically, the empowerment of local communities and the workers in organizations, i.e., in all senses of empowerment (e.g., skills, knowledge, information, participation, social insurance, legitimization of the new forms by the state) as an approach to building employment capacity and as a solution to the current crisis.

Christos Kanellopoulos and Sotiria Liakaki, after an almost exhaustive review of the concept of "full citizenship" in the relevant literature (that includes not only political but also social rights), focus on the state of "full citizenship" and social [welfare] rights in the Greek society. In Greece, the notion of citizenship does not imply automatically access to social rights. Social rights (e.g., social and health insurance, unemployment benefits, access of workers to training, etc.) have been connected to employment and types of employment. In addition, a history of multiple social insurance systems depending upon sector, along with the "noble" social insurance systems and clientelism, is responsible for the "particularistic" social insurance systems that culminate in a non-productive labour force and non-sustainable welfare systems (See also G. Tsobanoglou). The attempts toward more "universalistic" notions of citizenship with social rights, dissociated from employment or a means tests and promoting the reproduction of a sustainable labour force (exemplified especially by the "Nordic models" of "full citizenship"), have not accomplished the desired results. The failure is primarily due to the austerity that accompanies these reforms, the compressed time-perspective for implementation and the negative impact on the cohesion of a society [social trust] already traumatized by the history of clientelism, compartmentalization of public/private labour and the resistance from the "noble" social welfare systems.

As almost everyone would agree, the banking system played a vital role in the current debt crisis, mainly as a cause but also as vehicle for recovering from the crisis. Following the perspective of mass emergencies and disasters as well as a systems model whereby the banks are interdependent with the other social systems (production, consumption, services, etc.), Antti Silvast views the banking/finance system as a "critical infrastructure" that must be protected from a breakdown, regardless of the event ("natural" or "social") causing the crisis. He reviews conceptualizations of "critical" or "vital infrastructure in the U.S., the European Union and Finland and the extent to which they include finance, banking or the economy in their conceptualization. In turn, he focuses on the Finnish strategies (2003, 2006 and 2010) where "banking and finance" are part of a "functioning economy". The strategies have stipulated various "threat scenarios" among which is one relating to a "serious disturbance in financial and payment systems". In addition, the 2006 strategy also stipulates that Finland has adopted the common security measures of the Eurozone against financial crises (in 2006 strategy), supplemented by national backup protection, although the 2006 strategy has no provisions for risks from bailouts within the Eurozone. In a sense, entry into the Eurozone was conceived as mitigation. Aside from the perception of the EZ as mitigation, the author also noted other limitations/omissions in the Finnish strategy, including the perception of a financial crisis as part of world business cycles (that could lead to a "normalization" of crises), an absence of details for bank failures despite the bank runs and bank-loan problems in early 1990s, and an inadequate investment of bank-system security with sociological conceptions of mass emergency management (e.g., resilience). Although fiscal and banking system integration on the EU level was viewed by the European Council (June 2012) as a potential solution to the fiscal crisis, the increasing interdependence that this union entails could open the road for new mega risks, which of course need commensurate resilience measures on both an EU- and a member-country level.

George Gantzias' contribution may constitute an answer not only to the questions raised by Silvast regarding the security of banking systems but also to the current economic crisis confronting the Southern European countries. Gantzias focuses on the latest developments in the new technologies—the "digital transaction [payment] culture" (DTC) that was facilitated after the arrival of 3rd and 4th generation mobile phones and cloud-computing services. The DTC, whose actors can include banks, investors, traders, entrepreneurs, NGOs, governmental departments, software providers and political parties, has been widely diffused, especially in North America and the European countries. According to the author, digital transactions have become routine in North Europe. They have comparative advantages over "physical-money" transactions, including, among others, the reduction of tax evasion, generation of new digital jobs, increase of investments in the private sector, transformation of bureaucratic systems, transparency and protection from cyberlaundering. Using comparative data, the author demonstrates how the adoption of the Digital Tax Payment Culture helped Sweden to reduce public spending, cut corporate taxes, reduce its public debt and its budget deficit and recover from the 2007-2008 fiscal storm. The economic crisis in Greece and other Southern European countries started in 1999, when the EMU lacked a provision for "a regulatory mechanism that would take into account the economic, political, cultural and social differences of… member states. More specifically, in the case of Greece, the "main reason" for the austerity measures and the high unemployment rates was the inability of "Greek politicians to understand the digital payments culture and their unwillingness to institute reliable regulative mechanisms in the public and private sectors…" Therefore, the wider adoption of the DTC could help Greece and other debt-ridden countries to mitigate the impact of the fiscal crisis.

Causes and factors generating the debt crisis. Several of the authors, whom we have referred to above, touch upon the causes of the debt crisis. For Georg Vobruba, the fall of the spreads during the decade before the crisis broke out, the constant flow of cheap money into the "less productive Euromembers, either via private credit or public debt" were main factors; this, in turn, facilitated imports, bank expansion, investments and consumption in the "less productive countries" as well as exports from the "more productive Euromembers". These came to an end "overnight" with the subprime crisis and the failure of Lehman Brothers.

Along similar lines, Dennis Smith views the "double-dip recession" as stemming from a "global crisis in the workings of capitalism". More specifically, it resulted, "in large part, from the collapse of confidence in debt creation as a means of managing market transactions…" and the "deliberate creation of risky sub-prime debt…" which, in turn, "weakened the credit and credibility of many large banks, leading to a widespread unwillingness of banks to lend to each other…" For Smith, the emphasis given in the media about the failures of politicians may have taken attention away for the "sometimes fraudulent behaviour of bankers and allied professions in and around the finance industry".

Sotiris Chtouris and DeMond Miller, arguing from the "Total Social Value Stock" perspective, point to the lack of social solidarity among "central powers…" toward peripheral countries, the disintegration of a "protective framework for national and regional economies…not deemed to have an adequate level of competitiveness", a "sharp increase in unemployment", the "longstanding deficit in social capital in South

Europe", and the "pervading black economy/corruption phenomena, especially in countries such as Greece and Italy…" as examples of social capital degradation. In short, the crisis results from a devaluation of social capital which according to Chtouris and Miller affects economic capital.

Ignacía Perugorria and Benjamín Tejerina noted that by 2007 Spain "…had a public account surplus of more than 2 percent of the GDP and the economy was growing by 3.5 percent". Within one year, however, "the surplus had become deficit, growth had fallen to less than 1 percent, and the Spanish economy was officially entering recession…" They continue: "Although the economic decline was related to a worldwide financial crisis, it also responded to clearly identifiable domestic facts: the bursting of a decade-long real estate bubble and the implosion of the associated lending market".

George Tsobanoglou chides the IMF—and by extension the troika—which expected the Greek economy to bounce back after a year of austerity but which, in early 2013, admitted the failure of this prediction, though there followed no corrective measures after a year of implementation, possibly because the "ordoliberalist" German decision-makers did not share the *mea culpa* of IMF. Nonetheless, Tsobanoglou does not overlook the internal factors such as the clientelistic relations, the hierarchization of private and private labour, the inequitable tax system, the lack of transparency in transactions, the asymmetries in information distribution and the administration deficiencies of labour/farmer organizations which have been abettors of the crisis.

Kanellopoulos and Liakaki view "ordoliberalism, a German version of neoliberalism…, in stark contrast to both Keynesianism and monetarism", which "rejects a fiscal *and* monetary stimulus in the face of a depressed economy" and which became an integral part of the "Eurozone monetary mechanisms" (read Maastricht), as the principal cause of the economic crisis and the continuing crisis in the Greek social insurance system. The austerity measures and a compressed time-table for the reforms made the bailout program counterproductive. However, they, too, do not overlook internal factors in Greek society such as clientelism, absence of a "welfare elite", etc. that compound the problem.

Magnus Ryner and Brigitte Young, who were the keynote speakers in the Lesvos conference, in their brief contributions, go into more depth with regard to the political-economic causes of the debt-crisis. Ryner views the Eurozone crisis as a "metamorphosis of the global financial crisis that started in the U.S. subprime housing markets in 2007… when the state bailout systems transformed private debt into public debt in an effort to save the financial system from meltdown". This, however, "put the public debt of some countries, namely, Portugal, Italy, Ireland, Greece and Spain, under stress as the confidence in their capacity to service their debt waned resulting in a deteriorating balance of payments and a spread in bond yields… that further increased "the costs of servicing the debt" and, hence, further undermined confidence with all its attendant consequences for these countries. The expectations for the "efficient market hypothesis", "self-equilibrating powers", "self-regulating financial markets" and "flexible labour markets" that would make for a "rational allocation of capital to business investments in high-tech and high valued-added sectors" and the neoliberal "economistic" rationality, both of which are integral in the European Monetary Union, have not materialized, threatening to perpetrate a disaster, as documented by other chapters in the present volume.

While Brigitte Young does not disagree with these finance-dominated processes ("financialisation") in the Eurozone, she locates the principal historical source of the problem in another genre of neo-liberalism—"German Ordoliberalism"—that dates back to the pre-WWII Freiburg School, which rejects government intervention championed by Keynesians to shore up indebted countries, since this would violate the independence of the European Central Bank to follow its mandate of price stability. The idea of price stability is strongly entrenched in German tradition and widely shared among the political elite, the economic profession, the media and the population at large. The present international demand for political intervention in fiscal and monetary policy to stabilize the euro crisis would be contrary to the long-term goals of ordoliberals to establish a legal system to force countries to adhere to strict fiscal discipline and for automatic sanctions if these rules are violated. This system gives priority to a "rule-based export-oriented, supply-side model" rather than a Keynesian demand-led growth model. However, the institutional framework of the Economic and Monetary Union (EMU) separating monetary and fiscal policies further exacerbated a successful crisis resolution. According to Young, "…setting monetary policy at the European level while leaving fiscal policy in the hands of individual member states was a huge gamble from the inception of the European Monetary Union and may have worked during 'normal' economic times, but became the Achilles heel during the financial crisis". The heated debate among German economists (between Keynesians and ordoliberals) demonstrates the divisiveness among the German economic profession in how to resolve the euro crisis. It may also account for the government's vacillation and Angela Merkel's "incremental and reactive steps" rather than providing a forward strategy for sustainable Eurozone growth.

Crisis management and resolution— some policy recommendations

The contributions to this volume presuppose a diversity of theoretical perspectives, so it is inevitable that the policy recommendations will vary; some wanted to separate the "scientific" and the "policy roles" and restricted themselves mainly to research recommendations which nonetheless they considered as vital documentation for policy makers. In a way, the consideration of various policy perspectives, though an eclectic approach, could also be viewed as an "integrated crisis management" approach, borrowed from the literature on disasters.

Poverty reduction. The principal source of poverty is unemployment which has increased dramatically during the implementation of the austerity program. Therefore, reduction of it through public investments, especially in alternative energies and high-tech occupations, in accord with more Keynesian/monetarist models, is an imperative (Ryner). A more systematic use of ESF funds, that focuses on training for general instead of specialized skills may also contribute to the reduction of poverty (Gräbener). During the phase of economic recovery and the restructuring of businesses and skills in the debt-ridden countries, there should be established a "universal safety net" through the granting of sufficient family benefits and a guaranteed minimum income (Kanellopoulos & Liakaki, Balourdos, Tsiganou).

Welfare Reforms. Reduction of unemployment will have positive impacts on the welfare system which is on the verge of bankruptcy in Greek society by increasing the revenue to the social insurance funds. There is a need to abandon the more "particularistic" structure of the Greek welfare system— legacy of clientelism, welfare benefits that don't allow for a social reproduction of labour, hierarchization of labour and social insurance funds—and move toward the adoption of the more "universalistic" system of Northern European countries, a system that is consistent with the concept of "full citizenship", is divorced from employment and can also cover "marginalized" groups. The implementation of the austerity/reform program—attendant to the "bailout" and "self-defeating" policies of the troica—has not expedited the development of social trust and the assimilation of social welfare reforms that may, otherwise, be in the right direction (Kanellopoulos & Liakaki, Tsobanoglou).

Labour market improvements. The development of "assembling sociality"—"…a form of interdependence" that arises "from exposure to common risk" and involves "shared participation in organizations and agencies in order to cope with the risk"—is a necessity during the current economic crisis. The devaluation of labour due to traditional factors and the erosion of the sociality-forms of assembly (e.g, collective bargaining) induced by the implementation of thc austerity program can be offset by new forms of assembling sociality (e.g., mutual-aid societies, cooperatives, social enterprises, movements without go-betweens, social economies, worker-controlled failed factories) which can contribute to the building of employment capacity at the local community level. While there have been sporadic movements in the direction of "assembling sociality", there is a need to legitimize and mainstream them (i.e., by state recognition) (Tsobanoglou).

Migration and social integration. As the large volume of irregular migration to Greece distorts the labour market and restricts the integration of migrants, more systematic regulations of non-dcomented migrants are called for. Border fences, migrant detention centers and Frontex services have not solved the problem. There is a need for a review of the Dublin II agreement but more importantly for "responsibility sharing" with the EU that could provide for a "relocation mechanism", perhaps on a proportional basis in the EU countries not so affected by large influxes of irregular migrants. Bilateral agreements between the vulnerable countries and the countries of origin would not only normalize the labour market and reduce irregular migration but would also allow the implementation of EU policy on skilled immigration and facilitate social integration of all migrants (Nagopoulos & Rontos). In addition, attacking the roots of irregular migration by restraining foreign interventions, encouraging the establishment of genuine democracies and supporting economic development in the countries of origin constitute the best preventive policies.

Reducing xenophobia and racism. The observations in the present volume suggest that economic recovery from the debt crisis and the reduction of unemployment and poverty would contribute to a reduction of intergroup prejudice, both in the native ["majority"] and the migrant ["minority"] groups (Kalogeraki, Iliou). Undoubtedly, a more rational migration policy, regarding non-documented migration, would reduce threat, check right-wing populism and improve intergroup relations (Nagopoulos & Rontos). A new legislative framework against racist and fascist acts may also undermine the institutional props of racism, though it, too, would not be sufficient. Intergroup attitudes are not determined only by economic conditions but are also the result of historical, cultural and psychodynamic factors that may predate the economic crisis (for the role of religion see Stathopoulou & Kostaki).

Political alienation. Restoration of trust in social and political institutions is a significant factor in reducing political disaffection. For one thing, this can be done when politicians, officials in government, celebrities, civil servants and plain citizens, who are involved in either "white-collar" or "blue-collar" crimes, receive the same treatment before the justice system (Tsiganou). Furthermore, the one standard of justice for parliamentarians (e,g., immunity) and another for the plain citizens must come to an end. Perhaps, the hand of justice should be less lenient against those who have a comparative economic/political/social advantage in society. Finally, movements of the "indignados in Spain and Greece", for "real" and "direct democracy"—as long as they remain non-violent in their ideology and tactics—are collective phenomena in the right direction. These can now be more feasible with "on-line" participation as Perugorria and Tejerina point out, though a minimum common ideological platform and somewhat more structure in leadership may increase their viability and make them more effective in bringing about changes.

Bank system resilience. Since banks are an important part of the economic system and interdependent with the other sectors of society, and can also be both causes of and agents for recovery from disasters and crisis, it is vital to treat them as critical infrastructures and develop appropriate emergency plans. The case study of the Finnish economy (finance and bank system), as "critical infrastructure", suggests that there is a need to develop more explicit plans, using the sociological models of resilience, against bank failures, bank runs, lack of liquidity etc. in case of crises. In addition, nations must guard against considering bank failures as parts of the "business cycle" as they run the risk of "normalizing" and being complacent about the current measures; moreover, higher levels of integration of member states in the EMU or an expanded political-economic-fiscal union do not guarantee resilience from crisis. They imply increased interdependence, risk for mega-crisis and a need for commensurate civil protection measures. The present case study needs to be supplemented by more quantitative analysis as well as by historical studies of bank failures during mass emergencies (wars, depressions, etc.) (Silvast).

The "digital transaction/payment culture" revolution. The DPC, as described by Gantzias, has comparative advantages over "physical" money. Therefore, countries, especially the debt-ridden ones, should rush to adopt this system of transaction. Although there are several digital payment alternatives, the bitcoin is the one of the most widely used. Yet, this digital payment system has not been adopted formally by any government or commercial organization. Moreover, it is vulnerable to "cyberlaundering". An alternative that is under development is the "Global Info-Cash" (GIC) that purports to overcome these problems (Gantzias). Undoubtedly, the DTC as a technological innovation has many benefits, but, like all innovations, there are social and cultural factors that facilitate and others that block the acceptance of this innovation. Needed are sociological studies, in the debt-ridden countries, to assess the situation and make policy recommendations to accelerate the diffusion of the digital transaction culture.

Structural and political-economic changes. Here,we rely heavily on the macro-economic recommendations made by Magnus Ryner and Brigitte Young—recommendations that challenge the current structures of EU and the EMU. Among others, Ryner recommends: (1) reducing the power and the size of the financial sector (e.g., separate commercial and investment banks, taxing of financial transactions, banning most derivatives, setting-up a public-owned credit rating agency) (2) formulating a common EU macroeconomic policy (e.g., making ECB a lender of last resort and implementing EU-wide fiscal transfer mechanisms) and (3) adopting an EU-wide incomes policy where wage growth is based on productivity growth equal to productivity growth in the deficit countries and above productivity growth in the surplus countries—the percentages to be determined. Without necessarily being in disagreement with Ryner's recommendations, Young recommends (1) accepting the June 2012 European Council proposal for deeper political, economic and fiscal integration of the EU with the introduction of a banking union (2) the formulation of social policy at the EU level rather than at the level of the member states (3) revision of the Lisbon Treaty to make it less economistic (4) strengthening the democratic dimensions of EMU governance and (5) abandoning the austerity approach for indebted countries. To these, we can also add Dennis Smith's proposal to "Europeanize" matters of corporate tax-evasion by transferring them to EU. For us, these proposals translate into more Europe, less market Europe, more social Europe, more solidarity among EU member states and, concurrently, a Europe friendly to social and economic development.

A Bourdieuian approach to crisis resolution. Working from the perspective of "Total Social Value Stock", Sotiris Chtouris and DeMond Miller propose that both the crisis *and* its resolution depend primarily on a better balance of the various forms of capital; specifically, an upgrading of social, human, cultural and natural capital will have a positive impact upon economic capital development, leading to a virtuous cycle for development and youth employment. The first four forms of capital, that have been jeopardized by economistic orientations on the part of the EU structure and by clientelistic policies in deficit countries, need to be revitalized. The Editors await with great interest the completion of the relevant cross-cultural study and the conclusions regarding the weight of the various forms of capital in the TSVS equation.

The positive functions of social conflict. As indicated by Vobruba, the Common Currency was responsible for the Europeanization of distribution conflicts and for a transformation from conflicts between nations to conflicts among peoples. The re-distribution of conflicts has led not only to conflicts of interest among various interest groups in EZ countries, it has also reinforced right-wing populist movements. Nonetheless, with the enlargement of the "public sphere", the "employment of more effective conflict-regulating mechanisms" and an increased sense of "solidarity" (not just interdependence"), among the European nations, the Europeanization of distribution conflicts should not be construed as a "danger" (or "risk") but as "manifestations of a society in the making".

The Editors hope they have made an objective presentation of the contributors' basic conclusions and policy recommendations. In accordance with the "integrated disaster management" approach, policy-makers should take into account all the policy recommendations. Nonetheless, there should be a prioritization. Although all of them should enter in the recovery equation, we *as sociologists* are of the opinion that the pivotal X factor in the recovery—or to be more exact in the reconstruction—equation are the "surplus" countries of the Eurozone, and especially Germany with the €188 billion trade surplus for 2012. Germany has a precedent: a debt restructuring plan based on the 1953 London Debt Agreement for Germany's war debts which was essential in restoring West Germany's debt sustainability after the Second World War. Finally, the Editors, *as participant-observers* of the "deficit" so-called "PIIGS" (or GIIPS as Brigitte Young would have it) societies, believe that the overwhelming majority of citizens of these societies do not want more "self-defeating" policies, are not content with the "*mea culpa*" of the IMF or the mere acknowledgement by creditors of sacrifices made by the peoples in the "deficit countries—and, especially, by their country, Greece. The members of these societies are not comfortable with the role of "guinea pigs" or *Iphigenias* for the salvation of Europe, and they definitely would hope that the "surplus" powers, which hold the fate of EU in their hands, would do their utmost to prevent a confirmation of Joschka Fischer's warning about the unintended collapse of the European order. The Editors recommend "atonement programs" that would help the "deficit" countries get out of the dire situation and would be worthy of the visions of the European Union founders.

CONTRIBUTORS

Dionyssis Baloudros (National Centre for Social Research, Greece) Dionyssis Balourdos is a Director of Research at the National Centre for Social Research (E.K.K.E). He holds a Ph.D. in Economics from the University of Panteion (Greece), an M.Sc. in population and poverty issues from the same University and a Bachelor's from the Uppsala University (Sweden). He has coordinated or participated in a large number of studies on issues related to social policy, social inequalities, discrimination, social welfare policy, labour market policy, human resources development, poverty, social exclusion, ageing problems and social inclusion policies for vulnerable social groups. Indicative projects are, among others, "Excellence in the research fields: Poverty, Social Exclusion and Social Inequalities" and "Establishment of an Observatory on Combating Discrimination in Greece". He has participated as an expert in numerous committees on the management and evaluation of the European Social Fund (ESF) programmes, development of academic curricula, evaluation of ESF interventions in Greece and the EU, etc. He has published on social inequalities, poverty, social exclusion and population-ageing issues. E-mail: dbalourdos@ekke.gr

Joanna-Despina Bergiannaki-Dermitzaki, (University of Athens, Greece) Joanna Bergiannaki has a Medical Degree from the University of Vienna and a specialization in Neurology and Psychiatry from the University of Athens. Currently, she is Associate Professor of Psychiatry at the University of Athens, 1st University Psychiatric Department, Eginition Hospital, Athens. She has made numerous presentations in International and Greek Congresses. More specifically, a significant number of these presentations dealt with the topics of PTSD and disaster consequences and were made in the capacity of an invited speaker. Among her publications are a number of articles and a book in Greek and English that deal with the topic of PTSD and natural, man-made and economic disaster research.
E-mail: bergian@otenet.gr

Sotiris Chtouris (University of the Aegean, Greece) Sotiris Chtouris is Professor of Sociology and Head of a Post-Graduate Programme in the Sociology Department at the University of the Aegean. His scientific

expertise and research interests involve the following fields: urban sociology and social reconstruction, social differentiation and inequality with an emphasis on the issues of poverty and social exclusion, cultural networks and cultural change, cultural models and technological culture, research methodology in the social sciences, information technology and social sciences and, more specifically, the use of geographic information systems in the social and cultural analysis of urban space.
Email: htouris@aegean.gr .

Alberto Cotillo (University of La Coruña, Spain) Alberto Cotillo is University Professor of Sociology and Professor of Methodology of the Social Sciences. He specialises in the sociology of scientific knowledge, has published several articles on the topic, and co-edited the volume *Sociología de la Ciencia y la Tecnología* (Madrid: CSIC). In recent years, his main research interests are the sociology of risk and environment and political sociology. E-mail: acp@udc.es.

Stefanos Dimitrakopoulos (University of Athens, Greece) Stefanos Dimitrakopoulos is a Psychiatrist and a Military Doctor. He has received his Medical Degree from Aristotle University of Thessaloniki and completed his specialization in Psychiatry in the 1st Psychiatric Department, Eginition Hospital, National and Kapodistrian University of Athens. He has also been an undergraduate student in the Faculty of Philosophy, Pedagogy and Psychology of the National and Kapodistrian University of Athens. Currently, he is Psychiatrist in the Department of the Psychiatric Clinic of 414 Military Special Diseases Hospital, Athens. His field of interest is mainly preventive psychiatry. He has published articles and books and made presentations in Greek and international conferences: some of those in relation to the topic of PTSD and Disasters.
E-mail: stefan_dimitrakopoulos@yahoo.gr

George K. Gantzias (University of the Aegean, Greece) George Gantzias is an Associate Professor in the Department of Cultural Technology and Communication at the University of the Aegean, Mytilene, Greece. He teaches Cultural Management, Cultural Policy, Administration, Advertising and Marketing, Cyberspace and Electronic Commerce, New Media and Communication Policy, Crisis Management, Digital Money. He has been involved heavily in administration, developing undergraduate and postgraduate studies in the University of the Aegean, The City University, and Open University in Greece since 2004. H has been a consultant to a variety of international companies, European

Community projects, Regulatory Institutions and Academic Research Centres. His books [and articles] are: (1) *The dynamic of regulation: Global control, local resistance,* Ashgate, Adershort UK, 2001 (in English) (2) *Cultural policy, sponsorship and corporate social responsibility*, Papasotiriou, Athens, May 2010 (in Greek) (3) "The Greek crisis and CO.D.TRA (Code of Digital Transactions): Mobile Payments and the Global Info-Cash (GIC)" in E.G. Carayannis and G.M. Korres (eds.), *European socio-economic integration, innovation, technology and knowledge management*, Springer, Business Media, New York, 2013 (in English). E-mail: ggantzias@aegean.gr and ggantzias@yahoo.gr.

Josua Gräbener (University of Grenoble, France) Josua Gräbener is a Ph.D. candidate in Political Science. He graduated in Political Sociology at the University of Lyon, with a Master's thesis on the role of NGOs in the Europeanization of the asylum policy in Cyprus. After an internship at the European Parliament, he was awarded a Ph.D. scholarship by the Rhône-Alpes Regional Council to investigate the role of Labour-Capital Joint Management Commissions in the Europeanization of lifelong learning policies in France and Italy. He was a teaching assistant on EU politics at the University of Lyon (Lumière Lyon 2) and a visiting student scholar at the European University Institute (Florence), during the fall 2013 term. E-mail: josua.grabener@iepg.fr.

Katerina Iliou (National Centre for Social Research, Greece) Katerina Iliou is a Social Psychologist, and a researcher at the National Centre for Social Research (EKKE). She has a Ph.D. in Social Psychology, in the field of "new forms of prejudice" (Panteion University of Political and Social Sciences) and an M.Sc. in the field of "social exclusion and minorities". Her research interest concerns are prejudice and racism, group relations, social inequalities, exclusions and discrimination against social groups. She has experience in planning and conducting research and has publications in the field of social exclusion. E-mail: kiliou@ekke.gr.

Stefania Kalogeraki (University of Crete, Greece) Stefania Kalogeraki holds a Ph.D. from the University of Reading, U.K., and is a lecturer in Quantitative Methods in Sociology. She has been involved as a quantitative social researcher in various projects and published articles in international and Greek journals. Her main research interests include comparative social research designs, questionnaire development and measurement errors, and social demographic analysis with a special focus on migration. E-mail: kaloge@social.soc.uoc.gr.

Christos Kanellopoulos (University of Athens, Greece) Christos Kanellopoulos is a PhD candidate in Political Science in the National and Kapodistrian University of Athens, where he acquired his Degree in Political Science and Public Administration and his Master's in Political Science and Sociology. His research focuses on the interplay of welfare states, political economy and corporatism and the Nordic case. He has published articles on welfare and Eurozone policies.
E-mail: cskanel@gmail.com.

Anastasia Kostaki (Athens University of Economics and Business, Greece) Anastasia Kostaki is Associate Professor in the Department of Statistics of Athens University of Economics and Business. She holds a Ph.D. from Lund University, Sweden. She is Scientific Coordinator of the postgraduate program "Statistics in Medicine" of the Department of Statistics, Athens University of Economics and Business. Author of numerous research papers published in peer-reviewed international journals, e.g. *Mathematical Population Studies, Demographic Research, Journal of Official Statistics, Biometrical Journa*l. Member of scientific associations, e.g., International Union for the Scientific Study of Population, European Association of Population Studies. Her main research areas are: development of statistical methodology for analyzing demographic data, statistical analysis of biomedical data and social statistics. E-mail: kostaki@aueb.gr.

Sotiria Liakaki (Independent Researcher, Greece) Sotiria Liakaki holds a Degree in Communication and Mass Media from the Panteion University, a Master's degree in Political Science and Sociology from the National and Kapodistrian University of Athens and a DEA in Philosophy from the University Paris Ouest Nanterre La Défense, where she also acquired her PhD in Philosophy. Her academic interests cover theories of institutional change, welfare states, citizenship and European integration.
E-mail: sliakaki2001@gmail.com.

DeMond Shondell Miller (Rowan University, United States) DeMond Miller is a Professor of Sociology in the Sociology Department of Rowan University, USA. He is also Director and Research Scientist in the Liberal Arts and Sciences Institute for Research and Community Service. Professor Miller has conducted several research projects on a wide range of issues: namely, vulnerable youth groups, emergency response to social and natural risks etc. Prof. D. Miller has acquired a vast experience in the organization of On Line Research. He has published numerous articles in international scientific journals. E-mail: millerd@rowan.edu.

Nikos Nagopoulos (University of the Aegean, Greece) Nikos Nagopoulos is Associate Professor in the Department of Sociology of the University of Aegean. He completed his studies in Sociology and Sociolinguistics at the University of Heidelberg. His main areas of research are Theory and Methodology of Social Sciences and Sociology of Knowledge. He was an academic national expert and researcher for the Ministries of Labor and Social Protection of Greece and Cyprus, for the purpose of modernising existing social structures, developing new social services and re-enforcing anti-exclusion mechanisms.
E-mail: n.nagopoulos@soc.aegean.gr.

Ignacia Perugorría (Rutgers University, USA) Ignacia Perugorria is a Ph.D. candidate in sociology at Rutgers University, working on the interaction between identity battles, social movement networks and political opportunity structures in the making of "participatory culture." She is a Fulbright scholar and has also been awarded fellowships by the Institute of International Education and the Graduate School at Rutgers University. She received her M.A. in sociology at Rutgers and her B.A. at the University of Buenos Aires, both with honors. She is affiliated to the Gino Germani Research Institute (University of Buenos Aires) and is currently a visiting researcher at the Collective Identity Research Center (University of the Basque Country). She has published in the areas of social movements, political culture, and cultural activism.
Email: ignacia.perugorria@fulbrightmail.org

Nicholas P. Petropoulos (formerly of the Pedagogical Institute, Greece) Nikos Petropoulos holds B. Sc. and M.A. degrees from Ohio State University and a Ph.D. from the University of Kentucky. He has academic specializations in social psychology, sociology, cultural anthropology, minorities, and collective behavior. After his return to Greece, he worked as a Special Scientist in the Ministry of Migration and at the Pedagogical Institute of Greece as Sociology Counselor. Dr. Petropoulos has served on the Board of the National Centre for Social Research and as member of a scientific committee at the Earthquake Planning and Protection Organization. He has played a decisive role in the founding of the "Hellenic Sociological Association", the "Emergencies Research Center" of Athens, the "Disaster, Conflict, and Social Crisis Research Network" of ESA and the "Hellenic Society for Psychosocial

Intervention in Mass Emergencies and Disasters". He has organized conferences/workshops/meetings on psychosocial response in mass emergencies, traumatic-stress training and the social impacts of the debt-crisis. He was founder and Editor of the *Journal of the Hellenic Diaspora* (US) and an editor of the DCSCRN electronic newsletter. He has publications on the social aspects of disasters, disaster education, EQ prediction, terrorism, school bullying, minority groups and migration.
E-mail: erc@otenet.gr

Kostas Rontos (University of the Aegean, Greece) Kostas Rontos is a Professor of Social Demography and Statistics in the Department of Sociology of the University of the Aegean. He is the President of the aforementioned Department. He is the Director of the e-learning program "Empirical Research on Social Sciences" and of the Summer School "Quantitative and Qualitative Research Methods for Social Sciences". During 2009-11, he was the Director of the postgraduate program "Research on local social development and social cohesion" and Vice President in the Department of Sociology. He is a former Director of the National Statistical Service of Greece. E-mail: k.rontos@soc.aegean.gr.

Magnus Ryner (King's College-University of London, United Kingdom) Magnus Ryner is Reader (Associate Professor) in International Political Economy at King's College, University of London. His publications include *Europe at bay: In the shadow of US hegemony* (Boulder: Lynne Rienner, 2007) and *A ruined fortress? Neoliberal hegemony and transformation in Europe* (Lanham: Rowman & Littlefield, 2003) (both with Alan Cafruny). E-mail: magnus.ryner@kcl.ac.uk.

Antti Silvast (University of Helsinki, Finland) Antti Silvast holds a Ph.D. (2013) from the University of Helsinki, Department of Social Research, Discipline of Sociology. The thesis, *Anticipating interruptions: Security and risk in a liberalized electricity infrastructure,* is available online (http://urn.fi/URN:ISBN:978-952-10-7683-1) and in print by the Helsinki University Print Unigrafia. His other recent publications include "Is the normal accidents perspective falsifiable?", *Disaster Prevention and Management,* vol. 22, no. 1, 2013 (with Ilan Kelman) and "Monitor screens of market risks: Managing electricity in a Finnish control room", *STS Encounters,* vol. 4, no. 2, 2011. He has served as the newsletter editor and the website manager of ESA's "Disaster, Conflict and Social Crisis Research Network" since 2010. E-mail: antti.silvast@helsinki.fi.

Dennis Smith (Loughborough University, UK) Dennis Smith is Emeritus Professor of Sociology at Loughborough University, UK, and does research on globalization and world-formation processes, the shaping of cities, the workings of capitalism and democracy, the development of Europe as a new kind of polity, current transformations of "the West", and the way people experience and cope with displacement and humiliation. He is one-time Vice-President of the European Sociological Association and has been editor of *Current* Sociology (2002-10).
E-mail: d.smith@lboro.ac.uk

Theoni Stathopoulou (National Centre for Social Research, Greece) Theoni Stathopoulou is Research Director at the National Centre for Social Research (EKKE) in Athens and Vice President of the Scientific Advisory Board. She has conducted European Social Survey (ESS) research in Greece as a member of the National Coordinating team and has also participated as an expert in the development of ESS Research Infrastructure. She has participated in various international and national research projects, and she is currently coordinating a project on religiosity and social capital. Her main research and teaching areas are: cross-national survey methodology, measurement of religious behavior, religion and politics, immigration.
E-mail: theosta@ekke.gr.

Benjamín Tejerina (University of the Basque Country, Spain) Benjamin Tejerina is Professor of Sociology and Director of the Collective Identity Research Center at the University of the Basque Country. His research interests include collective action and social movements, living conditions, precariousness and transformations in work culture, sociology of language and ethnolinguistic movements, collective identity, social conflict and youth transitions, and sociological theory. He has published extensively in these areas. In 1990, he received the National Ph.D. Dissertation Award in Sociology and Political Sciences from the Sociological Research Center (CIS, Spain). He is the President of the Research Committee on Social Movements, Collective Action and Social Change (RC48) of the International Sociological Association.
E-mail: b.tejerina@ehu.es.

Joanna Tsiganou (National Centre for Social Research, Greece) Joanna Tsiganou is Director of Research at the Greek National Centre for Social Research (EKKE). She holds a Ph.D. degree in the field of the Sociology of Crime and Deviance (University of London, LSE 1988). For the last 25 years, she has published articles, monographs and books on

issues of law and social change. Within this area of research, she has also been devoted to the study of social exclusion and social inequalities against women and children. She has been actively involved in the strategic planning of research at EKKE as Acting Director of the Institute of Political Sociology for almost a decade (2003-2012). She participated as leader, project manager and co-coordinator in a significant number of national and European/international competitive research projects and as a member of the research team in several national and European/international competitive research projects. She has delivered numerous papers in national and international conferences (mostly upon invitation). She has published a significant number of articles in national and international refereed journals and collective volumes following an invitation. She has written and/or edited and co-edited a number of books.
E-mail: jtsiganou@ekke.gr.

George Tsobanoglou (University of the Aegean, Greece) George Tsobanoglou is Associate Professor in the Department of Sociology of the University of the Aegean. He is serving a third term as President of the Research Committee on Sociotechnics/Sociological Practice of the International Sociological Association (ISA-RC26). He received his Ph.D. (Sociology) from Carleton University and he worked as researcher at the Oslo Institute for Social Research and the London School of Economics. He was visiting Professor at the Universities of Leeds and Newcastle-upon-Tyne. He has engaged in research on social/institutional governance issues, management in different work cultures, local employment development issues, the politics of empowerment and social-economy development issues such as the role of qualifications in cooperative labour forms. He is the author of *Divisions of Greece*, Saarbrucken and the editor of *Women, Livelihoods and Socio-Economic Growth,* Delhi, and of *The Politics of Participation and Empowerment: Current Issues and Practices*, Hildesheim. He has published numerous articles; some of his latest include "Sociological practice and the sociotechnics of governance', in A. Dennis and D. Kalekin-Fishman (eds.), *The ISA handbook in contemporary sociology*, Sage, London and "Aspects of European socio-economic integration: Labour conditions in Greece", *Journal of Knowledge Economy*, Springer Science-Business Media, New York, 2013.
E-mail: g.tsobanoglou@soc.aegean.gr.

Georg Vobruba (University of Leipsig, Germany) Georg Vobruba studied law, economics and sociology at Vienna and Freiburg. He has worked at the Austrian Television and the Science Center Berlin—an

Hamburg Institute for Social Research. Since 1992, he is Professor of Sociology at the University of Leipzig. Main fields of research are: labour market and social security, European integration, theory of society. The latest books include: Kein *Gleichgewicht. Die Ökonomie in der Krise* (No equilibrium. Economics in crisis). 2012 and *Der postnationale Raum. Transformation von Souveränität und Grenzen in Europa.* (The postnational space. Transformation of sovereignty and borders in Europe). 2012. E-mail: vobruba@sozio.uni-leipzig.de.

Brigitte Young (University of Münster, Germany) Brigitte Young is Professor (em.) of International Political Economy at the University of Münster, Germany. Her research interests are finance with a special emphasis on the European sovereign debt crisis, global financial reforms, financialisation, IPE theories (ordoliberalism/neoliberalism). She is currently a Working Group leader in the EU-COST project on "Systemic risks, financial crisis and credit". Young has published widely on the Eurozone debt crisis and the role of Germany in the crisis resolution. She is presently working on a manuscript "Germany and the Future of the Eurozone", and with Bob Jessop/Christoph Scherrer on "Varieties of Financial Cultures". E-mail: byoung@uni-muenster.de.

INDEX